THE PAPERS OF ULYSSES S. GRANT

THE PAPERS OF

ULYSSES S. GRANT

Volume 27:

January 1–October 31, 1876

Edited by John Y. Simon

ASSISTANT EDITORS
William M. Ferraro
Aaron M. Lisec

TEXTUAL EDITOR
Dawn Vogel

SOUTHERN ILLINOIS UNIVERSITY PRESS

CARBONDALE

Library of Congress Cataloging in Publication Data (Revised)

Grant, Ulysses Simpson, Pres. U.S., 1822–1885.
 The papers of Ulysses S. Grant.

 Prepared under the auspices of the Ulysses S. Grant Association.
 Bibliographical footnotes.
 CONTENTS: v. 1. 1837–1861.—v. 2. April–September 1861.—
v. 3. October 1, 1861–January 7, 1862.—v. 4. January 8–March 31,
1862.—v. 5. April 1–August 31, 1862.—v. 6. September 1–
December 8, 1862.—v. 7. December 9, 1862–March 31, 1863.—
v. 8. April 1–July 6, 1863.—v. 9. July 7–December 31, 1863.—v. 10.
January 1–May 31, 1864.—v. 11. June 1–August 15, 1864.—v. 12.
August 16–November 15, 1864.—v. 13. November 16, 1864–
February 20, 1865.—v. 14. February 21–April 30, 1865.—v. 15.
May 1–December 31, 1865.—v. 16. 1866.—v. 17. January 1–
September 30, 1867.—v. 18. October 1, 1867–June 30, 1868.—
v. 19. July 1, 1868–October 31, 1869.—v. 20. November 1, 1869–
October 31, 1870.—v. 21. November 1, 1870–May 31, 1871.—
v. 22. June 1, 1871–January 31, 1872.—v. 23. February 1–
December 31, 1872.—v. 24. 1873.—v. 25. 1874.—v. 26. 1875.—
v. 27. January 1–October 31, 1876.
 1. Grant, Ulysses Simpson, Pres. U.S., 1822–1885. 2. United
States—History—Civil War, 1861–1865—Campaigns and battles—
Sources. 3. United States—Politics and government—1869–1877—
Sources. 4. Presidents—United States—Biography. 5. Generals—
United States—Biography. I. Simon, John Y., ed. II. Ulysses S. Grant
Association.
E660.G756   1967   973.8′2′0924   67-10725
ISBN 0-8093-2631-0 (v. 27)

The paper used in this publication meets the minimum requirements
of American National Standard for Information Sciences—Perma-
nence of Paper for Printed Library Materials, ANSI Z39.48-1992. ⊚

Published with the assistance of a grant from the National Historical
Publications and Records Commission.

Contents

———

Introduction

In EARLY 1876, Congress balked at appropriating the necessary funds to commemorate the nation's centennial. By late March, Ulysses S. Grant wrote of "the present embarrassments" facing the government and successfully urged funding "to carry out the undertaking in a creditable manner." In May, Grant opened the exhibition in Philadelphia. He voiced pride in the nation's achievements, noting that while "necessities have compelled us to chiefly expend our means and time in felling forests, subduing prairies, building dwellings, factories, ships, docks, ware houses, roads, canals, machinery, etc. . . . we yet have done what this exhibition will shew in the direction of rivaling older and more advanced nations in law, medicine and theology—in science, literature, philosophy, and the fine arts." Subsequent Centennial proclamations urged citizens to compile local histories and to include religious observances in their Fourth of July festivities.

While the nation celebrated, Grant confronted scandals within his administration. In February, Grant's private secretary, Orville E. Babcock, stood trial at St. Louis for his alleged involvement in the "Whiskey Ring." Indignant at prosecutors' offers of immunity or leniency to procure testimony against Babcock and others, Grant directed Attorney General Edwards Pierrepont to discourage the tactic in a circular letter to United States attorneys. Babcock intercepted this letter and leaked it to the press, telling Pierrepont: "I was

drowning. They were trying to destroy me, and I had a right to anything that I could get hold of." Pierrepont related this to Grant, who
"treated it as he frequently treats things, with entire silence." When
the cabinet dissuaded him from testifying in person on Babcock's
behalf, Grant protested that the trial "was aimed at himself, & that
they were putting him on trial; that he was as confident as he lived
of Babcocks innocence, referred to his long association with him, the
entire confidence he had in him, and that he knew he was not guilty."
Grant's deposition in Babcock's defense helped win acquittal. Nonetheless, Grant soon replaced Babcock as private secretary with his
son, Ulysses, Jr.

The Treasury Department directed the Whiskey Ring prosecutions, and Grant turned on Secretary of the Treasury Benjamin H.
Bristow, believing that he "had become possessed with the idea of the
complicity of the President, and was using his office for the purpose
of annoying him." Grant also distrusted Bristow's presidential ambitions. When Republicans nominated Rutherford B. Hayes in June,
Bristow resigned, but hard feelings lingered. Called to testify about
the Whiskey Ring before Congress, Bristow invoked executive privilege, as the cabinet had previously agreed. Grant now took offense,
and publicly relieved Bristow "from all obligation of secrecy on this
subject; and desire not only that you may answer all questions asked
relating to it, but wish that all the members of my Cabinet" would do
likewise. Months later, Grant told Secretary of State Hamilton Fish
that "Bristows nature was one of intense selfishness and ambition
and of extreme jealousy and suspicion and that from the time he entered the Cabinet he had set his eye on the Presidency with a distrust
and hostility to himself . . . He said he should not attempt to influence
Hayes but he Should be extremely sorry were he to offer Bristow an
appointment which he thought was what Bristow was seeking."

Grant faced a major new scandal in March. Secretary of War
William W. Belknap resigned abruptly, hours ahead of impeachment
for taking bribes from post traders. By accepting the resignation,
"with great regret," Grant appeared to shield Belknap. The House
of Representatives voted to impeach anyway. Grant told the cabinet
that he had "been unable to comprehend its magnitude & importance

the surprise was so great, that it was really not until evening that he could realize the crime, and its gravity." He had acted, he said, "under the wrong impression, . . . he did not know that acceptance was not a matter of course." The Senate acquitted Belknap because he had resigned, thus vindicating Grant's critics. An investigation of the post trader system that uncovered influence peddling by the president's brother Orvil L. Grant provided more ammunition for the administration's detractors.

Belknap's interim successor, Secretary of the Navy George M. Robeson, was himself under investigation for corruption in the Navy Department. Grant promptly chose Alphonso Taft, a Cincinnati lawyer, as the new secretary of war. Taft soon brought General William T. Sherman and his army headquarters back to the capital from St. Louis, where Sherman had gone to avoid Belknap and other politicians. Another scandal prompted a larger government shuffle. Robert C. Schenck, who held the country's premier diplomatic post as minister to England, had targeted British investors in the notorious Emma Mine swindle. After a lengthy search, Grant settled on Pierrepont to replace Schenck. Taft took Pierrepont's seat as attorney general, and James D. Cameron, son of the powerful Pennsylvania senator, replaced Taft as secretary of war. Later, Grant picked U.S. Senator Lot M. Morrill of Maine to replace Bristow at the Treasury. Finally, Grant removed meddlesome Postmaster General Marshall Jewell in favor of James N. Tyner, next in line at the post office. By summer's end, only Fish and Robeson had served more than a year at their posts.

In an election year, the Democratic House of Representatives voted in April to reduce the president's salary. Grant vetoed the bill. "I do not believe the citizens of this republic desire their public servants to serve them without a fair compensation for their services. Twenty-five thousand dollars does not defray the expenses of the Executive for one year, or has not in my experience." Asked to account for his frequent absences from the capital, Grant responded that what Congress "may require as a right in its demand upon the Executive for information, is limited to what is necessary for the proper discharge of its powers of legislation or of impeachment."

When a committee sought to investigate a United States marshal in Texas, Grant refused to recognize its authority "to call to account either for grounds of apt. or retention in office of this official."

Grant's temper flared as budget negotiations grew heated. He refused to leave the capital for Fourth of July festivities in Philadelphia, partly to protest a protocol blunder at the opening in May, but also to make the point that Congress had not yet agreed to a budget. Grant drew a sharp line between legislative and executive branches, forbidding even the transmission of routine information, and reacted angrily to a breach. "This action is in direct violation of my orders to the heads of departments, was extra officious, and shows plainly that this office[r] was in communication with some one of the Committee . . . I will be obliged if you will dismiss Mr. Jones, by my order, from this date." Unwilling to veto a necessary appropriations bill, Grant still deemed "it a duty to show where the responsibility belongs for whatever embarrassments may arise in the execution of the trust confided to me." Battling over a public works bill, Grant wrote: "Without enumerating, many appropriations are made for work of purely a private or local interest, in no sense national—I cannot give my sanction to these and will take care that during my term of office, no public money shall be expended upon them." Even a minor bill to pave Pennsylvania Avenue provoked a veto. "Experience shows that where contractors have unlimited time to complete any given work they consult their own convenience and not the public good."

Amid upheaval and struggle, Grant welcomed the nomination of his successor, telling serenaders outside the White House: "I know Governor Hayes personally, and I can surrender with unfeigned pleasure my present position to him, as I believe I shall do on the 5th of March, next year, with a guaranteed security for your rights and liberties under the laws of the land." Grant was more diplomatic about Hayes's stated intention to serve only one term. "I am not aware of any feeling personal to myself on account of your allusion to your determination not to be a candidate, under any circumstances, for a second term. Whether it was wise to allude to the subject in a letter of acceptance is a question about which people might differ. But in this you have largely the advantage of your competitor. You say distinctly what course you will take, without condemning what the people have done on seven distinct occasions—re-elect the incumbent."

Hayes's election depended largely on Grant's ability to protect Republican voters in the South. That July, in Hamburg, South Carolina, whites summarily executed members of a black militia. Petitioners wrote "to tell you that our people are being shot down like dogs, and no matter what democrats may say; unless you help us our folks will not dare go to the polls." Grant deplored the "barbarous massacre of innocent men . . . as cruel, bloodthirsty, wanton, unprovoked, and as uncalled for as it was." Expanding on the theme, he singled out Mississippi, "governed to day by officials chosen through fraud and violence, such as would scarcely be accredited to savages, much less to a civilized and christian people." Grant warned that "Too long denial of guaranteed rights is sure to lead to revolution, bloody revolution, where suffering must fall upon the guilty as well as the innocent." Speaking to blacks, Grant vowed that "to the extent of the power vested in him, it was his purpose to see that every man of every race and condition should have the privilege of voting his sentiments without violation or intimidation. When this was secured we would then, and only then, deserve to be called a free Republic." As the election approached, a black man in Georgia wrote to ask "if there is any part of the Goverment that we could emigrate to or Colonise or where we could have equal justice . . . we are Willing to do what you think is best and where is the best place that we Could emigrate to or be Colonnised." In October—very late in the campaign—Grant issued a proclamation to disperse the South Carolina rifle clubs, "who ride up and down by day and night in arms, murdering some peaceable citizens and intimidating others, which combinations, though forbidden by the laws of the State, cannot be controlled or suppressed by the ordinary course of justice." An overstretched army left Grant with limited means to enforce his words.

In May, amid growing tension over white incursions into the Black Hills, Lieutenant General Philip H. Sheridan had written to Sherman: "We might just as well settle the Sioux matter now; it will

be better for all concerned." In June, the Sioux destroyed Lieutenant
Colonel George A. Custer's veteran command at the Little Big Horn.
Grant later called the massacre "a sacrifice of troops, brought on
by Custer himself, that was wholly unnecessary—wholly unnecessary." He proposed a modest increase in the current cavalry force to
help subdue the Sioux and resisted a clamor for volunteers. "I would
not order out any volunteers unless, in my opinion, based upon reports from the scene of war, I deemed it absolutely necessary, and
then only the smallest number considered sufficient to meet the
emergency."

Grant encouraged new ministers from Costa Rica and Nicaragua to pursue negotiations for an interoceanic canal. Grant's own
interest in this project dated back to his crossing of the isthmus in
1852. He wanted a canal "made free to the use of all powers and built
by the funds of all who may be willing to unite." Great Britain attempted to add new conditions to an existing extradition treaty,
prompting Fish to protest in cabinet. "The President says thats exactly right, we cannot allow another power to put without our assent
its construction on our Treaty, changing it from the interpretation
which both had put upon it for a series of years." Failure to resolve
this issue was partially balanced by the successful extradition from
Spain of Democratic chieftain William M. "Boss" Tweed, who had
been convicted on graft charges before escaping from a New York
City prison.

Grant took steps to prepare his family financially for private life.
In January, he sold stock in an outmoded Chicago horse railroad and
purchased shares in Nevada mining companies. Grant bantered with
his friend and fellow investor Adolph E. Borie. "I am sorry you were
not lucky enough to have purchased Mining stocks a few days later.
But as it is I have no doubt but California will be from $1:25 00 to
$150 00 pr. share before the end of the year, and will be paying divi-
dends of $3 00 pr. share." Grant planned a postpresidential trip based
on future profits. "I shall go to Europe, but I shall have no set programme and go just where I like. When I go to a place I shall stay
there just as long as I like and take my time leisurely." Afterward, "I
suppose I shall settle in Washington. I feel at home there. I feel more
identified with it than any other city."

Grant believed that he had served faithfully as president, an office that he had not sought and always found onerous. He eagerly awaited the time when he would again become an ordinary citizen.

We are indebted to J. Dane Hartgrove and Howard H. Wehmann for assistance in searching the National Archives; to Harriet F. Simon for proofreading; and to Dana McDonald and Robyn Rhoads, graduate students at Southern Illinois University, for research assistance.

Financial support for the period during which this volume was prepared came from Southern Illinois University, the National Endowment for the Humanities, and the National Historical Publications and Records Commission.

JOHN Y. SIMON

July 4, 2004

Editorial Procedure

1. Editorial Insertions

A.   Words or letters in roman type within brackets represent editorial reconstruction of parts of manuscripts torn, mutilated, or illegible.

B.   [. . .] or [— — —] within brackets represent lost material which cannot be reconstructed. The number of dots represents the approximate number of lost letters; dashes represent lost words.

C.   Words in *italic* type within brackets represent material such as dates which were not part of the original manuscript.

D.   Other material crossed out is indicated by ~~cancelled type~~.

E.   Material raised in manuscript, as "4th," has been brought in line, as "4th."

2. Symbols Used to Describe Manuscripts

AD	Autograph Document
ADS	Autograph Document Signed
ADf	Autograph Draft
ADfS	Autograph Draft Signed
AES	Autograph Endorsement Signed
AL	Autograph Letter
ALS	Autograph Letter Signed

ANS	Autograph Note Signed
D	Document
DS	Document Signed
Df	Draft
DfS	Draft Signed
ES	Endorsement Signed
LS	Letter Signed

3. *Military Terms and Abbreviations*

Act.	Acting
Adjt.	Adjutant
AG	Adjutant General
AGO	Adjutant General's Office
Art.	Artillery
Asst.	Assistant
Bvt.	Brevet
Brig.	Brigadier
Capt.	Captain
Cav.	Cavalry
Col.	Colonel
Co.	Company
C.S.A.	Confederate States of America
Dept.	Department
Div.	Division
Gen.	General
Hd. Qrs.	Headquarters
Inf.	Infantry
Lt.	Lieutenant
Maj.	Major
Q. M.	Quartermaster
Regt.	Regiment or regimental
Sgt.	Sergeant
USMA	United States Military Academy, West Point, N.Y.
Vols.	Volunteers

4. Short Titles and Abbreviations

ABPC   *American Book Prices Current* (New York, 1895–)

Badeau   Adam Badeau, *Grant in Peace. From Appomattox to Mount McGregor* (Hartford, Conn., 1887)

CG   *Congressional Globe.* Numbers following represent the Congress, session, and page.

J. G. Cramer   Jesse Grant Cramer, ed., *Letters of Ulysses S. Grant to his Father and his Youngest Sister, 1857–78* (New York and London, 1912)

DAB   *Dictionary of American Biography* (New York, 1928–36)

Foreign Relations *Papers Relating to the Foreign Relations of the United States* (Washington, 1869–)

Garland   Hamlin Garland, *Ulysses S. Grant: His Life and Character* (New York, 1898)

Julia Grant   John Y. Simon, ed., *The Personal Memoirs of Julia Dent Grant* (New York, 1975)

HED   *House Executive Documents*

HMD   *House Miscellaneous Documents*

HRC   *House Reports of Committees.* Numbers following *HED, HMD,* or *HRC* represent the number of the Congress, the session, and the document.

Ill. AG Report J. N. Reece, ed., *Report of the Adjutant General of the State of Illinois* (Springfield, 1900)

Johnson, Papers LeRoy P. Graf and Ralph W. Haskins, eds., *The Papers of Andrew Johnson* (Knoxville, 1967–2000)

Lewis   Lloyd Lewis, *Captain Sam Grant* (Boston, 1950)

Lincoln, Works Roy P. Basler, Marion Dolores Pratt, and Lloyd A. Dunlap, eds., *The Collected Works of Abraham Lincoln* (New Brunswick, 1953–55)

Memoirs   *Personal Memoirs of U. S. Grant* (New York, 1885–86)

Nevins, Fish   Allan Nevins, *Hamilton Fish: The Inner History of the Grant Administration* (New York, 1936)

O.R.   *The War of the Rebellion: A Compilation of the Offi-
                        cial Records of the Union and Confederate Armies*
                        (Washington, 1880–1901)

O.R. (Navy)   *Official Records of the Union and Confederate Navies
                        in the War of the Rebellion* (Washington, 1894–
                        1927). Roman numerals following *O.R.* or *O.R.*
                        (Navy) represent the series and the volume.

PUSG   John Y. Simon, ed., *The Papers of Ulysses S. Grant*
                        (Carbondale and Edwardsville, 1967–)

Richardson   Albert D. Richardson, *A Personal History of
                        Ulysses S. Grant* (Hartford, Conn., 1868)

SED   *Senate Executive Documents*

SMD   *Senate Miscellaneous Documents*

SRC   *Senate Reports of Committees.* Numbers following
                        SED, *SMD*, or *SRC* represent the number of the
                        Congress, the session, and the document.

USGA Newsletter   *Ulysses S. Grant Association Newsletter*

Young   John Russell Young, *Around the World with Gen-
                        eral Grant* (New York, 1879)

5. Location Symbols

CLU   University of California at Los Angeles, Los An-
                        geles, Calif.

CoHi   Colorado State Historical Society, Denver, Colo.

CSmH   Henry E. Huntington Library, San Marino,
                        Calif.

CSt   Stanford University, Stanford, Calif.

CtY   Yale University, New Haven, Conn.

CU-B   Bancroft Library, University of California,
                        Berkeley, Calif.

DLC   Library of Congress, Washington, D.C. Num-
                        bers following DLC-USG represent the series
                        and volume of military records in the USG
                        papers.

DNA	National Archives, Washington, D.C. Additional numbers identify record groups.
IaHA	Iowa State Department of History and Archives, Des Moines, Iowa.
I-ar	Illinois State Archives, Springfield, Ill.
IC	Chicago Public Library, Chicago, Ill.
ICarbS	Southern Illinois University, Carbondale, Ill.
ICHi	Chicago Historical Society, Chicago, Ill.
ICN	Newberry Library, Chicago, Ill.
ICU	University of Chicago, Chicago, Ill.
IHi	Illinois State Historical Library, Springfield, Ill.
In	Indiana State Library, Indianapolis, Ind.
InFtwL	Lincoln National Life Foundation, Fort Wayne, Ind.
InHi	Indiana Historical Society, Indianapolis, Ind.
InNd	University of Notre Dame, Notre Dame, Ind.
InU	Indiana University, Bloomington, Ind.
KHi	Kansas State Historical Society, Topeka, Kan.
MdAN	United States Naval Academy Museum, Annapolis, Md.
MeB	Bowdoin College, Brunswick, Me.
MH	Harvard University, Cambridge, Mass.
MHi	Massachusetts Historical Society, Boston, Mass.
MiD	Detroit Public Library, Detroit, Mich.
MiU-C	William L. Clements Library, University of Michigan, Ann Arbor, Mich.
MoSHi	Missouri Historical Society, St. Louis, Mo.
NHi	New-York Historical Society, New York, N.Y.
NIC	Cornell University, Ithaca, N.Y.
NjP	Princeton University, Princeton, N.J.
NjR	Rutgers University, New Brunswick, N.J.
NN	New York Public Library, New York, N.Y.
NNP	Pierpont Morgan Library, New York, N.Y.
NRU	University of Rochester, Rochester, N.Y.
OClWHi	Western Reserve Historical Society, Cleveland, Ohio.

OFH	Rutherford B. Hayes Library, Fremont, Ohio.
OHi	Ohio Historical Society, Columbus, Ohio.
OrHi	Oregon Historical Society, Portland, Ore.
PCarlA	U.S. Army Military History Institute, Carlisle Barracks, Pa.
PHi	Historical Society of Pennsylvania, Philadelphia, Pa.
PPRF	Rosenbach Foundation, Philadelphia, Pa.
RPB	Brown University, Providence, R.I.
TxHR	Rice University, Houston, Tex.
USG 3	Maj. Gen. Ulysses S. Grant 3rd, Clinton, N.Y.
USMA	United States Military Academy Library, West Point, N.Y.
ViHi	Virginia Historical Society, Richmond, Va.
ViU	University of Virginia, Charlottesville, Va.
WHi	State Historical Society of Wisconsin, Madison, Wis.
Wy-Ar	Wyoming State Archives and Historical Department, Cheyenne, Wyo.
WyU	University of Wyoming, Laramie, Wyo.

Chronology

January 1–October 31, 1876

JAN. 2.   USG sought to sell shares of Chicago railroad stock to pay debts.

JAN. 7.   In a cabinet meeting, USG condemned published reports that falsely connected his brother, Orvil L. Grant, and son, Frederick Dent Grant, to the Whiskey Ring.

JAN. 8.   USG told a rally of Union veterans that he would "find a place for any of your comrades that may be discharged from the Capitol," as the new House of Representatives Democratic majority rewarded supporters with patronage jobs.

JAN. 26.   At USG's urging, Attorney Gen. Edwards Pierrepont discouraged U.S. attorneys from granting immunity for testimony in Whiskey Ring cases.

FEB. 8.   Cabinet members convinced USG not to testify in St. Louis on behalf of his private secretary Orville E. Babcock, an alleged Whiskey Ring conspirator. Instead, on Feb. 12, USG gave a deposition that helped acquit Babcock.

FEB. 14.   USG complained privately that Secretary of the Treasury Benjamin H. Bristow "had become possessed with the idea of the complicity of the President" in the Whiskey Ring.

FEB. 16.   USG signed a bill appropriating $1,500,000 to complete Centennial buildings in Philadelphia.

FEB. 27.   USG received evidence implicating Babcock in the 1869 "Black Friday" gold scandal.

FEB. 28.   USG urged Congress to fund emergency provisions for the Red Cloud Agency, declaring that delay "will cause great distress and be likely to provoke raids on white settlements, and possibly lead to a general outbreak of hostilities."

MAR. 2.   Secretary of War William W. Belknap resigned to avoid impeachment over alleged payments from post traders.

MAR. 3.   Displacing Babcock, USG appointed Ulysses S. Grant, Jr., as his private secretary, "some one whom he could absolutely trust to open letters."

MAR. 6.   USG learned of possible frauds involving Secretary of the Navy George M. Robeson.

MAR. 7.   USG nominated Alphonso Taft to replace Belknap. USG told the cabinet that he believed in Belknap's innocence.

MAR. 9.   Orvil Grant testified before a congressional committee on his role in distributing post-traderships.

MAR. 9.   USG ordered the military to suppress border incursions along the Rio Grande in Tex.

MAR. 17.   Troops under Brig. Gen. George Crook attacked Crazy Horse's camp on the Little Powder River, Montana Territory.

MAR. 21.   USG said that a future interoceanic canal should be neutral, "made free to the use of all powers and built by the funds of all who may be willing to unite."

MAR. 27.   In *United States* v. *Cruikshank*, the Supreme Court weakened civil rights enforcement in a case stemming from an 1873 massacre of blacks in Colfax, La.

APRIL 3.   The House of Representatives voted five articles of impeachment against Belknap. The Senate later acquitted him on all charges.

APRIL 6.   USG issued orders reestablishing army hd. qrs. at Washington, D.C., and clarifying the chain of command.

APRIL 14.   USG unveiled the Freedmen's Memorial Monument to Abraham Lincoln in Washington, D.C.

APRIL 18.   USG vetoed a bill to reduce the president's salary from $50,000 to $25,000.

APRIL 22.   USG inspected Centennial facilities in Philadelphia.

APRIL 28.   USG relieved Lt. Col. George A. Custer from command of an upcoming expedition against the Sioux, but later allowed him to join under Brig. Gen. Alfred H. Terry.

MAY 4.   In answer to a congressional resolution, USG defended his absences from the capital.

MAY 10.   USG opened the Centennial Exhibition and toured exhibits with Emperor Pedro II of Brazil.

MAY 21.   USG's grandson Grant Sartoris died in England.

MAY 22.   Reshaping his cabinet, USG nominated Pierrepont as minister to Great Britain, Taft to succeed Pierrepont, and James D. Cameron to replace Taft.

MAY 25.   USG urged Americans to prepare local histories as part of Centennial observances.

MAY 25.   USG ordered limited protection for miners and others trespassing in the Black Hills.

JUNE 6.   USG encouraged Sunday school children to "Hold fast to the Bible as the sheet-anchor of your liberties."

JUNE 7.   USG's granddaughter Julia Grant was born at the White House.

JUNE 9.   USG attended the consecration of Adas Israel synagogue in Washington, D.C.

JUNE 14.   USG postponed efforts to change a treaty governing Chinese immigration.

JUNE 15.   At the College of Notre Dame of Maryland in Baltimore, USG conferred diplomas on graduates, including niece Bessie Sharp.

JUNE 16.   At Cincinnati, Republicans nominated Governor Rutherford B. Hayes of Ohio for president.

JUNE 17.   Crook's troops battled Sioux and Cheyenne along Rosebud Creek, Montana Territory.

JUNE 17.   USG urged Congress to pass stalled appropriations bills.

JUNE 21.   USG nominated Lot M. Morrill as secretary of the treasury to replace Bristow, who had resigned on June 17.

JUNE 23–25.   USG, Julia Dent Grant, and Gen. William T. Sherman spent the weekend in Harrisburg, Pa., as guests of Cameron.

JUNE 25.   Sioux and Cheyenne overwhelmed Custer's command at the Little Big Horn River, Montana Territory. News reached the capital on July 6.

JUNE 26.   USG asked the nation to observe the Fourth of July with "some public religious and devout thanksgiving."

JUNE 29.   At St. Louis, Democrats nominated Governor Samuel J. Tilden of N.Y. for president.

JUNE 30.   USG signed the first of several bills extending appropriations for ten days to meet expenditures.

JULY 4.   A bill to open homestead lands for public sale in five southern states became law without USG's signature.

JULY 8.   In Hamburg, S.C., whites attacked a black militia co. and summarily executed five. On July 26, USG condemned the "barbarous massacre of innocent men."

JULY 11.   USG nominated James N. Tyner as postmaster gen. in place of Marshall Jewell, who resigned because USG "could stand his annoyance no longer."

JULY 12.   USG released Bristow "from all obligation of secrecy" after he had cited executive privilege before a committee investigating whiskey frauds.

JULY 14–17.   USG visited the Deer Park Hotel in western Md., a resort operated by the Baltimore and Ohio Railroad.

AUG. 1.   Colo. became the thirty-eighth state.

AUG. 2.   USG approved $200,000 over four years to construct the Washington Monument.

AUG. 14.   USG signed a bill to improve rivers and harbors but told Congress: "Under no circumstances will I allow expenditures upon works not clearly National."

AUG. 19.   USG and family left the White House for Long Branch.

SEPT. 1.   In an interview, USG blamed Custer for the "sacrifice of troops" at Little Big Horn.

SEPT. 9.   Troops attacked a Sioux camp at Slim Buttes, Dakota Territory.

SEPT. 20–23.   USG and Julia Grant visited Philadelphia friends and toured the Centennial grounds.

SEPT. 26–28.   In Ithaca, N.Y., USG and Julia Grant visited their son Jesse, a junior at Cornell University.

SEPT. 30.   USG greeted a black marching club in Washington, Pa.

OCT. 6.   USG and Julia Grant returned to the White House.

OCT. 7.   USG ordered that William M. "Boss" Tweed, recaptured in Spain after escaping from a New York City jail, be delivered to N.Y. authorities.

OCT. 12.   In New York City, USG told Secretary of State Hamilton Fish he had "great confidence" in Hayes's election.

OCT. 17.   Citing diplomatic protocol, USG refused to accept a Centennial address carried by Irish nationalists Charles Stewart Parnell and John O'Connor Power.

OCT. 17.   USG ordered S.C. "rifle clubs"—armed whites organized to intimidate blacks—to disperse within three days.

OCT. 18.   USG spoke at an Army of the Tennessee reunion in Washington, D.C., where a statue of James B. McPherson was unveiled.

OCT. 31.   USG welcomed the Nicaraguan minister, who spoke of his country's desire to expedite canal treaty talks.

The Papers of Ulysses S. Grant
January 1–October 31, 1876

To J. Russell Jones

Jan.y 2d /76

DEAR JONES:

Seeing no chance of extinguishing my private indebtedness during my term of office without the sale of property of some discrip-
tion, and having nothing els apparently available at this time as my
Chicago horse-rail-road stock, I have determined to dispose of ~~that~~
it if it will bring a fair price. May I ask you what it will bring at this
time? If as much $150 you may dispose of my 277 shares and tele-
graph me and it will be expressed at once already transfered. This
will releave me almost entirely and leave me with an income that will
enable me to live in Galena until some of my real estate becomes
available.

I have no special news to write, but you will no doubt receive
abundence of it as soon as Congress assembles.

Yours Truly

U. S. GRANT

ALS, IHi. In 1864, USG invested in the Chicago West Division Railway Co., J. Russell
Jones, president. See *PUSG*, 9, 406, 409, 496; *ibid.*, 16, 136–37; *ibid.*, 19, 110; *ibid.*, 25, 265;
letter to J. Russell Jones, Feb. 22, 1876; George R. Jones, *Joseph Russell Jones* (Chicago,
1964), pp. 36–37.

To Emperor of China

TO HIS MAJESTY THE EMPEROR OF CHINA.

GREAT AND GOOD FRIEND:

I have made choice of George F. Seward, Esquire, one of our distinguished citizens to reside near Your Majesty in the quality of

Envoy Extraordinary and Minister Plenipotentiary of the United States of America.

He is well informed of the relative interests of the two countries [1] and of our sincere desire to cultivate and strengthen the friendship and good correspondence between us and from a knowledge of his fidelity, probity and good conduct I have entire confidence that he will render himself acceptable to Your Majesty. I therefore request Your Majesty to receive him favorably and to give full credence to whatever he shall say on the part of the United States and most of all when he shall assure your Majesty of their friendship and good wishes for your prosperity.

And I pray God to have Your Majesty always in His safe and holy keeping.

Your Good Friend,
U. S. GRANT.

WASHINGTON, JANUARY 10, 1876

Copy, DNA, RG 84, Despatches, China. On Dec. 23, 1861, President Abraham Lincoln nominated George F. Seward (Secretary of State William H. Seward's nephew) as consul, Shanghai, a post later reclassified as consul gen. On Nov. 26, 1875, Secretary of State Hamilton Fish recorded in his diary a discussion with USG held while riding to Vice President Henry Wilson's funeral. "I mentioned to the President the death of Mr Avery our Minister to China and suggested the appointment of Mr Geo F. Seward stating that the revision of the treaties will soon take place and Mr Seward understood the question of our interests and relations with China better than any other man; that he was a man of ability and had been a faithful officer The President replied with great promptness—I do not think I will appoint Seward, he is not much of a Republican and I do not like any of the family I remarked, I suggested the name in public interest, that although I had no special reason for being fond of Gov Sewards family I should still think this the best appointment that could be made. I then dropped the subject." DLC-Hamilton Fish. On Dec. 3, U.S. Senator Aaron A. Sargent of Calif. telegraphed to Fish. "Please send to me by mail letter of Avery I left this morning. I spoke to President about Seward. He seemed doubtful. If Seward is not to be appointed which I desire to be done I wish to be heard again before final action. China is now only California mission. I Consider Seward substantially a Californian." Copy, DNA, RG 59, Letters of Application and Recommendation. On Dec. 7, "Merchants of New York and Boston" petitioned USG "to suggest Mr George F. Seward, our present Consul General in China, as a person eminently fitted by his character, abilities, and long experience in Chinese affairs, to represent our Country in Peking." DS, *ibid.* Illness delayed Seward's assumption of duties as minister to China in place of Benjamin P. Avery. See *PUSG,* 24, 382–83; *HMD,* 45-2-31, part 2, pp. 550–57. On March 21, 1876, Fish wrote to USG exonerating Seward from allegations that he had sold the right to fly the American flag to Chinese vessels. Copy, DNA, RG 59, Reports to the President and Congress. See *PUSG,* 19, 524; *HRC,* 45-3-141.

On Dec. 2, 1875, Joaquin Miller, New York City, had written to USG. "I learn that Mr. Avery, U S Minister to China is dead. I suppose the vacancy will be filled from the Pacific Coast. I desire that place. I have in mind a great work and want to retire from the world and begin it. I can never work while compelled to write things to *sell*, and to LECTURE, and the like for a living. I ask for this place with some confidence. I think I deserve it. I shall not complain however if I do not get it but shall go on bravely in the battle, proud and independent, as I have lived. I shall make no further effort for the place than this. I shall not write to any of the Senators or ask any one to speak for me. But let me assure you Mr President, when I want a place bad enough to ask for it *I realy want it*; besides I think the Pacific Coast would be proud and pleased to have me get this place." ALS, DNA, RG 59, Applications and Recommendations, Hayes-Arthur. Related papers are *ibid.*

On Dec. 3, Frederick MacCrellish, *Alta California*, San Francisco, wrote to USG. "Please allow me to suggest name of Govr Romualdo Pacheco present Governor California [as Minister to China] his term expires Dec sixth he is a native born Californian educated and accomplished his appointment would be gratifying to our peope and tend to harmonize the Republican and Independent parties Begging pardon for this intrusion . . ." Telegram received, DLC-USG, IB. On Dec. 7, Maj. Gen. John M. Schofield, San Francisco, wrote to USG. "The friends of Governor Pacheco, whose term has just expired, propose to submit his name for the vacant Chinese Mission, and ask me to join in recommending him for that place. I have enjoyed the most pleasant personal and official relations with the Governor during his term of office, have found him an accomplished, dignified and courtly gentleman, quite of the diplomatic cast of character, and have no doubt he would represent the United States at the Chinese Court in an entirely satisfactory manner." ALS, DNA, RG 59, Letters of Application and Recommendation.

On Dec. 3, John A. Dix, New York City, had written to USG. "Private. . . . I observe that Mr. Avery, our Minister to China, is dead. My son-in-law, Thomas Walsh, who addressed a letter to you, afterwards printed by Congress, on Japanese affairs, was sixteen years in China and is thoroughly acquainted with its condition & with our relations to that important Empire. I doubt whether a fitter person could be found for the post of Minister. He is about 45 years of age, and a man of great intelligence, extensive information and untiring industry. It would gratify me very much if you could find it consistent with the public interests to give him the appointment, and I am confident he would do credit to your administration." ALS, *ibid.* See *PUSG,* 21, 311–17.

On Jan. 14, 1876, Fish recorded in his diary. "I show the President a letter from T B. Swann of Charleston West Virginia stating he had telegraphed to the President asking the Mission to China and me to ascertain whether he had received it. He says it was received and desires me to answer and say that it was received after the filling of the vacancy was determined" DLC-Hamilton Fish. See *PUSG,* 24, 318–19.

1. On April 17, Columbus Delano, Mount Vernon, Ohio, wrote to USG. "I take the liberty of sending to you herewith, a letter from J. H. C. Bonté of Sacramento Cal. in regard to the Chinese population in that State Mr Bonté is an Episcopalian Clergyman. He is a man of education and culture and feels a deep interest, an no small anxiety in regard to the subject of his letter I had considerable conversation with him on this subject during my late visit to Cal While I do not feel at liberty to offer either suggestions, or advise in regard to the matter referreed to by Mr Bonté I nevertheless deem it advisable to forward his letter for your information With sincere friendship and high regard . . ." ALS, DNA, RG 59, Miscellaneous Letters. On April 3, John H. C. Bonté, Sacramento, had written to Delano of fears that anti-immigrant sentiment might lead to the "wholesale

slaughter" of Chinese in Calif., and suggested that USG address the problem in a message. ALS, *ibid.* On May 5, Fish discussed Bonté's letter with USG, who "did not think it required any action on his part." Fish diary, DLC-Hamilton Fish. See *New York Times*, April 5, 10, 1876.

On April 24, T. N. Stone, Elko, Nev., had written to USG. "Inclosed I hand you a copy of the Preamble and Resolutions adopted at a Mass meeting of the citizens of Elko, which are in perfect harmony and unison with the sentiment of the entire coast—" ALS, DNA, RG 59, Miscellaneous Letters. "*Whereas* The present unobstructed and free emigration from the Chinese Empire has brought to our shores during the past twelve or fourteen years over 200.000 of degraded Pagans, which number is being daily increased by fresh arrivals of these aliens and enemies to civilization, whose manners, customs, filthy habits and semicivilization are at variance with our onward progress and prosperity—to free government and free institutions founded upon inteligence, patriotism, and mutual moral responsibility. That in a sanitary point of view, they are dangerous propagators of disease and their dens are but the nurseries of fearful and fatal epedemics, that the presence of these people in large numbers is calculated to degrade all kinds of industrial occupations, drive white labor from the market, multiply idlers and paupers, demoralize society, and corrupt our people, therefore be it *Resolved*, That we the citizens of Elko County, State of Nevada, in Mass Meeting assembled, without distinction of party, do *hereby* enter our solemn protest against the further importation or immigration of Chinese or Coolie labor, as the same is detrimental to the commercial, Mechanical and laboring interests of our Country, and we hold that the educated and well paid laborer is necessary to the general prosperity of our country as well as to the maintenance and support of the Government. And that we are in favor of such National Legislation upon this subject by the Congress of the United States, and the treaty making power thereof as will give ample protection to the great interest above referred to from the hordes of Asiatics that are now crowding to our shores . . ." DS (adopted April 17), *ibid.*

At about this time, Lee Ming How, president, Sam Yup Co., and six others, "Representative Chinamen in America," petitioned USG. "In the absence of any Consular representative, we, the undersigned, in the name and in behalf of the Chinese people now in America, would most respectfully present for your consideration the following statements regarding the subject of Chinese immigration to this country: I. We understand that it has always been the settled policy of your Honorable Government to welcome immigration to your shores from all countries, without let or hindrance. The Chinese are not the only people who have crossed the ocean to seek a residence in this land. II. The Treaty of Amity and Peace between the United States and China makes special mention of the rights and privileges of Americans in China, and also of the rights and privileges of Chinese in America. III. American steamers, subsidized by your Honorable Government, have visited the ports of China, and invited our people to come to this country to find employment and improve their condition. Our people have been coming to this country for the last twenty-five years, but up to the present time there are only 150,000 Chinese in all these United States, 60,000 of whom are in California, and 30,000 in the city of San Francisco. IV. Our people in this country, for the most part, have been peaceable, law abiding, and industrious. They performed the largest part of the unskilled labor in the construction of the Central Pacific Railroad, and also of all other railroads on this Coast. They have found useful and remunerative employment in all the manufacturing establishments of this Coast, in agricultural pursuits, and in family service. While benefiting themselves with the honest reward of their daily toil, they have given satisfaction to their employers, and have left all the results of their industry to enrich the State. They have not displaced white laborers from these positions, but have simply multiplied the industrial enterprises of the country. V. The Chinese have neither attempted nor desired to interfere with the established order of things in this country, either of politics or religion. They have opened no whiskey saloons, for the purpose of dealing out poison and degrading their fellow men. They have promptly paid their duties, their taxes, their rents, and their debts. VI. It has often occurred, about the time of the State and general elections, that political agitators have stirred up the minds of the people in hostility to the Chinese, but formerly the hostility has usually subsided after the elections were over. VII. At the present time an intense excitement and bitter hostility against the Chinese in this land, and against further Chinese immigration, has been created in the minds of the people, led on by His Honor the Mayor of San Francisco, and his associates in office, and approved by His Excellency the Governor, and other great men of the State. These great men gathered some 20,000 of the people of this city together on the evening of April the fifth, and adopted an address and resolutions against Chinese immigration. They have since appointed three men (one of whom we understand to be the author of the address and resolutions) to carry that address and those resolutions to your Excellency, and to present further objections, if possible, against the immigration of the Chinese to this country. VIII. In that address numerous charges are made against our people, some of which are highly colored and sensational, and others, having no foundation whatever in fact, are only calculated to mislead honest minds and create an unjust prejudice against us. We wish most respectfully to call your attention, and, through you, the attention of Congress, to some of the statements of that remarkable paper, and ask a careful comparison of the statements there made with the facts of the case; and (*a*) it is charged against us that not one virtuous Chinawoman has been brought to this country, and that here we have no wives nor children. The fact is that already a few hundred Chinese families have been brought here. These are all chaste, pure, keepers-at-home, not known on the public street. There are also among us a few hundred, perhaps a thousand, Chinese children, born in America. The reason why so few of our families are brought to this country is, because it is contrary to the custom, and against the inclination of virtuous Chinese women to go so far from home, and because the frequent outbursts of popular indignation against our people have not encouraged us to bring our families with us against their will. Quite a number of Chinese prostitutes have been brought to this country by unprincipled Chinamen, but these, at first, were brought from China at the instigation, and for the gratification of white men. And, even at the present time, it is commonly reported that a part of the proceeds of this villainous traffic goes to enrich a certain class of men belonging to this Honorable nation—a class of men, too, who are under solemn obligation to suppress the whole vile business, and who certainly have it in their power to suppress it, if they so desired. A few years ago our Chinese merchants tried to send these prostitutes back to China, and succeeded in getting a large number on board the out-going steamer; but a certain lawyer of your Honorable nation, (said to be the author and bearer of these resolutions against our people,) in the employ of unprincipled Chinamen, procured a writ of 'habeas corpus,' and brought all those women on shore again, and the Courts decided that they had a right to stay in this country if they so desired. Those women are still here, and the only remedy for this evil and also for the evil of Chinese gambling lies, so far as we can see, in an honest and impartial administration of Municipal Government in all its details, even including the police department. If officers would refuse bribes, then unprincipled Chinamen could no longer purchase immunity from the punishment of their crimes. (*b*) It is charged against us that we have purchased no real estate. The general tone of public sentiment has not been such as to encourage us to invest in real estate, and yet our people have purchased and now own over $800,000 worth of real estate in San Francisco alone. (*c*) It is charged against us that we eat rice, fish, and vegetables. It is true that our diet is slightly different from the people of this Honorable country; our tastes in these matters are not exactly alike and cannot be forced. But is that a sin on our part, of sufficient gravity to be brought before the President and Congress of the United States? (*d*) It is charged that the Chinese are no benefit to this country. Are the railroads built by Chinese labor no benefit to the country? Are the manufacturing establishments, largely worked by Chinese labor, no benefit to this country? Do not the results of the daily toil of a hundred thousand men increase the riches of this country? Is it no benefit to this country that the Chinese annually pay over $2,000,000 duties at the Custom House of San Francisco? Is not the $200,000 annual poll tax paid by the Chinese any benefit? And are not the hundreds of thousands of dollars taxes on personal property, and the Foreign Miner's tax, annually paid to the revenues of this country, any benefit? (*e*) It is charged against us that the 'Six Chinese Companies' have secretly established judicial tribunals, jails and prisons, and secretly exercise judicial authority over the people. This charge has no foundation in fact. These Six Companies were originally organized for the purpose of mutual protection and care of our people coming to and going from this country. The Six Companies do not claim, nor do they exercise any judicial authority whatever, but are the same as any tradesmen or protective and benevolent societies. If it were true that the Six Companies exercise judicial authority over the Chinese people, then why do all the Chinese people still go to American Tribunals to adjust their differences, or to secure the punishment of their criminals? Neither do these Companies import either men or women into this country. (*f*) It is charged that all Chinese laboring men are slaves. This is not true in a single instance. Chinamen labor for bread. They pursue all kinds of industries for a livelihood. Is it so then that every man laboring for his livelihood is a slave? If these men are slaves, then all men laboring for wages are slaves. (*g*) It is charged that the Chinese commerce brings no benefit to American Bankers and Importers. But the fact is that an immense trade is carried on between China and the United States by American merchants, and all the carrying business of both countries, whether by steamers, sailing vessels or railroad, is done by Americans. No China ships are engaged in the carrying traffic between the two countries. Is it a sin to be charged against us that the Chinese merchants are able to conduct their mercantile business on their own capital? And is not the exchange of millions of dollars annually by the Chinese with the banks of this city any benefit to the banks? (*h*) We respectfully ask a careful consideration of all the foregoing statements. The Chinese are not the only people, nor do they bring the only evils that now afflict this country. And since the Chinese people are now here under solemn treaty rights, we hope to be protected according to the terms of this treaty. But, if the Chinese are considered detrimental to the best interests of this country, and if our presence here is offensive to the American people, let there be a modification of existing treaty relations between China and the United States, either probibiting or limiting further Chinese immigration, and, if desirable, requiring also the gradual retirement of the Chinese people, now here, from this country. Such an arrangement, though not without embarrassments to both parties, we believe, would not be altogether unacceptable to the Chinese Government, and, doubtless, it would be very acceptable to a certain class of people in this Honorable country. With sentiments of profound respect," Printed in *The Other Side of the Chinese Question in California: Or a Reply to the Charges Against the Chinese . . . By the Friends of Right, Justice, and Humanity* (n. p., n. d.), pp. 20–24.

On June 6 and 14, Fish recorded in his diary. "I read a letter addressed to me by Alex R. Beeker of Okland Cal May 24th on the subject of Chinese in California describing them as generally industrious and inoffensive and that the hostility to them comes from the Irish who are competing for labor and that the politicans sided with them who had votes against the Chinese who had none. The President says that with the exception of the importation of Chinese women for immoral practices he has no objection to their emigration." "I brought up a resolution of the House of Representatives passed on the 3d April requesting the President to open negotiations with the Chinese Government for the purpose of modifying the provisions of the Treaty between the two countries and refer to the letter of Aexander R. Beeker which I read to the Cabinet I read also a letter of Genl Henry M Naglee dated San José March 31st speaking of the peaceful and industrious character of the Chinese and their valuable labor; also Mr Sewards #34 dated Hong Kong March 22d 1876 on the subject of Chinese emigration, some conversation follows on the subject, but the conclusion reached is that it is inexpedient to take any measure at present for the modification of the Treaty." DLC-Hamilton Fish. See Annual Message, Dec. 7, 1875; Andrew Gyory, *Closing the Gate: Race, Politics, and the Chinese Exclusion Act* (Chapel Hill, 1998), pp. 76–91.

To Thomas P. Shallcross

To THOMAS P. SHALLCROSS.

Whereas, it appears by information in due form by me received, that Charles Worms, charged with the crime of forgery, committed in the State of Pennsylvania, is a fugitive from the justice of the United States, in the Dominion of Canada;—

And whereas, application has been made for the extradition by the British Authorities, of said fugitive in compliance with existing treaty stipulations between the United States of America and Great Britain;

And whereas, information has been received that, in compliance with such application the necessary warrant is ready to be issued by the authorities aforesaid, for the delivery of the above-named fugitive, into the custody of such person or persons as may be duly authorized to receive the said fugitive and bring him back to the United States;

Now, therefore, you are hereby authorized and empowered, in virtue of the treaty aforesaid, and in execution thereof, to receive the said Charles Worms, as aforesaid, and to take and hold him in your custody, and conduct him from such place of delivery in the Dominion of Canada, by the most direct and convenient means of transportation, to and into the United States, there to surrender the said Charles Worms, to the proper authorities of the State of Pennsylvania.

For all which these Presents shall be your sufficient warrant.

In testimony whereof, I have hereunto signed my name and caused the seal of the United States to be affixed.

Done at the City of Washington, this Twentieth day of January, A. D. 1876, and of the Independence of the United States the one hundredth.

U. S. GRANT.

Copy, DNA, RG 59, General Records. On Jan. 29, 1876, Thomas P. Shallcross and another postal agent arrested "Dr. Charles Worms, the Indian contract forger, in Montreal, . . . Worms is a native of Lille, in France, and came to this country in 1861. He enlisted in the Fifty-eighth Regiment, National Guard of this State, and was appointed Commissary Sergeant, and rose to the rank of Lieutenant. In February, 1863, he was appointed Assistant Quartermaster, with the rank of Captain, . . . In October last, Worms appeared in Chicago, and went to board in a hotel kept by Mr. William L. Newman. He speedily gained Mr. Newman's confidence, and informed that gentleman that he could procure him a lucrative contract to furnish supplies and clothing to the Indian Department, from which a large sum could be realized. . . . They went to Philadelphia and put up a second-class hotel. Worms informed Newman that if the contract was awarded him and his partner, John Keller, he must forward, with the signed contract, $5,000 for President Grant. Newman agreed to do so. On the following day Worms sent the hotel boy to the Post Office for a letter addressed to him. The boy came back saying that the Post Office clerk refused to give him the letter, as it was registered. Worms then went to the Post Office and came back with a registered letter, which he opened in presence of Newman, and took from it what purported to be a contract signed by Hon. Zachariah Chandler, and a large envelope addressed 'His Excellency U. S. Grant, President United States.' Worms told Newman to sign the contract, . . . Worms then told Newman to put $5,000 into the envelope for the President. Mr. Newman did so. Worms then asked Newman to get him some sealing wax. The latter left the room to do so and while he was absent Worms substituted for the envelope containing the $5,000 one containing newspaper scraps, addressed to the President, which he had in readiness. This letter was mailed and received at the Executive Mansion on Nov. 22. When opened its contents considerably astonished the President, who read over the newspaper scraps, and wondered who had sent them to him. . . . Mr. Newman went home, and on arriving in Chicago told an intimate friend of the affair. His friend happened to be a man of common sense, and at once said, 'You have been robbed by a swindler. You had better go to Washington with me.' They went to Washington and saw the President and Secretary Chandler. Mr. Chandler at once pronounced his signature a forgery, and the swindle was laid bare. . . ." *New York Times*, Feb. 1, 1876. USG wrote an undated memorandum. "Capt. Chas. Worms, representing himself as Inspector of Indian purchases, induced Mr. Wm L. Newman & John Keller—Chicago—to accept a contract for purchasing goods. Contract—bogus—was handed the latter and they were induced to go to Phila before depositing the $5,000 00 forfeiture. From there it was mailed in a registered letter to U. S. Grant Washington, D. C. Receipt was taken for the letter, ~~in the following words~~. It purports to have reache[d] Washington and to having been receipted for by Thos Dolan, Messenger at the Ex. Mansion Meads Block, Georgetown is a place where Worms took his victim and stated that that was the place where Cowen did his business of letting Indian Contracts." AD, Connecticut Historical Society, Hartford, Conn.

On June 8, Postmaster Gen. Marshall Jewell telegraphed to USG. "I have information from Phila this morning that Worms is Convicted, but not yet sentenced, I am im-
mensely delighted at this, as I feared our Cause was a doubtful one, It has been fought
with great vigor on both sides & the victory is ours," Telegram received, DNA, RG 107,
Telegrams Collected (Bound). See Hamilton Fish diary, Dec. 29, 1875, Feb. 17, 1876,
DLC-Hamilton Fish; *New York Times*, March 6, 1880; P. H. Woodward, *Guarding the Mails;
or, The Secret Service of the Post Office Department* (Hartford, 1876), pp. 385–416.

To House of Representatives

To The House of Representatives.

I transmit to the House of Representatives in answer to their
resolution of the 17th instant a report from the Secretary of State
with accompanying documents.

U. S. Grant.

Washington 21st Jany. 1876

Copies, DNA, RG 59, Reports to the President and Congress; *ibid.*, RG 130, Messages to
Congress. *HED*, 44-1-90. On Jan. 21, 1876, Secretary of State Hamilton Fish wrote to
USG. "The Secretary of State to whom was referred the resolution of the House of Representatives of the 17th January, instant, 'That the President be required to furnish to this
House all correspondence between the government of the United States and Spain in relation to the Island of Cuba, which is not incompatible with the public interest,' has the
honor to lay before the President certain documents and correspondence furnishing the
information called for by said resolution. As correspondence between the government of
the United States and Spain in relation to the Island of Cuba has on several occasions
heretofore been communicated to Congress, as well as that touching particular questions
which have arisen between the United States and Spain in Cuba, the correspondence now
transmitted is limited to the late correspondence upon the subjects referred to in the resolution, and which has not been previously communicated to Congress. . . . Negotiations
are still in progress between the government of Spain and the United States, in reference
to complaints arising from trials of citizens of the United States in violation of treaty provisions, and from the confiscation or embargo of the property of citizens of the United
States in Cuba. For such reason the correspondence on such questions is not transmitted
herewith." Copy (undated), DNA, RG 59, Reports to the President and Congress; *HED*,
44-1-90. See Fish diary, Jan. 17, 1876, DLC-Hamilton Fish. On Jan. 25, USG wrote to the
House of Representatives. "In answer to the Resolution of the House of Representatives
of the twenty second of January, instant, I herewith transmit a report from the Secretary
of State." Copies, DNA, RG 59, Reports to the President and Congress; *ibid.*, RG 130,
Messages to Congress. *HED*, 44-1-100. On the same day, Fish had written to USG "that
no correspondence has taken place during the past year with any European government,
other than Spain, in regard to the island of Cuba. . . ." Copy, DNA, RG 59, Reports to the
President and Congress. *HED*, 44-1-100.

On Oct. 26, 1875, Fish had recorded in his diary. "The President enquires of me the
condition of affairs in Cuba This evidently comes from the inspiration of the Cuban bond-

holders who have been at work at Long Branch and at the Office of the Washington Republican all summer I enter into a general explanation stating among other things what Consul Hall said namely that the Spanish Officers are really at heart sustaining the insurrection as a means of pecuniary advancement; that the Military officers by agreement and secret understanding with the insurgent leaders furnish them with Arms, Munitions, and supplies. The President remarks that he thinks it would be necessary to say something decided in a message to Spain with regard to their Legislature imposing heavy burdens on the property of Americans and high export duties while we consume a larger part of their productions and they take next to nothing from us The following article appeared in the New York Graphic of the same day." DLC-Hamilton Fish. On the same day, a correspondent reported. ". . . The views of the President in regard to the conflict which has so long been urged in Cuba have never been concealed. Not only in his annual messages to Congress and diplomatic correspondence, but also in his private conversation has he indicated his opinion that the Government should not stand aloof and view the contest with passing indifference. He has refrained from official action solely through the influence of the Secretary of State, for there has been no time within the last three years that Congress would not have endorsed his recognition of Cuban belligerency. One year ago the President used very strong language in regard to this subject in the original draft of his message but subsequently, through the representations of the Secretary of State, he was induced to modify it. Latterly the President has become more confirmed in his views that it is neither politic nor just for the United States to remain longer silent. . . ." Clipping, *ibid.* The cabinet discussed Cuban bonds held by the John A. Rawlins estate. Largely through Fish's efforts, USG did not recognize Cuban belligerency or independence. See *PUSG*, 26, 420–21; Fish diary, Oct. 29, Nov. 5, 1875, DLC-Hamilton Fish; Nevins, *Fish*, pp. 874–85.

In Nov., James S. McMurtry, St. Louis, wrote to USG. "An uncompromising third term Republican Desiers the favour of your attention for about five minutes Many Republicans in Missouri as well as myself are for President U S Grant as the Standard Bearer of the Republican Party in the next Presidential Race—for the following (to my mind) conclusive Reasons 1st Because your Excellancy Has made and will make *a model President* . . . 5th *War with* Mexico, or *Spain* for the Posession of *Cuba* (the Latter Being geologically an out flow of the Missippi, the washing By Rain and flood of your farm and my farm ~~other~~ and other mens farms we ought to Have It) is the only Sure Safe and Direct Road out of Present financial *and Political Bankruptcy*—men of all Parties would Hail with Satisfaction the Inauguration of a war that would give Employment and money to thousands out of work as well as to those Engaged in Every useful ocupation at the Same time that It would Enable the farmer and Buisness man—to overcome their Money Dificulties, a foreign war would not only Bring general and Universal Prosperity But would unite the People of all Sections In Heart as well as in name—federal and confederet would strive in friendly competition for the Honour of carrying the old flag—farthest into the Spanish Lines, . . ." ALS, USG 3.

To Chester A. Arthur

———

Jany 22, 1876

Dear Sir:——

Mr J. O. Williams of your office has, I understand suffered from the reduction of salary imposed in common on Custom House employees.

I desire to say with a view to his receiving a promotion when a vacancy shall occur, that while I was General of the Army, he was the Senior clerk at Head Quarters, after that when Gen. Rawlins became Secretary of War, he went with him and served until the death of the Secretary, in the capacity of Private Secretary.

In both of these positions of trust he was faithful reliable, and competent.

Very truly yours
U. S. Grant.

Genl. C. A. Arthur, Col. of Customs, N. Y. City.

Copy, DLC-USG, II, 3. In Sept., 1877, John V. Williams, New York City Customhouse clerk since 1871, received $1,800, the same as his starting salary.

To Adolph E. Borie

———

Jan. 25th /76

My Dear Mr. Borie:

I am sorry you were not lucky enough to have purchased Mining stocks a few days later. But as it is I have no doubt but California will be from $1:25 00 to $150 00 pr. share before the end of the year, and will be paying dividends of $3 00 pr. share. Dr. Linderman [1] is not in the city to consult with. But as soon as he returns from Columbus, where he has gone to examine a building tendered to the govt. for a new mint,[2] I will see him and inform you of the result. I send you a report of the Con. Va for the last year which will give you some idea of the richness of those mines.[3] I hope you will run down again during the winter.

Please present our kindest regards to Mrs. Borie and the family
Yours Truly
U. S. GRANT

ALS, PHi. On Jan. 26, 1876, USG wrote to Adolph E. Borie. "In writing yesterday I forgot to send you a commission to order some Champagne for me, which you were kind enough to offer to do. Will you please order 15 cases qts, 2 pts. for Sec. Fish; 10 qts. & 10 pts for Sec. Bristow, 5 qts & 5 pts for Sec. Belknap, 15 qts & 5 pts for Sec. Robeson, 15 qts & 5 pts for Sec. Chandler, 10 qts for General Sheridan, and 50 qts & 5 pts. for myself. The entire bill for the wine, and duties, with all other charges may be sent to me." ALS (facsimile), Sothebys.com, June 2001. On March 30, Secretary of State Hamilton Fish wrote to USG enclosing a check for $414.16 to pay for his wine. ALS (press), DLC-Hamilton Fish. On April 17, Lt. Gen. Philip H. Sheridan wrote to Culver C. Sniffen. "Enclosed I send you draft for $122 65 in payment for the five boxes of wine which came duly to me. With my thanks to the President for his kind consideration, . . ." Copy (press), DLC-Philip H. Sheridan.

1. Henry R. Linderman practiced medicine in Pa. before serving at the Philadelphia mint as chief clerk (1853–65) and director (1867–69). On Dec. 3, 1873, USG nominated Linderman as the first director of the mint. See *HED*, 43-1-2, 463–83; Linderman, *Money and Legal Tender in the United States* (New York, 1878).

2. On Feb. 3, 1876, USG wrote to the Senate. "In answer to the resolution of the Senate of the 19th of January instant, requesting the examination with a view to ascertaining their suitableness for the purposes of a mint building and grounds situated in Columbus Ohio, known as the 'Capital University' and proposed to be donated to the United States by F. Mitchell of said city—I have the honor to transmit herewith the report of the Director of the Mint, accompanied by a diagram of the building and lot." Copy, DNA, RG 130, Messages to Congress. *SED*, 44-1-23. On Feb. 2, Secretary of the Treasury Benjamin H. Bristow had written to USG transmitting Linderman's report. Copy, DNA, RG 56, Letters Sent to the President. *SED*, 44-1-23. On Feb. 7, William H. Crook wrote to Bristow. "The President directs me to say, that, he will see you & Dr Linderman at any time you may call." ALS, DLC-Benjamin H. Bristow. No action followed.

On Jan. 6, USG had written to the Senate. "In reply to the resolution of the Senate of the 27th of February last, requesting the President to institute inquiries as to the proper place for the establishment of a branch mint at some point in the Western States or in the Mississippi Valley, I transmit herewith the report and accompanying papers of the Director of the Mint, who was charged with the duty of making the inquiries called for by said resolution." Copy, DNA, RG 130, Messages to Congress. *SED*, 44-1-11; *HRC*, 48-1-1549, 12–13. On Jan. 5, Bristow had written to USG transmitting a report from Linderman recommending St. Louis, with related papers. Copy, DNA, RG 56, Letters Sent to the President. *SED*, 44-1-11; *HRC*, 48-1-1549, 2, 13.

3. For the misleading character of the Consolidated Virginia report, published Dec. 31, 1875, see Grant H. Smith, *The History of the Comstock Lode 1850–1920* (Reno, Nev., 1943), pp. 194–95.

To Adolph E. Borie

Jan.y 27th /76

MY DEAR MR. BORIE;

Senator Jones has returned and spent last evening with me—as Chandler & Dr. Norris did once or twice whilst you were here. He gives a very glowing account of Con. Va & California and sustains the judgement of Dr. Linderman & Sheridan in saying the latter is the richer of the two. He says that California will be dividend paying as soon as their works are ready to extract the metal from the ore, probably about Apl. next. At present they are only working around the ore bed, and what metal they get from this is reduced at Mills of other companies, and yiealds more than expenses. By the end of the year he thinks the stock will be worth from $150.00 to $200 00 pr share beside paying nine or ten months dividends,—of not less than $3 00 pr. share—in the mean time. Mrs. Grant & I have taken 500 shares of this at whatever the price may be to-day.

I write this thinking you may be interested in the latest and most reliable news from the scene of your late investment.

My kindest regards to Mrs. Borie.

Yours Truly

U. S. GRANT

ALS, PHi.

On March 7, 1876, Lt. Gen. Philip H. Sheridan, Chicago, twice wrote to USG. "Permit me through the medium of this note, to introduce Col. James G. Fair, one of the owners and the Superintendent of the Consolidated Virginia and California mines. Col. Fair can give you much interesting information of mining interests in Nevada, and their coming influence in the settlement of the financial problem of the country." "I gave to-day to Col. James G. Fair a letter of introduction to you. He wants to see you about the exhibition of the Ten millions of bar silver from the Bonanza mines, at the Centennial. He thinks the importance of the Nevada mines has never been fully appreciated, either in this country or abroad, and if this exhibition could be arranged, that it would not only be of striking importance to the Exposition at Philadelphia, but it might have a great influence in causing the world to more fully appreciate the mineral resources of this country, the development of which has only begun. Hoping, my dear General, that you will further his project, and begging for him kind consideration when he calls, . . ." Copies, DLC-Philip H. Sheridan. See Sheridan to James G. Fair, Jan. 27, 1876, *ibid.*; Oscar Lewis, *Silver Kings: The Lives and Times of Mackay, Fair, Flood, and O'Brien, Lords of the Nevada Comstock Lode* (New York, 1947), pp. 115–215.

On March 10, Secretary of State Hamilton Fish recorded in his diary. "The President states that a proposition has been made by the Virginia Consolidated Company and the California to furnish silver at the rate of about $2.000.000 a month for the purpose of issuing bullion for the taking up of the fractional currency, the parties proposing to take U. S. Bonds at a premium. The President states that he owns 150 shares of the Virginia consolidated and several hundred shares of the California which he had purchased some time since as a permanent investment; that he thinks the stock will advance very much beyond its present price; that he has repeatedly said he would not sell; and the question now arises, in view of this contract, whether he should not divest himself of his interests in the Company Jewell thinks it better for him to do so; Pierrepont talked on both sides, Chandler said he would not, I said I thought it a question for him to decide that probably he would be criticised if he made a contract with a company in which he was a stockholder and especially if, as he expected, the stock should advance in consequence of the contract; that the public would charge that he was making a contract with himself—Bristow concurres." DLC-Hamilton Fish.

To Gen. William T. Sherman

[*Jan. 29, 1876*]

DEAR GENERAL,

Senator Conkling advised me that you had written him a letter giving your recollection of what I had said in relation to your book on our way to the house of Judge Hunt, of Utica, and asking, substantially, for his endorsement of your recollection. I said to the Senator that I did not think that recollections of a conversation should be made a matter of record, particularly when I had reflected so seriously upon one person, but that I would write you my views upon the "Memoirs." I read the book—or commenced the reading—with great prejudice. It was criticised with great severity before I had an opportunity of even seeing the volumes. I read all these criticisms and supposed, as a matter of course, that they were founded upon statements in the book. From another than you, and a few others who I esteemed so highly for their services in the rebellion, I would not have felt badly even if the criticisms had proven just. But from you I did feel agrieved, and started with the intention of writing the severest criticism in my power—not for publication—but to shew to friends. After reading the book however, with these feelings to commence with, I laid it down saying that if I had not read these criticisms I should have none of my own to make, except as your friend.

I do think that if you had subjected the book to friendly criticism before publication—to your brother John for instance—you would have been induced to leave out some things that have subjected you to much harsh feeling and severe—though unjust—criticism. ~~His~~

Historically ~~you are~~ there is no more correct ~~than any other writer upon the war whos books I have read~~ account of that portion of the war treated of by you than is contained in "the Memoirs." I think You make a mistake in trying to prove that Halleck was the author of the march upon Ft. Donaldson. I think also You make ~~another by attempting to prove that you were the author of the plan to march to Savanah~~ a mistake in arguing the question of authorship of the ~~march~~ plan of the march "through Georgia" ~~In a~~All history ~~you would have credit for the latter, as you are entitled, but for this attempt. As~~ would have credited you with it without question, ~~as you are entitled to~~ only dividing with the brave army you commanded. As to the former it was a plain proposition that that the enemy was to be struck where he could be harmed most with the least risk to ourselves. My mind was made up from the time I went to Cairo— before Halleck assumed command of the Dept.—where that point was—Before your Planter's House interview with Halleck I had communicated my views to him both orally and in writing. You state however an actual occurrence. Again: you are unjust to Burnside. It is true that every word you state in regard to hardships endured by your troops in going to his rescue was endured. ~~by~~ It is true that you found the sumptuous repast at Knoxville on your arrival, and the abundanc of supplies for man and beast. But recollect that about sixty hours before your arrival—forty-eight at least—Longstreet knew that your coming was assured; knew that he could not remain in your company; made a final assault without much hope of its success, and departed. The moment he did so supplies poured in from the whole neighborhood of Knoxville. Burnside felt greatful for the relief your coming had given his command and taxed the entire loyal portion of the city to do you honor. He ~~got~~ borrowed plate & knapkins from one house, preserves & various sweet meets from another, and in that way made up his table to do you honor after your fatiguing march. He was exhibitin no show of the abundance of ~~hi~~ supplies previously enjoyed by his command, but it was in honor of you who had opened the way for such supplies to reach his otherwise destitute command. Burnside was really more destitute of the means to keep up ~~res~~ armed resistance to the enemy from scarcity of Ammunition than from scarcity of provisions   So too I think you made a mistake in attributing selfish motives to Blair & Logan for going into the war. You may be wright but who has the right to judge other mens motives? when their actions are right? In your Memoirs you speak highly of their services—deservedly—but wind up with a "fling." at the inducements that actuated them to the course they pursued. Both were members of Congress when the war broke out. Both were democrats at that time—a party that, as a political organization was not then giving much support to the govern~~me~~ment. How much better it would have been to let "History record itself," and said nothing about motives. How still better it would have been to have stated that these two generals were members of Congress when the war broke out; that they left their seats to enter the field in their countries cause, thereby illustratin a ~~general~~ patriotism which was so general that it enabled the government to suppress a rebellion such as the world never witnessed hebefore.

I will repeat that I do not believe a more correct history can be given of the events recorded by you in "The Memoirs." The mistakes, in my judgement, are entirely in speculations. If you are right you have made enemies and critics where there was no necessity for it. If wrong you have done unintentional injustice. It may be too that ~~you~~ many of your deserving subordinates feel that they should have received more attention: but I confess that I should never have thought of this criticism had it not been made by others. These are not all the criticisms that might be made, but they embrace all the classes which, to my mind, the book is fairly subject to.

I have written this very hastily, without any reference to the book except from memory of its contents from reading it in June last. Attention enough has not been paid to these statements to justify authorizing their publication. But if you wish to read this to any friend, in a semi confidential way—a friend who will not state the contents for publication further than the general tone of this letter—I have no objection.

I have written this as a ~~continued~~ friend, and if there is any thing in this letter where you think I am wrong I will be glad to hear it and to correct the impression. I believe on the whole the book does you great credit. I think it would have taken but very little to have made its reception by the public a greater success. That your second addition will correct many of the statements that have called forth unfavorable comments I do not doubt. That it will ultimately receive the commendation which it is justly entitled to I believe.

Very Truly yours
U. S. Grant

Gn. Wm T. Sherman.

ADfS, USG 3; LS (dated Jan. 29, 1876), DLC-William T. Sherman. On Feb. 2, 1876, Gen. William T. Sherman, St. Louis, wrote to USG. "I acknowledge receipt of your letter of Jan 29, and thank you for it cordially. The only reason the allusion to Genl Halleck's claim to originating the thought of the movemt up the Tennessee, was introduced into the Memoirs was because long ago, about the close of the War, I had made the same statemt, which then went unquestioned. I will so alter the language as to make it refer to a belief at that date, but not *now.* I certainly in most emphatic language give you the credit of the execution which was every thing. I certainly did not want to make a fling at Generals Blair and Logan—No allusion is made to their being in Congress at the outbreak of the War—but they did embarrass our movemts much at the Atlanta Campaign—You remember that when I was trying hard to reinforce McPherson at Huntsville with the 16th Corps assembling at Cairo, Gnl Blair was still at Washington in Congress, and I could not be certain that he would Come at all.—So both he and Gnl Logan were away, when Hood took the initiative & forced us to move back to Alatoona & Resacca. I do not wish to reflect on them personally, but on the habit of trying to be both Soldier and Politician in the midst of War and Battle. I did subject the Memoirs to the perusal of a Gentleman usually extremely careful, (not my brother whom I do not wish to compromise), but he failed to detect much that has been severely criticised, because he says it is not there.—Still minds look at words in every possible shade of difference, as you know. As ever your Friend" ALS, USG 3. See next letter; *PUSG,* 26, 327–28.

On June 16, 1875, Henry Van Ness Boynton, *Cincinnati Gazette,* Washington, D. C., had written to Orville E. Babcock, Long Branch, seeking corroboration for his contention "that the campaign to the sea originated with Gen Grant, & was carried out only so far modified as ~~the~~ events made necessary." ALS, USG 3. Related papers are *ibid.* On June 19, Babcock wrote to Boynton. ". . . The fact is Grant and Sherman talked of that march at Cincinnati—though Grant may not have used the words—'March to the Sea'—I know from personal knowledge obtained from Grant in Nashville—before he was made Lieut. Genl. that he expected to move South from Chattanooga and cut through the Confederacy for he told me he wanted some one in command in the East who would co-operate with him when he moved South and asked my opinion of Baldy Smith as such commander. . . ." Copy, *ibid.* On June 28, 29, and 30, Boynton again wrote to Babcock concerning Sherman's *Memoirs.* ALS, ICN. On Dec. 6, Gen. William T. Sherman, St. Louis, wrote to U.S. Senator John Sherman of Ohio asserting that Secretary of War William W. Belknap "put up Boynton to his work. Of course my Memoirs give them ample opportunities, and Genl Grant is too selfish to interpose. At Utica he told me in the presence of Senator

Conkling that he had carefully read the Memoirs and did not find in them any cause for the bitter criticisms that had been brought to his notice. . . ." ALS, DLC-William T. Sherman. On Dec. 10, John Sherman wrote to Gen. Sherman. ". . . Boynton is universally regarded here as a liar and a l[i]beller—of rather better character than Donn Piatt—but far more malicious. It may be that he wrote the book from ill will but far more likely that he wrote for money—& to gratify the ill will of others. . . . I am satisfied that Boyntons book has done you no harm but it has excited remark upon the singular spectacle of the archives of the War Dept. being placed open to the inspection of your avowed enemy—assisted by numberless Clerks & employees of the Government, and all to assail the General of the Army, their chief officer. . . . Grant has to several persons recently spoken strongly and kindly in favor of your Memoirs as fair and just to all. I have heard of this from several persons. . . ." ALS, *ibid.* In 1875, Gen. Sherman wrote to Belknap. "Gen. Grant told me he had read my memoirs with intense interest, and he thought them so correct that he had no corrections to suggest. . . . In time I will make a second edition that will stand," *The Collector*, No. 208, Nov., 1905, p. 6. See H. V. Boynton, *Sherman's Historical Raid. The Memoirs in the Light of the Record. A Review Based Upon Compilations from the Files of the War Office* (Cincinnati, 1875); DNA, RG 94, Letters Received, 3476 1875; Adam Badeau to Babcock, Sept. 30, 1875, NjR.

To Gen. William T. Sherman

Jan. 29th /76

Dear General:

Your letter of more than a week ago requesting one from me, either for publication or to be held as strictly private, as I might elect, was duly received. I have had company every day and night since so to-day is the first opportunity that has presented itself when I could comply with your request. I have read over the note which I had hastily written—in pencil—after my conversation with Senator Conkling—refered to in it—and send you what I then wrote, copied by a Secretary.

It would be impossible for me to do full justice to the subject without again reading the Memoirs which I have not the time to do now.

Very Truly Yours,
U. S. Grant

Gen. W. T. Sherman, U. S. A.

ALS, DLC-William T. Sherman. On Jan. 19, 1876, Gen. William T. Sherman, St. Louis, wrote to USG. "You were kind Enough to say that you were willing to give me in writing the benefit of your Criticism of the Memoirs. I am fully conscious that they are subject to correction & and I propose to correct them, Especially in omitting Expressions that have given offence. Any thing you please to write me shall be regarded absolutely Confidential if you so wish it: but of course I would prefer something that I could use in a Preface, to a New Edition." ALS, MoSHi. See previous letter.

To Edwin D. Morgan

Jany 30th 1876.

DEAR GOVERNOR:

By the death of Genl. Rawlins I was left the guardian of his children, three in number, the oldest now a young man in his twentieth year. He is I believe, a young man of excellent habits and character, writes a good hand and composes well. He is anxious to get employment to fit him for future usefulness, and through his Uncle, H H. Smith, now an employee in the New York Custom House, expresses a desire to get into some good shipping house like that of "Maitland, Phelps & Co. or E. D. Morgan & Co." Not being acquainted with the gentlemen of the former ~~firm~~ house I take the privilege of writing to you. Salary, until he progresses sufficiently to earn it, is not so important as employment to fit him as a business man. He has one third of the income from over $30.000 U. S. 6 pr. ct. bonds and one third of the rent of two houses, one in this city & one in Brooklyn. If you will be kind enough to answer me I will be obliged & if your answer is favorable I will feel as though the young man's future was well provided for.

Very truly yours
U. S. GRANT

HON. E. D. MORGAN
NEW YORK CITY

Copy, DLC-USG, II, 3. On Feb. 14, 1876, USG wrote to Edwin D. Morgan. "This will introduce Jas. B. Rawlins, son of Gen. Rawlins, formerly chief of my Military Staff, and at the time of his death Sec. of War. He is the young man in whos behalf I wrote you recently and to which letter you so kindly replied." ALS (facsimile), Early American History Auctions, Inc., June 10, 2000, no. 81.

On Dec. 5 and 8, 1875, Levi P. Luckey had written to James B. Rawlins, West Point, N. Y. "I trust you will pardon me for writing to you upon the subject that I do, but my great interest in your success must plead my excuse. Your uncle & I are warm friends & he feels the greatest anxiety that you should not quit the Academy, but no more doubtless than I feel certain the President would feel if he knew you had any such thin[g] in contemplation. I know it would disappoint him greatly if you should resign, I am confident you yourself would regret it, & look back upon it as having been all unnecessary. I don't doubt your being all right in Jan. and at any rate if you should fail then you would be far better satisfied to know you had stood up to it than to feel you had shirked it before you did know what the result might be. You will, after you find you have been successful, be glad that your friends encouraged you to keep going ahead. I have seen so many doubt their own ability & get disheartened, & in the end come out better than if they had been too self confident, that I appreciate just how you feel; but at any rate stand square up to the rack & do all you can, & then if you should fail you have nothing for which to take yourself to task, nor can others do it. But should you, as I feel quite confident, succeed, no one would know you had even doubted it yourself—I hope you will accept this advice as [I] most heartily mean it in the best of feeling for your welfare and success." "Your letter is at hand & I am very glad you received my advice so kindly, & that you are determined to go ahead, I don't believe you will fail in January. Peg away & trust to luck." ALS, Stephanie Koppmann, Lake Forest, Ill. On Jan. 12, 1876, William T. Barnard, War Dept., telegraphed to Col. Thomas H. Ruger, superintendent, USMA. "The President accepts resignation of Cadets Rawlins and Sands, at large, which should be tendered you, in writing, *immediately*—Please telegraph me answer—" ALS (telegram sent), DNA, RG 107, Telegrams Collected (Bound). For Rawlins, see *PUSG*, 20, 97–99; *ibid.*, 24, 144–48.

On Jan. 17, USG wrote. "Geo. H. Sands asks to be appointed as his own successor to West Point. If elegible for such apt. it may be given to him" ANS, DNA, RG 94, Correspondence, USMA. On Dec. 9, 1874, Maj. Cyrus B. Comstock, New Orleans, had written to USG. "Mr G. H. Sands aged 18; a son of Admiral B. F. Sands U. S. Navy, is desirous of an appointment as Cadet at the Military Academy. He is of excellent character, a[n]d I believe proficient in his studies. It is not necessary for me to speak to you, to whom they are so well known of his father's services during the war, at sea, & since its close at the Naval Observatory. Should his son's claims be deemed sufficient to secure him an appointment it would give me much pleasure, and I trust a good officer to the service" ALS, *ibid.* Related papers are *ibid.* George H. Sands reentered USMA and graduated in 1880.

On March 30, 1875, Tuesday, Morgan, New York City, had telegraphed to Orville E. Babcock. "Please inform the President that Thursday is agreeable, and also favor us with your company at dinner" Telegram received, DLC-USG, IB. On March 31, "President Grant and wife, Lieut. Col. F. D. Grant and wife, and Mr. and Mrs. Sartoris arrived at the Fifth Avenue Hotel . . ." *New York Times*, April 1, 1875. On the same day, a correspondent reported from Washington, D. C. "John Sherman, Jr., the head of the Washington banking-house of Sherman & Co., left here to-night to join President Grant and party at the Fifth Avenue Hotel, New-York." *Ibid.*

On Oct. 21, 1876, Morgan wrote to USG. "I commend the application of Mr Leland for the appointment of his nephew—Hamilton Wells aged 21 years and son of George Wells of Buffalo—to a second Lieutenancy in the U. S. Army. Such application I understand has the endorsement of Mr Spaulding Mr Rogers and of Bishop Cox—I am told that young Hamilton Wells held the position of Captain in the Volunteer service for two years and that he is in all respects worthy. The Messrs Lelands have always been our political friends and I shall be pleased, other things being equal, to have their request granted—" LS, DNA, RG 94, Applications for Positions in War Dept. Related papers are *ibid.* No appointment followed.

On Nov. 23, Ulysses S. Grant, Jr., wrote to Morgan. "Lieut Dowd cannot be transferred to the Engineers unless he has been recommend for that Corps in his West Point
Diploma. The President is busy with his message, but bids me make the above reply."
ALS, New York State Library, Albany, N. Y. 2nd Lt. Heman Dowd, 3rd Art., had graduated USMA in 1876, second in his class.

To Horace Porter

[*Feb. 5–6, 1876*]

GEN. HORACE PORTER:

Gen Babcock understands perfectly my position and will make it
known to his council on arrival in St. Louis, and ~~and~~ they will then
determine on a course of action.

AN, USG 3. On Feb. 4, 187[6], Horace Porter, New York City, wrote to USG. "Confidential . . . Judge Porter, Babcock's senior counsel, left for St. Louis last night after devoting
four solid weeks to preparing the defence He says he never had a case in his life which
made such an appeal to his heart and in which such gross and outrageous injustice was
attempted. If Babcocks lips were unsealed for five minutes, he feels that the case would be
dismissed in an hour, but by the cruelty of the law in Mo. this is not possible. He fears
from what he learns that the prosecution bases the guilt almost entirely upon alleged as-
sertions that Babcock urged and controlled the appointments and changes of the Convicted Revenue officers and he feels that with your personal testimony on these points *an
honorable acquittal will absolutely follow*, but without this the scoundrels out there may divide the jury which would be most unfortunate. The judge is so earnest and anxious about
your going, in case the prosecution takes this shape, that he begged me to go on and see
you Sunday next, but I am so busy with Rapid Transit affairs that I can ill spare a day Besides I know the goodness of your heart better than most people, and I feel assured that
you would not omit any proper act that could secure justice to as noble a man as Babcock.
The Judge says he will not summon you unless it is of vital importance to the case. My
only fear is lest some unwise friend or covert enemy may be cruel enough to try and dis-
suade you from going. Counsel say they could not use a deposition, for even if accepted by
the Court it is such an unusual thing in a criminal trial that it would be of no avail. I feel
so much in earnest on this subject that I beg that if it is still your intention to obey this
call of one in such distress as Babcock, knowing as you do his absolute innocence, and if
summoned go in person as a witness, to telegraph me on receipt of this the word 'yes.' and
I shall then feel that I shall not neglect a sacred duty to a friend by not going on to Washington to see you in person I have ordered a car to be in readiness any time you notify
our agent in Washington which will take you out comfortably. There is not a person who
ever served with you, nor a member of the Republican party who is not directly interested
in seeing justice done in this trial, and while I know full well your intention as you expressed it me when I last saw you still I cannot help writing to you and asking you to telegraph me 'yes,' when I shall feel assured of Babcock's entire triumph, and you will have the

satisfaction of knowing that you have added one more to the many noble deeds of your life." ALS (misdated 1875), *ibid.*

On Feb. 5, Saturday, a correspondent reported from St. Louis. "Gen. Babcock, George H. Williams, ex-Attorney General; Levi P. Luckey, the President's Private Secretary; and W. O. Avery, arrived here from Washington this morning and took rooms at the Lindell Hotel. Other friends of the accused will arrive to-morrow and for several days to come. Judge Porter, of New-York, of counsel for Gen. Babcock, will probably not reach here till to-morrow or Monday, owing to sickness." *New York Times,* Feb. 6, 1876. On Feb. 8, opening arguments began in the trial of Orville E. Babcock, charged with conspiracy to commit revenue fraud. See *PUSG,* 26, 375–85; Deposition, [*Feb. 12, 1876*].

On Jan. 3 and Feb. 1, David P. Dyer, U.S. attorney, St. Louis, wrote and telegraphed to Attorney Gen. Edwards Pierrepont. "The moment that I get the notes of the testimony taken before the Grand Jury written out I will transmit according to the request contained in your letter of the 30th ult, so much as relates to the case against Gen'l Babcock." "Krum declines to stipulate to waive the presence of the attaches of the mansion in regard to receipt of despatches by general Babcock I therefore order Subpoenas advise the president" ALS and telegram received (at 5:30 P.M.), DNA, RG 60, Letters Received, Mo. See *HMD,* 44-1-186, 42; Dyer to Chester H. Krum (2), Jan. 24, 1876, DNA, RG 118, Letters Sent, U.S. Attorneys, Eastern District, Mo.

On Jan. 7, Secretary of State Hamilton Fish recorded in his diary. "The President referred to an article in the Chicago Times of the 3d and the New-York Herald of the 5th Jany charging that O. L. Grant & Fred D. Grant (brother and son of the President) were implicated in the Whiskey Frauds in St Louis or Chicago, that he wished instructions given to the District Atty to summon the parties publishing these statements before the Grand Jury and requiring them to expose any charges or ground for suspission against either of them and that if there be any ground for the rumor that he thoroughly investigated and proceedings instituted He directs the Attorney General to carry this out to its fullest extent, that if the rumors are true the parties should be prosecuted and if not the authors should be disclosed." DLC-Hamilton Fish. On July 28, Bluford Wilson, former solicitor of the treasury, testified concerning USG. "On the 25th of December he sent for me and confronted me with the charge that it was reported to him that I was trying to have his brother, Orvil Grant, and his son, Col. Fred. D. Grant, indicted for complicity in the frauds; and in the course of the conversation, he again asserted to me his earnest belief in Babcock's innocence and his sense of the great outrage that had been perpetrated on him by Henderson and Dyer in refusing to send to the military court at Chicago the original evidence contained in the records of the civil tribunal at Saint Louis. As illustrating the personal attitude of the President to myself, I may mention that Colonel Grant told the reporter of the New York Herald, in December, that Babcock's indictment was the result of a conspiracy between a prominent Treasury official, naming myself, and Carl Schurz. This I state because the reporter, Mr. Meeker, told me so the same evening, as did also Mr. Nordhoff, because I brought the attention of the President himself to it, and on the 2d day of January the attention of Col. Fred. D. Grant." *HMD,* 44-1-186, 366. On Feb. 10, Wilson had written to USG. "My attention has been called to an article in the 'Inter Ocean' which is said to place me in the attitude of having subörned perjury and of being a deliberate conspirator against your own good name and that of your relatives. I have not seen the article in question, but understand that I am also charged as having pursued Senator Logan and Mr. Farewell by the same methods. As to these two gentlemen I am not called upon to make any explanation further than to say that I have no ill-will towards them personally. I hope, however, that if they have aided or abetted in any way in the commission of frauds upon the revenue at Chicago, they will be caught and punished. In ref-

erence to your relatives, I ask a favor that you will read the enclosed copies of letters written to Col. Matthews, Supervisor of Int. Revenue at Chicago. These copies have been in
Judge Pierrepont's possession as you will see by my pencil endorsement thereon. In addition to what I have said there in, & they embody every reference direct or indirect to the
subject, I desire to add that every allegation in the article as far as reported to me is un-
qualifiedly false, whether it emanates from Mr. Tutton or from whatever source. Before
making up your mind in relation to any statement that reflects upon me, I trust you will
have the kindness to permit me to be heard. I have done no act since I have been in public
office than I am afraid to own, and none which I am sure you will not endorse when you
understand the circumstances and facts leading up to that action. . . . P. S. C. S. Bell was
in this morning with a remarkable story about his connection with Babcock, Luckey and
Avery." Copy, DLC-Benjamin H. Bristow. *HMD*, 44-1-186, 368. See *PUSG*, 26, 284–90.
On Feb. 7, a correspondent had reported from Washington, D. C. ". . . It is given out to-
day that the President remarked casually to Secretary Bristow that the Solicitor of the
Treasury shows a great deal of zeal in circulating statements concerning his family and
friends. A United States Senator the other day repeated to the President a conversation
which he had with a prominent subordinate of Secretary Bristow's, in which the subordinate stated that, when the whole truth about the whisky frauds was known, Orville
Grant, the President's brother, and Colonel Grant, his son, would be smutted as badly
as McDonald or McKee. The President says he has heard enough through talk like this
from Treasury officials, and wanted it either stopped or proven true." *Chicago Inter-Ocean*,
Feb. 8, 1876. See *ibid.*, Feb. 7, 1876.

On March 31, Charles S. Bell, former special agent, Post Office Dept., testified that
USG had given him a card. ". . . I think it ran something like this: 'Hon. Z. Chandler, Secretary of the Interior: I commend to you the bearer, Mr. C. S. Bell, for an appointment;
he has rendered valuable service during the war and since.' I know it covered one full side
of the card and a portion of the other. I handed it to the Secretary of the Interior. . . . I know
that the President and Mr. Luckey both spoke to him personally about appointing me. I
received the appointment January 5. . . . Q. Under that appointment in the Interior Department were you interested in the Babcock case in Saint Louis?—. . . A. No, sir; not under this appointment. . . . I was employed by Mr. Luckey, the private secretary of the President. . . . I was to look into the hands of the district attorney there, Colonel Dyer, and see
what evidence there was against General Babcock. . . . Q. Did you go there and get hold of
it?—A. I did. Q. With the consent of the district attorney?—A. No, sir. . . . Q. Did you furnish what you got to Colonel Luckey?—A. I did; that was in November, at the Lindell Hotel. . . . It was intended that I should be appointed special agent in the Attorney-General's
Office and sent to Saint Louis to continue my work, . . . and I had a card from the President
to Attorney-General Pierrepont similar to the one I had to Secretary Chandler. . . . it said,
'This is the man of whom I spoke for that appointment,' or something to that effect. . . .
That was about the 15th of December, and the Attorney-General delayed the appointment
from day to day, . . . I reported to the President two or three times that the appointment
had not been made, and I finally found out that the Attorney-General was in consultation
with the Treasury officials, and he said that he had ascertained that Mr. Dyer would not
consent to my working in his office any longer. . . . I reported that to the President, and it
was decided that I could not be of any service under the circumstances if I was appointed
in the Attorney-General's Office. . . . Q. When you got that card from the President was it
understood between you and him that the purpose of it was to get you an appointment?. . .
A. The object, as I understood it, was to ascertain whether there was any reasonable
ground for believing General Babcock guilty, and that, if that was so, the President wished
to know it, and if he was innocent and an attempt was being made to make political capi-

tal out of it, or, in other words, to persecute an innocent man, the President wished to know
it; but he trusted in my judgment and I was not report to him but to the Attorney-
General. . . . I had three or four interviews with the President. Up to the time I had my last
interview I was firmly of the belief that Babcock was innocent. When I proved to my satisfaction that he was guilty, from what he desired me to do, and remarks that were made,
and talk with the counsel and himself and myself, I attempted three times to send to the
President, or see him, and failed. . . ." *Ibid.*, pp. 358–60, 362, 364, 367. On April 25 and 26,
Bell again testified. ". . . My understanding was when I got this appointment in the Interior Department that it was not intended that I should do any service as a special penson
agent until the Babcock matter was ended, but was to watch matters and obtain information for him. That was the understanding between General Babcock and myself. Q. Had
the Secretary of the Interior Department any knowledge of that understanding?—A. I
will state this: I mentioned to him several times that the President had spoken to him and
given me a card to him, and I said, 'I suppose you know what duties I have to perform before going to my regular work?' He said, 'Yes.' Said I, 'It is not necessary to enter into details,' and he said, 'No.'. . . Q. What was the understanding you had with General Babcock
as to your duties at Saint Louis?—A. I was to obtain all the evidence that I could; that is
to say, everything that was going on, and report to him so that he would know what their
line would be, . . . Q. Were you to obtain this information with the consent of the district
attorney, or without his knowledge?—A. Without his knowledge. That was the desire. I
would state here that after General Babcock talked with me and admitted that he wanted
the evidence stolen out of the office, I told him I was not prepared to go that far, and I
dropped the case that time, . . . Q. Prior to your dismissal, did you have a conversation with
the President?—A. I did not. I tried to see him and failed. I sent a New York Herald in,
with a copy of the cipher and some printed matter connected with it, that would indicate
to him fully, I thought, who sent it. . . . The President knew that I had been employed by
General Babcock, and Mr. Luckey had talked with him a good deal about it, and I had met
him myself. There are circumstances connected with it that I do not know that I could explain clearly, but I am perfectly satisfied that he would know what it was, and I am more
than satisfied that some one knew what it was, from the fact that I was immediately removed from the service. . . ." *HMD*, 44-1-186, 113–14, 134. Secretary of the Interior
Zachariah Chandler testified that USG had recommended Bell for Interior Dept. agent.
". . . One day General Hurlbut was sitting at the table with me when the card of Mr. Bell
came in. I threw it carelessly on the table and told the waiter to say I was engaged, and
General Hurlbut said: 'Bell, Bell—C. S. Bell? I know that fellow; he was a spy for me; he
enlisted in the rebel army and was promoted to be a sergeant;' and, I think General Hurlbut said, served seven months in the rebel army while he was his paid spy. I said, 'If he
could keep his neck out of the halter as long as that in the rebel army, I think he would
make a good detective, and I will try him for a month;' and on that day, or the next, I gave
him his appointment on trial. . . . Q. What were the causes which induced the dismissal of
Mr. Bell?—A. I went into the Cabinet meeting a little in advance of the others; the President had the name of Mr. Bell upon the table before him, and he asked me if Bell was in
my employment? I said I believed he was. He said he believed him to be a scoundrel, and
that I had better dismiss him, and I went directly from the Cabinet meeting and dismissed
him at once. . . ." *HRC*, 44-1-799, 379. Attorney Gen. Edwards Pierrepont testified concerning his contacts with Bell, and conversation with USG about Bell. *Ibid.*, pp. 383–85.
Luckey testified that he had met Bell in Nov., 1875, at St. Louis, and refused Bell's offer to
remove evidence in the whiskey fraud prosecutions; and that Bell visited the White House
in Dec. ". . . I asked the President to see Bell, and he saw him. . . . Mr. Bell had represented

himself to me as having been a scout for General Grant, and my impression is that he had shown me a small piece of paper signed 'U. S. Grant,' given him during the war to enable him to pass the lines, and I asked the President if he recognized him as such a man, and he said he did. . . ." *Ibid.*, p. 395. Babcock testified that he saw Bell in late Dec. ". . . I remember Mr. Bell telling me this, that it had been a big mistake that the Attorney-General had not given him an appointment to go out to Saint Louis, because if he had gone out there he might have been of a great deal of service to me; but the Attorney-General had consulted, he thought, with the Secretary of the Treasury, and it was all known, and he could not be of any service to me now any way. He came to my house six or eight times. He generally came along about ten or eleven o'clock at night, and he used to tell his story, and tell us how circuitous a route he had to take to get there without being observed by the detectives of the Treasury Department, who, he said, were watching him and me and every one in my interest. . . . I told him, when he came again, that unless he had something positive for me, I thought it would be of no use for him to come there. He again urged on me that he was poor, and that he had got no appointment. . . ." *Ibid.*, p. 398. See *ibid.*, 376–78, 408–12; *HMD*, 44-1-186, 44–45; *New York Herald*, Feb. 10, 16, 1876; Endorsement, May 25, 1875; *PUSG*, 10, 386–87.

Deposition

————

[*Feb. 12, 1876*]

Question. How long have you known General Babcock, and how intimately?

Answer. I have known him since 1863, having first met him during the Vicksburg campaign, in that year. Since March, 1864, I have known him intimately

Q. Please state the various capacities in which he has been employed, and what positions he has held since 1863.

A. From about March, 1864, to 4th March, 1869, he was an Aide-de-Camp on my military staff. Since that time he has been acting as my Private Secretary; and continued in that position until his indictment. He has also, for several years past, been superintendent of Public Buildings and Grounds.

Q. As your Private Secretary, please state what were his general duties.

A. They were to carry to Congress all communications from the President, and to have charge of and supervision over all correspondence—particularly that of an official character. In his capacity as Private Secretary, he received my mails, opened my letters, and referred them to the appropriate Departments, submitting to me all such as required any instructions or answer from myself.

Question.—His relations with you were confidential?

Answer. Very.

Q.—Do you know whether, during the time General Babcock has been your Private Secretary, he has had frequent applications, from persons throughout the country, to lay their special matters before you, or before the various Departments?

Answer. That was of very frequent occurrence; indeed it happened almost daily.

Q. In what manner, so far as you have observed, with reference to the public interests, has General Babcock discharged his duties as your Private Secretary?

Ans. I have always regarded him as a most efficient and most faithful officer.

Q Are you acquainted with the general reputation of General Babcock in the city where he now lives, and in the places where he has lived, among his associates and acquaintances, and in the army and elsewhere, for honesty and integrity?

A. I am acquainted with his reputation in the army and in this city.

Question. Please state what that general reputation is and has been.

Ans. If an intimate association of twelve years with a man gives one an opportunity of judging what others think of him, I have certainly had not only ~~only~~ an excellent opportunity of knowing his character myself, but of learning the general reputation he sustains—

Q. From these opportunities, what has been his reputation.

Ans. Good.

Q. Were you acquainted with C. W. Ford, of St. Louis, in his life time? and what, if any position did he hold at the time of his death?

Ans. I was intimately acquainted with C. W. Ford—first in the State of New York, when I was a Lieutenant in the army, and he a young lawyer residing in the same town where I was stationed,[1] and subsequently, from 1854 to 1860, when we were both living in St. Louis county. He was from 1854 until his death connected with the United States Express Company in St. Louis; and from 1869—though I am not sure of the date—was collector of internal revenue for the first district of Missouri, which position he held when he died.

Q. State, please, what, if any applications, were made at the time of his decease as to the appointment of his successor.

Ans. It is impossible for me to remember all the applications that were made for the place. I do recollect, however, that General Babcock brought to me a despatch, addressed to him by John A Joyce, in which the latter practically applied for the position.

Q What other, if any applications were made as to the appointment of a successor? But first let me inquire if you have the despatch to which you have just made reference?

Ans. I do not know.

Q. Do you know where it is?

Ans. I do not, but presume it could be found. I think it very likely that it is in possession of Genl Babcock's counsel or of the District Attorney.

Question. Were there any requests or communications with regard to the appointment of Mr. Ford's successor from his sureties?

Ans. When Genl Babcock exhibited to me the despatch from Mr Joyce, I said to him that as Mr Ford had died away from home and very suddenly, I would, in the selection of a successor, be to a great extent guided by the recommendation and wishes of his bondsmen. I thought they were at least entitled to be heard respecting the person to be selected, and upon whom would devolve the settlement of the affairs of the office.

Q. What did you decide to do with reference to to the appointment, and to whom, if to any one, did you decide to leave the nomination of Mr Ford's successor?

A. That information is embraced in the answer just given.

Q. Whom did the bondsmen actually recommend?

Ans. Constantine Maguire.

Q. And on their recommendation exclusively he received the appointment?

Ans. I could not say exclusively, because he was well recommended, and was satisfactory to the bondsmen of Mr. Ford.

Q. Did Gen. Babcock ever, in any way, directly or indirectly, urge, or request, or seek to influence the appointment of Mr. Maguire, or did he ever exchange a word with you upon the subject which indicated that he desired his appointment?

A. I do not think he ever did. Nor do I believe that he was aware of the existence of Constantine Maguire prior to his ~~appointment to succeed~~ recommendation as the successor of Mr. Ford.

Q. Did you inform Genl. Babcock that you intended to leave the naming of Mr Ford's successor to his bondsmen? Did you request him so to notify the parties?

A. The question has I think already been answered.

Q. It embraces perhaps this addition: did you request him to notify the parties?

A. I do not remember.

Q. Are the telegrams now shown you the ones received by you in relation to the appointment of Mr. Maguire?

A. I have no doubt that these are the despatches, or copies of the despatches, I received If they are not, despatches similar in tenor were received.

Q. Connected with these telegrams is a letter dated January 4, 1876, from D. D. Pratt, Commissioner.[2] Will you be kind enough to explain how that letter was received by you, and why, and what connexion it has with these telegrams?

A. The communication to which you refer from the Commissioner of Internal Revenue is in answer to a request made in my name to be furnished with the telegrams recommending Mr. Maguire for the office of Collector.

Q. Did General Babcock, so far as you know, ever seek in any way to influence your action with reference to any charges made or proposed to be made against Joyce or McDonald, or either of them?

A. I do not remember of his ever speaking to me upon the subject. ~~except that~~ He took no lively interest in the matter, or I should have recollected it.

Q. Did General Babcock, so far as you know, ever seek in any way to influence your action in reference to any investigation of the alleged whiskey frauds in St. Louis or elsewhere?

A He did not. I will state at this point that I do not remember but one instance where he talked with me on the subject of these investigations, excepting since his indictment. It was then simply to say to me that he had asked Mr. Douglass why it was his Department treated all their officials as though they were dishonest persons, who required to be watched by spies, and why he ~~did~~ could not make inspections similar to those which prevailed in the army, selecting for the purpose men of character, who could enter the distilleries, examine the books, and make reports which could be relied upon as correct. Genl Babcock simply told me that he had said this to Mr Douglass.

q If I understand correctly the answer, Gen. Babcocks conception was that in making the investigation it would be wiser to have it done by men of superior character than by men of inferior and suspicious character.

A Yes Sir.

q Do you remember the circumstance of John McDonald being in the city of Washington on the 7th day of Feby [*Dec.*] 1874?

a I do not remember the particular date. I remember the time in ~~the~~ question.

q Did you ride with him on or about that date or occasion and was anything whatever said by him to you with reference to the investigation of alleged frauds in his district

A. I picked him up on the sidewalk as I was taking a drive and invited him to go with me. I have no recollection of any word or words on any matter touching his official position or business.[3]

q Did Gen. Babcock at or about that time say anything to you with reference to such investigations, and to your knowledge did he in any way undertake to prevent them?

A I have no recollection of his saying anything about that Certainly he did not intercede with me to prevent them.

q Do you recollect the circumstances attending the promulgation of an order transferring the various supervisors from their own to other districts?[4]

A I do.

q State fully with whom the idea upon which that order was based originated and the particular reasons which induced you to direct it to be issued?

A Sometime when Mr. Richardson was Secretary, I think at all events before Secretary Bristow became head of the department Mr. Douglass in talking with me expressed the idea that it would be a good plan occasionally to shift the various Supervisors from one district to another. I expressed myself favorably toward it, but it ~~would~~ was not ~~do~~ done then, nor was it thought of any more by me until it became evident that the Treasury was being defrauded of a portion of the revenue it should receive from the distillation of spirits in the west. Secretary Bristow at that time called on me and made a general statement of his suspicions when I suggest~~ing~~ed to him this idea. On that suggestion the order making these transfers of supervisors was made. At that time I did not understand that there was any suspicion at all of the officials but that each official had his own way of transacting his business. These distillers having so much pecuniary interest in deceiving the officials learn their ways and know how to avoid them   My idea was that by putting new Supervisors acquainted with their duties over them they would run across and detect their crooked ways. This was the view I had and explains the reason why I suggested the change.

q Can you state whether Mr. Douglass at that time Commissioner of Internal Revenue was aware of the fact that you suggested or made the order?

A I do not know that he knew anything about it.

q After the order had been finally issued were any efforts made to induce you to direct its revocation or suspension?

A Yes Sir. Most strenuous efforts.

q Were such efforts made by prominent public men?

a They were.

q Did you resist the pressure which was made upon you for the revocation or suspension of the order, and if you finally decided to direct the revocation of that order, will you please state why you were induced to do so and by whom?

A I resisted all efforts to have the order revoked until I became convinced that it should be revoked or suspended in the interest of detecting frauds that had already been committed. In the conversation with Supervisor Tutton he said to me that if the object of that order was to detect frauds that had already been committed he thought it would not be accomplished. He remarked that this order was to go into effect on the 15th of February This conversation occurred late in January, and he alleged that it would give the distillers who had been defrauding the Treasury nearly three (3) weeks notice to get their houses in order and to be prepared to receive the new supervisors. That he himself would probably go in a district where frauds had been committed and he would find everything ~~going on~~ in good order, and he would be compelled so to report That the order would probably result in stopping the frauds at least for a time but would not lead to the detection of those that had already been committed. He said that if the order was revoked it would be regarded as a triumph by those who had been defrauding the Treasury. It would throw them off their guard and we could send special Agents of the Treasury to the suspected distilleries—Send good men, such a one as he mentioned a Mr. Brooks They could go out, and would not be known to the distillers and before they would be aware of it, the latters frauds would be detected. The proofs would be all complete, the distilleries could be seized and their owners prosecuted.

I was so convinced that his argument was sound, and that it was in the interest of the detection and punishment of fraud that this order should be suspended that I then told him that I would suspend it immediately, and I did so without any further consultation with anybody. My recollection is that I wrote the directions for the suspension of the order on a card in pencil certainly before leaving my office that afternoon and that order was issued and sent to the Treasury signed by one of my secretaries.

q Did Gen Babcock ever in any way directly or indirectly seek to influence your action in reference to that order.

A I do not remember his ever speaking to me about or exhibiting any interest in the matter.

q From anything he ever said or did do you know whether he desired that the order should be revoked or suspended?

A That question I think has been fully answered.

q Has Gen. Babcock so far as you know or any one for him undertaken to prevent any investigation of his alleged connection with wha[t] is known as the whiskey ring at St Louis or elsewhere?

A To my knowledge he has not. Gen. Babcock complained very bitterly of the treatment that he was receiving after the speech made by Mr. Henderson made in the Avery trial was delivered[5]

q Since his Endictment has any effort been made to your knowl-
e[dge] to dismiss the indictment found against him or to enter a
"nolle prosequi" or in any way to interfere with or prevent his trial?
A No.

q Has Gen. Babcock so far as you know ever used any effort with
yourself or anyone else to prevent the finding of indictments against
any person suspected of complicity with the whiskey ring at St. Louis
or elsewhere.

A He has not.

q Since the finding of the St Louis indictments against these persons,
has Gen. Babcock so far as you know ever exhibited any desire to interfere with or prevent their trial or exhibited any ~~such~~ interest or
wish in that direction.

A He has not to my knowledge.

q At the time the Court of Inquiry was ordered at Gen. Babcocks request was it not understood by yourself and so far as you know by
him that no indictments were to be found against him. If so why did
you so understand?

A No indictment had been found against him and I supposed none
would be because I understood from the Attorney General that
the Grand Jury then in session would adjourn in a day or two. That
was the only course then apparently left ~~to me to benefit him~~ for his
vindication.

q Was not that Court called because it was supposed that Gen. Babcock could not in any other way vindicate himself?

A I so understood.

q Was it not called very soon after he was informed that he could not
be heard as a witness in the Avery case.

A It was

q Do you know whether he was anxious to appear as a witness in that
case

A I cannot say any further than his dispatch to the District Attorney
requesting to be heard.

q Do you know whether he dispatched to the District Attorney for
the purpose of being heard as a witness in the case.

a I know it must have been so because I saw the answer he received from the District Attorney.

Q So far as you know what was the substance of the answer of the District Attorney, Mr. Dyer, to the telegram of General Babcock desiring to appear as a witness in the Avery case?

A He in substance informed him that there would be no more criminal prosecutions until sometime, I think, in the following month. I do not remember the date accurately.

Q And I presume his desire could not be complied with?

a It amounted to a statement that his desire could not be complied with.

Q Have you ever seen anything in the conduct of General Babcock, or has he ever said anything to you which indicated to your mind that he was in any way interested in or connected with the whiskey ring at St Louis or elsewhere?

a Never.

Q In what manner as regards the public interests, and as evincing his fidelity and integrity has he performed his duties as your private secretary?

A Always to my entire and full satisfaction.

Q Have you in any form observed or learned of anything in connection with General Babcock's conduct which has tended to diminish your confidence in his fidelity and integrity, and is that confidence in his fidelity and integrity still unimpaired and undiminished.

A I have always had great confidence in his integrity and his efficiency; and as yet my confidence in him is unshaken. I have never learned anything that would shake that confidence. Of course I have heard of this trial that is progressing

Cross-examination.

By MR EATON of counsel for the Government.

Q General, of course you do not suppose, do you, that while General Babcock has been your private Secretary and in intimate and confidential relations with you any one would voluntarily come to you with statements injurious to his reputation?

A I do not know any such thing.

Q Perhaps you are aware, General, that the Whiskey Ring have persistently tried to fix the origin of that ring in the necessity for funds to carry on political campaigns. Did you ever have any intimation from General Babcock, or any one else in any manner, directly or indirectly, that any funds for political purposes were being raised by any improper methods?

A I never did. I have seen since these trials intimations of that sort in the newspapers, but never before.

Q Then let me ask you if the prosecuting officers have not been entirely correct in repelling all insinuations that you ever had tolerated any such means for raising funds?

A I was not aware that they had attempted to repel any insinuations.

Q Speaking of C. W. Ford, I presume, General, that your confidence in him continued up to the time of his death?[6]

A I never had a suspicion that anything was wrong.

Q Did you regard his knowledge of men and affairs in St. Louis as trustworthy?

A I had as much confidence in him that way as any person I knew in St. Louis.

Q When did you cease to reside in St. Louis General?

A In May 1860.

Q From 1860 down to the time of Mr. Ford's death, Mr. Ford's residence was also in St. Louis?

A Yes, sir.

Q Did you have private correspondence with Mr Ford during the time that he was Collector?

A I did.

Q Did you preserve that correspondence?

A No, I never kept a copy of a letter that I sent to him in my life.

Q Did you preserve letters that you received from him?

A No, sir; I did not preserve those. We corresponded regularly, because I had such confidence in him that I left him to conduct my own affairs there, and I had to be constantly sending him money. I would send checks to him of five hundred dollars, one thousand dollars and twelve hundred dollars at a time, and he would pay out the money and account to me for it. My confidence in him was such that I did that without even saving the letters.

Q Do you remember a letter of Mr. Ford to yourself dated May 30, 1870, in which he spoke of McDonald as a bad egg, and ~~his~~ as saying to you that he was a discredit to the administration?[7]

The WITNESS. Was that before or after McDonald's appointment?

Mr EATON. I think it was shortly after. McDonald was appointed very early in that year if I recollect.

A I have no recollection of such a letter. I have an indistinct recollection that when McDonald was first recommended for the position he [Ford] told me either in a letter or in a conversation that McDonald would not do. My recollection is that finally he united with others in recommending McDonald. I have a general knowledge that about the time McDonald was being pressed for the appointment Ford thought it was not a suitable appointment, but my recollection is that ~~the~~ he ~~officers~~ afterwards acquiesced in it and possibly either joined in the recommendation, which was written and will be found on file in the Treasury Department, or else he told me in a conversation.

Q Do you remember whether John A. Joyce was recommended to you as Ford's successor by General Babcock?

A He was not.

Q Was anything said to you by General Babcock between the time of the death of Ford and the appointment of Constantine Maguire touching Joyce's fitness for the place?

A General Babcock presented me a dispatch that he had received from Joyce saying that he was an applicant or making application for it. I do not remember the words of it. The substance of it was that he wanted to be Ford's successor. My reply to him was that I should be guided largely in selecting the successor of Mr. Ford by the recommendations of his bondsmen. He having died suddenly, unexpectedly and away from home I thought they were entitled to be at least consulted as to the successor who should settle up his accounts.

Q Did you advise General Babcock to telegraph to Joyce to get the bondsmen of Ford to recommend Joyce for Collector?

A I made the statement in substance that I have ~~heretofore~~ given in answer to a former question. Whether I told him to so telegraph or not it would be impossible for me to say. That might be regarded as at least authority to so telegraph.

Q Did you see any telegram of that character from Babcock to Joyce at that time?

A I do not remember to have seen any.

Q Did General Babcock at that time show you a dispatch ~~from~~ from Joyce in these words:

"St. Louis, October 28, 1873. See dispatch to the President. We mean it. Mum.

JOYCE"[8]

A I do not think that my memory goes back to that time. Since these prosecutions were commenced I have seen that.

Q I ~~will~~ am asking you in regard to that time

A I do not call it to memory.

Q Did you receive a protest against the appointment of Constantine Maguire signed by James E. Yeatman, Robert Campbell and others?

A I do not remember such a letter. If such a one was received it is no doubt on file in the Treasury Department. Such a protest may have been received.

Q Your purpose ~~of~~ in leaving the nomination of Mr. Ford's successor to his bondsmen was because they were liable on his bond for the administration of his office, was it not?

A Yes, sir; further than that some of them were men that I knew very well and had great confidence in.

Q Speaking of Ford's objection to McDonald were you aware that in the matter of education McDonald when he was appointed was an ignorant man and barely able to write his name?

A I was aware that he was not an educated man, but he was a man that had seen a great deal of the world and of people. I would not call him ignorant exactly. He was illiterate.

Q Did you receive a protest against McDonald's appointment signed by Carl Schurz, G. A. Finkelnburg, R. T Van Horn and other men in Missouri?

A I do not remember. It is a matter of record if it was received. I do not know that it would have had any particular weight with me if I had received it, his endorsements being good.[9]

Q Was not that objection based on the ground of his entire unfitness for the place?

A I do not remember. If it was received it is no doubt a matter of record and can be obtained.

Q Did you ever see the paper now shown you?[10] If so state in whose handwriting it is.

A As to handwriting I do not pretend to be an expert. I have had a great many letters from Mr. Ford. That looks like his signature. I do not remember to have ever seen that before, and I do not think I ever did.

Q Do you know the other signatures to the paper?

A No, I know all the parties, but I don't know their signatures.

Q Did you see, at or about the time of its date, the affidavit now shown you made by James Marr, taken from the files of the Treasury Department, a copy of which, marked "Exhibit No 7", is hereunto annexed.[11]

A If I ever did see that paper it has passed entirely from my memory, and I think it would be impossible that such a document as that could be read by me and I do not remember it.

Q Do you remember at this distance of time on whose recommendation Mr Joyce was appointed?

A My recollection is that when McDonald was appointed Supervisor he asked the Commissioner of Internal Revenue to give him an assistant from his office—some man that was acquainted with the duties. I think that there was no acquaintance existing at all between Joyce and McDonald at that time. That is my recollection. I never had heard of Joyce myself and did not know of the existence of such a man until he was appointed on the recommendation, as I understood, of the then Commissioner, who thought him to be the most capable man in his office.

q Will you please to state whether Gen. Babcock showed you on or about the time of its date a dispatch to him in these words:—

"St. Louis, February 3, 1875. GEN. O. E. BABCOCK, Executive Mansion, Washington, D. C. We have official information that the enemy weakens. Push things. SYLPH."

A I do not remember of ever seeing that dispatch until since these ~~transactions~~ prosecutions have commenced.

q Did you know that Gen. Babcock was at that time in correspondence with Joyce about the transfer of supervisors.

A I knew that he received frequent letters from Joyce, for I saw a number of them myself; and those that I did see were generally as to what he was doing in the way of writing editorials for the different papers, and enclosing editorials which he would say in his letters he had written, and asking how he liked the tone of them, and so on. I recollect of him saying in one letter that some papers in the State of Missouri, and perhaps in Arkansas—at different points, at all events—were willing to publish as editorials, matter that he would write for them.[12]

q Do you remember that Gen. Babcock, prior to May 1875, talked with you about the propriety of sending detectives into the several districts to detect frauds?

A I do not. I remember of his telling me at one time of what he had proposed to Mr. Douglass, but the date of it I do not remember. And that was not a suggestion to me; it was merely telling me what he had suggested to Mr. Douglass; and this is the same that I have before stated.

q Did you have any conversation with Gen. Babcock prior to May 1875 in reference to a letter written by J. J. Brooks to Deputy Commissioner Rogers?[13]

A I do not remember dates; but I remember of his ~~saying~~ showing me a letter that had been handed to him from somebody in Philadelphia to Mr. Rogers; and he said that that appeared to his judgment to be simply blackmailing. And I think that was the occasion when he told me what he had said to Mr. Douglass; that is as I remember now.

q Do you remember when that conversation was?

A No; I do not. My recollection is that he had shown that letter to Mr Douglass before he did to me, and that was the occasion ~~of~~ when he told me of this suggestion.

q Did Gen. Babcock about the time of its date show you a dispatch in these words: "St. Louis, October 25, 1874. GEN. O. E. BABCOCK, Executive Mansion, Washington, D. C. Have you talked with D? Are things right? How? [signed] J."

A I do not remember anything about it.

q Did Gen. Babcock, at or about the time of its date, show you a dispatch in the following words:—"St. Louis, December 3, 1874. GEN. O. E. BABCOCK, Executive Mansion, Washington, D. C. Has Secretary or Commissioner ordered anybody here? [signed] J."

A I do not remember particularly. I know that, as a general rule, when he got dispatches that required an answer he would get from me the answer that he ought to send.

q You have no recollection of that?

A I have no particular recollection of the wording of the dispatch?

q Did Gen. Babcock at or about the time of its date show you a dispatch from himself to John A. Joyce in the following words: "Washington, D. C. December 5. 1874. COL. JOHN A. JOYCE, Care of John McDonald, St. Louis, Mo. Can not hear that any one has gone or is going. [signed,] O. E. BABCOCK."

A I do not remember to have ever seen that dispatch until it was Shown here after these ~~defe~~ developments. I recollect then of Gen. Babcock making an explanation of these dispatches.

q Did Gen. Babcock on or about the 13th of December 1874, show you a dispatch from himself to John McDonald in the following words: "Washington, December 13. 1874. GEN. JOHN McDONALD, St. Louis. I suceeded. They will not go. I will write you. [Signed] SYLPH."

A No. I have no recollection of it at that time.

q Did Gen. Babcock on or about April 23, 1875, show you a dispatch in these words: "St. Louis, April 23. 1875. GEN. O. E. BABCOCK, Executive Mansion, Washington, D. C. Tell Mack to see Parker of Colorado; & telegram to Commissioner. Crush out St Louis enemies. [Signed] GRIT." [14]

A I did not remember about these dispatches at all until since the conspiracy trials have commenced. I have heard Gen. Babcock's explanation of most or all of them since that. Many of these dispatches may have been shown to me at the time and explained, but I do not remember it.

q Did you know at the time that during the Fall of ~~1865~~ 1875, subsequent to your visit to St. Louis, that Gen. Babcock corresponded with John McDonald after the latter was indicted, and sent his letters to McDonald under cover to Maj. E. B. Grimes.[15]

A No; I was not aware of it at the time.

q Did you know at the time that Gen. Babcock sent cypher dispatches to Major Luckey at St. Louis, over his own and over a fictitious signature, on the 17th or 18th of last November?

A I do not remember as to particular dates; but we have an Executive Mansion cypher so that when myself and Secretaries are separated, dispatches can be sent without being read by the operators. We always have had such a cypher. I have no particular knowledge, but I know in a general way that they were corresponding while Mr. Luckey was there during the A[ve]ry trial, he having gone there as a witness for the defence as I understood.

q Did you see the dispatches before they were sent?

A I do not think I saw the dispatches.

q Have you any objection to stating the meaning in that cypher of two words only—the words "Hamlet" and "bandage?"

A I never keep the cypher, & I never write a cypher dispatch. I never travel without having a Secretary with me.

q You do not know what those words mean?

A I do not know. When I want to send a dispatch in cipher, I give it to one of my secretaries in the ordinary form and he transmits it.

q On or about December 5, 1873, did Gen. Babcock show you a dispatch from Joyce to himself in these words: "Is there any hitch in sending Maguire's name to the Senate? [signed] JOYCE."

A I can not remember particularly. I think, however, that Gen. Babcock did ask me if there was any reason why Maguire's name should not be sent. I have an indistinct recollection of his asking me the question.

q You have said that you resisted the pressure brought to bear upon you by prominent public men in regard to the suspension or revocation of the order transferring Supervisors. If you have no objection, will you please state the names of those prominent men who brought that pressure to bear upon you?

a There were many persons, and I think I could give the names of several Senators and probably other Members of Congress, but probably I should have to refer to papers that are on file. I do not know that it is material. I know that the pressure was continual from the Supervisors and their friends.

q Can you from memory name any Senators or Representatives?

A I could name two or three, but I do not believe it is necessary.

Mr. Eaton. I will not press it, then.

q Did Gen. Babcock at the time tell you he had endeavored to influence Commissioner Douglass to revoke that order?

A No.

q Since you say that Genl. Babcock has not manifested to you any desire to interfere with or prevent the trial of the indictments against himself and others, will you be so good as to state whether any of his friends for him have at any time since those indictments were found endeavored to prevent the trial of the indictments against him or any other indicted parties? If so, please state who have made such efforts.

A They have not with me.

q Will you please state why the order for the Court of Inquiry in Gen. Babcock's case was made before the adjournment of the grand jury which found the indictment against him, if you know?

A It was made because he applied for it, and I thought he was clearly entitled to vindicate himself, if he was innocent. He had been denied that opportunity before the grand jury.

q Did Gen. Babcock show you a telegram from District Attorney Dyer, saying that the next conspiracy case would be tried on December 15th 1875?

A He did; I do not remember about the dates particularly.

q Now I suppose, Mr. President, that the substance of your testimony is—what we all know to be true—that if there has been any misconduct on the part of Gen. Babcock, it has not come to your knowledge? [16]

A Yes, sir; that is true.

q You do not know, of course, do you, whether Mr Douglass suggested to Secretary Bristow the same thing about the transfer of Supervisors which you say he originally suggested to you?

A I do not know anything about it, except from the Secretary himself.

q Do you recollect that Supervisor Tutton was ordered from Philadelphia to St. Louis under this order for transfers?

A That is my recollection, that he was ordered to St. Louis.

q You say that Gen. Babcock has made no efforts with you to avoid a trial; but you do not know of your own knowledge, of course, whether he has made any efforts with others?

A No; I do not.

Re-Direct Examination.

By Mr. COOK.

q [Handing witness copy of a telegram.] I wish you would state what you know in relation to that.

A This dispatch seems to be dated "Washington, October 27th; To WM H. BENTON, WM. McKEE and JOHN M. KRUM. Your request in regard to Collectorship will be complied with. [signed.] U. S. GRANT." [17] Those are gentlemen are a part of the bondsmen of Ford, and they had recommended Constantine Maguire for Fords place as Collector.

q The original of that, I believe, is in your handwriting?

A Yes, I wrote that myself. I saw the original this morning.

q What was the character of the correspondence between Mr. Joyce and Gen. Babcock as exhibited to you?

A My answer to that is the same as has been given and objected to.

q What was the general character of the explanation of the nature of the dispatches to which your attention has been directed, as given to you by Gen. Babcock?

A The explanations which he gave seemed to me to clear up all grounds of suspicion against him.

q What was the general character of those explanations?

A It was generally a statement of their meaning, and what they were in response to; but I could not probably give at this time his explanation of any one of them.

q But the explanations, as given at the time, were such as to satisfy you?

A They seemed to me to be entirely satisfactory.

U. S. GRANT

DS (brackets in original), DNA, Central Plains Region, RG 21, Records of District Courts. Printed in newspapers and in John McDonald, *Secrets of the Great Whiskey Ring* . . . (Chicago, 1880), pp. 246–65. Frequent objections by counsel for both sides have been omitted. Editing of USG's answers by counsel and the trial judge has been ignored.

On Feb. 12, 1876, a correspondent reported from Washington, D. C., that Chief Justice Morrison R. Waite had acted as notary for the deposition. "Next to the Chief Justice sat Mr. Bristow, Secretary of the Treasury, and a little further along the table Mr. Pierrepont, the Attorney General. To the right of the President, and occupying the other side of the table, were the attorneys, Messrs. Lucien Eaton, of St. Louis, government counsel, and William A. Cook, of Washington, who submitted the questions, on behalf of General Babcock." *New York Herald*, Feb. 13, 1876. See *ibid.*, Feb. 14, 1876. On Feb. 17, lawyers for Orville E. Babcock concluded their case by reading USG's deposition. See *St. Louis Globe-Democrat*, Feb. 18, 1876.

On Feb. 8 and 9, Secretary of State Hamilton Fish had recorded in his diary. "Before the Cabinet adjourned the President asked the members to meet at 4 o'clk in the afternoon when the Attorney General could be present. At that hour all assembled and the President stated that he wished to consult with reference to some of the papers which he had received from St Louis He proceeded to read several telegrams from Babcocks counsels addressed to a lawyer by the name of Cooke, whom he says is also appointed Counsel; also a long letter addressed to himself, not signed, enclosed in one written by John K. Porter saying that it was written with the intent of being signed by all the Counsel but their absence at the last moment before the departure of the train prevented. These telegrams & letter urge the importance of his presence at St Louis as a witness on the trial; while we were in session another telegram to Cooke was brought in, stating in substance that the opening speach of the prosecution indicated the absolute necessity of his testimony on certain pont The President manifested a great-deal of excitement and complained that they had taken from him his Secretaries, & Clerks, his Messengers, & doorkeepers; that the prosecution was aimed at himself, & that they were putting him on trial; that he was as confident as he lived of Babcocks innocence, referred to his long association with him, the entire confidence he had in him, and that he knew he was not guilty; that were he guilty it would be an instance of the greatest ingratitude and trechery that ever was. He said he proposed to have interrogatories prepared by the prosecution which he should answer before the Chief-Justice or some other person authorized to take his deposition. The telegrams however show that no such proposition had been made by Babcock's Counsel who had assumed that if made, it would not be assented to by the prosecution. The President expressed his determination to go to St Louis, to start either this evening or tomorrow morning, and said he should like to take at least two members of the Cabinet with him; and enquired of the Attorney General whether he would accompany him. Pierrepont replied that he might so arrange his business as to go, but that the subject was a serious one, and needed very grave consideration; that it would attract the attention of the Community and would be the subject of very serious investigation and criticism; he stated that it was on the eve of an election when every act done would be commented upon with all the severity which might properly attach to it, and generally might be assumed as very great injustice; that the fact of the President of the United States appearing in Court was without precedent and would naturally be regarded with great suspicion. For the purpose of having the answer made I asked the Attorney General if a sub-poena could be served on the President, to which he of course replied in the negative. I then remarked should the President go, it would be a voluntary offering himself as a witness for the defence, in a criminal prosecution instituted by the Government of which the President is the Representative and embodyment; that it would therefore place him in the attitude of volunteering as a witness to defeat the prosecution which the law made it his duty to enforce. Robeson suggested that he might be sub-poenaed on an order of the Court to request his presence and that the Attorney General might telegraph to that effect Pierrepont replied that by law he was the Prosecuting Officer and could not suggest a line of defense: or the summoning of witnesses for the defendant. Bristow sustained this view. The President suggested that Robeson should communicate to Cooke that application should be made to the Court either for a continuance of the case until he might be able to attend or for an order to take his testimony. Pierrepont & Bristow remarked that that would be a subject in the discussion of the Court which might not feel disposed to allow it in as-much as the actual presence of the witness in criminal prosecutions is always required. I objected to the form of suggestion proposed in-as-much as it intimated that the President might at a future time attend in case the case was postponed to another time; that I did not think that the President of the United States should in any case, allow himself to be brought into court as a witness, and put on the stand to testify, I refer to the trial of Aaron Burr, when an effort was made to bring Mr Jefferson as a witness in Court The Cabinet were unanimous in the opinion that the President ought not to leave Washington during the session of Congress to be made a witness of and there was no dissent expressed to the position which I took, that he ought not under any circumstances to consent to appear in Court as a witness. Various suggestions as to the mode of conveying the conclusion, that the President would not appear as a witness, and it was finally determined that Mr Cooke who it appeared was in the house and had brought the request for the Presidents appearance should be referred to the Attorney Genl who would answer that it was impossible and unseemly for the President to appear as they requested him that he should be reminded that the defense had made no effort or proposition to obtain his testimony under a commission and that should such commission be issued the President would be ready to make reply. While the discussion was going on the President wrote in Pencil what he suggested as an answer, at first, with a view of sending it to the Counsel for the defense but this was objected to, on the ground that the government could not advise the line of the defense; some of his expressions were excepted to and a part of it was rewritten by him; it finally assumed the form of the reply which Pierrepont was to give to Cooke. During the discussion the President stated that in Justice to the Counsel for the defense it should be mentioned that he had given them to understand before they left that he would attend. It appeared also that he had spoken with Conkling on the subject who had intimated to the President a doubt as to the propriety of his appearing as a witness; but the President did not state that he had directly disuaded him. After two hours consultation the meeting broke up with the understanding that Mr Cooke who had brought two telegrams during the meeting should call upon the Attorney General who would remain at home until

9 oclock. Later in the evening I saw Pierrepont at Judge Swaynes who remarked that it was quite strange that Cooke had not called upon him although he had remained at home until after 10. o'clock." "Call upon the President and he reads me in confidence part of a letter which he had received from the Counsel of Babcock in St Louis which he had not read to the Cabinet but only to the Attorney General. He speaks of Bristow and his prospects and says that he thinks that he himself is perfectly right, but that he is being pushed along by too large a number of zelous young friends" DLC-Hamilton Fish. See Nevins, *Fish*, pp. 792–99.

On Feb. 24, James F. Casey, collector of customs, New Orleans, telegraphed to Secretary of the Treasury Benjamin H. Bristow. "The following special despatch from Washington was published in the N Orleans times of this morning 'Leading papers in Baltimore Chicago & Cincinnati will publish a statement to-morrow morning to the effect that evidence has been forwarded here sufficiently to indict West & Casey for complicity in the whisky ~~frauds~~ rings Bristow it is said will if possible have these cases tried in Tennessee instead of La. As many papers in the N & W. have published time and again that I was mixed up in the whisky ~~frauds~~ ring and had been or would be indicted I think it time to take notice of the malicious persecution & knowing that such reports are a base calumny and circulated for malicious purposes I ask you to say to the public whether or not you have any information implicating me in fraudulent whisky or cotton transactions please show this to the President & Atty Genl" Copy, USG 3. Bristow replied to Casey. "your message just received gives me the first information of the despatch alleged to have been sent from here I have inquired of the Commissioner of Internal Revenue and Solicitor of the Treasury and find no evidence here involving you or Mr West in complicity with whiskey frauds in New Orleans. Neither I nor the Officers named know where the alleged information came from" Copy (undated), *ibid.* On March 3, Ulysses S. Grant, Jr., wrote to Bristow. "Enclosed please find the telegram from New Orleans and the reply which you wished to have returned to you when the President had read them. They have just come in from the President's table" ALS, DLC-Benjamin H. Bristow.

On Feb. 24, jurors had found Babcock innocent of conspiracy to commit revenue fraud. On Feb. 26, John McDonald wrote to Babcock. "This will be presented you by Mr. Walsh my brotherinlaw—He was my chief clerk in Supervisors office—When yourself and Krum called last evening, I forgot to mention to you that *he* (Walsh) is an applicant for a special agency—It is needless for me to say, that which every body already knows who is acquainted with Walsh, that he is one of the smartest Post office Men in the Western Country—He is strongly endorsed by Genl A J Smith Late Postmastr here—and also Col. *Schaurte* who is head of the Division of Special Agents and, by the way the man Schaurte has been *one of the most* determined and zealous workers *for* you in your troubles here—Schaurte is a whole team, and to my knowledge, has rendered you *excellent service*—in fact he has been untiring in his efforts in your behalf all along before, and since your arrival here—He knows Walsh intimately, and is very anxious for him to get the position—In regard to my own affairs and *yours* Walsh has been my Confidential agent—You can get him the position and in doing so you will oblige . . ." ALS, ICN. See McDonald, *Secrets of the Great Whiskey Ring*, pp. 268–74.

On July 28, Bluford Wilson, former solicitor of the treasury, testified. "On Sunday night, February 27, statements were submitted to the President of the United States, by which it appeared that Orville E. Babcock, the private secretary of the President, had been engaged in the Black Friday transactions; that he and others lost in that transaction $40,000; that the money was lost to Jay Cooke & Co., of whom Fahnestock seemed to be the party through whom the transactions were had; that to make good his own losses and that of his associates, Babcock had made a trust deed of his property, creating Asa Bird Gardner, of West Point, subsequently the judge advocate of the military court of inquiry ordered at Chicago, his trustee. The statement was made to the President while Babcock was *en route* from Saint Louis to Washington. It was, I believe, subsequently verified by competent evidence satisfactory to the President. The result was that neither General Bristow nor myself went out of the public service, and that the President of the United States and the Secretary of the Treasury, in a manner highly creditable to both, were reconciled. . . . Because the President then, for the first time, comprehended, in all its significance, the fact that he had been betrayed by Babcock, and that if he (Babcock) had betrayed him in the Black Friday transactions, he was quite capable of betraying him in connection with the whisky frauds, and of becoming a party thereto; and the President recognized that the prosecution against General Babcock had had its full warrant and justification. . . . The President sent for me not long after this, and we had a full and very friendly conference, covering all the questions of difference between us, and the result was that I supposed I left him entirely satisfied with myself. . . ." *HMD*, 44-1-186, 369–70. See Asa Bird Gardiner testimony, *ibid.*, pp. 421–37; Appointment, March 3, 1876; letter to Benjamin H. Bristow, June 19, 1876.

On Aug. 9, Roger M. Sherman, asst. U.S. attorney, New York City, wrote to USG. "I enclose a copy of a communication addressed to the Attorney General upon a subject personal to me. After serving three years in the Office of the Attorney General under my kinsman Judge Hoar, and Attorneys-Generals Akerman, & Williams I was appointed an assistant in this office. For the past year and a half I have had entire charge of Internal Revenue business in this office, and have succeeded in many important and difficult cases, as the records of the Office of the Commissioner of Internal Revenue will show. At the time the excitement in the Whiskey cases in the West reached its climax, I was selected to go West to get evidence for use in cases here against spirits sent from the West, and also to secure evidence, which I believed existed, of the complicity of dealers here in the frauds. In spite of opposition and abuse from Mr Dyer, then U. S. Attorney at St Louis—abuse that was circulated through the press of the country, I succeeded in obtaining such evidence that all the cases against such spirits here, were subsequently tried upon that evidence by me, and verdicts obtained for the Government. Besides I obtained evidence upon which I obtained from a Grand jury here 32. indictments for conspiracy by dealers here with the Western rings. All this labor has been done by me. It is beyond my province and duty. I performed it upon assurances that I should be adequately compensated. I am expected to try those indictments in November. Incidentally to my labors in St Louis, I had the opportunity to place genuine and relevant evidence in the hands of General Babcocks counsel, which showed that the information which he was accused of giving the ring, was given by Revenue agent Hogue. This evidence Mr Dyer endeavored to obtain from me, but I was firmly impressed with the belief, which was unavoidable to anyone situated as I was, that General Babcock was being made a pretext for reflections & attacks upon yourself. I believed that Mr. Dyer would take any step to carry out that purpose, even the destruction of this evidence. I declined therefore to give it up to him, but offered him every facility to use it; he refused to do so, & the abuse which I have mentioned followed. Since that time I have felt myself opposed in reasonable endeavors in the Internal Revenue Office, and in the Attorney Generals Office, to obtain credit and recognition for my labors, by the disposition on the part of the Internal Revenue Office to claim in the face of glaring facts to the contrary, that all the success of the Government against the Whiskey rings was the work of a few exceptionally honest and competent officers, and by a corresponding blindness to what had been done by others, and also by the feeling that I had thwarted the plans which depend, as certain persons in those offices appeared to think, upon General Babcock's conviction. General Bristow who had to that time been very considerate and kind to me, has gone out of the way to unjustly and untruly stigmatize me. The letter to that effect, mentioned in my letter (herewith) to the Attorney General is an example. I beg to submit to your judgment, that I did only what any honorable man was bound to do, independently of the innocence or guilt of a defendant—afford him the use of the evidence in his favor, and refuse to suppress it, and that I ought to receive just compensation for my services, without hindrance for such a cause. I respectfully ask that if the Commissioner of Internal Revenue shall be of the opinion that my present request to the Attorney General is in the interest of the Government, you will make some direction in the premises. I enclose also a copy of a letter from the U. S. Attorney here to the Attorney General showing my functions in this office. It is on file with the Attorney General, and also with the Commissioner of Internal Revenue" ALS, DNA, RG 60, Letters from the President. The enclosures are *ibid.* See David P. Dyer to Edwards Pierrepont, Feb. 12, 14, 19, 1876, Dyer to Roger M. Sherman, Feb. 14, 1876, and Dyer to Bluford Wilson, Feb. 14, 1876, *ibid.*, RG 118, Letters Sent, U.S. Attorneys, Eastern District, Mo.; *HMD*, 44-1-186, 13–19, 93.

1. Sackets Harbor, N. Y.
2. On Jan. 4, Daniel D. Pratt, commissioner of Internal Revenue, had written to Levi P. Luckey. "Enclosed herewith I send you the papers which you ask for in your note of the 3rd instant viz: telegrams from Henry T. Blow, Wm McKee, Wm. H. Benton, and John M. Krum recommending the appointment of Constantine Maguire as Collector of Internal Revenue for the 1st District of Missouri vice C. W. Ford, deceased, referred to this Department by the President October 28th 1873." LS, DNA, Central Plains Region, RG 21, Records of District Courts. See note 16 below.
3. See McDonald, *Secrets of the Great Whiskey Ring*, pp. 106–13.
4. See *PUSG*, 26, 235–36.
5. See *ibid.*, pp. 375–76.
6. Lucien Eaton, special U.S. counsel for the St. Louis trials, later testified concerning Charles W. Ford. See *HMD*, 44-1-186, 106–7.
7. See *PUSG*, 20, 149–50.
8. See *ibid.*, 24, 232.
9. See *ibid.*, 19, 253.
10. On Feb. 16, 1870, Chester H. Krum, Charles W. Ford, and Carman A. Newcomb, St. Louis, had written to Columbus Delano, commissioner of Internal Revenue. "Private . . . If the change contemplated in change of Supervisor in [this] District is not fixed. I would suggest that the character of the new appontee [should] be investigated here & at Memphis." LS (torn), DNA, Central Plains Region, RG 21, Records of District Courts; *St. Louis Globe-Democrat*, Feb. 18, 1876. On Feb. 14, McDonald, supervisor of Internal Revenue for Ark. and Indian Territory, had been assigned jurisdiction over Mo., previously part of the district supervised by James Marr. See McDonald, *Secrets of the Great Whiskey Ring*, pp. 27–29.
11. On Feb. 19, Marr filed an affidavit in St. Louis charging that McDonald had repeatedly sought to involve him in corruption; that McDonald ". . . told me that he had made $250.000 in Memphis during the war, out of his position there in the Military Service, and he said that that was the only opportunity of the kind he had ever had, and that he improved it, and that I ought now to improve my opportunity to help myself and friends as he had done in Memphis. That I need not be afraid of him, that he would never tell or 'go back on me.' That a very respectable gentleman, a merchant in high standing in this city

told me only a few days since, that he knows that this McDonald had, ~~and~~ himself made, a contract with the rebel Genl Roddy at one time during the war, and while McDonald was in Memphis to deliver cotton inside our our (the union) lines to said McDonald or his agents at $50 per bale. That he (McDonald himself) went outside our lines and met Genl Roddy and made the contract above named. That I have now in my possession a letter from a well known, and reliable gentleman in Memphis stating that the career of McDonald in that city during the war was such that if known would send him to the pennitentiary." Copy, DNA, Central Plains Region, RG 21, Records of District Courts.

    12. See *PUSG*, 21, 351.

    13. James J. Brooks, asst. secret service chief, Treasury Dept., and Henry C. Rogers, 1st deputy commissioner of Internal Revenue, both testified at Babcock's trial. See *St. Louis Globe-Democrat*, Feb. 12, 16, 1876; *HMD*, 44-1-186, 466–77.

    14. See *PUSG*, 26, 237. On July 10, 1869, Daniel Sayer, Denver, had written to USG. "Col W. H. Parker who formerly commanded one of the Military Posts in this Territory, and now a resident of Denver, desires the appointment of Collector of Internal Revenue of this Territory. It affords me pleasure to commend him to your favorable consideration for the position, knowing him to be a suitable and deserving person for the office." ALS, DNA, RG 59, Letters of Application and Recommendation. On the same day, Governor Edward M. McCook of Colorado Territory favorably endorsed this letter. AES, *ibid.* On Aug. 10, William H. Parker, Washington, D. C., wrote to USG seeking appointment as consul, Brindisi. L, *ibid.* On Aug. 11, USG endorsed this letter. "If vacancy occurs please call special attention to this application." AE (initialed), *ibid.* Related papers are *ibid.* On June 11, 1874, USG nominated Parker as collector of Internal Revenue, Colorado Territory. On April 13, 1876, Parker appeared before the select committee to investigate whiskey frauds and denied that he had helped to procure a witness for Babcock's defense. See *HMD*, 44-1-186, 91, 108–10. On April 19, Bristow wrote to Parker that his resignation had been accepted. Copy, DNA, RG 56, Letters Sent. On May 20, USG wrote a note. "If the Atty. Gen. sees no good reason for contrary action I would be glad to have Col. W. H. Parker, of Colorado, apt Asst. Dist. Atty of that territory." ANS, InU.

    15. Capt. Edward B. Grimes, asst. q. m., St. Louis, testified at Babcock's trial. See *St. Louis Globe-Democrat*, Feb. 12, 1876; *Secrets of the Great Whiskey Ring*, pp. 180–82.

    16. On Feb. 12, David P. Dyer, U.S. attorney, St. Louis, had telegraphed to Wilson. "Tell Eaton that he must show on cross-examination that the President had no knowledge of the secret correspondence of Babcock with Joyce and McDonald. Let no matter of delicacy stand in the way of a full and complete examination." ALS (press, telegram sent), DNA, RG 118, Letters Sent, U.S. Attorneys, Eastern District, Mo.

    17. See *PUSG*, 24, 232. On Oct. 27, 1873, Henry T. Blow, St. Louis, had telegraphed to USG. "It would be gratifying to your friends and the republicans of our city if Constantine Maguire could be appointed Collector of Revenue of the Dist, He is on Mr Ford's bonds, has the Confidence of Mr Fords friends and is really an honest straightforward man as well as capable," Telegram received, DNA, Central Plains Region, RG 21, Records of District Courts. On the same day, William H. Benton, William McKee, and John M. Krum twice telegraphed to USG. "As your personal & Political friends we urgently request the appointment of Constantine Maguire as successor to our friend the late C W Ford" "If you rec'd telegram from us please answer" Telegrams received (both at 6:25 P.M.), *ibid.* USG's telegram in reply was received at 6:52 P.M. *Ibid.*

    On Oct. 25, Benton, Krum, and McKee had telegraphed to USG. "Please see our despatch of this day to Delano and tell us how we as securities of our friend C W Ford can protect ourselves from any wrong action of his deputies" Telegram received, *ibid.*

USG endorsed this telegram. "Will the Com. of Int. Rev. please answer this dispatch." AES (undated), *ibid.*

To J. Russell Jones

Feb. 22d /76

DEAR JONES:

I rec'd your letter and one from Ovington yesterday relating to Horse R. R. affairs, but have misplaced them. I want to write however to say that I can not take the certificates awarded to me unless by not doing so I loose the $1,662 00 awarded to me. I presume the bonds, or certificates, will readily bring par, or there about, and if so any one may take my share by giving me the difference.

It is almost certain that I shall be compelled to sell my stock in the road. I may be able to hold on for sixty or ninety days however by borrowing on them for that time. Will you be kind enough to advise me whether it would be better to let it go now, or wait the time specified above?

My kindest regards to Mrs. Jones & family.

Yours Truly
U. S. GRANT

ALS, IHi. See letter to J. Russell Jones, Jan. 2, 1876.

To Ministers and Consuls

February 22d, '76.

To Diplomatic and Consular Representatives:

It affords me pleasure to introduce to your acquaintance and invite your good offices to Rev. Wm. H. Milburn, "the blind preacher," who visits Europe and purposes to lecture while there. Mr. Milburn is well known in this country and by his countrymen abroad as an eloquent and learned Methodist preacher. His loss of sight has not diminished his pursuit of knowledge; and but few persons are more capable of imparting their knowledge to others than he is.

Again asking your good offices for Mr. Milburn in any proper way, I subscribe myself,

Very respectfully,

U. S. GRANT.

Jacksonville (Ill.) *Journal,* July 31, 1885. William H. Milburn, blinded in childhood, studied at Illinois College (1841–43) and became a Methodist preacher, lecturer, and writer. See William Henry Milburn, *Ten Years of Preacher-Life: Chapters from an Autobiography* (New York, 1859); *Washington Post,* April 11, 1903.

On Feb. 12, 1873, Harper & Brothers, New York City, wrote to USG. "Our friend, the Rev. *William Henry Milburn* desires a diplomatic position or Consul-Generalship in Europe or at Alexandria—& should you make any changes in your appointments to these positions, we venture to ask that you will bear in mind Mr Milburn's application. . . ." L, DNA, RG 59, Letters of Application and Recommendation. No appointment followed.

On Feb. 10, 1874, USG and twenty-eight others, including the entire cabinet, wrote to Milburn. "The undersigned unite in the request that at some early date you will deliver in this city your very admirable and justly popular lecture on Aaron Burr. We are confident that by so doing you will gratify a large number of personal friends." Handbill, DLC-Alexander R. Shepherd.

To Congress

———

Feby. 28. 1876

TO THE SENATE AND HOUSE OF REPRESENTATIVES:

I lay before you herewith a communication from the Secretary of the Interior, of date 26th instant upon the subject of the deficiency of supplies at the Red Cloud Agency, Nebraska.

This matter has already been presented to you by the Secretary, and the House of Representatives has requested an investigation by a military officer of the cause of this deficiency. I have taken proper steps to comply with the request of the House; but the present need of supplies is not disputed. A prolonged delay in furnishing provisions to these Indians will cause great distress and be likely to provoke raids on white settlements, and possibly lead to a general outbreak of hostilities.

I therefore deem it proper to invite your attention to the importance of early and favorable action upon the estimates heretofore and herewith submitted.

These estimates and the views of the Secretary in regard to this emergency meet with my full concurrence, and I recommend that the appropriation asked for be made at the earliest day practicable.

U. S. Grant.

Copy, DNA, RG 130, Messages to Congress. *SED,* 44-1-30. On Feb. 26, 1876, Secretary of the Interior Zachariah Chandler wrote to USG. "I have the honor to lay before you a copy of a communication this day received from the Commissioner of Indian Affairs in regard to the condition of affairs at the Red Cloud agency. The Commissioner reports that further supplies are needed there at once, and gives at some length the reasons for the deficiency now existing. These reasons may be briefly stated as, first, diminished appropriations; and, secondly, unusual issues to Indians visiting the agency to meet the Black Hills commission in September last. An estimate for this appropriation was submitted by this Department to the House of Representatives on the 10th ultimo, and attention was again called to the subject on the 26th ultimo. On the 3d instant the House of Representatives requested you to detail a military officer to investigate the cause of this deficiency. But the report of that officer cannot be made under some days or weeks, and the emergency is reported by the Commissioner to be pressing. The case has additional urgency from the fact that over one thousand members of Sitting Bull's band, heretofore defiant and actively hostile, have come in to this agency in compliance with messages previously sent to them, and it is important that any measures looking to the disintegration of this heretofore united band, and the destruction of Sitting Bull's authority, should have proper encouragement. The Commissioner is prohibited by law from taking any steps toward supplying the agency in the absence of further appropriations by Congress, and deems it imperative to the best interest of the Indians and of the white settlers alike, that early steps should be taken toward placing supplies at the Red Cloud agency. He recommends an appropriation of $50,000, in addition to that previously called for, on account of the probable submission of Sitting Bull's band to the Government, and their possible arrival at an agency where supplies are lacking. I fully concur with the Commissioner in the views expressed in this communication, and transmit herewith copies of all my previous communications to Congress on this subject, with the recommendation that they be laid by you before Congress and that the urgency of the case be again brought to its notice." *Ibid.,* pp. 1–2. The enclosures are *ibid.,* pp. 2–12. On April 6, USG signed into law a $150,000 deficiency appropriation. See *U.S. Statutes at Large,* XIX, 28; *CR,* 44–1, 1637–38, 1911–12; message to House of Representatives, March 23, 1876.

To *William W. Belknap*

Washington, D. C., March 2, 1876.

Dear Sir: Your tender of resignation as Secretary of War, with the request that it be accepted immediately, is received, and the same is hereby accepted with great regret. Yours, &c.,

U. S. Grant.

New York Tribune, March 4, 1876. *HRC*, 44-1-186, 10, 44-1-799, 13. On March 2, 1876, Secretary of War William W. Belknap wrote to USG. "I hereby tender my resignation as Secretary of War, and request its immediate acceptance. Thanking you for your constant and continued kindness . . ." ALS, USG 3. *HRC*, 44-1-186, 11, 44-1-799, 14. On the same day, Secretary of State Hamilton Fish recorded in his diary. "While in bed this morning the Secretary of the Treasury calls and informs me of the Genl Belknap Affair After some conversation I advise him to call upon the President, and suggest that he send immediatly for Mr Bass to give him some information and the particulars" DLC-Hamilton Fish. Also on March 2, 12:45 P.M., U.S. Representative Hiester Clymer of Pa. wrote to USG. "The Committee on Expenditures in the War Department finding it necessary in the progress of their investigations to have a copy of the letter of resignation of W. W. Belknap of the office of Secretary of War, stating the time as nearly as may be, the hour at which it was received by you on this day, have requested me to ask the same of you—" ALS, USG 3. On the same day, USG endorsed this letter. "Time of acceptance of resignation about 10 20 this a. m." AE, *ibid.* Also on March 2, Culver C. Sniffen wrote to Clymer transmitting the requested information. Copy, DLC-USG, II, 3. *HRC*, 44-1-186, 11, 44-1-799, 14. On March 3, U.S. Representative James A. Garfield of Ohio recorded in his diary. ". . . The President gave me a minute account of his part in the Belknap resignation. He had not heard a word of the case until he was at breakfast when Bristow called. The day before, he had promised to give Ulke, the artist, a sitting for a portrait, after his breakfast Friday morning. So he brought his coat and hat down stairs when he came to breakfast. After Bristow's call, he ordered a note sent to Mr. Bass, asking that gentleman to call at 12. Having finished breakfast, he started to go out, when he was met at the door by Belknap and Chandler. The former was nearly suffocated with excitement; made an incoherent explanation and offered his resignation. The President, still being bent on going to the artist's, did not go up stairs, but sent up to have a letter of acceptance written. When it came down, the language did not suit him, and stepping to the mantel he wrote the letter as it now appears. . . ." Harry James Brown and Frederick D. Williams, eds., *The Diary of James A. Garfield* (East Lansing, Mich., 1967–81), III, 243–44.

On March 1, Clymer had written to Belknap. "At a meeting of the Committee on Expenditures in the War Department held yesterday, testimony of a character important to yourself was taken—There will be a special meeting of the Committee to day at 11. Oclock A. M. at which time you are hereby invited to attend to cross examine the witness if you desire to do so." ALS, NjP. On Feb. 29, Caleb P. Marsh, a New York City merchant, had testified to the House Committee on Expenditures in the War Dept. that his friendship with Belknap's deceased wife and current wife (who were sisters) had induced Belknap to assist him in making an irregular contract with John S. Evans, post trader at Fort Sill, Indian Territory. Belknap, or his wife, then accepted payments from Marsh between 1870 and 1875. See *HRC*, 44-1-186, 3–9.

On March 2, a correspondent reported from Washington, D. C. "The discovery of the Belknap frauds has created a very great excitement here, and it takes rank as one of the most stirring events Washington has seen. . . . About one o'clock a rumor was started in the House that Belknap had shot himself, and for a while it was believed. It was known by noon that he had resigned, and it was then reported that the President had nominated Treasurer New to be Secretary of War. . . ." Clymer "read first the report of the committee, accusing William W. Belknap, late Secretary of War, of high crimes and misdemeanors, and proposing, in the name of the House and of the American people, articles of impeachment. The impressive wording of such a report had a solemn effect. When this was done he retired to his seat, and for a moment there was an awful sense of disgust in the House and galleries at the supposition that he was done; but he immediately asked leave to read, also, the testimony on which the report was based and all the documents accompanying it. . . . When the letter of the President was read, stating that he had accepted the Secretary's resignation at half-past ten o'clock, there was a murmur of amazement at what looked to everybody then like an act deliberately intended to shield Mr. Belknap, but when the terms of the letter were read, in which the President tells Mr. Belknap that he accepts his resignation with great regret, people turned to each other with indignation at something which seemed to them an open defiance of decency and of public opinion. . . . The discussion turned mainly on the question of the power of the House to impeach a person who had resigned office, and Mr. Blackburn, with great spirit, but in an admirably impartial tone, asserted the power and dignity of the House, and brought down a burst of applause when he said that, if it were true that the House in such a case as this was powerless, then it must be on the old ground that 'the King can do no wrong,' for it gave the President the power to shield offenders by accepting their resignations; but, he said, though it may be true that the King can do no wrong, we have not yet, in this country, heard it asserted that the President can do no wrong. . . . Finally the vote was taken *viva voce*, and there were no nays. Thereupon the Impeachment Committee was named by the Speaker, and the House adjourned after one of its most eventful and exciting sessions. . . . Senator Logan made no concealment of his regret at the Secretary's downfall. He characterized it as a most terrible calamity and said that his resignation ought not to have been accepted by the President. . . . Senator Cameron repeated the words, 'Terrible, terrible.' 'This comes,' said he, 'from Grant's system of appointments.' He frequently told him that he ought not to put obscure men in high positions. He always had a lot of these unknown characters around him. . . ." *New York Herald*, March 3, 1876. See also *CR*, 44–1, 1426–33; *Chicago Inter-Ocean*, March 4, 1876.

On March 3, Fish recorded in his diary. "The President spoke of Belknaps defection saying that yesterday he had really, in the first part of the day been unable to comprehend its magnitude & importance the surprise was so great, that it was really not until evening that he could realize the crime, and its gravity, he spoke of his long continued acquaintance with Belknap in the Army, of his having known his father as one of the finest Officers of the Old Army, when he himself was a young lieutenant. He directed the Attorney General to examine the law with a view to consider what action could be taken against the late Secretary, either criminal, or civil   He said that he had accepted the resignation on its being tendered and under the wrong impression, as he did not fully understand the statements of Belknap, who was very much overcome and could scarcely speak; he did not know that acceptance was not a matter of course. There was some conversation as to the right of a public officer to resign, and thereby to absolutely terminate his official tenure. Pierrepont & Bristow seemed to think that he had such right. It was not however clearly established that he had; the case was suggested of an officer giving a bond, and other instances and justice might be jeoparded by the admission of such right. . . ." DLC-Hamilton Fish.

On March 4, Secretary of the Treasury Benjamin H. Bristow wrote to USG. "I hand you a message just received from Mr Eaton of St Louis. I suppose the man Robinson named in the message is the person who has been giving to the newspapers all sorts of stories about the Belknap affair. I deem it prop[er to] hand you the message for your information" ALS, USG 3. The enclosure is a telegram of the same day from Lucien B. Eaton, St. Louis, to Bristow. "Irrespective of his grievances his means of information and his actual knowledge if any that Captain Robinson late tenth Cavalry who is bemirching the President is totally unworthy of belief generally is a bad man and probably half crazed by intemperance" Telegram received (at 10:40 A.M.), *ibid.* For the allegations of George T. Robinson, cashiered as capt., 10th Cav., as of April 15, 1875, see *New York Tribune*, March 3, 1876. On Sept. 26, 1874, Robinson, St. Louis Barracks, had written to USG. "Although personally unknown to you I have the honor to forward to you this my petition hoping by the Enclosed letter to call your attention to the fact that friends of mine are also firm friends of yours—On the 11th day of September I was placed in arrest at this post by order of the Hon Secretary of War—but as yet no charges have been received by me   I only Suppose that they relate to debts that I have unfortunately contracted most of them unavoidably—I have a large family to Support beside the care of an aged Father & Mother— I respectfully ask that my Resignation may be accepted to date on the 30th day of November 1874 giving me also a leave of absence to that date to Enable me to adjust my liabilities with my Creditors—. . ." ALS, DNA, RG 94, ACP, 3705 1873.

On March 4, 1876, Gen. William T. Sherman, St. Louis, wrote to U.S. Senator John Sherman of Ohio. "Now that Belknap has shown his hand, it is no longer a subject of regret that he did not share his confidence with me but on the Contrary that he availed himself of this very fact, to carry on for years this system of selling & taxing officers which Congress took from the General of the Army to give the Secretary, and at the time almost relieving him of all restraints and Checks—The fault lies with Congress, which by special legislation has almost invited this very system. I feel sorry for Belknap—I dont think him naturally dishonest, but how could he live on $8000 a year in the style that you all beheld? I am glad the explosion has come—for he acted towards me without frankness & meanly—gradually usurping all the power which had been exercised by Genl Grant— leaving me almost the subject of ridicule: and he took advantage of the publication of my Memoirs to create the impression that I had belittled Genls Thomas, McPherson & my old comrades in arms, a thing that is not in the Book—he used that Scamp Boynton to rake among the records for Scraps to antagonise with my positive assertions—The whirlwind that is now let loose in Washington will do good—There is more waste in army matters in Washington, than in all the land beside—Our Posts are models of simplicity and economy—but the Staff in Washington, NewYork &c control the Press & Congress, always at the expense of the Fighting part of the army. I think I see the dawn of better times. I pity Belknap—and regard him as the 'effect' and not the 'Cause'—Grant is not blameless; he could have given an impetus in the right direction in 1869,—meant to; but saw or thought he saw the danger—and made up his mind to let things *run* The result was inevitable." AL (initialed), DLC-William T. Sherman.

On March 5, Henry H. Wells, U.S. attorney, Washington, D. C., wrote to Attorney Gen. Edwards Pierrepont. "At. 1. o'clock this morning information was brought to me by Mr. Washburne Chief of the Secret Service to the effect that Gen. Belknap. was making his preparations to flee from this City. I thereupon requested that officer to procure from the Police Magistrate in case the information proved to be correct, a warrant for Gen. Belknap's arrest and to take such other steps as seemed proper to prevent an escape. I am just now informed by one of Mr. Washburne's subordinates that a watch was placed and kept about Mr. Belknap's house from about one o'clock until this time and that if he did not leave before one o'clock he has not left. On recieving this last information I requested the officer bringing the same to procure the warrant but not to execute it unless some attempt is made to escape. It seems to me that the fact should be speedily ascertained whether Gen. Belknap. is still in his house and if there that the house should be constantly guarded to prevent the possibility of an escape. I have however no power to issue such directions to the Secret Service force. I should be glad to receive instructions from you and if you deem proper that some instructions should be given to Mr. Washburne of the Secret Service. I assume that the dispatch sent to you by me from the Capitol at three o'clock yesterday afternoon as well as my letter written latter giving the result of the application to the Hon. J. Proctor Knott, have reached you and therefore I do not repeat the same." LS, DNA, RG 60, Letters Received, D. C. See *Washington Evening Star*, March 6, 8, 9, 1876.

On March 7, Wells again wrote to Pierrepont. "On yesterday morning I issued subpoenas for witnesses to attend before the Grand Jurors in the case of the United States vs.
Gen. Belknap and others. Among these witnesses was the Honorable Hiester Clymer,
J. C. S. Blackburn and W. M. Robbins, members of the House of Representatives. All these
three gentlemen appeared this morning in open Court and desired permission to make a
statement, which having been granted they said in substance that they denied the authority of the Court to require them to testify to what had been testified to by witnesses before
the Committees of Congress of these gentlemen were members, and informed the Court
that if they answered before the Grand Jury it would be under protest, which they would
not only make in Court, but also enter upon the records of the House of Rep. To which I,
as District Attorney, replied that so far as I knew it was not the purpose, nor was it my
wish to interrogate either of these gentlemen as to any matter which had been testified
to before them as members of such Committees. And that to obviate any personal inconvenience which their presence here might occasion, the grand jury would, I had no doubt,
arrange their sessions so as to suit the convenience of these gentlemen. Mr. Clymer and
his associates then stated further that in their judgment their presence before the grand
jury as witnesses in relation to any matter which had come or might come before their respective committees would prevent the proper prosecution of such inquiries by the Committees themselves. . . . I should be glad to receive instructions as to what course I shall
take in relation to the examination of the members of the Committees above referred
to. My purpose was simply to obtain from them any statements or confessions of guilt
made to them or either of them by Gen. Belknap. . . ." LS, DNA, RG 60, Letters Received,
D. C. Fearing prosecution, Marsh had gone to Canada after his controversial discharge
by the congressional committee, and his absence hindered legal proceedings. See *CR*,
44–1, 1523–39, 1566–74, 1632–37; *New York Times*, March 4, 6, 1876; *New York Tribune*,
March 11, 1876.

On March 7 and 14, Fish recorded cabinet discussions in his diary. "Reference was
made to proceedings against Genl Belknap, the President said he believed he was entirely
innocent to which no response of assent was made by any one present, but the remark was
made that it was important that the proceedings be so conducted as to afford no possible
opportunity for suspicion of collusion or want of earnestness in the proceedings" "Judge
Pierrepont says that he has very substantial reasons for saying that if Marsh could be protected against legal proceedings he could be brought to Washington to testify in the proceedings against Belknap; he was disinclined to state the source of his information but said
there was a person in the City who had come to see him who was prepared to go to Canada,
leaving tonight and who professed to speak by authority that Marsh could be brought here
within a very few days; the opinion was unanimous that the effort to bring him back should
be made." DLC-Hamilton Fish.

On March 17, U.S. Representative J. Proctor Knott of Ky. wrote to USG. "On Thursday the 2d inst. the committee of the House of Representatives on Expenditures ~~of~~ in the
War Department, laid before the House the testimony of Mr Caleb P. Marsh, which with
certain accompanying papers, was considered sufficent by the House to warrant the immediate impeachment of William W. Belknap, ~~the~~ late Secy. of War, for high crimes and
misdemeanors in office, and the Committee ~~of~~ on the Judiciary of which I have the honor
to be Chairman, was directed to prepare, and report to the House, without unnecessary delay, sutiable articls in support of the same. The facts disclosed by the evidence which was
referred to the Committee ~~of~~ by the House, are briefly as follows:— ~~1~~1—That at the suggestion of the then wife of Mr Belknap, Marsh applied to him as Secretary of War, for an
appointment as post trader, and was promised by the Secretary the position of post Trader
at Fort Sill, Indian Territory. 2—That after having received that promise, Marsh on the

8th day October 1870, entered into a written agreement with one John S. Evans, to the Effect that Evans should receive the appointment, in consideration of which he was to pay Marsh annually, the sum of $12.000, quarterly in advance, the amount subject to be increased or diminished after the first year in certain proportions upon the the happening of one or the other of certain contingiencies provided for in the agreement. 3—That Marsh promised to pay Belknap or Belknap's wife—one half of whatever sums he should receive from Evans under their agreement; and that in pursuance of this corrupt arrangement, Evans was appointed Post Trader at Fort Sill, Oct. 10th 1870. 4—That sometime in the month of November 1870, Marsh paid to Mrs. Belknap, $1.500—one half of the first quarterly instalment received by him from Evans, and that Mrs Belknap having died in December 1870, Marsh paid one half of the next and each subsequent quarterly instalment *directly to Belknap himself* until the last one which was paid some time in December 1875 to the present Mrs. Belknap. Upon these facts the Committee on the Judiciary proceeded to frame such articles of Impeachment as seemed to them to be necessary; but before they had an opportunity to report them to the House, they were advised of the fact that Marsh, the only witness within their knowledge, by whome the most material facts upon which the impeachment had been predicated and the articles drawn, could be proven, had gone beyond the ~~jud~~ jurisdiction of the United States, and that under the circumstances then existing, his attendance As a witness before the senate sitting as a court of Impeachment could not probably be procured. The Committee therefore deemed it their duty to report these facts to the House with a resolution recommitting the subject to them with instructions to hear farther evidence, which was accordingly done, and the resolution adopted. Proceeding under this resolution the committee have been able to discover evidence (and will beyond doubt find much more) strongly corroborative of the testimony of Marsh— the character of which is indicated to some extent by the following letter addressed by ~~the~~ Col. B. H. Gierson of the 10th Regiment U. S. Cavalry to the adjutant General of the Army of the United States, ~~and~~ and forwarded by the latter to the Secretary of War, immediately upon its receipt, together with the application which Marsh had originally filed for the position of Post Trader at Fort Sill, . . . I have not called your attention to this letter and the endorsement thereon, for the mere purpose of showing that, to this manly appeal of a gallant and distinguished officer in behalf of the soldiers under his command, the Secretary of war turned a deaf ear, but simply to indicate ~~as~~ one of the many methods of corroborating the *vital fact*, to which (so far as is yet known,) *Marsh alone can testify*—not merely that Mr. Belknap was a party to a deliberately planned conspiracy to plunder the officers and soldiers of the Army whose interests he was under every obligation that the law, honor, or morality could impose to protect, and defend; *but that quarter by quarter for full five years he received into his own hands his full share of the ill gotten spoils of the infamous combination*; and to show moreover that the accumulation of corroborative evidence which the Committee has already obtained and will doubtless still further develop, renders the testimony of Marsh as to the facts to which he alone is competent to testify, of the very highest importance; and that the attendance of Marsh as a witness, should be secured if possible; if ~~If~~ it is expected that Belknap shall be successfully prosecuted, for ALL the offences involved in the facts above recited—either before the Senate on impeachment, or in the Criminal courts of the Country. . . . I have been repeatedly told that Mr Marsh is now in the City of Montreal, Canada, but that upon your assurance as President of the United states that he shall not be punished for his complicity in the offences charged against the late secretary of war, if he will as a witness on behalf of the government make a true statement of all the facts within his knowledge, he will appear and so testify before any tribunal to which he may be summoned. I do not pretend to know whether he would do so or not, but my firm conviction is that he would. At any rate the importance of his testimony is in my judgement sufficient to justify such an attempt to procure it; and feeling that no one can possibly entertain a deeper interest in seeing the laws faithfully executed I have, after consultation with several of my colleagues on the committee which has the matter in charge, taken the liberty of laying before you the foregoing suggestions, and of suggesting further—with the utmost possible respect that you extend to the witness Marsh the assurance of immunity, and on the condition above indicated. Should this meet your approval a brief note to me giving such assurance will quite sufficient. I will undertake to have the proposition communicated to Marsh, and if he shall fail or refuse to avail himself of it you will at least be entitled to the approbation of the country for having done all in your power to secure the ends of justice and to vindicate the dignity and integrity of the government of which you are the Executive head—" LS, DNA, RG 60, Letters from the President. On the same day, Ulysses S. Grant, Jr., wrote to Pierrepont. "The President desires that you should *to day* acknowledge to the Hon. J. Proctor Knott, Chairman of the Judiciary Committee, the receipt of the enclosed 'referred to you by the President,' and make such reply as you deem proper." ALS, *ibid.* Col. Benjamin H. Grierson's letter of Feb. 28, 1872, linked exhorbitant prices charged by the post trader at Fort Sill to the contract with Marsh.

On March 21, 1876, Fish recorded in his diary. "The Attorney General has a subject which he wishes regarded as confidential viz: That tomorrow morning Marsh and wife will be here and at his house at about 10 oclock. He wishes advice as to whether he had better take them before the Grand Jury, or to put them at the disposal of the Committee. After a good deal of consultation it is concluded that he had better write to Proctor Knott Chairman of the Judiciary Committee informing him of Marshs presence and that he desires to have him before the Grand Jury; that arrangements are made whereby he can be examined so as to be able to appear before the Committee of the House by eleven; and submitting to the Chairman of the Commitee whether Marsh shall first appear before the Grand Jury or before the Committee. Pierrepont states that there are reasons to apprehend that there may be efforts made to get the witness away after the Committee may have obtained such evidence as they desire As I was going into Cabinet the Messenger told me Mrs Grant desired to see me when the Cabinet was over—I found that the same invitation had been extended to all, and on meeting her I found that I was slightly late. Mrs Grant was much excited by sympathy in behalf of the Belknaps—I had not heard what she said before I entered the room but inferred she had made some appeal to those present asking them and their wives to call upon them   She says that Mrs Belknap was very much distressed and had expressed a wish to see her and that she would come so as not to be either seen or recognized. Mrs Grant had refused to let her come in secret; but had seen her when she called on Sunday last during the day. Robeson, Jewell and Chandler had been to see Belknap. I told Mrs Grant that I had not called because I thought it better for both the Belknaps and the Administration that I should not. Robeson stated that his call had been on account of his having been fellow student with Belknap; that the second was yesterday in consequence of a request from Belknap to see him. Robeson expressed regret that Mrs Grant had seen Mrs Belknap in which we all concurred, he stated very clearly and frankly the embarrassment which might result and the advantages both to Belknap and his wife that they should see and speak to no person except their Counsel on the subject of their trouble. Mrs Grant overcome and in tears said she supposed this was right—but she felt so sorry for them." DLC-Hamilton Fish. See *Julia Grant*, pp. 189–92; *Evening Star*, March 3, 1876.

On March 24, Marsh testified before the committee investigating the War Dept. concerning his flight to Canada. *HRC*, 44-1-799, 109–10. On March 31, Fish recorded in his diary. "The Attorney General refers to the instruction given by the President some 3 weeks ago today to institute proceedings against General Belknap   he refers to the fact of

Marshs escape, of his being brought back by the action of the government his having appeared before the Committee of the House of Representatives and of his now being in New York   He asks whether he is to proceed in accordance with the instructions thus given. The President asks me my opinion—I reply that under the circumstances I thought that the administration would be held up to much criticism should it fail after the announcement it had made of its intent to prosecute, institute and press, such proceedings; that if Marsh's testimony had been correctly reported and if there was no other evidence against Belknap than such as had been made public before the Committee I did not suppose he could be convicted, but that the Administration owed it to itself and the country to press the indictment   Robeson and others concurred and the Attorney General was directed to proceed" DLC-Hamilton Fish. On April 1, Saturday, Wells wrote to Pierrepont. "In pursuance of the instructions received from you today I at once telegraphed Mr. Marsh requesting the presence of himself and wife as witnesses in Genl Belknaps case before the Grand Jury on Monday next, at 11 o'clock, and at the same time sent to the U. S. Marshal, N. Y. a subpoena for their attendance accompanied with a letter giving their address, requesting immediate service to be made and the payment or tender of their fees." LS, DNA, RG 60, Letters Received, D. C.

On April 3, the House of Representatives adopted five articles of impeachment against Belknap. *CR*, 44–1, 2159–61. On April 5, the Senate set April 17 for the start of Belknap's trial. *Ibid.*, pp. 2215–16. On April 12, Wednesday, Belknap wrote to his sister Anna M. Belknap. "No news. Everything going on well. The feeling changing rapidly. Some men sorry that they made fools of themselves by being in a hurry & some *remaining* fools, because they are ashamed to acknowledge their error. The Impeachment will begin on Monday without fail. I don't think that the Senate will take up the case. I don't care whether they do so or not. In any event I shall beat them. . . ." ALS, NjP. On April 17, Belknap appeared in the Senate to request dismissal of his case on the ground that his impeachment had occurred after he had resigned as secretary of war; the senate approved a motion by the House managers to adjourn until April 19. *CR*, 44–1, 2502–3. On April 19, Belknap wrote to his sister. "If I had *not* appeared in the Senate I would have been censured because I did not. Now that I *have* appeared the newspaper men censure me because I have.—But I told Judge Black—while in the Senate—that I did not desire to show a spirit of bravado—& I wished to act modestly—but, for my life, I could not look frightened because I did not feel so. . . ." ALS, NjP. On the same day, the House managers refuted Belknap's plea for dismissal, and the Senate adjourned until April 27, when the impeachment trial began in earnest. *CR*, 44–1, 2578–79; *Proceedings of the Senate Sitting for the Trial of William W. Belknap,* . . . (Washington, 1876).

On [*May 2*], Belknap wrote to his sister. ". . . I enclose some slips from hostile papers to show you how I am gaining. The Grand Jury will indict me if they possibly can but they have no testimony but Marsh's & he has told so many stories that they don't know which to believe. The managers (especially McMahon—a son of Hon. Jno. V. L McMahon of Baltimore, by a dissolute woman) have examined witnesses to find out how much it cost me to live—where I bought my clothes—where my underclothes—where we bought marketing—whether I supported you—&c &c all to find whether I had lived beyond my means. Their questions went beyond the bounds of decency, as I hear, but I have no means to prevent it. Barnard was the witness to whom they put these questions. I shall beat them on the question of jurisdiction, I think, without doubt. If not, I shall beat them on the trial & if indicted I shall beat them in the Criminal Court. Gen'l. Hazen is here & is trying to make it appear to my friends that he is not unfriendly to me. Custer is trying to brow-beat the President. He *may* succeed. Anything seems possible now-a-days. I believe that I am the only man in Washington—except Carpenter among the Republicans who is not stam-

peded. They accuse me of everything now, which is illustrated by the fact that some Belknap seduced a girl in Jones Co. Iowa twenty years ago, & the papers are saying that I am
the man—The good fortune of that is that the women are fast coming to my side & soon
I'll be as popular among them, as Beecher!—. . ." ALS (dated "Tuesday"), NjP. In his closing argument on July 24, Jeremiah S. Black, counsel for Belknap, compared USG's receipt
of gifts to Belknap's alleged misdeeds. ". . . That the present Chief Magistrate has taken
large gifts from his friends is a fact as well known as any other in the history of the country. He did it openly, without an attempt at concealment or denial. He not only received
money and lands and houses and goods amounting in the aggregate to an enormous sum,
but he conformed the policy of his administration to the interests and wishes of the donors.
Nay, he did more than that; he appointed the men who brought him these gifts to the highest offices which he could bestow in return. Does anybody assert that General Grant was
guilty of an impeachable crime in taking these presents even though the receipt of them
was followed by official favors extended to the givers?. . ." *Trial of William W. Belknap*,
pp. 972–73. On Aug. 1, the Senate acquitted Belknap on all five articles of impeachment.
Ibid., pp. 1049–97. See William Belknap to Anna Belknap, Aug. 3, 1876, NjP; Ben: Perley
Poore, *Perley's Reminiscences of Sixty Years in the National Metropolis* (Philadelphia, 1886), II,
306–13; Nevins, *Fish*, pp. 804–10; William N. Brigance, *Jeremiah Sullivan Black: A Defender
of the Constitution and the Ten Commandments* (1934; reprinted, New York, 1971), pp. 271–
72; E. Bruce Thompson, *Matthew Hale Carpenter: Webster of the West* (Madison, Wis., 1954),
pp. 243–46; Richard E. Welch, Jr., *George Frisbie Hoar and the Half-Breed Republicans*
(Cambridge, Mass., 1971), pp. 51–54; Mark Wahlgren Summers, *The Era of Good Stealings*
(New York, 1993), pp. 133–34, 261–62.

On Jan. 19, 1877, Matthew H. Carpenter, Washington, D. C., wrote to USG. "In the
prosecution, United States vs. W. W. Belknap, there is in my opinion no foundation for the
prosecution on the facts. Nevertheless a trial would be annoying and expensive to Genl
Belknap; and after all he has suffered for *nothing*, he ought not to be *persecuted*, by a trial if
there is no expectation of conviction   May I ask you to refer it to the Attorney General,
to be by him referred to the District Attorney, to ascertain whether the Dist Atty thinks
conviction can be had, and if not to discontinue the proceedings," ALS, DNA, RG 60, Letters from the President. USG endorsed this letter to Attorney Gen. Alphonso Taft. AE
(undated), *ibid.* On Jan. 26, Henry H. Wells, U.S. attorney, D. C., reported to Taft. "I have
the honor to return herewith a letter addressed to the President, dated Jan'y 19, 1877, by
Matt H. Carpenter, counsel for Gen. Belknap, and by you referred to me on the 23d of this
month. In the report of the impeachment trial of Gen. Belknap there is a very lengthy report of the testimoney on both sides, which I presume may fairly be supposed to exhibit
the proofs against the accused at least as conclusively or strongly as we could expect the
evidence to appear on a trial before a common law jury. I see it was maintained on that trial,
that to convict the accused it was not necessary to establish his guilt of a statutory offence,
nor was it requisite that the proof should show his guilt of every material element in the
offence 'beyond all reasonable doubt.' But whatever the correct rule on an impeachment
trial may be, there can be no doubt whatever that the presumption of innocence in this case
will go with the defendant until by the verdict of a jury he is actually found guilty. And
that he cannot be thus found guilty unless the testimony establishes that conclusion in the
mind of every juror to the exclusion of all reasonable doubt. A careful examination of
the testimony as found in that report can not, I think, fail to impress any one who reads
the same, notwithstanding the rather contentious light in which Mr. Carpenter regards it,
not only with the gravity of the charge, but that the testimony in support of it is of very
great weight. That the accused held office, and appointed the post-Trader, and that a regular stipend amounting to many thousands of dollars was paid as a consideration for the

appointment to and continuance in the place, and that a definite portion of that sum went to the family of the accused, if not to him in person, cannot be doubted. Nor do I see how in the presence of that testimony a trial on such a charge can be said 'to be for nothing' or be denominated 'a persecution.' I cannot, however, when called upon, as thus I am, to express my opinion as to the probable result of such a trial occurring after a trial and acquital on some ground ground by the Senate, say that I have no doubt of the result. Not only so, but I do believe that a conviction is very improbable. It is highly probable that a number of the jurors might have grave doubts as to whether the money was paid to the defendant and received by him with knowledge or belief that it was a price for the appointment already made or a consideration for continuing the person in the position. And under those doubts they would not convict. I believe on the other hand that others of the jury would conclude without doubt that the receipt of so large a sum of money from the person holding the appointment and who was personally known to the defendant, was inconsistant with innocemce, and conclusive Evidence of guilty knowledge. They, therefore, doubtless, would not agree to a verdict of acquital. And I, therefore, should have very little expectation of an agreement by the jury in a verdict of either guilty or not guilty. My expectation would be that a long, expensive and laborous trial would result in a disagreement." LS, *ibid.*, Letters Received, D. C. On Feb. 1, USG endorsed this report. "In view of the within statement of the District Attorney for the District of Columbia in the case of the United States against W. W. Belknap, to the effect that he believes a conviction improbable, and in view of the long suffering of the accused, and the great expense already subjected to, I think the District Attorney should be directed to dismiss the suit." Copies (2), *ibid.* On Feb. 8, Belknap's case was dismissed. See *New York Times*, Feb. 9, 1877.

To George M. Robeson

March 2d 1876.

Sir:

The resignation of the Secretary of War having been tendered and accepted this day, you are hereby directed to assume and perform the duties pertaining to the office of Secretary of War, in addition to those of your own office, until otherwise directed.

Very truly yours
U. S. Grant.

To The Secretary of the Navy.

Copies, DNA, RG 94, Letters Received, 1239 1876; *ibid.*, RG 153, Letters Received, 96 BMJ 1876; DLC-USG, II, 3.

On March 6, 1876, Secretary of State Hamilton Fish recorded in his diary. "While waiting for the President at the White House I met Genl Hurlbut who told me that there were rumors seriously affecting the Navy Department that Mr Whittehorn, Chairman of the Naval Committee had one day last week mentioned to an officer of the Navy who boards at the same house with Hurlbut, that by Wednesday next they would have the Head of the Navy Department in a worse fix than Belknap Kasson came to my house last night and mentioned that Burleigh of Maine a Republican, very hostile to Robeson, had said with a good deal of bitterness speaking of Robeson 'damn him we have caught him' and that some one in the Navy Department had testified, or was ready to testify that $92.000 awarded on the Secor Claim had been paid to Mrs Aulick now Mrs Robeson. In my interview with the President I confidentially told him what had been confidentially told me. . . . After returning to my Office I send to Mr Robeson asking him to come in to see me. He calls and I tell him what I have heard. He says that all is false." DLC-Hamilton Fish.

On March 18, Admiral David D. Porter, Washington, D. C., wrote to Gen. William T. Sherman, St. Louis, concerning William W. Belknap's resignation as secretary of war, gossip surrounding Kate Williams (wife of the former attorney gen.), and impending revelations involving Robeson. ". . . Our cuttle fish of the navy although he may conceal his tracks for awhile in the obscure atmosphere which surrounds him, will eventually be brought to bay and in less than two weeks will create a greater sensation than ever did the illustrious Tweed. . . . There are some thirty misdemeanors, each punishable by separate fine and imprisonment that will be brought home to the Secy and a most perfect confusion in the accounts of the Department. In the Bureau of Construction alone, out of fifty six millions disbursed fifteen millions cannot be accounted for and I think I can safely say that the impression left upon the minds of the members of the Committee is that it has been stolen by—somebody! As the Cuttle fish is responsible for it all and has drawn drafts right and left for objects never contemplated by the law; it is fair to suppose he must have pocketed a large share of the deficiency. The Committee are very close and try to keep things to themselves as much as possible, but from hints dropped now and then about houses that I hear have been presented other real estate and presents of all kinds which the Cuttle fish has gobbled up, it is certain that there will be more than enough to hook him. . . . How the President could have been deceived in this person I do not know, but he certainly has been to a most astonishing degree He ought not to have been deceived a great while for he has had advantages which other people do not have to find out the truth. He has Ammen at his right hand and if Ammen has been a true friend he must have satisfied the President of the Cuttle fish's dishonesty—or else he should have left the Department and not become a party to it. . . ." LS, DLC-William T. Sherman. See Sherman to Porter, March 15, 1876, MoSHi. U.S. Representative Washington C. Whitthorne of Tenn., chairman, House Committee on Naval Affairs, oversaw hearings on the Navy Dept. that did not lead to any formal charges against Robeson. See *HMD*, 44-1-170, parts 1–9; *HRC*, 44-1-784; *CR*, 44–1, 4942–63, 5016–28; Mark Wahlgren Summers, *The Era of Good Stealings* (New York, 1993), pp. 128–29, 262–66.

Appointment

I hereby appoint Ulysses S. Grant Jr. to be Private Secretary to the President of the United States to date from the first day of March 1876.

U. S. GRANT

EXECUTIVE MANSION
MARCH 3D 1876.

DS, USG 3.

On Feb. 22, 1876, Secretary of State Hamilton Fish recorded in his diary a conversation with USG. "He then spoke of Genl Babcock and said he supposed he would be acquitted but that he could never return to his office, that both he and Luckey must leave it, that it was very hard for Babcock that he did not know whether he would wish to return but he should say to him that it was better for himself and necessary for the President that such should be the case" DLC-Hamilton Fish. On Feb. 24, a jury in St. Louis acquitted Orville E. Babcock on conspiracy charges. On Feb. 25, Friday, and subsequently, Fish recorded in his diary. "The President said now that the Babcock trial is over the question to be considered was whether Mr Dyer was to be retained This created a conspicuous silence The President then said that he after mature consideration had come to the determination to make a change in his entire Official Family, and should make his son his Private Secretary; he said it was hard on his son as it would put him back a year, but he was compelled to have some one whom he could absolutely trust to open letters, and if he did that he could do nothing else. Judge Pierrepont thought no one could doubt the wisdom of that course. The President then made some other remark about Dyer and Pierrepont said that the question of compensation of Counsel in these cases would have to be considered, that he had received extravagant bills from special counsel. Hendersons bill was about $26.000, and that the whole question must be considered either by the Cabinet or President and that probably a special appropriation would have to be asked for. The President said he would not pay Henderson one cent but would leave him to the Court of Claims; he asked Pierrepont if he thought Henderson rendered any service to the Government Pierrepont thought he rendered good service, and a good deal of money had been returned to the Government. Bristow concurred—The President spoke of Dyer and Pierrepont suggested that it should come up before full Cabinet and receive careful consideration. The President said that he would let the matter stand until Tuesday." "Feby 29th . . . I tell him I hear that Babcock has resumed his seat in his office and express my regret thereat He says he is only there temporarally but that an Article in the New York Tribune had stated that he was to be ejected, and that seeing that he had allowed him to take a message to the Senate; but it would not occur again" "March 1st . . . Another conversation takes place about Babcock and his resignation. The President said he would resign today and that he had appointed his son as his Private Secretary, and there was no place for Babcock in the Office; that he had promised his resignation today and the President had waited a half hour before coming to see me for it, but it had not come I told him he had nothing to resign; after a moments pause he smiled and said 'thats true hes only got to stay away'" "March 4th . . . I speak of Genl Babcocks still occupying the place in the adjoining room he says it is but temporary and only to get together his papers which are in the office. I ask him if Babcock is to continue as Commissioner of Public Buildings He says the designation of the officer rests with the head of the Engineer Corps that he thinks it would be well for Babcock to withdraw. He says that Babcock seems to feel agrieved at not being allowed to occupy the next room." DLC-Hamilton Fish. See letter to Alphonso Taft, Sept. 16, 1876; Adolph E. Borie to Zachariah Chandler, Feb. 26, 1876, DLC-Zachariah Chandler.

On March 8, Levi P. Luckey wrote to Elihu B. Washburne. "This letter is principally about my own affairs but I know the kind interest you take in them and I wish you to know the facts in connection with my resignation at the White House. . . . While I was in St. Louis in November parties came to me & told me of a great many things on the part of Dyer & Henderson & also of officers of the Treasury which looked like treason to the President. I took it all in, kept my own counsel, & when I got home told the President, as I considered it my duty to do, all that I had heard & from whom. He said it coincided with other information. Just at that time came Henderson's speech in the closing of Avery's trial, for which the President removed him. In all this nothing had occurred on my part with which the President was not perfectly satisfied. . . . Upon our return after Babcock's trial I saw at once that Fred & Buck, who had been acting while we were away in St. Louis three weeks, were anxious to stay & that the family wished them to. The second day after our return I had a talk with the President when he informed me that he and Mrs. Grant would like to keep Buck & Fred with them the last year of the Administration & he could not afford to keep Buck without the salary; also that he knew that the Democrats intended to keep right on attacking Babcock & me too, though he knew there was nothing upon which they could harm me, yet if he had his own sons there they could make no attack except upon him personally. I told him I could not complain that he should wish to give my place to his son, but just upon our return from the triumphant issue of Babcock's trial, to leave then would throw a reflection upon us, (though I spoke particularly of myself.). The President said no one could reflect upon me in any way for both he & Mr Chandler were desirous that I should take charge of the Indian division of the Secretary's Office of the Int. Dept. which Mr Chandler considered the most responsible place under him, as he signed away millions during the year upon the initials of the one in charge. That A. S. H. White who had held the place for over 20 years had been dismissed by Mr Chandler two months ago & he had been unable to find anyone he would trust in the place. That the plan was for me to take that position & if Cox (D. C.) whose re-nomination had been in the Senate two months nearly for Pension Agent here, should be rejected on the charges preferred against him before the Senate Committee that he would give me that place. I was in hopes he would withdraw Cox & nominate me, but he would not do that as Cox had been a fair officer for four years past. He said he would do anything for me he could that I wished but recommended me to take the Indian office now. So here I am, and pitching in to learn all about the Indian business I can. Cox's nomination is yet in the Senate & I believe the Committee is examining witnesses &c yet. I presume if he is rejected I shall be nominated in his place, if not I shall have to look around for something else or try and find some business opening, which no doubt would be best of all. I can't say I like the prospect of staying in this place & having the responsibility, which I must assume, for $2.000 a year. The Pension Agency pays about $4.500. I understand. My Secretaryship paid $3.500. and it is a good plunge to come down to about one half. I told the President that I should like to know if I had lost any of his confidence in any way or if he had any cause to be dissatisfied with my administration of his office. He replied he never had more confidence in me in his life than right now, & never in the seven years I had been with him had had occasion to find fault with a single thing. . . . P. S. I have just heard that the Senate confirmed Cox last evening, so that matter is out of the question." ALS, DLC-Elihu B. Washburne. See Washburne to Luckey, March 27, 1876, *ibid.* On Jan. 8, 1877, USG nominated Luckey as secretary, Utah Territory.

To Lt. Gen. Philip H. Sheridan

Washington, D. C. March 6th *1876.*
GEN. P. H. SHERIDAN, CHICAGO, ILL.
You ~~may~~ [will] notify post trader at Fort Sill that his trade license are revoked to take effect as soon as his successor is ready to furnish

supplies. In the mean time direct the Council of Administration at
the post to meet and fix prices at which the present post trader will
be permitted to sell goods while allowed to remain at the post, and
also direct them to recommend to the Sec. of War, through the
proper Military channels, a suitable successor for the present incumbent. Also direct Military commanders at all posts[1] to report
whether there is reason to believe that ~~reasons exist for~~ change
should be made in their Post Traders, and ~~through~~ where they recommend a change let the Council of Administration recommend to
the Sec. of War in like manner suitable person for the places.[2]

U. S. GRANT

ALS (bracketed word not in USG's hand), DNA, RG 94, ACP, 1067 1876. On March 6,
1876, Secretary of State Hamilton Fish recorded a conversation with USG. "I suggest to
him the propriety of issuing an order to the Officer at Fort Sill to take control of the Post
Traders establishment there and to recommend a new trader in the place of Evans and to
fix the prices at which articles should be furnished until a new trader should take possession. He had given orders for the removal of Evans but it had not yet been issued. I suggested that the removal of Evans without further order might close the store and subject
the garrison and others to great inconvenience—he said he would himself prepare an order and have it issued at once. I then suggest that as there were charges affecting more
or less all of the post trader establishments whether it would not be well to anticipate
any movement in Congress and direct the post-Council or Advisory Board at each post to
investigate the affairs of the Post Traders. To which he assented saying he would direct
such order to be sent out. I urge expedition and care in the preparing of the order" DLC-
Hamilton Fish. On the same day, Ulysses S. Grant, Jr., wrote to George M. Robeson, act.
secretary of war. "The enclosed is an order the President wishes you to give 'at his direction.'" ALS, DNA, RG 94, ACP, 1067 1876. On March 7, AG Edward D. Townsend addressed commanding officers. *"By direction of the President of the United States, you will immediately report whether or not you have reason to believe it would be for the public interest to
revoke the appointment of the present Post Trader at your post. In case you deem such action advisable, you will forthwith convene a Post Council of Administration, in order to a nomination of a
suitable person to receive the appointment, which nomination will be endorsed with your views as
to its approval. You will transmit the report and any papers pertaining thereto to this Office through
military channels, for the action of the Secretary of War."* D, *ibid.* Related papers are *ibid.*
   Also on March 7, Oliver R. McNary, Leavenworth, Kan., wrote to USG. "Confidential . . . If it is desirable to make a full and complete Expose of Corruption on the part of
the Late-Sect-of War—You should have certain parties—from here or Ft Leavenworth as
witnesses. . . ." ALS, *ibid.,* Letters Received, 1536 1876. A related letter is *ibid.*
   On March 14, Secretary of War Alphonso Taft wrote to U.S. Senator John Sherman
of Ohio. "Since my advent into the War Office many applications have been made for the
Post-Tradership at Fort Sill, to all of which I have replied that, as the President, previous
to my appointment, had referred the subject of the selection of a trader for Fort Sill, to the
Council of Administration there, I did not feel at liberty to take any action in the premises.
But on account of your commendation of Colonel Nigh, and other recommendations in his
favor, I have directed the Adjutant General to refer the whole matter, through the Com-

manding Officer at Fort Sill, to the Council for its consideration." Copy, *ibid.*, RG 107, Letters Sent, Military Affairs. On the same day, Taft wrote to Elias Nigh, former lt. col. and q. m., Ironton, Ohio, concerning his application. Copy, *ibid.* On March 18, Lt. Col. James W. Forsyth wrote to Bernard Laiboldt, St. Louis. "I am instructed by Lieut. Gen. Sheridan to acknowledge the receipt of your letter of 7th inst., making application for the Tradership at Fort Sill, and to inform you in reply thereto that he has nothing to do with the appointment of Traders at military posts, nor does he intend to have anything to do with them. . . ." Copy (press), DLC-Philip H. Sheridan. See *PUSG*, 24, 381–82. On March 31, Fish recorded cabinet deliberation. "The Secretary of War has received from the Officers of the Post, at Fort Sill an application for the reappointment of Evans at post-trader. Genl Pope disapproves of the reappointment in transmitting it to the Department. It is determined not to reappoint him, but to instruct the post council to recommend some other person." DLC-Hamilton Fish. On May 22, Col. Ranald S. Mackenzie, Fort Sill, wrote to Gen. William T. Sherman concerning post-trader problems. ALS, DLC-William T. Sherman. See *HRC*, 44-1-799, 105–6. Joseph K. Byers, former 1st lt., 42nd Inf., replaced John S. Evans as post trader, Fort Sill.

On July 19, Evans testified at the impeachment trial of William W. Belknap concerning his tenure as post trader and business arrangement with Caleb P. Marsh, elaborating on testimony he had given in March to the House Committee on Expenditures in the War Dept. *Proceedings of the Senate Sitting for the Trial of William W. Belknap,* . . . (Washington, 1876), pp. 836–51, 854–63; *HRC*, 44-1-799, 76–88. The House managers prosecuting this impeachment probed the history of post-trader appointments. See letter to William W. Belknap, March 2, 1876; DNA, RG 94, ACP, 2124 1876.

Orvil L. Grant's involvement in post-trader irregularities implicated USG and heightened interest in congressional investigation. On July 3, 1874, Secretary of the Interior Columbus Delano had written to USG. "Durfee and Peck have trading licenses as follows; Cheyenne River Agency, Dakota, which expires January 22. 1875. Fort Berthold in Dakota, which expires December 22. 1874. Grand River Agency, Dakota, which expires September 19. 1874. Fort Belknap and Fort Peck in Montana expire September 11. 1874. These embrace all their licenses and they have been instructed to close them up at the earliest possible day, not later than September 22. next." Copy, Delano Letterbooks, OHi. On March 9, 1876, Orvil Grant testified before a House committee examining expenditures in the War Dept. ". . . Q. Did you ever show to Mr. Bowen, in Orange, a letter purporting to be from the President of the United States, in reply to one addressed by you to him applying for the trading-post at Fort Peck, the substance of which was that he had given orders for no more trading-posts to be given out until he should so order, and that he did not know what that post at Fort Peck was worth?—A. I don't think I ever showed that to Bowen. . . . I presume I have destroyed it; I never save my letters. Q. Can you state about the date of that letter?—A. No, sir. . . . I suppose that it must have been—I don't remember—it must have been in 1874, . . . I think it must have been in the summer of 1874. . . . Q. Was this the only letter you had from the President of the United States relating to post-traderships?—A. I think so. . . . I think he wrote me once that there were going to be some vacancies created—some persons to be removed. Q. Why did he write you that letter?—A. Because I had told him that I would like to get a trading-post. Q. At the time he wrote you that there were vacancies in trading-posts, did you make application to him for one?—A. I spoke to him about it previous to that. Q. But after he wrote you that there were vacancies did you obtain one?—A. Yes, sir; I obtained Fort Peck. . . . Standing Rock, also. Q. They were both given after the President had informed you that there were to be vacancies?—A. Yes, sir. Q. Did you ever make application to him for any other posts than these two—Fort Peck and Standing Rock?—A. I don't remember that I ever did. . . .

Q. Do you know when Durfee & Peck were removed? You said a while ago in 1874; can you tell the time exactly?—A. No; I cannot tell exactly. Q. Did the President notify you before or after they were removed?—A. I think he notified me that they were going to be removed. Q. So that you could make application before anybody else did?—A. I don't know that that was what it was done for. . . . If I had not known there was going to be a vacancy of course I should not have made an application; because I would never try to get any one removed. . . . Q. Did you say to the reporter of the Philadelphia Times that you got men appointed to posts through your influence with the President?—A. I did not state as much to the Philadelphia Times man as I have stated here. . . . I suppose I feel grateful to my brother, and indebted to him for getting that post at Standing Rock. . . . Q. You consider, then, that you do have influence with the President to manage these matters to some extent?—A. To some extent I have; though I am sorry to say that they are of very little profit to me. . . ." *HRC*, 44-1-799, 26–29. See *ibid.*, pp. 23–32, 49–65, 155–56, 236–38, 240, 249–54, 259–65; *HMD*, 44-1-167, 328–35, 341–44. On March 14, U.S. Representative Hiester Clymer of Pa. wrote to USG. "I have the honor to request that, you will please furnish for the information of the Committee on expenditures of the War Department certified copies of *all Orders*, issued by the Executive since March 4th 1869, relating to the extension of certain Indian Reservation, with special reference to that of Standing Rock Agency. An early compliance with this request is respectfully solicited." Copy, DNA, RG 130, Register of Congressional Inquiry. On March 21, USG wrote to Clymer transmitting "copies of all the papers received this day from the Secretary of the Interior to whom your request was referred." Copy, DLC-USG, II, 3. *HRC*, 44-1-799, 549. See *ibid.*, pp. 549–58. On March 22, Culver C. Sniffen wrote to Clymer. "The accompanying map should have been handed in yesterday afternoon with the communication to you from the President in the matter of the 'Standing Rock Agency.' I overlooked it." Copy, DLC-USG, II, 3.

    Probably in 1879, Orvil Grant wrote letters to L. D. Randall & Co., Dubuque, Iowa, and John Thompson & Co., Standing Rock, Dakota Territory, concerning payments for trading posts. ALS, OFH. On Sept. 10, 1879, Ezra A. Hayt, commissioner of Indian Affairs, telegraphed to John Thompson, Dubuque. "Have you agreed to sell your trading Post To Grant." Telegram received, *ibid.* On the same day, Thompson telegraphed to Hayt. "Have not Agreed to sell any thing to Grant   he is a fraud and not worthy of beleif" Copy, *ibid.* By 1879, Orvil Grant's mental health was considered unsound. See *New York Times*, Sept. 5, 1878, Jan. 28, 1879, Aug. 7, 9, 1881; *The History of Dubuque County, Iowa*, . . . (Chicago, 1880), pp. 863, 888.

    Reportedly in late Nov. or early Dec., 1874, John H. Charles, Washington, D. C., had written to USG. "Regretting very much that circumstances compel me to trouble you with the subject-matter of this letter, I only do so because my all is at stake; and as I have failed to obtain just relief from your subordinates, the President and Congress are the only tribunals left to which I can appeal for justice, and as this lies within your jurisdiction. I was granted licenses to establish trading-posts at certain points on the Missouri River. Under those licenses I went on, purchased stocks of goods, erected or purchased the necessary buildings and warehouses, and prepared for trade. While prosecuting my business, without a single charge having been preferred against me, my licenses were revoked and Mr. Orvil L. Grant was given the sole right to trade on the river. The law nowhere contemplates that this right of trade shall be made a monopoly. I was and am still willing to withdraw from that country and give up the trade, provided that Mr. Grant will pay a reasonable price for my buildings and stock on hand; we to agree upon the prices wherever we can, and to leave the prices of all things upon which we cannot agree to be settled by arbitrators, appointed in the usual manner. To such an arrangement I was and am willing to agree, and to break up my business and withdraw from trade in that country, upon any basis that will not involve my total ruin. If Mr. Grant, coming in with exclusive powers and privileges, will not do this, then I hope and entreat that as a matter of fairness and justice you will order the Secretary of the Interior to carry out the law, to renew my licenses, withdraw the interdiction on my trade, and allow me to carry on my business in fair and honorable competition." *HRC*, 44-1-799, 121. On March 25, 1876, Charles testified before the committee examining the War Dept. "Q. Did you tell the President also the substance of that letter in your interview with him?—A. Yes, sir; Senator Allison was present when the interview took place. Q. What did the President say?—A. Well, he said he had fixed that thing, and was not going to change it, and he bit the end off his cigar, as if he didn't like me a bit. . . . My impression is that when I came here and had an interview with the President, it was about the 1st of December, 1874, . . ." *Ibid.*, p. 122. On the same day, George W. Felt testified concerning his appointment "as Indian trader at Cheyenne agency" in 1874. "I made the application for it in August, I think, and the appointment came about the 5th of September. Q. Who was the occupant of the place at the time you made application?—A. John H. Charles. . . . Q. Had you any conversation with the President on that subject?—A. I had. . . . He said I should receive an Indian appointment. . . . Q. You paid nothing for your privileges there?—A. Not a cent. Q. What did you pay for political purposes?—A. Not a cent. No demand ever has been made upon me. . . ." *Ibid.*, pp. 131–32. See *ibid.*, pp. 123–25. Also on March 25, Felt, "age, thirty-eight; residence, Sioux City; occupation, grocer and Indian trader up the river," testified on the same subject before the Committee on Indian Affairs. ". . . I was acquainted with General Grant before the war, when he was as poor as I am now, probably, and we had traveled together collecting. We lived in the same town, Galena, Ill., and I had been somewhat unfortunate in my business matters at Sioux City, and went to General Grant and asked him if there was a trading-post at his disposal that I could have. He said that he would reflect upon it and let me know. He told me that I could have a post. I applied for Cheyenne. I got the license; it went through in regular form. . . . The long and short of it is, I never paid a cent, and not even gave a cigar, not because I am too mean to do it, but because the circumstance never arose where I could do it with propriety. I knew that he would not thank me particularly for a cigar or a box of them or a thousand of them. . . ." *HMD*, 44-1-167, 347–48. On Aug. 4, 1874, Belknap had telegraphed to Orville E. Babcock, Long Branch. "A Mr. Felt from Sioux City is at Long Branch trying I am informed to effect the removal of the trader lately appointed at Fort Lincoln. It would be great injustice to the new trader ~~to have~~ to interfere with him now. If it comes to your attention please say ~~so to t~~ this to the President" ALS (telegram sent), DNA, RG 107, Telegrams Collected (Bound). On Feb. 18, Felt, Sioux City, Iowa, had written to USG recommending Lewis Candee for army paymaster. ALS, *ibid.*, RG 94, Applications for Positions in War Dept. On Feb. 23, U.S. Senator George G. Wright of Iowa wrote to Babcock concerning Felt's letter. ". . . be good enough to lay it before the President. Mr. Felt is one of my very best friends and constituents, and his wishes, I trust, may be carried out." ALS, *ibid.* No appointment followed.

On Jan. 13, 1875, Orvil Grant's involvement with post-trader licenses came under attack during House debate on Indian appropriations. *CR*, 43-2, 440–44. On Jan. 27, George A. Fitch, Chicago, wrote to Orvil Grant. "I want to see you 'the worst in the world.' I have a matter of the *greatest possible importance* on hand, in which I want you to join me, and which I have neither time or space to explain. Suffice it to say, that no money will be required of you—only a brief amount of your time, your influence, and your work. Let me know *immediately*, and by *telegraph*, where I can meet you and lay the whole matter before you. I *know* that when you are informed of the project, you will take hold of without a moment's hesitation. And if there was not a large amount of money in it for you, and for me,

I would not trouble you about it. Let me hear from you *immediately*, and by *telegraph*, where I can see you." ALS, Babcock Papers, ICN. Grant endorsed this letter, presumably to Babcock. "Will you please write Mr Fitch and tell him you do not know where I am I leave the city tomorrow morning and if you write him tomorrow you can safely say you do not know where I am. I dont want him to come here and annoy me in trying to get me to use my influence and I have lost all aspirations to make a fortune so suddenly as Fitch would like me to do." AE (initialed, undated), *ibid.*

On July 29, 1874, Mrs. M. T. Crapser, Evanston, Ill., had written to USG. "Excuse the liberty I take addressing you, but the great trouble I am in must be my excuse Three years ago, I came to this place. I am a widow with two daughters, and I brought with me six thousand dollars to invest it was my all. My Brother-in law J H Smith said his friend O L Grant would take the money and [g]ive me ten per cent I asked him what security he would give. he said that he Smith had a guarantee from the President U. S. Grant that he would be security for O L Grant, and he gave me the paper to read. I was satisfied, and let him have the money, and took O. L. G. notes for the same, with J H Smiths name on the back also for security, and I have received the interest till within the last year and also have drawn one thousand of the principal the notes came to maturity one, last July, the other the twenty six of May, and the interest was due, and when time past by, and I neither got interest or principal I wrote to O. L. Grant, by the advice of my Lawyer Mr G. Ide, and he wrote me word that he had never had a dollar of my money in his life. Mr Ide took the notes to Mr Small of Chicago and he recognized the signature as that of O. L. Grant, and Mr Grant does not deny the signature, but says he never had my money, says he signed the notes in blank but did not know it was for my money, and he also says that Mr Smith had no right to that Guarantee. now will you please explain how J. H. Smith come by that guarantee (a copy of the same I will send you) I would not trouble you but I have two children dependent on me for support and that was my all, and I know not what to do. now my desire to clear up this mystery and recover my money if possible is very great, and if you will explain to me about the guarantee, you will greatly oblige a wronged family." ALS, USG 3. The enclosure is a purported note dated March 5, 1867, from USG, New York City, to J. H. Smith. "I will be responsible for my brother O L Grant to the extent of $15,000 00" Copy, *ibid.*

1. On Sept. 11, 1874, Belknap had written to Lt. Gen. Philip H. Sheridan, Chicago, concerning the appointment of Robert C. Seip as post trader, Fort Abraham Lincoln, Dakota Territory, in place of Samuel A. Dickey. ". . . I had nothing to do with the removal of the trader at Lincoln; he was ordered to be removed by the President, and was permitted to resign. The order came to me in the President's handwriting, and is filed with papers in the case. The order refers to the fact that Dickey is charged with violation of the revenue laws, and of introducing whisky among the Indians. It further states that the office is held in the name of Dickey, but really for the benefit of Robert Wilson, formerly sutler at Fort Riley, driven from there for disloyalty. All of this is in the President's handwriting, and that is all I know about the removal of Mr. Dickey, excepting that the commanding officer at Fort Lincoln, General Custer, was called upon for a report, which he made, . . ." *HRC*, 44-1-799, 153. On March 29, 1876, Lt. Col. George A. Custer testified before the House committee investigating War Dept. expenditures. ". . . Mr. Seip then became the trader, and the prices that were charged the officers and soldiers became so exorbitant that as many as could, purchased what they desired elsewhere. They did so until Mr. Seip made a written complaint and forwarded it to the Secretary of War, claiming that under the privilege which he held as trader, nobody, no officer even, had a right to buy anything else-

where or bring it there, but must buy everything through him. . . . Q. Have you ever had any conversation with Orvil Grant, or his partner, Bonnafon, with regard to their interest in military and trading posts?—A. Yes, sir; I have had several conversations with Mr. Bonnafon and with Mr. Grant. . . . The first time I met them I was traveling from Saint Paul to my post, Fort Abraham Lincoln, four or five or six hundred miles, and Mr. Bonnafon and Mr. Grant were on the same train, and as they desired to travel from Fort Lincoln by wagon, or other similar conveyance, and about the only means of conveyance were those in possession of the military, they explained to me that they were then on a visit to certain Indian trading-posts, in which they were interested. They mentioned the posts, four or five in number; I don't know that I can state them accurately; but Fort Belknap, Fort Peck, Fort Berthold, and Standing-Rock I think were the four posts they named, and Mr. Grant asked me if I would furnish him an ambulance to make the trip. . . . I told him I would not give it to him as a trader, but that to any member of the President's family visiting there, out of courtesy to the President of the United States, I would render any facility I could." *Ibid.*, pp. 153, 155. Custer testified that he discovered fraud involving 8,000 bushels of corn purchased for Indians at Fort Peck, Montana Territory. "Q. Do you know anything about the traders at Fort Peck having anything to do with that corn fraud, or was there any complicity on their part?—A. The only way that there could have been fraud would have been by complicity on the part of the agent. The agent would have to relieve the contractor in some way, by certifying that this corn had been delivered. Q. I mean complicity on the part of the traders?—A. My experience has been that the traders and the agents are interested with each other very generally. . . . Q. You do not know positively whether such an arrangement existed at Fort Peck or not?—A. No, sir; I do not." *Ibid.*, pp. 160–61. Recalled on April 4, Custer testified that Belknap had issued orders in 1873 that effectively barred individual army officers from reporting such frauds to Congress. See *ibid.*, pp. 162–63.

On April 5, 1876, Forsyth wrote to Belknap. ". . . I have yet to meet a single officer of the Army who approves of the action of either Custer or McCook—As to their testimony, it is nothing but hearsay, which is largely made up of frontier gossip, and stories—The English English language, as known in polite society, will not permit of my doing full justice to the subject—but if I were with you, for a few moments, I think that I might illuminate the subject *some*—. . . The fact of the matter is; that both Hazen, and Custer, are now working to make capitol with the Democratic party—*they want stars.* As for McCook he is a damn fool who thinks too little and talks too much, . . ." ALS (press), DLC-Philip H. Sheridan. On April 10, Forsyth wrote to Belknap requesting that these remarks on Custer and other officers be kept private, adding, "I understand that Custer is on his way out here, the (3) three Companies of the 7th Cavly have been orderd up from the south, and I understand that an Expedition will go out from Lincoln. ~~and~~ I have no doubt but that Custer will go in Command. If you are going to want him, you had better make your application at once, and have the War Dept: telegraph and call Custer back There is no use of asking who will go in command of any troops, or Expedition sent against Indians in Dakota: for if Custer is available he is *certain to have the command.*" ALS (press), *ibid.* On April 28, Gen. Sherman telegraphed to Sheridan. "The President has just sent me instructions through the Secretary of War, to send some one else than General Custer in command of that force from Fort Abe Lincoln. Detail and instruct some one else. If you have no one that you want, indicate the man and if subject to my orders you can have him." Copies, USG 3; DNA, RG 108, Letters Sent. On April 29, Sheridan telegraphed to Sherman. "Your dispatch in reference to the Command of the Expedition from Fort Lincoln was duly received, I propose to send Genl Terry the Department Commandant in Custers place" Telegram received, *ibid.*, RG 94, Letters Received, 2347 1876.

On May 1, Custer wrote to USG regretting that his request for an interview had not been granted. "I desired this opportunity simply as a matter of justice . . ." Parke-Bernet Galleries, 1963, no. 44. On May 2, Sherman telegraphed to Sheridan. "I am this moment advised that General Custer Started last night for St Paul and Fort Ab. Lincoln. He was not justified in Starting without Seeing the President or myself—Please intercept him at Chicago or Saint Paul and order him to halt and await further orders. Meantime let the Expedition from Fort Lincoln proceed without him." ALS (facsimile, telegram sent), W. A. Graham, *The Story of the Little Big Horn: Custer's Last Fight* (Harrisburg, 1945), between pp. 104–5; copies, USG 3; DNA, RG 108, Letters Sent. On May 4, Ulysses S. Grant, Jr., wrote to Sherman. "The President wishes that you and the Secretary of War should see the enclosed newspaper clipping. After you have seen it will you please show it to the Secretary" ALS, USG 3. The enclosed clipping originated in the *New York World.* "President Grant has to-day performed an act which appears to be the most high-handed abuse of his official power which he has perpetrated yet. As is well known, General Custer gave important testimony before the investigation committees relative to the post-tradership frauds, and was subpœnaed by the House managers as a witness in the impeachment trial. In obedience to that subpœna he came on, and has been here for some days. To-day the President relieved him from his command. When the news came to General Sherman and Secretary Taft, both went to the President and protested that it would not do. General Sherman went further, and said that Custer was not only the best man, but the only man fit to lead the expedition now fitting out against the Indians. To all their entreaties Grant turned a deaf ear, and said that if they could not find a man to lead the expedition he would find one; that this man Custer had come on here both as a witness and a prosecutor in the Belknap matter to besmirch his administration, and he proposed to put a stop to it. By advice of General Sherman and Secretary Taft General Custer went to the White House to call on the President, although he said he did not believe it would be of any use, for he had done nothing but his duty, nothing that he had any apologies to make for doing, and nothing but what he would do again under the same circumstances. He had come on here in obedience to law. Nevertheless, in deference to their judgment, he went to the White House and sat in the waiting room unsent for until the President's calling hour was over, although he repeatedly sent in his card. Finally he wrote a letter to the President and left it, in which he stated that he called for the purpose of disabusing the President's mind, if he had heard any statements that he (Custer) had said or done anything against the President personally. It is understood that the President will publicly assign as his reason for relieving Custer that he is here and will not be back to his command in time to take charge of the expedition now getting ready to start against the Indians; but it is also understood that General Custer will be back in time, for the managers have relieved him from their subpœna, and General Grant will have to make some other excuse to the people." *Ibid.* Also on May 4, Thursday, Sherman wrote to Grant, Jr. "I am glad to receive your letter of this date enclosing the newspaper slip which I had seen before, because it enables me to state officially the facts of the case. Last Friday Genl. Custer came to my office and stated that he was extremely anxious to get away from Washington to join his command at Fort Abe Lincoln. He asked me to write a note to Mr. Clymer to the effect that he was much needed with his command on the point of taking the field. I explained to him that I could not properly communicate with the Committee, but would explain his case to the Secretary of War who could. I saw the Secretary when he was in the act of starting for the Cabinet meeting of that day, and he said he would attend to it as soon as he got back to his office. When he, the Secretary of War, came back, he said the President was not pleased with General Custer, and that he wanted the expedition started out from Fort Lincoln without him. I at once sent the enclosed despatch marked A to General Sheridan and received the answer B. On Saturday General Custer again called and I told him what had been done, and showed him the record of my despatch to General Sheridan. He was much troubled and I advised him to see the President in person. On Saturday night I went to New York and did not return till Tuesday. I called to see the President that same morning and was then of opinion that General Custer was still in Washington, and did not learn till near night that he had actually started west for his post. I at once sent to General Sheridan the despatch (C) and have received his acknowledgment of it. So that General Custer will be stopped at Chicago or St. Paul to await further action or orders. I say most emphatically that General Custer though relieved as a witness by the Committee was not justified in leaving Washington under the circumstances of the case, and that the enclosed newspaper paragraph gives a wrong statement of the whole case. I surely never 'protested' to the President or to any body, nor did I ever intimate that General Custer 'was not only the best man, or the only man fit to lead the expedition &c.' I believe the Army possesses hundreds who are competent for such an expedition and I knew that General Terry who is perfectly qualified for the highest military duty had already been chosen to conduct the same expedition. I will show this letter and its enclosures to the Secretary of War, and most respectfully report that General Custer is now subject to any measure of discipline which the President may require. Whether he is responsible or not for the enclosed newspaper paragraph I have not the means of knowing and I surely cannot believe that he could so mis-represent the case." LS, *ibid.* On the same day, Secretary of War Alphonso Taft wrote to Grant, Jr., concerning the clipping. ". . . These statements are entirely untrue. . . ." LS, *ibid.* Also on May 4, Sheridan telegraphed to Sherman that "General Custer is in this City and will remain until further orders are received from higher authority." Copy, *ibid.* Sherman telegraphed in reply. "Have received your dispatch of today announcing General Custer's arrival. Have just come from the President who orders that General Custer be allowed to rejoin his post, to remain there on duty—but not to accompany the expedition supposed to be on the point of starting against the hostile Indians under General Terry." Copy, DNA, RG 108, Letters Sent.

Also on May 4, Custer, Chicago, twice telegraphed to Sherman. "I have seen your dispatch to Genl Sheridan directing me to await orders here and am at a loss to understand that portion referring to my departure from Washington without seeing you or the president as I called at the white House at ten o'clock A. M. Monday sent my card to the President and with the exception of a few minutes absence at the War Department I remained at the white House awaiting an audience with the President until three (3) Pm when he sent me word that he could not see me, I called at your office about two (2) P. m. but was informed by Col McCook you had not returned from New York . . ." "I desire to further call your attention to your statement to me in your office that I could go in command of my regiment also to your reply when I enquired if the president or other parties had any charges against me in leaving washington I had every reason to believe I was acting in strict accordance with your Suggestions and wishes I ask you as General of the army to do me justice in this matter" Telegrams received (at 2:45 and 3:46 P.M.), DLC-William T. Sherman. On the same day, Sherman telegraphed to Custer. "Before receipt of yours had sent orders to General Sheridan to permit you to go to Abe Lincoln on duty, but the President adheres to his conclusion that you are not to go on the expedition" Copy, DNA, RG 108, Letters Sent.

On May 7, Sheridan telegraphed to Townsend. "The following dispatch from Genl Terry is respectfully forwarded I am sorry lieutenant Colonel Custer did not manifest as much interest by staying at his post to organize & get ready his regiment & the expedition as he does now to accompany it; on a previous occasion in eighteen sixty eight (1868) I asked executive clemency for Colonel Custer to enable him to accompany his regiment against the indians & I sincerely hope if granted this time it will have sufficient effect to prevent him from again attempting to throw discredit on his profession and his brother officers" Telegram received (at 4:00 P.M.), *ibid.*, RG 94, Letters Received, 2347 1876. Sheridan enclosed a telegram dated May 6 from Brig. Gen. Alfred Terry, St. Paul, to the AG, Dept. of the Mo., Chicago. "I forward the following to his excellency the President through military Channels 'I have seen your order transmitted through the General of the Army directing that I be not permitted to accompany the expedition about to move against hostile indians' As my entire regiment forms a part of the proposed expedition and as I am the senior officer of the regiment on duty in this department I respectfully but most earnestly request that while not allowed to go in command of the expedition I may be permitted to serve with my regiment in the field   I appeal to you as a soldier to spare me the humiliation of seeing my regiment march to meet the enemy & I to not share its dangers   Singed—G. A. CUSTER Bv't Maj Genl USA   In forwarding the above I wish to say expressly that I have no desire whatever to question the orders of the president or of any of my military superiors.   whether Lieutenant Colonel Custer shall be permitted to accompany my column or not I shall go in command of it. I do not know the reason upon which the orders already given rest but if these reasons do not forbid it Lieutenant Colonel Custers services would be very valuable with his regiment." *Ibid.* On May 7, Custer, St. Paul, telegraphed to Sherman. "By permission of Dept Commander I telegraph to request you to telegraph Genl Terry direct owing to Sheridans absence informing him whatever action is taken on my telegram of yesterday to the President" Telegram received (at 6:33 P.M.), DLC-William T. Sherman. On May 8, Sherman telegraphed to Terry. "The despatch of General Sheridan enclosing yours of yesterday touching Genl Custers urgent request to go under your command with his Regimnt has been Submitted to the President who sends me word that if you want Genl Custer along he withdraws his objections   Advise Custer to be prudent, not to take along any newspaper men who always work mischief, and to abstain from any personalities in the future. ~~He has taxed~~ Tell him I want him to confine his whole mind to his legitimate office, and trust to time. That newspaper paragraph in the New York World of May 2, compromised his best friends here, and almost deprived us of the ability to serve him." ALS (telegram sent), DNA, RG 94, Letters Received, 2347 1876. See Edgar I. Stewart, *Custer's Luck* (Norman, 1955), pp. 120–39.

2. On Aug. 31, a council of administration at Standing Rock Agency, Dakota Territory, recommended Henry F. Douglas as post trader. Copy, DNA, RG 94, ACP, 5049 1876. On Sept. 23, U.S. Senator William Windom of Minn., Winona, wrote to USG. "I beg to introduce my nephew, Mr Henry F. Douglas, who was recently elected Post Trader at Standing Rock. He is very anxious that action may be taken as speedily as possible, in order that, if appointed, he may be able to transport his goods to the Post before the river closes. If it awaits the return of the Secretary of War he fears it will be too late to avail himself of river transportation, in case you should favor him with the appointment. I have known him from his childhood and cheerfully give him the most unqualified endorsement as a young man of integrity and business ability. I am very sure he will give entire satisfaction in all respects. If you will be kind enough to act upon his recommendation at an early day, you will very greatly oblige . . ." ALS, *ibid.* On Oct. 14, USG endorsed this letter. "Referred to the Sec. of War. If Mr. Doulass apt. as Post Trader is in accordance with law I see no reason why his commission should be withheld." AES, *ibid.*

To Alphonso Taft

Dated WASHINGTON DC MCH 7 *1876*
To JUDGE ALPHONZO TAFT CIN O.

I have just sent your name to the Senate for the Office of Secretary
of War. I with my Entire Cabinet sincerely hope you will accept the
trust.

U. S. GRANT

Telegram received (at 1:36 P.M., facsimile), Lewis Alexander Leonard, *Life of Alphonso Taft*
(New York, 1920), p. 157. Born in 1810 in Vt., Alphonso Taft earned undergraduate and
law degrees from Yale, moved to Cincinnati, and promoted the city's business and civic development as a lawyer and judge. On March 7, 1876, Secretary of State Hamilton Fish
recorded in his diary. "President states that Sen Morrill declines nomination of Secretary
of War. A very long discussion followed Chandler suggesting John M. Forbes of Boston
Pierrepont suggesting Wayne Mac Veagh of Phila Chandler says that Mac Veagh is an
able man but an uncomfortable one—The President says he finds more fault with his
friends than with his enemies and that it would not affect the Penna disaffection; Chandler says that if they are going into the Cameron family they had better take the best and
that would be Don Cameron. Bristow suggests Judge Hoar, which I endorse strongly. The
President, with a good deal of feeling, said he would not appoint him, that he had just appointed one Massachusettts man as Minister to England and he was not willing to admit
that Mass alone could furnish men fit for places Robeson asked me what I thought of John
Forbes I replied that he was a man of ability and of great integrity with the training of a
Merchant who thought every consul who imposed a tax on any of his ship-masters was either a fool or a scoundrel on whom he would vent pretty hard epithets. I asked the President if he had thought of Judge Taft he said he had been frequently suggested but he
would not think of him C. C Washburne of Wis. had been suggested by Judge Howe and
for a time his name seemed very favorably entertained but the question arose whether in
the controversy between him and Carpenter there had not been some charges made of
his being connected, with some speculations in lumber. Bristow and I returned to the name
of Judge Hoar and said that this selection would probably effect the elections in N H. on
Tuesday next. The President then spoke kindly of Hoar but said his appointment would be
offensive to some two or three promanent Senators—I urge the strong hold he had on the
people and that that ought to out weigh the prejudices of any half dozen men Pierrepont,
Robeson & Jewell all spoke kindly of his appointment but without any great earnestness.
The name of Judge Taft was again brought up and the President suddenly changed his position with regard to it, Pierrepont Bristow and myself strongly urging it, and enquired
whether he had not been tainted with liberalness We all thought not, Bristow thought he
was the strongest kind of a hard money man. Jewell spoke of his strong hold on the people
of the East, neither Robeson nor Chandler, knew him personally. The President suddenly
said, suppose we send in his name? we all assented and the nomination was made out and
signed, and the President prepared a telegram to him informing him of the appointment."
DLC-Hamilton Fish. Probably on the same day, USG wrote a note. "Nominate Alfonso
Taft [of Ohio] for Sec. of War." AN (undated; bracketed words in another hand), DLC-
William H. Taft. Also on March 7, USG telegraphed a second time to Taft. "If you qualify

before the Expiration of the ten days for which the acting Secretary is Eligible to serve it will make no material difference—I will be glad to see you here however as soon as your convenience will admit of" Telegram received (at 7:28 P.M.), *ibid.* See Note, May 22, 1876; Henry F. Pringle, *The Life and Times of William Howard Taft: A Biography* (New York, 1939), I, 4–16.

On March 3, Fish had recorded in his diary cabinet deliberation over William W. Belknap's replacement as secretary of war. "The President said he must consider the question of a successor that Sen Morton had suggested Mr New (U. S. Treas) but he felt little inclination to bring into his Cabinet any one who entertained the Indiana platform. Chandler asked him if he had thought of Don Cameron, he replied he had among the first name which had occurred to him—after some pause I said I hoped he would not be in a hurry to determine upon any name, that the public would demand now a very different selection, from that which it would be satisfied on ordinary occasions, and that the effort should be made to select the person whose name would go far to relieve the administration, and the country of the scandal which had been brought upon both. A general concurrence in this view was expressed The President then said he would be willing to appoint Morrill of Maine All present seemed to think that such would be a very good selection but all doubted whether he would be willing to leave his place in the Senate to take one in the Cabinet. Bristow said he would venture to suggest a name which would strike the whole community favorably, and named Judge Hoar, the President doubted whether he would be willing to accept, and added that when in the Cabinet he had made himself very unpopular. Bristow thought not but that his very high character would command the confidence of all, and his devotion to the Party, and affection for the President, would make it the best appointment which could be made; in answer to the question the President said he would not regard the geographical position of the appointee. Jewell thought Hoars appointment would be very well received. I said that with regard to unpopularity in his various appointments that Judge Hoar, came in at the beginning of the Administration, to a Department with a large amount of patronage, and had possibly been some-what intolerant of the efforts of politicians, to force into judicial positions, persons whom the Judge, with his high appreciation of the importance of those positions, and his knowledge of the requisites to fill them, knew to be incompetent, and it was his rejection of such improper nominations that had possibly offended parties who endeavored to impose improper conditions upon him; that in the War Department there were no such importunities and no such patronage, and that it would afford a field for those high qualities, which the Judge so emanintly possesses, that no name occurred to me that would command more confidence and restore the Republican Party in the country more than the appointment of Judge Hoar. I asked the President whether he had thought of Gov Hayes of Ohio—He had not but said it would be a most excellent nomination though he was satisfied he would not accept Washburnes name was suggested and was pressed very strongly by Robeson and Pierrepont. I was asked my opinion and replied that it would be a most excellent appointment, and I thought it would satisfy the country, but doubted whether he would accept; being asked why? I said that he had refused the Treasury which had been offered him, that he was before the country as a candidate for the Presidency, and I thought for the last year had been manifesting the determination to avoid everything which might call upon him for any action, or exact criticism. Pierrepont suggested that we might telegraph to him; and the President rather impatiently replied it would be time enough when *he* was ready. The President finally directed a message to Sen Morrill of Me requesting him to call and see him; he directed that no mention should be made of any names suggested in connection with the office" DLC-Hamilton Fish.

On March 8, U.S. Senator Lot M. Morrill of Maine wrote to USG. "Refering to our interview of yesterday and deepely impressed with the expressions of your confidence and with every disposition to comply with your wishes, I still feel constrained to decline the proffered hon[or] for reas[o]ns expressed to you then." ALS, USG 3. On March 5 and 6, Fish had recorded in his diary. "Sen Lot M. Morrill calls and says he has had an interview with the President who has offered to him the position of Secretary of War; after expressing gratification at the confidence proposed he said the acceptance of the place would involve a sacrifice of feeling and interest and a change in his relations towards his constituents at home which would require of him much deliberation and the necessity of explanation to his friends in Maine; that nothing but a sense of high duty, and the peculiar circumstances in which Belknaps conduct involved the country, and the Republican Party, could induce him to make these sacrifices, that he could say to me in confidence that he was not in harmony with the personal surroundings of the President, that he had a great mistrust of Shepard and Babcock and the influences which he supposed shaped the Presidents course and had brought discredit upon the Country and administration, and that if these influences were to remain he would be unwilling to come into the Cabinet. I told him of the conversation I had had with the President with regard to Babcock and of the Presidents assurances to me that Babcock should no longer remain at the White House, that I had myself indicated Shepard as one of those whose influence with and through Babcock had been prejudical and should be gotten rid of, which the President had accepted without dissent, although he had not expressed assent further than with a seeming approval of my suggestion that Babcock should be sent away from Washington on some duty as an officer of the Engineer Corps. I urged his acceptance of the appointment and he left me with the enquiry whether it would be necessary for him to give an answer this evening I told him it would be sufficient if he would let the President know before twelve oclock tomorrow." "At 12 oclock I go to see the President who signs nomination of Dana and Fox; he had not yet heard from Morrill but requested me to send in Nomination of Secretary of War in blank and he calls his son and directs him to register the other two nomination and to go to the Senate and see Senator Morrill to inform him that he has the nomination and ask in the Presidents name if it shall be sent in; if so to deliver it to the Senate, otherwise to bring it back." DLC-Hamilton Fish.

On March 10, Gen. William T. Sherman, St. Louis, wrote to U.S. Senator John Sherman of Ohio. ". . . Even since Belknap's fall the President telegraphed his orders about the Trader Evans at Fort Sill, to Genl Sheridan, & not to me. In the NY Herald of Mch 8, is a paper headed the 'Army Ring' which is substantially true, and I cannot imagine where the writer got his information. When Genl Grant sold me that house for $65,000, ~~that~~ (which he had bought of his brother in Law Corbin for $30,000 on a ten years credit), he knew that I could not maintain the establishmt except at fearful cost, & yet he made no suggestion that I know of, when the Committee insisted on the reduction of my pay.—I can account for every cent of the donation out of which came the $65,000. Genl Grant made me repeated promises to bring Belknap and me together, to arrange amicably our respective fields of duty, but he *never* did. When I relieved him, I took on my Staff three of his Aids—Dent, Porter and Comstock & left the two former with him in the White House—Comstock is a fine honorable officer, but soon gave me voluntarily his place for 'Poe,'—Dent hung on till the President thought fit to send him away when I gave his place to an officer from the Frontier. Porter hung on till the last when I notified him I wanted his place for another Frontier Officer (Tourtelotte) he never thanked me for the favor I had extended to him for years, but on the Contrary was false to me, & formed one of that Cabal so well described in the Herald. He is a treacherous fellow, but is no longer in the Army. It was then that Mrs Grant applied to me, to put Fred on my Staff—You remember I took him with me to Europe & nursed him as well as I could but there is an Army Regulation, now construed as 'Law,' which reads as follows, 'An officer shall not fill any Staff appointmt or other situation, the duties of which will detach him from his Company Regiment or Corps until he has served at least three years with his Regm't or Corps; nor shall any officer (aides de camp excepted) so remain detached longer than four years.' I told the President and Mrs Grant of this law, and that if Fred would go on and serve his three years with his Regm't (4th Cavalry then in Texas now at Fort Sill) I would cheerfully put him on my Staff. But Mrs Grant was unwilling to wait that long, and Sheridan told me he had put him on his Staff, to reconcile 'Mrs Grants difficulty with me.' It is a positive violation of law: and even were there no law or Regulation on the Subject it would be construed as an act of toadyism, by evry honorable man. Fred Grant had and has no claim to military distinction other than being his father's Son. I know that Genl Grant feels as I do on this matter, but he may have some reserved thought that I knowing Mrs Grants feelings for her children, ought to have deferred in this matter for his peace in his family: But as these Army Regulations were always held up to me as a legal barrier to my exercising any authority remotely under the jurisdiction of the War Secretary, I had no alternative but to Construe this clause as binding on me. The time has come, when even Genl Grant must admit my action was right, and that he evinced a weakness in allowing Sheridan to do that for which he must now blush. . . . A set of flatterers clerks & orderlies will cringe & bow to the new Secretary just as they did to Stanton & Belknap, and make others do as they did, look on army officers as men to be snubbed—denied even the privilege of beholding the Capitol for whose safety they fought, unless they explain the reasons of their presence—as though they were enemies. There will remain the same Townsends, Myers, Ingalls, Lyforts &c &c no more representatives of the real army, that Congress provides for liberally, than your doorkeeper and folders are Representatives of Senators. No officer worth his weight in salt, will stay in that atmosphere, and this is the Augean stable that some Secretary must cleanse—. . ." ALS, DLC-William T. Sherman. See Rachel Sherman Thorndike, ed., *The Sherman Letters . . .* (New York, 1894), pp. 348–49; *PUSG*, 19, 118–19, 122–23. On March 10 or 11, Julia Dent Grant wrote to [*Gen. Sherman*]. "If the enclosed emanates from Gen. Sherman, then [h]is memory is greatly [at] fault. I did say once, during a social call at your house, having learned that one of your staff would resign soon, that if it were not contrary to Etiquette that I should be petitioning for a staff appointment for my son. Upon hearing of this the President reproached me, saying that I had compromised Fred, and he hoped I would never do so again." L, DLC-William T. Sherman. The enclosure is a clipping. "GENERAL SHERMAN, having been asked whether he had ever refused a request of President Grant to give his son Fred a place on his staff, replied: 'General Grant has too much sense to make such a request. Mrs. Grant asked me to give her son a place, but I refused because he was not fitted for it. He lacked age and experience. I believe in promoting men to official position for past services, and for the proficiency they have acquired. General Grant himself would never have asked me to do such a thing.'" *Ibid.* See *PUSG*, 23, 294.

On March 14, John Sherman wrote to Gen. Sherman. "Your letter of the 10th is rec'd and read with interest   I have felt for years that you had been treated by the sett of officers that surrounded and ruled Belknap with discourtesy, and that they were bringing discredit upon the Gov't. Still as long as they have been backed by Grant you could do nothing and therefore was 'frozen' out of Washington. For myself I felt that I was ignored except in Ohio local matters where I would not be, and was often inclined to openly arraign what I could not defend. The Admin was so purely personal that we felt the proper power of the

Rep. Party was wasting away under its influence, and obscure men of doubtful character and conduct were thrust into high office Still I had faith in Gen Grant and did not wish to join the malcontents who arraigned him and therefore bore in silence many things I did not like—My discontent however was well known in the Senate and I was not regarded as one of his friends or as one having influence with him—When Belknap was exposed I did not feel free to go to Grant about his successor but indirectly through Morrill & other Senators I did all I could for Taft. . . . If it is agreable to you I could readily suggest to Taft to ask you to come which he would do, but might not unless he knows it is agreable to you. I am told that Grant is much discouraged and your presance I think would have a good effect upon him. . . . Would it not be well for you to write a kindly letter to Grant and ask him if you had better not come on? If you do not choose to do this but are willing to come let me know and I will make the occasion for you to come—If you do not you will drift into unpleasant relations to the President & the Department which ought to be avoided . . . John & Fred Grant have dissolved partnership, by mutual consent & with my concurrence—They have made nothing but have lost but little & that in depreciation of personal assets. John is at Sea but I will try & get him employment away from Washington. All well with us" ALS, DLC-William T. Sherman. On March 16, Gen. Sherman wrote to John Sherman. "I have just received your letter of Mch 14, . . . I am ready at a minutes notice to fulfil any duty that may be assigned me, even if it carries me to Washington, but I cannot again risk the removal of my family back to Washington, because the Same end may be reached as soon as the present tempest is over. Th[e]re are two ways to govern the Army, one *through* its Generals, and the other through the Staff. If orders and instructions are made to individuals composing the Army, *direct*, by the Adjt Genl—and not *through* the Comdg General, the latter is not only useless but an incumbrance, and had better be away: but if Secretary Taft is willing to trust me to execute, and carry into effect his orders & instructions, all he has to do is to so order, and he will find me ready. . . . I of course know that Fred Grant could not be relied on in business matters, and am glad John is free of him so easily. . . ." ALS, *ibid.* USG had deposited his salary with the bank of Sherman & Grant. On March 15, USG wrote to Secretary of the Treasury Benjamin H. Bristow. "I have to request that hereafter the warrants for my salary may be issued to the Citizens National Bank of this city." LS, DNA, RG 56, Letters Received from the President. On May 18, Ulysses S. Grant, Jr., wrote to Attorney Gen. Edwards Pierrepont. "The President wishes you would send in to-day the nomination of John E. Sherman Jr. as Marshall of New Mexico—" ALS, *ibid.*, RG 60, Letters from the President. See *PUSG*, 26, 190; Larry D. Ball, *The United States Marshals of New Mexico and Arizona Territories, 1846–1912* (Albuquerque, 1978), pp. 79–106.

On March 16, Culver C. Sniffen had written to Taft. "The President desires me to say that he would be pleased to see you at his office this morning, as soon as you can make it convenient." LS, DLC-William H. Taft. On March 19, John Sherman wrote to Gen. Sherman. ". . . Last evening Judge Taft with Gen McCook of your staff called on me & spent the evening—He is evidently very desirous that you come to Washington to which I said that he could easily call you here. He said you and he could readily arrange the questions in dispute as to your proper respective duties & powers but as the subject had been much mooted he thought it best to have a full talk with the President and then he will write you—. . ." ALS, DLC-William T. Sherman. See Gen. Sherman to Jacob D. Cox, March 19, 1876, Oberlin College, Oberlin, Ohio; Cox to Gen. Sherman, March 29, 1876, DLC-William T. Sherman.

On March 21, Fish recorded in his diary. "As I was leaving the White House the Secretary of War asked me if I supposed the President was still disengaged—He wished to speak to him about General Sherman and the importance of having his Head Quarters (as General of the Army) established at Washington." DLC-Hamilton Fish. On March 22, Wednesday, Gen. Sherman telegraphed to John Sherman. "Will start for washington this Evening expect me Friday morning" Telegram received (at 12:28 P.M.), DLC-William T. Sherman.

On March 29, Gen. Sherman, Washington, D. C., telegraphed to Lt. Gen. Philip H. Sheridan, Chicago. "I am convinced that the President and Secretary of War desire my presence here and that every reasonable concession will be made that should be, consistent with law. I think the part of the Army I am designed to command should be clearly defined. That no orders should go to any part of it except through me. That the entire Adjutant General's Department should be under the control of the General in Chief . . ." Copy, DNA, RG 108, Letters Sent. On April 1, Saturday, Gen. Sherman wrote to Sheridan. ". . . The President has been unwell really sick, but I have seen him daily, and today though he denied himself to all others he admitted me, and I sat and gossiped with him nearly two hours. I have also been much with the new Secretary, who is a man of good feeling and an excellent lawyer & judge but utterly innocent of Army knowledge. I have just parted with him, and he said emphatically 'I must have you here.' I have told him repeatedly that I wanted nothing for myself, would rather return to St Louis as President of the 5th Street RRoad, than remain in W. on any terms—but that if he would define what was the Army of the US, and leave me to command it, of course my duty was to conform. He says he is more than willing to concede that the Line and Adjt Genls Dept entire shall be subject to my orders and that no order shall go to the Army, except through me—. . . Meigs reenters his office today, and Ingalls goes to NewYork & Easton to St Louis—But the President today agrees to retire Allen, send Ingalls to San Francisco & leave Easton at NewYork, the vacancy to be filled by young Heintzelman. The President had settled on an Inspector Gnl to be Supdt of West Point. I asked him why he did not select one of our Genls citing the precedent of Porter at the Naval Academy & of even Lt Genls in Europe, and mentioned Schofields name—He said if Schofield would accept he would cheerfully grant it. I telegraphed Schofield and he is willing to accept, and will be detailed, the change to occur this summer, and I will be named as Inspector, to close the door to Shriver, or Some Engineer applicant. Thus the Academy will become a school for the whole army, in fact a part of the Army. . . ." ALS, DLC-Philip H. Sheridan. On April 3, Sheridan wrote to Gen. Sherman. "Confidential. . . . The Army is now very feverish under the apprehension of consolidation, and reduction of pay, as threatened, and is liable to excitement and confusion and demoralization under many and important changes, and I think it would be best to go slowly. . . ." LS, DLC-William T. Sherman. On April 6, USG issued General Orders No. 28. "The Headquarters of the Army are hereby re-established at Washington City, and all orders and instructions relative to military operations, or affecting the military control and discipline of the Army, issued by the President through the Secretary of War, shall be promulgated through the General of the Army, and the Departments of the Adjutant General and the Inspector General shall report to him and be under his control in all matters relating thereto." Copy (printed), DNA, RG 94, Letters Received, 1892 1874.

On Feb. 23, Belknap had telegraphed in cipher to Brig. Gen. Alfred H. Terry, St. Paul. "Confidential. After consultation with President of the United States I desire to know if you are willing to accept appointment of Superintendent U. S. Military Academy. . . ." Copy, *ibid.*, Correspondence, USMA. On Feb. 24, Terry telegraphed to Belknap his declination. Telegram received (at 10:40 P.M.), *ibid.* Related papers are *ibid.* On March 29 and 30, Gen. Sherman telegraphed to Maj. Gen. John M. Schofield, San Francisco, concerning his appointment as USMA superintendent. Copies, *ibid.*, RG 108, Letters Sent. Schofield accepted the assignment with misgivings. See Schofield to Gen. Sherman, March 30, 1876, DLC-William T. Sherman; Gen. Sherman to Schofield, April 8, May 25, June 1, 1876, DNA, RG 108, Letters Sent; Schofield, *Forty-Six Years in the Army* (New York, 1897), pp. 439–45.

On May 20, Gen. Sherman wrote to Lt. Col. Frederick T. Dent. ". . . You need not fear my being tempted to become a Candidate for any Civil office, however exalted, for I knew personally Genl Harrison, Genl Taylor &c besides Gnl Grant—The latter has more nerve than I profess, and still if the thing were to do over again I doubt if he would stand the racket, for the price again. I dine with the family tomorrow. Mrs Grant and all are in excellent health. I never saw them look in better health—. . ." ALS, Mrs. Gordon Singles, Arlington, Va.

To Benjamin H. Bristow

March 20 /1876

TO THE HONORABLE SECRETARY OF THE TREASURY
DEAR SIR:

I desire to call your attention to a young gentleman in the Architects branch of your Dep't who is deserving for every reason of your most favorable consideration, His record as an official is one of which he and his intimate friends feel justly proud, He comes of an historic family, his grandfather a Revolutionary officer and the first Adj't Gen'l of the State of NewYork. His father Genl G W. McLean and his brother Major Wm McLean were among the Nations bravest defenders, in its last struggle, It is to be hoped that the merits of this young man, whom I personally know, may not be overlooked when the time comes for you to reward honest faithful and efficient service

Sincerly yours
U. S. GRANT

Copy, DNA, RG 56, Applications. Harry C. McLean continued as a clerk in the supervising architect's office, Treasury Dept.

To Alphonso Taft

———

March 20th /76

Hon. Alphonso Taft:

Sec. of War:

Dear Sir:

You may if you please nominate Capt. F. W. Perry—the bearer of this—as 2d Lt. in the Army with the view of having him placed on the retired list immediately after confirmation. The papers which will be submitted with this letter will show the justice of such action and should be submitted to the Military Committee of the Senate,— with a letter stating that the appointment is made with the view of immediate retirement—at the time the nomination is sent in.

Respectfully &c.

U. S. Grant

ALS, DNA, RG 94, ACP, 3402 1871. On March 24, 1876, USG nominated Frank W. Perry for reappointment as 2nd lt.; on April 10, the Senate rejected this nomination. On June 21, Secretary of War James D. Cameron wrote to USG that Perry had died on June 18. LS (press), *ibid.*

A court-martial convened at San Antonio on June 2, 1871, had cashiered Perry for drunkenness; on Aug. 3, USG mitigated "his sentence to suspension from rank for the period of eighteen (18) months, and from pay for the same period, excepting fifty dollars ($50) per month." D (printed), *ibid.* Perry resigned as capt., 24th Inf., as of Feb. 1, 1873, while under charges. On Nov. 20, 1874, Perry, Washington, D. C., wrote to Orville E. Babcock. "I have the honor to solicit, through you, from his Excellency, the President, an appointment as U. S. Consul or re-appointment into the U. S. Army as 2nd. Lieutenant, with a view to retirement, on account of wounds received in action which daily give me more or less annoyance. This request is based upon services rendered by me during the war. Having, before 21 years of age been engaged in some 25 battles, fights &c, in fact participating in all the campaign's of the Army of the Potomac, including the entire campaign of the Wilderness, except when disabled by wounds; either in command of a Company of the 14th. U. S. Infty., or on Staff Regular Brigade,—wounded 3 separate times and twice brevetted for personal gallantry on the field of battle; sinc[e] which time I have been employed in different T[er]ritories against Indians. My Father, late Capt. John S. Perry, 15th. U. S. I[*nf.*] lost his life in 1850, from disease contracted during the Mexican War. The record of service which I forward herewith, w[ith] endorsements, is an application for a commission i[n] the Egyptian Army, which I failed to obtain, the[re] being no vacancy. General Stone's reply is also forwarded." LS, *ibid.*

Speech

———

[*March 21, 1876*]

Mr Peralta:

I am happy to receive you in the character in which you present yourself. It may be regarded as an earnest on the part of the government of Costa Rica to strengthen the friendship between that Republic and the United States, a purpose which I heartily reciprocate.

The relations of all maritime States and especially of this country with yours, are of particular interest at this juncture, from the impression destined as I believe to become general, that the canal between the two oceans, must, in part at least, pass through the territories of Costa Rica.

I thank you for your kind expression towards me personally and towards the people of whom I am the Chief Magistrate. It is not to be doubted that you will discharge the functions of the trust committed to you according to the spirit in which it has been conferred.

D, DNA, RG 59, Notes from Foreign Legations, Central America. USG responded to Manuel M. Peralta, Costa Rican minister. ". . . The President of Costa Rica, being desirous to draw closer and diligently to cultivate the friendly relations which fortunately exist between his Government and the Government of the United States, has done me the honor to charge me to tell you, in his name and in the name of the Costa Rican people, that your welfare and happiness, as well as the prosperity of the American people, are as dear to him as are those of his own country. The interest taken by your wise and far-seeing Government in the construction of the proposed Inter-oceanic Canal through the territories and waters of Costa Rica and Nicaragua, her neighbor and sister, is a further bond which unites us to you personally. . . ." DS (in Spanish, undated), *ibid.*; translation, *ibid.* Related papers are *ibid.* On March 16, 1876, Thursday, Secretary of State Hamilton Fish wrote to USG. "I return Commodore Ammens note, & the letter to him from Mr Benard—As it is possible that the new Minister from Costa Rica (to be presented on Tuesday) may have some instructions, with regard to the Canal, I presume that you will think it best to await his presentation, and ascertain what he may be authorized to do in the matter—If he has authority, it will be better to negotiate with him, here, than in Costa Rica, which has (for some unreasonable cause) taken offence with Mr Williamson." ALS (press), DLC-Hamilton Fish. See Fish diary, March 16, 1876, *ibid.*

In 1872, USG had appointed a commission to survey potential canal routes. See *PUSG,* 23, 46–50. On Dec. 29, 1875, Felix Belly, Brussels, wrote to USG. "The construction of an interoceanic canal, via Nicaragua, for which I have labored for ten years, is about to be courageously undertaken by your glorious administration, it having been decided, by those who have made a special study of the matter, that this route is at once the most practicable and the most salubrious of all that have been proposed during the last half century. This truth, which is now triumphant, has been sustained by me since 1858, ~~not~~ in opposition not only to the American routes which public favor protected out of pure Chauvinism, but also to the party which supported Mr. Buchanan's administration, and subsequently, to the official science of the Washington Observatory, whose publications in favor of the Darien route have hitherto been regarded as law, even in France and England. As regards the construction of the Nicaragua canal, I have, therefore, been systematically thrust by the North Americans into the same position into which Mr. Lesseps has been thrust by the English, with this difference, that the hostility of the United States, in depriving me of the support of my own Government and the confidence of those European groups that were ready to take part in this great work, has left me nothing but ruin as the reward of my labors, which were performed for the good of the world at large. I know, Mr. President, that these iniquities are inevitable in the course of human events, and that the *sic vos non vobis* of the poet is not applicable in the case of an entire nation. The point in question here, however, is an official denial of justice, and a systematic conspiracy upheld by the authority of the Government of the United States. You will consider, in the spirit of justice which characterizes you, whether this unfortunate intervention in favor of an erroneous thesis, in opposition to the rational solution which I advocated, does not now authorize me to ask for some compensation in return for new services. . . ." ALS (in French), DNA, RG 59, Miscellaneous Letters; translation, *ibid.* See Felix Belly, *A Travers L'Amérique Centrale: Le Nicaragua et le Canal Interocéanique* (Paris, 1867).

On Feb. 10, 1876, Fish recorded in his diary. "Called on the President, who has received the report of the Commission on the Survey of the different routs for the Inter Oceanic Canal which is unanimous in favor of the Nicaragua Route. He consults as to the best mode of proceeding; whether to present the report to Congress, with or without a recommendation I suggest a doubt of submitting it to Congress but that probably the report may show the expediency of entering into negotiations with Nicaragua I refer to the various negotiations which have heretofore been held and mention that we are now examining and collecting all the facts connected there with which we can find in the State Department. He says he is uncertain in his own mind whether we should attempt to make a Canal in common with other Nations, throwing it open to the Commerce of the whole world, and perpetual guarantee of neutrality, or should secure it to ourselves and regulate the terms on which it could be used. He manifests a great deal of interest in the subject & requests me to obtain all the information I can. I advised him to request the Commissioners, if they have not given expression to the conclusion which they have reached, not to give publicity to it which might lead Nicaragua and Costa Rica to impose exorbitant conditions which otherwise they would not do. I take back with me the report and leave with him the separate report of the survey on which the board had reached their conclusion." DLC-Hamilton Fish. See *PUSG*, 23, 221–23; *ibid.*, 25, 123–24. On Feb. 18, Fish wrote at length to USG. "The Secretary of State to whom has been referred the Report of the Interoceanic Canal Commission in favor of the Nicaraguan route, has the honor, by the President's direction, to state such material antecedents in regard to the proposed communication, as may be necessary or desirable for a proper understanding of the subject. . . . Though the practicability of the work may have been most clearly shown by the recent surveys and though the Nicaraguan route has been decided as preferable by the Commission, it may be apprehended that the enterprise will not command the confidence of capitalists without a treaty providing for its protection, to which not only the Republics through whose dominions the canal must pass, but the chief maritime nations of the globe and especially those whose territories are washed by both oceans, shall be parties." Copy, DNA, RG 59, Reports to the President and Congress.

Probably before March 20, Brig. Gen. Andrew A. Humphreys, Carlile P. Patterson, and Commodore Daniel Ammen, commissioners, prepared a "Private memorandum for the consideration of the President." ". . . In the common interest of all Nations and Peoples, and to insure the security of Nicaragua and adjacent states, as well as for the security and interests of the constructors of an inter-oceanic ship canal, a guaranty of neutrality and protection seems necessary on the part of all Nations who ~~wh~~ wish its benef[its,] making neutral approaches so wide and so well defined as to forbid a close of effective blockade, and that the Government of Nicaragua should guarantee that both ports adjacent to the sea should be free and without port charges, or let or hindrance. . . . It would be essential that the constructors should maintain an armed police to preserve order on the neutral territory during the period of construction, and that should laborers or others pass beyond the neutral belt into adjacent territories, that at the request of the Government concerned it should be the duty of the constructors to pursue, apprehend and bring to justice marauders or other culprits, but under no other condition to cross over, tresspass, or interfere in any way beyond the limit of the neutral territory. . . . It is thought worthy of consideration whether it might not serve as a guarantee to stockholders, as well in relation to the progress of the work as to the proper application of the means [employed] for its execution, if the Nations specially [interested] in this construction of the canal were to [appoint] 'examiners' who should form part of the Board of Directors or Honorary members of it—these examiners to be officers of the respective Governments, paid by them, and not allowed to receive any compensation from the canal constructors." Copy, *ibid.,* Report of the Commission to Consider an Isthmian Canal; *SED,* 46-1-15, 7–9. On March 20, Ammen, Washington, D. C., wrote to USG. "I have looked over the history of the early canal projects given by the State Dept with a great deal of curiosity. It is somewhat singular that until Childs made a survey about '51 none existed of any value & even he got his level of Lake Nicaragua from the Pacific and after levelling down on our slope perhaps half way to Graytown, put down the other parts by proportion. The Senate resolution of March 3rd '35 seems apropos, indicating the advantage of having all the great nations as well as those near Nicaragua, interested in the construction. Had Biddle gone to Nicaragua instead of to Panama, as he was first directed, it is possible that a canal might now be in existence via the Nicaraguan Lake. The actual treaty with Nicaragua establishes the right of canal or land transit in common with her own citizens and also the sea coast ports should be free of duty and that duties cannot be collected on goods not intended for or left on Nicaraguan territory. It seems to me that the general provisions contained in your private memorandum would be necessary as a preliminary and would be advantageous to the broad interests of Commerce.—There may be other points not perceived by the Commission but they have not occurred to me. If Costa Rica was not willing to subscribe to a proper treaty, as the construction of the canal would only involve the abutment of three or four dams on her territory and that entirely wild & uninhabited it would seem to me to be carrying National rights to a foolish extent to regard them at all.—No interest of that Nation would be injured or compromised by the construction of the canal & any demands on her part would seem to me to be absurd. Nicaragua, if not acted upon by unreasonable instincts or pretensions, will be able in a passive way to aid the construction of a canal a great deal, and through its construction without any other advantage would become stable & rich. I suppose that at present no Nation would be disposed to endeavor to retard or prevent the construction of a ship canal unless it was assumed or supposed that it was intended to be specially an advantage to ~~other~~ another Nation, in a discriminating manner. If left to us wholly, the Panama R. R. would spend a good deal to destroy the project and would probably be abetted, stupidly, by the Pacific R. R. companies. It seems on this account still more desirable to make it the work for the world since all will & should enjoy common advantages. If the idea in the memorandum in relation to 'examiners' should be thought favorably of, would it not be worth while that they should be one Army & one

Navy man from every Nation sufficiently interested to subscribe to a joint Treaty & ~~was~~ disposed to appoint them?—This would admit of a semi-anual inspection by different parties of persons who could not be stock jobbers & would have none other than a general or government interest in this matter?. A number of years ago, you may remember that a joint Commission of Army & Navy men went to Mexico to ascertain *simply the facts* of the 'Gardner claim' which proved to be fraudulent.—It was either by request of the Court of Claims or by Congressional resolution. Admiral, then Lieut DuPont, spoke to me about it at the time, remarking that it was significant that they had to call upon Army & Navy men simply to get at a truth. Among Army & Navy men, officers of special professional training may be found to serve as canal examiners, and their presence or duties as such it seems to me, would be a great prevention for attempt at fraud & a great corrector of it should it be found to exist. I hope that you will be able to bring about the Inauguration of this great work, which will serve as a lasting monument of your labors as President." ALS, DNA, RG 59, Miscellaneous Letters. On March 21, Fish recorded in his diary. "The President returned to me the report on the Inter-Oceanic-Canal which I had left with him some days since and requested me to speak with the representatives of the foreign governments in favor of the construction of the Canal He evinces great earnestness that the work be done during his Administration He wishes the neutralizing of the Canal and its being made free to the use of all powers and built by the funds of all who may be willing to unite." DLC-Hamilton Fish. See Fish diary, March 23, 24, April 6, June 22, 29, 1876, *ibid.*; Peralta to Fish (confidential), March 31, June 26, 1876, DNA, RG 59, Notes from Foreign Legations, Central America.

On July 10, Aniceto Esquivel, Costa Rican president, San José, wrote to USG. "Señor Don Manuel Maria Peralta, Minister Resident of this Republic near the Government of your Excellency, has been separated for some years from his country; and it is just that he should return to it to serve it in another honorable capacity, and for this reason the mission which has been confided in him is terminated. . . ." Copy (in Spanish), *ibid.*; translation, *ibid.* On Aug. 10, Vicente Herrera, San José, wrote to USG. "A popular movement which took place on the 30th of last month, and which was supported by the army, put an end to the Administration of the Licentiate Don Aniceto Esquivel, and proclaimed me at the same time Provisional President of the Republic. I deem it a pleasing duty to bring this fact to Your Excellency's knowledge, assuring you that the relations which happily exist between Costa Rica and the United States of North America shall be faithfully and carefully preserved, and that I shall endeavor to draw them closer and strengthen them more and more each day in the interest of both nations. Permit me to offer my best wishes for your Excellency's happiness and for the prosperity of the great people which you so worthily govern, . . ." LS (in Spanish), *ibid.*; translation, *ibid.* Peralta continued as minister. See Speech, [*Oct. 31, 1876*].

To House of Representatives

———

To The House of Representatives

In answer to the resolution of the House of Representatives of the 3d of February last, requesting the President "to require a competent and experienced military officer of the United States to execute the duties of an Indian Agent so far as to repair to the Red Cloud Agency, and in his discretion other Sioux Agencies with instructions, to inquire into the causes of 'the exhaustion of the appropriation for the subsistence and support of the Sioux Indians, for the present fiscal year,' as also his opinion, whether any further, and what amount should be appropriated for the subsistence and support of said Indians for the remainder of the current fiscal year," I have the honor to transmit herewith the report of Lieutenant Colonel Merritt, of the 9th Cavalry, who was charged by the Secretary of War with the duty of making the inquiries called for by said Resolution.

U. S. GRANT.

EXECUTIVE MANSION
MARCH 23D 1876.

Copy, DNA, RG 130, Messages to Congress. *HED*, 44-1-145. On March 22, 1876, Secretary of War Alphonso Taft wrote to USG responding to the resolution. LS (press), DNA, RG 94, Letters Received, 942 1876. *HED*, 44-1-145. On March 17, Lt. Col. Wesley Merritt, Chicago, had reported to AG, Military Div. of the Mo. ". . . I would premise that in making this investigation I was forced to rely on such statements as were made by the Indian Agent and his employes, and that because of their lack of information on many points, with reference to which all knowledge is confined to the Indian Department in Washington, my report in some particulars may be incomplete. . . . All my inquiries convinced me that the Department at Washington must know more of the causes of the deficiency and the management of the supply department than the Agents do, or at least more than they are willing to tell. The Agent at Red Cloud could not tell me how much had been appropriated to the support of his Agency during the year, nor how much had been expended. He reported all records of the Agency bearing on these points, if there ever had been any, either lost, destroyed, or carried away by his predecessor in the Agency. I could not discover that estimates for supplies are made in any regular manner. The Indian Agent it appears reports the number of Indians at his Agency and the supplies are apportioned and forwarded by the Department. It also appears that though quarterly returns of the supplies on hand are required at the Indian Department, from the Agencies, that no regular form of return is prescribed and that no retained reports are kept, at least, at the Red Cloud Agency. I mention these matters to indicate how difficult it is to make an intelligent investigation under the circumstances. . . . As I have intimated, it is difficult to arrive at the exact figures of the amount to be appropriated to cover the deficiency and to feed the incoming Indians. I think I can safely say that the estimate given below is not too small, as it is based on figures and facts given me by those who are sufficiently interested in making the sum as large as it can properly be made. Besides when in doubt I have erred, if at all, in favor of the appropriation rather than agains[t] it. I find the amount needed to supply the Thirteen thousand Indians now at the Red Cloud Agency, estimating from the time of expiration of present supplies, as reported by Agent, to be One hundred and thirty four thousand seven hundred and eleven ($134.711) dollars: . . . The Agent at Red Cloud informed me that the Indians at the Agency had considerably increased in numbers since his predecessor's last issues. These indicated the presence of from eight to ten thousand Indians at the Agency. The Agent now claims, as has been stated, thirteen thousand. He estimates that two thousand more will probably come into the Agency to be fed. The cost of supplies for this number of Indians for four months is found to be, Twenty two thousand five hundred and forty five dollars ($22.545) which should be appropriated for the support of the Indians coming to the Agency from the north. As no new Indians had arrived at the Agency not included in those reported at the Agency, it would seem that the above amount is not too small. In addition to the causes, given in the foregoing, for the deficiency at the Red Cloud Agency I would respectfully call attention to the fact that these Indians have never been properly counted. They are estimated by lodges the numbers in which are reported by the Indians. This being the case the number of Indians reported at the Agency is more or less factitious, depending on the quantity of stores on hand, the character of the weather, and resulting from the character of the Agent and of the Indians. If supplies are plenty the Agent is perhaps not so careful of restricting the number of Indians reported to the least possible, if the weather is inclement the Indians exaggerate their numbers in order to secure a more abundant supply of food for consumption and barter. . . . When I proposed to have the Indians at the Agency counted I was told by both Military and Indian officials that it would be impracticable without a larger force of troops than was available. The Indians should be carefully counted and their numbers verified at least once a month. A great loss of supplies as food results from issuing flour instead of hard bread to the Indians. I am told that the Indians underrate the value of flour as food because they do not understand how to use it properly and that they will give a sack of their flour for a few pounds of hard or other bread. The truth is they dispose of their flour and get little or nothing in return for it. . . ." LS, DNA, RG 94, Letters Received, 942 1876. *HED*, 44-1-145, 3–6. See message to Congress, Feb. 28, 1876.

To House of Representatives

To The House of Representatives

I have the honor to transmit herewith a communication received from the chairman of the Board on behalf of the United States Executive Departments containing in detail the operations of the Board and setting forth the present embarrassments under which it is now laboring in the endevor to conduct the participation of the Government in the Centennial Exhibition and showing very clearly the necessity of additional funds to carry out the undertaking in a creditable manner.

U. S. Grant

Executive Mansion
Mch. 27, 1876

Copy, DNA, RG 130, Messages to Congress. *HED*, 44-1-148. On March 27, 1876, Maj. Stephen C. Lyford, Washington, D. C., wrote to USG explaining that the cost of erecting a building for government exhibits had been deducted from the appropriations for each dept. "... It thus appears that but little more than half of the amounts required for the War and Navy Departments and the Smithsonian Institution are available for the preparation, transportation, and display of the articles and materials to be contributed by them; while, in the case of the Interior Department, the amount available is considerably less than one-half...." *Ibid.*, p. 3. On Feb. 16, following extensive congressional debate, USG had signed a bill appropriating $1,500,000 "to complete the Centennial buildings and other preparations." *U.S. Statutes at Large*, XIX, 4. On May 1, USG signed legislation allocating an additional $73,500 among the depts. *Ibid.*, pp. 45–46. See *PUSG*, 26, 76–77, 414–15; message to Congress, May 1, 1876; *HRC*, 44-1-1; *SED*, 45-3-74, 9–13.

To Congress

To THE SENATE AND HOUSE OF REPRESENTATIVES—

I have the honor to transmit herewith for your information a communication from the Secretary of the Interior, of this date, upon the urgent necessities of the Pawnee Indians—This tribe has recently been removed to the Indian Territory and is without means of subsistence, except as supplied by the Government. Its members have evinced a disposition to become self supporting and it is believed that only temporary aid will be required by them—The sums advanced by the U. S. for this purpose, it is expected will be refunded from the proceeds of the sale of the Pawnee Reservation in Nebraska.

The present destitute condition of these Indians would seem to call for immediate relief, and I recommend the subject to your early and favorable consideration—

U. S. GRANT.

EXECUTIVE MANSION—
APRIL 3D 1876.

Copy, DNA, RG 130, Messages to Congress. *HED*, 44-1-154. On April 10, 1876, USG signed an act to authorize the sale of the Pawnee reservation in Neb. and to appropriate $300,000 to defray expenses of moving the tribe to the Indian Territory. *U.S. Statutes at Large*, XIX, 28–30. See *HED*, 44-1-1, part 5, I, 823–24, 44-1-80, 44-2-1, part 5, I, 398, 459–60; Clyde A. Milner II, *With Good Intentions: Quaker Work among the Pawnees, Otos, and Omahas in the 1870s* (Lincoln, Neb., 1982), pp. 84–94.

Veto

———

[*April 18, 1876*]

To the Senate of the U. States.

Herewith I return Senate bill No 172 entitled "An Act fixing the Salary of the President of the United States, without my approval.— I am constrained to this course from a sense of duty to my successors in office, to myself and to what is due to the dignity of the position of Chief Magistrate of a nation of more than $40.000.000 of people.—When the salary of pPresident of the United States was fixed by the Constitution at $25,000 per Annum we were a nation of but 3.000.000, of people, poor from a long and exhaustive war, without commerce or manufactures, with but few wants and those cheaply supplied. The salary must then have been deemed small for the responsibilities and dignity of the position, but justifiably so from the impoverished condition of the Treasury, and the simplicity it was desired to cultivate in the Republic.—The constitution at the same time fixed the Salary of Congressmen at six dollars per day for the time Actually in Session—an average of about 120 days to each session—and milage at the rate of one days salary for each twenty miles traveled in coming to and returning home for each session.

Fixing the average distance traveled by members of Congress in reaching the National Capitol, and returning home, for each session of Congress, at 750 miles—probably quite up to the actual ~~dif~~ distance traveled at the time when there were but thirteen states—we have the actual compensation to Congressmen of nine hundred & [forty-]five dollars pr. annum, or less than one twenty-seventh part of the salary of the President. Congres have legislated upon their own salaries from time to time since that date until finally it reached $5,000 00 pr annum,—or one fifth that of the President—before the latter was ~~changed~~ increased.—No one having a knowledge of the cost of living at the National Capitol will contend that the present salary of Congressmen is to high unless it is the intention to make the office one entirely of honor when the salary should be abolished entirely, a proposition ~~entirely~~ repugnant to our republican ideas and institutions.

I do not believe the citizens of this republic desire their public servants to serve them without a fair compensation for their services. Twenty-five thousand dollars does not defray the expenses of the Executive for one year, or has not in my experience. It is not now what it was when fixed by the constitution in reality, nor one fifth of it in purchasing power when increased demands or taken in consideration together with increased cost ~~of~~ [of] all supplies.

Having no personal interest in this matter I have felt myself free to return this bill to the House in which it originated, with my objections, believing that in doing so I meet the wishes and judgement of the great Majority of those who indirectly pay all the salaries and other expenses of government. If I ~~have~~ [do] not I will bow to their judgement no matter how expressed.

ADf (bracketed material not in USG's hand), DLC-USG, III. *SED*, 44-1-49; *SMD*, 49-2-53, 394. The draft includes two pages of calculations in USG's hand. See Hamilton Fish diary, April 18, 1876, DLC-Hamilton Fish. Senate Bill No. 172 reduced the president's salary from $50,000 to $25,000. See *CR*, 44–1, 1696–98, 44-2, 1747; *PUSG*, 24, 12.

On April 12, Culver C. Sniffen had written to Attorney Gen. Edwards Pierrepont. "The President directs me to say that he will be pleased if you will have prepared and sent to him a statement showing the compensation of Members of Congress from the foundation of the Government to the present time; the date of each law effecting changes in their salaries and the amounts of salary received by them under each change of law." ALS, DNA, RG 60, Letters from the President. On April 15, Pierrepont wrote to USG at length as requested. Copy, *ibid.*, Letters Sent to Executive Officers.

On April 19, George A. Peltz, *Sunday School Times*, Philadelphia, wrote to USG. "Permit me, as one who has enjoyed your society, who keeps an eye on you continually, and who believes in you, to express my pleasure at your Veto of the President's Salary Bill. Many of my friends feel as I do also upon the point. God Bless you!" ALS, USG 3.

To Roscoe Conkling

———

Confidential

Apl. 19th /76

DEAR SENATOR

Do you know any reason why Col. Brady,[1] of Norfolk, Va should not be appointed Pension Agt. in place of Chandler, deceased?

Brady is a native of the state; an original Union man, and republican, and seved in the Union Army.

He is also highly recommended for the position.

Yours Truly

U. S. GRANT

HON ROSCOE CONKLING

ALS, DLC-Roscoe Conkling. On [*April 26, 1876*], USG wrote to [*Culver C. Sniffen*]. "Write Sec. of the Int. that I favor the nomination of Saml L. Annable for Pension Agt. in place of Chandler deceased. If the nomination is sent up in time ~~I~~ [it] will get ~~it~~ in [to the Senate] to-day." AN (bracketed material in another hand), Wayde Chrismer, Bel Air, Md. On the same day, USG nominated Samuel Annable as pension agent, Norfolk, replacing Lucius H. Chandler.

On [*May 20, 1875*], USG had written. "Write note to Sec. of the Int. saying that I approve the transfer of Richmond Pension Agcy to Norfolk" AN (undated), *ibid.* On May 21, USG ordered this change. ES, DNA, RG 48, Miscellaneous Div., Letters Received.

1. Born in 1843 in Va., James D. Brady moved to New York City, enlisted in the 37th N. Y., rose to lt. col., 63rd N. Y., and settled in Va. after the war. On Oct. 24, 1876, Brady, secretary, Va. Republican State Central Committee, Richmond, wrote to USG. "As a Virginian who was loyal to the Government during the war, and whose every interest is with the South, I tender you my most grateful thanks for your timely proclamation as to South Carolina. I am in the position to know the real sentiments of the people of Virginia as well perhaps as any other man in the State, and I am satisfied that there is not a truly loyal man within her borders who does not thank you from the bottom of his heart for your noble action in this matter. You have and do understand the condition of affairs South. Your proclamation gives strenght and encouragement to every patriotic american in this section. We hope to have the protection of the government in exercising our rights as free citizens ~~of~~ in a free country. The loyal masses of the Country will, I believe, sustain you." ALS, *ibid.*, RG 60, Letters from the President. See Proclamation, Oct. 17, 1876. On Dec. 16, Brady, "Maj Genl Comd'g Dept," "Army of the Boys in Blue," Portsmouth, wrote to USG. "*Confidential* . . . In view of the fact that many of the leading Democrats in all parts of the Country and many of the most influential Democratic papers openly threaten war in the event of Tilden not being declared President I deem it proper to invite your Excellency's attention to the existence of the organization of the 'Boys in Blue,' composed exculsively of the vetrans of the Union army during the late war, in this state. Should the Democratic Members of the House of Representatives attempt to declare Tilden President contrary to law and in opposition to the decision of the Senate,—they mean war—and in that event, it is likely that an effort may be made to capture the government property at this naval station—We have thorroughly organized about fifteen hundred vetrans in Portsmouth, Norfolk and Norfolk County, and should it become necessary this force can be relied upon to assist the naval authorites in charge of the yard—I sincerely trust that there will be no truble, but should it come we shall be prepared to defend ourselves, and to serve our country in any manner that may be deemed requsite by the Commander in chief of the Army and Navy." ALS, USG 3. On Jan. 29, 1877, USG nominated Brady as collector of Internal Revenue, 2nd District, Va. On Feb. 5, USG withdrew the nomination. See John S. Mosby to John Sherman, Jan. 31, 1877, DLC-John Sherman.

To Congress

TO THE SENATE AND HOUSE OF REPRESENTATIVES—

I transmit herewith, for the information of Congress, a report of the President of the Centennial Commission upon the ceremonies to be observed at the opening of the Exhibition, on the 10th instant— It will be observed that an invitation is therein extended to Senators and Representatives to be present on that occasion—

U. S. GRANT.

WASHINGTON. MAY 1ST 1876.

Copies, DNA, RG 59, Reports to the President and Congress; *ibid.*, RG 130, Messages to Congress. *SED*, 44-1-54. On April 20, 1876, Joseph R. Hawley, president, Centennial Commission, Philadelphia, wrote to USG submitting a schedule for opening ceremonies on May 10. ". . . Programme. 1. Centennial Inauguration March by Richard Wagner of Germany 2. Prayer by the Rt. Rev. Bishop Simpson 3. Hymn by John G. Whittier, music by John K. Paine of Mass Orchestral and organ accompaniment. 4. Cantata, the words by Sidney Lanier of Georgia, Music by Dudley Buck of Connecticut Orchestral and organ accompaniment. 5. Presentation of the Exhibition by the President of the Centennial Commission. 6. Address by the President of the United States. . . ." LS, DNA, RG 59, Miscellaneous Letters. *SED*, 44-1-54. On April 27, Ulysses S. Grant, Jr., wrote to Hawley. "In your letter to the President some days ago you wrote that you would send him a copy of the remarks you intended to make at the Centennial Opening. As he has not yet received a copy referred to, he wishes me not to let the matter escape your memory. The President's remarks will no doubt be brief but he would prefer having them as appropriate as possible." ALS, Gilder Lehrman Collection, NNP. See Address, May 10, 1876.

On Feb. 8, USG had written to the Senate. "I transmit to the Senate in answer to the Resolution of that Body of the 18th ultimo, a report from the Secretary of State with accompanying papers." Copies, DNA, RG 59, Reports to the President and Congress; *ibid.*, RG 130, Messages to Congress. Secretary of State Hamilton Fish reported on diplomatic preparations for the Centennial Exhibition. Copy, *ibid.*, RG 59, Reports to the President and Congress.

On Feb. 14, James S. Davis, Oakville, Ontario, wrote to USG. "My attention has been drawn to a Paragraph—Which appeared in the *Toronto Globe*—Dated Decer 24th 1875 Stating that yourself—and Secretary Belknap had ordered at the Mint in Philadelphia Gold Medals—To be given to the surviving Soldiers—Who served in the Mexican War of 1846 & 7—I have had the pleasure of serving twelve months in that Campaign Was present at the Battle of Monterey and other minor engagements I have been induced through Friends to make application—To you by Letter For one of those—Medals Which I should Prize much—above its intrinsic value . . ." LS, *ibid.*, RG 94, Letters Received, 1046 1876. Related papers are *ibid.* On May 5, Secretary of War Alphonso Taft wrote to James W. Denver, president, National Association of Veterans of the Mexican War. "The President has referred to me your application for such further quantity of condemned material as will compensate the United States Mint, at Philadelphia, for 5000 additional medals, for issue to Veterans of the Mexican War, and that discretionary authority be given to the Chief of Ordnance to provide further material from time to time to be devoted to this purpose, as occasion may require, and in reply thereto, I regret to inform you that there is no authority of law under which your request can be favorably considered. The Department is ready to turn over to your Association such number of bronze guns as Congress may authorize" Copy, *ibid.*, RG 107, Letters Sent, Military Affairs.

On Feb. 24, Governor John F. Hartranft of Pa. had written to USG. "I am informed that the gentlemen charged with the management of the Centennial Exhibition are very desirous of having an United States Officer detailed to assist them in perfecting the arrangements for and in the reception of foreign Officers, as well as the various military organizations of this Country, and I believe some of the gentlemen most prominently connected with the Commission are anxious that General Lewis Merrill should be detailed for this special duty. I beg leave therefore to ask that your Excellency will be pleased to designate this Officer for the position named who I feel assured is eminently qualified therefor, and whose selection will be particularly gratifying to Pennsylvanians, and will personally oblige . . ." LS, *ibid.*, RG 94, ACP, M103 CB 1863. On March 21, Taft wrote to AG Edward D. Townsend. "After conference with the President upon Lieut. General Sheridan's representation that officers of his command had been detailed to other duty without his assent, it is ordered that Major Merrill, 7th Cavalry be relieved from his assignment to duty with the centennial exposition." LS, *ibid.* On March 24, Maj. Lewis Merrill, Philadelphia, wrote to Townsend. ". . . Since 1871 I have had the most onerous and obnoxious duty to discharge in the South which has in that time fallen to any officer of my regiment. Because of the faithful and efficient discharge of this duty I have been subjected, up to the present time, to the most bitter and violent partisan attacks in the newspapers and even in Congress. As much as I have had to cultivate patience under this unjust and outrageous assault to which I could not reply, I have never yet become so thickskinned that it has ceased to be very annoying. I submit that I have had my full share of it and should have relief from it. For this reason quite as much as any other, my detail to Philadelphia was peculiarly pleasant inasmuch as I am sure that a condition of sentiment exists about my late station which will make peace impossible during the coming political campaign. I think I am not immodest in saying that I am entitled to the consideration of being relieved from that sort of duty. For the reasons given the revocation of the order detailing me is a very great hardship and I beg that I may not be subjected to it. I have no wish to shirk legitimate duty nor to seek what are called soft places, but I most earnestly wish to avoid any more of the millstone of debt." LS, *ibid.* See *PUSG*, 23, 102. Also on March 24, Ward H. Lamon, Philadelphia, wrote to USG. "Yesterday the centennial commission at a regular session of the Board decided, without one dissenting voice, to have as one of the great features of the Exhibition, a citizen military encampment—under the auspices of the commission, in order to give it a national character—and it is suggested that the military control & command of it be under the nominal if not the actual direction of the General of the Army. To this end, it is very important to have an experienced military officer upon the Staff of the President of the Commission—Major Merrill had been detailed for this duty and there seems to be a general sentiment of regret that he has been relieved from duty here, by an Order from the War Department—Major Merrill is a most popular officer—he has suceeded in winning the esteem of the people here and is universally regarded as an efficient and experienced officer—and a frank and courteous gentleman. . . ." ALS, DNA, RG 94, ACP, M103 CB 1863. USG endorsed papers on this subject. "War I have no objection to Maj. Merrill's retention but not at the expense of revocation of the orders detailing other officers. His retention will make three instead of two officers for that duty." AE (undated), *ibid.* See Hawley to Gen. William T. Sherman, April 4, 1876, DLC-William T. Sherman. Merrill and Lt. Col. Luther P. Bradley, 9th Inf., represented the army at the exhibition; Commodore Edward Calhoun, Commander George D. Ryan, and Lt. Harrison G. O. Colby represented the navy.

On March 9, USG had written to Adolph E. Borie, Philadelphia. "I take pleasure in introducing to you Mr Henry Ulke an artist of high reputation in this city who purposes to exhibit some of his paintings at the 'Centennial' I commend him to your kind offices." Copy, DLC-USG, II, 3. USG wrote a similar letter to George W. Childs. See *Julia Grant*, p. 190; Charles E. Fairman, *Art and Artists of the Capitol of the United States of America* (Washington, 1927), p. 356.

On March 30, John C. Dawson, "Giles Mills," Sampson County, N. C., wrote to USG. "your Petitioner prays that letters of Commissions may be Granted to him for *one* of the Commissioners of this State to be appointed by you to attend to the National Centennial . . . I have Some very important inventions if I can get the money to take out the Patent for them if the Goverment or Some privat individual will loan me the money I will make them Safe for the money I feel that I am doing a wrong to keepe Such and invetntions hide from the world it is for the like of money the inventions I speak of is viz Perpetual Motion a 2 Giant Gun Batery that it is such that it is imposiable for and Armey of men to take it One man can Shoot 1.00.00 times per minute . . ." ALS, DNA, RG 59, Letters of Application and Recommendation. No appointment followed.

On April 5, Joseph N. Bourassa and two others, Silver Lake, Kan., wrote to USG. "We pray and hope what we write, will not be deemed as dictating, by your excellency, but as an humble suggestion; of men of Indian blood; who have witnessed your *Policy* for years, and who know the Indian Character for fifty years. And more over we have had the honor to serve the Government for many years, as Interpreters, and also in other Capacities. We desire your Excellency, to invite some delegates from most tribes, especially from those that have been refractory for years back, to your Great Celebration next July, the Centennial of the American people. We humbly believe it would have a more pacific effect on all those tribes, more so, than the many treaties of *Peace*, which have been made with them: to witness such an august assemblage of your Nation; and also to see the *Heads* of other Powers of the world meet with you. We are sure, from what we know of the transatlantic Nations, it would be a great Curiosity, and gratification to them, to see the Indian as he is, as most of them never have seen an Indian of North America, in his wild costume and uniform. The expense of transportation would only be a trifle, in our day of improvement. The above is our candid opinion and real conviction. We give the above intimation because we love our *people*, and our adopted *Government.* Your Red children" LS (one by mark), *ibid.*, RG 75, Letters Received, Centennial Exhibition. On June 19, Bourassa wrote to USG. "I am an Indian, was educated at Transylvinia University Lexington. Ky. and graduated in 1837, Bachelor of the Laws, by the aid of the Government, for which I am thankful. Since that time, I have been writing a work which is an exposition of the Customs of my nation, the Pottawatomies; with about 12 biographies of our *Chiefs* and *Braves.* A vocabulary of their language. A *tree* of their heaven and religion. A Hebrew scroll, containing parts of Exodus and Numbers. And a work on the Indian Meteria Medica, which I have been composing for over 40 years, with valuable recipes for the cure of many diseases. Also I have a wonderful Horse Powder, to enliven jaded horses; and to increase the speed of Race horses. So that one of less speed with the use of this powder can out run one of greater speed. I have a great desire to bring my work, before the Pulic, to be dedicated to the people of the U. S. But I cannot, because I am too poor. I want the President to help me, in the above, by ordering me, as Interpreter of the Pottawatomies, to the Centennial Ground, at Philedelphia, which will enable me to sell my work at once—I want my nephew to accompany me as I am old—The fare, will be but a small consideration with your great and rich Government—An attention to the above will be thankfully received by your red son—" ALS,

ibid. See *HED,* 44-1-148, 34–35; Dorothy V. Jones, "A Potawatomi Faces the Problem of
Cultural Change: Joseph N. Bourassa in Kansas," *Kansas Quarterly,* 3, 4 (Fall, 1971), 47–55;
J. N. Bourassa, "The Life of Wah-bahn-se: The Warrior Chief of the Pottawatamies,"
Kansas Historical Quarterly, XXXVIII, 2 (Summer, 1972), 132–43.

On April 6, William Quinn, "Plumber & Gasfitter," Troy, N. Y., had written to USG.
"Having lost my health in the late war, which disables me from working at my trade, for
the support of my family, I most respectfully request that you have me appointed to some
position under the government, at the Centennial, at Philada, or in any capacity where, as
a writer, a watchman, clerk, Doorkeeper, or Detective or in any light business, I may be
useful. . . ." ALS, DNA, RG 59, Letters of Application and Recommendation. On April 7,
Joseph R. Carter, Philadelphia, wrote to USG seeking "a situation in some one of the various departments in the U. S. Gov't Building at the Centennial grounds as correspondent,
clerk, messenger, guard, or any place where I can be of service to the enterprise either in
this, or the Custom House department at the Centennial grounds." ALS, *ibid.*

To House of Representatives

To the House of Representatives:

I transmit herewith, in answer to the Resolution of the House of
Representatives of the 15th. March last, a report from the Secretary
of State, and accompanying papers.

U. S. Grant.

Washington, May 1, 1876.

Copy, DNA, RG 59, Reports to the President and Congress. *HED,* 44-1-161. On May 1,
1876, Secretary of State Hamilton Fish wrote to USG. ". . . Early in the year 1872 Commander Meade, of the United States Navy, entered into an agreement, with the Great Chief
of the Bay of Pago Pago, of the Island of Tutuila (one of the Navigator's Islands,) whereby
the latter granted to the United States the exclusive privilege of establishing in said harbor a naval station, for the use and convenience of the vessels of the United States Government. About the same time, the attention of this Government was directed, by highly
respectable commercial persons, to the importance of the growing trade and commerce of
the United States with the Islands in the South Pacific Ocean, and to the opportunities
of increasing our commercial relations in that quarter of the globe. The Samoan, or Navigator's Islands lay precisely in the track of such trade; and this fact, taken in connection
with their reported good harbors, supposed fertility, and the friendly disposition of their
inhabitants manifested towards this Government, led to a desire to secure more reliable
information in reference to them. With this object in view, Mr. Steinberger was, in March
1873, instructed to proceed to the Islands, make a thorough examination in regard to all
the points on which it was desirable that the Government should be informed, and report
the result of his observations. In compliance with these instructions, he proceeded to the
Islands, and in due time submitted his report, a copy of which was transmitted to Congress
by the President, on the 21st of April, 1874, and published by the Senate in Executive Document No. 45, First Session of the Forty-Third Congress. In December, 1874, Mr. Stein-

berger again proceeded to the Islands, in the capacity of a Special Agent, to convey to the Chiefs a letter from the President, and certain presents, which it was deemed advisable to send them. He has submitted a second report of the result of his observations and the course pursued by him in the Islands. After submitting this report, Mr. Steinberger resigned his position as Special Agent of the Government, which resignation was accepted on its being received, on the 10th. of December last. In the meantime, reports had been received at the Department, to the effect that Mr. Steinberger had exceeded the limits of his instructions, in various ways, and that, among other things, he had, promised to the Samoans the protection of this Government. On the receipt of these reports, instructions were at once sent to him, (on 6. May. 1875.) calling his attention to the limited nature of his instructions. In the latter part of 1875 further reports were received, from Mr. Foster, the Consul of the United States at Apia, in relation to the course pursued by Mr. Steinberger, and on the 12th. of January, last, it was deemed advisable, in order to put an end to all doubt in regard to his status, to address to Mr. Foster an instruction, to the effect that Mr. Steinberger's visits to the Islands were simply for the purpose of observation and report, that his mission had no diplomatic or political significance whatever, and that he had never been authorized to pledge the United States to the support of any government he might form or assist in forming" Copy, DNA, RG 59, Reports to the President and Congress. *HED*, 44-1-161. See *PUSG*, 25, 297–302.

Also on May 1, the "Taimua and Faipule" (upper and lower houses) "of the Samoan Government who are left," Mulinu'u, wrote to USG. "We bring again to the knowledge of Your Excellency and of the Chiefs and Rulers of your Government, an account of the difficulties we now experience, and principally of the obstacles which have impeded the march of our Government. On the 13th of March last a fight took place at Mulinuu between the Samoans and seamen of H. B. M. Ship Barracouta. On that day there were present at Mulinuu Captain Stevens R. N., Mr. S. S. Foster, United States Consul, and Mr. S. F. Williams, British Consul. The presence of these gentlemen was not anticipated by us. We were taken by surprise, when English sailors made efforts to take our arms from us and a shot was fired at a Samoan soldier, who was killed. Then began the bloodshed of the Samoans and the British sailors. Eight Samoans were killed—one Taimua, one Faipule and six soldiers—Only three Englishmen died. Three Faipule of our Government have also been taken as hostages and have been kept since then on an Engish Ship-of-war. Our arms were also taken away, and our guns spiked on the day which we were so much alarmed. We are greatly pleased and very thankful in having met Captain J. N. Miller, of the U. S. Ship-of-war 'Tuscarora.' He has shown great love for us and we have had him many days in Samoa. We think he knows everything about the troubles that have been brought upon our Government. There was no cause for the opposition to our Government, and we know very well that it came from a great jealousy of foreigners living in Samoa who saw the Samoans advancing to civilization by the teaching and love of Colonel Steinberger. There is also another cause why we are so grieved, as Colonel Steinberger our Premier, has been taken away from us by secret means, by some bad hearted people living in Samoa, but we have patience in our troubles and have hope in the friendly aid of the United States Government. We, and the Samoan Government in our actions during the recent difficulties have had no wish to join any other nation. Our only wish was to keep fast our friendly relations with your Government and be under your good care, and we wished to treat as friends the Agent of the United States and all American citizens. We can never forget our love for Colonel Steinberger. He was as the lamp of Samoa, which is now extinguished, and since he has been taken away from us some persons living in Samoa have seemed to try to spread darkness again. He has never said a word in Samoa by which he tried to bring it under the power of the United States. This is true. On the day we appointed him Premier he gave his solemn oath and made his speech saying that he intended to give up his Agency from your Government and work for us as if he were a Samoan in the formation of our Government, and indeed he did so until the day he was seized and taken away from us. It was also the will of all Samoa that he should form laws for our Government according to the laws of civilized Governments. We know very well that everything done by him in Samoa was right. Therefore we declare now to Your Excellency that we wish still to have Colonel Steinberger as our Premier, because he has done right with a true love and great patience in the darkness which we have been in. If agreeable to Your Excellency and the representatives of your Government, please to send to us Colonel Steinberger so that he can work again with us in our Government as he did when we had him with us. Our wishes expressed in our previous letter in regard to him have not changed, they will remain the same until his death. We would be troubled if you could not accept our request; but if your intention is that he should not come back, we then humbly pray to Your Excellency to appoint another gentleman as good and as skillful as Colonel Steinberger to teach our Government. We will support him, pay him well, and after our Government is well instructed he can then return to America if he so desires. We have confidence in your kindness and in the Government of the United States of America, that you will consent to the wishes which we have expressed and that by the friendly helping of your Government our country will yet be safe. We pray also that your nation may always, be glorious, in the love of God. We are forever your most affectionate, . . ." D (in Samoan), DNA, RG 59, Despatches from Special Agents; translation, *ibid. HED*, 44-2-44, 71–72.

On May 5, Richard L. Ogden, commercial agent, Samoa, San Francisco, wrote to USG. "I have the honor to transmit herewith a communication from Col A B Steinberger to the Hon Sect. of State which I address to you to ensure its coming under your notice at an early day. The action of S S Foster under authority of the United States has been of a character so outrageous and I may say unparalled, that I but express the desire of Every respectable unbiased american, that he may no longer be permitted to disgrace the goverment that he professes to represent. I beg most respectfully to suggest the name of J. M. Coe formerly commercial agent of the U. S. and at various times acting consul as qualified to perform the duties of consul, he having been a resident of the Islands for twenty five years. speaking the language, and in every way acceptable to the native Goverment. The continuation of S. S Foster as consul would be considered by the native Goverment as inconsistent with the good wishes heretofore expressed by your Excellency for their succesful Efforts to establish a goverment in accordance with the Example of civilized nations, as well as being considered an Endorsement of the late proceedings calculated to overthrow and destroy the effort to maintain such a Goverment. The salary of a consul at the port of Apia would be inadequate to the Support of any person not a resident. I recommend Mr Coe for the position as being the most Eligible under the circumstances to fill the position and do so at the request of such of the american residents of Samoa as have taken no part in the effort to overthrow the native Goverment. In asmuch as the opportunities for communicating direct with the Samoan group are not frequent, and the regular packet having sailed a few days since, I beg to say that a vessel now loading at a point on the coast above will sail the latter part of the month, by which I can forward any dispatches the State Department may desire to send, if addressed, to my care—I beg to mention also, that Mr Coe is now in this city having been imprisoned on board the British man of war and subsequently taken out of the country and landed at the Figi Islands, by order of Mr Foster, to whom he was obnoxious by reason of his sympathy with Steinberger and the native Goverment—The Fipula or native Congress are unanimous in their desire to have

Steinberger return to them and are determined to maintain at all hazards the goverment he formed for them—as shown by their determined resistance and obstinate refusal to abandon it, even under the best efforts of the missionaries, and intimidations of the commander of the British man of wa[r.] The dethroned King (Malietoa) repudiated by reason of his consent without the eassent of the chiefs, to the arrest of Steinberger, has but three native followers to count as his support in his claims for restoration—while the native congress in favor of Steinberger, numbers some one hundred & fifty chiefs—and the Entir native population of thirty six thousand These facts prove conclusively that the banishm[ent] of Steinberger was only at the instigation of the foreign residents who bitterly oppose anything American . . . May 6th P. S. I take the liberty of enclosing Slips from the Alta California newspaper, of this morning. The article expresses the general feeling of the people here, who are strongly in favor of some measures to restore Steinberger to the position from which he was so unjustly deposed, and any steps to that End would be heartily Endorsed. The feeling here, is, that the English seek the possession of these Islands. seeing their commercial value We also see the great value they would be to *this* coast. The trade already since Steinbergers arrival there has increased ten fold—As coaling stations they are invaluable, lying immediately in the track of the line of Australian steamers, The natives are anxious to come under American rule and influence—and the late outrages have created a predjudice against the English that would greatly facilitate obtaining any concessions Americans might ask. I trust your Excellency will pardon the liberty I take in offering a suggestion based upon my intimate knowledge of the real facts of this matter, and feeling of the native population of Samoa, in regard to Mr Steinberger. It is this, that some slight countenance and moral support shown Mr Steinberger at this critical moment would completely and firmly Establish him in his former position, and utterly defeat the attempts of his enemies to overthrow the Samoan Goverment—The simple pestige of the protection of a man of war requiring no special action or involving responsibility, would be sufficient—If Steinberger returned to the Figii Islands the nearest point to Samoa and could there avail himself of the opportunity to return to Apia in a man of war landed there under the simple honors paid him on a former occasion involving the expenditure of a few pounds of powder to the Samoan Flag. The natives would receive him with the wildest delight and the opposing element be forever silenced, The alacrity with which the Hon Secretary of State declared Mr Steinberger in no way accredited by the U S was construed into an intimation that he would receive no protection that an ordinary american citizen might expect and went far to bring about the present condition of affairs. Especially the part played by the U S Consul who openly declares that he has acted under instructions Should it be considered of sufficient importance to order a man of war to any port in Australia New Zealand or the Figiis with instructions to take Col Steinberger on board and land him at the port of Apia—I will communicate with him and see that he is at the appointed point in time to meet the vessel—provided I can have Early intimation to that effect to Ensure a connection. A more popular step in the Estimation of leading men of this coast could not be taken and would be heartily Endorsed by the people at large irrespective of party or politics" ALS, DNA, RG 59, Despatches from Special Agents. *HED*, 44-2-44, 73–74. On Nov. 28, 1875, and on May 7, 1876, Ogden wrote to Orville E. Babcock. "I enclose slips cut from the local papers here by which you will see that our friend Steinbergers stock is gradually appreciating and in *this* locality it begins to dawn upon the public mind that Samoa will yet pan out advantageously—. . ." "I presume you will have seen all the row and doings in Samoa—I enclose you extracts from recent news—The consul S S Foster must be *immediately suppressed*! He is about the d__dst scoundrel unhung and all this has come about from that miserable old Scare crow Fish not having any back bone—If he had not been so frightened as to go down on his knees and swear that Steinberger had no friends in Washington all this would not have occurred. It was on the strength of a letter from Fish to Foster saying he (S.) would not be protected by the Govt—that he was in no way accredited, that produced the row—Foster said, this man has no friends at court Ill go for his scalp—Had Mr Fish exhibited a decent regard for facts and said Mr Steinberger altho not officially accredited as an Agent or Comr of the Govt., is nevertheless acting in sympathy and harmony—Foster would not have dared to do it—The highhanded outrage in seizing all of his private papers, and letters, should be noticed, *He has all of your letters* and is showing them about—He showed one letter to Capt Stevens of the Barracouta wherein you say 'In a shorttime you will have the Islands'—. . . *It is for the interest of all concerned* that immediate steps be taken to restore Steinberger & arrest Foster. . . ." ALS, ICN. The enclosures are *ibid.*

On May 8, Albert B. Steinberger, Auckland, New Zealand, wrote to USG. "I arrived in this port on the 2[8]th ult an[d] found H. M. Steamers 'Pearl', Flag ship, C[o]mmodore Hoski[ns] 'Sappho', 'Nymphe' and 'Barracouta' I was disappointed upon arrival [to] find that telegraphic communication was int[er]rupted [and] that I could not communicate [wi]th the Departments at Washington—And that nothing further than a preliminary investigation was held in the case of Capt Charles E. Stevens R. N. commanding H. M. Steamer 'Barracouta'—And that he is ordered to England for court-Martial The letters furnished myself by your Excellency, for the benefit of the Samoan people, and others (autograph) addressed to Foreign ministers, Consul and other representatives of the United States, wi[th] other and certain letters from the Hon. Sec of the Navy have been seized with all of my personal effects. That some of the said letters have been wantonly exhibited to colonial officers in the Fijis and published in the Press of these colonies in a manner calculated to cast discredit upon your Excellency, but especially to fa[s]ten odium upon myself; not as an individual American, but upon the presumption that I was a duly accredited agent of the United States. The illegal seizure of my person and the consequent strife and bloodshed in Samoa my prevent the sudden acquisition of that group [of islands by Her Majesty's government. The lodgment effected, and the native sentiment as to America, with the hearty feelings evinced upon the receipt of Your Excellency's letters by the] chiefs has made the name of America dominant throughout the group. I do now charge the American Consul at Apia, S. S. Foster, with aiding and abetting a Foreign power, displaying an inimical sentiment and action to the U. S. of America—For the furtherance of his views he deemed in necessary to seize and participate in the seizure of my personal property, as well as property of the U. S. Government, furnished me by the Navy Department for personal use in the Samoan Islands. All of which has been squandered by public and private sale in the Port of Apia, while I was a prisoner upon H. M. Str 'Barracouta' H. M. Str 'Pearl' Com'dr Hoskins accompanied by H. M. Str 'Sappho' has left this port for Samoa and I am kept in profound ignorance of the object of such expedition—certain it is that the Samoan Government and chiefs will resist every attempt of H. M. Government for the the annexation or even diplomatic control of the Islands—It is of the utmost importance that I be for a certain period in the Samoan Islands, to take such testimony as will vindicate the action of the U. S. Government, and fairly refute the aggregation of material accumulated by Capt Charles E. Stevens, which he has availed himself of in a surreptitious and dishonorable manner, during my imprisonment upon the 'Barracouta', when, for a period of sixty three (63) days, I had no means of communication with the Native Government or friends upon shore. I find, upon my arrival here, American Vice Consul H. P. Barber in re[ceipt] of despatches from S. S. Foster, U. S. Con[sul] at Apia, inimical to myself and o[f a] most malicious character—Hence I a[m in] the painful position of being prejudged by a[n] American representative, whose business and associations are purely foreign and Anti-

Americ[an.] May I ask that your Excellency will give to me such aid and comfort as will enable me to refute the unnatura[l] charges made against myself and supp[ort] the fervent desires of the Samoan people. Believing this to be for the honor of m[y] country . . ." LS, DNA, RG 59, Despatches from Special Agents. *HED*, 44-2-44, 96, 101.

On May 23, Fish recorded in his diary. "Spoke to the President of the Steinberger case and suggest the importance of the appointment of a new Consul and remark on the difficulty of finding a suitable man to go to that district on the Salary attached—The Secretary of the Treasury asked if I had thought of G. W. Griffin—I doubt whether Griffin would take the place but am quite willing to offer it and authorize Mr Bristow to ask if he will. I also mention the importance of sending a vessel of war with some discrete commander to investigate matters. Robeson says that the Tuscarora is now on her way there." DLC-Hamilton Fish. See *PUSG*, 22, 401.

On Aug. 18, Steinberger, Suez, Egypt, wrote to USG. "I beg to notify your Excellency that the London Standard (official organ) announces officially that H. M. Ship 'Barracouta' is ordered to England in the case of Steinberger—I am still without advices from Washington but confident of Judge Pierrepont having definite instructions, as well as finding certified copies of my official correspondence with your Excellency and the Hon: Secy of State—Plundered of my Commission, Passport, Letter from the Hon: Secy of Navy addressed to Commanders of Fleets and War Vessels of the U. S. Navy in the Asiatic, North, and South Pacific Stations as well as your Excellency's personal autograph letters addressed to Ministers Consular and other U. S. representatives abroad—the loss of the latter I most keenly feel not only for the inconvenience to which I am subjected, but I had treasured such papers as being evidence of my official character and the confidence of the President of the United States of America—If duplicates of these papers have not yet been forwarded to London, may I ask that your Excellency be pleased to forward the same—I shall at once place myself in the hands of the U. S. Minister upon arrival in London and withhold despatches to the Hon: Secy of State until such time as I can reach the Admiralty and Foreign Office—The testimony of the Officers and Seamen of the 'Barracouta' will justify the previously expressed opinion in former despatches from Fiji and New Zealand—I expect in Sixty days from this date full testimony from Samoa from Special agent whom I sent from Auckland N. Z.—particulars of this mission furnished to the Hon Secy of State in official despatch dated 1st June 1876.—Without a decided expression from the United States addressed to Her Majestys Government, Samoa will fall into the hands of England or Germany—of movements in this direction I will be able to advise my Government at quick intervals" LS, DNA, RG 59, Despatches from Special Agents. *HED*, 44-2-44, 105–6. On Nov. 14, Steinberger, London, wrote to USG. "Communicating witnessed document from the Taimua and Faipule, the Government of Samoa—I have the honor to state that this is one of many papers forwarded to me from Auckland, New Zealand, through an agent whom I sent to the Samoan Islands from the said Port, originals and copies of which will be forwarded to the Honorable Secretary of State, all of which will have an important bearing on my case—I wish to assure Your Excellency that my action is prudent and conservative, prompted by a desire to maintain the friendly disposition of the English people and submit to the enlightened judgment of the Honorable Secretary of State.—I now beg to present to your Excellency my thanks for the prompt recognition of my letter of the 18th August, inclosing certified copies of my commissions letters of instructions &c, and herewith beg to state that the decided action of the English Government will depend much upon the repudiation of the acts of S. S. Foster United States Consul for Samoa and the maintenance of my integrity as an ex-United States official—" LS, DNA, RG 59, Despatches from Special Agents. *HED*, 44-2-44, 106–7.

On Nov. 30, Pa'u Lauaki and three others, "appointed by all the chiefs and Rulers of our Government of Samoa to prepare this letter," Apia, wrote to USG "and all the chiefs appointed to rule over the United States of America." "We address your Excellency and your Government in Order that you may know of the troubles which have arisen in this our Country, Samoa on account of what was done by Steinberger up till the present time some of the Chiefs and people of our Group are believing in him. But we now know that it was not under Authority from you and your Government that Steinberger came for for the purpose of establishing laws in this our Group of Samoa. That is why we wish to inform you that we have no desire for that Gentleman to return, nor for any other to come, but we wish to be allowed to carry on our own Government of Samoa, only let us have friendly relations with one another and be on good terms; in the same way as we are with other great Governments, that are represented in Samoa, viz—England & Germany—our relations with them are friendly and we are on good terms with them We desire to be on the same friendly terms with your Excellency and your Government, that no Gentleman be again sent down here, but that we be left to carry on our own Government as we please. At the present time our Country is devided because we know that the Government established by Steinberger and those that we appointed as Taimua is bad. Their laws are carried out in a tyrannical manner and many bad things are done which greatly distress our Nation There is no peace for our Country. We wish you to know that we have broken off from those whom we appointed as Taimua—in our Government,—and from the laws which were framed by Steinberger And now we are called by them rebels—and bad people, but it is not so,—it is they who are the rebels, for they have broken the Constitution & all the laws of our Government. But now we have turned to the old flag was hoisted by our whole group of Samoa,—the flag which was hoisted on the 2nd October 1873 That is why we beg of you not to be offended, but if any letters have been sent to you by those whom we appointed as Taimua, please do not agree to their proposals, because they have been missled in trusting still to the bad schemes set on foot by Steinberger. They whom we appointed as Taimua of the Government are still holding to these things It is indeed our desire to carry on our own Government and that only friendly relations should subsist between us and the great and enlightened Nations Another thing that we wish to inform you of is the bad things that have been done by the Consul whom you appointed to Samoa in place of Mr Foster. His Instructions to the Taimua are as follows 'I am going back to America to leave on the 12th Novr 1876, but will return to Samoa in six weeks with eight ships of War and troops. Let the Taimua be strong in holding to their present opinions and to all that Steinberger did'—On account of the instructions of this Gentleman whom you appointed as Consul in Samoa, some of those chiefs and others whom we appointed as Taimua of the Government are still the more obstinate in their opinions Since these Instructions were given by that Consul certain parties who have been misled by him are more obstinate then ever. We consider that the said Consul is quite as bad as Steinberger and consequently certain people of our group are still being led astray—Graciously send us a quick reply to this letter—May your Excellency the President have health as also all the chiefs appointed to rule over the United States of America." Translation, DNA, RG 59, Despatches from Special Agents.

On Jan. 8, 1877, Steinberger wrote to USG. "May I hope that your Excellency will take cognizance of my case—the 'Barracouta' will arrive here in Feby and my papers, as well as the Archives of the Samoan Govt having been seized or destroyed—my defense is in the Copies of these papers in the State dept. Surely I am an American Citizen—I could not be expatriated—after some service to my Country—because I had accepted service among an Aboriginal people, and an unrecognized govt. May I respectfully ask for Copies of the 'Investigation of the Mulifanuu plantation' in Samoa:—the 'Alaaua & Asu' trial in

Tutuila Samoa; the Samoan Constitution, my address to the govt; Capt Erben's address to the Chiefs; the petition of the white residents—and Capt Millers (USS Tuscarora) report. Recently the Samoan Govt and High Chiefs have forwarded me much valuable material evidence—the govt is still intact, and the devotion of all the people remains the same. In the unfortunate state of affairs in the US I am loath to intrude my own matters upon your Excellency, but I feel that I am fairly entitled to just weapons of defense." ALS, DNA, RG 59, Despatches from Special Agents.

On Feb. 24, USG wrote to the House of Representatives transmitting correspondence concerning Steinberger and Samoa. Copies, *ibid.*, Reports to the President and Congress; *ibid.*, RG 130, Messages to Congress. *HED*, 44-2-44. See R. P. Gilson, *Samoa 1830 to 1900: The Politics of a Multi-Cultural Community* (Melbourne, 1970), pp. 321–31; George Herbert Ryden, *The Foreign Policy of the United States in Relation to Samoa* (New Haven, 1933), pp. 142–47; *New York Times*, May 4, 1894.

To House of Representatives

To THE HOUSE OF REPRESENTATIVES:

I have given very attentive consideration to a Resolution of the House of Representatives, passed on the 3d. day of April, requesting the President of the United States to inform the House whether any Executive offices, acts, or duties, and, if any, what, have within a specified time been performed at a distance from the seat of government established by law, &c.

I have never hesitated, and shall not hesitate, to communicate to Congress, and to either branch thereof, all the information which the Constitution makes it the duty of the President to give; or which my judgment may suggest to me, or a request from either House may indicate to me will be useful in the discharge of the appropriate duties confided to them. I fail, however, to find in the Constitution of the United States the authority given to the House of Representatives (one branch of the Congress in which is vested the legislative power of the government) to require of the Executive—an independent branch of the Government, co-ordinate with the Senate and House of Representatives—an account of his discharge of his appropriate and purely executive offices, acts, and duties, either as to when, where, or how performed.

What the House of Representatives may require as a right in its demand upon the Executive for information, is limited to what is necessary for the proper discharge of its powers of legislation or of impeachment.

The inquiry in the resolution of the House as to where executive acts have, within the last seven years, been performed, and at what distance from any particular spot, or for how long a period at any one time, &c., does not necessarily belong to the province of legislation. It does not profess to be asked for that object.

If this information be sought, through an inquiry of the President as to his executive acts, in view or in aid of the power of impeachment vested in the House, it is asked in derogation of an inherent natural right, recognized in this country by a constitutional guarantee which protects every citizen, the President as well as the humblest in the land, from being made a witness against himself.

During the time that I have had the honor to occupy the position of President of this Government, it has been, and while I continue to occupy that position it will continue to be, my earnest endeavor to recognize and to respect the several trusts and duties and powers of the co-ordinate branches of the Government, not encroaching upon them nor allowing encroachments upon the proper powers of the office which the people of the United States have confided to me, but aiming to preserve in their proper relations the several powers and functions of each of the co-ordinate branches of the Government, agreeably to the Constitution, and in accordance with the solemn oath which I have taken to "preserve, protect, and defend" that instrument.

In maintenance of the rights secured by the Constitution to the executive branch of the government, I am compelled to decline any specific or detailed answer to the request of the House for information as to "any executive offices, acts, or duties, and, if any, what, have been performed at a distance from the Seat of Government established by law, and for how long a period at any one time, and in what part of the United States."

If, however, the House of Representatives desires to know whether, during the period of upward of seven years during which I have held the office of President of the United States, I have been absent from the seat of Government, and whether during that period I have performed or have neglected to perform the duties of my office,

I freely inform the House that from the time of my entrance upon my office I have been in the habit, as were all of my predecessors, (with the exception of one who lived only one month after assuming the duties of his office, and one whose continued presence in Washington was necessary from the existence at the time of a powerful rebellion,) of absenting myself, at times, from the seat of Government, and that during such absences I did not neglect or forego the obligations or the duties of my office, but continued to discharge all of the executive offices, acts, and duties which were required of me as the President of the United States. I am not aware that a failure occurred in any one instance of my exercising the functions and powers of my office in every case requiring their discharge, or of my exercising all necessary executive acts in whatever part of the United States I may at the time have been. Fortunately, the rapidity of travel and of mail-communication, and the facility of almost instantaneous correspondence with the offices at the seat of government which the telegraph affords to the President, in whatever section of the Union he may be, enable him, in these days, to maintain as constant, and almost as quick, intercourse with the Departments at Washington as may be maintained while he remains in the capital.

The necessity of the performance of executive acts by the President of the United States exists, and is devolved upon him, wherever he may be within the United States during his term of office, by the Constitution of the United States.

His civil powers are no more limited, or capable of limitation, as to the place where they shall be exercised, than are those which he might be required to discharge in his capacity of Commander-in-Chief of the Army and Navy; which latter powers, it is evident, he might be called upon to exercise, possibly even without the limits of the United States. Had the efforts of those recently in rebellion against the Government been successful in driving a late President of the United States from Washington, it is manifest that he must have discharged his functions, both civil and military, elsewhere than in the place named by law as the seat of Government.

No Act of Congress can limit, suspend, or confine this constitutional duty. I am not aware of the existence of any Act of Congress which assumes thus to limit or restrict the exercise of the functions of the Executive. Were there such acts, I should nevertheless recognize the superior authority of the Constitution, and should exercise the powers required thereby of the President.

The act to which reference is made in the Resolution of the House, relates to the establishment of the seat of government and the providing of suitable buildings, and removal thereto of the offices attached to the government, &c. It was not understood at its date and by General Washington to confine the President in the discharge of his duties and powers to actual presence at the Seat of Government. On the 30th of March, 1791, Shortly after the passage of the act referred to, General Washington issued an executive proclamation, having reference to the subject of this very act, from Georgetown, a place remote from Philadelphia, which then was the seat of Government, where the Act referred to directed that "all offices attached to the seat of Government" should for the time remain.

That none of his successors have entertained the idea that their executive offices could be performed only at the seat of Government is evidenced by the hundreds upon hundreds of such acts performed by my predecessors in unbroken line from Washington to Lincoln, a memorandum of the general nature and character of some of which acts is submitted herewith; and no question has ever been raised as to the validity of these acts, or as to the right and propriety of the Executive to exercise the powers of his office in any part of the United States.

U. S. GRANT.

WASHINGTON MAY 4, 1876.

Copy (with memorandum), DNA, RG 59, Reports to the President and Congress. *HED*, 44-1-162. On May 4, 1876, Secretary of State Hamilton Fish wrote to USG. "I send the copy of the Message—having taken a press-copy of it, which I will bring to you tomorrow for the purpose of your records if you desire it—" ALS (press), DLC-Hamilton Fish. On May 5, Fish recorded in his diary. "The Presidents letter refusing to answer the enquiry of the House of Representatives with regard to the preformance of Executive acts having been sent in I ordered the draft of it in my hand writing to be distroyed whereupon Mr Brown the Chief Clerk asked that he be allowed to retain it—I said he could provided he would promise not to show it—Which he did. . . . The message of yesterday was commented upon and is said to have been received with great enthusiasm by the Republicans and that the Democrats were incensed at the introduction of a Resolution which gave the President an opportunity of writing such a letter." *Ibid.* Also on May 5, U.S. Senator Oliver

P. Morton of Ind. wrote to USG. "I cannot refrain from expressing my gratification at your message to the House yesterday in regard to your absence from the city of Washington. It was a complete answer to a multitude of slanders. While there have been some complaints of the absence of some of your subordinates, whose duties were more local than yours, no sensible person ever beleived for a moment that the public interest suffered in the least because of your absence at Long Branch or elsewhere." ALS, USG 3.

Address

MY FELLOW COUNTRYMEN:

It has been thought appropriate, upon this Centennial occasion, to bring together in Philadelphia, for popular inspection, specimens of our attainments in the industrial and fine arts, and in literature, science, and philosophy, as well as in the great business of agriculture and commerce.

That we may the more thoroughly appreciate the excellencies and deficiencies of our achievements, and also give emphatic expression to our earnest desire to cultivate the friendship of our fellow members of the great family of nations, the enlightened agricultural, commercial, and manufacturing [people] nations of the world have been invited to send hither corresponding specimens of their skill to exhibit, on equal terms, in friendly competition with our own. To this invitation they have generously responded: for so doing we render them our hearty thanks.

The beauty and utility of the contributions will this day be submitted to your inspection by the managers of this Exposition. [Exhibition.] We are glad to know that [a] view of specimens of the skill of all nations, will afford to you unalloyed pleasure, as well as yield to you a valuable practical knowledge of so many of the remarkable results of the wonderful skill existing in enlightened communities.

One hundred years ago our country was new and but partially settled. Our necessities have compelled us to chiefly expend our means and time in felling forests, subduing prairies, building dwellings, factories, ships, docks, ware houses, roads, canals, machinery, etc. etc. Most of our schools, churches, libraries & assylums have been established within an hundred years. Burthened by these great primal works of necessity which could not be pretermitted [delayed], we yet have done what this exhibition will shew in the direction of rivaling older and more advanced nations in law, medicine and theology—in science, literature, philosophy, and the fine arts. Whilst proud of what we have done, we regret that we have not done more. Our achievements have been great enough however to make it easy for our people to acknowledge superior merit wheresoever found.

And now fellow citizens, I hope careful examination of what is about to be exhibited to you will not only inspire you with a profound respect for the skill and taste of our friends from other nations, but also satisfy you with the attainments made by our own people during the past one hundred years. I invoke your generous co-operation with the worthy commissioners to secure a brilliant success to this [Inter] National Exhibition, and to make the stay of our foreign visitors—to whom we extend a hearty welcom— at once both profitable and pleasant to them.

I declare the Centennial International Ehibition now open.

U. S. GRANT

PHILADELPHIA, PA
MAY 10TH 1876

ADfS (bracketed words interlineated by USG—except for [a]), PHi. *SED*, 45-3-74, 37–38. Joseph R. Hawley, president, Centennial Commission, spoke before USG. ADf, DLC-Joseph R. Hawley. *SED*, 45-3-74, 36–37. "... The President read his reply from a printed copy, in an ordinary conversational tone. I was within 20 feet of him, and I could not catch a single word. When he pronounced the Exhibition opened, the signal was given. A flag ran up the staff on the main building, the chimes began, the cannon boomed from George's Hill, and the orchestra and chorus pealed forth the majestic Hallelujah Chorus. . . ." *New York Tribune*, May 11, 1876. Accompanied by Emperor Pedro II of Brazil, USG then toured the Main Building and proceeded to Machinery Hall where the two started the Corliss engine. See Dee Brown, *The Year of the Century: 1876* (New York, 1966), pp. 110–31.

On May 2, Lt. Gen. Philip H. Sheridan had telegraphed to USG. "Letter received all right Fred will be in Philadelp with me Tuesdy morning." ADfS (telegram sent), DLC-Philip H. Sheridan. Sheridan left for Philadelphia on May 7, indicating that he intended to arrive on Tuesday, May 9.

On May 5, Friday, Horace Porter, Jersey City, telegraphed to Ulysses S. Grant, Jr. "I shall take pleasure in furnishing the car you desire on Tuesday" Telegram received (at 10:20 A.M.), DLC-USG, IB.

On May 7, Secretary of State Hamilton Fish wrote to USG. "The Brazilian Minister has this moment called to say that the Emperor has arrived in Washington and desires to pay his respects to you tomorrow at such hour as may be agreeable to you. . . ." Copy (press), DLC-Hamilton Fish. See Fish diary, April 5, May 6–8, 1876, *ibid.* On May 11, a correspondent reported from Washington, D. C. "Senators who have returned from the Centennial represent the President as not altogether pleased with the manner in which he was received. He was compelled to wait a considerable time for Dom Pedro, who insisted upon stopping and talking to all the mechanics." *Chicago Tribune*, May 12, 1876. See *Julia Grant*, pp. 187–89; Proclamation, June 26, 1876.

On May 10, Thomas M. H. Flynn, Philadelphia, wrote to USG. "In passing through the British section to-day will you look at the exhibit of granite from Bestbrook [*Bessbrook*] the model village of Ireland, out of which granite as there is nothing like it in America I will have pleasure in donating a centennial memorial stone for the National Monument at Washington when remodelled if you as President will accept the same from Ireland;" Copy, DNA, RG 59, Miscellaneous Letters. See U.S. Centennial Commission, *Reports and Awards* (Washington, 1880), III, 125, 429.

On May 23, John Sewart, "The National School," Lastingham, England, wrote to USG. "All the world knows that you and your people are about to hold high festival in honour of the centenary of your National Birth. In common with my countrymen of every degree I respectfully tender you my hearty congratulations. But I've another motive for encroaching upon your privacy & time. In the ancient Churchyard of Sedbergh, Yorkshire, there is still standing the family gravestone of the Washingtons. It is now rapidly decaying, as the stone is of a perishable nature. The Washingtons belonged to Howgill, a township in Sedbergh Parish, & the name Washington is still borne as a Christian name, altho' as a surname it has died out. Would it not be a graceful act at this particular time were that monument restored?. . ." ALS, DNA, RG 59, Miscellaneous Letters.

Also on May 23, H. G. Leisenring, Philadelphia, addressed USG. "The honor of your company is respectfully requested on the evening of May the 29th at 8 o'clock at the Hall 609 Chestnut St. north side, at the unveiling of the life-like representation of the Signers of the Declaration of Independence executed in wax full size, by distinguished artists. . . ." DS, USG 3.

On Sept. 23, S. P. Sallandrouze, Philadelphia, wrote to "President Grand." "I am the only man in this country as understends the manufacture of plate glass. I have on Exhibition the man Building a Splendid Specimen, that measures 16 ft by 8 ft at section *T. 45 . . .*" ALS, DNA, RG 48, Miscellaneous Div., Letters Received.

On March 30, S. J. Anderson, Waterford, N. Y., had written to USG. "I take the liberty of writing to you concerning a matter over which you have control, viz. the American consul in Siam. Gen. Partridge has on many occasion[s] '*mis*represented' the U. S. Gov. thereby causing a stigma to be attached to the name 'America.' And now he has done a *great* wrong in the matter of Siam's contributions to the Centennial Exhibition; . . ." ALS, *ibid.*, RG 59, Miscellaneous Letters. On May 16, Fish recorded in his diary. "The Secretary of the Navy read a telegram from Adml Reynolds to the effect that the Siamese Government desired to send things to the Exposition if we would transport them in one of our vessels. I advise that orders be given to bring them as I think that the effect would be good on the Siamese government which had had a difficulty with our Consul   The Secretary is to telegraph Adml Reynolds to this effect and I our Consul in Bankok." DLC-Hamilton Fish. On Aug. 2, USG nominated David B. Sickels as consul, Bangkok, replacing Frederick W. Partridge. See Fish diary, June 23, 1876, *ibid.*; *PUSG*, 25, 322; *Foreign Relations, 1877*, pp. 480–81; Lisa McQuail Taylor, "'Articles of Peculiar Excellence': The Siam Exhibit at the U. S. Centennial Exposition (Philadelphia, 1876)," *Journal of the Siam Society*, 79, part 2 (1991), 13–23.

On Sept. 5, 1881, Partridge, Sycamore, Ill., wrote to USG. "Under ordinary circumstances an apology would be necessary for obtruding myself and my affairs upon your attention; but, as I beleive you to have done me unwittingly, I do hope and beleive, a considerable injury, I am certain you will admit that none is needed. It has lately come to my knowledge that at a dinner-party given at Rockford by Mr. Emerson or Talcott, I am not certain which, in July 1880, you discussed my official conduct as consul. Stated that at Bangkok I had disobeyed instructions, disappointed your administration, and brought home a considerable amount of money, which your hearers were left to infer had been improperly acquired. My informant, who claims to have been present and participating in the conversation, says, your manner at the time indicated some feeling and resentment. From another source I have learned that you had said that you kept a gun-boat six months in the bay of Siam watching me! I have been for 20 years an ardent admirer of Genl Grant. Only a little month before the happening of this reported conversation, had spent my days and nights in this city & county working in his political interest & had in fact been the rallying point of the Grant friends, receiving the unstinted abuse, even of my intimates, for my refusal to work for Mr. Blaine—and now to learn that such charges are industriously circulated as coming from the General himself! Am I not entitled to an explanation? I, too, am an old soldier, and can show beside disabling wounds a clan record. When in April 1869 I was appointed by you Consul for Siam at Bangkok I had not seen you since the close of the war. I did not see you *after* my appointment in fact to this day I have not met you. . . . When there, as everywhere, I was proud of my Birth-right as a citizen of the United-States, and for the honor of my country, entertained handsomely; especially Tourists and American Naval officers, and in Seven years did not save *$5000.00* out of my salary— Being Episcopal in religious beleif, and unwilling to be *used* by any Sect represented by American Missionaries at B. I was not popular among them; and have lived to know by experience, that as 'There is no fury like a woman scorned,' so there is no *liar* less unsparing than an American Missionary who fancies his Craft in danger. Still I always labored for the *true* interest of those Missionaries, and at a critical moment by my firmness, absolutely saved the *lives* of Several of them at 'Cheangmai', as well as the Mission and Property there; and this *several* of them have had the grace to acknowledge Three months before I left Bangkok for the United-States there seemed some dissatisfaction at Washington with my supposed course in relation to the representation of Siam at the 'Centennial Exposition.' But in this my government was misinformed I had from the first urged this representation, and had several satisfactory personal interviews with the First King in regard to it, and if, near ~~the time~~ the time the Siamese contribution was about to be sent to Pa., I wrote a letter to His Majesty which was not approved by my Gov't, the *Act* of writing was warranted by my intimate relations with the King & Foreign Office. I have often been consulted by his Majesty and by the Foreign office in matters of the highest importance, and touching as they beleived the very existance of the Kingdom; and not unfrequently have written first [*drafts*] of Dispatches to Queen Victoria, to the French and to the Austrian Governments. To me, General, it seems as though I had spent about 7 of the best years of my life in a lonely, little interesting foreign Consulate, without adequate reward—To find my conscientious discharge of poorly paid official duty, characterized and misunderstood by one whose eminent services, and spotless integrity, give added weight to every utterance is too bitter to be borne with equanimity. I ask your immediate assistance . . ." ALS, DLC-Hamilton Fish.

To Ministers and Consuls

————

May 13th 1876.

Sir;

This will introduce to you Dr Charles McMillan of New York— Dr McMillan has recently been appointed Consul General to Italy ~~and~~ and is proceeding to his post   I take pleasure in commending him to you as a gentleman worthy of such courtesies as you may be able to extend while he remains near you

Very Truly Yours—

U. S. Grant.

To U S Ministers and Consuls in Europe.

Copy, DLC-USG, II, 3. A clerk wrote "Void" across this letter. On March 27, 1876, Charles McMillan, New York City, wrote to USG. "I have the honor, herewith, to make application for appointment to the Consulate Generalship at Rome, made vacant by the death of Paul Dahlgreen Esq. I most respectfully refer to my record in the War Department, an abstract of which is herewith enclosed, and to the officers under whose command the various & responsible duties were performed. . . ." ALS, DNA, RG 59, Letters of Application and Recommendation. Related papers include a letter of the same day from U.S. Senator Angus Cameron of Wis. to USG. "I am advised that Dr. Charles McMillan of New York City is an applicant for the position of Consul at Rome—Dr. McMillan and I were 'boys together'—I have known him for thirty years and I take great pleasure in stating that he is a gentleman of the highest character and by education and habits is peculiarly qualified to discharge the duties of the office he seeks—" ALS, *ibid.* On April 4, USG nominated McMillan as consul gen., Rome. See *PUSG*, 7, 392; *ibid.*, 8, 322.

On March 25, J. Schuyler Crosby, New York City, had written to USG. "I have the honor to apply for the position of Consul General at Rome, and enclose herewith letters of recommendation from Lieut General Sheridan, Ex Gov John A Dix. E. D. Morgan, C. A. Arthur, Thurlow Weed and others." ALS, DNA, RG 59, Letters of Application and Recommendation. The enclosures are *ibid.* On May 15, Lt. Gen. Philip H. Sheridan, Chicago, wrote to USG. "Col. J. Schuyler Crosby, for a long time a member of my staff, wishes the appointment as one of the Commissioners to visit the Sioux Indians during the coming summer. I believe him to be a suitable person for such appointment and recommend him to your kind consideration." Copy, DLC-Philip H. Sheridan. On June 27, Secretary of State Hamilton Fish recorded in his diary. "This morning the President handed me a letter from Sen Cameron recommending Schuyler Crosby for the Consulate at Florence. I laughlingly said that is Conkling's. He said yes & added that he had a letter from Conkling. I told him of the conversation of yesterday and said that under these circumstances I did not wish to appoint Crosby as Conkling was ungrateful and unjust—The President handed me his letter saying he says he has no Consular appointment but added he cannot say he has not parties appointed in other Departments. The President gave me the letters of Conkling & Cameron and from them it is evident that they are working together and Conkling had gone to see the President to try to commit him. I called the President attention to it and commented somewhat sharply he withdew the notes and said there was no use of filing them." DLC-Hamilton Fish. See Fish diary, June 28, July 13, 1876, *ibid.* On Aug. 15, USG nominated Crosby as consul, Florence. See letter to J. Schuyler Crosby, [*April, 1878*].

On March 25, Finley Anderson, Washington, D. C., had written to USG. "I have the honor to apply for the position of Consul General to Italy recently made vacant by the death of Mr. Dahlgren. My home is in NewYork, whence I was appointed Assistant Adjutant General in the Army by Mr. Lincoln. I served until the close of the war, having been wounded at Spottsylvania Court House, and twice promoted for gallant and meritorious services. I may add that this is the first position I have ever solicited from the Government." ALS, DNA, RG 59, Applications and Recommendations, Hayes-Arthur. On April 2, Admiral David D. Porter wrote to USG. "Col Findley Anderson having applied to me to give him a letter in view of obtaining an appointment as Consul at Rome I take pleasure in stating that I knew him during all the time I was on the Mississippi and can give testimony to his honorable character as a gentleman and as a brave loyal Citizen and am certain that he fill creditably the Post in question, excuse the liberty I take . . ." ALS, *ibid.* Related papers are *ibid.* On June 3, 1865, USG had approved Anderson's promotion from capt. to maj., as recommended by Maj. Gen. Winfield S. Hancock. ES, *ibid.*, RG 94, ACP, A217 CB 1865. Prior to his commission, as war correspondent for the *New York Herald*, Anderson was captured aboard the *Queen of the West* and imprisoned by C.S.A. authorities.

On March 27, 1876, William W. Nevin, Philadelphia, wrote to USG. "You may recollect my having met you as an officer [a. a. G.] in Nashville during the war and as the editor of *The Press* in Philadelphia I retire from the Editorship of The *Press* on the return of Mr. J. W. Forney from his two years in Europe I would like to spend some time in Europe and take the liberty of suggesting my name for the U. S. Consul generalcy just vacated at Rome . . ." ALS (brackets in original), *ibid.*, RG 59, Letters of Application and Recommendation. Related papers are *ibid.*

On March 28, George P. A. Healy, Washington, D. C., wrote to USG. "I regret not being able to have seen your excellency before dinner yesterday. My business was to impress on your mind the fitness of appointing Mr. D. M. Armstrong as Consul General to Rome, who gave complete satisfaction to the U. S. Government & American residents in Rome; this I can answer for, having resided there during the three years Mr. Armstrong officiated in that city, his artistic qualities endeared him to the artists & lovers of art; I feel sure Mr. President, this gentleman's high character & high connections, for his wife is a Niece of Mr. Secretary Fish, will make this appointment approved of by all. He wrote me a note which I think proper to enclose to you and trust if this post is not already promised, that your Excellency will consider my friend Mr. Armstrong in connection with this mission to Rome." ALS, *ibid.* The enclosure is a letter of March 27 from David M. Armstrong, Washington, D. C., to Healy outlining his qualifications for a second appointment as consul gen., Rome. ". . . I should mention, that I was not removed, but voluntarily resigned my office on account of affairs ~~in America~~ which required my presence here. . . ." ALS, *ibid.* Related papers are *ibid.*

On March 28, Thomas B. Swann, Charleston, West Va., wrote to USG. "A letter from Mr A. F. Gibbens requests me to ask Your Excellincy to make him Consul General at Rome, Italy. Mr Gibbens is now a clerk in the Treasury Department at Washington. Until lately he was Senior Editor of The West Va Journal, an ably conducted republican paper at this Place. . . ." ALS, *ibid.*, Applications and Recommendations, Hayes-Arthur. Related papers are *ibid.* On Dec. 12, USG nominated Alvaro F. Gibbens as postmaster, Kanawha Courthouse, West Va.

On April 3, Adolph E. Borie and George W. Childs, Philadelphia, had written to

USG. "We take an especial interest in the appointment of Richard L Willing of this city to
the consul general ship at Rome; he is an educated gentleman, 34 year of age, in independent circumstances, acquainted with the Italian and French languages, and we think in
every way well fitted to the post; he has always been an earnest republican." LS, *ibid.*, Letters of Application and Recommendation. Related papers are *ibid.*

To Seth J. Comly

May 16th 1876—

DEAR SIR;

As intimated, while on a recent visit to Philadelphia, I would
write to you, or inform you, if your resignation as Collector of the
port should be desirable, I now write to say,—and it is with great reluctance that I do so—that it will be agreeable to me to have your
resignation—The resignation might be worded "to take effect on
the qualification of your successor"—This could not be before the
first of June—I beg to say that I have no complaints of you on which
to rest this request; but it is in response to numerous recommendations, and my promises that I would do so—and believing that the
office had no special attractions to make it desirable of retention by
you, this promise was made—There was also the desire to place in
it a valued officer of the Revenue service, who has been connected
with that service from the foundation of the present system of collecting revenue from internal sources   I believed, as I told you, that
you would care nothing for remaining in the office—I was pleased
at the assurances you gave, and hope that you will not feel disappointed that I should now make this request—

You have my assurances of the greatest satisfaction with your
official conduct while holding position under this administration,
and of my great esteem for you personally—

With great respect,
your obt servant—
U. S. GRANT

S. J. COMLEY ESQ
COLLECTOR OF PORT—PHILADELPHIA—

Copy, DLC-USG, II, 3. On April 25, 1876, Adolph E. Borie, Philadelphia, wrote to George
W. Childs, Philadelphia. "Mr Comly has told me that he has told you all about his matter,
and especially of how very kindly 'The President' received his last visit to him—the poor
fellow is really very much distressed and seems to look to you and me to interfere on his
behalf and try to induce 'The President' to give up his first intention. Now as I always am
most loth to let any matter come between The Prest and myself or the close relations
of friendship and esteem which exist mutually between us, and as in spite of that, I did,
at once upon my return from St Louis write to him from New York, from the deep interest I felt in the possible appointment of Mr Tutton and did therein give him my views
adverse to such an appointment, and as he still persevered in it, it would ill become me
now to re-iterate these views altho' I still entertain them, apart from all and *the great*, interest I take in Mr Comly We all must know that 'The Prest' is actuated simply by the desire to reward a faithful officer but this ought not to be done in opposition to many sound
reasons to the contrary; and another position might be sought for Mr Tutton I think it
would be well for you to write to 'The Prest' on the subject and in doing so, you may say
that you know that I feel as you do, but for the reasons given above, will not say another
word to him about it." ALS, USG 3. On Feb. 18, USG had nominated Seth J. Comly to continue as collector of customs, Philadelphia; on May 31, USG nominated Alexander P. Tutton to replace Comly. See *PUSG*, 23, 7; *ibid.*, 26, 235–36; letter to Edwards Pierrepont,
July 29, 1876.

Endorsement

I would say to Mr. Caulfield substantially that the Marshal of Texas
was aptd. by the President, by and with the advice and consent of the
Senate, in accordance with the provisions of the Constitution; That
we do not recognize the authority of a Committee of one House of
Congress to call to account either for grounds of apt. or retention in
office of this official

U. S. GRANT

MAY 18TH /76

AES, DNA, RG 60, Letters from the President. Written on a letter of May 17, 1876, from
Attorney Gen. Edwards Pierrepont to USG. "I very respectfully refer to you herewith a
letter of the 13th inst. addressed to me by Hon. B. G. Caulfield, Chairman of the Committee on Expenditures in the Department of Justice." LS, *ibid.* On May 20, Pierrepont wrote
to U.S. Representative Bernard G. Caulfield of Ill., Democrat from Chicago, concerning
Thomas F. Purnell, U.S. marshal, Western District, Tex. ". . . As to the affidavits and reports, on file in my office, of which you speak, I referred the same to the Solicitor General,
who examined witnesses, and after careful investigation, reported that the charges were
not sustained." Copy, *ibid.*, Letters Sent to Executive Officers. See *PUSG*, 26, 171–73.
   On March 17, Edmund J. Davis, Austin, had written to U.S. Senator Morgan C. Hamilton of Tex. "I have to acknowledge receipt of yours of March 1st. In regard to the Purnell matter, there is no question that the two sons who attacked me at the U. S. court

House, being then armed with revolvers, and their Father and other Deputies being within call, in the Court House, and also coming to the scene before it was through—*were then his deputies.* I do not suppose that Purnell (though I know he will unhesitatingly tell an untruth to serve his purpose) has, or will have, the hardihood to deny the fact that they were such deputies, . . . You say that Purnell is being investigated. Well, if he were an honest or sincere Republican, that investigation might mean something, but as he is a Democrat in disguise, and has always played into their hands, so as to get their protection against Republicans who might make bold to expose his swindlings and [p]eculations, I have an idea he will not be investi[g]ated much to hurt by a Democratic House of Representatives. Everything told against him will be quietly ignored or squelched. . . . I saw Purnell in 1869 at his Farm in Harrison County. He appeared broken and penniless, and that was also his reputation. *Now,* with an office that, legitimately, can bring him but $6000. a year and a considerable family to support, he is a large Stockholder in two National Banks, has Plantations, Houses, Farms &c. . . . I note what you say about A. M. Bryant for Purnell's place if a change can be made. Mr. Bryant is undoubtedly a good man, and I would like to see him appointed. But my object is to get an honest man in the office and therefore will make no issue as to who should have it. If Purnell's successor, whoever he may be, has even *a moderate* share of honesty decency and Republicanism, he will be an improvement on the present incumbent. I do not think the President has ever seen any of the evidence against Purnell, and I believe he would at once remove him if his time allowed him to examine the charges and proofs himself. Would it be asking too much of you to see him and ask him to glance at this letter and the enclosed printed statements?" ALS, DNA, RG 60, Records Relating to Appointments.

On June 24, Col. Joseph J. Reynolds, Washington, D. C., wrote to USG. "I have just learned that there are some efforts on foot for the removal of *Mr Purnell* as U. S. Marshal in Texas. I ~~am~~ was well acquainted with Mr Purnell and knew him in Texas as one of the very best representatives of the administration in that part of the Country—What *specially* his opponents may have against him I do not know, but, without his knowledge, I have felt it but simple justice to an absent man that one who knows him Should say a word for him" ALS, *ibid.* Purnell remained as marshal until Jan., 1878. See *New York Times*, Aug. 11, 14, 1877.

Note

Edwards Pierrepont Minister to England vice Schenck resigned, Alphonso Taft to be Atty. Gen. vice Pierrepont apt. Min. &c. J. Donald Cameron [1] [of Pa.] Sec. of War vice [Alphonso] Taft apt. Atty. Gn. [MAY 22D 76—]

AN (bracketed material not in USG's hand), OHi. On May 20 (Saturday) and 22, 1876, Secretary of State Hamilton Fish recorded in his diary. "Mr Monroe member of the Committee on Foreign Affairs says that Mr Hewett has prepared the report on the Emma Mine had read it to the Democratic Members and then submitted to the Republicans; that it acquitted Schenck of intentional wrong, but charges him with great impropriety and proceeds to criticise the Administration for retaining him and calls for his removal; that the Republicans were willing to assent to the report so far as the general statement of facts and the condemnation of Schencks 'improprieties' but objected to the censure of the President in suggesting as to what should be his conduct; that Hewett had objected in-as-much as he had strong reasons for believing that Schenck would be allowed to return, saying that Judge Pierrepont had told him that he was present at a conversation between Schenck and the President in which Schenck deplored the hardness of his position, and entreated to be allowed to return to London, that after Pierrepont left the room Schenck returned to the President imploring him not to allow him to be sacrificed, or unjustly judged as he would be if he was not allowed to go back. The President and Pierrepont had each narrated to me this interview very much as repeated at third hand by Monroe. I urge on Monroe to insist on exclusion of the objectionable parts of the message assuring him that Schenck was not to return, but that the President had decided to send in another name in a day or two, probably on Monday." "Called upon the President on my way to the Office (he having requested me to see him this day with reference to the nomination of Minister to Great Britain) and he expressed a wish to nominate Mr Patterson of Phila, saying that Sen Cameron and his son Don were very anxious for it. I remonstrate saying that with the exception of the Camerons and the gentlemen in Philad (Chlds Drexel & Borie) there was probably no one who had thought of him in that connection and that I was satified that the public would not receive the nomination favorably; that I was told that he was a Democrat and during the war had been opposed to it and that he did not at present profess to be a Republican, although I understood he had voted for the President in 1872 and possibly in 1868. He spoke of the appointment of Pierrepont to Great Britain, Judge Taft to the Attorney Generalship, and Don Cameron as Secretary of War. I suggested the appointment of Courtland Parker to Great Britain adding that while he knew my friendship for Pierrepont I thought him very indiscrete and imprudent, that he was too communicative for a Diplomat. I mention what Monroe had told me of Pierreponts communication to Hewett and the report which Hewett proposed to make in the Schenck case. I reminded him of Pierreponts disobedience of instruction from the Attorney General and myself in reference to the Cuban question. He thought he said that he would be prudent in this and decided to send in the nominations, forthwith giving directions to have them made out at the White House. I told him that I thought it important that he should caution Pierrepont of the necessity of obedience of any instruction which he might receive not to go beyond or fall short in any particular and to be careful to communicate nothing whatever of his official affairs. Judge Pierrepont calls to speak of the trial of Lawrence and how far he should be allowed immunity for being used as a witness—I mention to him his nomination to England—He professes surprise—I then speak of his communication to Hewett and point to him the consequences. He claimed that Hewett should not have repeated the conversation as it occurred at a Private House. I tell him his conversation was also at a private House also—He seemed worried and said he would see Hewett and try to have the objectionable part expunged from the report. Which he did . . ." DLC-Hamilton Fish. In 1871, Robert C. Schenck, U.S. minister, London, had taken stock and a directorship in a co. formed to promote the Emma Mine, in Utah Territory, to British investors. Soon forced to resign as director, Schenck faced persistent attacks from angry investors after the mine failed in 1872. Beginning in March, 1876, U.S. Representative Abram S. Hewitt of N. Y. led an investigation of Schenck's role in the scandal. See *HRC*, 44-1-579; *PUSG*, 24, 179; Nevins, *Fish*, pp. 814–15.

On Dec. 8, 1875, Thomas O. Hague, New York City, had written to USG. "Will your Excellency pardon the liberty the writer takes in venturing a suggestion   I think the impression is very general in this city, that the best interests of this country are not served in the continuance of Genl Schenck as our minister to London. I believe the best and most satisfactory appointment to that office, and one that would greatly strengthen confidence in the Republican Party would be to appoint Elliot C Cowdin of this city. His unwavering constancy, and devotion to the nation's best interests, in Politics, Finance, Industry, and Commercial prosperity, has won for him the esteem and confidence of men of every party." ALS, DNA, RG 59, Letters of Application and Recommendation.

On Feb. 8, 1876, John W. Forney, London, telegraphed to USG. "Without consultation with schenck implore you not sacrifice useful Minister to his personal foes and yours," Telegram received, *ibid.*, Miscellaneous Letters. On the same day, Schenck telegraphed to Fish. ". . . If on account of the malignant and calumnious misrepresentations with which I have been pursued the President considers that I embarrass his administration and am no longer useful in my position, grateful for his past confidence and support, I shall cheerfully accept his judgment and will resign . . ." Copy, Fish diary, Feb. 9, 1876, DLC-Hamilton Fish. On Feb. 11, Fish recorded in his diary. "Genl Schencks telegraph was referred to and the President directed me to telegraph him that his resignation would relieve him from embarrassment." *Ibid.* See *ibid.*, Feb. 14, 15, 1876; Schenck to Fish, Feb. 19, 1876, *ibid.* On Feb. 22, Fish recorded in his diary. "Called upon the President as he was about to review the Military Procession. After it had passed I entered the house with the President and showed him Schencks telegrams received last evening asking leave to return home to attend the Committee on Inquiry, of the House of Representatives. I told the President that there was no occasion for his presence in London and possibly it might be a means of enabling Schenck to leave Great Britain without the annoyance of a law suit and that it had better be allowed To all of this he assented" *Ibid.* Fish subsequently spoke of Attorney Gen. Edwards Pierrepont as a replacement for Schenck. "I said that while I should be quite satisfied with the appointment of Pierrepont, I thought it would be better for him and the Administration that he should not leave the Cabinet; in view of all the clamor which had been raised against Schenck I thought it better to appoint some man not much of a politician, but who might be known to the country from his general character or his social standing—some man of letters. That I had no person in view but if there was some one of the position which Washington Irving, his appointment would be favorably received and would strengthen the Republican Party. He said some such person might be found in Mass or in the East and thought such selection might be good adding Richd H. Dana for instance I told him I had not thought of him but he struck me very favorably. He said he would not offer it to Dana until he knew whether Pierrepont desired it, that he would talk with Judge Pierrepont on the subject" *Ibid.* See *ibid.*, Feb. 29, March 1, 1876. On March 2, Schenck telegraphed to Fish. "I tendered my resignation when the action of the Executive was questioned. As my conduct is now the subject of charges, and investigation, I assume the Presidents decision on my offer will be suspended while this proceeding is pending." Copy, *ibid.*, March 3, 1876. On March 3, the cabinet met. "I showed the President Schencks telegram received last evening and he very promptly and earnestly said No! we have scandals enough without assuming any more. I read him the following telegram which he directed me to send 'President has taken steps to fill the place immediatly, and on that account and for other reasons cannot delay acting on resignation'" *Ibid.* On March 6, USG nominated Richard H. Dana, Jr., as minister to Great Britain. See Dana to Fish, March 3, 1876, *ibid.* On March 13, in answer to a resolution, Fish wrote at length to U.S. Representative Thomas Swann of Md., chairman, Committee on Foreign Relations, detailing Schenck's hesitant moves toward resignation. Copy, DNA, RG 59, Reports to the President and Congress.

On March 14, Fish recorded in his diary. "The President stated that the Chairman of the Committee on Foreign Relations and a Democratic Senator had been to see him on the subject of Mr Dana's going to England. I mentioned what I had heard of the complaints against Dana and denounce them as malicious & vindictive that it seemed to be a litigation between Beach Lawrence who with all his ability and cleverness, had been an arrent copperhead, and secessionist during the war, taking sides in all cases against the government; and a man who had written some of the ablest essays, and most loyal ones on International Law, and that General Butler had come on to Washington, as he told me, for the purpose of defeating the nomination of Dana who had run against him for Congress. Bristow, Jewell, Taft, & Robeson, express themselves strongly in favor of Dana. Pierrepont is more qualified, Chandler not at all; while conversing on the subject Sen Cameron called and sees the President in an adjoining room and tells him that the Committee had decided to report adversely The President requested the report to be withheld until tomorrow and desired me to see the two Senators from Mass with reference to this subject." DLC-Hamilton Fish. On the same day, Fish wrote to USG. "Since the Cabinet Meeting it has occurred to me that it would not be fair or just that the Committee on Foreign Relations of the Senate should visit a Genteman of Mr Dana's high character and position with its disapproval on the exparte statements which may have been presented to it without affording an opportunity to him to reply or to explain. Should not the Committee inform him of the charges made against him before determining to report adversely to his nomination I shall endeavor to see the Massachusetts Senators this Afternoon or Evening as you request" Copy, *ibid.* On April 4, the Senate rejected Dana. See Dana to Fish, March 18, 25, 1876, *ibid.*; Nevins, *Fish*, pp. 829–31; Samuel Shapiro, *Richard Henry Dana, Jr. 1815–1882* (East Lansing, Mich., 1961), pp. 164–70.

On March 7, William A. Tell, New York City, had written to USG. "Hoping you Injoy the best of helth. I do not understand. this coolness to mee. I requisted first for the mission to england. befor that swelhead from boston I was at boston last somer. I saw know better than. me if as good. thare. I acted as good through the as a genreal of the armey. three Hon. Discharges. the rest Independ. please condecend & give mee that little mission to London as a favor. i will be good. . . . P. S. I do not lie. or beag Adieu" ALS, DNA, RG 59, Letters of Application and Recommendation.

On March 14, Edward Winslow, Boston, wrote to USG. "If you wish to do Credit to your adminstration & to the Country please nominate Hon Robt C Winthrop as Ambassador to England even if he does not accept, or he is opposed it will shew your disposition to make a good selection" ALS, *ibid.* A related letter is *ibid.*

On March 22, R. S. Gould, Newark, N. J., wrote to USG. "Should Mr. Dana not be confirmed as Minister to England, I would most Respectfully sugjest the name of the Hon Courtland Parker of the City of Newark N. J. he is of the old School Republicans, has laboured more faithfully for our principals I believe than any one in the State, and recd less consideration, I don't think their is a more fit person in the *Relm*, one of the best Lawyers in the State and an Honest man Genl If you are not acquainted with Mr. Parker you can with out much trouble knou all about him" ALS, *ibid.* On April 27, William S. Sharp, *Weekly Public Opinion*, Trenton, wrote to USG. "Having supported you with my paper and otherwise while you were at the head of our armies in the field, and also during the campaigns of 1868 and 1872, when you were a candidate for the Presidency, I feel that I can with propriety make a suggestion or recommendation, which I do without the knowledge or consent of the gentleman in whose interest I make it. If Gen. Schenck is not to return to England as Minister, I do not think that you could select a more suitable person to fill his place than the appointment of Cortlandt Parker, Esq., of this State. He stands at the head of his profession as a lawyer—is a man of the highest culture and refinement—one who would give dignity and tone to the position—and what is better still—is a gentleman of unimpeachable integrity. His appointment would be an honor to you and to the Nation. I think that Secretaries Fish and Robeson, and Senator Frelinghuysen and Justice Bradley would endorse Mr. Parker to this extent, at least. I hope that you may be persuaded to look

at this matter, as Mr. Parker's many friends do, if you intend to make any change at all."
ALS, *ibid.*

On March 31, James Harding, *Berkshire County Eagle*, Pittsfield, Mass., had written to USG. "Stick to Dana; he's a good man. But if he is impossible, at the end of the fight, give the place to Gen. W. F. Bartlett, of this town and state. By birth, breeding and education Gen Bartlett is just the high toned gentleman to represent us with courtesy and dignity at the court of St James. His ability and culture fit him for its responsibilities and duties; there is no question about his capacity in brains for the largest requirement of the place. He is a fellow soldier of yours, and like yourself gave his heart and hand to the glorious cause of the Union, and his name, like your own will be on the pages of the nation's history, not as the great leader, as your fame is secure, but as a faithful, enthusiastic, patriotic soldier, one of the fingers, so to speak, of your mighty right arm. He went into the service from Harvard College, a captain, in 1861. He lost a leg at Yorktown; had his arm splintered at Port Hudson, was wounded in the *face* at in the Wilderness and was discharged in 1865 a brigadier, brevet Major, General. Massachusetts loves and honors him. The Nation can trust him, and he merits a share of in her rewards. Brave, patriotic, pure and able is Gen. Bartlett; make him Minister to England. Wishing you long life and happiness . . . Gen Bartlett is now in Europe seeking rest and health. He was in Danville and Libby prisons for a time, receiving shocks to his health that have made the tour abroad a sad necessity." ALS, *ibid.* William F. Bartlett died Dec. 17 at Pittsfield.

On March 16, R. Ogden Doremus, Bellevue Hospital Medical College, New York City, had written to USG. "I see by this morning's paper that the name of Hon: E. W. Stoughton is mentioned in connection with the English mission. As an old New Yorker I take the liberty of expressing my hearty wish that he shall receive this most honorable appointment at your hands. Mr Stoughton is beloved and most highly esteemed by members of his own Profession, by those of the other learned Professions, as well as by the Public. No one could more fitly or more elegantly represent our Country in old England." ALS, *ibid.* On March 25, Lt. Gen. Philip H. Sheridan, Chicago, telegraphed to USG. "Hope you will do the best you can for Judge Stoughton as Minister to England" Telegram received, *ibid.* On April 5 (Wednesday) and 6, Fish recorded in his diary. "I talk to the President of the action of the Senate in the rejection of the nomination of Mr Dana—He suggests Schenck again—I tell him that with a sincere regard for Schenck I do not think it would answer; that the criticism for retaining him has not been confined to the Democratic Press but has been equally strong in a large majority of the Republican Papers He speaks of Mr Stoughton of New York and refers to the scandal which has been associated with his name—Judge Pierrepont had told him some things respecting it but he does not appear to have all the facts, as Pierrepont told them to me. I tell the President that independent of these stories a positive objection exists at the present time to Mr Stoughtons appointment; that we had a grave question with Great Britain in relation to the Extradition clause of the Treaty; that Mr S—is counsel for Lawrence and went to England in his interest, and has it is understood to have received large fees for opposing the government. The President expresses himself as very decided that if the British government adhere to the position which they have taken on the Extradition Treaty he will regard the Treaty as broken by them and refuse any further Extraditions. He says that Stoughton's connection with this case is conclusive against his appointment of Minister to England. In relation to the appointment of a Minister to England he says he wishes to appoint one who has been a Republican without faultering, or complaint, and who shall be free from all scandal To my inquiry whether he has any particular person in view, he says no! although he has thought of several. I tell him Judge Bradley has suggested the name of Courtland Parker —He says he is one of whom I have thought, and he believes it would be altogether a fitting and good appointment. He says he will bring his name up in Cabinet on Friday." "Judge Pierrepont calls and states that he understands that Stoughton has arrived here and is pressing his case for Minister to England, and that Conkling had called on him yesterday in his behalf. He states that a Mrs Ker sent up her card to him today and turned out to be the woman who is persecuting Mr Stoughton and exhibited a letter from John D. Townshend of New York stating that if he (Stoughton) were appointed the whole story would be made public." DLC-Hamilton Fish. On May 1, Edwin W. Stoughton, New York City, wrote to USG. "Your great kindness to me, and the tender consideration shown by you and Mrs. Grant to Mrs Stoughton when upon a late occasion she sought an interview with Mrs. Grant in Washington, convince me that you will cheerfully read and consider what I am about to write, upon a subject which I am free to confess, deeply concerns me and mine. On saturday I saw Genl. Ingalls who informed me in substance, that when he last saw you in Washington, you spoke most kindly of me, and referring to the appointment of Minister to the Court of St. James, gave him the impression, that the objection made by the Secretary of State to my appointment was, my action in the case of Lawrence as his counsel: And this conversation the Genl. said I might allude to, in any communication I should make to you. You are familiar with the views which as counsel for Lawrence I considered it my duty to ~~make~~ present, with a view to Executive action in his behalf. It may, I believe be said of all the most eminent of my profession, who have ever lived, that ~~that~~ at different periods of their professional career they have been compelled by their duty as Counsel, to advance in some cases—arguments not in harmony with those presented in others—nor indeed with their personal opinions: and I feel confident the Secretary of State—a distinguished member of the legal profession, will not suggest that I should be the less able to present and enforce upon the British Government his views as to the true construction of the Extradition clause of the treaty of 1842 because they may differ from those urged by me as counsel; . . ." ALS, USG 3. See Message to Congress, June 20, 1876; letter to Edwin W. Stoughton, [*Dec. 27, 1880*].

On April 7, Nathaniel A. Cowdrey, New York City, had written to USG. "Permit me to suggest to you the name of Theodore D. Woolsey of New Haven, Conn: as a suitable man for the position of Minister to England from the U. S—Mr. Woolsey was for many years the President of Yale College and in attainments as a Scholar and International Lawyer is unsurpassed   His appointment in my belief would do great credit to you and to your administration." ALS, DNA, RG 59, Letters of Application and Recommendation. On the same day, C. Augustus Haviland, New York City, telegraphed and wrote to USG. "I suggest Benj J Lossing the historian for English Mission." "I take the liberty to suggest the name of one *not a politician* for the English Mission. I name *Benson J. Lossing* Esq, the Historian. His residence is Dover Plains N. Y. A more estimable man does not live in America. By such a nomination you will satisfy the whole country." Telegram received and ALS, *ibid.* Also on April 7, George W. Childs, Philadelphia, wrote to USG. "We all regret Mr. Dana's rejection so much. I wrote some time since suggesting Mr. Joseph Patterson's name. You know something of him, and I can add; in every way, he would make a creditable appointment. He has ability, high character, and is beyond reproach. His appointment would be received as a grateful recognition by Pennsylvanians, not only by the strict party men, but by the general public. If you have no other name more deserving, and you should consider the matter, satisfactory evidences of his confirmation can be furnished you. Regretting to hear of your recent indisposition, and hoping you are now quite well . . ." ALS, *ibid.* On the same day, Peter Walsh, Boston, wrote to Fish recommending James Russell Lowell as minister to Great Britain. ALS, *ibid.* Also on April 7, Stephen M. Allen, Boston, wrote to USG. "Permit me in behalf of New England, and the country, to suggest to your

Excellency, another illustrious name as minister to England. Gen' Joshua L. Chamberlain, of Maine; the well tried souldier, citizen and scholar, could not fail to satisfy the expectations of both countries in these trying, and perplexing times. . . ." ALS, *ibid.* On April 7 and 8, George H. Gordon, Boston, telegraphed and wrote to USG. "If Massachusetts is to have the appointment of Minister to England might I suggest a representative of the soldiers of the late War Col Charles R. Codman of Boston. Col Codman is an able and experienced legislator a man of high social standing in our community . . ." ". . . I think the nomination of Col Codman would be received here, and throughout the country by the Republican party, with satisfaction; because: it would be a recognition of the young and staunch element of the party, in the place of the conservative old fogy leaders, who are doing so much to destroy us—. . ." Telegram received (at 4:00 P.M.) and ALS, *ibid.* Related papers are *ibid.* On April 15, Jerome F. Manning, "of Worcester Mass," Washington, D. C., wrote to USG. "*Confidential* . . . Permit me to suggest the name of Hon. A. H. Bullock—of Worcester, Mass—as a proper one to be sent in to the Senate in place of that of R. H. Dana as Minister to Great Britain. He was 3 years Governor of Mass—& for some years previous was Speaker of the House. He has since passed some years in Europe—is a ripe scholar & possessess those *natural* qualities preeminently fitting him for *diplomatic* service. I write this of my own motion—consulting no one—& if you may desire further information, shall be glad to call on you & give it—I am engaged in some law business in Washington—with Messrs. Corwine—for a few days—Excuse my intrusion—" ALS, *ibid.*

On April 26, Fish recorded in his diary a conversation with USG. "I showed Pierreponts note suggesting his willingness to accept the British Mission and urge upon him the importance of filling the place without delay. He expresses a willingness to appoint Pierrepont   I enquire whether it was expedient to make a change in the Cabinet at present— He says he will see Pierrepont and talk with him on the subject. He asks whether I know Jas Patterson of Philadelphia and said that several person were anxious for his appointment as Minister to Great Britain—I told him I knew that Childs and Drexel were but I did not know of any others; but that Robeson had said that he was a Democrat. He enquired whether I thought that Stoughton would answer for Attorney General if Pierrepont were sent to England. I told him I feared it would give rise to a great deal of scandal and I thought it very inadvisable at present to incite any more criticism of public men than possible." DLC-Hamilton Fish. See *ibid.*, April 11, 20, 28, 1876.

1. Born in 1833, James D. Cameron graduated from Princeton, entered banking, and served as president, Northern Central Railway Co. (1866–74). On May 1, 1876, Fish reported a conversation with USG. "He says Judge Pierrepont came to see him last night and spoke of the Mission to Great Britain—that Pierrepont has gone to New York to be absent for 2 or 3 days and professes a desire to do whatever may be deemed proper with reference to remaining in the Cabinet. He tells me he has spoken to Sen Cameron on the subject of Wayne MacVeagh as Attorney General before he had spoken to me and told him he wished it to be confidential, but that he had started for Harrisburg, had a family council no doubt, and had told Conkling and a dozen others that he was to be appointed. He said he would however not decide until he had had a conversation with Don Cameron who he says is a wiser man than his father." *Ibid.* See Wayne MacVeagh to Fish, April 8, 1876, *ibid.* On May 22, Cameron, Harrisburg, Pa., telegraphed to USG. "Please accept my thanks for the honor you have conferred upon me   I am now confined to the house and my physician protests against my going out before the end of the week. as I wish to confer with you before deciding to accept or decline will it cause any inconvenience for me to delay my decision until that time" Telegram received (at 4:42 P.M.), DLC-USG, IB. On [May] 31, USG

wrote a note. "Ask Judge McArthur, Sup. Court of the Dist, if he will be kind enough to come to the Ex. Mansion to-morrow morning at 10 O'clock to [administer the] swear in [oath of office to] the new Sec. of War" AN (bracketed material not in USG's hand), Wayde Chrismer, Bel Air, Md.

Proclamation

———

Whereas a Joint Resolution of the Senate and House of Representatives of the United States was duly approved on the 13th day of March, last, which Resolution is as follows:

"Be it resolved by the Senate and House of Representatives of the United States of America in Congress assembled, That it be, and is hereby, recommended by the Senate and House of Representatives to the people of the several States that they assemble in their several counties or towns on the approaching Centennial Anniversary of our National Independence, and that they cause to have delivered on such day an historical sketch of said county or town from its formation, and that a copy of said sketch may be filed, in print or manuscript, in the Clerk's office of said county, and an additional copy, in print or manuscript, be filed in the office of the Librarian of Congress, to the intent that a complete record may thus be obtained of the progress of our institutions during the First Centennial of their existence."

And whereas it is deemed proper that such recommendation be brought to the notice and knowledge of the people of the United States;

Now therefore, I, Ulysses S. Grant, President of the United States, do hereby declare and make known the same, in the hope that the object of such resolution may meet the approval of the people of the United States, and that proper steps may be taken to carry the same into effect.

Given under my hand at the City of Washington, the twenty-fifth day of May, in the year of Our Lord, one thousand eight hundred and seventy-six, and of the Independence of the United States the One Hundredth.

U. S. GRANT

DS, DNA, RG 130, Proclamations; DfS (facsimile), Sotheby's, March 27, 1985, no. 172. *Foreign Relations, 1876*, p. 2. On May 17, 1876, U.S. Representative James A. Garfield of Ohio and nine others wrote to USG. "The within Joint Resolution having passed both Houses of Congress by a unanimous vote & approved by you it is thought its Proclamation by you would call the attention of the Country to ~~its~~ an observance of its provisions" LS, DNA, RG 59, Miscellaneous Letters. The enclosure is *ibid.* On May 18, USG wrote to Secretary of State Hamilton Fish. "I herewith send you an outline of my Centennial Proclamation which I will broadcast throughout the Nation in several days. Have you any suggestions or improvement to make on it, or add anything to it? If so kindly do, and return the document as soon as possible." Sotheby's, March 27, 1985, no. 172. See Fish diary, May 19, 1876, DLC-Hamilton Fish.

Veto

To THE HOUSE OF REPRESENTATIVES:

I return herewith without my approval House bill No. 1922 entitled "An Act providing for the recording of deeds, mortgages and other conveyances affecting real estate in the District of Columbia."

The objection to affixing my signature to this bill may be found in the communication addressed to me by the Attorney General and which accompanies this message.

U. S. GRANT

EXECUTIVE MANSION,
MAY 26TH 1876.

DS, DNA, RG 233, 44A-D1. *HED*, 44-1-165; *SMD*, 49-2-53, 395. On May 23, 1876, Attorney Gen. Edwards Pierrepont wrote to USG. "In reply to your note of the 19th instant, . . . I have the honor to state that the Bill seems to me objectionable because of indefiniteness and uncertainty, as to the *time* which it purports to fix when deeds of trust, mortgages, etc., shall take effect and be valid as to creditors and subsequent purchasers for valuable consideration without notice. Although there is no constitutional objection to the Act, yet for the reason above stated, I hesitate to advise its approval." LS, DNA, RG 233, 44A-D1. *HED*, 44-1-165; *SMD*, 49-2-53, 395. See *U.S. Statutes at Large*, XVIII, part 2, pp. 52–53.

On April 5, William B. Moore, Washington, D. C., had written to USG. "Two years ago I asked for the appointment of Recorder of deeds for the District. I based my supposition that a change would occur, upon rumors then in circulation. To day, testimony is to be given before a congressional Committee charging the incumbent with infamous action. I respectfully state that I will renew my application for the position at once, and beg that you will excuse this informal method of reminding you of the interview referred to" ALS, DNA, RG 48, Appointment Div., Letters Received. See Note, [*July 1, 1876*]. On April 6, Ferdinand S. Winslow, Washington, D. C., wrote to USG. "I have the honor herewith to submit my petition for appointment as Recorder of Deeds of the District of Columbia, and would further state, that I held Commission during the late war as Captain & Assistant Quartermaster, serving from 1861 to 1864, first as Chief Quartermaster of the Army of the Southwest, Major General S. R. Curtis commanding,—was afterwards Chief Quartermaster of the Department of Missouri. Having been transferred to Nashville I was assigned to duty there as Disbursing Officer and Chief Officer of River Transportation, in which charge I remained until forced to resign on account of poor health. Referring to the endorsements on this application . . ." ALS, DNA, RG 48, Appointment Div., Letters Received. Related papers are *ibid.* On April 7, Joseph F. Wilson, Washington, D. C., wrote to USG. "Should any change in the Office of Recorder of Deeds for this District be in contemplation, I hope you will remember me in connection therewith. If a change is made and I should receive the appointment, I will give my entire time and attention to the business of the office, and endeavor to so conduct the same as to give entire satisfaction to the whole community. Refering to the accompanying testimonials, . . ." ALS, *ibid.* A related letter is *ibid.* Simon Wolf, who continued as D. C. recorder of deeds, denied accepting money to promote a candidate for post trader. See *HRC*, 44-1-799, 14–15, 177–78, 192, 194–201.

To Editor, Sunday School Times

WASHINGTON, *June* 6, 1876.
To the Editor of The Sunday School Times, Philadelphia:
Your favor of yesterday, asking a message from me to the children and youth of the United States, to accompany your Centennial number, is this moment received.

My advice to SUNDAY-SCHOOLS, no matter what their denomination, is: Hold fast to the Bible as the sheet-anchor of your liberties; write its precepts in your hearts, and PRACTISE THEM IN YOUR LIVES.

To the influence of this book are we indebted for all the progress made in true civilization, and to this we must look as our guide in the future.

"Righteousness exalteth a nation: but sin is a reproach to any people."

Yours, respectfully,
U. S. GRANT.

Sunday School Times (Philadelphia), June 17, 1876. H. Clay Trumbull edited the weekly, published by John Wanamaker. See Herbert Adams Gibbons, *John Wanamaker* (New York, 1926), I, 192.

On May 10, 1876, John M. Henderson, Elmira, Ill., wrote to USG. "I know it will seem utterly presumptuous in me—an obscure pastor of an obscure country congregation (Presbyterian)—to address you a letter of encouragement. But I well remember how Lincoln was sometimes lightened in heart by words of cheer received from *the people*. . . . In behalf of not a few of the people and in behalf of *Christianity* I want to thank you most heartily for your truly valuable efforts and services in behalf of suffering humanity, especially in these three things   1. the cause of justice to the despised and abused Negro, 2. the cause of justice against fearful opposition to the Indian,   3 the cause of Peace consistent with justice and honor in our relation to foreign nations.—to which I will add, though generally set in account against you, your faithful and honorable standing by those public servants whom you *suppose* to be wronged by the public voice. . . . And now let me express the gratification that would be afforded to many of the people if along with these services you could add that of ~~a decided~~ an example for good in a decided personal regard for the sacredness of the Sabbath and, after the manner of Henry Wilson & Colfax, of abstinence from stimulants. May we not hope that such example will yet be given? Assuring you that you are and will be not only earnestly but charitably remembered in the prayers of many of the people . . ." ALS, USG 3.

USG signed a certificate awarded at the Centennial Exhibition to Lizzie Fortman, age 8, of Clay Public School, St. Louis, "for Punctual Attendance at School 200 days Sep. 5, 1875, to June 15. 1876." DS, MoSHi.

To James D. Cameron

Refered to the Sec. of War with suggestion that the tenor of this be telegraphed to Gen. Sheridan to the end that he may take such action as he deems proper.

U. S. Grant

June 13th /76

AES, DNA, RG 94, Letters Received, 3322 1876. Written to accompany an undated petition from James E. Boyd and forty-three others to Secretary of War Alphonso Taft. "Your petitioners respectfully represent that they are citizens of Nebraska and Wyoming and largely interested in raising cattle. That their herds in number as hereinafter stated are located at various points west of the junction of the North and South Platte Rivers in Nebraska. Besides the cattle of your petitioners a large number of other herds belonging to frontier settlers range and graze through the same country. Your petitioners represent that their property interests, the development and settlement of North-Western Nebraska and eastern Wyoming, the lives of those in their employ and of the families of actual settlers are now greatly endangered by threatened Indian attacks. The danger is imminent and unless speedy steps are taken, great and irreparable damage will result. The troops of the Department of the Platte are entirely inadequate in number and are so placed as to afford no protection from the threatened danger. Experience has shown that Infantry Stationed at posts are not available as safeguards. The presence of Cavalry is absolutely required. Your petitioners respectfully pray that at least three companies of eCavalry shall be placed through the stock-grazing country described at such places as may be designated by the General commanding this Department" DS, *ibid.* On June 13, U.S. Senator Phineas W. Hitchcock of Neb. presented this petition. E, *ibid.* On June 23, Lt. Gen. Philip H. Sheridan, Chicago, endorsed these papers. "In accordance with a telegram received on this subject I directed the Commanding Officer at Red Cloud Agency to keep the road open and protect the country down as far as Chimney Rock. I moved a company from McPherson north of the Platte, on the Sidney road, to protect the country as far up as Chimney Rock, and stationed a detachment of infantry at the bridge across the North Platte to protect it. This will give two companies of cavalry and one of infantry for the protection of the stock raising interests mentioned herein." ES, *ibid.*

On Jan. 4, Sheridan had written to Gen. William T. Sherman, St. Louis, concerning possible "military operations against sioux indians, in case, they refuse to occupy the reservation assigned them by the Indian Bureau on or before the 31st day of January 1876. . . . General Terry is of the opinion that Sitting Bull's band of hostile Indians is encamped at or near the mouth of Little Missouri . . . I earnestly request, should operations be determined upon that directions to that effect be communicated to me as speedily as possible, so that the enemy may be taken at the greatest disadvantage" Copy (press), DLC-Philip H. Sheridan. *HED*, 44-1-184, 11–12; *SED*, 44-1-52, 7–8. On Jan. 15 and 24, Charles W. Darling, Indian agent, Fort Berthold Agency, wrote to John Q. Smith, commissioner of Indian Affairs. "I have the honor to state that on the night of the 11th or morning of the 12th instant a band of Hostile Sioux Indians succeeded in stealing 25 horses from the Gros Ventres winter quarters at the mouth of the Little Missouri river about 25 miles above this Agency. . . . That these Indians were from Sitting Bulls camp of Hunpapa I beleive as they were making direct for it on the Yellowstone . . . From the best information possible to get here Sitting Bull has about 500 lodges of lawless ruffians with him, in fact the home of the very worst Indians in the northwest. . . . I was in hopes the Government would put its strong and heavy hand upon this band of red rascals who seem to defy and laugh at every effort made to compel good behavior. I think a good thrashing would do them good and save lives in the end" "I have the honor to report that the large band of hostile Sioux under the leadership of Sitting Bull, are still encamped on the reservation of the Indians of my Agency. . . . I would respectfully, but strongly urge on the Department the absolute necessity of driving Sitting Bull and his band of lawless Indians off the reservation of the Indians of my agency with as little delay as practicable" Copies (press), DLC-Philip H. Sheridan. *HED*, 44-1-184, 22–23. See *ibid.*, 44-2-1, part 5, pp. 433–34. On Jan. 26, Henry W. Bingham, Indian agent, Cheyenne River Agency, wrote to Smith that no reports indicated trouble from Sitting Bull. Copy (press), DLC-Philip H. Sheridan. *HED*, 44-1-184, 22. On Jan. 31, Smith wrote to Secretary of the Interior Zachariah Chandler recommending military operations against Sitting Bull. Copy (press), DLC-Philip H. Sheridan. *HED*, 44-1-184, 18. On Feb. 1, Chandler wrote to Secretary of War William W. Belknap authorizing military action. Copy (press), DLC-Philip H. Sheridan. *HED*, 44-1-184, 17–18; *SED*, 44-1-52, 9. On Feb. 12, Bingham wrote to Smith with recent information from "the Camps of 'Sitting-Bull' and other wild bands, . . . They are now Camped on the Yellowstone river, and my informants say that they are not only peaceably inclined, but deny the statements so extensively circulated that they intended to make war on the frontier on the approach of Spring. I cannot determine how much importance to attach to this information but until something transpires to convince me that hostile movements are intended, I must adhere to my present opinion, that there is no danger to be apprehended." Copy (press), DLC-Philip H. Sheridan. *HED*, 44-1-184, 26. On Feb. 21, Chandler forwarded Bingham's communication to Belknap. Copy (press), DLC-Philip H. Sheridan. *HED*, 44-1-184, 25–26. See *SED*, 44-1-52; *HED*, 44-2-1, part 2, I, 28–29, 440–42.

On Jan. 30, William Fielder, interpreter, Cheyenne Agency, Dakota Territory, wrote to Fanny Kelly, Washington, D. C., seeking her assistance in explaining Indian "greivances to the officials at Washington. The idea of the Indians is, that as you are living at Washington near the President, and are a friend to them that you may be able to do for them, a great amount of good. There is at this Agency about six or seven thousand Indians, . . . In the first place the government wished to obtain from the Indians that portion of their country known as the 'black hills' and for that purpose a commission was appointed from among our best men and I know, as I was interpreter for said commission, that it was as much the fault of the commission, as it was of the Indians that the negotiation for the black hills was not successfully concluded. . . . In the face of this an order comes from Washington, which of course the Agents are in duty bound to see obeyed, which prohibits the sale of arms and amunition to Indians, upon the reservations. There is more room for argument upon this question than I have time or space to write I will however say: that, in the first place the rations allowed by the government is not sufficient for the Indians to subsist on entirely. The balance of their subsistance is obtained by hunting. Take the gun an amunition away from an Indian, and it is much the same as taking the plow and seed grain away from a farmer. . . . Before this order came here, all that was said by the Indians in regard to the whites going to the black hills, was, let them go; we will not harm them; we want peace and must regard them as our friends. But since this order came among them, it has been the cause of arousing the warlike spirit of the young hostiles, and will I am afraid cause the loss of many a poor white man; who but for this order, might have passed unharmed. . . . The Indians boast of the peace and happiness they have enjoyed during the seven years of President Grant's administration and look to him with pride and confidence, believing that he will see that they have their rights, which their actions during his administration entitles them to. Hoping you may attend to this matter at your earliest convenience . . ." ALS, DNA, RG 75, Letters Received, Cheyenne River Agency. See Fanny Kelly, *Narrative of My Captivity among the Sioux Indians* (Cincinnati, 1871).

In a fictitious letter docketed March 31, probably authored by a white person, "Red Wing" had written to USG. "Red Wing, from the Dakota country of the Black hills, one of the Sioux, comining from the upper hunting grounds of the good Spirit, makes this appeal in behalf of his red brothers. . . . Send chiefs to look after the wants of the wh red children, send out talking sheet over the country forbidding white man invade Black hills in search of shiners, send words to chiefs at forts, no to allow braves to fire on red skins, This what Red Wing want, this what great Spirit want, the good father at Washington to make his council, a council of Peace, what him to protect Red man, then the Indian troubles will subside, and the Red man will pass away, quite and natural from his lodges, to the hunting ground of Manota beyond the setting sun, leaving the country to the pale face, and the Glory of father Grant, Will surround his life, like the glory of the sun at noon day heat." L (undated), DNA, RG 75, Letters Received, Dakota Superintendency.

On May 24, C. Dormey, Cedar Bluffs, Kan., wrote to USG. "The Indans are Geting quite sasey out heer thay are killing Lots of the settlers through the contry an I ask it as A favor of you to put A compny of solgers on the head of Beaver crick or furnish the setler with arms to portect thamselves the farmer are Working hard this sumer and it Looks hard to see tham shot down in thare fields & the poor childern slotered Like the Wilde Beasts of the fields   pleas get us some infer maishon What will bee done" ALS, *ibid.*, Letters Received, Miscellaneous.

On May 25, Sherman telegraphed to Sheridan. "Have just been to the President with Governor Thayer—after reading the papers and some discussion the President said: that the people who have gone to the Black Hills of Dacota inside the Sioux Reservation, or who may hereafter go there, are there wrong-fully, and that they should be notified of the fact; but the Government is engaged in certain measures that will probably result in opening up the country to occupation and settlement. Meantime the Indians should not be allowed to scalp and kill anybody, and you are authorized to afford protection to all persons who are coming away or who are conveying food and stores for those already there. I understand that arrangements are now in progress with Red Cloud and Spotted Tail to remove—and meantime the agency Indians should be kept near their agencies. If satisfactory arrangments are not concluded, then new orders will be made as to the whites who have intruded on the Sioux Reservation." Copy, *ibid.*, RG 108, Letters Sent. On June 1, Sherman twice telegraphed to Sheridan. "A communication of the Secretary of the Interior to the Secretary of War is referred to me. It recites that the Sioux Reservation is invaded by Black Hill emigrants from Fort Pierre, and that a regular stage line has been established, and the Secretary of the Interior requests that military force be used to prevent these violations of the treaty. This letter is endorsed by the President himself with an order to execute the request of the Secretary of the Interior. Please order that this intrusion must stop and enforce the same as far as possible. The original papers will come to you by mail." "Your dispatch of yesterday is received, and I understand the orders of the President concerning the route through the Reservation to the Black Hills from Fort Pierre and Yankton, to be absolutely prohibitory. The route from Laramie lies mostly west and outside of the Reservation, and military protection there is only in the cause of humanity. General Vandever is here direct from Spotted Tail and Red Cloud Agencies and he insists that these Indians are, in the main, disposed to peace. I doubt if the Civil Agents will be relieved of their Control unless the law for transfer is passed, of which I have grave doubts. If by any means you can aid in keeping the bulk of them at peace, whilst operations are in progress against the hostiles, I know it will meet the sanction of the authorities here. The Interior Department still construe the Sioux treaty to be in full force." Copies, *ibid.* On June 5, Governor John L. Pennington of Dakota Territory, Washington, D. C., telegraphed to USG. "The following received signed J. C. KIDDER 'Yankton D. T. to HON J C KIDDER Washn D. C. June 4th Is Sherman's order forbidding all travel to Black Hills general and does it apply to all routes or does it apply only to route from Ft Pierre to Hills while Cheyenne route is left open Large quantities of provisions at Pierre for Hills stopped by order. people here very much exasperated and insist that all routes be closed or in justice to them the Pierre route be opened" Telegram received, *ibid.*, RG 107, Telegrams Collected (Bound). On June 5 and 8, Sherman telegraphed to Sheridan. "Just came from conference with Sectys Chandler and Cameron. The former says he thinks a bill will pass today appointing Commission to confer with Red Cloud and Spotted Tail, with a view to obtain the consent of the peaceful indians to release their rights to Black Hills to emigrate to some other reservation. . . ." Copy (press), DLC-Philip H. Sheridan. "Judge Kidder of Dakota represents that there are about a hundred tons of provisions at Fort Pierre ready for the Black Hills and that the Commanding Officer forbids their going. We have just seen the President who consents that these provisions may be hauled out but that no escort can be given. You may instruct accordingly. The Commanding Officer should see that the parties who go out with the train are armed and prepared to defend the train and to prevent its falling into the hands of Hostile Indians. Judge Kidder has been very zealous in this matter in the interests of his Territory." Copy, DNA, RG 108, Letters Sent.

On May 29, Joseph P. Root, Washington, D. C., had written to USG. "Having been somewhat intimate with the leading men of the Sioux tribe of Indians for many years—including Red Cloud and Spotted Tail, and having been in correspondence with parties of influence connected with said indians since the failure to make a treaty with the Sioux last year, I am convinced that at no time for many months—as well as at the present time—would it have been a difficult thing to make a satisfactory arrangement with these indians. From what I deem reliable information the reason of the failure of last falls Commission was not all the fault of the indians. It does seem as though something ought to done and that right seepdily to prevent further murders on the part of either whites or indians and I am positive that the *indians* if *reached properly* will not be found objecting to an equitable treaty. More than a hundred whites—including many good men from my own state (Kansas) have recently been massacred near the 'Black Hills' and I sincerely hope measures may be speedily adopted which shall result in permanent peace to all parties" ALS, *ibid.*, RG 75, Letters Received, Dakota Superintendency.

On June 10, Albert G. Boone, Washington, D. C., wrote to USG. "Permit one who has had considerable experience among the Indians of the West to present, most respectfully, for your consideration, the following plan of treating the hostile Indian tribes. My object is principally to save money and the effusion of blood. Already a great deal of money has been expended and over two hundred whites killed by the Indians in the Black Hill country. It is quite certain that the many commissioners who have been sent out there, have produced nothing but voluminous reports of their attempts and failures to carry out the wishes and intentions of the Government. Now to avoid any more trouble and the shedding of blood, I propose to try 'moral suasion,' by sending out to those hostile Indians a person who has a knowledge of the habits and customs of the Indians, and who shall be permitted to select one civilized Indian from each of the friendly tribes, who are also friendly to the Sioux, to accompany him on the mission. They should go there without any ostentation, and pay the Sioux a friendly visit, as Indians often do. . . . The delegation to the hostile Indians should be authorised to treat with the Sioux tribe for their lands, but the subject should not be alluded to until their confidence is gained. And in order to gain their confidence, they should be assured that the visit is solely for their good, and that the delegation is authorised to pledge them the friendship and protection of the United States Government. It is folly to send officers of the Army to these people on a peaceful mission. They know nothing of the habits and customs of Indians. The Indians should be met and treated as friends, and every thing so simplified that they may understand. Language should not be used that neither the Indians nor interpreters can understand or comprehend." ALS, *ibid.*

On June 24, Patrick E. Connor, Salt Lake City, telegraphed to USG. "If volunteers are required in the Sioux Country I respectfully tender my services" Telegram received (at 3:55 P.M.), *ibid.*, RG 94, Letters Received, 3755 1876.

On May 29, Sheridan had written to Sherman, Washington, D. C., concerning troop movements against the Sioux. ". . . As no very accurate information can be obtained as to the location of hostile Indians, and as there would be no telling how long they would stay at any one place, if it was known, I have given no instructions to Generals Crook or Terry, preferring that they should do the best they can under the circumstances and under what they may develop, as I think it would be unwise to make any combinations in such a country as they have to operate in. As hostile Indians in any great numbers, cannot keep the field as a body for a week or at most ten days, I therefore consider, and so do Terry and Crook—that each column will be able to take care of itself, and of chastening the Indians should it have the opportunity. . . . The result of the movement of these three columns may force many of the hostile Indians back to the Agencies on the Missouri river and to the Red Cloud and Spotted Tail Agencies on the northern line of Nebraska, where nearly every Indian, man woman and child, is at heart a friend. It is easy to foresee the result of this condition that as soon as the troops return in the fall, the Indians will go out again, and another campaign with all its expenses, will be required, as was the case with the Cheyennes, Arapahoes, Comanches and Kiowas of the Indian Territory. To obviate this, I advise that the two posts recommended by me be established on the Yellowstone, and that the military be allowed to exercise control over the Indians at the agencies to such an extent as to prevent any friendly Indians from leaving to join the hostile Indians, and the latter or any of their families from coming in, except by unconditional surrender, the ringleaders to be punished, as were the southern Indians, by having them sent to some distant point until they and their people are willing to behave themselves. I hope that good results may be obtained by the troops in the field, but am not at all sanguine unless what I have above suggested be carried out. We might just as well settle the Sioux matter now; it will be better for all concerned." Copy (press), DLC-Philip H. Sheridan. *HED*, 44-1-184, *53–54*. See *ibid.*, 44-2-1, part 2, I, *29–30*; message to Senate, July 8, 1876.

To Congress

To The Senate & House of Representatives

The near approach of a new fiscal year and the failure of Congress up to ~~provide~~ this time to provide the necessary means to continue all the functions of government makes it my duty to call ~~th~~ your attention to the embarrassments that must ensue if the fiscal year is allowed to close without remedial action on your part.

Article 1 Sec. 9 [of the Constitution] declares . . .

To insure economy of expenditures and security of the public treasure Congress has from time to time enacted laws to restrain the use of public moneys except for the specific purpose for which appropriated, & within the time for which appropriated; ~~from~~ [and to prevent] contracting debts in anticipation of appropriate appropriations.

Rev. Stat, Sec. 3679 provides, . . .

Sec. 3732 provides . . .

Sec. 3678 as follows . . .

3690 that

The effect of the laws quoted, taken in connection with the Constitutional provision refered to is, as above stated, to prohibit any outlay of public money toward defraying even the current and necessary expenses of government after the expiration of the year for which appropriated,—excepting when those expenses are provided for by some permanent appropriation, and excepting in the War & Navy departments under Sec. 3732

The number of permanent appropriations are ~~but~~ very limited, and cover but few of the necessary expenditures of the govt.

Copy marked matter in here.[1]

A careful examination of this subject will demonstrate the embarassed condition all branches of the govt. will be in—and especially the Executive—if there should be a failure ~~by~~ [before] ~~the 1st of July~~ to pass the necessary appropriation bills. [before the 1st of July, or otherwise provide.]— ~~I commend~~ I commend this subject most earnestly to your consideration, and urge that some measure be speedily adopted to avert the evils which would result from non-action by Congress. I will venture the suggestion—by way of remedy—that a joint resotution, properly guarded, might be passed through the two houses of Congress, extending the provisions of all appropriations for the present fiscal year to the next, ~~when~~ in all cases when there is a failure on the 1st of July ~~next~~ to supply such appropriation, ~~to hold until~~ each appropriation so extended to hold good until Congress shall have passed a corresponding appropriation applicable to the new fiscal year, when all moneys expended under laws enacted for this fiscal year shall be deducted from the corresponding appropriation for the next.

To make my ideas on this subject more clear I have caused to be drawn up a "Joint Resolution" embodying them. [more fully.

U. S. Grant

Ex Man. June 17th 1876]

ADf (ellipses in original; bracketed material not in USG's hand), DLC-USG, III. *SED*, 44-1-75; *HED*, 44-1-177. A proposed joint resolution accompanied the message. ". . . Be it resolved by the Senate and House of Representatives of the United States of America in Congress assembled, That in case any of the following appropriation bills for the fiscal year ending June 30, 1877, shall not have passed by the commencement of such year, so that the funds to be appropriated thereby may then be available for expenditure, that is to say, the bill providing for the legislative, executive and judicial expenses—; the bill providing for the consular and diplomatic expenses; the bill providing for the service of the Post Office Department; the bill providing for the support of the Army and the bill providing for the naval service, the appropriation Act for the current fiscal year corresponding in its general description and object to such appropriation bill shall extend to the fiscal year next ensuing until such appropriation bill is enacted and takes effect, to the end that the provisions of such appropriation Act which apply to the ordinary and necessary expenses of the public service for the current fiscal year shall in like manner be applicable to similar expenses which may accrue during the period intervening between the end of the current fiscal year and the time when such appropriation bill for the next ensuing fiscal year shall be enacted and take effect" Copy, DLC-USG, III. *SED*, 44-1-75, 3; *HED*, 44-1-177, 3.

On June 27, 1876, Tuesday, Secretary of State Hamilton Fish recorded in his diary. "No business was transacted except a general discussion on the condition of the Departments in case of a failure of the appropriations to pass before 1st July. Jewell said he would continue to run his department law or no law, and repeated it once or twice—the President remarked we must act under the law; whereupon Jewell repeated he would go on the same unless ordered to the contrary. I mention the circular I had issued to the Consuls cautioning them in the event of the appropriations to fail to pass. Robeson spoke of the impossibility of his giving orders to the squadrons now in the different parts of the world. The Solicitor General was sent for in absence of the Attorney General and requested to prepare an opinion on the question by Friday next." DLC-Hamilton Fish. See *ibid.*, June 30, 1876. On June 30, USG signed the first of several successive bills extending appropriations for ten days to meet government expenditures. See *U.S. Statutes at Large*, XIX, 65; *CR*, 44–1, 3854–71, 4286–87; messages to House of Representatives, July 31, Aug. 14, 1876.

On May 23, Ambrose W. Thompson, New York City, had written to USG. "Confidential . . . I have hesitated to write you, but feel that I should hesitate no longer. The opposition in the House has done so much to scandalise the Country, and so little—or, nothing to relieve it from its financial distress, that the people are disgusted, and the immediate political future is in your control if you strike as promptly and boldly an adverse political mistake, as you would a military one. A brief clear message to Congress pointing to the House resolution to adjourn at an Early day—calling attention to the fact that nothing has been done to alleviate distress; that industry is paralyzed; manufactures and Commerce, nearly destroyed—failures of Corporations, Bankers, & merchants, although of greater than any former proportion in numbers—are daily on the increase—*all this*, because Congress has failed to form and pass a System of finance which could bring relief—That deeply impressed with your Obligation to the Country, you conceive it will be your duty to it, if Congress shall adjourn without some measure which can restore confidence and prosperity—to call an immediate Extra Session for this Express and only purpose. That in the hope of being spared this resort you now suggest a plan which it is believed will restore immediately, confidence throughout the land—will reduce the taxes over thirty millions Annually, provide for Early Specie payments, create a Sinking fund to redeem the whole amount of National, and National Bank notes, giving in their stead a government issue of Specie Value, and a funding of the various loans of the government into one fund of low interest rate for fifty years, by which the credit of the Government will stand on an [equality] with that of any Country in Europe. . . ." ALS (press), DLC-Ambrose W. Thompson.

1. "They are nearly all, if not quite all, embraced in Sections 3687. 3688, and 3689 of the Revised Statutes. That contained in Section 3687 is applicable to *expenses of collecting the revenue from customs*; that in section 3688 to the payment of interest on the *public debt*; and that in section 3689 to various objects too numerous to detail here. It will be observed that while section 3679, quoted above, provides that *no* Department shall in any one fiscal year involve the government in any contract for the future payment of money in excess of the appropriation for that year, Section 3732, also quoted above, confers by clear implication upon the heads of the War and Navy Departments full authority, even in the absence of any appropriation, to purchase or contract for clothing, subsistence, forage, fuel, quarters, or transportation, not exceeding the necessities of the current year. The latter provi-

sion is special and exceptional in its character, and is to be regarded as excluded from the operation of the former more general one. But, if any of the appropriation bills above enumerated should fail to be matured before the expiration of the current fiscal year, the Government would be greatly embarrassed for want of the necessary funds to carry on the service. Precluded from expending money not appropriated, the departments would have to suspend the service, so far as the appropriations for it should have failed to be made." Taken from an undated memorandum by Attorney Gen. Alphonso Taft, titled "*Constitutional & Legal provisions as to Appropriations.*" DS, DLC-USG, III. *SED*, 44-1-75, 2; *HED*, 44-1-177, 2. USG wrote "Copy" in the margin opposite the quoted text. Taft's memorandum also supplied the statutory sections indicated by USG's ellipses. On June 15, Ulysses S. Grant, Jr., wrote to Taft. "Will you please send to the President those papers you brought him yesterday and carried off again by mistake: The papers related to the laws of appropriations." ALS, DLC-William H. Taft.

Speech

[*June 19, 1876*]

Gentlemen, after all the speaking you and I have listened to tonight, for I was with you at your ratification meeting, you cannot wish, even if I was a speaker, to hear anything from me. But I cannot withhold my approval of the excellent ticket given you by the National Republican Convention at Cincinnati—a ticket that should receive the cordial support of all races in all sections. I know Governor Hayes personally, and I can surrender with unfeigned pleasure my present position to him, as I believe I shall do on the 5th of March, next year, with a guaranteed security for your rights and liberties under the laws of the land.

New York Herald, June 20, 1876. "The serenaders from the ratification meeting at the City Hall, after paying Mr. Blaine the compliment of a visit, directed their course to the White House, on the balcony of which the President soon appeared in response to the music of the Marine Band and the cheers of the crowd." *Ibid.* On June 16, 1876, Republicans convening in Cincinnati had nominated Governor Rutherford B. Hayes of Ohio on the seventh ballot, 384 to 351 over U.S. Representative James G. Blaine of Maine. On the same day, USG telegraphed to Hayes. "I congratulate you and feel the greatest assurance that you will occupy my present position from the Fourth of March next" Telegram received (at 10:10 P.M.), OFH.

Also on June 16, Joseph H. Millard, Omaha, telegraphed to U.S. Senator Algernon S. Paddock of Neb. "For ratification meeting here tomorrow night please get authority from Secty of War telegraphed Genl Davis tomorrow to furnish us two guns with squad for firing" Telegram received, DNA, RG 94, Letters Received, 3428 1876. On June 17, USG

endorsed this telegram. "The Sec. of War may authorize Comd.g officer at Omaha to furnish the Artillery reques[ted] but not the squad unless they volunte[er] for the service and
with the consent of the Comd.g officer." AES, *ibid.*

On June 26, W. H. Mason, Atlanta, Ill., wrote to USG. "I was pleased with reading
the contents of your dispatch to Gov. Hayes your chosen successor and I have no doubt but
what your prediction 'that he will be your successor' will be proven true this fall at polls
if the signs of times are correct. But I think for the Republican party to be successful it
is necessary that the laws be ridgidly enforced in the South so that the Negroes may vote
and not be intimidated or driven away from the polls. Louisiana Mississippi Florida and
N. Carolina will give republican majorites if they are allowed to vote and I hope you will
enforce the laws and let us have a fair and legal election. I see in the reports of the proceedings in Congress that the Democrats are trying by unfair means to have the Registra-
tion laws repealed so that they can by fraudulent votes carry the election. It is necessary
that these appropriation bills should pass but if they cannot be passed by no other means
it is to the best interests of the Nation that they be not passed if by so doing the Registry
laws are repealed and the Democratic party to again gain controll of the Government but
I have no fears of the Senate will pass those bills and if they should I know that you would
veto them at once as any man with a little common sense can see their object in thus attaching such measures to bills that should be immediately passed. With a fair and legal
election in N. York city the Republicans will carry that State and I hope the laws will be
ridgidly enforced in that corrupt city. Set Davenport to work and we are all right. We have
a good ticket men whom the people can trust and with work and a fair legal election they
will be triumphantly elected. See to it that the laws are enforced and that the Registry laws
are not repealed and the people will endorse your action heartily all over this broad beautiful land of ours. wishing you success and prosperity . . ." ALS, DNA, RG 60, Letters from
the President. On July 10, Mason again wrote to USG. ". . . The nomination of Tilden the
partner of Boss Tweed shows conclusively that they intend to try to carry this election by
fraud and with money . . ." AL (incomplete), *ibid.*

On May 20, Mannen Gore, "Ex Corporal of Co. F. 40th Mo Volunteer Infty," Honey
Bend, Ill., had written to USG. "Having with much anzxiety been a close wacher of the administrations for the Past 20 years and Seeing an effort within the Past few years to stiga-
matize *yourself with* the *corruptions* of these *times* allow me as one of the common People and
one that served under you to offer you the congratulations and ashurance that the good
honest people of all classes still have faith in you as they did when you led them against
Donaldson Vicksburgh in the *wilderness* and at *Richmond* Hoping you will live long to Enjoy the blessings of a Free Country that you have done so much to save and with My Best
wishes for you and all that is near and Dear to you and offering you my sincere thank as
an humble Citizen . . ." ALS, USG 3.

On May 22, Ellery P. Ingham, Philadelphia, wrote to USG. "I want to write to you in
these times of Democratic Investigations and Democratic calumnies, and tell you how
much I honor, admire and respect you. Nearly every day in reading the newspapers I find
some suspect and slanderous article written by some 'out' who desires greatly to be an 'in'
and who throws mud on every clean object the better to disguise his own garments. It
makes my blood boil to read them,—so mean, so scurrilous, so unjust—To think that
these mongrel curs who only a few years back were writing editorials in Richmond, or issuing 'Peace Proclamations' from the depths of Canadian woods, should now assail the
honor and criticise the actions of the one who was chiefly instrumental in saving the
Union, and in preserving 'our lives and sacred honor' One thing, President Grant, is certain, and that is that your name is deeply engraven on the hearts of the American people,
and so long as the Union lasts so long will the names of Washington, Lincoln and Grant

be remembered with affection and spoken of with pride—Now please do not consider this *flattery* for it is not, and I have no 'axe to grind' or nothing to ask of you, except not to think me so very silly in writing this. If you do think it so, please lay it to my youth; for I am not a voter yet, and will not be next fall, 'miserabile dictu.' But I wanted to let you know that you *are* loved by the people, and that such papers as the N. Y. *Herald* and *Sun,* or the Phila *Times,* do not express the ideas of their readers at all. Again please do not consider this flattery, or even fulsome praise for I assure you that it comes from the heart and not from the head. If I thought you would consider it obsequious or any thing like it, I would not write at all, for I am a true American and do not faun. But an American can see greatness and admire it, and feel goodness and cherish it. I do not expect or ask any notice of this, for I am not even an autograph hunter. . . . (I feel easier now)" ALS, *ibid.*

On June 2, James F. Chaffee, Washington, D. C., wrote to USG. "In company with two other Methodist ministers, Rev. Mr. McKinley of Winona, and Rev. J. Stafford of St. Paul, I was presented to you this morning by Senator McMillan. As there were several present we were perhaps unduly afraid of taking your time for a moment, even; and therefore omitted to say to you, what we all feel, that we are alike proud of your valor in war, and of your administration in peace. We are satisfied that the great mass of the American people still have confidence in the integrity of your motives, and, for the most part, in the wisdom and justness of your measures; and notwithstanding the clamor of politicians, we are satisfied that the Republic will yet be ever generous in its expressions of gratitude to her greatest soldier and faithful President, U. S. Grant. May heaven protect your Excellency, that no untoward event may tarnish the lustre of your record or the honor of your name, . . ." ALS, *ibid.*

On June 12, Robert Frost, Winchester, Ill., wrote to USG. "Allow me to adopt as familliar a stye of adress as I can, to say that I am an Englishman but a citizen of the U. S. since 1842 that I have never sought office, & want none, but that if you should be a candidate for the Prescidency for a *third* term I shall take great pleasure in doing what I properly can to help you I have always admired your consistant course and often defended you in private conversation as I *now* do when occasion requires, I have also some influence with many men who like myself were born across the Sea. Trusting this information will not be unpleasant to you and asking your forgiveness if it is . . ." ALS, *ibid.*

On June 14, A. S. Lane, "Dealer in Butter & Eggs," Hiawatha, Kan., wrote to USG. "I have watched the political Horisson and I See no man in the country that will make So good a President as Yourself—I am a democrat but I am for You heart and Soul. For God Sake run So that we can have a man for our President that the nations of the Earth can respect—and at the Same time fear, and as true as their is a god above! You can be Elected againe. I would Spend the last dollar I had on Earth to have You. from the bottom of my heart I feal this. I know how the people feal." ALS, *ibid.*

On June 17, Isaac H. Sturgeon, collector of Internal Revenue, St. Louis, wrote to USG. "My heart bids me repeat to you what you already know that I am your well wisher in all that concerns the happiness and welfare of you and yours at all times and when the rest that you so much need of private life shall come to you my heart will follow you with its prayers to God for His Choicest blessings to you and all near & dear to you The present Rebel congress and their Democratic sympathizers will now I suppose give you some peace and rest—Their vile efforts to tarnish your good name will re coil on their own heads You have passed through a fearfully trying time in the history of our Country— The Rebellion—The Reconstruction after the war—The settlement of a most delicate question with England & all the varied questions growing out of these issues and all your vilest enemies can say is that your good heart was imposed upon and here and there out of the thousands of office holders your confidence was abused by them—Your record is the grandest and proudest of any public man since the days of Washington and now as you retire to private life you crown the whole by asking that our Common school system be protected by a Constitutional amendmt. With the watch words of Hard money, protection to our Common school system, Loyalty to the front—treason & its sympathizers to the rear I think we shall triumph and perpetuate our Governmt in the hands of those who fought to preserve it and the loyalists of the Country—If it were possible that the people of this Governmt could remit its control to those so lately in arms to destroy it & their Democratic sympathizers then will the war have been fought for the Union in vain & every life lost & dollar spent worse than wasted   May God avert such a calamity—With sentiments of the highest regard & always holding myself ready to serve you if I can personally or publickly . . ." ALS, *ibid.*

On June 23, William B. Wright, *Boston Post*, wrote to USG. "I write to send a word of encouragement and gratitude to you. I used to think General, that you were a good deal of a political schemer and a man who dishonored his position, but having seen your face several times of late and watched you closely I have come to think much better of you than ever and indeed an old batchelor friend of mine has often suggested to me that you were not the man whom the press has cried down and maligned so much during the past four years. I mean no flattery, General, seek no reply to this note, wish no office and am but spontaneously giving you a kind word now that you have ceased to be the attraction to the crowd. . . ." ALS, *ibid.*

On July 6, Henry K. Johnson, clerk, Post Office Dept., wrote to USG. "I have the honor to enclose an article appearing in the columns of the Daily chronicle of to day in which I have the satisfaction of indicating my views of the manner in which you have carried out your pledges of economy in the administration of the Government. In the face of such a statement as this the public cannot be blind to the marked improvement you have secured in every department of the service. Your enemies Sir, have succeeded to some extent in obscuring your just fame, but it is only for a brief time, and that it may shine more brightly. You may look confidently forward to the *most* gratifying appreciation of your great deeds; the future will show that you are still first in the hearts of the people. I would not venture to offer this word of faith but when calumny is so common it seems a good office on the part of even the humblest citizen to state his belief in the purity of your purposes & the wisdom of your course." ALS, *ibid.*

To Benjamin H. Bristow

Washington, D. C. June 19th *1876*

Hon. B. H. Bristow, Sec. of the Treas.

Dear Sir:

I am in receipt of your resignation of the office of Sec. of the Treasury, tendered on the 17th, to take effect on the 20th of this month.

In accepting it, for that date, permit me to hope that our personal relations may continue as here-to-fore and that you may find that peace in private life denied to any one occupying your present official position.

Your obt. svt.

U. S. GRANT

ALS, DLC-Benjamin H. Bristow; copy, USG 3. On June 17, 1876, Benjamin H. Bristow wrote to USG. "In mentioning to you on the fifth instant my purpose to retire from the office of Secretary of the Treasury on a day in this month not later than the twentieth I but expressed a wish entertained by me for some months and of which you were advised. Acting upon that intention I now have the honor to tender my resignation to take effect on the twentieth of this month Thanking you, Mr President for the honor you did me in calling me to the office, and with my best wishes for your future welfare, . . ." ALS, *ibid.* Bristow drafted another version. "It must be apparent to ~~yourself~~ as it is to myself that my longer continuance in the office of Secty of Treasury ~~is is not~~ can but bring increasing embarrassment to both of us. ~~You will remember that I have repeatedly expressed to you my~~ ~~Having assured you when I accepted this office that it was against my interest to do so~~ Having repeatedly advised you of my earnest desire to retire from official life and return to my private business, I need not now assure you that ~~there is~~ considerations of ~~pri-vate~~ personal interest invite my ~~personal~~ retirement. ~~When on~~ Early in September last I ~~have tendered~~ asked you to accept my resignation, but was induced to withdraw the request upon your statement that my resignation at that time would be charged to alleged disagreement between you & myself growing out of the active movements of officers of this Deptmt in detecting & bringing to punishment violators of the Internal revenue laws. In view of the many false and malicious rumors that have been put in circulation on that subject by the conspirators against the revenue, their friends & allies, to which you seemed to attach some importance, and of the firm belief on my part that you desired as earnestly as any one, the complete exposure of ~~th~~ all the frauds on the revenue and especially that those who had been entrusted with official duties & responsibilities, or who claimed that they had high influence to protect them should be brought to the bar of justice, I yielded to your request to withhold ~~those~~ my resignation. Now however the ~~duty~~ chief duty imposed on the Secty of Treasury by law ~~on~~ & the nature of his office in respect of these [—] & unprecedented frauds ~~on~~ has been performed & the cases arising therefrom have been brought into the courts where they ~~are under the~~ are beyond the control or direction of this Department, ~~the objection~~ it seems no longer necessary for me to forego personal interest & desire on this account. Moreover it is due to perfect candor to add that I am not unconscious of the fact that the persistent efforts of ~~guilty men~~ persons charged with crime, their abettors & friends ~~to e~~ by the most unscrupulous means to convince you that ~~the prosecutions against the revenue~~ certain prosecutions which have grown out of the developments referred to, are really aimed at you and are prompted by ~~b~~ a mixture of base & ambitious motives have not been without effect. Utterly false as I know such statements to be so far as they relate to the head & subordinate officers of this Deptmt, and absurd as they seem to me, it is painfully apparent that they are not so regarded by you. The withdrawal of your confidence & official support, to say nothing of the manifest disturbance of personal relations, renders me as the head of a Departmt powerless for the accomplishment of the important duties imposed on ~~mye~~ by law satisfactorily or creditably to your Administration Regretting that ~~our earnest &~~ my efforts to expose & punish frauds on the govmt— ~~which~~ should have been tortured by interested parties into ~~to~~ schemes for the advancement of personal ambitions, which I have never felt, and of base ~~revenge~~ desire to injure others against whom I have had neither ~~nor~~ personal hatred nor political enmity, I

~~nertheless~~ nevertheless, feel that a ~~just~~ proper regard for my own comfort, and character, requires me to withdraw from your Cabinet. without further delay. Whatever misrepresentations may have been made ~~or may hereaft~~ or however this step on my part may ~~have~~ be miscontrued, I feel impelled to it by a sense of self respect, & shall at least carry with me to private life, a consciousness of having been actuated by no other motive than a sincere desire to perform faithfully, & the duties of the office reluctantly accepted at your hands, & to contribute by all means in my power to the promotion of good Government & ~~honest administration~~ If there be those who have not desired these thing 'such have I offended,' ~~but not without purpose to do so.~~" ADf, DLC-Benjamin H. Bristow.

On Dec. 15, 1875, "Argus," Washington, D. C., had written to USG. "The writer is a personal and political friend of yours—He heartily indorses your past administration and and goes in for you for the 3d term—He keeps both eyes open, and thinks he sees which way the *cat* is aiming to jump—My Dear Sir—allow me to suggest that you have a bitter, unrelenting, insidious enemy in your own household—Don't be startled—The writer understand himself perfectly well, and knows what he says to be so—his means of knowledge will not be stated—Your Secretary *Bristow* is the man I refer to—Bristow is working for the nomination in 1876—He intends to take all the credit of the Whisky prosecutions to himself—your indorsement is to be neutralized by connecting your confidential & Private secretary, with the alleged frauds—This friendly warning will most likely go to the waste basket—be it so I have discharged my duty—Bristow should be made to git up and git—Remember, the 'Ides of March'—" L, USG 3.

On Dec. 29, Bristow wrote to J. Russell Jones, Chicago. "*Personal*. . . . Your kindness in sending me the article from the *Tribune* in reply to the slanderous charges of the *Inter Ocean* against me, gives another proof of your friendship, for which I am deeply grateful. I beg to assure you that these infamous lies not only do not disturb my equanimity, but will not be permitted to abate my zeal in the prosecution of the thieves, or to divert me from the plain path of duty. So far as I can control the prosecutions there will be no 'let up' until every revenue thief who can be reached has received the punishment provided by law for such scoundrels I care nothing for the attacks on myself, for I know there is no part of my record in this regard that is vulnerable. [']Let the galled jade wince, My withers are unwrung'. I am glad to know that in the determination to enforce the law we have your earnest sympathy and support." LS, ICHi. See *Chicago Inter-Ocean*, Dec. 25, 1875, Jan. 1, 1876.

On Feb. 6, Secretary of State Hamilton Fish recorded in his diary. "Received a letter from Bristow Secretary of the Treasury that he wished a confidential talk with me, and accordingly in the afternoon he called at my house. He says that his position in the Cabinet is a painful one, that the embarrassments have been increasing from time to time, that he thinks the President does not entertain the same confidence that he once did, that in the prosecutions for violation of the Revenue Laws, he had endeavoured only to do his duty and has not given any special instruction, although the Statute places all such cases under his control, yet from delicacy he has allowed the Attorney General to direct. That the President has manifested impatience and dissatisfaction at the course pursued in Chicago, where the prosecuting officers have made use of the testimony of some guilty parties in order to convict others. He refers to the conversation which took place a short time since at Cabinet with reference to such course, when in answer to a suggestion from parties in Chicago it was determined to leave the subject in the hands of the prosecuting officers, with instructions to them to act according to law. He has a newspaper slip from which he reads a letter of the Attorney General to those officers in Chicago, and criticises very severely the last paragraph, and says that the public will think that it is intended to fetter the trial of Genl Babcock. He proceeds at some length to refer to his own connection with these prosecutions and his relations with the President, and his desire to retire from the Cabinet. In the course of his remarks he alludes to his position as a possible candidate for the Presidency. . . . He reminded me that last summer he had proposed to resign, and that in September he went to Long Branch having his resignation in his pocket and had handed it to the President, who had told him that he did not wish to accept it, that he was throwing away a great opportunity that he was more likely than any one person to be named as his successor, and that there was no one whom he would prefer, and he begged him to take back his resignation, which he did; and that the President added that he would be in Washington about Oct 1st, when they could consider the subject again if necessary; that the President did not return until some weeks after the time named and that nothing further had been done on the subject. He spoke of the rumor now prevalent of a disagreement between him and the President, which he says was without foundation, although the Presidents manner was *cold*, distrustful and at times offensive, and severe in his insinuations and his remarks. . . ." DLC-Hamilton Fish. See note to Horace Porter, [*Feb. 5–6, 1876*]; letter to Edwards Pierrepont, July 29, 1876; Nevins, *Fish*, pp. 801–2. On Feb. 14, Fish described a conversation with USG. "He then said he wished to say some things in confidence which I was not to repeat even in confidence to any one and alluded to the relation to certain parties with himself which were to him painful and embarrassing. I abstained from making any memorandum of what was said in consequence of his request for entire confidence. (Confidential memorandum given on March 6th, attached in margin) . . . The President spoke of the Babcock trial which he said was a prosecution aimed at himself not Babcock; that the Secretary of the Treasury had become possessed with the idea of the complicity of the President, and was using his office for the purpose of annoying him. That he had been watched by detectives when in St Louis and while going there, and that these detectives were endeavoring at the present time to collect evidence that a subscription had been made, by the parties charged with the Whiskey Frauds in St Louis, to raise money to pay his Hotel and travelling Bills, and all sorts of small devises were being resorted to to annoy him, and hold him up to public condemnation; that he did not so much charge this upon the Secretary himself as upon a number of men who were attaching themselves on him, in the hopes of his elevation to the Presidency, but that he was yielding to it and allowing himself to be made a party to these proceedings. He spoke very bitterly of Bluford Wilson who he said was manipulating and controlling these movements; that the law vested the entire control of prosecutions in the office of the Attorney General, but that Bristow and Wilson were attempting to assume their direction. I told him I understood that the law gave the control of suits for violation of Internal Revenue Laws to the Treasury Department. He said no, that he had examined the law together with the Attorney General and that the Attorney General had the entire control of it; that the Babcock trial would soon be over and that as soon as it was the Secretary of the Treasury should leave the Cabinet. I asked if he had made up his mind as to the successor. He said he thought he had, and that he would transfer the Attorney General to the Treasury Department, and asked my opinion. I said I understood his question to apply to his having come to a decision to make a change; if so, he knew my relations with Pierrepont and would understand that I would have no personal objection, but I thought the fact of change should be well considered—He said upon that he was determined that Bristow should not remain in his Cabinet." DLC-Hamilton Fish. On Feb. 22, Fish urged USG to keep Bristow in the cabinet. ". . . He said that efforts were being made to secure to Bristow the Democratic nomination. . . . He thought that the Democrats would adopt him as they had Greely. I thought not 1st because of their ill success in the Greely movement 2d because they could ensure the election of their own candidate by inducing Bristow's friends to nominate and support him and 3d that I had too much confidence in Bristows integrity, and believed he would under no circumstances accept a Democratic Nomination that I believed him firmly attached to the Republican Party and I had reason to know he felt most painfully his present position. He finally assented and said he would do nothing intended to lead to Bristow's withdrawal. I then spoke of Bluford Wilson whom I told him I did not know by sight, but who from what I heard might I heard have been led into doing things personally unfriendly to the President; that Sen Conkling told me there was written evidence to that effect, that if this be so it might be well presented as a reason, but the relations of the Solicitor to the head of the Department were of such confidential a nature that the removal of the Solicitor on rumors and without absolute proof of disloyalty to the Administration would be a movement against the Secretary himself. He said that no movement should be made against Wilson on mere rumor or without proof. He then proceeded to say that he scarcely saw how the Secretary could remain and doubted whether he would and asked what I thought in the event of his resigning of the transfer of Judge Pierrepont to the Treasury; saying he is thoroughly sound on the Currency question and that he could fill his place with a District Attorney from Ohio or from the West. I replied assenting to Pierreponts soundness on the financial question and added that I knew he had given the subject a great deal of study and had on one occasion said to me that he understood that business better than any other Department of the Government. I then told him Schencks place was about to be vacant and that it had once been offered to Pierrepont and that since the intelligence had been received of Schenck's resignation he had spoken to me on the subject and had intimated more than a willingness to have it, saying that while he should like, it he would not seek it, or accept it, if either the President or myself thought he had better not" *Ibid.*

On March 7, Bristow wrote to Bluford Wilson, solicitor of the treasury. ". . . The President sent for me yesterday to say that he was continually told of unfriendly acts and speeches of yours and Adams. He says it is represented that your room is the rendezvous of unfriendly newspaper correspondents, and that on the day the announcement of Belknap's crime was made you exclaimed in the presence of a member of Congress, 'Well, there is a God in Israel yet,' as if you rejoiced at the announcement; he also said that he was told that you said some days ago, 'If I go out the Secretary will go too.' I told him that I knew nothing of these matters and had never heard of them, but advised him to send for you and talk with you upon the whole subject, which he promised to do after to-day. . . ." *HMD*, 44-1-186, 370. On March 9, Wilson wrote to USG. "I forward the inclosed letter from General Wilson because I am too unwell to deliver it in person and too weak to write you in detail. He writes you, doubtless, because of a note from me that you were again troubled by stories touching my fidelity to you and your administration. I regret that you are subjected to such annoyance on my account, but I believe if you could see your way either to confront me with those who run to you with their idle inventions, or to give me their names, that I could safely promise there would soon be an end of the whole matter. I have for now nearly seven years waged persistent warfare upon your enemies and those of your administration whenever I had just cause to suspect dishonesty and wrong. I have tried always to keep the facts under my feet and right on my side. I do not claim that I have not made mistakes; doubtless I have made many. I have also made many enemies, some of them having power and influence. I do not ask you to protect me against them, but I do ask that you will at least give me equal opportunity to be heard in my own defense." *Ibid.* On March 8, James H. Wilson, New York City, had written to USG. "*Personal . . .* I take the liberty of writing to you, because I cannot spare the time to visit you for a personal interview. I am informed that you have again expressed dissatisfaction with the Solicitor of the Treasury, on the Ground that he has expressed himself gratified at the discovery of Belknap's crime, and that his office is 'a rendezvous of the correspondents.' I recognize the fact that I have no right to interfere in this matter except as your friend and Major Wilson's; but this is a grave crisis in your affairs as well as in his, and I therefore beg of you to consider well, whether you can afford to cut off a friend, much less an able and efficient officer at the instance of those who are mean enough to fill your ears with lies against him. If he were assailed by such men as Judge Edmunds, or Mr Morrill instead of by such as Logan and West, I might well exclaim 'Strike and Spare not,' but as he enjoys the confidence of good men wherever known, I trust you will not condemn him unheard. Please send for him to explain, whatever needs explanation, or shut your ears and *doors* against those who take up your time in misrepresenting him. One word more. The end of all the rascality has not been reached yet, and I beg of you, do not stay the hands of those whose duty it may be to hunt it down & bring it to punishment. You can well afford to forgive an excess of zeal in friends or foes, if they only help you in the great work of reforming the public service, and enforcing the laws. Your good name, is equally with the country, concerned in the course you may choose now, and I for one have the greatest confidence that you will turn your back upon mere politicians and time servers, and give your counsel & support to honest men and good officers in the performance of their duties. Every man who helps you punish or expose a thief, is entitled to your support and countenance. I know Maj. Wilson has been your firm and loyal friend always and has done no act to merit your displeasure. Please send for him & confront him with the men who accuse him! I trust that you will call to your assistance in all the high offices of your administration, the wisest & purest men you can find & that you will get rid of all who have lost or never had the public confidence. Genl Sharpe will be in Washington by the time this reaches you. I hope you'll talk further with him. I will not trouble you with renewed assurances of my own fidelity, for if our friendship of fifteen years will not stand the assaults of those who charge me with having 'talked against you,' I have only to express my unfeigned regret, . . ." ALS, USG 3. Bluford Wilson later testified that he asked USG for the names of his accusers. ". . . He refused to do that, although I asked him; but I knew full well, upon information entirely satisfactory to me, who they were. . . . They were, first and above all, Charles B. Farwell, of Chicago; John A. Logan, of Illinois; Senator Spencer, of Alabama, and Stephen Hurlbut, of the House, . . ." *HMD*, 44-1-186, 372. On June 20, Wilson wrote to USG. "For the reasons explained to you, at our interview this morning, I have the honor to tender my resignation, as Solicitor of the Treasury, to take effect on the first day of July next. Permit me to express my gratitude for the opportunities for public usefullness which you have been kind enough to give me, and to renew the assurance of my high personal regard." ALS, USG 3. *HMD*, 44-1-186, 372. On July 15, Simon S. Davis, Cincinnati, telegraphed to USG. "The appointment of C. H. Blackburn as Solicitor of the Treasury would meet the hearty approval of Cincinnati Republicans I trust you will favorably consider his application. He will call upon you in person on Monday." Telegram received (at 2:10 P.M.), DNA, RG 56, Appointments Div., Treasury Offices, Letters Received. On July 17, Benjamin Eggleston, Cincinnati, telegraphed to USG recommending Charles H. Blackburn. Telegram received (at 3:54 P.M.), *ibid.* No appointment followed. On July 22, USG nominated George F. Talbot to replace Wilson.

On April 5, Fish had recorded in his diary a conversation with USG. "He refers to some testimony, which has been given before one of the Committees, with much feeling, and asks if I have seen the testimony of Henderson of St Louis. I had only seen a brief allusion to it in one of the Washington papers which is all that he has seen; but he says that Mr Broadhead late 2d Comptroller of the Treasury had told him this morning that Henderson's testimony was very personal and he is evidently impressed with new suspicion against Bluford Wilson & Bristow. He has been induced to believe that they had employed detective Bell to abstract papers, important to the defense of Babcock, and to create prejudice against the President. I suggest to him that there may be an object in pursuading him of such feelings—He admits this but says he intends to know, and if such feelings do exist he is determined to have a clearing up." DLC-Hamilton Fish. On May 15, Fish spoke with Bristow. "He said . . . that his continuance in the Cabinet was excessively irksome and disagreeable to him; that the President was again under the influence of the Whiskey Ring and accepts their statements and was about to remove one of Commissioner Pratt's most trusted officers, that he had made up his mind to ask the President to fix a day when he should retire from the Cabinet that he was undecided whether to ask him to name the first of June or the end of the present fiscal year, but he would not remain longer; that he was being charged with circulating reports against others when in point of fact there was a band of detectives who were dismissed persons from the Department for fraud and improper conduct who were persecuting him in every possible way, visiting every part of the country, where he had ever lived or practiced law or done any business, hunting up every case, in which he had been employed and every transaction in which he had been engaged, misrepresenting them and maligning him; that these persons were impecunious had an office in Washington and were supported by funds drawn from New York and directed by those hostile to himself, that he could and would no longer endure the annoyance of his position. . . ." *Ibid.*

On June 6 and subsequently, Fish recorded in his diary. "During the session of the Cabinet the President requested me to remain after its close. He then told me confidentially that Bristow had been to see him yesterday after I had left and had a long conversation during which he said he wished to retire from the Cabinet on the 20th instant, he named that day as it would be his birthday when he would be 44 years old. The President said that he had thought of but two persons in connection with the succession viz. Courtland Parker of N J. and Kasson of Iowa asking my opinion with regard to them and whether I had thought or could think of any one else. I told him I was not prepared to express an opinion. He requested me to think of it and see him again in a few days that he wished nothing said of it, as he had not mentioned the fact and probably would not until after the Cincinnati Convention." "June 18th . . . The President called during the afternoon to talk about Bristows resignation and the appointment of a successor. He suggested the transfer of either Chandler or Cameron to the Treasury. Washburnes name was again spoken of and he evidently does not want him; he says while he is honest & able he is self-willed and would run the Department according to his own pleasure regardless of the President, the Cabinet or Congress. He says that Kasson should not leave the House. He then asks what I think of another change referring to the Post master General. I express my opinion that it is not advisable unless for good reason. He however seems strongly inclined to make the change." "Monday June 19th . . . He does not wish to consider the names of Washburne & Kasson for the Treasury Department and thinks that Chandlers transfer from the Interior Department not entirely satisfactory but that Cameron from the War Department would be. I find he had an interview last night with Senator Conkling & Jones. I ask if he is sure of Cameron being sound on the currency question, saying that his father is a little shakey and that it is most important should not only be strong but aggressive. The name of Sen Morrill of Maine was proposed and he assented very cordially saying he would write to him for an interview this evening He spoke of a change in the Post Office Department and added if Morrill would accept the Treasury it would be easy to ask Jewells resignation on geographical grounds." *Ibid.* On June 21, USG nominated and the Senate confirmed Lot M. Morrill to replace Bristow. On June 28 and 29, Fish recorded in his diary. "Receiving a message from the President I called to see him and he referred to his trouble with regard to the Secretaryship of the Treasury saying that several Senators had called on him urging the importance of Mr Morrills remaining in his present position and that he was at a loss who to appoint. He suggests the name of Onslow Stearnes late Governor of New Hampshire but did not himself think the appointment would be satisfactory he begged me to suggest some name and said he would send for Morrill and explain the necessity of a decision. I named Kasson of Iowa, he said he had spoken of him with some Senators who admit his ability and friendship to the Administration but say there are things connected with his history which will be embarrassing, among other things he has brought a libel suit in which he failed in obtaining a verdict and has gone no further in the case. I remarked that he might be forced to make the transfer he had spoken of on a former occasion—He replied that he did not think, that he had thought it over and given up the idea. He spoke of Genl Garfield but said he was from Ohio and that the stories of the Credit Mobilier stuck to him although he believed him to be innocent of any improper conduct. He spoke of James Wilson of Iowa as being as thoroughly competent as any man in the United States but entirely disqualified by his identification with speculative Rail Roads." "Called on the President on my way to the Office at his request. The names of person for Secty of the Treasury were discussed I told him I had been unable to think of any one except Gov Rice of Mass beyond those names we had previously talked of He expresses a fear that if Gov Rice were appointed he might not be willing to make all the changes in the internal of the Department which he thinks necessary The only other name spoken of was Courtland Parker and when I left his inclination seemed, in case Morrill declined, (whom he sent to ask to call at about noon today) towards Parker" *Ibid.* On July 7, Morrill resigned as U.S. Senator from Maine.

On July 5, Silas Reed, Boston, had written to USG. "*Personal* . . . I beg you to accept, Mr President, my very sincere congratulations because of the recent changes in the Treasy Dept. In all your eventful life you never suffered a tenth part of the harm & ingratitude from false friends, that you have recd from the late head of that Dept—My long political experience does not furnish me with so gross an instance of base ingratitude towards a benefactor, as this, & all from personal ambition—The Yaryan case creates a sensation which I hope Mr Woodward of St. L. (& perhaps Mr Douglass) can now aid in counteracting by his or thier experiences with those detectives a year ago." ADf (initialed), CtY. See Note, [*July 1, 1876*].

On July 16, John A. Joyce, Jefferson City, wrote to Orville E. Babcock. "*Confidential* . . . I see that Bluford Wilson is going before the Committee, proposing to know a great deal and will raise the devil if he can with the Republican party and the Administration. Now: here is a piece of unwritten history that can be given to the world if McD. and myself are placed in the air of freedom, and before any tribunal where we can show the *conspiracy* put up & carried out by the subordinates of the President to ruin himself & the Party. Just after the seizures in St. Louis last May, a year ago, Wilson visited the city to see Hawley & Dyer—McDonald and myself met him at the Lindell Hotel—this was before any indictments were found—Wilson conversed with McD & self very earnestly and walked with us from the Lindell Hotel up 6th street to the Southern Hotel; and this is the guts of his conversation. 'I know that you gentlemen have been faithful politicians, are more sinned against than sinning, and if you have done anything wrong, they are sins of omission and not of commission—We want to get at the bottom and *top* of this thing, and Bristow and myself have full charge of everything now—We know that Grant & Babcock & others know all about this fraud and we want to catch them—Bristow is determined to get at the *Top* and if you gentlemen join us, all will be right and you shall have no trouble—What we want is to show up the White House and burst the Third Term. Now this is strictly confidential and I hope you will go right in with us, and if Bristow is elected President as he will be, if he gets the nomination, you men can have front seats' Many other things of this same character were said, when McD & Wilson got in a carriage and drove to the Depot on the Illinois side—Before leaving Wilson, we told him that we knew nothing of the W. H. but what was square & honest and if we had to purchase our liberty by perjury, he might as well crack his whip. Now, Genl. if we are put in position we will put this damnable conspiracy before the country & show that the whiskey prosecutions were not for the sake of law & right, but for ambition & vengeance." ALS, Babcock Papers, ICN.

On Aug. 1, John Tyler, Jr., Clifton, Md., wrote to USG. "In relation to the testimony of Bluford Wilson before the Investigating Committee of the House of Representatives, it is not a little Singular that in various conversations here as to its character and bearings, that I should invariably have assumed and said that it made patent to my mind, through my past habits as a lawyer, that a Conspiracy existed between Bristow, Wilson and Webster, at least, and in all probability embraced Jewell, to seize upon your thunder in respect to the Whisky frauds, although acting under your orders and instructions, so that Bristow and Jewell should be presented to the Country as a Republican Reform Presidential ticket, diverting and directing the prosecution of the business in such manner as to stab you under the fifth rib through the implication of Babcock and others of your household and near your person and confidence. My intimate knowledge of the elements entering into the Kentucky and Tenessee and Mississippi Valley and Cotton states character contributed also not a little to this conclusion of my mind—Selfish, false and treacherous in the extreme as that Character is, after the Gambling, Land-Speculating and horse-trading order in all things, while affecting to be every thing that it is not. I am led to these remarks by a Paragraph in the 'Sun' of this morning upon the subject from which it appears that 'the president is preparing a statement to show, as he believes, that Bristow and Wilson entered into a Conspiracy to injure him, so that Bristow might be prominently before the public as a Presidential Candidate.' If this statement be true as to yourself it is singular how truly I should have divined that which you believe and have reason to know. Will you pardon me for adding that this led me to take out of my trunk the Copy I had preserved of the letter I addressed you on the 29th October 1873, 'on the political status of Florida,' in reply to which General Babcock wrote on the 13th November 1873 as follows—'Your letter is at hand. I will place the paper you send in the hands of the president as you request. I shall always be pleased to attend to your requests.' If you still have that Communication in your office, Mr President, and desire to save Florida this Fall to the Republican Party, seeing that the National success of the Party may even hang upon the four votes of that state, it might be well at some leisure moment, if, indeed, you ever have leisure, for you to recur to it as I have done. It is truthful so far as it goes and has much in it still precisely applicable to the political Condition & situation there, particularly in reference to the false and treacherous political attitude of *Senator* Conover—. . ." ALS, Tyler Papers, College of William and Mary, Williamsburg, Va. See *PUSG*, 26, 452–54.

On Aug. 2, James M. Tomeny, Washington, D. C., wrote to USG. "Having for a number of years, through the Departments and the Courts, made efforts to recover to the United States Treasury, a large sum of money due from the Mobile and Ohio Railroad Company, and finally having, on the eve of success, been defeated by the extraordinary, unjust, and perhaps corrupt, action of the late Secretary and Solicitor of the Treasury, I beg to lay before you the facts in the case, for such action as it may be deemed proper for the President to take. . . . Wm Butler Duncan (of Duncan Sherman & Co) President of the Road, came to Washington, wined and dined with the Secretary (as I am informed) and from that date the U. S. Court at Mobile lost jurisdiction of the M. and O. R. R. case and Mr. Bristow took it under his special charge. Before the next term of the Court Mr Duncan had *persuaded* the Secretary, and late Solicitor, to accept $22.564.80, instead of $114,674.91, in gold, which latter sum, would, beyond all question, have been the amount of the judgment of the Court in favor of the United States, the collection of which could have been readily enforced against the Company. The loss to the Government was just $92,110.11 in gold coin, and this by one single official act of the late reform Secretary of the Treasury. If this wrong can be made to appear right, by any of the arts of sophistry, Messrs Wilson and Bristow, will doubtless be found equal to the emergency, but you, Mr. President, in my humble judgment, should cause the whole case to be re-examined, Mr. Bristow's compromise to be set aside, if that can legally be done, and the payment of this ninety two thousand dollars ($92,000) into the Treasury of the United States to be enforced through the proper judicial tribunals. . . . I have intimated, Mr President, that the compromise was corruptly obtained. The justification for this opinion, is found, not only in the extraordinary circumstances under which the decision was made, but also in the fact, communicated to me in Mobile, on January 20. 1875, by United States Attorney Duskin, that a direct proposition was made to him, to pay him several thousand dollars, if he would merely recommend a compromise. This bribe he indignantly spurned, and from first to last, opposed the compromise, which was finally made by Mr. Bristow, without consultation with, or recommendation from the Attorneys prosecuting the case, or from any agent of his own Department, so far as I am able to ascertain. The question naturally arises—If this Company, or some one for them, were willing to pay so large a bribe to the U. S. Attorney at Mobile, merely to obtain his recommendation of a compromise, which they failed to get, how much would they pay here for the compromise itself? Hence my conviction that the settlement was corruptly procured, and should be set aside." ALS, DNA, RG 206, Closed Cases. On Aug. 5, USG endorsed this letter. "Refered to the Sec. of the Treas. Please have these papers carefully examined." AES, *ibid.* On April 2, 1869, David A. Nunn, former U.S. Representative from Tenn., Washington, D. C., had written to USG concerning Tomeny. ". . . He was Earnest active and unwavering in his loyalty to the Government all through the War,   He worked constantly and faithfully for the reorganization of a loyal State Government, for emancipation by State action in Tennessee; was amoung the first to advocate the equality of all men before the law, the removal of all disabilities on account of race or color, and every progressive measure of the National Republican party, and has at all times contributed largley of his private means for these purposes. . . ." ALS, *ibid.*, RG 60, Records Relating to Appointments. Related papers are *ibid.* See Johnson, *Papers*, 6, 299–300; *ibid.*, 16, 696.

On Aug. 2, 1876, Benjamin F. Butler, Boston, endorsed to USG a letter of Aug. 1 from John D. Sanborn concerning "the use of the Government funds to run the 'Bristow machine.'" "The writer of this communication is a man who knows as much about the workings of the Internal Revenue Bureau as a political machine as anybody, and I would recommend that he be allowed to see the records to ascertain what use has been made of the funds in the late Presidential Campaign." ES (facsimile), R. M. Smythe & Co., Inc., June 12, 1997, no. 320. On Aug. 9, USG endorsed this letter. "Refered to the Sec. of the Treas. for such action,—and examination into alleged abuses,—as he may deem proper." AES (facsimile), *ibid.*

On Aug. 12, Charles E. Dailey, former clerk, Treasury Dept., Washington, D. C., wrote to USG. "I beg the favor to be heard in my own behalf in a matter concerning which an unfortunate controversy occurred in your presence between Ex-Secretary Bristow, the Hon. B. F. Wade and myself, about one year and a half ago. It will occupy too much of your valuable time to restate here the circumstances which lead me to solicit another interview; suffice it to say, Mr. Bristow did me a great injustice on an unwarrantable pretext, and condecended to pursue and misrepresent me to you, and to my friend Mr. Wade, notwithstanding every fact and presumption of truth cleary showed him to be in error, as shown by the word of Genl Spinner *then*, and *since*. As his administration of the Treasury demonstrated, Mr. Bristow labored hard for supremacy, no matter what the consequences to friend or foe. No man did more to bring into disrepute the Administration and its Head than Mr. Bristow, and whoever, in whatever position, he esteemed inimical to him or his interests, he determined to crush. Why he should disregard your expressed desire to have me dealt fairly with, and so tyrannically and unjustly pesist in doing me an injury, to say nothing of added abuse, can be accounted for only on the ground of his extravagant desire to rule. He abused his high office, and not only that, he abused the confidence of the President, and maltreated those subordinate to him. My hard earned experience in the public service entitles me to respect, and should merit better treatment than that had at the hands of Mr. Bristow. Trusting you will grant me the interview I ask, and hoping for that assistance which my necessities alone prompt me to seek.—" ALS, DNA, RG 56, Letters Received from the President.

On Aug. 16, Henry E. Wrigley, Titusville, Pa., wrote to USG. "I have no axe to grind or favors to ask—but I have just read the acct. of your 'interview' in N. Y Herald. and it occurred to me that were I in your place it might be pleasant to know that not only as an old member of your Staff with you as Engineer for a short time before Vicksburg—but as a born and bred democrat voting that ticket except in your case for the past fourteen years, I cannot refrain from expressing my *utter detestation* of the attacks and the *manner* of attack which the leaders of our party have thought fit to make upon you. . . ." ALS, USG 3. On Aug. 14, a correspondent had interviewed USG at the White House about "the attacks upon him recently, and those particularly in the evidence adduced before the Committee on the Whisky Frauds, . . . The names of ex-Secretary Bristow and ex-Solicitor Wilson came up, of course, most prominently. . . ." *New York Herald*, Aug. 15, 1876. On Aug. 16, J. R. Bailey, public school principal, Homewood, Pa., wrote to USG. "You will pardon, I hope, the presumption of a young man who desirs to thank you for the *honorable, able,* and *honest* policy you have pursued in the administration of the public affairs of this great people. A close observation of your career in Military and Civil life, compels me to render *honor* and *gratitude* to *you,* as the preserver of the unity of this nation. And when I see men so quickly forgetting, or ignoring your noble services, and who, to make political capital, and to gain political ends, hesitate not to apply to you epithets the most vile, charges maliciously false, and charges monstrously absurd, I blush that I am an American Citizen. Noble President, go forward in the path you have pursued from the beginning; never heed the storm of abuse, of slander, of bellowings and ravings uttered by traitorous, rebellious, and ungrateful tongues and pens, but rest assured that deep down in the American heart there is remembered, and ever shall be remembered, the name and fame of the *patriot Soldier* and *Statesman*—U. S. Grant—who conquered *Secession* and *Rebellion,* and who preserved the *American Union.*" ALS, USG 3.

On Oct. 12, Fish recorded in his diary a conversation with USG. "He expressed great confidence of Hayes election and that in the event of his election he had no one to ask him to appoint or to retain in office though he felt interest in many but he did hope he would not appoint one person and that was Bristow who was the only person who had been associated with him in his Cabinet who on parting had left an unpleasant impression who he shaid had been trecherous in the Cabinet and after he left it and went into several details some of which were in accordance with what I knew others were perfectly new to me but of a nature to call fourth much of the feeling which the President manifested. I expressed regret to learn these things and the state of feeling they had produced on the President. He said Bristows nature was one of intense selfishness and ambition and of extreme jealousey and suspicion and that from the time he entered the Cabinet he had set his eye on the Presidency with a distrust and hostility to himself (the President) and to every member of the Cabinet adding not less to you than to the others although he never dared to

manifest it to you as he did toward them. I remarked that I never had known of any disagreement between Bristow & Belknap or Robeson that for a period he had been extremely
intimacy with Jewell & Pierrepont though I was aware that latterly he had withdrawn his
confidence from both of them and he never had any respect for Belknap that I had never
heard Bristow say anything unkind of Robeson though Robeson had told me of his dislike
and mistrust of Bristow and that Bristows conduct to me had always been kind and
friendly to the very last. The President replied yes! not because he loved you any better
than the others but because he feared you: to which I said I knew no cause why he should
hear me. The President added he feared to differ with you on account of your general character and sought to appear in harmony with you before the public but would have turned
upon you as quick as the others but for that cause. He said he should not attempt to
influence Hayes but he Should be extremely sorry were he to offer Bristow an appointment
which he thought was what Bristow was seeking. The conversation was a sad and painful
one to me for personally I liked Bristow although I think that he has given the President
much ground for his present feelings." DLC-Hamilton Fish. See Ross A. Webb, *Benjamin
Helm Bristow: Border State Politician* (Lexington, Ky., 1969), pp. 219–52; H. V. Boynton,
"The Whiskey Ring," *North American Review*, CXXIII, CCLIII (Oct., 1876), 280–327.

To Congress

To THE SENATE AND HOUSE OF REPRESENTATIVES:

By the tenth Article of the Treaty between the United States and
Great Britain, signed in Washington on the ninth day of August,
1842, it was agreed that the two governments should upon mutual
requisitions, respectively made, deliver up to justice all persons, who
being charged with certain crimes therein enumerated, committed
within the jurisdiction of either, should seek an asylum, or be found
within the territories of the other.

The only condition or limitation contained in the Treaty to the
reciprocal obligation thus to deliver up the fugitive, was, that it
should be done only upon such evidence of criminality as according
to the laws of the place where the fugitive or person so charged
should be found, would justify his apprehension and commitment for
trial, if the crime or offence had there been committed.

In the month of February last a requisition was duly made in
pursuance of the provisions of the Treaty by this government upon
that of Great Britain for the surrender of one Ezra D. Winslow,
charged with extensive forgeries and the utterance of forged paper,
committed within the jurisdiction of the United States, who had

sought an asylum, and was found within the territories of Her Britannic Majesty, and was apprehended in London. The evidence of the criminality of the fugitive was duly furnished and heard, and being found sufficient to justify his apprehension and commitment for trial if the crimes had been committed in Great Britain, he was held and committed for extradition.

Her Majesty's Government, however, did not deliver up the fugitive in accordance with the terms of the Treaty, notwithstanding every requirement thereof had been met on the part of the United States, but instead of surrendering the fugitive demanded certain assurances or stipulation not mentioned in the treaty, but foreign to its provisions, as a condition of the performance by Great Britain of her obligations under the Treaty. In a recent communication to the House of Representatives, and in answer to a call from that body for information on this case, I submitted the correspondence which has passed between the two governments with reference thereto. It will be found in Executive Document No. 173, of the House of Representatives of the present session, and I respectfully refer thereto for more detailed information bearing on the question.

It appears from the correspondence that the British government bases its refusal to surrender the fugitive, and its demand for stipulations or assurances from this government on the requirements of a purely domestic enactment of the British Parliment, passed in the Year 1870.

This Act was brought to the notice of this government shortly after its enactment, and Her Majesty's government was advised that the United States understood it as giving continued effect to the existing engagements under the treaty of 1842, for the extradition of criminals—and with this knowledge on its part, and without dissent from the declared views of the United States as to the unchanged nature of the reciprocal rights and obligations of the two powers, under the Treaty, Great Britain has continued to make requisitions and to grant surrenders in numerous instances, without suggestion that it was contemplated to depart from the practice under the treaty which has obtained for more than thirty years, until now, for the first time, in this case of Winslow, it is assumed that under this Act of

Parliment Her Majesty may require a stipulation or agreement, not provided for in the treaty, as a condition to the observance by her government of its treaty obligations towards this country. This I have felt it my duty emphatically to repel.

In addition to the case of Winslow, requisition was also made by this government on that of Great Britain for the surrender of Charles J. Brent, also charged with forgery, committed in the United States and found in Great Britain. The evidence of criminality was duly heard and the fugitive committed for extradition.

A similar stipulation to that demanded in Winslow's case was also asked in Brent's, and was likewise refused.

It is with extreme regret that I am now called upon to announce to you that Her Majesty's government has finally released both of these fugitives, Winslow and Brent, and set them at liberty, thus omitting to comply with the provisions and requirements of the treaty under which the extradition of fugitive criminals is made between the two governments.

The position thus taken by the British government, if adhered to, cannot but be regarded as the abrogation and annulment of the Article of the treaty on Extradition.

Under these circumstances it will not, in my judgment, comport with the dignity or self-respect of this government, to make demands upon that government for the surrender of fugitive criminals, nor to entertain any requisition of that character from that government under the treaty.

It will be a cause of deep regret, if a treaty which has been thus beneficial in its practical operation; which has worked so well, and so efficiently, and which, notwithstanding the exciting, and at times violent political disturbances of which both countries have been the scene during its existence, has given rise to no complaints on the part of either government against either its spirit or its provisions— should be abruptly terminated.

It has tended to the protection of society, and to the general interests of both countries, its violation or annulment would be a retrograde step in international intercourse.

I have been anxious, and have made the effort to enlarge its scope, and to make a new treaty which would be a still more efficient agent for the punishment and prevention of crime. At the same time I have felt it my duty to entertain a proposition made by Great Britain, pending its refusal to execute the existing treaty, to amend it by practically conceding by treaty the identical conditions which that government demands under its Act of Parliment. In addition to the impossibility of the United States entering upon negotiations under the menace of an intended violation or a refusal to execute the terms of an existing treaty, I deemed it inadvisable to treat of only the one amendment proposed by Great Britain, while the United States desires an enlargement of the list of crimes for which extradition may be asked, and other improvements which experience has shown might be embodied in a new treaty.

It is for the wisdom of Congress to determine whether the Article of the treaty relating to extradition is to be any longer regarded as obligatory on the government of the United States or as forming part of the Supreme Law of the Land.

Should the attitude of the British government remain unchanged, I shall not, without an expression of the wish of Congress that I should do so, take any action either in making or granting requisitions for the surrender of fugitive criminals under the treaty of 1842.

Respectfully submitted,
U. S. GRANT.

WASHINGTON, JUNE 20. 1876.

Copy, DNA, RG 59, Reports to the President and Congress. *SED*, 44-1-79; *HED*, 44-1-178; *SMD*, 49-1-162, part 2, II, 786–89; *Foreign Relations, 1876*, pp. 253–55. On June 10, 1876, USG wrote to the House of Representatives. "I transmit, herewith, in answer to the Resolution of the House of Representatives of the 30th. day of March last, a report from the Secretary of State with accompanying papers, which presents the correspondence and condition of the question up to the day of its date." Copies, DNA, RG 59, Reports to the President and Congress; *ibid.*, RG 130, Messages to Congress. *HED*, 44-1-173. On June 16, Friday, Secretary of State Hamilton Fish recorded in his diary. "I mention the discharge of Winslow and a discussion was held as to the proper course to pursue The President was inclined to give notice of the termination of the Treaty I thought no notice was necessary, but suggested that the President send a message to Congress simply stating the facts, declaring his intention not to execute the Treaty in the future unless an expression of Congress be had to that effect, but recommending that it be declarred by Congress annulled and broken by the Act of Great Britain. . . . I read the rough draft of an act of repeal which was approved and the President requested me to prepare a message to be sent to Congress on Monday" DLC-Hamilton Fish. See *ibid.*, June 18, 1876; message to Senate, Dec. 23, 1876.

On March 3, 1875, USG had authorized James Mooney to extradite Charles L. Lawrence, "alias George G. Gordon," charged with forgery, from Great Britain. Copy, DNA, RG 59, General Records. On May 18, Lawrence, New York City, petitioned USG claiming that charges of smuggling and conspiracy had been added after he had been returned to the U.S., in violation of the 1870 British extradition act. DS, *ibid.*, RG 60, Letters Received, N. Y. On May 20, USG endorsed this petition. "Respectfully refered to the Atty. Gen.l" AES, *ibid.* On May 21, Col. James B. Fry, asst. AG, New York City, telegraphed to Col. Rufus Ingalls, care of Orville E. Babcock. "Burnside telegraphs that he will forward letter in Case of Lawrence today, So you can mention it as made," Telegram received (at 10:00 A.M.), DLC-USG, IB. Also on May 21, Fish recorded in his diary a lengthy cabinet discussion of the Lawrence case. ". . . I further expressed the opinion that this question was not properly of executive consideration but a Judicial one and must be raised if at all before the Courts Pierrepont thought it rather of a political nature to which I replied that if so it could only be raised by the British Government to be presented through its representatives and could not be brought before the Executive by an American Citizen charged with crime, or by his counsel . . . The President is of opinion that as a political question it cannot be entertained as now presented; that the question is for the courts and that the Attorney General refer the case to the Solicitor General assigning on the reference the reason for so doing viz that he had been Counsel for the prisoner previous to his (Attorney Genl) appointment: that the District Attorney of New York who is conducting the case be advised to suspend the proceedings on the charge of smuggling (the case being set down for tomorrow) until either the trial be had on the charge of forgery or until it be satisfactorally ascertained that the indictment for forgery cannot be maintained in which case the question will again come up for consideration." DLC-Hamilton Fish. On the same day, USG issued an order. "In the matter of Charles L Lawrence the Dist Atty of the Southern Dist of New York is directed to stay all proceedings except upon the charges upon which said Lawrence was extradited and until the report of the Solicitor General to whom the matter has been referred is made and until further order. And the Dist Atty may exercise his option as to the time when he will proceed upon the charges mentioned in the Warrant of Extradition" Copy, Columbia University, New York, N. Y. On July 16, Samuel F. Phillips, solicitor gen., addressed to USG a lengthy opinion on the Lawrence case. ". . . Upon the whole I am of opinion: I. That as there has been no promise, or conduct by any person who represented the United States in the proceedings for the Petitioner's extradition which modifies the operation of the Treaty upon his present condition that condition is here a question of *law*, not of *policy*. II. Therefore, that the President cannot interfere in the civil suit pending against the Petitioner; and, III. That no ground has been laid for an order to discharge the Petitioner from further prosecution upon the criminal matters specified in the petition. . . ." DS, DNA, RG 59, Miscellaneous Letters; copy, *ibid.*, RG 60, Opinions. *Official Opinions of the Attorneys-General*, XV, 500–15; *HED*, 44-1-173, 58–66. See Fish diary, Aug. 21, 1875, DLC-Hamilton Fish. On Oct. 26, Attorney Gen. Edwards Pierrepont wrote to USG. "I am obliged to be in the Supreme Court to-day and therefore absent from the Cabinet. I send the Opinion in the Extradition Case which [t]he Solicitor General prepared, the con[s]ideration of which, as you will remember, was defered until the return of the Secretary of State. I can say nothing about Lawrence, whose friends once retained me, but as this case will be a precedent for future action between two great Governments I wish to suggest that Lawrence [o]ught *first* to be tried upon the [c]harge for which he was extradited. If he is convicted on that charge no complications can arise; if he is aquitted, there will then be time enough to consider whether he can be tried upon a charge which is not extraditable. This latter question is a grave one, and as the decision of it will form a precedent, it would seem prudent to delay action which a conviction on the extradited charge may render wholly unnecessary . . . If the President desires this can be read in Cabinet" ALS, DNA, RG 59, Miscellaneous Letters. On Oct. 26 and 29, Fish recorded in his diary. "The President spoke to me about the case of Charles L. Lawrence whose extradition was obtained from Great Britain on the charge of forgery   he stated that Col Bliss the District Attorney thought he could not convict him of the charge of forgery but wishes to convict him on the charge of smuggling; that he (Genl Grant) was opposed to having him tried on other than the charge named in the Extradition; that Great Britain might then obtain the surrender of parties from this country and try them for other charges than those for which their Extradition is asked. . . ." ". . . I expressed my concurrence in the conclusion reached by the Solicitor General; that the United States were not restricted to the to the trial on the single charge of forgery, named in the requirementsition and warrant of Extradition; but were at liberty to proceed against him, on any other criminal charges, and also and also to continue the prosecution of a civil suit which which had been instituted against him for the recovery of several hundred thousand dollars, of duties on goods alledged to have been fraudulently introduced by his practices; but I thought that on the first warrant instance; in duty to ourselves, the prosecution should be '*bona fide*' and vigorously pressed, on the complaint named in the papers of Extradition; that there was no authority or justification on the part of the government, or claim of right on the part of the defendant for the suspension of proceedings in the civil suit; and that the government should take such steps as it saw fit with regard to other charges or complaints as to the criminality of Lawrence   Bristow said he concurred in this view; the President then directed the Attorney General to instruct the District Attorney in New York *first* to proceed vigorously and *bona fide* in the prosecution of Lawrence on the complaint named in the Extradition papers; *Second* to continue the civil proceedings now pending, and on which he is under arrest; *third* to await instructions as to the prosecution of the other indictments and complaints against Lawrence   Pierrepont said that this was his own opinion, 'as had been expressed by him some time previously'; though until now I had supposed his opinion was the reverse" DLC-Hamilton Fish. See *ibid.*, Oct. 27, Nov. 27, Dec. 9, 1875.

On Jan. 30, 1876, Mayor Samuel C. Cobb of Boston telegraphed to USG. "E D Winslow a forger to an immense amount has fled to Rotterdam   will arrive there early this week   Can you waive official etiquette & use your good offices to have him delivered up to us & thus greatly subserve the cause of justice   mess Pierce & Harris of massachusetts know the facts" Telegram received (at 1:30 A.M.), DNA, RG 59, Miscellaneous Letters. On Feb. 17, USG authorized Albion P. Dearborn to extradite Ezra D. Winslow from Great Britain. Copy, *ibid.*, General Records. On March 9, USG authorized James E. Wilkinson to extradite Charles I. Brent, also charged with forgery, from Great Britain. Copy, *ibid.* On March 3, Fish had recorded in his diary. "I spoke of the demand made by the British Government that Winslow should simply be tried upon the offense named in the Warrent of Extradition   Jewell thought that the demand was right which I contested with great earnestness; Jewell said it was conceded by the Treaties of all other governments; whereupon I told him he knew but little of those treaties, that the fact that it was conceded by Treaty in this instance, and not in others showed, that it was a question of conventional agreement and not one of right, that for 30 years our treaty with Great Britain had existed and each government had under it felt at liberty to try surrendered fugitives for other crimes than those named in the warrant. That the question now is whether Great Britain can by act of Parliament impose new conditions, beyond those required by the Treaty—which I emphatically deny. The President sustains this view with great decision & promptness I then submit the form of reply which the President and all except Jewell approve Jewell remaining silent. On reading it Jewell asks what will be the result, to which I reply, they will either give up Winslow, or we shall regard the Treaty as terminated by the refusal of Great Britain to comply with it. The President says thats exactly right, we cannot allow another power to put without our assent its construction on our Treaty, changing it from the interpretation which both had put upon it for a series of years. The President directed the Telegram sent." DLC-Hamilton Fish. See *ibid.*, Feb. 17, 1876; *HED*, 44-1-173, 5; *Foreign Relations, 1876*, p. 208.

On April 7 and subsequently, Fish recorded in his diary. "The attitude taken by Great Britain on the subject of the Extradition of Winslow was discussed at length—I reading my instruction to Hoffman of the 31st March, which was approved and the President determined that the Treaty must be regarded at an end should Great Britain refuse to surrender Winslow on the ground assumed. Few questions have been more thoroughly discussed in Cabinet than this one was today." "Monday May 15th . . . found Bristow in conversation with the President and shortly there-after Pierrepont came in—On Wednesday last while in Philadelphia at Mr Childs shortly before going to the Exposition Bristow spoke to me of the instruction to Hoffman in the Winslow Extradition Case, of March 31 complimenting it very warmly, and said that Pierrepont had told him that he had arranged that Lawrence should be Extradited on only one of the thirteen indictments which had been sent against him. I took occasion therefore, the two being present, to express to the President . . . that General Schenck had told me that he thought Mullens, the Lawyer he had employed to present the case in London, had been tampered with; that I had received intimamations that the influences to induce the presentation of only one of the thirteen indictments had proceeded from this country in Lawrence's interest and I wished to be prepared to know how far to charge a want of good faith on the British Government in my reply and that as Judge Pierrepont had been a Counsel of Lawrence at the time he possibly might be able to advise. The Attorney General denied having been associated in the case at that time but said that when upon first learning that he had been extradited on only 1 of the 13 indictments he had expressed gratification in that it made it an easier case for Lawrence. Bristow and myself left the room together leaving Pierrepont with the President [I] asked Bristow if I had correctly understood him in Philadelphia that Pierrepont had claimed the origination of the plan for having him surrendered on only the one indictment; he repeats that he had not only said so distinctly but spoke of it with great exultation as a clever argument on his part, adding that he was not surprised at Pierreponts denial in the presence of the President for that Pierrepont could not tell the truth on any subject." "May 23d . . . Attorney General among other things referred to the pending trials against Lawrence in NewYork and states that Mr Webster has been employed as special Counsel and that he has received reports from both Messr Bliss & Webster but they do not agree in their conclusion—He reads part of the reports of each. The Secretary of the Treasury expresses a doubt whether Bliss will succeed in obtaining conviction. I refer to the fact that Mrs Lawrence as well as her husband is supposed to be in possession of information with regard to the circumstances attending his Extradition, which may be of very great political importance, that I am very desirous to obtain what they are supposed to be in possession of. Mr Bliss' proposition in the opinion of Judge Pierrepont, would not lead to the obtaining of this information. The President suggests to leave the matter in the hands of Mr Webster—To which I object as overlooking Mr Bliss and placing Mr Webster in a delicate position toward him and the case. The President proposes that it be left to the Court to decide what may be the value of the information given after that Lawrence should have plead guilty. Bristow remarks that the information would be of little value to the Treasury or to the prosecution of suites, that it is the political information which is to be of value if any and that the Court should not judge. I advise that it be left to the Attorney General and as Judge Taft yesterday was nominated and confirmed as such, but has not yet received his commission the result of the discussion was that Taft and Pierrepont should go to New York with power to decide the question They are to leave tomorrow morning—" "May 26th . . . Judge Taft has returned from New York where he has been with Judge Pierrepont to look after the Lawrence case. Lawrence he says pleads guilty with the understanding that he shall not be sentenced to more than two years imprisonment and has given some information which Taft considers as very important. He hands me some papers which he has brought back but they do not amount to much it strikes me." "June 6th . . . I read the telegram from Gov Bagley received yesterday in relation to Smith the murderer now in Canada and also my telegram to Mr Hawley the substance of which had been agreed upon yesterday with the President. He approves the telegram that pending the Winslow case we should have no more requisitions. This led to the consideration as it stands between Great Britain and the United States and the course to be pursued with regard to the two men in Boston concerning whom the proofs are being taken and of whom Sir Edward Thornton had addressed me a note some short time since, my judgment was that they should not be surrendered until the Winslow case has been decided, but the President was of a different opinion and was sustained by all of the Cabinet, holding that until Great Britain actually broke the Treaty by a refusal to surrender or by the actual discharge of Winslow the United States would comply on their part. I called attention to the fact that Lord Derby had refused the surrender, but the President considered that the remanding of Winslow was equivolent to still holding the question under advisement and that until Winslows release we should hold ourselves bound by the Treaty." DLC-Hamilton Fish. See *ibid.*, April 5, 28, June 8, 15, 1876, Feb. 23, 27, 1877; Sidney Webster to Fish, May 17, 1876, *ibid.*; *HED*, 44-1-173, 8–16; *Foreign Relations, 1876*, pp. 210–18, 305–6; *Foreign Relations, 1877*, p. 287.

On Aug. 12, Adam Badeau, consul gen., London, wrote to USG. "*Private* . . . I am determined for once to write you a letter in which I bother you with none of my own affairs. I want to tell you how universally the English press, and English statesmen (except those sworn to support the Government) approve the position of your administration on the Extradition matter. Govr Fish's arguments are pronounced incontrovertible, and he will find no difficulty in negotiating a new treaty with Lord Derby; for this nation desires and demands it. *I hope it may be undertaken at once,* so that a matter once taken up by your government may be brought *by it* to a successful conclusion. The diplomacy of the last eight years will bear a comparison with that of any previous period of the same length in American history; And I have never doubted that when the heat of party and the mists of personal interest have abated, the whole administration will be regarded as quite as successful as any that preceded it. When one considers the enormous difficulties it had to encounter, arising from the war—the conflict of races, the questions of finance, the dangers of foreign war—it will be held to have done wonders. As to the abuse which has been lavished on it, it will be forgotten, and men will be ashamed that they were ever opposed to its chief. There is just as much corruption, in instances, in England as in America, only here they hush it up, while in the U. S. it is spread out for the world to see. The English underrate, the Americans overrate their own faults. I have always thought that if I lived, it would be a worthy task hereafter, to clear away the clouds of abuse that have obscured the truth (in some quarters) about your civil administration, and a volume written or published when no possible motive but truth can be ascribed to the writer—may do much to accomplish this. Meanwhile the military history will be completed in *less* than six months if it goes on as it does now. It occupies and almost absorbs my mind, and is a good medicine for mind and body. I feel like my old self as I study the old scenes and talks and letters, and recall the old times, the old trials, marches, battles—and above all the chief by whose side the happiest hours of my life have been passed. Please dear General, make my best and kindest regards to Mrs Grant . . . Judge Pierrepont has been most cordially received, and appears to have made a capital impression" ALS, USG 3. See Badeau to Fish, Aug. 12, 1876, DLC-Hamilton Fish.

To John A. Logan

June 22. 1876—

DEAR GENERAL—

I should like it very much if you can manage to push through, as soon as possible, the bill authorizing General Emory to retire with the rank of Brigadier General—

General Sheridan is anxious to have Colonel Merritt—who will be promoted by Emorys retirement—take command of an expidition now started—

Yours Very Truly

U. S. GRANT—

GENL JOHN A. LOGAN. U. S. SENATE.—

Copy, DLC-USG, II, 3. On June 22, 1876, U.S. Senator John A. Logan of Ill. spoke in favor of a bill to retire Col. William H. Emory as brig. gen. ". . . This officer is the oldest officer in the Army of his rank. He has served forty-three years, and has been ten years in command according to the rank which he will hold if he is retired under the bill, but he has been jumped by appointments all the time and kept in the rank of colonel. . . ." *CR*, 44–1, 4005. On the same day, the Senate passed the bill; USG signed it on June 26. See *PUSG*, 26, 32–33.

On May 5 and June 22, Gen. William T. Sherman telegraphed to Lt. Gen. Philip H. Sheridan, Chicago. "The President seems loth to make the order about Emory, but promises that he will do so, before it is possible anything can happen to prejudice the rank of Merritt. If you have special and strong reasons for immediate action, give them and I will urge the matter again." "General Emory has appealed in person to the President to withhold the order for his retirement, for a few days, but you may act on the assurance that the order promoting Merritt will be made by July 1st" Copies, DNA, RG 108, Letters Sent. On July 8, USG nominated Wesley Merritt as col., 5th Cav., to date from July 1. See Paul L. Hedren, *First Scalp for Custer: The Skirmish at Warbonnet Creek, Nebraska, July 17, 1876* (Glendale, Calif., 1980), pp. 47–48.

Proclamation

———

The Centennial Anniversary of the day on which the people of the United States declared their right to a separate and equal station among the Powers of the Earth seems to demand an exceptional observance.

The founders of the Government at its birth and in its feebleness invoked the blessings and the protection of a Divine Providence, and the thirteen colonies and three millions of people have expanded into a nation of strength and numbers commanding the position which then was asserted and for which fervent prayers were then offered.

It seems fitting that on the occurrence of the hundredth anniversary of our existence as a Nation a grateful acknowledgment should be made to Almighty God for the protection and the bounties which He has vouchsafed to our beloved country.

I therefore invite the good people of the United States on the approaching Fourth day of July, in addition to the usual observances with which they are accustomed to greet the return of the day, further, in such manner and at such time as in their respective localities and religious associations may be most convenient, to mark its recurrence by some public religious and devout thanksgiving to Almighty God for the blessings which have been bestowed upon us as a Nation during the century of our existence, and humbly to invoke a continuance of His favor and of His protection.

In witness whereof I have hereunto set my hand, and caused the seal of the United States to be affixed.

Done at the city of Washington, this twenty-sixth day of June, in the year of our Lord one thousand eight hundred and seventy-six, and of the Independence of the United States of America the one hundredth.

U. S. GRANT

DS, DNA, RG 130, Proclamations. *Foreign Relations, 1876*, p. 3.

On June 24, 1876, Joseph R. Hawley, chairman, Centennial Commission, Philadelphia, telegraphed to Secretary of State Hamilton Fish. "The President sent letter yesterday regretting that he will not be able to attend the ceremonies of the fourth of July. We expected he would preside. His absence would be subject of universal criticism, and be considered national mortification. He would not be called to severe labor. It is hoped he will occupy a stage in front of Independence Hall while the troops march by in the morning, and sit two or three hours on the platform in Independence Square, beginning at 10 o'Clock, during the Oration Poem and Music. No exercises in the afternoon. Pray tell me what embarrassments can be removed. Dom Pedro was not invited to the opening as Emperor. Cards were sent to Dom Pedro de la Cantara and wife a distinguished Brazilian family at the request of the Brazilian Commission, the same course will be taken now. Pray induce the President to reconsider." Copy, DNA, RG 59, Miscellaneous Letters. See Address, May 10, 1876; *Julia Grant*, pp. 187–89.

On March 28, Frank M. Etting, Philadelphia, had written to USG. "A committee, composed of the Presidents of Councils of the City of Philadelphia, the Chairman of the Committee on the Centennial Anniversary, the Commissioner of City Property, and myself, have been, under the authority of an ordinance, engaged for the past three years in restoring Independence Chamber to its appearance in July, 1776. The original chairs used by the Members, the chair occupied by Hancock as President, the table upon which the Declaration of Independence was signed, even the silver inkstand used upon the occasion,—all have been restored to their positions; while the walls of the chamber exhibit portraits duly authenticated of nearly all who debated and signed our Magna Charta. I respectfully transmit for your examination the three reports duly made as the work progressed. We beg most respectfully but earnestly to request that you will sanction the deposit in this room of the Original Declaration of Independence, now in custody of the Patent Office; that it may be exhibited to the citizens of the United States generally, and to people from all parts of the world, in the very chamber where that document was originally discussed and signed. We have already taken every precaution that the most experienced Insurance Inspector could point out to secure this building against fire; and desire to express ourselves ready and willing to adopt whatever mode you may point out to ensure the *perfect* safety of this inestimable document. A fire proof safe, so constructed as to contain an inner door of heavy plate glass with secure lock and key, the usual outer doors closed by night and opened by day, will place the safety of the precious document beyond the possibility of harm. The key of the inner or glass door could be retained by the present custodian, who might himself be induced to bring the Declara[tion] to Philadelphia; thus the actual possession would not pass from the Department to which it has been long entrusted. The Councils of Philadelphia would no doubt take additional action if it should be so desired, and declare Independence Chamber subject to the United States government during 1876, precisely in the same way as it was placed at the disposal of Congress during 1776. The Committee or its Chairman will personally proceed to Washington and carry out your instructions; or will take such action as you may deem desirable or expedient." LS, DNA, RG 48, Miscellaneous Div., Letters Received. On March 30, George W. Childs, Philadelphia, wrote to USG on the same subject. LS, *ibid.* On April 13, Secretary of the Interior Zachariah Chandler wrote to USG. ". . . While I recognize the eminent fitness of the exhibition of the Declaration of Independence in the Chamber wherein it was adopted and signed, I do not feel at liberty to permit it to pass from my custody, unless authorized by Congress to do so. I have the honor, therefore, to suggest the propriety of submitting the proposition, touching such transfer, to Congress, for such direction as that body may see fit to authorize. Should this suggestion meet with your approval, I will prepare the necessary letters and transmit them, with copies of the correspondence already had in the matter, to Congress; unless you shall prefer to make the proposition for such transfer the subject of an Executive communication to that body." LS, *ibid.* USG endorsed this letter. "Return to Sec. of the Int. The request to have the original draft of the Declaration of Ind. placed on exhibition at the centennial may be granted under such regulations as the Sec. of the Int. may choose to make" AE (undated), *ibid.* On July 4, Mayor William S. Stokley of Philadelphia addressed a crowd at Independence Hall. ". . . Impressed with a sense of the magnitude of an occasion such as the one which we to-day celebrate, the President of the United States recently intrusted to my care the original of the Declaration of Independence of the United States, that the same might be read and exhibited to the people in this place . . ." *SED*, 45-3-74, 47. Richard Henry Lee then read from the original manuscript. See James D. McCabe, *The Illustrated History of the Centennial Exhibition,* . . . (Philadelphia, 1876), pp. 666–72. On Feb. 6, 1877, USG endorsed a letter of the same date from Secretary of State Hamilton Fish to Chandler. "The custody of the original Declaration of Independence, of the Commission and treaties referred to in the within letter appearing to be by law placed with the Secretary of State, I approve of the request made by him for their return to the Department, and hereby authorize such return to be made by the Hon. the Secretary of the Interior." Copy (unsigned), DNA, RG 59, Domestic Letters. See John H. Hazelton, *The Declaration of Independence: Its History* (New York, 1906), pp. 290–92.

On June 12, 1876, Jesse D. Jernigan, Morgan, Ga., had written to USG. ". . . Dear Father or step Father of our Country i Write to you bcause it is Sentenial year and I hope your honer is in a good heumer ~~and its one~~ and in concequenc of its being and hundred years sinc the declaration of independanc was assigned I hope you will answer my letter and give me your address and tell me how to address my letters to you and by so doing you will grateley oblige . . ." ALS, USG 3.

On June 14, Ulysses S. Grant, Jr., wrote to Samuel S. Rickly, Columbus, Ohio. "The President directs me to acknowledge the receipt of your favor of the 9th inst, enclosing an invitation from the citizens of Columbus, to attend their Centennial Celebration on the 4th of July next, and express his thanks for the courteous attention—He regrets, that, his engagements will not permit him to accept." Copy, DLC-USG, II, 3.

On June 15, Henry C. Dane, New York City, wrote to USG. "I have been informed by Father Nicholas Bjerring, Priest of the Russian Greek Church of this city, that the Turkish Commissions to the Centennial Exposition, find themselves in very embarrassing circumstances, in consequence of the late sad Revolution in their Empire, viz:—that they are without money, and consequently unable to release their consignments from the Custom House, and also unable to pay their laborers. In view of those facts—if they be so, it has occurred to me that in consideration that they are the *invited guests* of this grand young Nation, it might be well for our Government to exhibit its usual spirit of hospitality, and voluntarily extend to the gentlemen who are placed in such a sad plight, its cordial assistance by advancing to them the needed funds to meet their painful wants. Pardon me for this boldness, but I appeal to you, as the one man, who can bring to our Republic a fresh glory in this Centennial year, by lending your aid to this matter." ALS, DNA, RG 59, Miscellaneous Letters.

On July 3, John L. Cadwalader, asst. secretary of state, recorded in Fish's diary. "The Presidents Private Secretary Mr Grant brought me a letter addressed to the President by Mr Borie which stated that Mr Seybert of Phila had presented a new bell for Independence Hall costing some $20.000 and that it had been suggested and was desired that some person in Philad sd be authorized to send a telegram, . . . to the effect that on the occurrence of the day &c &c the President sent greeting to all the Nations of the Earth with some quotation from scripture added. . . . the President said he did not think it proper himself but he desired to send it here to know whether it was proper. I told him what I had said in which he acquiesced and drew a short telegram to Mr Borie declining to accede to his request which was given to Mr Sniffen to be copied and sent. He said he should not go to Philadelphia, would be here tomorrow and would receive the German Minister at half after ten o'clock." DLC-Hamilton Fish. See letter to William I of Germany, July 18, 1876.

Endorsement

———

Refered to the Sec. of War. If the protection asked for Mr. Roberts[1] can be given without detriment to the service I suggest it be given. Mr. Roberts goes, as I understand on a scientific research in which the whole country is interested, his labors therefore may be regarded as National.

U. S. Grant

June 28th /76

AES, DNA, RG 94, Letters Received, 3683 1876. Written on a letter of June 26, 1876, from Amos Clark, Jr., Elizabeth, N. J., to USG. "Personal:—. . . The Revr. Dr. Roberts of Westminster Church Elizabeth N. J called at my office a few days since and stated that he contemplated visiting the National Park during his vacation in July, and that you had kindly offered, when he mentioned his intention of so doing, on meeting him at my house last fall, to send and escort with him from *Fort Ellis.* I have taken the liberty to write you, stating these facts, and would say that the Doctor is very desirous of making the trip and if the President can send an escort with him to protect him from the Indians, we shall feel under very ~~on~~ great obligations. We are very much attached to our Pastor and do not care to have him scalped just now." ALS, *ibid.* On June 28, Ulysses S. Grant, Jr., wrote to William C. Roberts conveying USG's endorsement. ". . . The President desires me to add, that possibly, on account of the Indian troubles in that region, it may be impossible to give you the escort—" Copy, DLC-USG, II, 3. On June 30, Frederick Dent Grant wrote to Roberts. "Yours of June 29 just received I do not think it safe to go to the Yellow Stone Country this year. The Indians are very bad this year. My love to my grand mother and aunt also to Mr eCorbin" ALS, NjP. On July 21, Secretary of War James D. Cameron wrote to Clark. ". . . General Sheridan reports that the constant application for troops to meet the demands on the frontier makes it extremely doubtful whether, if required, an escort could be furnished from the forts in Montana. But he scarcely considers as escort necessary, as a great number of people are constantly going into the park, and the route to it, up the Madison fork, is quite a thoroughfare. Besides there are no Indians on the route named, and none are in, or will go to the park, except a class that is perfectly harmless. To which, General Sherman adds—agreeing as to the impracticability of furnishing escorts to travellers— 'No escort is necessary; hundreds of the curious pass over this route every summer, via the Pacific Railroad, to Corwin, Stage to Helena and Fort Ellis, Montana; a hired poney the balance of the route. See the late publication, the "Great Divide," by the Earl of Dunraven, London, 1876.'" LS, *ibid.*

1. Born in 1832 in Wales, William C. Roberts emigrated to the U.S. in 1849, graduated from Princeton Theological Seminary (1858), and was ordained a Presbyterian minister. See letter to William C. Roberts, Dec. 19, 1880.

To Simon Wolf

June 28, 1876.

MY DEAR MR. WOLF:

Your letter in the matter of the Statue to be dedicated to Religious Liberty in Fairmount Park, Philadelphia, on the 4th of July, has been duly received.

It has impressed me deeply and I congratulate you and all concerned for this splendid contribution on the part of American citizens who at all times in war and in peace, have shown their loyalty and patriotism on and in behalf of the Republic.

I sincerely regret that official duties will prevent my attendance.

Sincerely yours,

U. S. GRANT.

Simon Wolf, *The Presidents I Have Known from 1860–1918* (Washington, 1918), pp. 89–90. On June 26, 1876, Simon Wolf, Washington, D. C., wrote to USG. "No doubt you are aware of the fact that the Independent Order of B'nai B'rith at its quinquennial Convention held in Chicago in 1874, unanimously voted the erection of a Statue to Religious Liberty, and that the same should be erected in Fairmount Park, Philadelphia. Now on this coming Fourth of July, the Statue having been completed by an American sculptor, Sir Mosely Ezekiel, will be dedicated and given to the people of the United States. This evidence of patriotism and of love of liberty on the part of American citizens of Jewish faith is in keeping with their history and their lofty ideals and conception of duty. No class of citizenship has been made happier by religious liberty than the Jew, for the denial of that liberty in other lands has been the cause of endless persecution and misery. We sincerely trust that this statue, typifying so grandly the separation of church and state, may be an inspiration and an example for all the generations of the future. Is it not possible for you to attend the unveiling?" *Ibid.*, p. 89.

On June 3, Isaac-Adolphe Crémieux, French senator, *et al.*, "Alliance Israélite Universelle," Paris, had written to USG. "The United States are about to celebrate the Centennial Anniversary of their independence by a grand and magnificent festival which unites all nations in the same sentiment of universal sympathy. In this celebration, the Universal Israelite Alliance requests that it may take part. Established for the support and elevation of the Israelites in the countries where they are still subjected to a persecution which our age cannot comprehend, the Alliance casts upon your country looks full of the liveliest gratitude. It especially behoves us to recall with gladness, that, first of all nations, yours has proclaimed without distinction of sect, the grand principle of religious liberty. As long as a century ago, while the countries of Europe subjected the Israelites to 'laws of exception', America invited them, as brothers, to the equality of political and civil rights. Under the protection of such laws, we see them in that generous country rapidly increasing; erecting large places of worship and grand institutions for the purposes of charity and instruction. Besides those born under your skies, the Israelites of our countries who have crossed the Ocean, have received at your hands this emancipation and have had their share of this great blessing. And in how many instances by their international policy, by their management and the choice of their diplomatic agents, has not the United States given to European Israelites the striking proof of their sympathy! President of the Republic of the United States, permit the Central Committee of the Universal Israelite Alliance to express to you, to Congress, and to the whole American people, their good-wishes for the prosperity of the great Union, which, during the century of its existence has conquered for itself so noble a place in contemporaneous history. Your flag carries the stars, which in our sacred literature are the symbols of divine benediction. With this auspicious emblem marching before you, may this divine benediction shed its rays over your beautiful Republic with increasing brilliancy during centuries of peace, useful works, and good will among men, and fraternity among nations." DS (more than 20 signatures, in French), DNA, RG 59, Miscellaneous Letters; translation, *ibid.* See *Foreign Relations, 1876*, pp. 120–21.

On June 30, Morris Cohen, secretary, Adas Israel congregation, Washington, D. C., wrote to USG. "The very pleasant duty devolves upon the undersigned to impart to Your excellency the foregoing—begging leave at the same time to enclose to you a receipt for the amount you kindly donated—We sincerely thank you, for your munificance and liberality—and humbly ask to please accept these, our sincere thanks accordingly." ALS, USG 3. Cohen enclosed an extract from the minutes of a June 11 meeting. *"Resolved,* that the Trustees—of this Congregation, on behalf of the members—hereby tender to His Excellency—*U. S. Grant,*—The President of the United States of America—their profound thanks for the kindness and courtesy shown, in honoring us with His Presence, on the occasion of the consecration of our synagogue June 9. 1876. *Resolved*—That the heartfelt thanks are hereby tendered to His Excellency—in donating the amount of Ten Dollars— for the benefit of this Congregation. *Resolved,* that the fact of such donation be spread separately upon the minutes of this meeting—and his autograph signature—to the subscription card be deposited in the archives of this Congregation as an everlasting remembrance. Resolved further, that the Secretary impart the foregoing under the seal of this Congregation to His Excellency, U. S. Grant. President of *the United States* of America." Copy, *ibid.* On July 7, Culver C. Sniffen wrote to Cohen. "Enclosed please find $10—the amount of Presidents subscription towards building a Synagogue for your Congregation." Copy, DLC-USG, II, 3. On July 10, Cohen wrote to Sniffen acknowledging receipt. ALS, USG 3. See Stanley Rabinowitz, *The Assembly: A Century in the Life of The Adas Israel Hebrew Congregation of Washington, D. C.* (Hoboken, N. J., 1993), pp. 144–46.

Note

———

[*July 1, 1876*]

The Sec. of the Treas will please order revoked the order dismissing W. B. Moore and reinstate him to his ~~position~~ former position. I am aware that this is an apt. by the Sec. of the Treas. but I am

anxious to have this done to correct an injustice that I believe has
been done a faithful officer

AN, OHi. On July 1, 1876, Culver C. Sniffen wrote a similar note to Charles F. Conant, act.
secretary of the treasury. Copy, DLC-USG, II, 3. William B. Moore served in the 2nd
Ill. Cav. and mustered out in Tex., where he stayed to publish the *San Antonio Express.* On
Dec. 6, 1869, USG nominated Moore as assessor of Internal Revenue, 3rd District, Tex.
Moore later transferred to Baltimore as a special Treasury agent.

On July 28, 1876, Bluford Wilson, former solicitor of the treasury, testified before the
select committee to investigate whiskey frauds. "I dismissed from the secret service, in the
spring of 1876, one William B. Moore, who was a special agent of the customs, for the reason that he left his post at Baltimore, without orders and without subpœna, and went to
Saint Louis as a witness in General Babcock's case. He was to swear that he was present in
General Babcock's room at the White House and saw General Babcock receive the letter
from Joyce referred to in the testimony of Everest, and that when opened it contained
nothing but a blank sheet of paper. He was not put up on the stand. On his return to Washington he came to me and made repeated requests that I should pay his expenses while
traveling from Baltimore to Saint Louis and returning. This I peremptorily refused to do,
and told him that the expenses of the trip must, of course, be paid by the defense, in whose
interest he was a witness; that for me to pay them would be misappropriation of the public moneys." *HMD,* 44-1-186, 370–71. On Aug. 12, Moore appeared before the committee. "I testified before this committee on the 26th day of April. On the 27th day of April I
received a communication from Mr. Wilson requesting me to resign, which was virtually
a dismissal from the service. He told me of it first himself. I met him on the street, and he
told me of it, and I went to the Department and received a copy of the request to resign. I
called upon Mr. Wilson and asked him if he had any personal reasons for making that demand, saying that if he had I did not propose to raise any issue with him, but if there were
any charges I would like to have myself put right upon the record. He stated to me that the
reason for my removal was that I had forced myself before a committee to testify against
his friend Mr. Yaryan. . . . Q. And not because you went to Saint Louis?—A. Not because
I went to Saint Louis. That was not mentioned at all. . . . Mr. Wilson said, when I presented
this account, 'If the President drags our officers all over the country he must pay them.'
My reply to that was, that there were at least a dozen other officers of the Government
who had been subpœnaed from the Treasury to Saint Louis, and all of them had received
their actual expenses, and I could not understand why I should not. . . . Q. When were you
removed from that position?—A. My removal was to date May 3. . . . Q. How did you get
back again?—A. I appealed to the President, by a written appeal. . . . The official action re-
voking my removal was taken July 8, by Secretary Morrill. . . ." *Ibid.,* pp. 551–52. See *New
York Sun,* July 3, 1876.

On Jan. 7, Homer T. Yaryan, chief of Internal Revenue agents, Washington, D. C., had
written to Daniel D. Pratt, commissioner of Internal Revenue. "Referring to the remark
I am charged with having made to Senator Geo. E. Spencer, namely, that 'I had traced the
whisky frauds to the White House and then turned the matter of further investigation over
to the Secretary and Solicitor' I have the honor to make the following statement. The expression quoted is not only false in the words used but is absolutely false in the meaning
it conveys. I have never directly or by implication reflected upon the President or his
household in any conversation with any living person. I *did* have a conversation with Mr
Spencer of his own seeking. It was a mere social chat and of too recent a date for me to forget what was said. After talking on various topics I was asked by the Senator 'Do you think
Babcock is guilty?' I replied to him, as I have to scores of others who have asked the same

question, 'that I could not say—it was a case too big for me to handle—that I had avoided taking part in his prosecution and the facts were all with the Secretary and Solicitor.' I do not pretend to repeat my exact language and may have said 'he was too big a fish for my net' but have conveyed the substance, and certainly the meaning, of what I said. I had hoped that Senator Spencer had been misunderstood but after seeing him I am convinced that it was a malicious attempt on his part to injure me with the President." ALS, USG 3. An undated memorandum discussing possible counter-allegations against Yaryan, written on stationery of the Yarbrough House, Raleigh, is *ibid.* See *HMD*, 44-1-186, 142–43. On July 10, Yaryan testified before the committee. "In February last, Secretary Bristow called at the Commissioner's Office, and had with him a note—a memorandum rather—in the handwriting of the President, which read as follows: 'Senator Spencer says Yaryan told him that he had traced the whisky frauds to the White House, and had then turned it over to the Secretary.' The Commissioner and the Secretary had a conference, and the Commissioner sent for me, and read the note to me. I said that it was entirely false, and I would like to have Senator Spencer sent for. The Commissioner went for him. He said to my face, in the presence of the Commissioner, that he had told the President that. . . . The President wanted me to call upon him, and desired the Commissioner to bring me over. I went over to the President and related to him my conversation with Senator Spencer, as it had occurred, and then told him my position was such as to excite some kind of enmity. I said that men would try to injure me; that my every act was aggressive, and that I hurt no one that did not have prominent friends; that I supposed he understood my position. I will remark here that he had had a great many complaints from prominent men, members of Congress and Senators. Q. About what?—A. About me. He did not say what, but complaining of me, and that was my answer to it. Q. When did this conversation occur?—A. My recollection now is that it was in February, just before the trial of Mr. Babcock; it may have been in January, . . . The President, after hearing me through, said, 'Mr. Yaryan, I am entirely satisfied. I am glad I have had this interview. I understand your position;' and then entertained us with conversation on social matters." *Ibid.*, pp. 328–29.

On June 29, Sniffen had written to Conant. "The President directs me to inform you that he will be pleased to learn from you, that, the resignation of Mr Yaryan of your department has been tendered and accepted, to take effect from the 1st proximo.—" Copy, DLC-USG, II, 3. On June 30, Yaryan wrote to Pratt resigning his office. ". . . I am not conscious of having done anything to warrant [t]his summary proceeding on the part of the President, but presume he has reasons which are satisfactory to himself. . . ." *New York Times*, July 1, 1876. On the same day, Pratt wrote to Yaryan. ". . . During all these long months in which so much has been accomplished in the purification of the service, the discovery of frauds, the punishment of wrong-doers, the breaking up of illicit distilleries, and the energetic collection of the internal revenue taxes I have ever found you in hearty cooperation with the Secretary and myself, and I have relied with unshaken confidence in your intelligence, judgment, zeal, and strict integrity, . . ." *Ibid.* See *ibid.*, June 30, 1876; *New York Sun*, June 30, July 1, 1876. On July 10, USG wrote to Secretary of the Treasury Lot M. Morrill. "I wish you would notify Mr Pratt, Commissioner of Internal Revenue, that his resignation is desired, and will be accepted to take effect as soon as tendered—" Copy, DLC-USG, II, 3. On July 11, a correspondent reported from Washington, D. C. ". . . It is known that the President is displeased with the letter of Mr. Pratt accepting Mr. Yaryan's resignation, and in an interview with the Commissioner the President referred to this letter, and Mr. Pratt reiterated its statements. When Mr. Morrill assumed the office of Secretary of the Treasury, Mr. Pratt called upon him and said he desired the Secretary to say to the President that while he would at all times receive with respect any suggestions the President had to make touching the general administration of the office, or the appointment and removal of officers, he desired it to be plainly understood that he could not be responsible for the proper enforcement of the laws unless he was left free in the full exercise of his legal functions and prerogatives, and that he would not permit any one to dictate the appointment and removal of his subordinates. . . . The resignation of Mr. Pratt is universally regretted, and his forced retirement at this time is charged upon the President by Republicans with expressions of condemnation. . . ." *New York Times,* July 12, 1876.

On July 8, a correspondent had reported from Washington, D. C. "The announcement has been authoritatively made that the President caused H. T. Yaryan, chief of the special agents of the Internal Revenue service, to be dismissed summarily because he had procured the removal of one W. B. Moore, a subordinate revenue officer. . . . Who is this W. B. Moore in whom the President manifests such deep interest? He has a history in which the public will be interested, and to make it perfectly impartial as well as complete, I must briefly refer to an old scandal. It will be remembered that the principal witness against the President and Gen. Babcock in the San Domingo investigation of 1871 was one Raymond H. Perry. . . ." *New York Sun,* July 10, 1876. On Aug. 14, Moore, Washington, D. C., wrote at length to Morrill. ". . . The facts with reference to the attempted arrest of Perry are briefly these: In Novr 1865, I was honorably mustered out of the service at San Antonio, Texas, while serving as Acting Assistant Adjutant General of the 1st Cavalry Division, Department of the Gulf. In December following I was employed by the government to look up captured and abandoned property between San Antonio and the Rio Grande on the Eagle Pass road, in Texas, and a company of the 3d Michigan Cavalry as guard and escort. While performing this duty, I was waited upon by the citizens of Castroville, Uvalde, and all along the route, who represented that they had been visited by a gang of mounted men who represented themselves as U. S. Troops, and had taken by force, horses equipments, money, arms, forage, subsistence, &c. and had committed every specie of outrage, ending, it was alleged, in murder. I had seen Major. R. H. Perry in San Antonio, a few weeks before, organizing a party from among the discharged soldiers of my Division of Cavalry, ostensibly, to join the liberals in Mexico. These were the men who had committed the depredations. There being no civil law, I took the witnesses and their sworn testimony and p[u]rsued Perry towards the Mexican border, recapturing some of the property, and hastening them into Mexico. When the constitutional convention of Texas, adjourned in May 1869, the republican party in the state was hopelessly divided. Ex Governor A. J. Hamilton leading the conservative wing and carrying the party organizations with him beside being backed by the ex-rebel element of the state, this wing wanted the election held on the day fixed by the convention i. e. Aug 12, 1869. Hon. M. C. Hamilton, brother of A. J. lead the other wing and his party wanted the election postponed to give them time to organize. I was sent to Washington by the Morgan C Hamilton party to urge the president to order a postponement. I arrived in Washington in May and visited the president at once laying our case before the president, who decided that he could not discriminate between such well known republicans as the two Hamiltons. Senator Sumner took me to Governor Claflin of Mass, on the 7th of July 1869, and the Governor, then chairman of the National Republican Executive Committee, gave me an official recognition of the Morgan C Hamilton party as the one identified with the national party. Senator Sumner telegraphed to Gov. Boutwell then Secretary of the Treasury, to stand by us and armed with Gov. Claflins letter of recognition I again called upon the president, and with Gov. Boutwell's coöperation induced him to order the postponement of the election. Mr Sumner gave me some credit for my action in getting the postponement; and in the fall of 1870 when I was again in Washington I became a frequent and welcome visitor at Mr. Sumner's residence corner of 'H' street and Vermont Avenue and often met Maj. Ben.

Perley Poore who was the senator's most constant visitor. During one of these Calls they discussed the San Domingo controversy and mentioned the name of Perry who had been Consul at San Domingo. At the conclusion of their conversation I inquired of Mr. Sumner, who this Perry was and the Senator gave me a printed and bound copy of the committee's report upon the San Domingo investigation, containing a history of Perry, from which I learned for the first time that he was the depredator I had persued on the Texas frontier in 1865. I communicated my discovery to the Senator, who was very strongly impressed with my story and he remarked to me, that if such could be proven as Perry's character he,—Mr Sumner,—had done the president an injustice, and if I was to establish the charges by law it ought to entirely relieve the public mind from its suspicion against the president with reference to the San Domingo treaty. I called upon Gen. O. E. Babcock, whom I had never known up to this date, and related my previous talk with Mr. Sumner. on his and Mr Sumner's advice I proceeded to the scene of Perry's depredations in 1865, obtained the proofs of his guilt, secured the necessary requisition, and would have arrested Perry had it not been for the fact that Perry got wind of my purpose and escaped. I never exchanged a word with President Grant, on the subject of Perry's arrest either before or since the attempt and do not know that he has ever had an intimation of it. In taking the steps I did, I acted, primarily upon a suggestion from Hon. Charles Sumner and had the hearty sympathy of Gen. Babcock, who felt a deep interest in the movement, because of the effect it would have upon Mr. Sumner and thro' him upon the public mind to impeach the testimony of the only witness, relied upon by the president's enemies to smirch him in the San Domingo affair. The only aid given me, by Gen. Babcock, in my efforts to arrest the alleged criminal, aside from his advice, was the letter of introduction to Col. Whitley. I will now show the relevancy of this somewhat extended statement to the subject of Col. Washburn's alleged participation in the Bristow conspiracy against president Grant. The correspondence between myself and Col. Whitley, referred to herein, was placed on file, in the archives of the secret service Division of the U. S. Treasury. no copies were kept, none are in existence except those so filed, except such as have been made from the originals, since Col. Whitley left the office. Therefore, the copies that appeared in the 'N. Y. Sun' of July 9th 1876 were furnished from the records of the Secret Service Division, at, or about the time of their publication, and must have been published with the connivance of Mr. Washburn or someone in his confidence. A wholly false and infamous inference is given the correspondence, whereby an attempt is made, to injure the character of the president in public estimation, by alleging that in restoring me, after my removal May 1st, 1876, by Secretary Bristow, on the pretext given by Mr Yaryan that he,—the president,—was awarding me for services in performing a disreputable job. . . . My delay in calling attention to the publication of the 'Perry letters' in the '*Sun*', was caused by my desire to ascertain positively, whether any copies of the letters were in existence outside of the Secret Service Division. I have obtained the proof, that there are none, from Ex Chief Whitley, which leaves no doubt from whence the '*Sun*' obtained its copies.—" ALS, USG 3. See *PUSG*, 19, 214−17; *ibid.*, 20, 162−63, 176; *ibid.*, 21, 407.

On July 5, A. N. Lowry, New York City, had telegraphed to Sniffen. "Say to the President he is right in Yaryans case as he was in Douglass and Hedricks—I know them all—Will accept office—" Telegram received (at 3:05 P.M.), DLC-USG, IB.

Also on July 5, Octavius H. Blocker, former collector of Internal Revenue, 3rd District, N. C., Fayetteville, wrote to USG. ". . . The abolition of my Dist was unwise as the receipts of the consolidated Dist. show. The people are inconvenienced as men of all parties testify. Petitions were sent up signed by presidents of banks and mayors of cities and by the people but of no avail for Mr Bristow, Mr Pratt and Mr YARYAN knew better than all of us. Knowing something of the past in this country and fearing for the future and being as patriotic and as loyal as Mr Bristow, Mr Pratt or Mr Yaryan, and I challenge them for honest zea[l] in support of this administration (believing the Treasury Department rotten as to fidelity and patriotism in this respect) and feeling as 'honest' as any of them, as my official conduct has shown—I beg . . . [to] congratulate you in your removal of *Yaryan,* . . ." ALS (damaged), USG 3. Blocker had also served as postmaster, Fayetteville, and assessor of Internal Revenue.

On Aug. 1, Francis O. Boyd, New York City, wrote to Orville E. Babcock. "I have just been informed by a friend that there is now a person in Washington who has been engaged in some frauds on the revenue together with that 'pup Yaryan' and that he is willing to go before the investigating Committee and testify as to what he knows. If one half of what I *hear* can be substantiated (and I have no reason to doubt it) it will place that scoundrel about where he should be. I have the name of the party, now in Wash who will give this testimony and would be glad to see him subpoened before the 'Whiskey investigating Come   And in case he did not tell *all* he knows, I have a friend here to whome this party has related in great detail his swindles with Yaryan while in Memphis & other places in Ten. I write to you knowing that Y. has been your enemy, as well as mine. I was indicted at *his* instigation & upon *false testimony*   If you will look into this matter & put it through I will give you the particulars. If you will ask Genl. Porter or some other friend of yours to call on me I will tell them all my information and I do not doubt Yaryan can be shown up to be, what I believe him to be an infernal scoundrel. Please give my kind regards to Mrs Babcock—. . . P S Please treat this letter as Confidential" ALS, Babcock Papers, ICN. See *New York Herald*, Jan. 9, 1876; *New York Times*, July 22, 1900.

On Aug. 19, Moore wrote at length to Morrill after investigating allegations of child molestation against Charles Robinson, former consul, Quebec (1868–70), and later clerk, Boston customhouse. ALS, USG 3. Robinson retained his position.

On Oct. 16, Moore wrote to USG. "Confidential. . . . I inclose a list, so far as I have positive information, of those who have been conspicuously engaged in defaming you, in the cause of Mr. Bristow, yet remaining in the Department. This information was obtained under pledges that it would not go on the official files, and names of informants are given who will appear to substantiate their statements. Gen. Sewell, Chief of Special Agents, Internal Revenue Bureau, will be glad to have Mr. Maddox in place of either of the three agents named in the report, and asks that you suggest the change to the Commissioner of Internal Revenue. I have conferred with Gen. Sewell in regard to those of the Internal Revenue Bureau and Acting Chief Clerk Kimball as to those in the Secretary's office, affected by this report, and they approve the allegations, so far as their information goes. A red line is drawn under the name of those to whom your attention is especially drawn in the report. Tuesday last, the day you left for New-York, I saw Mr. Morrill by appointment at his residence, and talked this subject about two hours. He will not ask for Mr. Conant's resignation nor remove the appointment clerk unless directed to do so. He has pledged Senator Wadleigh of New-Hampshire that he will retain Conant. Wadleigh so stated to Collector Simmons of Boston, a month ago. When at Augusta, Me., 11th ult., I repeated to the Secretary your emphatic statement to me four days earlier, at Long Branch, respecting Mr. Conant. The Secretary telegraphed Mr. Conant assurances of confidence and his purpose to retain him. Mr. Conant showed the telegram to Gen. McDougall of New-York. Senator Wadleigh has been your bitterest enemy and one of the loudest Bristow men in the country. He lives in Conant's family, in Washington, and led the New-England charge in the Bristow ranks at Cincinnati. Mr. Conant has made repeated overtures to me in the last few days, through Major Stuart, with intimations of rapid advancement. Secretary Morrill asked me to cultivate Conant, and coöperate with him. This I mention to show my disinterested motives, and further show that the Secretary cannot himself see that a man can be so false, and yet protest his innocence with the unblushing effrontery now assumed by Conant. I have no doubt of Mr. Morril[l]'s loyalty to you, and am far from wishing to plant a doubt in your mind, but you will have to place your prerogative before him in dealing with these two men (I say 'two,' because he is not pledged for the others) if you expect justice toward your memory or your friends after you shall have surrendered your high office." *New York Tribune*, May 31, 1877. Charles F. Conant continued as asst. secretary of the treasury. On Jan. 18, 1877, Moore wrote to USG. "The Secretary of the Treasury has consented to a change in the force of special agents, by which Col. Chamberlin can be reappointed. If Gen. Pollock is confirmed as General Appraiser of Customs, another vacancy will occur. Mr. Maddox has done more valuable service under my direction, and the internal revenue people do not like to have an officer working outside of their special line. If you would ask Gen. Raum to appoint Gen. Mosby's brother in Maddox's place, the Secretary will appoint the latter vice Pollock. This will provide for the two gentlemen you have named for appointment, and also place Maddox satisfactorily." *Ibid.*

To Rutherford B. Hayes

Washington, D. C. July 4th *1876*

DEAR GOVERNOR:

With the adjournment of Congress I shall *adjourn,*—with my family,—to Long Branch, the enquiries of Congress as to my right to do so notwithstanding.[1] When there I should be much delighted to have a visit of a week from you and Mrs. Hayes. Mrs. Grant & I will do all we can to make your stay pleasant, and with the aid of the genial sea breeze, fine roads and beautiful surrounding villeges, and pleasant and hospitable neighbors, I have no doubt but we will succeed.

There is no ~~immed~~ indication of an immediate, nor very early, adjournment, but I feel that some how a solution will be found for the present *dead lock* on the appropriations, and that when it is, Congress will soon leave. If I can have your acceptance I will inform you at the earlyest day when we will be at the Brance, and will fix a time when it will be agreeable for you to go on.

With great respect,
yr. obt. svt.
U. S. GRANT

GOV. R. B. HAYES,

ALS, OFH. On July 7, 1876, Governor Rutherford B. Hayes of Ohio wrote to USG concerning this invitation. Parke-Bernet Sale No. 2235, Dec. 3, 1963, no. 118. See letter to Rutherford B. Hayes, Aug. 16, 1876.

1. See message to House of Representatives, May 4, 1876.

To City Council, Birmingham, England

MY GOOD FRIENDS,

I have received the address which, under date the twelfth of last month, you have been pleased to communicate, congratulating me, and the Nation of which I am Chief Magistrate, on the celebration of the first centenary of the independence of this country.

I thank you for the sympathies which you express, for our trials, and for your joy in our prosperity.

As one of the main purposes of the international Exhibition to which you advert, was to enable its visitors to compare the various productions of mankind, there is reason to hope that that comparison will tend to promote commercial intercourse, and to strengthen friendly relations.

The reception given by me, to your countrymen, to which you refer, was due to their personal characters, and to their eminence in their callings at home.

Acknowledging, however, the strength of those ties of kindred and interest which connect the United States and Great Britain, I cordially hope, that these may be improved in every needful way, as an example of Righteousness, Peace, and good-will to all other nations.

Written at Washington, the fifth day of July, in the year of our Lord, one thousand, eight hundred and seventy-six.

U. S. GRANT

Copy, DNA, RG 59, Domestic Letters. On June 12, 1876, Mayor Joseph Chamberlain of Birmingham, England, wrote to USG extending his city's congratulations on the approaching Centennial. DS, DLC-USG, IB. On July 1, John L. Cadwalader, asst. secretary of state, met with Frank Wright, appointed to present the letter to USG. "... I mentioned the facts to the President as I had occasion to go there and informed him that it struck me as improper for a town councellor of Birmingham unaccompanied or accredited by his Minister to make any formal presentation and that I felt quite sure the Queen would under no circumstances receive a Member of the Washington Common Council. He did not seem struck with the impropriety of it and said he could not receive him on the 4th July but would if he desired it afterwards. . . ." Hamilton Fish diary, DLC-Hamilton Fish.

To Rutherford B. Hayes

———

July 5th /76

DEAR GOVERNOR:

This will present to your acquaintance Hon. S. W. Dorsey, U. S. Senator for Arkansas, and Chairman of the Republican state Committee. The Senator desires to talk with you about efforts that are being made by a few self styled republicans—but who have sustained the democratic party since 1872—to insure defeat of the republicans in that state at the presidential election. The Senator will explain to you their plan, and how far they are using your name in the execution of their designs.

I am Dear Governor,
Your obt. svt.
U. S. GRANT

GOV. R. B. HAYES

ALS, OFH. Stephen W. Dorsey, born in 1842 in Vt., attended Oberlin, served during the Civil War as an art. officer, moved from Ohio to Ark. (1871), and entered the U.S. Senate in 1873. See *PUSG*, 26, 52–54.

To Senate

———

TO THE SENATE OF THE UNITED STATES.—

I have the honor, herewith to transmit a report from General W. T. Sherman, together with the most recent reports received from Brig General A. H. Terry, as a response to the Resolution of the Senate of the 7th instant, a copy of which is attached to this message—

U S. GRANT—

EXECUTIVE MANSION
JULY 8. 1876.

Copy, DNA, RG 130, Messages to Congress. *SED*, 44-1-81. A note on the copy indicates that this message was not delivered until July 10, 1876. On July 7, the Senate had resolved to ask USG "whether the Sioux Indians made any hostile demonstrations prior to the invasion of their treaty reservation by the gold hunters.—Whether the present Military operations are conducted for the purpose of protecting said Indians in their rights under the Treaty of Eighteen hundred and sixty eight, or of punishing them for resisting the violation of that treaty; and whether the recent reports of an alleged disaster to our forces under General Custer in that region are true.—" Copy, DNA, RG 130, Register of Congressional Inquiry. *SED*, 44-1-81. On July 8, Gen. William T. Sherman wrote to USG, appending Secretary of War James D. Cameron's name. "To enable you to answer the enclosed Resolution of the Senate of July 7, I have the honor to submit the following brief statemt of facts as exhibited by the Records of this Departmt. The Sioux, or Dakota Nation of Indians embracing various tribes as the Yanktons, Yanctonnais, Brulés, Ogalallas, Minne-Conjou Sans Arcs, Two-Kettles &c have long been known as ~~of~~ the most brave and warlike Savages of this Continent. They have for centuries been pushed Westward by the advancing tide of Civilisation till in 1868 an arrangemt or Treaty was made with them by a Special Commission named by Congress, whereby for certain ~~Conditions~~ payments and Stipulations they agreed to surrender their claim to all that vast Region which lays west of the Missouri River and north of the Platte; ~~and~~ to live at peace with their neighbors— and to restrict themselves to a territory bounded East by the Missouri River, South by Nebraska, West by the 104° ~~degree of Longitude~~ meridian, and north by the 46th ~~degree of Latitude~~ parallel, a territory as large as the State of Missouri. The terms of this treaty have been liberally performed on the part of the United States, and have also been complied with by the Great Mass of the Sioux Indians. Some of these Indians however have never recognised the binding force of this Treaty, but have always treated it with contempt, have continued to rove at pleasure, attacking scattered settlemts in Nebraska, Wyoming, Montana & Dakota, Stealing horses & Cattle, and murdering peaceful inhabitants and travellers. On the 9th of November 1875, U. S. Indian Inspector E. C. Watkins made an elaborate Report to the Commissioner of Indian Affairs in which he uses this language, 'I have the honor to address you, in relation to the attitude and condition of certain Wild and hostile bands of Sioux Indians in Dakota and Montana that came under my observation during my recent tour through their Country, and what I think should be the policy of the Govt toward them. I refer to Sitting Bulls band, and other bands of the Sioux Nation under Chiefs or "head-men" of less note but no less untameable and hostile. These Indians occupy the Center, so to speak and roam over Western Dakota and Eastern Montana, including the rich vallies of the Yellowstone and Powder River, and make War on the Arickarees, Mandans, Gros Ventres Assinaboines, Blackfeet, Piegans, Crows and other Friendly tribes on the Circumference. From their Central position they strike to the East, North and West, steal horses, and plunder from all the Surrounding tribes, as well as Frontier Settlers and luckless White hunters or Emigrants, who are not in Sufficient force to resist them'. after describing at great length their character and supposed numbers given at a few hundred he says 'The true policy in my judgmt is to Send troops agaist them in the Winter, the sooner the better and whip them into Subjection. They richly merit punishmt for their incessant warfare, and their numerous murders of white settlers and their families, or white men wherever found unarmed.' The force estimated as necessary to whip them was one thousand men. This communication was submitted by the Commissioner of Indian affairs Hon Edwd. P. Smith to the Hon Sec of the Interior Z. Chandler, who in turn submitted it to the then Secretary of War Genl Belknap for his 'Consideration and action' In a Subsequent Communication of the Secretary of the Interior of Dec 3, 1875, to the Secretary of War, occurs this language, 'I have the honor to inform you that I have this day directed the Commissioner of Indian Affairs to notify Said Indians (Sitting Bull, & others outside their Reservation) that they must remove to the Reservation before the 31st day of January 1876, that if they neglect or refuse so to remove, that they will be reported to the War Departmt as Hostile Indians and that a military force will be sent to Compel them to obey the orders of the Indian office.' On the 1st day of February the Secretary of the Interior further notified the Secretary of War, 'The time given him (Sitting Bull) in which to return to an agency having Expired and the advices received at the Indian Office being to the effect that Sitting Bull still refuses to Comply with the directions of the Commissioner the said Indians are hereby turned over to the War Departmt, for such action on the part of the Army as you may deem proper under the Circumstances.' During all the stages of this Correspondence the General of the Army and his Subordinate Commanders were duly notified, and were making preparations for striking a blow at these hostile savages in mid-winter, an enterprise of almost insurmountable difficulty in a Country where in winter the thermometer often falls to forty degrees below Zero, and where it is impossible to procure food for man or beast—an expedition was fitted out under the personal command of Brig Genl Geo Crook, an officer of great merit & experience which in March last marched from Forts Fetterman & Laramie, north to the Powder River and Yellowstone vallies This expedition struck & destroyed the village of Crazy Horse one of the hostile bands referred to by Indian Inspector Watkins but the Weather was found so bitter cold, and other difficulties so great arose that Genl Crook, returned to Fort Laramie in a measure unsuccessful so far as the main purpose was concerned. These Indians occupy parts of the Departmts of Dakota and Platte, Commmanded by Brig Genls, Terry & Crook respectively—but the whole is immediately commanded by Lt Genl Sheridan, who has given this matter his special attention. Preparations were then made on a larger scale, and three columns were put in motion as early in May as possible from Fort Abe Lincoln on the Mo River under Genl Terry: from Fort Ellis in Montana under Genl Gibbon: and from Fort Fetterman, under General Crook. These Columns were as strong as could be maintained in that inhospitable region or could b be spared from other pressing necessities and their operations are not yet concluded—nor is a more detailed Report further needed than deemed necessary to Explain the subject matter of this Inquiry—The present Military operations are not against the Sioux Nation at all but against certain hostile bands that parts of it which defy the Governmt, and and are undertaken at the Special request of that Bureau of the Governmt charged with their Supervision and wholly to make the civilization of the remainder possible. No part of these operations are on or near the Sioux Reservation. The accidental discovery of Gold on the Western border of the Sioux Reservation, and the intrusion of our poeple thereon have not caused this War, and have only Complicated it in [*minor*] details by the uncertainty of numbers to be encountered. because tThe young warriors love war, and frequently escape their agents to go on the hunt or War Path their only idea of the object of life. The object of these Military Expeditions was in the interest of the peaceful parts of the Sioux Nation, supposed to embraced at least nine tenths of the whole and not one of these peaceful or Treaty Indians has been molested by the Military authorities. The recent reports touching the disaster to which befell a part of the 7th Regular Cavalry led by General Custer, in person are believed to be true. For some reason as yet unexplained, Genl Custer who commanded the 7th Cavalry and had been detached by his commander Genl Terry at the mouth of Rosebud to make a wide detour with the Regimt up the Rosebud, a tributary to the Yellowstone—across to the Little Horn, and down it to the mouth of Big Horn the place agreed on for the Concentration of all the troops of Generals Terry and Gibbon meeting, attacked en route a large Indian village, with only a part of his Command force, having himself detached the rest with a view to intercept the Expected retreat of the Savages, and experienced almost an utter annihilation of his immediate Command. The force of Genls Terry & Gibbon reached the field of battle the next day, rescued fifty two wounded men, and buried two hundred and sixty one dead men including Lt Col Geo A. Custer, Captains Custer, Keogh Yates, ~~and~~ Lts Cook, ~~and Lieuts~~ Smith McIntosh Calhoun, Hodgson, Reilly, Porter, Sturgis, all of the 7th Cav and Crittenden ~~all of the 7th Cavalry~~ of the 20th Infantry. Lieut Harrington ~~and~~ asst Surgeon Lord and Acting Ass't Surg DeWolff are missing. The wounded were Carried back to the Mouth of the Big Horn in the Yellowstone River, which is navigable, and where there were two Steamboats one of which was sent down the River to Fort Abe Lincoln with the Wounded and to ~~carry back supplies:~~ Communicate these sad facts. General Terry is therefore at the Mouth of the Big Horn refitting and will promptly recieve reinforcemt, and Supplies, and will resume his operations immediately. Meantime General Crook had also advanced from Fort Fetterman and on the 17th of June, Eight days before Genl Custers attack had encountered this same force of Warriors on the head of the Rosebud, with whom he fought ~~four~~ several hours, driving the Indians from the field, losing nine men in killed ~~and~~ one officer & twenty men wounded—General Crook reports his camp as on Tongue River Wyoming. Reinforcemt and supplies are also in route to him and Every possible means ~~are~~ have been adopted to accomplish a concert of action between these two forces which are necessarily separated, and are only able to communicate by immense distances around by their rear. The task committed to the military authorities is one of unusual difficulty, ~~but it~~ has been anticipated for years, and must be met and accomplished. It ~~and~~ can no longer be delayed and Every thing will be done by the Dept to ensure success, which is necessary to ~~ensure~~ give even an assurance of comparative safety to the important but scattered interests ~~that~~ which have grown up in that remote and almost inaccessible portion of our National Domain. It is again Earnestly recommended that the appropriation asked for repeatedly by Genl Sheridan of $200,000 be made to build ~~a~~ two Posts on the Yellowstone at or near the Mouths of the Big Horn and Tongue Rivers Enclosed herewith please find cop~~iesy~~ of Gen. Terry's report just received by telegraph, since the preparation of this letter" ADf, DNA, RG 94, Letters Received, 3770 1876. A clerk's press copy of this draft, signed by Cameron, is *ibid.* SED, 44-1-81, 1–4; HED, 44-1-184, 2–4. See CR, 44–1, 4470–78. On July 22, USG signed a bill appropriating $200,000 for construction of military posts on the Yellowstone and Muscleshell rivers. See *U.S. Statutes at Large*, XIX, 95–96; CR, 44–1, 3007–8, 3233–34, 4518, 4546.

On July 8, Col. Richard C. Drum, asst. AG, Chicago, had telegraphed to AG Edward D. Townsend. "The following is a copy of general Terrys report of the action of June twenty fifth 25 Camp on little Big Horn River June twenty seventh 27th . . . It is my painful duty to report that day before yesterday the twenty fifth 25th instant a great disaster overtook genl custer & the troops under his command at twelve 12 oclock of the twenty second 22 he started with his whole Regt & a strong detachment of scouts & guides from the mouth of the Rosebud proceeding up that River about twenty 20 miles he struck a very heavy Indian trail which had previously been d[is]co[vered] & pursuing it found that it led as it was supposed that it would lead to the little big horn river Here he found a village of almost unexampled extent & at once attacked it with that portion of his force which was immedy at hand Maj Reno with three Cos A. G. and M of the regiment was sent into the valley of the stream at the point where the trail struck it. Gen Custar with five companies C E F I & L attempted to enter it about three miles lower down. . . . of the movements of Genl Custer & the five companies under his immediate command scarcely anything is known from those who witnessed them for no officer or soldier who accompanied him has yet been found alive. His trail from the point where reno crossed the Stream passes along & in the rear of the crest of the bluffs on the right bank for nearly or quite three miles then it comes down to the bank of the river but at once Diverges from it as if he had unsuccessfully attempted to cross then turns upon itself almost completes a circle & closes It is marked by the remains of the Officers & the bodies of his horses some of them dropped along the path others heaped where halts appear to have been made   there is abundant evidence that a gallant resistance was offered by the troops but they were beset on all sides by overpowering numbers. . . . The scouts were set out at half past four in the morning of the twenty sixth 26   the scout discovered three 3 Indians who were at first supposed be sioux but when overtaken they proved to be Crows who had been with general custer they brought the first intelligence of the battle   their story was not Credited it was supposed that some fighting perhaps severe fighting had taken place but it was not believed that Disaster Could have overtaken so large a force as twelve 12 Companies of Cavalry— The infantry which had broken Camp very Early soon came up and the whole Column Entered and Moved up the valley of the Little Big Horn during the afternoon   Efforts were made to send scouts through to what was supposed to be general Custers position and to obtain information of the Condition of affairs but those who were sent out were driven back by parties of Indians who in increasing numbers were seen hovering in general Gibbons front . . . Major Reno & Capt Benteen both of whom are officers of Great Experience accustomed to see large masses of mounted men Estimated the number of indians Engaged at not less than twenty five hundred 2500   other Officers think that the number was greater than this   The Village in the Valley was about three miles in length and about a mile in width   besides the lodges proper a great number of temporary brushwood shelter was found in it indicating that many men besides its proper inhabitants had gathered together there—Major Reno is very Confident that there were a number of white men fighting with the indians   It is believed that the loss of the indians was large—I have as yet received no Official reports in regard to the battle but what is stated as gathered from the Officers who were on the ground—Then and from those who have been over it since   signed ALFRED H TERRY Brig General" Telegram received, DNA, RG 94, Letters Received, 3770 1876. *SED*, 44-1-81, 4—6.

On July 6, Drum had telegraphed to Henry T. Crosby, chief clerk, War Dept. "Despatch from General Terry dated from his camp at Mouth of Big Horn July second (2d) confirms the news-paper reports of a fight on the twenty fifth 25 of June on the Little Big Horn and of Custers death. Terry has fallen back to his present camp. I have sent full despatches to Lieut Genl who will probably communicate them. I have not yet received Genl Terrys report of the action or a list of the casualties." Telegram received (at 1:52 P.M.), DNA, RG 94, Letters Received, 3770 1876. On the same day, 3:10 P.M., a copy of this telegram was made for USG. E, *ibid.* Also on July 6, Sherman, Philadelphia, telegraphed to Lt. Gen. Philip H. Sheridan, Philadelphia. "Dispatch about Custer received. Let me have the full message of Genl. Terry to transmit to Washington, as there will be terrible anxiety there." Copy, *ibid.*, RG 108, Letters Sent. On July 7, Sherman, Washington, D. C., telegraphed to Sheridan. "Will you advise the raising of any volunteer Cavalry to assist in your operations against the Sioux. Answer immediately." Copy, *ibid.* On the same day, Sheridan twice telegraphed to Sherman. ". . . I have ordered already six 6 companies of infantry from the msouri to yankton & thence by steamboat to Terry on Yellowstone   The eight companies of the fifth Cavalry on powder River trail were ordered either to go over to Red Cloud agency or to Return to Fort Laramie when I can send them to Crook if necessary—As soon as I get home I will take the campaign full in hand & will push it to a successful termination sending every man that can be spared   All will be right" "Your dispatch received. I think it premature to think of asking for Volunteer Cavalry with the attendant expense. If the six companies of the 22d Infantry are given Terry he will have about 2000 men. Crook in a few days will have 1500 men, and I send him Merritts eight companies of the fifth Cavalry, four hundred strong, which will make him over two thousand strong. We are all right. Give us a little time. I deeply deplore the loss of Custer and his officers and men. I fear it was an unnecessary sacrifice due to misapprehension and superabundance of courage, the latter extraordinarily developed in Custer. . . . It should be remembered that the loss of Custer and the men with him, must have been attended by at least a corresponding loss on the part of the Indians." Telegram received and copy, *ibid.*, RG 94, Letters Received, 3770 1876. Also on July 7, a correspondent reported from Washington, D. C., that USG, Cameron, and Sherman "have been in consultation in Cabinet to-day, and again at the White House this evening with a view to provide reinforcements for the troops now operating against the Indians. General Sherman, who seems to counsel great caution and secrecy as to what is being and will be done, was interviewed to-night. He says that, so far as any additional news is concerned about the Custer massacre and what has transpired in the past, the public are fully informed, but as to what is being done and what may be done in the future, that is a matter in which concealment is necessary, . . . General Grant gave a dinner this evening to some friends, among whom were Secretary Cameron, General Sherman, Messrs. G. F. Hoar, of Massachusetts, and Lapham, of New York. . . ." *New York Herald*, July 8, 1876. On July 8, Sherman wrote to Sheridan, Chicago. "Your despatches from Philadelphia embracing those of General Terry have all been received, have been furnished the Secretary of War and the President, . . . We can better spare Companies of Artillery from the Coast, than troops from the South, and I will back you with all the men you want. Offers of Volunteers come pouring in, but we all agree that they should not be accepted, if it can possibly be avoided. . . ." Copies (2), DLC-William T. Sherman. See Sherman to Elizabeth B. Custer, Aug. 11, 1876, *ibid.*; *HED*, 44-2-1, part 2, I, 30–39, 442–47, 459–87.

On July 6, Governor John L. Routt of Colorado Territory had telegraphed to USG. "Can raise one regiment of frontiersmen in ten days for service against Indians if Govt. will arm & equip them if you accept telegraph orders" Telegram received (at 4:10 P.M.), DNA, RG 94, Letters Received, 3830 1876.

On July 7, U.S. Senator Algernon S. Paddock of Neb. wrote to USG. "I hand you resolution of Ingalls and aetbill afterwards introduced by myself I shall want to call up my aetbill tomorrow morning if you think its passage advisable. Three regiments can be raised in three weeks at outside. Would like to hear from Gen'l Sherman, Sec'y of war, or yourself as to insufficiency of present military force, Long continued hostile acts of Siouxs, inability of Indian Dept to bring them upon reservations peacefully, &c &c" ALS, *ibid.*, 3770 1876. Paddock's proposed bill authorized the president "to accept the services of volunteers from the State of Nebraska, and the Territories of Wyoming, Colorado, Dakota and Utah, or either of them, to be employed as a part of the Army of the United States against the tribes of hostile Sioux, in the North West, who have for years defied the authority of the Government, and by whose hands, recently, several hundred soldiers—Citizens of the United States—have been slaughtered—Provided; that not more than five regiments of Cavalry or Infantry, or both. shall be accepted and that the term of service shall not extend beyond nine months from the date of enlistment—" Copy, *ibid.* On July 8, Sherman drafted a reply to Paddock for Cameron. ". . . We believe that in a short time the troops now in the Field with such reinforcements as will be drawn from the points where they can best be spared these hostile bands of Indians will be subjugated, disarmed or killed." ADf, DLC-William T. Sherman. A press copy of this letter signed by Cameron is in DNA, RG 94, Letters Received, 3770 1876. Paddock's legislation died in committee. See *CR*, 44–1, 4438, 4514.

On July 7, Joseph O. Shelby, former brig. gen., C.S. Army, Kansas City, Mo., had telegraphed to USG. "Gen Custer has been killed. We who once fought him propose to avenge him should you determine to call volunteers allow Missouri to raise one thousand"

Telegram received (at 4:48 P.M.), DLC-USG, IB. On the same day, Robert A. Friedrich, Topeka, Kan., wrote to USG. "Taking it for granted that the disastrous defeat of our troop in their late engagement with the indians will call for prompt and summary retaliation on the part of the government, I take the liberty of tendering you my services, together with from one hundred to one thousand men, all skilled, and enured to border war-fare, among whom would be a number of the finest indian scouts in the world, of the Pottawottamie tribe of indians, and who are old enemies of the sioux . . ." ALS, DNA, RG 94, Letters Received, 3830 1876. Also on July 7, William Weste, Cheyenne, wrote to USG. "The rumor here is that there is an order from Washington to organize a Regiment of Volunteer. I take the liberty of offering my service and blood if required to the U. S. of America. . . ." ALS, *ibid.* On the same day, J. B. Barford, Philadelphia, wrote to USG. "I beg leave to ask your permission to rise one company to go west to fight the indians that have killed Gen: Custer and his command we have about 3 hundred young men ready to go out any moment we have all been in the late war from the begining to the end and are ready to go again please do not say no as we will a wait your answer verry impataintly" ALS, *ibid.*

Also on July 7, J. T. Atkinson, Geneseo, Ill., wrote to USG. "May the peace policy inaugurated in your administration, toward the Indians, *wards,* of the nation, not be abandoned, but carried out to success, and we as a people, not stand before *God,* and the world, as a nation of treaty breakers, and oppressors of the weak." ALS, *ibid.*, RG 75, Letters Received, Miscellaneous.

On July 8, A. J. Bell, Rawlins, Wyoming Territory, wrote to USG. "Allow an humble private citizen to claim your attention a few moments, and when I tell you that 22 years of life has been on the frontier, and much of the time among the sioux, I am sure you will give some thought to my suggestions. I am led to venture this letter while reading over the list of brave men whose mutilated corpses now lie at Little Horn Calling for an avenging from thousands of as brave men, ready at your Command to do and dare—I have watched the movements of the sioux ever since the spirit Lake Massacre in 1857, at which time I tendered the Gov. of Minnesota a body of frontiersmen to overtake and chastise Inkpadutah and his band, but was not accepted; again in the New Ulm Massacre by Little Crow and his associates, I was Camped on the big sioux in Dakota, at the time of the Massacre and surrounded two nights by a band of sioux and again requested Gov Jayne of Dakota to allow me to take the four Companies Dakota Volunteers and inetercept the retreating sioux at foot of Big stone Lake, at a point they would surely cross in their retreat when Gen. sibley was pursuing them but was again frustrated. subsequent events proved that I was correct in my judgement as to time and place of crossing. I merely make mention of these facts to convince you I know something of the habits and haunts of the sioux.—As it is known to the sioux that the Utes have been ~~soli~~ solicited to join in the fray by Gen. Crook, it must be plain to your practical mind that this region is in iminent peril, sitting Bull has proved himself no mean foe, how easily for him to send a band to chastise and cut off the 300 utes that is preparing to go north, this being what Indians call neutral ground, the poor settler is between two fires, this point is now the outfitting place for the snake River Mines, where Miners are scattered over the new rich placers recently opened up, teams leaving daily for there liable to be cut off by these bands of Indians, and while the Utes have behaved quite well ever since the chastisement given them at sand creek by Col. Chivington, yet I think these great sioux victories will have the effect of uniting many tribes supposed to be friendly—I submit why not allow the Govs. of Colorado Wyoming, Montana and Utah, each to raise a Batallion or Regiment, and place under command of one of your best Generals, and settle this sioux question, it does seem as if repeated acts of kindness only adds to this great Tribes insolence, and nothing but a terrible chastisement will save the frontier from utter abandonment. I feel sure you desire to do what is best" ALS, *ibid.*, RG

94, Letters Received, 3830 1876. On the same day, Thomas S. Mather, Springfield, Ill., wrote to USG. "As one of your personal friends I take the liberty of tendering to you the servics of a Regiment of Volunteers for service against the Indians Enough old soldiers have already signified there desire to go to make the complement If possible give the Illinois boys a chance They will promptly respond to the call of their trusted Commander of the Army of the Tenn" ALS, *ibid.* Also on July 8, T. M. Hope, Alton, Ill., wrote to USG. "I offer you for the Sioux War a Battalion of five hundred Illinoians We will furnish our own horses, and their Equipments. Give our Illinois boys a chance. When and where we meet the Red Skins, you may be sure, that you will hear that we have done our duty" ALS, *ibid.*

On July 10, William R. Mattison, postmaster, Newton, N. J., wrote to USG. "I respectfully tender my services to raise such number of recruits from the late volunteers of General Sheridan's Cavalry Corps, as may be necessary to fill up the Seventh Cavalry. . . ." ALS, *ibid.*, Applications for Positions in War Dept.

Also on July 10, delegates at a Universal Peace Union convention in Philadelphia telegraphed to USG "a request that the spirit of justice, humanity and fairness, and not of revenge, be manifested in the treatment of the Black Hill Indians." *Voice of Peace*, III, 5–6 (Aug.–Sept., 1876), 74. The convention also considered a resolution that "does not regard the late unhappy massacre of U. S. troops under General Custer as requiring, or justifying any departure from the pacific policy inaugurated by the President of the United States. They believe this event, on the contrary, to have been the result of an attempt on the part of our troops to occupy by force a territory formally ceded to the Indians, and already long occupied by them; and they would respectfully request the Government either, to complete the purchase of the disputed territory, or to secure to the Indians its peaceable possession." *Ibid.*, p. 86. For related resolutions and discussion, see *ibid.*, pp. 79–80. On June 30, a presidential secretary had written to convention organizers. "The President directs me to acknowledge the receipt of your favor of the 27th inst., and express his regrets that he is unable to accept your kind invitation to attend the Convention of the Friends of Peace, in Philadelphia, from the 10th to the 15th of July next." *Ibid.*, p. 67.

On July 11, Richard M. Kirtland, Little Rock, wrote to USG. "I most respectfully request authority to raise a Company of Cav or Mounted infantry from Arkansas to assist in suppressing the 'Indian War' I formerly was a Commissioned officer in 2nd Iowa Cav Vols Maj Genl Edward Hatch's old regiment." ALS, DNA, RG 94, Letters Received, 3830 1876. On the same day, Z. D. Carter, Canandaigua, N. Y., wrote to USG. "in Just gitting Back from the Black Hills Countray i thought i Would Write you a few Line 9 nine of us Went to the Black Hills last September 1875 We Spent all our time Revuing the hull Country know about all the indians Camps in the mount of may as we was Camp on Point Creek 6 out of 9 was Shot Dead my Self and T Jones & Brown Ran Cross the Creek and thire we was taken By 15 indians and Cept all Night in the morning tuck us to thire Camp and Robes us all We had Jones & Brown had about $600.00 in green Back my Self $900.00 in green Back the other 6 Boys had about $2000.00 in green Back ~~with~~ and tuck Jones & Brown and Sclp them in my Presents Expecting my turn Every minuet and thay Lived about ½ an houre with Paine and then tuck me and Cut my mustash thay Ware very Long and Stuck them to thire face and Dance and kick arond the Circul and spt in my face and kick me fore about 2 hours thay tide my hands and thay Painted my face and then made me under Stand Leve the Camp I did So and on my Way Came through 14 Camp of indians and made my Way to the Sioux City and from thire to here With out money Walk Part of the Way I intended to go to Washington first and Report but getting a Post from Detroite to Buffalow i Came here Being on my Way to Schenectady, N. y Ware i Left from for the West Dear Sir thire is but one Way to have Paece Let us go all in a Boday and butcher them all No youse in going there Not knowing Whare to find them i tell your Sire thay are Strong in thire hole thire is thousand indians hiding under Brushes you Can Not see anany thing around you in a minuet thay Will Raise up and kill three time thire Number i am Whilling to volunteare and mount a horse and go thire and Lead a boday of men through the Hills fore Revenge of my Countray man . . ." ALS, *ibid.*

On July 12, George Rossman, Lakeview, Mich., wrote to USG. "Will you give me the priviledge of raizing 100 men or a regiment ready to march in 10 days, to avenge the deth of Gen Custer who was killed by the Indians. I enlisted in the 2d Mich Cavelry on the 10th of Sept 1861 &and served during the rebellion. Please answer as soon as convenient . . . P. S. Can Raize Regiment in 20 days" ALS, *ibid.*

On July 17, Governor Benjamin F. Potts of Montana Territory wrote to USG. "I respectfully suggest that all trading posts on the Missouri River, from Sioux city to Fort Benton, be at once closed for the sale of arms or ammunition to white men or Indians, and all arms and ammunition now on hand seized and held by government agents until after the Sioux war is over. If traders are permitted to sell arms and ammunition to whites and half breeds, the Indians can obtain all they want. I earnestly ask your respectful attention to this suggestion. I am busy placing our people in a condition to defend themselves, if the Sioux make a raid into our settlements. The Crow Indians on the Yellowstone remain steadily loyal to us. The Sioux camp attacked by Custer was on the Crow reserve, in Montana, about 170 miles from Fort Ellis. Our people are very much excited over the Indian situation. I shall keep you and the Departments advised of the situation here." Copy, *ibid.*, RG 75, Letters Received, Montana Superintendency. On Aug. 5, Cameron replied to Potts by communicating Sherman's views. ". . . 'Of course this ought to be done, indeed it never should have been tolerated for a day—But the authority to seize and confiscate private property consisting of arms and ammunition, does not exist; especially at Agencies under the control of the Interior Department. This power is now supposed to exist at the Agencies in the Sioux Reservation, but not at the Agencies and trading posts above Standing Rock.'" Copy, *ibid.*, RG 107, Letters Sent, Military Affairs. See Sherman to Potts, July 17, 1876, DLC-William T. Sherman.

On July 18, James F. Fagan, former maj. gen., C.S. Army, Washington, D. C., wrote to USG. "If it be necessary to employ volunteer troops in the present Campaign against the hostile Indians I have the honor to tender my services to raise a Battalion or Regiment, or if necessary a larger force to be composed of the veterans of the late war now residing in the state of Arkansas and the Indian Territory adjacent." ALS, DNA, RG 94, Letters Received, 3830 1876. All four U.S. Representatives from Ark., and Elias C. Boudinot "in behalf of the Indian Territory," favorably endorsed this letter. ES (undated), *ibid.*

On July 18 or 19, John Winch, Walsingham, Ontario, wrote to USG. "Having read some accounts of the U. S. War, with the Indians, your severe losses &c &c. and the expression of General Sherida[n] to drive the Indians to reserve, or exterminate them, the idea came to my mind of offering myself as a mediator first, then as teacher, trader or anything that I might consider to the Indians advantage or the benefit of both parties. I am an Englishman having been in Canada about 30 years I have had a good business experience, . . ." ALS, *ibid.*, RG 75, Letters Received, Miscellaneous.

On July 21, John G. Lindsay, Garnett, Kan., wrote to USG. "I beg leave respectfully to propose to the War Department of the Government to furnish fifty (50) recruits for the regular Army ready for muster at any designated point within fifteen days after notice— the same to be all selected from among men who served in the Cavelry during the late war and who have spent many years on the plains among the Indians. I had the honor to Serve as an officer in the late war from May 1861 until Sept. 1865 the last year commanding a Squadron of Cavelry on the plains operating against the Indians. I have resided all my life on the frontier a part of the time among the Indians and am familiar with the language of several of the wild tribes—. . ." ALS, *ibid.*, RG 94, Letters Received, 3830 1876.

On July 22, Sherman telegraphed to Sheridan. ". . . We must not have another massacre like Custers and Congress is now in Session willing to give us all we want. I can send you three battalions of Artillery from the Atlantic and Pacific coasts but the troops of the south cannot be spared. Do you want Volunteers say the word and no doubt Congress will give them. if we fail to have force enough the country will blame us. . . ." Copy (press), DLC-Philip H. Sheridan. On July 23, Sheridan wrote to Sherman. ". . . The events which have occurred to the troops and my best knowledge of Indian strength and affairs at the Agencies and in the field, will not warrant me at the present time in asking for Volunteers. I have no objections to asking for them as soon as I conscientiously believe their services necessary; but from the disaster which came to Custer from a divided command, I do not feel warranted to take the responsibility of asking for Volunteers now, thereby entailing on the Government an enormous expense. . . . If Congress will increase the companies of the 2nd 3rd 4th and 5th Cavalry to one hundred men, as was done for the two regiments on the Rio Grande, we can fill them up at once, and they will be large enough to meet the wants of the service and relieve the public mind of the constant fear of disaster to our present insufficient force in the Indian country. This could be done at much less expense than by calling for Volunteers, as the organizations are already prepared, and the winter would be on us before we could get Volunteers fairly in the field. . . ." Copy (press), *ibid.* See Sherman to Sheridan, July 25, 31, Aug. 1, 1876, *ibid.*

On July 24, Thomas J. Berry, gauger, 1st District, Tenn., Lee Valley, wrote to USG. "I have heard of the massacree of Custer, and hereby ask the privilege of raising one hundred East Tenneseans, to assist you in avenging him. I have seen service among the Indians of the west as a California Volunteer during the war; as to character, I refer to Maj. Gen'l. Irwin McDowell, U. S. Army, who knows me personaly. . . ." ALS, DNA, RG 94, Letters Received, 3830 1876.

On July 26, Va. Representative T. Spicer Curlett, Litwalton, wrote to USG. "Should the U. S. call for volunteers I ask an appointment as 1st Lieut. and for authority to raise my own company which I can do in fifteen days after notice—" ALS, *ibid.* See *PUSG*, 22, 390–91.

On July 31, William L. Tryon, Port Gamble, Washington Territory, wrote to USG. "In regard to the war, in the Black hills and the many Union Soldiers that have Been killed at the hands of the Savags, I feel it my duty to help bring the Indiens to Justice. I ask you for permission to raise a company of Scouts or Sharp Shooters, out of the Warm Spring Indiens in Oregon and report to the commanding Ofiser in Montanna for active duty I Survsed through the Rebellion in the Army of the cumberland was Honorable Discharged, at the close of the War. am Wel drilled in Artillery, Infantry & Skirmish Drills. at the close of the War I came West have Been a Scout on the plains and on the fronnteer up to the present date. and wel know what it is to Fite the Red man thoes Indiens I want for Scouts have proved them Selves Equal to any and all the Modocks in California 3 years Since. as they are on friendly turms With the U S government, I have no dout they would gow. any time to fite for the Same, if you wil give me permission. to take thoes Scouts I would prefur to arm them with the latest Improved Buffalo Rifle Breeck loeding. Caliber 44/100 I have killed Buffalo with them at one Shot. ~~ove~~ over 1.200 yards actuel measure. . . . P S As this is the only letter I ever tryed to write to the president of the U S I Beg you to give me Some place in the Ranks if nothing Better and forgiv my poor Writing." ALS, DNA, RG 94, Letters Received, 3830 1876. Other communications to USG during July related to avenging Lt. Col. George A. Custer's defeat are *ibid.*; *ibid.*, Applications for Positions in War Dept.

On July 31, Isaac N. Morris, Quincy, Ill., wrote to USG. "I have watched with no ordinary interest your treatment of the Indian question, and have not discovered anything to justify me in the belief that you are unkindly disposed towards the Indian people. On the contrary it has been evident to my mind that you are desirous of doing them justice. Yet the singular anamoly is presented of a hundred soldiers to one civilian being employed in the Governmental supervision over them. This I have not exactly comprehended, nor do I see any evidence of its termination. A mixed polity, part military and part civil, may be the best course of treatment but I have always had the impression, from my earliest manhood, that it would, in the end, be advantageous to both races if none but civil rule was exercised over the Indians. However this may be I am not able to comprehend, (nor do I believe hundreds of thousands of others are) why the present Indian war was made a necessity, or what was really the origin of it, or why so many additional troups are being sent to the Indian country. By the latter remark I mean to say, why cannot peace be effected— Are these Indian wars to continue, and are we to acknowledge the fact before the civilized world that our bayonets are to be continually employed in their extermination? A full letter from you on this subject, which I hope to receive with permission to publish it, would be, beyond all doubt, of great value and read with intense interest by the whole nation— There must be, in time, some permanent solution of this question, and why not that time now. When the event transpires it will not be brought about by bloody massacres on either side, but by the observance of justice, and the teachings of peace and good will. Does the Government of the United States now keep its faith with the Indians? What statesman dare rise in his place and say it does? Does the Indian violate his faith with the Government? Let the indictment be presented against him—The troubles arise between the two races from wrongs committed somewhere, and these wrongs should be traced to their source, (and it seems to me they might be) and the evils corrected. You can certainly do nothing, as President, that would shed more glory upon your administration than to reconcile the conflicting elements between the Indian and the white man, and establish justice and good will between them. I have seen a good deal of the Indian character, both barberous and civilized, so called, and availed myself of every possible opportunity to familiarize myself with it. I have found it sensitive to wrong and yielding to kindness as in other men. Let me relate to you, Mr President, one instance of this, presented by one who is called a barbarous chief. When Red Cloud was in Washington some five or six years ago, I called upon him for the purpose of having a friendly talk with him. It was the day before he started home. I had called upon him two or three times before—We took a seat together upon the side of his bed, and I said to him, through his Interpreter, that I deeply regretted he had not been successful in the accomplishment of his mission to Washington—that I had been informed that he was greatly dissatisfied with his failure, and the fear was expressed that when he returned to his people he would commence a war upon the whites— that war was a very bad thing both for the white man and the Indian, and he should deliberate long, and consider well before he took a step of that kind—I impressed upon him every consideration that presented itself to my mind why he should not take it, assuring him that while there were bad white men, the greater and better part of them would do the Indian no injustice, but in due time redress all their wrongs. This is the substance of what I said to him, but expressed of course in greater detail than I have given here. While his Interpreter was delivering to him my words he manifested the most intense interest, and I thought I saw a tear in his eye. As soon as the Interpreter had finished, Red Cloud sprang instantly to his feet, and commenced an energetic and rapid enunciation, which he continued for, I should think, twenty minutes. As soon as he concluded his remarks he took a seat beside me again—Of course I understood nothing at all he said, nor did he understand anything I said, but our words were repeated to each other by his Interpreter who addressed me as follows—'Red Cloud directs me to say to you that it is so long since a white man has spoken kindly to him that what you have said i̶s̶are apples of gold to his eyes and words of comfort to his heart. He wants you to know that he fully understands that war is a bad thing for his people and for the white people, and that he has always tried to cultivate the blessings of peace and good will between them,—that he calls upon the Great Spirit to bear witness that he has never commenced a war upon the whites, but they have always commenced the war upon him by acts too hard to be borne—that the Indian claims the same right to his property that the white man does to his, and must defend it—that the Indian gets hungry as well as the white man, and must defend his hunting grounds, or go without food to eat—that when he came to the big city (meaning Washington) to talk with his Great Father about the troubles of his people, he would send him to his little chiefs, and when he saw them they would say neither yes nor no—that he had been looking all over Washington for some one who would say yes or no to him, but had found no one. The little Chiefs, he says, wanted him to say something, but did not want to say anything themselves—Still he will go to his people and tell them to shake the hand of friendship with the white man, and will still hope that justice will be done them—the clouds of heaven, he says, will still give them water to drink, and the earth supply them with food and clothing, if their country is not taken from them by white men, without compensation, or if purchased without paying therefor—' This is, in substance, what Red Cloud said, and almost all of it in his very words though more in detail. Although, Mr President, Red Cloud is an unlettered savage, and unacquainted with the details of your great office, and expected you to perform duties pertaining to other officers, he was still a man, could shed a tear of sorrow or sympathy, and understand the rights pertaining to persons and things. Let me repeat, I cannot understand the origin of the present war, from any information I have been able to obtain upon the subject, unless it grew out of the forcible seizure by the whites of the Black Hills, (which belonged to the Indians) contrary to your published admonition, and in violation of the warnings of Gen. Sherman to keep away from them—" LS, *ibid.*, RG 75, Letters Received, Dakota Superintendency. Morris also wrote an undated "Private Note" to USG. "My eldest Son, Edgar R, is at Fort Peck where he went with the Indian Agent T. J Mitchell to instruct the Indians in farming, of which he has much practical knowledge, as my pecuniary losses have been such that I could not assist him. His wife and two Sons are with me and are, of course, uneasy for fear something will happen him growing out of the Indian war. His youngest boy, under seven, was standing by when I was dictating the letter to you to his mother, who was writing it down, and he rushed down stairs of his own accord and with great demonstrations of joy exclaimed 'Grand Mother Grand Pa is writing a letter to General Grant to stop the war.' That is just what I was doing. The child understood me, and I repeat it to impress my purpose in writing. Let the war stop—borrowing your idea Let us have peace" ALS, *ibid.*

On July 31, Bishop Henry B. Whipple, Washington, D. C., wrote to USG. "You are aware of my deep interest in the welfare of the Indians and I am sure will pardon this letter. We have entered upon another Indian war, which I fear will be one of the most memorable in our history—I do not fear the few thousands of hostile Indians but I do fear that eternal law of a righteous God 'whatsoever a man soweth, THAT shall he reap'—a nation which sows broken faith, injustice & wrong will reap a harvest of blood—Thousands cry for extermination—There is ONE who can exterminate, and a people who have more than half a million of soldier's graves within i̶t̶s̶ their borders ought to know that God is not blind. I t̶u̶r̶n̶ yield to no man in my sympathy for the brave men of the border who are always the first victims of savage hate—Every generous feeling of my heart goes out for the brave soldiers who without one thought of self go ~~out~~ to die, & yet I can but feel that for every life lost in such a war the nation is guilty, which for one hundred years has persisted in a policy which always ends in massacre & war—Every friend of the Indian owes you a deep debt of gratitude for honestly trying to give us a better policy. The so called peace policy was commenced when we were at war. The Indian tribes were either openly hostile or sullen & turbulent The new policy was a marvellous success. I do honestly believe that it has done more for the civilization of the Indians than all which the government had done before—Its only weakness was that the system was not reformed. The new work was fettered by all the faults & traditions of the old policy—The nation left 300,000 men living within our own borders without a vestige of government, without personal rights of property, without the slightest protection to person, property or life—we persisted in telling these heathen tribes that they were independent nations—we sent out the bravest & best of our officers, some who had grown grey in the service of the country, men whose slightest word was as good as their bond—we sent them because the Indians would not doubt a soldiers honor—They made a treaty and they pledged the nations faith that no white man should enter that territory—I do not discus its wisdom. The Executive & Senate ratified it— ~~The~~ By the Constitution of the United States these treaties are the Supreme law of the land and are binding upon the individuals & states who compose the nation. The Constitution vests the power of making treaties in the Senate & Executive—This treaty was so made & it was in all of its provisions the Supreme law of the land—It was a question for ~~them~~ the Senate & Executive to decide whether they should or should not make such a treaty—but when once made, it was a solemn compact to the fulfilment of which the nation by its own organic law was pledged. A violation of its plain provisions was an act of deliberate perjury—In the words of General Sherman (see report) 'civilization made its own compact—with the weaker party—It was violated but not by the savage'— It was done by a civilized nation—The treaty was approved by the whole nation—The people & the press approved it—because it ended a shameful Indian war which had cost us 30 millions of dollars & the lives of ten white men for every Indian slain. The whole world knew that we violated that treaty and the reason of the failure of the negociations of last year was that our own commissioners did not have authority from Congress to offer the Indians more than one third of the sum they were already receiving under the old treaty—The peace policy has never been understood by the people. They suppose it was some vague plan to give immunity to savages who commit crimes—when the first thing which the friends of the Indians ask is law to punish crime. You did all that you had the power to do & that was to provide for honest men to fill the agencies You said to all the religous bodies of the country who had executive committees to manage their missionary & ~~eleyomosanary~~ charitable work, if you will nominate to me a man for this Indian agency and your church will be responsible for his fidelity, I will appoint him—You provided for the honest purchase of Indian Supplies—There have been mistakes—In a few instances dishonest & incapable men have been appointed, but not one where there was a score under the old system—You look in vain for the shameless robberies which were common when an Indian agent was appointed as a reward for political service, and a fortune was made in four years upon $1.500 a year—There are no records (see Senator Doolittles report) of blankets made out of shoddy & glue, no best brogans with paper soles; no steel spades made out of sheet iron—There are no tales of Indians fed upon the soup made out of the Entrails & diseased meat of dead cattle—no stories of christian women picking over the dung of cavalry horses to get half digested kurnels of grain to save their children from death—The peace policy did not fail—It was a success until our faith was broken—It was difficult to find the men fitted for this work who would go to a distant agency upon a salary of 1,500 year, but many of the best men in the land have done this work and been rewarded by leading many of the Indians to christian civilization. I have feared to have the Indian Bureau changed to the War Department, because it would be a condemnation of the peace policy—It was a make shift—Nothing was reformed—It was the old system in another office. You Cannot make a bad bank note good ~~simp~~ by changing pockets My own conviction is that the Indian Bureau ought to be an independant Department of ~~It~~ civilization, with one of the best men in the nation at its head—If this was done & we then gave to the Indians the protection of law, personal rights of property, a place where they can live, by the cultivation of the soil, if required to labor, if provided with necessary aid in the work of civilizati[on] if christian schools & missions were ~~encourade~~ protected, and plighted faith kept sacre[d] we should solve the Indian problem & bring down upon ourselves the blessing of God—I sometimes almost despair and then I think it is so plain the people will see—Here are two pictures—On one side of the line a nation which has spent 500 millions on Indian war, a people who have not 100 miles between the Atlantic & the Pacific which has not been the scene of an Indian massacre—a government which has not passed 20 years without an Indian war, not one Indian tribe ~~which~~ to whom it has given christian Civilization—and which Celebrates its Centennial year by another bloody Indian war—On the other side of the line there is the same greedy dominant Anglo Saxon race—and the same heathen—They have not spent one dollar on Indian wars, they have had no Indian massacres. why? In Canada the Indian treaty calls these men 'the Indian subjects of her Majesty'—when civilization approaches them they are placed on ample reservations they receive aid in civilization they have personal rights of property, they are amenable to law and protected by law, they have schools & christian people delight to give them their best men to teach them the religion of Christ—we expend more than one hundred dollars ~~for~~ to their one, in caring for Indian wards—Will you pardon me ~~a suggestion~~ if I suggest a ~~remedy~~ plan which may obviate some of the evils until Congress provides a remedy—I doubt whether Congress will adopt any new system or appoint a commission to devise one—The end may be reached by a simple method—1 Concentrate the Indian tribes—viz place all of the Indians in Minnesota on the White Earth Reservation, the Indians of New Mexico Colorado & Sioux in the Indian Territory—The Indians on the Pacific Coast upon two reserves. The Sioux cannot be removed at once, but probably 20 bands would consent to go at once & their prosperity in their new homes would draw others—If the goverment adopt the plan the end can be reached—2. Whenever an Indian in good faith gives up his wild life & begins to live by labor give him an honest tittle by patent of 160 acres of land and make it inalienable—so long as the reserve is held by the tribe it offer's a premium to the greed of white men—The certificates of occupancy are not as titles worth the paper upon which they are printed—3 Provide government for every Indian tribe placed upon a reservation. Congress might authorize the President to appoint any Indian agent exofficio a United States Commissioner with full powers to administer law on the reservation—[T]he United States marshal in whose district this reserve is, might be authorized to appoint the requisite number of civilzed Indians or men of mixed blood to act as a constabulary force—The United States judge might be required to hold one session of his court on the reserve each year—It requires no new machinery, no great expence. There are 40 reservations where this plan could be ~~introdu~~ inaugurated at once—As it is now, the civilized & christian Indian is pitiably helpless—Two years ago a brute killed an Indian woman on the White Earth reserve in open day—The Indians arrested him—He was taken to Fort Ripley. After two months the Secretary of war ordered him to be discharged because there was no law to punish an Indian—I believe I can count one hundred murders by Indians which have taken place in Minnesota in the past 17 years. No one asks any questions more than if they were severe—They have almost uniformly been committed while under the influence of 'fire water', ~~and~~ furnished in violation of law by white men—when an Indian has become a perfect Ishmelite we quietly allow him to join some hostile sovreign like Sitting Bull ~~and~~ to murder our soldiers—Pardon this long letter. You have often aided us in this work & if you can aid in this simple remedy I shall be deeply grateful . . . ~~and~~ I do believe that a just and humane policy worthy of a great christian nation will save our poor Indian wards and bring upon us the blessing of God   assuring you of my kind regard . . ." ALS, *ibid.*, Letters Received, Miscellaneous.

On Aug. 1, Secretary of State Hamilton Fish recorded in his diary. "*Cabinet.* . . . A long and very interesting conversation followed on the policy of treatment of the Indians not in reference to any immediatly pending question but in reference to their general treatment and policy. The absence of sufficient appropriation probably brought on the present war; it is thought that during the present summer the war will be terminated, and the government will be able to direct the movements of the Sioux in the Indian territory. The President has had a conversation with Bishop Whipple and tells me that he approves the Bishops policy who has promised to give him a memorandum in writing of the points of legislation which he thinks necessary." DLC-Hamilton Fish. See message to Congress, Aug. 11, 1876.

Note

[7/11. 76.]

Nominate Jas. N. Tyner [of Indiana] as Postmaster General vice Jewell resigned.

AN (bracketed material in another hand), OHi. On July 11 and 12, 1876, Culver C. Sniffen wrote to James N. Tyner, 2nd asst. postmaster gen. "The President directs me to say that he will be pleased to have you call at his office at half past one oclock this afternoon." "The President will be pleased to have you call at his office at 4 o'clock this afternoon to subscribe to the oath of office." ALS, Robert L. Markovits, Middletown, N. Y. A lawyer and U.S. Representative (1869–75), Tyner had also served as Ind. senate secretary (1857–61) and a special postal agent (1861–66). See *PUSG*, 25, 140–41.

On July 10, 1876, Secretary of State Hamilton Fish recorded in his diary. "Returned yesterday from New York and called on the President this morning and found him talking with Jewell of some appointments. The President manifested much impatience and to several questions which Jewell put answered he would attend to it himself. He then requested Jewell to leave the room and wait as he wished to speak to me. As he left the room the President said he intended to ask him for his resignation as he could stand his annoyance no longer and asked me whether I knew Mr Thompson of Indiana whom he thought had been in Congress while I was in the Senate I asked if he meant Dick Thompson He looked up his card and found it was Richd W. Thompson   I told him he was I knew an uncommonly eloquent man but I was under the impression that there was some stories connecting his name with some land affairs which were not satisfactory. He said he thought of appointing him or Tyner as PostMaster General. I thought Tyner's appointment would be unexceptionable, he said he thought he would appoint him as it would be in the line of promotion. He requested me to ascertain if I could enquire about Thompson." DLC-Hamilton Fish.

See Fish diary, June 18, 28, 1876, *ibid.*; *Julia Grant*, p. 187. On July 11, a correspondent reported from Washington, D. C. "The announcement made this morning about the Capitol and elsewhere that Postmaster General Jewell had resigned caused a great deal of surprise. . . . Gov. Jewell himself says that he knows no cause, and asked for no reason for the President's request that the resignation should be presented. He went to the White House yesterday to transact some business pertaining to his department. While there the President quietly stated his desire for a change in the head of the Post Office Department, without any manifestation of feeling or giving any explanation. Gov. Jewell accordingly sent in his letter of resignation last evening, . . . The true reason for the President's action is probably to be found in the expressions of some of his friends that Gov. Jewell made too many apologies for the administration, and was not disposed to stand before all the world as a member of it, sharing to the full all its responsibilities and standing by all its acts. One member of the Cabinet is mentioned as having referred to the secret-service force of the Post Office Department as hostile to the President and throwing mud upon his administration. . . ." *New York Times*, July 12, 1876.

On July 13, L. Cass Carpenter, Greenville, S. C., telegraphed to USG. "Republicans of the South Congratulate you on recent appointments to Cabinet" Telegram received (at 9:15 P.M.), DLC-USG, IB.

To Lot M. Morrill

Washington.
July 12th /76

MY DEAR MR. SECRETARY,

I send you herewith copy of a letter sent by Wm Hemphill Jones, Depty. Compt to a chairman of a Committee of Congress.[1] This action is in direct violation of my orders to the heads of departments, was extra officious, and shows plainly that this office[r] was in communication with some one of the Committee before. It is impossible that he should have been able to compile the information in the time that has seemed to elapse between the request for information and when it was given. I will be obliged if you will dismiss Mr. Jones, by my order, from this date.

Your obt. svt.
U. S. GRANT

HON. LOT. M. MORRILL, SEC. OF THE TREAS.

ALS, DNA, RG 56, Applications. William Hemphill Jones graduated from Yale (1833), practiced law in Philadelphia, served as mayor of Wilmington, Del., and began a long tenure in the first comptroller's office during President James Buchanan's administration.

See *PUSG*, 26, 435; *New York Times*, May 1, 1880. On Aug. 24, 1876, Jones, Washington, D. C., wrote a letter of resignation to USG. ALS, DNA, RG 56, Applications.

1. On April 8, Jones had written to U.S. Representative William Mutchler of Pa., chairman, Committee on Expenditures in the Dept. of the Interior. "As requested in your note of yesterday's date, I send herewith the 'accounts of Govt Insane Asylum from the year 1868 to present fiscal year.'—Mr. Dickinson who will hand you this note, may be able to explain any apparent obscurities." Copy, *ibid.* See *HRC*, 44-1-793.

To Benjamin H. Bristow

July 12th 1876.

HON. B. H. BRISTOW:
DEAR SIR:

Through the press I learn that the Committee of Congress investigating *whiskey frauds* have summoned you as a witness, and that you—with great propriety as I think—have declined to testify, claiming that what occurs in Cabinet, or between a member of the Cabinet and the Executive, officially, is privileged; and that a Committee, or Congress, have no right to demand answer. I appreciate the position you have assumed on this question, but beg to relieve you from all obligation of secrecy on this subject; and desire not only that you may answer all questions asked relating to it, but wish that all the members of my Cabinet,—and all ex-members of the Cabinet since I have been president—may also be called upon to testify in regard to the same matters.

With great respect,
your obt. svt.
U. S. GRANT

ALS, DLC-Benjamin H. Bristow. On July 13, 1876, Benjamin H. Bristow, New York City, twice wrote to USG. "I have the honor this moment to receive your letter of yesterday in which after referring with approval to my refusal to testify before a Committee of the House of Representatives to what occured between the President and myself while I held the office of Secretary of the Treasury you are pleased to add that you wish to relieve me from all obligation of secrecy and to express your desire that all the members of your Cabinet may be called upon to testify fully. When I appeared before the Committee last week in obedience to their summons I refused to answer any and all questions which required me to state any conversation between you & myself touching official matters whether such conversation took place at a meeting of the Cabinet or at another time, saying however to the Committee that no inference adverse to any one should be drawn from my refusal to answer their questions I took the position distinctly that I considered all conversations between the President and Heads of Departments on official matters confidential and privileged, and that the privilege existed not so much for the protection of the parties immediately concerned as for the interest of the public service. If I was right in this view of the matter it would seem to follow that the privilege cannot be waived by either or both of the parties. Indeed I said to the Committee that I would not feel at liberty to answer their question with your consent. Although I have not had an opportunity to examine authorities on this subject I am still of opinion that the obligation of public duty to treat such conversations as confidential and privileged is not removed or modified by your consent that I should make full answer to the questions. If the privilege were merely personal it might be waived, but I place it on higher ground. I respectfully suggest that the appearance of the several Heads of Departments before a Committee of Congress to testify to conversations between the President and themselves running through a period of many months would almost inevitably lead to the disclosure of differences of recollection and present to the country an unseemly conflict to which I would not willingly be a party. Besides it seems to me that such an inquiry by a Committee of Congress tends to the absorption, if not the complete destruction of Executive power and to the establishment of a purely Legislative government. In any view I am able to take it seems to me that duty requires me to adhere to my announced purpose not to answer the questions propounded to me by the Committee. I beg to remind you that my opinion on this subject was repeatedly stated to you and the members of your Cabinet and, as I understood met your and their approval. My withdrawal from office does not alter or modify my duty in this respect, nor have my own views undergone any change. I hope I will not be recalled by the Committee, but should they see proper to call me again I cannot consent as at present advised to testify to conversations held with the President on official business." "Personal . . . Since my letter was written I have seen your letter to me printed in an afternoon paper. In view of the publication of your letter I trust you will not think it improper to give my answer to the press, as I do not feel at liberty to do so at present." ALS, USG 3. On July 7 and 8, Bristow had appeared briefly before the select committee to investigate whiskey frauds. *HMD*, 44-1-186, 322–28.

On April 18, Secretary of State Hamilton Fish had recorded in his diary a cabinet discussion of executive privilege. "Mr Bristow said that he had made up his mind to state (if he were called before a Committee) that he should not state any thing transpiring at Cabinet, before the examination begun; that when Mr Johnstons impeachment was impending certain Cabinet Officers, Mr Stanton &c did state without objection what took place on different occasions; but that he thought it had been done inadvertantly, and that Mr Speed who was very delicate, and right minded in such things had spoken to him about it lately and had said he had called Mr Stantons attention to it, who said he had not considered it, but that he agreed with him. The Secretary of War & Attorney General took part and it was agreed without dissent that consultation whether in Cabinet, or not actually in Cabinet, between the President and the Heads of Departments, and between heads of Departments themselves, were previleged, and that it would be proper hereafter for any such officer to decline to state what occurred and to advise the Committee of his determination before the examination begun" DLC-Hamilton Fish. On July 11, USG read to the cabinet the draft of a letter releasing Bristow from secrecy considerations. Fish responded. "I objected to that part of the letter which authorized communication on any other than the one

subject on which the Committee had interrogated Mr Bristow, as a concession of a principle which it was important to retain, of the confidence of the Cabinet relations, that there
certainly are questions especially with our Foreign Relations which must be observed as
confidential and that it would not be wise to throw open all the questions between the
President & the Cabinet or the Members themselves; that as the object of the inquiry
doubtless was to produce the impression of some improper interference by the President
with the Whiskey trials it was quite sufficient to throw that open to the inquiry of the
Committee. The President and all present assented to this view and he was to alter his letter accordingly" *Ibid.*

Also on July 11, Ulysses S. Grant, Jr., wrote to U.S. Representative John A. Kasson
of Iowa. "Your note of today asking to have sent you a decision of a previous Atty Genl as
regards the right of a Committee of Congress to inquire of a Cabinet Minister or Ex Cabinet Minister as to what took place in Cabinet is received. The President has referred your
letter to The Attorney General for an answer. He wishes to have you know that he has
written a letter to Ex Secretary Bristow, which will be delivered to him to morrow on his
return to the city—absolving him from all secrecy as to matters in question, and also all
other members of The Cabinet and Ex Members, with the desire with the desire that the
whole of them should testify to all the facts within their knowledge." ALS, IaHA. On
Dec. 29, 1893, Kasson endorsed this letter. ". . . Nothing shows so clearly the consciousness of innocence on the part of the President as this letter avowing his resolution to give
the fullest scope to his Enemies' investigation." AE (initialed), *ibid.*

On July 14, 1876, Henry A. Bowen, New York City, had written to USG. "You require
no meed of commendation from me but as a supporter of you and of your administration I
cannot refrain from expressing my liveliest satisfaction for your recent action in causing
certain removals in various departments at Washington. The people of the United States
saw fit to elect you President for two consecutive terms and thereby conferred upon you
[under the constitution] the right to make appointments and removals at will. In common
with others I am glad to see you exercise your perogative. Your recent letter to Mr Bristow more than realize the expectitations of your friends." ALS (brackets in original),
USG 3.

To William I of Germany

WASHINGTON, *July* 18, 1876.

GREAT AND GOOD FRIEND: Your letter of June 9, in which you
were pleased to offer your cordial congratulations upon the occasion
of the Centennial anniversary which we have recently celebrated,
was placed in my hands on the 4th of July, and its contents were pe-
rused with unfeigned satisfaction.

Such expressions of sympathy for the past progress of this country and of good wishes for its further welfare, as are contained in that

communication, are the more gratifying because they proceed from the head of a great empire with which this Republic during the whole century of its existence has maintained relations of peace and friendship, which have been conspicuous alike in prosperity and in adversity, and have become continually firmer with the increasing progress and prosperity of both countries. It is my sincere desire that this mutual cordiality and this prosperity, which have been the lot of the two countries during the first century of our Independence, may be vouchsafed to them during the century which is to come. Wishing you a long reign of health and happiness, I pray God that He may have Your Majesty in His safe and holy keeping.

U. S. GRANT.

Foreign Relations, 1876, p. 173. On June 9, 1876, Emperor William I of Germany wrote to USG. "It has been vouchsafed to you to celebrate the Centennial Festival of the day upon which the great Republic over which you preside entered the rank of independent nations. The purposes of its founders have, by a wise application of the teachings of the history of the foundation of nations and with insight into the distant future, been realized by a development without a parallel. To congratulate you and the American people upon the occasion affords me so much the greater pleasure, because, since the Treaty of Friendship which my ancestor of glorious memory King Frederick II, who now rests with God, concluded with the United States, undisturbed friendship has continually existed between Germany and America, and has been developed and strengthened by the ever increasing importance of their mutual relations, and by an intercourse becoming more and more fruitful in every domain of commerce and science. That the welfare of the United States and the friendship of the two countries may continue to increase is my sincere desire and confident hope. Accept the renewed assurance of my unqualified esteem." DS (facsimile, in German), USGA; translation, DLC-Joseph R. Hawley. *Foreign Relations, 1876*, p. 173. On June 29, Ulysses S. Grant, Jr., wrote to Secretary of State Hamilton Fish. "The President directs me to say that he will be pleased to receive the Minister from Germany at 10.30 A. M. on the Fourth of July here unless Congress adjourns to meet in Phila on that day. In that case he will receive it in Phila on the Fourth of July or here at a later day" ALS, DNA, RG 59, Miscellaneous Letters. See Fish diary, June 29, 1876, DLC-Hamilton Fish.

On May 19, President Thomas F. Burgers of the South African Republic, Pretoria, had written to USG. "On the approach of the first centenary of your independence Your Excellency will be greeted and hailed from all parts of the world and from countless lips with the most heartfelt congratulations. Amongst so many good wishes, those of this, Your young Sister Republic, may not be wanting and I feel convinced, will not be unwelcome. Africa greets America with a thrill of joy on this auspicious event. You celebrate the hundredth anniversary of your Great Republic founded on the broadest and most liberal principles and on the sacred rights of the people. By that you celebrate the triumph of modern civilization, as it displays itself, in social religious and political liberty. I congratulate Your Excellency   I Implore upon you, your Country and people the blessing of heaven. May your States, may your people be prosperous and maintain their well merited fame. Glorious is your past, brilliant be your future. I pray God to have your Excellency in His safe and holy keeping" Copy, DLC-Joseph R. Hawley. On June 11, King Victor Emanuel II of Italy wrote to USG on the same subject. Translation, *ibid.* USG received similar letters from Tsar Alexander II of Russia (June 17), Emperor Franz Joseph of Austria-Hungary (June 19), and Princess Isabella of Brazil (July 4). Translations, *ibid.* For USG's replies, see *Foreign Relations, 1876,* pp. 16, 28, 441.

On June 18, Marc Joseph Albertelli, Piacenza, Italy, wrote to USG. "The fourth of July rapidly approaches, the day of the anniversary of the glorious and immortal independence of the United States of America; and as all generous hearts, on this joyous occasion, hasten to present their respectful offering of congratulation have the goodness and kindness if you please Mr. President to permit a citizen of Plaisance (Italy) on his part to do the same . . ." ALS (in French), DNA, RG 59, Miscellaneous Letters; translation, *ibid.*

On June 19, Elihu B. Washburne wrote to USG. "I take great pleasure in presenting to you Mr. Frederic Gaillardet, a distinguished French citizen, for many years a resident of New York city and the founder of the French Journal, 'Le Courier des Etats-Unis.' For nearly a quarter of a century he has been the Paris correspondent of that paper. He now visits the United States to see the Exposition and see what progress we have made as a nation during the last twenty years. He will visit Washington and while there will desire to pay you his respects. Commending him to you as a gentleman of the highest character and intelligence, . . ." ALS (press), DLC-Elihu B. Washburne.

On July 4, Adalbertus Mielcuszny, pastor, St. Stanislaus Church, New York City, and many others, addressed USG. "We the undersigned Polish residents of the United States join with our fellow countrymen in Europe in presenting the following greeting to the American People: Americans! A hundred years has passed away since you attained by your spirit and arms your independence, one of the dearest national treasures, and you have begun to build up the land of your fathers, which has attained such great prosperity. In this immeasurable undertaking Poles took part and the Poles of today, who keep in their hearts a fervent love for these treasures are struggling for the same. The Polish people, wrestling during a hundred years with their enemies, who are trying to extirpate them, see in your progress their own, and they have manifested their sympathy to you in your national struggle. The grateful American people have immortalized the memory of mutual feelings by the erection of monuments to Pulaski and Kosciusko, whose names are engraved deep on the hearts of all. Happier than ever, you have reached a new world: you are the vanguards of liberty, and you give an example of adherence to faith and opinions to all men. Europe may well be jealous of you in this matter. In the present festival time of your national jubilee, the Poles in the midst of their ruin and oppression, but full of faith in the restoration of the liberty of their fatherland, reach the fraternal hand to you, wishing you a splendid existence, and a still greater development of your national life. United with you through the ties of national efforts in the holy cause of independence, we say, may the United States of America long prosper!" DS, DNA, RG 59, Miscellaneous Letters. A related document, printed in Polish, is *ibid.* Also on July 4, Charles Edmond *et al.*, Paris, addressed USG. "We esteem it an honour and we consider it as a duty to offer you as the worthy President of the great American Republic in the name of Poland, our Fatherland, a medal struck to celebrate the Centenary of the Independence of the United States of North America. We cannot remain indifferent to the solemnity which reminds the present generation of the brilliant triumph of Justice and Liberty in the New World, and on this commemorative medal, we are happy to place next to the immortal name of the Founder of your Republic, those of two Poles, his heroic fellow-soldiers, Kosciuszko and Pulaski. Champions of Right on the old Continent, they became afterwards the patriotic offering of Poland to America while struggling for her independence; the former perished in your holy cause, the latter fought for it until its final success. We found our hopes on the universal establishment of the two great principles of Liberty and Justice, for which Poland has fought so many battles. You have proved their omnipotence by succeeding in giving to them victory, and in thus assuring their future reign over the whole world. We form ardent wishes for the everlasting strength and prosperity of your Republic, founded as it is for the guidance, the example and the edification of all nations. May Europe in time, realize the full practical force of those immutable laws dictated by human conscience, and which are destined to destroy that unnatural state of society that consists of oppressors and of oppressed." DS (5 signatures), *ibid.*, Diplomatic Despatches, France. See *Foreign Relations, 1877*, pp. 127−28.

On July 7, Jeronymo Simoes *et al.*, Brazilian Literary Society of Rio de Janeiro, wrote to USG "congratulating him on the glorious Centennial of the North American people. The fruitful political existence of a nation which has labored so much for progress and for popular education could not be viewed with indifference by the Brazilian youths who form the Society; and the board of Officers take pride in being the interpreter of these sentiments, which the country of Beecher Stowe and Longfellow awakens in all minds which regard with enthusiasm noble enterprises and philanthropic achievements." DS (6 signatures, in Portuguese), DNA, RG 59, Miscellaneous Letters; translation, *ibid.*

On Jan. 26, 1877, USG vetoed joint resolutions instructing the secretary of state to acknowledge Centennial congratulations received from the Argentine Republic and Republic of Pretoria because "their adoption has inadvertently involved the exercise of a power which infringes upon the Constitutional rights of the Executive." Copy, *ibid.*, RG 130, Messages to Congress. *HED*, 44-2-32; *SMD*, 49-2-53, 406−8. See *CR*, 44−2, 227−28, 568.

Note

[*July 18, 1876*]

Withdraw nomination of [Thos W.] Bennett, at his own request, as Gov. of Idaho. Nominate Mason Brayman, of Wis.

AN (bracketed material in clerk's hand), OHi. On July 12, 1876, USG nominated Thomas W. Bennett as governor of Idaho Territory; on July 18, USG nominated Mason Brayman in place of Bennett, who had previously held the position (1871−75). See *PUSG*, 2, 250; *ibid.*, 10, 239−40; *ibid.*, 21, 108, 160−61.

On Jan. 27, 1875, Anna M. Bennett, Boise, had written to USG. "I hope I may be pardoned for reminding you of an interview which I had the honnor to have with you a year ago in referance to a change of position for my husband, T W Bennett, Governor of Idaho. In that interview I told you I felt assured that their was no future to this teritory worth waiting for and that I could not think of raising my family in this far off and desolate region isolated from the world with no prospect of a change. I asked you if possiable to change his position to Colorado or Utah if only to a Judgeship for I know that such a position there would in the end be far more advantage than the one he holds here. You replied that there were no vacancies then but kindly promised to remember my request. I see by the papers that there are probably vacancies in Colorado now. Could you not appoint my husband to one of these and let some one of the many aspiring persons enjoy the honnors of being Goveror of Idaho for awhile?. . . If it is not possiable to give him a place in Colorado and the new Teritory of Penbina should be organized it being on the N P R. R will have a future to it, and I submit whether the experiance popularity and merit of my husband would not pecurlarly fit him to organize that Teritory as Govenor?. . ." ALS, DNA, RG 60, Letters Received, Idaho Territory.

On April 30, Thomas W. Bennett wrote to USG. "I was elected Delegate to Congress from this Territory, last Fall. My seat is contested. I have not yet determined to accept the position. In the meanwhile, I learn that applications are being made for the appointment of my successor as Governor, in anticipation of my resignation. Some of the applicants are totally unfit—notably one Jonas W. Brown of this Territory. Before I resign, if I do so, I will see you personally, and shall be greatly pleased to confer with your Excellency, in reference to my successor, the more especially, if he should be chosen from among the citizens of this Territory." ALS, *ibid.*, RG 48, Appointment Papers, Idaho Territory. On July 6, James M. Jameson, Boise, wrote to John P. Newman, Washington, D. C. ". . . What I want to say to the president is this: We aught to have another man for Governer, whether Mr. Bennett is admitted as our Deligate or not. I do not object to Mr. Bennett politicaly or executively, but to his morral character and deportment. He is profain, a drunkard, and a gambler; and his morral influance on society is a shame to the Government—We have a man, Jonas W. Brown, of Idaho City, who would mak us a good Governer. He is a Repulican in politicts, a Lawyer by profession, a thorough temperance man, and a decided *Christion gentleman*—And has been for years a citizen of Idaho. I would like to ask the President to nominate him if I knew how to reach him—If I were as intimate with President Grant as I was with the late Chief Justice Chase, I should find no trouble in addressing him personaly. How can I approach him? Could you do any thing in such a case? We are bad enough in Idaho, in all conscience, without being led by our Governer in our crimes— Mr. Brown is worthy and qualified for the Office: He is an active Steward in the Church, and one of the most active Sunday School men in the Territory—Why can we not have such man in office? He is identified with all the interests of of the territory as one of her oldest citizens—If you can do any thing in the case do it, please—" ALS, *ibid.* Newman referred this letter to USG. AES (undated), *ibid.*

On Dec. 4 and 9, Bennett, Washington, D. C., wrote to USG. "Having been elected Delegate, to Congress from the Territory of Idaho, I most respectfully beg leave to resign the office of Governor of that Territory, to take effect this day. . . ." "Having objected to the appointment of Hon D. P. Thompson as Governor of the Territory of Idaho; upon the grounds, that as I believed his appointment would be unsatisfactory to the people of that Territory; and calculated to disturb the harmony which now exists there among the Federal officers, and among the people; and since making such objections, having examined the recommendations of Mr Thompson, now on file in the Interior Department, and finding them signed by so many prominent and representative men of the Territory, and having myself no personal objections to Mr Thompson, and a very high regard for the gentlemen who endorse him, and especially for Mr Mitchell the Senator from Oregon, I beg leave to withdraw my objections to the appointment. And for the reason that I am not clearly satisfied of the propriety of the appointment, I will make no recommendation whatever." ALS, *ibid.* On Nov. 6, John Hailey *et al.*, Boise, had petitioned USG. "In the event that a vacancy should occur, in the Governorship of Idaho Territory, We the undersigned, would most respectfully, recommend the Hon. David P. Thompson as a suitable person for Governor, his large acquaintance with the people of Idaho, and her material interests preeminently fit him for the position." LS (12 signatures), *ibid.* Related papers are *ibid.* On

Dec. 11, U.S. Senator Oliver P. Morton of Ind. wrote to USG. "From the fact that I am not sure that General Colgrove will accept the position of governor to Idaho, I will change the recommendation to Gen Reuben Williams of Fort Wayne. . . ." ALS, *ibid.* On Dec. 15, USG nominated David P. Thompson as governor of Idaho Territory. On Jan. 5, 1876, USG nominated Reuben Williams as deputy 2nd Comptroller, Treasury Dept.

On May 17, U.S. Senator John H. Mitchell of Ore. telegraphed to USG. "David P. Thompson Governor of Idaho been selected delegate to Cincinnati Convention desires leave of absence for one month commencing June first, I hope it may be granted, no pressing reason for his present presence in Idaho," Telegram received, *ibid.* On July 1, Thompson, Washington, D. C., wrote to USG. "Enclosed you will find my resignation of the Office of Governor of Idaho. Territory—I was appointed in December last to the Office of Governor without any Solicitation on my part—The people of the Territor[y] without distinction of party asked the assistance of the Oregon Senators to have me appointed and they did So. I think there is not a resident of the Territory that has been dissatisfied with my administration So far—I have *not* been absent from the Territory without leave. I have taken no contracts either as a Surveyor or as a mail contractor Since my appointment as Govenor I have presented no claims for Settlement as a claim Agent Since I was appointed Govenor nor received a fee for collecting claims Since then—I am Satisfied that representations however of that character have been made to you—in regard to myself—but not by any resident of Idaho Territory—I make this statement to you in justice not only to myself but to Senators Mitchell and Kelley who recommended me to you for appointment as Govenor. I have been in former years largely interested in Government Contracts all of which I have completed I believe to the Satisfaction of the Officers of the Government—It was my intention to soon resign the Office of Governor of Idaho Territory *had no* complaints been made against me—as I am entirely ignorant of the parties who have made complaint against me—'for absence without Leave with having interests in Sureying contracts in the Territories. mail contracts &c' I have not the opportunity to confront them and prove their statements to be unfounded. I was Elected a Delegate to the Republican Convention at Cincinnatti. I asked for and obtained leave of absence until first of July—My resignation being required I have not deemed it necessary to Either return at that time or apply for an Extension of leave of absence—my reason for not returning direct from Cincinnatti was Sickness ~~was Sickness~~ I shall return at once to Idaho and await the appointment and qualification of my Successor—and turn over the Office to him—" ALS, *ibid.*

On July 2, James S. Reynolds, San Francisco, wrote to USG. "The telegraph announces that Governor Thompson of Idaho, will resign. So it seems to be as difficult as ever to find a Governor who will stay in that Territory. Well, the office does not seem so desirable to me now as it once did, still I would like to have it. You may remember the reference had to the matter in our conversation at Washington when Governor Bard was appointed, and also at Galena when Governor Bennett was appointed. As to how my appointment would be received in Idaho, refer to any you may see from the Territory, also to senators Mitchell and Kelly of Oregon also to senator Sargent. If you find it possible to make the appointment I will not abuse the trust, but will honor it to the best of my ability, . . ." ALS, *ibid.* See *PUSG*, 21, 161.

On July 6, Ben Holladay, Washington, D. C., wrote to USG. "Since my return to the City yesterday, I am told 'Governor Thompson of Idaho will resign. I most earnestly recommend for the position 'Smith Kearny' resident and former Marshall of Washington Territory. He has always been a straight republican, and to my knowledge a warm devoted friend of yours: Has a thorough knowledge of the wants of the Territory, and above all a character above reproach, and honest man." ALS, DNA, RG 48, Appointment Papers, Idaho Territory.

On July 17, Godlove S. Orth, Washington, D. C., wrote to USG. "It affords me pleasure to join the friends of Hon M. L. Bundy of Indiana, in recommending his appointment to the position of Governor of Idaho. Mr Bundy is well qualified for such position, a man of strict integrity and high character—and his appointment would be very gratifying to the people of Indiana." ALS, *ibid.* Morton favorably endorsed this letter. AES (undated), *ibid.* Also on July 17, U.S. Representative Milton S. Robinson of Ind. and eight others wrote to USG recommending Martin L. Bundy for governor of Idaho Territory. LS, *ibid.*

To Lot M. Morrill

July 19. 1876.

DEAR SIR:

Will the Secretary of the Treasury be kind enough to give Hon: Mr Plaisted, the letter of Mr W. D. W. Barnard to me, written in the Summer of 74, and sent by me to the Secretary of the Treasury with the endorsement "to let no guilty man escape"? Mr P. is a Member of the Committee of the House, investigating "Whiskey frauds"—Any other information from the files of the Treasury Dept. which Mr Plaisted may want, may also be furnished at the discretion of the Secretary.

Respectfully &c

U. S. GRANT.

HON: LOT M. MORRILL. SECY OF THE TREASURY.

Copy, DLC-USG, II, 3. See *PUSG*, 26, 231–41. On Aug. 2, 1876, Bluford Wilson, former solicitor of the treasury, testified that on July 24 Treasury Dept. officials seeking to locate this letter and endorsement had refused him access to boxes containing his private papers. On July 25, Wilson went to the White House. ". . . I called upon the President of the United States, and after stating the case substantially as I have stated it to the committee, I asked the President to be good enough to give me an order on the Secretary of the Treasury for the boxes. To this he replied that he thought the boxes ought to be examined before they went out of the Treasury Department. He said that Mr. Morrill would designate some one man, and the Solicitor of the Treasury perhaps another, and that he saw no objection to my being present at the examination. To this I replied that I could not give my assent. I told the President that I thought it was putting me in the attitude of being a suspected party; that after careful inquiry I was assured by both the young men who had to do with packing the boxes that they contained nothing of a public character of which copies were not left on file, and as to the Barnard letter, I said to him that their assurance was definite that it was not in the boxes, but that if it was there he might rely upon my promptly returning it as soon as I could make the proper examination to ascertain if it was contained in the boxes. Quite a long conversation ensued between the President and myself, in which I endeavored to satisfy him that my record, both professional and official, was of a character that entitled me to the courtesy of being treated as an honorable man. I appealed to the President in the strongest terms I could employ to deliver the boxes to me, after such an examination as he and the Secretary of the Treasury (without just warrant under the circumstances in my judgment) seemed to think necessary to subject them to. He told me that he would see the Secretary of the Treasury, and after I had asked him again specifically for an order on the Secretary, and had been refused, our interview closed. On my return to my room I wrote the President a note . . ." *HMD*, 44-1-186, 403–4. On the same day, Tuesday, Wilson wrote to USG. "Genl Wilson & your son U. S. Grant Jr have my permission to go through my boxes of private papers, now in the Solicitors Office of the Treasu Dept—unless on reflection you can see your way to order them to me for the examination which ~~you~~ it seems to be thought proper to subject them to before I can have them The Genl—Will no doubt come on telegram from me tonight, and, I hope that your son could find a half hours time to give to the matter, if the Genl could see his way to incur the expense and loss of time to him Please be good enough to let me hear through U. S. G. Jr what your conclusion may be. I would be glad to see & talk with him further about other matters touched upon between us this AM . . . P. S. I must recall your attention to the fact that on Saturday I told the Treasury officials in writing to examine the boxes themselves—that I had not packed them, and that the young men who did could ~~make~~aid the Search—My instructions were explicit to put in nothing but my private papers." ALS, USG 3. *HMD*, 44-1-186, 404. On the same day, Culver C. Sniffin wrote to Wilson. "The President directs me to say that he sees no objection to General Wilson or yourself being parties to the examination of the papers referred to in your note just received—But the other party, or the party on the part of the Treasury Department, should be the new Solicitor or some one designated by the Secretary of the Treasury." Copy, DLC-USG, II, 3. *HMD*, 44-1-186, 404. On July 26, Wilson wrote to USG. "I am in receipt of your note of yesterday through Mr Sniffin in reply to mine of same date and after conference with Gen Wilson have requested him to see you upon the subject thereof" ALS, USG 3. Wilson testified. "I then sent word to the Solicitor's Office that I did not want the boxes searched unless I was present, either in person or through a friend. That night, as it seemed evident to me that I was to be put in the attitude of doing a suspected part and of taking public papers, I telegraphed to a mutual friend of my own and the President to come down. He came, and on the next day called upon the President, and the result was an order to the Secretary of the Treasury directing him to submit the boxes to my friend and to Mr. Robinson for examination. When the examination was made I was present. They contained what I always supposed they did—my original office drafts of my operations against the whisky ring, the safe burglary, and some other matters of a highly confidential and private character, which I thought then and still think the Administration was quite as much concerned in keeping secret as I was, and that was really the reason why I suggested that the boxes be examined by the President's private secretary and General Wilson. The Barnard letter was also found by myself, as the gentlemen who were making the search had overlooked it, it being marked 'Private and confidential' on the outside, which is doubtless the reason why it was overlooked by the young man who did the packing. . . . Q. Who was the mutual friend who examined the papers with you and Robinson?—A. My brother, General Wilson." *HMD*, 44-1-186, 404–6.

On July 26, James H. Wilson wrote to USG. "Mr Robinson & myself found the Barnard letter endorsed by you—in an envelope marked in your handwriting '*Private &*

Confidential,' and that wrapped up in the parcel of letters, relating to the same matters—
just as they had been left after they had been shown you by Maj. Wilson, last. The clerk
who packed the bundle was present—recognised ~~theit bundle~~when found and declares
that seeing ~~theit marked~~ contained private & confidential papers put it into the box, without opening or examining ~~theit parcel~~ & consequently without knowing that the Barnard
letter was one of them. He further asserts that Maj Wilson knew nothing about its being packed up, having left it entirely to him to separate personal from official papers.
Mr. Robinson admitted to me & the Secretary that Maj. Wilson had authorized him in
writing & had proposed to him personally to go through the papers, and that he (the act
Solicitor) had declined to accept either of these propositions, because he did not consider
himself authorized under ~~his~~the instructions of the Secretary to do so. No other papers of
~~any~~ value to anybody—were found—& none which had not been fully and clearly copied
into the official records. I leave to night at 9 30, but can call before that time if you desire
it. . . . I am at the Riggs House." ADfS, IHi.

On July 27, a correspondent reported from Washington, D. C. "There has been some
anxiety here within a few days in regard to the whereabouts of the original manuscript of
the President's famous order, 'Let no guilty man escape.' Yaryan testified that the letter
was forced out of the President by Bristow and Wilson, who had to represent to the President the necessity of his saying something so as to deceive the people into thinking he was
in sympathy with the prosecutions. Those who saw the original letter knew that it would
be sufficient evidence in itself of the falsity of Yaryan's story, and an anxious search was
made among the records of the department for the document, but it was not to be found.
Your correspondent remembered distinctly that Bluford Wilson told him last August he
intended to keep the document for the historical value it would some time have, and this
fact was stated to the President. He sent for Wilson and asked for the document. Wilson
denied having it, saying that he had not seen it since last August. Another search was made
through the records of the office without result, and it was then reported to the President
that there were stored in the office of the Solicitor several boxes of papers nailed up and
addressed to 'Bluford Wilson, Springfield, Ill.,' which Wilson had packed before he retired.
Wilson insisted that they were his private papers, but the President ordered that Wilson
be sent for and the boxes opened and the papers examined in his presence by Mr. Talbot,
the new Solicitor. This was done this morning, and among many other papers of importance to the department was found the original manuscript of the President's letter written on the back of a private communication from a Federal official in St. Louis, as described
in these despatches about two weeks ago. Wilson had no explanation to make, except that
the letter must have slipped in the boxes by mistake. The discovery places both Wilson
and his associate Yaryan in a very disagreeable position." *New York Daily Graphic,* July 27,
1876. On Aug. 7, U.S. Representative Harris M. Plaisted of Maine, Republican committee
member, cross-examined Wilson and placed into evidence the Barnard letter bearing
USG's endorsement. See *HMD,* 44-1-186, 484–85.

Endorsement

———

Refered to the Atty. Gen. The resignation will be accepted. The
~~name~~ nomination of Hoffeckr is this day withdrawn leaving the Dist.

Attyship of Delaware vacant. I suggest the name of Wm C. Spruance
as Mr. Higgins successor.

U. S. GRANT

JULY 20TH /76

AES, DNA, RG 60, Letters from the President. Written on a letter of July 20, 1876, from
Anthony Higgins, Wilmington, resigning as U.S. attorney, Del. ALS, *ibid.* Higgins, a
Wilmington lawyer, had graduated from Yale (1861) and studied law at Harvard. On
July 20, 1876, USG wrote a note. "~~Will the~~ Withdraw nomination of Hoffecker as Dist.
Atty. for Delaware." AN, OHi. On July 11, USG had nominated James H. Hoffecker, Jr., as
U.S. attorney, Del.; on July 20, USG withdrew this nomination in favor of William C. Spru-
ance, who graduated from Princeton (1852) and studied law at Harvard. See *PUSG*, 26,
217–19.

Endorsement

―――――

Refered to the Sec. of War. This is one of the apts. I expected to make.
The name therefore may be marked for *special attention* after the appointment of one whos name was sent to the Dept a few days since
urged by Senator Oglesby.[1]

U. S. GRANT

JULY 24TH /76

AES, DNA, RG 94, ACP, 5503 1875. Written on a letter of July 24, 1876, from Commodore
Daniel Ammen, Washington, D. C., to Ulysses S. Grant, Jr. "Unofficial . . . Mr Bogardus
Eldridge the young gentleman to whom this note is given, is the son of Doctor Eldridge,
whose father was a physician in practice at Huntsville, Alabama, and was driven out in the
early part of the rebellion and served as the Surgeon of a colored Regiment for some time
and in other professional capacity throughout the War. He is the nephew of Commodore
Parker, of the Navy who called a month ago and saw the President in behalf of Mr Bogardus Eldridge. I have reason to believe that he is a gentleman of capacity and character,
and if appointed to a Lieutenancy in the army would acquit himself well." ALS, *ibid.* On
Dec. 4, USG nominated Bogardus Eldridge as 2nd lt., 10th Inf.
     On July 21, U.S. Representative William Lawrence of Ohio had written to USG. "Or-
son C Knapp of Bellefontaine Ohio desires an appointmt as Second Lieutenant in the Infantry service. . . ." ALS, *ibid.*, Applications for Positions in War Dept. No appointment followed. Orson C. Knapp, former capt., 33rd Inf., died on April 16, 1877.
     On Aug. 4, 1876, Charles W. Ferguson, Montgomery, Ala., had written to USG. "I
have tried in vain to get in the West Point Military Academy, and being anxious to get in
the army, otherwise than as a private, I come to you to assist me in my undertaking, . . ."
ALS, *ibid.* No appointment followed.
     On Aug. 9, Retired Lt. Col. Samuel B. Hayman, USMA 1842, Washington, D. C.,
wrote to USG. "In accordance with your suggestion I have the honor to request, that when

a vacancy occurs among the commissioned officers of the Army, that you you will favorably consider the application of my son Wayne Hayman for an appointment in the military service" ALS, *ibid.* No appointment followed.

On Aug. 15, Culver C. Sniffen wrote to Secretary of War James D. Cameron. "The President directs me to say that if the Board for examining Candidates for admission to the Army has not adjourned—Mr James T. Keegan may be examined to take his chances for appointment hereafter—" LS, *ibid.*, ACP, 6104 1876. On Sept. 18, AG Edward D. Townsend wrote to USG, Long Branch, that James F. Keegan "failed badly before the Board; and, besides, has established for himself a ~~bad~~ record not Creditable in other respects, as will appear from a copy of the office memorandum herewith. As he has boastingly said that he will receive his appointment despite the Board's Action, I have deemed it proper to advise you as herein. The Secretary of War ~~a~~is aware of his failure & adverse record." Df, *ibid.* A memorandum dated Sept. 2 condemned Keegan for "prevarication and attempts at deception sufficient to prevent him from becomg an officer of the Army—" D, *ibid.* An undated memorandum with specific charges is *ibid.* On Jan. 23, 1872, Keegan, New York City, had written to USG. ". . . I served throughout the rebellion, in the rank's of the Union Army, and I am at present desirous of once more re'entering the service. I would request an appointment as 2d Lieutenant in the Regular Army, or Marine Corps. I was educated in Georgetown College, . . ." ALS (written on *Army and Navy Journal* stationery), *ibid.* On Jan. 24, USG endorsed this letter. "Respectfully refered to the Sec. of War. I am of opinion however that all the Army appointments have been made that can be made until after the apt. of the next graduating class at West Point." AES, *ibid.*

On Aug. 24, 1876, Thomas W. Wyman, Washington, D. C., wrote to USG. "Desiring to enter the Army of the United States, I most respectfully ask of you a permit to be examined as to my qualifications for a 'Citizens' appointment. I am the Son of Commodore Robert. H. Wyman U. S. Navy; Am twenty years and Seven Month old, having been born at Annapolis Md' on February 3d 1856." ALS, *ibid.*, Applications for Positions in War Dept. Favorable endorsements from Commodore Robert H. Wyman, S. Ledyard Phelps, Basil Norris, and Ammen are *ibid.* On Jan. 12, 1877, Commodore Wyman, Washington, D. C., wrote to Ammen concerning his son. ". . . Very recently I was told that Lieutenant Grant, told Assistant Surgeon Beirne that the President would make no Appointments other than at the instance of very intimate friends. . . . I cannot but beleive that the President has forgotten me, but without presumption or encroaching on him I do not see how I can with propriety bring it to his mind again—" ALS, *ibid.* On Jan. 13, Ammen endorsed this letter to USG. "at the risk of being regarded importunate and officious, I take the liberty of referring this note to you, to recall to your notice the application of the son of Commodore Wyman and the long and meritorious services of his forefathers." AES, *ibid.* Related papers are *ibid.* No appointment followed.

On Aug. 24, 1876, Robert P. Finley, Davenport, Iowa, had written to USG. "I have the honor to make the following statement. I was born in Missouri and am the fifth son of Bv't. Brig. Genl. C. A. Finley Surg. Genl. Ret'd. I have been in the Hardware business for several years but discouraged by want of success and the dullness of the times I am anxious to change my vocation and respectfully and earnestly request an appointment in the Army of the United States, preferring the Cavalry but submitting to your decision. . . ." ALS, *ibid.* On Aug. 25, Clement A. Finley, retired surgeon gen., West Philadelphia, wrote to USG on the same subject. ALS, *ibid.* On Oct. 9, Anthony J. Drexel, Philadelphia, wrote to USG. "My friend & neighbor Dr Finley is very desirous to have his son appointed in the Army & asks me to forward you the application which I do enclosed herewith & I will be very glad if you are able to grant the request or aid it in any way." ALS, *ibid.* No appointment followed. See *PUSG*, 25, 445.

1. On July 22, U.S. Senator Richard J. Oglesby of Ill. had endorsed papers to USG. "I again call your attention to the Recommendation of Mr Isaac Hamilton Rapp of Carbondale Ills for appointment as 2d Lieut in the Army and add my personal request for the appointment his Father was a good soldier I am informed and the young man posseses in his own right a good character and fine Qualities added to good sense and Industry. I shall be much pleased If you shall be able to gratify his wishes by an appointment" AES, DNA, RG 94, ACP, 4447 1876. On the same day, USG endorsed these papers. "Refered to the Sec. of War. If an opportunity occurs, through failures on the part of appointees already named, or from more vacancies occurring, I would like to have this apt. made." AES, *ibid.* No appointment followed. See Henry F. Withey and Elsie Rathburn Withey, *Biographical Dictionary of American Architects (Deceased)* (1956; reprinted, Los Angeles, 1970), p. 497.

Memorandum

[*July 26, 1876*]

Enclosure

No (1) Letter of July 22d from Gov. D. H. Chamberlain of S. C

No (2) Answer to above

No 3 Report of Hon. Wm Stone, Atty. Gn. S. C

No 4 Report of Gn. H. W. Purvis, Adj. & Inspt. Gn. S. C.

No 5 Copy of evidence before Cor. Jury

No 6 Printed Copy of statement by M. C. Butler

No 7 Printed Copy of letter by M. C. Butler

    8 Letter from Gov. Chamberlain to Hon. T. J. Robertson

    9 An address ~~by~~ to the American people by the colored people of Charleston, S. C.

    10 An Address by a Committee appointed at a Convention of leading representatives of Columbia, S. C on the 20th inst.

    11 Letter of July 15th /76 from Dist. Att'y Thos. Walton of Miss

    12 Letter of July 16 from Dist. Att'y Thos. Walton of Miss

    13 Report of Grand Jury lately in session in Oxford Miss.

AD (tabular material expanded), DLC-USG, III. Written on a Senate resolution dated July 20, 1876. "Resolved:, That the president be requested to communicate to the Senate, if in his opinion not incompatible with the public interest, any information he may have in regard to the recent slaughter of American Citizens at Hamburg, South Carolina." Copy, *ibid.* On July 26, Wednesday, Secretary of State Hamilton Fish recorded in his diary. "I call on the President and he reads to me the draft of a letter to Gov Chamberlain of South Carolina in reply to one to him about the Hamburg massacre also the draft of a message to the

Senate in answer to their call for information on that subject. The drafts contain some pretty sharp expressions which I advised him to omit. He is to revise them and submit the whole to Cabinet on Friday." DLC-Hamilton Fish. See following letter; message to Senate, July 31, 1876.

To Daniel H. Chamberlain

Washington, D. C. July 26th *1876*—

DEAR SIR:

I am in receipt of your letter of the 22d of July—and all the enclosures enumerated therein—giving an account of the late barbarous massacre of innocent men at the town of Hamburg—South Carolina—The views which you express as to the duty you owe to your oath of office—and to the citizen—to secure to all, their civil rights, including the right to vote according to the dictates of their own consciences, and the further duty of the Executive of the nation to give all needful aid, when properly called on to do so, to enable you to insure this inalienable right, I fully concur in—The scene at Hamburg, as cruel, bloodthirsty, wanton, unprovoked, and as uncalled for as it was, is only a repitition of the course that has been pursued in other Southern States[1] within the last few years— notably in Mississippi and Louisiana—Mississippi is governed to day by officials chosen through fraud and violence, such as would scarcely be accredited to savages, much less to a civilized and christian people—How long these things are to continue, or what is to be the final remedy, the Great Ruler of the Universe only knows— But I have an abiding faith that the remedy will come, and come speedily, and earnestly hope that it will come peacefully.—There has never been a desire on the part of the North to humiliate the South— nothing is claimed for one State that is not freely accorded to all the others, unless it may be the right to Kill negroes and republicans without fear of punishment, and without loss of caste or reputation —This has seemed to be a privilege claimed by a few States.—I repeat again that I fully agree with you as to the measure of your duties in the present emergency, and as to my duties—Go on, and let every Governor where the same dangers threaten the peace of his

State, go on in the conscientious performance of his duties to the
humblest as well as proudest citizen, and I will give every aid for
which I can find law, or constitutional power.—Government that
cannot give protection to the life, property and all guaranteed civil
rights (in this country the greatest is an untrammeled ballot,) to the
citizen, is in so far a failure, and every energy of the oppressed should
be exerted, (always within the law and by constitutional means,) to
regain lost privileges or protection—Too long denial of guaranteed
rights is sure to lead to revolution, bloody revolution, where suffering must fall upon the guilty as well as the innocent—Expressing
the hope that the better judgment and cooperation of the citizens of
the State over which you have presided so ably, may enable you to secure a [f]air trial and punishment of all offenders, without [d]istinc-
tion of "race, color, or previous condition of [ser]vitude"—and without aid from the federal government—but with the promise of such
aid on the conditions named in the foregoing—I subscribe myself

Very respectfully.

Your obedient servant—

U. S. GRANT

HON: D. H. CHAMBERLAIN—
GOVERNOR OF SOUTH CAROLINA.—

LS, South Carolina Archives, Columbia, S. C. *SED*, 44-1-85, 5–6; *SMD*, 44-2-48, III, 483;
HRC, 44-2-175, part 2, p. 17. On July [22], 1876, Governor Daniel H. Chamberlain of S. C.
wrote to USG. "The recent massacre at Hamburg in this State is a matter so closely connected with the public peace of this State that I desire to call your attention to it for the
purpose of laying before you my views of its effect and the measures which it may become
necessary to adopt to prevent the recurrence of similar events. It is in the first place man-
ifestly impossible to determine with absolute certainty the motives of those who were engaged in perpetrating the massacre at Hamburg. The demand which was made by the mob
upon the militia company for the surrender of their arms, taken in connection with the fact
that the militia are not shown to have committed or threatened any injury to any person
in that community, would seem to indicate a purpose to deprive the militia of their rights
on account of their race or political opinions. It seems impossible to find a rational or adequate cause for such a demand except in the fact that the militia company were composed
of negroes or in the additional fact that they were, besides being negroes members of the
Republican party. Those who made the demand were, on the other hand, white men and
members of the Democratic party. The lines of race and political party were the lines which
marked the respective parties to the affair at Hamburg. I mention this as a fact, and as apparently the most trustworthy index of the motives and aims which inspired those who
brought on this conflict. As affecting the public peace, however, the *effect* of this massacre

is more important than the motives which caused it. Upon this point I can speak with more confidence. It is not to be doubted that the effect of this massacre has been to cause wide-spread terror and apprehension among the Colored race and the Republicans of this State. There is as little doubt that, on the other hand, a feeling of triumph and political elation has been caused by this massacre, in the minds of a considerable part of the white people and Democrats. The fears of the one side correspond with the hopes of the other. I do not intend to overstate any matters connected with this affair. It is certainly true that most of those who have spoken through newspapers or otherwise upon this matter on the white or Democratic side have condemned the massacre. Their known and expressed opposition to such conduct has not, however, sufficed to prevent its occurrence, nor do I see any greater reason for beleiving that it will do so in the future. That class which now engages in this cruel work certainly disregard the expressed sentiments of those who assume to speak for the most part for their communities and go forward without fear of public opinion or pun-ishment. It is sometimes asked why do not the negroes or Republicans return violence with violence? why do they suffer themselves to be thus terrorized when their numbers greatly exceed those of their enemies? The answer is not difficult. The long habit of com-mand and self-assertion on the part of the whites of these Southern States, their superior intelligence, the fact that four-fifths at least of the property of these States is in their hands, are causes which contribute to give them an easy physical superiority thus far over the recently emancipated race which still exhibit the effect of their long slavery in their habit of yielding to the more imperious and resolute will and the superior intelligence and material resources of the white men. Add to this that in almost every Southern commu-nity their may be found a considerable number of daring, lawless, reckless white men, ac-customed to arms and deeds of violence, over whom the restraints of the better and more conservative classes of society have little, if any, power, who are inspired by an intense and brutal hatred of the negro as a free man and more particularly as a voter and a Republican, and you have the elements which would naturally give rise to, and in point of fact do give rise to nearly all the scenes of bloody violence which occur in the Southern States. Besides this, such events are sure to result in what is thought to be political advantage to the Dem-ocratic party and thus the communities are to a considerable extent, induced to overlook the naked brutality of the occurrence and seek to find some excuse or explanation of con-duct which ought to receive only unqualified abhorrence and condemnation followed by speedy and adequate punishment. In this way it often happens that a few reckless men are permitted or encouraged to terrorize a whole community and to destroy all freedom of ac-tion on the part of those who differ from them in political opinions. In respect to the Ham-burg massacre, as I have said, the fact is unquestionable that it has resulted in great im-mediate alarm among the colored people and republicans in that section of the State. Judging from past experience, they see in this occurrence a new evidence of a purpose to subject the majority of the voters of that vicinity to such a degree of fear as to keep them from the polls on election day and thus reverse or stifle the true political voice of the ma-jority of the people. But the Hamburg massacre has produced another effect. It has, as a matter of fact, caused a firm belief on the part of most republicans, that this affair at Ham-burg is only the beginning of a series of similar race and party collisions in our State, the deliberate aim of which is believed to be the political subjugation and control of this State. They see, therefore, in this event what foreshadows a campaign of violence and blood,— such a campaign as is popularly described as a campaign conducted on the 'Mississipi plan.' From what I have now said it will not be difficult to understand the feeling of a majority of the citizens in a considerable part of this State. It is one of intense solicitude for their lives and liberties. It is one of fear that in the passion and excitement of the current political campaign, physical violence is to be used to overcome the political will of the people. I confine myself here to a statement of what I beleive to be the facts of the present situation in this State as connected with the public peace and order, without any expression of my individual feelings or opinion. My first duty is to seek to restore and preserve public peace and order, to the end that every man in South Carolina may freely and safely enjoy all his civil rights and privileges, including the right to vote. It is to this end that I call your attention to these matters. I shall go forward to do all in my power as Governor to accomplish the ends above indicated, but I deem it important to advise you of the facts now stated and to solicit from you some indication of your views upon the questions presented. To be more specific, will the general government exert itself vigorously to repress violence in this State during the present campaign, on the part of persons belonging to either political party, whenever that violence shall be beyond the control of the State Authorities? Will the General Government take such precautions as may be suitable, in view of the feeling of alarm already referred to, to restore confidence to the good people of both races and political parties in this State by such a distribution of the military forces now here as will render the intervention of the general government, if it should become necessary, prompt and effective in restoring peace and order. It seems proper to add that I am moved in making this Communication to you by no motive or feeling save such as should animate me as the Chief Executive of this State, bound to do justice to all and to oppress none. I venture to say that I have given evidence by my whole conduct in this office that as Governor I am guided by my oath of office and my duty to all the poeple. I deem it my solemn duty to do my utmost to secure a fair and free election in this State, to protect every man in the free enjoyment of all his political rights and to see to it that no man or combination of men of any political party shall overawe or put in fear or danger any citizen of South Carolina in the exercise of his civil rights. And I trust you will permit me to add that I know no official duty more binding, in my judgment, on the Chief Executive of the United States than that of exercising the power with which he is invested by the Constitution and the laws, for the protection of the States against domestic violence and for the protection of the individual citizen in the exercise of his political rights, whenever a proper call is made upon him. I understand that an American citizen has an indefeasible right to vote *as he pleases*, to vote wrong as freely and safely as to vote right, and I know that whenever upon whatsoever pretext large bodies of citizens can be coerced by force or fear into absenting themselves from the polls or voting in a way contrary to their judgment or inclination, the foundation of every man's civil freedom is deeply and fatally shaken" Copy, USG 3. *HED*, 44-1-85, 2–5; *SMD*, 44-2-48, III, 480–82. On July 23, Chamberlain again wrote to USG. "*Personal*... I have mailed to you today the letter upon which we agreed, together with several documents which will give information concerning the massacre. In due course of mail the package should reach you on Tuesday morning, the 25th. It may be that one or two of the Enclosures will not be copied in time for today's mail and if not I will send them by the next mail. You will see that I have made a few changes in the letter to you from the copy which you now have, but they are not considerable." ALS, USG 3. See message to Senate, July 31, 1876.

On July 12, Wednesday, Chamberlain had written to Secretary of War James D. Cameron. "A riot occurred in the town of Hamburg in this State on the evening and night of the 8th. inst. which resulted in the killing of one white man and six colored men. The disturbance arose from the demand of a band of unauthorized white men for the surrender of their arms by a colored militia company located in Hamburg. This demand not being complied with a fire was opened upon the militia while assembled in the building used as an arsenal and drill-room, first with musketry and subsequently with artillery brought across the river from Augusta, Ga., and loaded with canister. The result was that one white man and one colored man was killed during the firing, and subsequently a considerable number of the militia were captured by the rioters and while held as prisoners, disarmed and defenceless, five of them were Called out one by one by name and shot dead in succession. Three more of these captured militia men were fired upon and wounded severely, if not mortally, in endeavoring to escape. If the accounts which have reached me up to this time are to be trusted,—and they are reports of eye-witnesses and officials who have investigated the affair on the spot,—the affair may be properly characterized as a cold-blooded butchery of unoffending and unarmed colored men by a brutal and blood-thirsty mob of white men. Of course, such an event excites wide-spread alarm. It is believed by many to have been a pre[c]oncerted demonstration to overawe and intimidate the colored people for political purposes. However that may be, there can be no doubt of the horrible atrocity of the occurrence and the necessity of such action as will give security against such occurrences in the future. I propose to endeavor to enforce the civil laws of the State against these murderers, and in all ways to do my duty as Governor of the State. At present the situation is not such as to enable me to call on the United States for active assistance but the request that I now make is, that a few United States soldiers be stationed at Hamburg, with a small detachments at Aiken and Edgefield Court House, the County seats of the two Counties concerned in this riot. There are at present six companies of United States Infantry here in Columbia, and if one company is ordered to be stationed at Hamburg, small detachments of an officer and ten or fifteen men can be sent thence to Aiken and Edgefield C. H. The moral effect of the presence of these troops will be all that is needed, I trust, to execute our laws, but in the present state of affairs I deem the presence of troops, as I have indicated, absolutely essential. I shall write to our Senators and ask them to call on you in reference to this matter on Friday, and if you agree with me I trust you will cause the necessary orders to reach here by telegraph on Friday next. If the military Commander here is directed to confer with me as to the proper disposition of the troops the arrangements will be made most satisfactorily. I wish to impress upon you my sense of the necessity of the action I have indicated. The President, when I was in Washington recently, stated to me that the troops here in Columbia could be stationed in different parts of the State, if it became necessary. Immediate action upon this request is respectfully and earnestly asked." Press copy, South Carolina Archives, Columbia, S. C. On July 14, Cameron wrote to Chamberlain. "If convenient for you to leave home I will be very glad to have you come to Washington, as early next week as possible." Copy, DNA, RG 107, Letters Sent, Military Affairs. See *CR*, 44–1, 4641–46, 4705–16. On July 19, Chamberlain arrived in Washington, D. C., for consultations with USG, Cameron, and Attorney Gen. Alphonso Taft. See *New York Herald*, July 13, 20, 1876; *New York Times*, July 14, 1876; *SMD*, 44-2-48, I, 27–90, 145–68, 695–714, II, 308–39, 490–98, 523–29, 602–19, III, 581–618. On Jan. 12, 1877, Chamberlain, Columbia, testified before a Senate investigating committee concerning his visit to Washington, D. C. *Ibid.*, II, 28–31.

On July 17, 1876, Robert M. Wallace, U.S. marshal, Charleston, S. C., had written to Taft. "The recent cruel murder, by a lawless mob, of a number of the members of a colored militia company, at Hamburg, S. C., calls for some action on the part of the United States Government, in order to aid in punishing the perpetrators and in preventing a repetition of such atrocities. I am not prepared to suggest any particular line of action at present, further than to recommend that a detachment or company of United States soldiers under an officer who is known to entertain republican sentiments be stationed at or near Hamburg, and that they be instructed to support the proper civil officers in any attempt to arrest the guilty parties who reside in that section of country. Their presence would have a good effect in restraining the disposition for turbulent outbreaks, which is manifested by the white citizens of that section, and it would restore confidence among the colored people, and give them an assurance that they were not to be abandoned to the swift destruction which was meted out to some of their friends and neighbors. . . ." *Ibid.*, III, 89; *HED*, 44-2-30, 94.

On the same day, John D. Bagwell, Plainfield, N. J., wrote to USG. "The unprovoked Massacre of unoffending citizens of Hamburgh S. C. on the 9th inst, dezerves the condemnation of all good citizens, and should evoke the strong arm of the law, in just punishment of the perpetrators. It is obvious now, if indeed there could have been before any doubts existing in the minds of the friends of the government, what is to be the policy of the Southren democracy to decrease the republican vote, and hand the government over to the same power that appealed to the arbitrament of the sword for its disruption. As in 1872 'Anything to beat Grant' So in 1876 anything to beat the Republican party, though it be the Massacre of a few thousand Republicans white and black is the evident ultimatam of the *reform Democracy* in the present campaign. I am confident that I utter the request of every patriotic man, and woman through out the length and breadth of the land, when I beg of you to vindicate the Supremacy of the law, and to exhaust every constitutional measure in the defence of the lives and liberties of the patriotic Citizens of the South. The late massacre at Hamburgh is unmistaably the first fruits of the Supreme Court decision, *declaring the enforcement act unconstitutional*, and which will be repeated again and again in almost every state in the South during the next three months; if the Supremacy of the law is not upheld, peacable if can be; forcible if must be. 'Let no guilty man escape' is the only course to be pursued in the total suppression of the wholesale murders, riots, and disorders, that have for the past eleven years been so prevalent in the South. In the name of the thousands of defenceless victims in the South who are already marked for their death: in the name of the Constitution that yet with impunity is trampled under the feet of the enimies of the government, I implore the execution of the law, in the protection of the lives of these people, and 'Let us have peace'—permanent peace, in the preservation of the Sacredness of the Constitution, in every part of our Common Country." ALS, DNA, RG 60, Letters from the President.

Also on July 17, John M. Carter, "an African and bans a slave," New York City, wrote to USG. "Not many mounth a go sixteen ar seventeen black men were arested in one of the southern states on mere suspicion of havng took part in the murder of a white man thay were lodged in jail About mid night a set of mounted white roughs road up to the jail overpowered the jailar took those poor inisont souls out in to a skirt of woods and did not gave them time to make peace with there God but ridled them with bulets And I venture to say not one of these roughs were braught to justice no for there is no justice for the poor black man in the south and very litle in the North I can call you atention to sevearl cases in the noth Far instance the two colored men returning from a picnic last fall who were asailed by a party of white Roughs and of the black men were killed instancly and the other dyed in a few days after wrds anothe case of a policman who shot and killed a black man in Brooklyen and was only put in prison for Twenty nine days And now in this Greet Centenial year when the whole nation are celerbrating there freedom and Rights We the black men are dagered to the very heart with the awful news from Hamburg of the butchury ten or twelve Black men by those law men. men who are a disgrace to the Comunity what were thay shot for Why thay were shot because thay were celerbrating the 4th of July I ask in the name of the whole popilation and evey black man in this country how long is this thing going to last we black men in the norther states due feel moast deeply for our people in the souther states will the president of the United

States Please for God sake look into this mater and stop the butchery of our people in South" ALS, *ibid.*

On Aug. 19, L. Cass Carpenter, collector of Internal Revenue, Columbia, wrote to USG. "*Personal* . . . I take the liberty of addressing you a few lines upon the condition of affairs here in this state. It has been evident to those who have had much to do with the politics of this state during the past six years or more, that the democrats were planning some scheme by which they were to capture this state at the next election in November. What that scheme was, has only been developed during the past ten days. The affair at Hamburg doubtless hastened the development, and the nomination of Wade Hampton, and a full ex-confederate military ticket have now made it as plain as noonday. Indeed, they do not hesitate to avow their purpose to carry the state at any, and every hazard. Their principal plan, is 'quiet intimidation,' by a 'show of force' at every republican meeting. Twice during the past week I have attended republican meetings, called for the purpose of ratifying the recent republican presidential nomination, one meeting held at Edgefield, and one at Newberry, at both of which there were present several hundreds of armed, mounted white men, members of rifle and sabre clubs of the respective counties who went theirre for no other purpose that to quietly intimidate the speakers, and the assemblage gathered to hear them. At both of these meetings the Governor of the state was present by invitation to address the republicans present, and at both meetings he was grossly, and wantonly insulted, jeered at and hooted by the white-line rifle clubs present for that purpose. At each meeting, we found, when we arrived at the public square where the procession usually forms to march to the grove, these rifle &. sabre clubs drawn up awaiting our arrival. At Edgefield I think there were not less than 800 mounted armed white men belonging to the democratic party, under the command of Gen Butler. At Newberry there were not less than 500 armed and mounted men present, who upon our arrival set up the same old 'rebel yell' that Union soldiers have so often heard upon the field of battle. Upon arriving at the stand where the speaking takes place, they usually entirely surround it, riding close up to the stand, as they did at Newberry, thus compelling the colored men to take positions in the rear of the horses, and farthest from the stand. At every point there were some of them present. They demanded half of the time, in which to reply to republican speakers, and to avoid trouble, and probable bloodshed, we allowed them their demand. The meeting was thus virtually under their control, for they were mounted and armed to the teeth, while the republicans were dismounted, and unarmed. In point of numbers there were probably quite as many democrats as republicans. While no threats were made outright against any one, it was plainly to be seen, that they were there for no other purpose than to over-awe the republicans by a 'show of force.' This plan they intend to carry out to the end. Should the republicans make any resistance to their demands to share the time with them, I am satisfied that no meeting could be held at all, and if an attempt should be made to hold one, blood would be shed. Although the county officials, such as Sheriff and Coroner, are republicans, their hands are virtually tied against such force. Should the sheriff, by any chance, succeedd in arresting a person charged with disturbing one of these meetings, no jury in this section could convict him against the testimony of he scores of willing witnesses who stand ready at all times to prove an alibi. In case of resistance to the sheriff, no posse-comitatus could be formed to assist him, except colored men, and these would stand no chance at all with the old, trained veterans of the confederacy. These are the reasons why the civil authorities are powerless to enforce their authority. When the civil authorities of a county fail, the Governor has no militia except negroes, and these are undisciplined, untrained, ignorant of military duties, and wholly unequal to cope with the white-liners on the other side. Many of the leading spirits in this movement are men who were charged with Ku Kluxing in 1870 &. 1871, and are more bitter today, than they were then, simply because they think the goverment will not punish them now, any more than it did then. The leniency and clemency of the national government have been mistaken for cowardice, and the longer they live, the bolder and more outspoken they grow. At the ratification meeting held here the 16th inst. some of the speakers openly advised their hearers 'to put out of the way' the white republicans first, then the mulattoes, and then the negroes. They said they did not fear the U. S. army, they had met it once without flinching, and they were ready to do so again. They were going to carry this state at whatever cost. Their intentions, it seems to me, are to keep up this 'quiet intimidation' until election day, and upon that day to keep perfectly quiet and peaceful that they may not come directly into conflict with the U. S. laws. If there is no way in which this species of 'intimidation' can be stopped, I see nothing to prevent them from carrying the election. Unless the government makes some show of force by sending the military to these infected counties, as a sort of moral support to the republicans, it will not only be useless to expect us to carry the election, but white republicans will not be permitted to live here in peace and quiet and express their political sentiments. Trusting Your Excellency will pardon this trespass upon your valuable time; . . ." ALS, *ibid.* *HED*, 44-2-30, 95–96. On Aug. 23, Carpenter wrote a private letter on the same subject to Secretary of the Interior Zachariah Chandler, who also served as chairman, Republican National Committee. ALS, DNA, RG 60, Letters from the President. *HED*, 44-2-30, 97–98.

On Aug. 21, David T. Corbin, U.S. attorney, Greenville, S. C., had written to Taft. "I have the honor to request that you will send to this State an intelligent and experienced detective to investigate the conspiracies being entered into in several counties to deprive the colored citizens of the right to vote at the coming election. . . . I have been retained by the attorney-general (Stone) to assist him in the prosecution of the Hamburgh murderers in the State court, and we expect to enter upon those trials on the first Monday of September, coming. I doubt very much whether the State can proceed now, on account of the lack of reliable accessible testimony. A practical bar exists in the terror of the witnesses to testify, the constant fear of assassination if they do. It is probable these cases will have to be postponed, or they will fail. Further, they will fail even with the best testimony just now, as the juries will not convict on any proof, however good. The State court is too weak. The only hope of effectually dealing with these troubles, in my judgment, lies in the vigorous prosecution of the offenders in the United States courts. To do this I must have something more than the ordinary means at the command of the district attorneys to work up the cases and prepare them for trial. It is accurate, reliable information that must be first had, and I trust you will furnish me the means of obtaining it. I desire that this letter may be treated as confidential, at present, as any indication of my views might warn the enemy and frustrate my plans." *SMD*, 44-2-48, III, 89–91; *HED*, 44-2-30, 96–97. On Sept. 6, William Stone, S. C. attorney gen., wrote to Chamberlain explaining that witness intimidation and political complications compelled him to postpone the trial of the Hamburg rioters. *SMD*, 44-2-48, III, 497–98.

On Aug. 26, Saturday, J. C. Grant, Abbeville, S. C., had written to USG. "I. will informe you of our Recencs truble in this Countey of abbeville South cala. on Last Tuesday the colorede Republicain a Large meetern at abbeville, C. H. S. C thay Democratic parttey Rushen on the Colored people a Rone The Stand and the Democraitic Speaker Siad When he got up that this Was a Republicean Meeten but Seme that we captide theme So that Want off very well and the Speachis was made and The Crowd all want off up towen the colored people carrede thay flaght that the Republician funish the Name of thay Nomanee as President of the united Steate as the colored man March a Rone the town of abbeville, the Democratic partey in force March up to the colored men and toll theme that thay must give up that flage and as the colored Men would Not give up the flage thay thern commence firen thay pistol and as Near to Theme as to Shoot holes in thay Clothing thay had on. Beetting one Colored man on the ~~and~~ head he blad Nelley to death but he is giten better thene he was and on Last friday the 25the The Democratic of a Large crowd of White Men want to a publice Shool Siad as the Riley Shool house and thay was a colored Man teachen publice Shool for the Govement and thay Rode up a Rone the Shool house whece he was teachen Shool thay Rown the and went in and hettin then the man with the Shool bell and Said to hime for you as a captin of the Milterrey Compney you must this get up theme guns in one week time if you Du not we Will take theme gunes a way frome you thay was Said to be a bout five hunderd mounted as all was Soperse to be arme a Rone the Shool Destution the govement teacher Now mr President we Say to you of hight Power of the u. S. Steats if you Exspeake for the colored men to du whate ~~what~~ thay coud to warse votein Seur you have to give ous Some protecetion and I bege you to du it Soon as the time will admite you to du So as hight power of our tone Steate. we ask your help in the Name of the Lord and I ask you to Exsquce bad ~~R~~Writen to Night all So I ask you to Not Wose my Name aney father this ase a Colored man that is Writen to you We have Ralley to the poles for your. Sopote for eaight Long years and Now What we ask that you will Sen help to abbeville. Soon I will come to a Close I ask you if you plece to answer to answer this Letter if you plece . . ." ALS, DNA, RG 60, Letters from the President. See *HMD*, 44-2-31, part 1, pp. 272–73; *SMD*, 44-2-48, I, 315–17, 428–30, 505–6, II, 86–89.

On Sept. 8, Arba N. Waterman, Chicago, wrote to USG. "If the telegraphic accounts are correct a great outrage has been perpetrated in Charlestown South Carolina upon a body of colored men, who it is said intend to vote the Democratic ticket. The right of every man to freely discuss political questions, to assemble with his fellows for political action and to exercise the elective franchise in the most perfect security should be maintained at all hazard and at whatever cost. It is a right which the people of the South, as a rule, practically have never enjoyed and without the enjoyment of which the formal republican goverment becomes as in the entire South it was prior to the suppression of the rebellion the merest farce. If there is but one black man in Charlestown who desires to vote the Democratic ticket he should be protected in so doing though it becomes necessay in order to afford him such protection to send there a fleet of war and ten thousand armed men. If there are three, fifty or five hundred negroes there who desire to parade the streets carrying Tilden banners, protect them in so doing though it be necessary to concentrate there a dozen regiments. If there is any portion of this country in which a citizen cannot express freely his political opinions and vote for whom he sees fit, unless such opinions and such vote ~~is~~are in accord with the sentiment of the community in which he lives, and the goverment of the United States cannot afford to him the security and protection to which the laws entitle him then the sooner ~~the~~ such imbecile goverment releases its claim to territory in which it cannot protect its subjects in the exercise of their dearest rights the better. For forty years white men had in the South no political rights which the local community respected. There was no more a republican goverment there than there was in Russia. The time has come for the goverment to assert itself and to make it prudent and safe for all men white or black to exercise all their political rights in Mississippi, Louisana, Texas Arkansas, Alabama Georgia The Carolinas and Florida even as they do in Illinois and Massachusetts. All other incidents and all other issues of this campaign sink into insignificance beside the importance of protecting every man in the enjoyment of the right of free speech and an unintimidated vote. Without these the election becomes a farce, the form of goverment a mockery, the law a reproach, and every evil which bad goverment engenders may be expected to follow. I trust that you will at once publicly assure the colored people of Charlestown that they shall be protected in meeting for political purposes and in voting for whom they see fit whatever may be the sentiment of the community in which they reside; and that you will make your assurance good." ALS, DNA, RG 60, Letters from the President. See Richard Zuczek, *State of Rebellion: Reconstruction in South Carolina* (Columbia, 1996), pp. 174–75.

On Sept. 14, L. M. Jordan, Edgefield Court House, S. C., wrote to USG. "I know we have never met but I write to inform you the kind of men we have to deal with in South Carolina. General Gary is advising the Rifle Clubs which have been formed by the old Rebel Democracy, to attack the United Soldiers now Stationed here and run them away from here   he says in all of his public speeches that he would not hesitate to lead a Company of men to attack them and kill the last one of them   I tell you Mr President that the Same old Rebel spirit is in these men yet and nothing but the strong arm of your Goverment will bring them to feel that they must obey the law. Genl Gary said the other day that he intended to carry the election or he would fill evry Street in Edgefield with dead Negros—" ALS, DNA, RG 60, Letters from the President. *SMD*, 44-2-48, III, 91–92; *HED*, 44-2-30, 99. See Proclamation, Oct. 17, 1876.

1. On March 5, James H. Brown, Beaufort, S. C., had written to USG. ". . . in these days & time it Seams that the poor & colored republican of this state & county has no chance for justice) dear President I. was in this city &. county for 10 years Sience I. was out of the war) & never had a black mark against me) & now I have had my own cart taken away from me by fals & briveary of money paid to the party to Sware falcly against me for to take my oawn property from me & cast me in to presen for one year) dear President— I. am heare in jail & expect Soon to go to the State Penetention at Columbia for one year & my poor wife & small children are suffering on wrong accouse) . . . do dear President if you will be so good to send me alittle means & trust it in to the hands of my friend Lieut Govr, R. H. Gleaves that he will give it to me when my time is ended in prisen if I had money to get me a good lawyer to defend me in this last court thy would never been able to take such advantage of me . . . thy are trying to brake up the republicans in this County by taken us & put us in presen without a cause . . ." ALS, DNA, RG 60, Letters from the President.

On June 14, J. H. Einen, Greensboro, Ala., wrote to USG. "i in form you to day a few Lines. of Bisnes. to ask you Can i get Me up a Millaintery Company, of Collor[d] Men. in this Little town of greens boro. the White Men has got one and i want to Do the same. and if you Will in sist Me in geting guns. for it. anCer Me as soon as you Can. i am antious to kNoW." ALS, *ibid.*, RG 59, Miscellaneous Letters.

On June 15, Frederick W. Sumner, postmaster, Sherman, Tex., wrote to USG. "Enclosed you will find an account of one of the most diabolical Murders on record. I fully concur in the statement of Dr W. H. Irving herewith inclosed. I was personally acquainted with Prof Gillyard, and no more civil, quiet and perfect Gentleman could be found anywhere, White or black. But his great crime was, that he belonged to the colored race, was educated, and going about raising funds to build a College at Austin Texas to educate the colored youths of this state. Van Zant County where he was so brutally murdered has been the nest and head quarters for Ku Klux ever since Andrew Johnson came clear in his Impeachment trial. I believe if Gen'l Sheriden could go down there with three companies of Troups and establish a Court Martial and punish the guilty parties as they justly deserve, that we would have very few men murdered hereafter on account of color." ALS, *ibid.*, RG 60, Letters from the President. Enclosed is a letter of June 1[4] from W. H. Irving, Sherman, to USG. "Enclosed please find a plain statement of Facts related to the Cold blooded murder that occured in this region on the 6 Inst. Mr Gillyard was well and favourably known in this place as a man of Letters & profound Litterature. The writer knew him years since in philadelphia shortly after the war, He was a True and ardent *Lover* of the *Cause* of his *race* for which they *fought* & died. His character was *unimpeachible*; unsullied, was murdered for his *collor* & *Loyalty* to the *Governent*, and in Every respect was acting within the circumpherance of the 15th Amendment & Its provisions, as well as the clause in ~~of~~ the Constitution '*That no person shall* be *deprived of life liberty* or *property* He fell a martyr To the noble cause for which we all took a part This is only one case of about 3000 in this state Since the Close of the war It most emphaticly demonstrates, as you stated to And Johnson in '67 when you were in command of the *U S Forces* as *Leut* Gnl, That 'more Union men were being killed in '66 '67 & 68 than during the war In La. & Texas, when you urged upon him To Declar 'Martial Law' in one or more Districts & give the Secess a True 'Idea' of the strong arm of the Government. This sir; is the begining of the campaign in Texas & all through the Extreme South, for '76 No man is Safe who is in any way prominent in Sustaining the Governent & will Stand Erect & upright for our cause 'Vengence is mine' I will repay Sath God' . . . refer to mr Fred Sumner the Efficient & much valued post master of this City." ALS, *ibid.* In a petition docketed June 28, Joseph R. Matthews *et al.* wrote to USG. "We the colored citizens of Sherman County of Grayson, State of Texas, We do most earnestly appeal to the Government for protection against violence on the part of the Democratic white people of this State, Predjdice is becoming so strong against colored people that they can't exercise the priviledge of a free people, if a colored man attempts to travel on the high way and preach the Gospel he is liable to be murdered at any time without provication or cause on his part. For instance professor Guilard (a colored Minis[t]er) was murdered without cause on his part more than that he was a Minster of the Gospel and an educated man and calculated to teach our people, which our Democratic friend can't or won't stand where they have power to prevent   an other inst.   Professor Ball was made an attempt upon to be murdered while lecturing at Bryan, We there fore ask protection from the general Government and if it denies us protection we have no recour[se] to apply too," DS (28 signatures, 27 by mark), *ibid.* Irving endorsed this petition. "the within named cittzens are all collored industreous peacible & True to the cause of Human rights, The times here are Such that immedeate help must be had or more bloood will shed from These innocent people Again we beg yourn immedate attention To This most important Subject" AES (undated), *ibid.* HED, 44-2-30, 137.

On July 29, Henry A. M. Bartley, "Near Orange C. H.," Va., wrote to USG. "*Private.* . . . I am aware of a well-planned plot against my life at the village of Orange C. H., Va, by WHITE LINERS—my offending being my opposition to the late war, and continued support of the Republican party since the war, and I prefer loosing my life in defence of my country to ~~being~~ becoming a martyr to principle. The republicans of Va, and I believe of the whole South, have been shamefully left to the tender mercies (?) of their enemies. Genl. Sheridan's reports from Louisana were the most correct I have seen of southern feeling and actions. Allow me again to insist that you will aid me in finding employment in Washington. . . ." ALS, DNA, RG 56, Applications. Related papers are *ibid.* No appointment followed.

On Aug. 26, G. F. Dihne, Pittsburgh, wrote to USG. "*Private Letter.* . . . Permit me to State in the Outsett that I am a Friend to the President, having had the pleasure to vote an two occations for You, as presedent of the U. S. having also voted twice for Our lemanted Lincoln, and Shall take pleasure to vote for Hays & Wheeler, . . . Permit me now to Say, that of late, I Seen a Publication in Some of the news papers, Emenating from the Secretary of War, Mr. Camron, to Gel. Sherman, recomending, to hold Troops in rediness, to Send South, for the protection of the People of the Southern States—against lawless bandes of men, and as I understand it, asking also Their Coopperation in the matter—permit me to Say, that I belive this to be a Wise plan, for unless, a number, a large body of Troops are Sent there—and distributed at the various Election Stations—at least at the most of them the Loyal White—as well as the collored Voter (the former but few now) dare not Venture to Vote the Republican Ticket—I was made aware of that fact, while I was South in november 1874. I was through the Several Southern States Spending upwardes of 60 deys (Selling goodes) and I was in the City of Atlanta Ga. on the day of the Ellection   I went to the State House, (or Court House) the onely place in that large City. for voting—at my arival at the place I found Small bandes of negros—outside the Enclosure on the Street—some few negro's in the State House Yard—but I found a large crowd of White People. I Supose from three to 500 men.   my attention was attracted by the great noice and Yelling of the Whites, and the Shoving about and the abuse of negro's. who were indevering to go up to Vote—I heard the Sharp noice of the 'Police mace' coming down on the negros head—a Sign for him to go back which they did—I Seen three (3) negro's get pushed up to the window, amidts Yells—their Hats picked off their heads. and thrown into the Crowd below.   the negros were Challanged—taken down bey Officers as 'repetors' and marched to 'Jail'   I Saw another pushed up—his coat all torne to Ribbons—. . . I seen as meny as from 10 to 15 negros maceed, knocked down—had the Poor fellows resisted—the Whites would have shot them on the spot—. . . While passing throgh the Several States Ky. Tenn. Ga. Miss. Ala. Louisana, seeing and hearing the people talk, and observing the Status of the cold. man, I have come to the conclusion, that unless Government Sends in the Several Southen States a large amout of Troops before the Election, So that Republicans can hold meetings—Explaning the Republican Platform and Republican princaples, and So as to be on hand in full force Even at meetings (for Should negros hold meetings, the Whites will report that these meetings are for an outbrake to murder Whites) So that free Speech as well as a free vote shall be accorded them—nothing will give these people so much Encouragment, as the sending in a lage amout of good and reliable Troops, who will fulley obey Instructions, to protect the large body of Voters in their rights—. . ." ALS, *ibid.*, RG 60, Letters from the President. *HED*, 44-2-30, 146–48.

On Aug. 27, Anonymous, Augusta, Ga., wrote to USG. "Lynch Law in Augusta Ga . . . we write to tell you that last night a colored man by the name of Thomas Williams was taken from the jail and mobbed ~~on~~ on account of assaulting a white woman by the nam[e] Mrs Bridges   although a general feeling of indignation in the neighborhood at the distardly outrage it was thought that the law would take its course and that there was no danger of the prisoner being dealt summarily with but last night between ten and eleven o'clock a large crowd numbering perhaps fifty person[s] none of whom were known to the officer or police in charge of the jail broke open the front gate and door with an axe when they demanded the keys of the jailor but he had secreted and after a vain search they then proceeded to break open doors leading the prisoner cell up stairs with an axe. Gaining entrance they took the prisoner from his cell and carried him about fiftey or a hundred yards from the jail and literally shot him to pieces besides cutting him in several places with axes and hatchets His head was cut from his body. this was done in the city it was impossible for that to be done and nobody know who they were   after he was killed he was carried to the hospital and from there to the poor-house and was no alarm made about it at all this makes the three men got killed from Augusta jail and nothing been done about it and they didnt have their trial even and Mr. B[r]idget keeps the jail and we have no Governor to protect us—the people in Georgia have no showing . . . they say it is no more to kill a nig-

ger than a hog they speak it boldy our lives are in stakes all the time and please send us
a strict military troop white and Colored for protection. all over Georgia our lives are not
safe no time and Augusta is the Capitol of all devilment . . ." L, DNA, RG 60, Letters from
the President.

On Sept. 15, Horace Booton, deputy U.S. marshal, Eastern District, Tex., Brownsville, wrote to USG. "Can I be of any service during the presidential campaign If I can am
willing to serve you at any time, will go any where, or enforce any trust that may be assigned *me* Address me at Galveston Txas care of U S Marshall after 15 Oct will remain
hear till then." ALS, *ibid.*

On Sept. 25, Mrs. George B. Wray, Bridgeport, Conn., wrote to USG. "Will you
please to excuse the liberty I am thus taking in addressing you, but from the importance
of the case I am induced to call your attention to a portion of a letter cut from a New York
paper, being part of an appeal from a southern born man (white) to the North for protection, in the coming general election. From the multiplicity of business you have to attend
to, this might escape your notice, hence, as we are all republicans, my husband and two
sons, defend your administration and feels deeply concerned for the colored people in the
south, therefore we urge you, for God's sake, to do all you can to protect those helpless
people. I wouldn't attempt to dictate, but allow me to suggest the propriety of bringing
the soldiers from the Mexican border and station them in Louisanna and South Carolina
and Mississippi and thus let the democrats reap the fruit of their doings for their termer-
ity in reducing the army this year. Also, some of those soldiers under Gen. Terry; instead
of bean disbanded might be stationed in some of those southern states until after the general election; by so doing many precious lifes may be saved. Again I would suggest: that if
any of those southern rebels should resist the United States Marshall or fire upon the
Union soldiers, such States should be placed under Martial Law and tried for high treason, and every one who has thus fought against this government, if not hung, should be
disfranchised for life and their property confiscated. With sincere desire and prayer to God
that hHis blessing may rest upon you and the nation . . ." ALS, *ibid.* A clipping is *ibid.*

Also on Sept. 25, Maggie Atkins, Bon Aqua, Tenn., wrote to USG. "Through the
great love which I have for my country, I now adress you with regard to important events
which are transpiring in this section of country. Through-out this line of railroad—the
Nashvill & Northwestern—the Democrats are forming clubs, and hoisting the rebel flag.
They have cast our dear old national banner to the fore wind, have, in its stead; planted
that ignominious emblem of treachery and treason. In the coming election they will control the colored vote, by their nefarious scheming and plotting. They have threatened the
life of our colored candidate for Gov. What in the name of all that is good, pure and holy,
will this state of things tend? If I posessed the means, I would go over the whole of Tenn.,
and impress this important idea upon the minds of the colored people, would place a flag
of truce beside that of the rebel flag, and thus, put them to shame. It is not for me, a woman;
to presume to be so officious, or egotistical; as to advise, or advance a subject of so much
importance, and that, to our honored President. But, casting this aside, I ask you, in the
name of our country, our flag and our Union; to send out troops over this section of Tenn.,
to guard the poll's, in the coming election, to suppress the breath of treason, which reigns
supreme here. They have already thrown out the 'gauntlet of war,' in the insolent act of
hoisting their rebel flag, which all true patriots, should look upon with contempt and disgust.—Should you not beleive the truth of this assertion, send a spy out into camp, and be
convinced of this treachery. I shall send this to a friend of mine, to be posted at Nashvill,
for fear it should not reach its destination, if posted here. In conclusion, I ask of you to save
our country, our fallag, and our Republic, in this impending crisis. That God may be with

you, in this struggle for liberty, is the prayer of," ALS, *ibid.* On Sept. 27, Frederic A. Chase, Fisk University, Nashville, wrote to USG. "The enclosed letter was sent to me by a southern lady, white, who has been very anxious to teach in this school, which you may know is a school for the education of colored people. Failing in that she has wanted to teach a colored common school. I should judge from one interview with her and several letters that she is a person of good character, but possibly a little unsettled in mind. Her former residence is Waverley Tenn. I have no knowledge of the contents of her note, beyond her note to me." ALS, *ibid.*

On Sept. 30, John Mercer, Orange Hill, Fla., wrote to USG. "may it Please your Honor I take the pivoledge of writing you A few Lines to let you know how things Are going on out here   there is A greadeat Deal of excitement out here   the Negroes have Become Demoralized from hearing so much speaking   they are forming Tildon clubs in Diferent parts of the Contry   I do not like to see this   I donot Like for us to give up the old Ship   She has glided on tolerable Smoothly for A long time   I think these Negro clubs might Be Bought in with A Little Money   in Washington and Jackson Counties, there is 5 or 6 thousand Negroes   if you think there is A chance to save this state see the officials and get them to throw in 50 cts or 1 dollar each and send out to me and I think I can work out Demoralized feeling   if you get aney Money of account you can send it to Bainbridge Georgia by express   also Drop me A few lines or send it in A Regestered letter   what is Done must be done Soon   Reflect on what I say   the old ship is in Danger   when you git this answer it if you Please . . . NB Let this Be privet   the time is short But there can Be A greadeal done in A short time with Money   I have no office and donot know whether it Ever will fall to my Lot or know   excuse me for writing so Long A letter to you" ALS, *ibid.*

On Oct. 2, L. M. Macksell, Towanda, Kan., wrote to USG. "you may think it strange to receive this note   I was at a Tilden and Hendricks meeting one night last week   the speaker got off considerble trash about you   I took all untill he said you was a thif and a coward   the I told him he was a damed liar   that raised cain in the camp   they tryed to scare me out but i told them I was a soldier under Grant to long to be scard at rebbles   after the meeting was over I come home went to bed   about 1 oclock a party come to my house on hore back called me up and told me they would give me two days to leave the contry   I told them positively I would not   they said if did not I would be sorry of it   when the time was out the thrd night the come and burnt my house and barn and all in both of them in all i have lost $2000   I have a Wife and six children nothing to eat nothing weare and no place to live no money no frinde this side of Scotland that I no of   now I do pray for you to have mercy on me and send me a draft on Newyork for you think you can sand solicit some of my old soldier friends to help me out this time Great need" ALS, *ibid.*

On Oct. 9, George S. Fisher *et al.*, Washington, D. C., wrote to USG. "At a meeting of the Central Republican Association of States, (which is composed of Delegates from all the Republican Associations of this District,) held on the 27th day of September last, the undersigned were appointed a Committee to present to you the following . . . Be it Resolved—That it is the solemn duty of the Government, by all means, to protect, defend, and shield every citizen without respect to Age, Sex, Color, or previous condition, and see to it that no man's, woman's, or child's blood—or rights of person, or property in any part of its wide domain, as well as abroad, shall be sacrificed without indemnity under the laws of God and man—especially the Statutory laws of the United States, and that every assassination for political opinions sake, calls for immediate and condign punishment, so that '*no guilty man shall escape*'. And, Mr. President, while we are Republicans and represent Republican Associations composed only of Republicans from almost every State in the Union, we disclaim any partisanship in offering this Resolution:—we come to you as citizens of our common Country—of this great Republic—having the best interests, honor, and common good of our whole Country at heart. That Country, too, can never be truly prosperous and happy until *every citizen* is protected in *every right* of citizenship in all sections alike. That this is not so now, in some of the States, is patent to every man. That the power is conferred upon you as the Executive Chief of the Nation, to protect every citizen at home as well as abroad, no one who comprehends the true theory of our Government will deny. These being facts, we respectfully but earnestly ask your attention to the condition of affairs in those States and Districts of the South, where thousands of citizens are being deprived of one of the highest and dearest rights of American citizenship—the rights of Elective franchise, the right of unrestricted suffrage. That this right is being denied by intimidation, outrage, and murder, practiced in the interest of a political party which claims to desire 'Reform' from alleged malpractices, only renders the crime greater, and the necessity of Executive interposition more urgent and apparant. It would, Sir, be a work of supererogation on our part, and task your time too greatly, to enumerate a tithe of the enormities and crimes alluded to. We can only speak of them in general terms, and ask you to extend the *aegis* of governmental protection, wherever it may be needed, to secure the freedom and security of the citizen of whatever political party, color, or condition. Aware that through the proper channels you are advised of the localities where such protection is needed, we do not propose to protrude advice upon that subject; our object being to assure you that the people of the whole Country—those whom you have led to victory in War, and wisely governed in Peace, will sustain you in the future as they have in the past, in every effort to uphold the honor of our Nations flag and to protect its citizens in every right. And could this grand object be effected by you, to the laurel wreath of the Victor, and civic crown of the wise Ruler, you will have added to you, ere you retire from public life, the crowning glory—the OLIVE BRANCH, which marks peace restored to a Nation of grateful people." LS (6 signatures), *ibid.*

Also on Oct. 9, Berry West, Morgan, Ga., wrote to USG. "I take this opportunity to rite you for information and that the Republican party in Calhoun County Geo has over two hundred majority of legal voters of Colored men but the most of the whites are democrats and they at the Elections defraud and Swindle the Republicans out of the Choice of men to represent them and we feel that we are Got Geting of rights as citizens of a Republican Goverment and if we have to remain in a free country under such rules as this we Respectfully request your advice to no if there is any part of the Goverment that we could emigrate to or Colonise or where we could have equal justice as the fundemental law and the Statuts of the Country Give us if can Get that that is all the colored people wants or exspects there is 750 colored voters of Calhoun County we desires of your we cant live at this rate of being defeated out of our rights we are Willing to do what you think is best and where is the best place that we Could emigrate to or be Colonnised we are abide by what ever you say do provided we have aid please rite to me at Morgan post office in Calhoun County Ga on the reception of this letter by so doing you will much oblige me and the Republican party" ALS, *ibid. HED*, 44-2-30, 149.

On Oct. 13, Daniel Joyner, Farmville, N. C., wrote to USG. "what I am going to state to you is this I am a poor republican Cold. Man havent got any thing in the world & havent got any thing been farming & they take all I make frome Me & I am a fraaid they are going to sell me out because I wont Vote for them & I wish you would if you please let Me have it for they have got Me charge with $200 100 in debt if you let Me have it I will thank you thank you. they tried to parish me so they could Make Me Vote for them but

I am going to Vote for Hayes & Wheeler & all the names on the Republican Tickets . . . Write soon for the time is most out. please please send it to me." ALS, DNA, RG 60, Letters from the President.

Also on Oct. 13, Timothy Russell, Mason, N. H., wrote to USG. "The condition of the souther portion of our country is such, that Rebublicans are not safe at the ballot box, or even at their home and If there ever was a time in the history of this Nation when five hundred thousand troops should be sent there to subdue rebellion that time is now. If Buchanan had acted promptly as he should have done in the fall of 1861, much Blood & treasure would have been saved. Your career as a General and as President has ben noble, and I hope you will take measures at once to save our Country from disgrace and ruin" ALS, *ibid.*

On Oct. 14, David Brundage, Milledgeville, Ga., wrote to USG. "Allow me to inform you of the Stupendous frauds committed at the Polls on wednesday the 4th inst—The Republicans could undoubtedly carry the Elections in this part of the State, if protected even by the Law, but the Law is dormant, & not executed. On the day of Election, a crowd of white men Stood at the Polls & knocked, kicked, pushed, pulled hair & Stuck pins & Small bladed knives in the col. voters, and would not let a col man vote unless he casted a Democratic ticket. The managers of the Polls would throw down the Republican tickets openly, or tear them up, & put in Democratic ones, and every Election day in Milledgeville, the old State Capital (or Polls) is filled with army Rifles & Shot Guns well charged. One time at the Polls, a difficulty Started between the Sheriff & a col man, but Soon Subsided. I happened to look up & Saw every window fairly darkened with cocked guns. This is the case in this Section. The Secession Democrats, are always the instigators, in all̶ every difficulty, and make it appear that it is the col man. I have known col men to be murdered in cold blood, & nothing done in the courts. Several col men have been Slaughtered outright by kukluxism, and Still nothing done. Now the col people are trying to assert their rights at the Ballot Box, which is about the only priviledge they have, & the kuklux are threatening them with death and the lash. At one time through this Section young drunken and unprincipled white men commenced lashing white men, and not long afterwards, the Roads were guarded & Some of the kuklux, left for the Spiritual world, & the matter Stoped, but threatened again. Tis true, I am b̶y̶ Southern born but proud to Say that my tender age prevented me from raising arms against the United States Government. I have been acting as a justice of the Peace for Several years, & always respected my oath, regardless of color. Here recently a great many of the white people & all the col in the counties Hancock Washington & Baldwin, run me for Senator, & I fairly beat the race, but cheated out of it. nearly all the white people turned against me because the col people Supported me, & the managers of the Election changed tickets right before my eyes. I tried to get the Sheriff to Stop the Election but to no use. I had to Submit & I[f] I commence a contest, my life is at Stake. Mr Peter O'Neal *c* run for Representative, & Mr Johnathan Norcross, for Governor & all treated in like manner. This is general evil through the recent Georgia Elections So far as I have heard. The Secession Democrats are So enraged that they openly declare to kill the man that the col people elect, & a man is in danger all the time. I do not See how matters can Stand under Such Circumstances. Some of the managers of the Polls are prominent church members, and dont Show any remorse of conscience, in Swearing to emphatical falsehoods. This is the State of matters without any exageration. About three years ago I wrote to you about kuklux depredations, but never heard from you, however if they Start again I will get Several to join me, & try to Stop them with powder & Ball. This the only thing that did Stop them. o̶n̶c̶e̶ Unless the Polls are Supported by troops, at the Presidencial Election I do not See how the col man will make out. one third of them dont go to the Polls from fear, & a great many have to remain at home, because the white man will turn him off, to keep his crop, or wages. This is often the case, & no chance to gain any thing in the Courts. No chance for the poor col man. The poverty Striken white men are the most eager to raise difficulties with the col man, & Still cling to the Secssion Democrats, as they did in the Rebellion. They will not hear reason, for their minds are inflated with poisonous Secession hatred. The col People as a universal thing, are obedient kind & industrious, and their complaint, which is true, they Cant get their wages even by Law— for the Courts will not do but little for them. A great many poor white men in this Country are more dependent than the col man, & yet they are So narrow minded, they will Sustain the Secession Democrats against their own interest. The recently elected men, threaten to Scale the Exemption Laws which will undoubtedly be the Case. Unless Hays & Wheeler are elected we poor class of people in the South are 'gone up.' I close. Please burn this. Write me a few words of advice,'" ALS, *ibid.* HED, 44-2-30, 149−50.

Also on Oct. 14, "meny of us," Louisville, wrote to USG. "By the Request of our log in new abllbany indiana last nite theay Enjoind it a pon me to Rite to you a gane and give you some of the facts in the case   one of our witnesses and he is the main one in the matter threw him we get the hole facts in the case   he was on the ground and saw them hang our people and now is drove off from his famaly and had to walk to louisville for the want of money   his the only man when somonds to louisville that ever said he was there out of 43   he told all he could tell and stay in Frankfort Ky and it turns out that he cant stay and now is drove from his wife and little children without a cent and we say he is one of the moast sensable clever poor men ever in the town of Frankfort   we can bet on any thing he says   the facts in the case is as he says and he can prove it buy 6 or 8 men that was on the ground at the time and the Reason he was there was to keep them from hanging Wm sneed hoo is now the debety U. S. Collecter at Frankfort and John L Scott James Saffell and Fielden Redish and because he objected and said if theay did he would Report them and theay have been down on him Ever sence and have in diferent ways drove him to louisville and he cant go back nor get his famaly a way   the staid in frankfort as long as theay would let him   theay gave him 4 notises in all to leave there but he has got a wife and 6 boys and 4 daughters and while meny and poor he has got the smartest and best Educated children in Frankfort to thear ages generly stated   his oldest are girls   now those partis swor to lies in the united states cort in Louisville when we had some of them arested   when the party went to the Jale the nite of the Elecion to take them out there was 2 black men in the Jail punt in for nothing Els but to keep them from voteing and theay come to louisville and Reported them and it was in this case that there was so meny of them swor to lies swaring theay were at home a sleep when at the same time were gethering up Ropes and hanging people   those four that was arested went to the Jail with others but did not get the Rops nor tie the not   when the ledgislator of Kentucky past the act that negros should tistify in common corts the united states cort at Louisville let the case go back to Frankfort to be tride but theay never tucht it and never will and those two black men that told on them could not go there to testify and if theay did theay would not do nothing with them but let a white Radical or a negro do the least thing if it is accidentle theay will send them to the pinetenchery as long as the law will let them and at Evry alecion theay Entemadate our voters in such a way theay are a fraid to vote for fear of beeing hung . . . those parties that swor to lies donit in the united states cort in Louisville   there is no sending that back to Frankfort for trial we have got them on that   if you give us any countence let us know hoo to go to   I am artherised to say if we cant get a hearing that we will hafto give up the party   this was the under standing at our log in newabaney last nite . . . Direct to R Sumonus Louisville Ky" L, DNA, RG 60, Letters from the President.

On Oct. 19, John D. Mallary, postmaster, Emerson, Mo., wrote to USG. "In this Locality It has become unsafe. for Loyal Citizens of the United states to Live. Without Some Protection from the united states The Following Will Give Some [Evid]ence Which is a Fact. this is cut from a Late *Quincy Paper* . . . Since the War, Jno L. Britendall & my self have come out, her from Western Pennsylvania & are in Business Here Both of us are Tax Payers & Pay License to the U S. & claim Protection. At the Election Some time ago We voted *to Enfranchise* To Give a vote to those that Did not have a vote Because they were *Rebels* Now the Same Parties Go around Carring Double Barrelled Shot Gun & Hollowing Hurrah for Jeff Davis & Swearing that No, Man Shall vote at the Polls Here unless he votes the Democratic Ticket, Shall that be the case . . . I. Jno. D. Mallary at the Verry Darkest Period of the War, Put in a Substitute for During the War & Loaned the Goverment, 13000. Thirteen Thousand Dollars, all the available means at my command then & I hold the *vouches* yet. 8000 in Reg. Bonds and 5000 in First Nat Bk Stock But Being a Grant. Administration Man With out Protection From the U. S. I will not Get to vote at the Presidential Electon Neither will any But Democrats at the Polls at Emerson, mo" ALS, *ibid.*

On Oct. 29, John Tyler, Jr., Washington, D. C., wrote to USG. "After officiating to Night in the Providence Chapel of the M E Church in the place of the Regular Minister of the blessed Gospel, I shall, God willing, start to Raleigh to meet the enclosed Telegraphic dispatch from the Republican State Central Committee. It may be and probaly is the turning point in that State. I shall address them from a stand-point unoccupied by any other man, and which no other man than myself could occupy. Believe me, Mr President, I have the most ominous forebodings that you will will be called upon, in all probability, this coming winter to play the most important Role of your life, as consequential as that you have played heretofore may have been, and all my Prayers are with you. And I feel that the Juncture is nigh at hand when, next to yourself, I myself, in all probability, will stand in relations of the highest value to the country. May God Preserve you for the issue in health and strength—" ALS, Tyler Papers, College of William and Mary, Williamsburg, Va.

On Nov. 1, N. W. Watson, Staunton, Va., telegraphed to USG. "I send this to do what can be done. They have put my brother in prison without a cause & want give bail nor let me pay his way out on the account of the election. please tell me what to do" Telegram received (at 12:51 P.M.), DNA, RG 60, Letters from the President.

On Nov. 2, N. Ellsworth, Martinsburgh, Va., wrote to USG. ". . . 'I am a minister of the Gosple Of the Babtice Church. I have labord Since the war as a missionary on the waubash River In Ind' My Dear Wife Lost hur health. I was compeld to bring hur back to Ver'. Sir, my Record for 30 year in the Ministry is pure as God knows. Oh Sir, I have Sufferd & made every Sacrafise in my power to promote the cause of Christ. I held meetings on my way back to this State. after I passed Bristol, near the State line My troubles began in this way. I found ministers of my our own church that opposed my Sistem of Praying for the Prosperety of our contry, & Espechaly, they told me, If I continued to pray for the President, the Brethern In Ver would not Lissen to my preaching—but, Sir, I kept on, as was my custem to pray for gods blessing on my contry, for god to give you wisdom in conducting the affairs of State, & Bless your Adminstrasion—& for this they made false reports about me through the papers. . . ." ALS, *ibid.* On Dec. 19 and on Jan. 6, 1877, the same person, writing from Va. as "Rev S. Nixon," warned USG against an undisclosed assassination plot. L, *ibid.*; L, USG 3.

Endorsement

Refered to the post-Master General. This applicant for a route agency is, I understand, an ex-Union soldier, discharged by the present House of representatives, and is there fore one of a class we have been trying to provide for even if some democrat should have to be removed to make place

U. S. GRANT

JULY 27TH /76

AES, DLC-USG, IB. Written on a letter of July 24, 1876, from Ferdinand H. Würdemann, Washington, D. C., to Postmaster Gen. James N. Tyner. "I would respectfully request to be employed at any work, such as you may select, I was a late employee of the U. S. House of Representatives: and a Union Soldier who served through the entire late rebellion. My family consists of five, whom, depend on my exertions for support. It is my earnest prayer, that you will find it convenient to give this application, an early, and favourable consideration." ALS, *ibid.* U.S. Senator Frederick T. Frelinghuysen of N. J. and two others favorably endorsed this letter. ES (undated), *ibid.*

On Jan. 8, USG had spoken from the White House in the evening to "ex-Union soldiers and sailors of the District" protesting "the employment of rebels in the public service to the exclusion of men who have served their country faithfully." "Gentlemen: I am fully in accord with the spirit of the resolutions offered by Messrs. Fort and Cason in the House of Representatives, and any measures that may be intended for your benefit. I will find a place for any of your comrades that may be discharged from the Capitol, and aid all others as far as lies in my power." *Washington Evening Star*, Jan. 10, 1876. Offices changed hands after Democrats assumed control of the House of Representatives in Dec., 1875. See *CR*, 44–1, 208.

On Jan. 12, 1876, U.S. Representative Thomas J. Cason of Ind. wrote to USG. "I have no knowledge of the Matters stated either in letter or clipping from Paper & know none of the parties named but from certain statements particularly in the extract from the paper I deemed it best to submit it to your judgement" ALS, DNA, RG 77, Letters Received. One enclosure is a letter of Jan. 7 from Samuel Sutter, Galveston, Tex., to Cason. "In the 'News' I see that you introduced a resolution in the House of Repr. in favour of former U. S. soldiers, and as I am one of them, to whom actual damage has been done by the Govt officers in charge of the harbour improvements here, as you will see by the following statements, I have the honor to pray you to recommend my case to his Ex. President Grant for investigation. . . . Before the War I used to teach school in Madison Co. Ills, and after the War in St Clair & Monroe Co's Ills. & 1½ year in Franklin Co. Mo. and in the Spring 1871 I went in the South and taught colored schools, first in Warren Co. Miss. and afterwards in Franklin & St Mary's Parishes, La, & last I taught a white school in Houston Tex. from Septr. 2nd 1872 until March 1873. But as there was a long law suit with the R. R. Co's about the school law, nobody could be compelled to pay the school tax; consequently teachers could not collect their wages; it was a year later when we got state warrants for our services. Therefore I gave up teaching and worked at whatever job I could get. As you know Sir, there is Govt work going on here, improving the harbour, and as there are the best wages paid, I tried to get a job there as early as last February, stating to Supt. Pease that I served in the U. S. Army during the last War. He said that he gave preference to nobody, but that if I was here if he wanted hands, he would employ me. Afterwards Lieut Quinn promised me a job for the 1st of June last. I was on the place at 5. o'clock a. m. on that day, but although about 25 to 30 men were employed I got no job. . . . I therefore wrote to the Secry of War, who gave orders to Lt. Quinn to find out w̶how many of the employed men served in eighther the U. S. or rebel Army. As I heard from a man there employed, with the name of Zweifel, the result was 12 former U. S. & 13 former rebel soldiers, while the greater portion had not served at all. . . ." ALS, *ibid.* A second enclosure is a clipping from the *Galveston Thunderbolt* of July 25 with allegations against 1st Lt. James B. Quinn, project superintendent, and R. M. Pease. ". . . If Lieut. Quinn will exhibit the pay-roll from May 1st, a fine mouse will be discovered; the men are forced to contribute $2 50 per month, the lord only knows for what purpose, and 'Overseer' Pease, who arrived in Galveston with a small carpetbag in hand, and was refused a drink of whisky on credit, by shrewd manipulations has been able to buy property, gives grand champagne suppers, invites women to his apartments, and makes night hideous with their lascivious songs and revellings, and does this on a small salary. Lieut. Quinn's salary is $130 per month, but manages to make away with over $500 over and above his board, etc. . . ." *Ibid.* On Nov. 16, 1875, Sutter had written to USG on the same subject. ALS, *ibid.* In May, 1876, 1st Lt. Charles E. L. B. Davis replaced Quinn. See *HED*, 44-1-1, part 2, I, part I, pp. 846–69, 44-2-1, part 2, II, part I, pp. 564–81.

On March 2, Clinton Lloyd, Washington, D. C., had written to USG. "I have the pleasure of commending to your favorable consideration my friend, Capt. Almont Barnes who desires an appointment in the Diplomatic Bureau of the State Department. Capt Barnes made a good military record in the late War, and for several years was closely associated with me in the Clerk's office of the House of Reps. where I had an oportunity to know him well. . . ." ALS, DNA, RG 59, Letters of Application and Recommendation. On Feb. 21, Almont Barnes, Washington, D. C., had written to Secretary of State Hamilton Fish requesting "appointment to the position of Chief of the bureau of Rolls and Library, in the Department of State, . . . I have, since the close of the war, been constantly in employment as a writer for the Republican press, including such papers as the N. Y. Times, Utica Herald, Iowa State Register, Chicago Post, and also for literary papers and magazines. I have been one of the enroling clerks of the House of Representatives for three years, and am this day displaced for no fault, but to make place for a Democrat. I respectfully submit that my army and political services, joined to my qualifications to creditably fill the position asked for, entitle me, a known Republican, to succeed, as I am succeeded by, a well-known Democrat." ALS, *ibid.* Related papers are *ibid.* On April 4, USG nominated Barnes as chief, Bureau of Statistics.

On May 31, USG endorsed a letter of Feb. 9 from U.S. Representative William W. Crapo of Mass. and three others to Bluford Wilson, solicitor of the treasury, recommending Henry H. Remington as a special agent. "Refered to the Sec. of the Treas. This applicant is a discharged soldier who has been dismissed from a place in the Capitol. I hope a place may be made for him." AES (facsimile), R. M. Smythe & Co., Inc., Oct. 30, 1997, no. 317.

To Edwards Pierrepont

———

July 29th 1876.

HON. EDWARDS PIERREPONT: MINISTER &C.
DEAR SIR:

I clip from the New York Herald of this date what purports to be the testimony of Maj. B. Wilson, late Solicitor of the Treasury, before a Committee of Congress. I invite your special attention to his reported interview with you in relation to the celebrated Circular letters to Dist. Attys   It is hardly nec-necessary for me to say to you that either he swears falsly or I have been grossly wronged. It is not true that you submitted to me the draft of the letter, and that it was not as strong as I desired. It is not true that I ever saw the letter, or knew aught of its contents until after it was published in the papers. I was not aware that a copy of that letter had ever been sent to me until long after its publication.

My recollection of the origin of the whole matter is this: I had learned that, through govt. counsel, or instructions from Washington, the Mass of the Chicago "Whiskey Ring" were being let off on condition that they would criminate some body else. I asked you about it. You confessed that you did not know about the management of these cases. I replied that they were being prosecuted with the machinery of the Dept. of Justice, and that you had a right to know, and that I had a right to know how the business was being prosecuted; that for information on such subjects I looked to you. To this you replied that you would write a letter to Bangs, the Dist. Atty. in Chicago, and ascertain what arrangements had been made with confessedly guilty parties who were turning "States evidence. You afterwards told me that you had received an answer from Bangs saying that he did not know what arrangements had been made, but excusing himself partially on the ground that the Asst. Counsel had managed those things their own way, and had had charge before he come into office. I said in reply to this that he ought to know, and should demand to know, all that had been done, or was being done, so that he could answer any question and that you should so direct him. You agreed that this was right, and said that instead of writing a letter to the Dist. Atty. in Chicago, which might look like a suspicion upon him you would send a circular letter to all the Dist. Attys [1] where these frauds were being tried. I am sure the idea of a circular letter had not occured to me, and that I saw no draft of your letter. Hoping that you will give me your recollection on these matters, I remain

Very Truly Yours

U. S. GRANT

ALS, CtY (clipping enclosed); copies, USG 3; ICN (Babcock Papers); DLC-USG, II, 3. On Aug. 22, 1876, Edwards Pierrepont, U.S. minister, London, wrote to USG. "Yours with enclosure is recd.—It is amazing that human recollection can be so at fault; it is even incredible. The matter happened some seven months ago, and I may not be able to gi[v]e exact dates as all my Washington p[a]pers are in Newyork, but I can give the substance of what occurred about the circular letter. I gave it in a report to a committee of which Mr Scott Lord was was chairman. I also gave it under oath before a committee of Congress:— both were published in the various journals of the day, and I never heard a suggestion from any one that they were not full and strictly accurate. I expressly stated that I never submitted a draft of the letter to you and that you never saw it until after it was published, that I sent you a copy after it was issued which, as I learned, you never received. *I now repeat the same.* Chicago was the place where complaints were gravest, but it was thought best to send the same letter to the three places where these frauds were being tried; complaints in Newspaps & otherwise were made from all the three places—Chicago, Milwaukie & St Louis—more especially from Chicago—Neither you or I got any official information as to what was being done. No official reports were made to me of these matters & when you called upon me for information, I could not give it We heard through NewPaper slips, ~~through~~ through letters & through personal communications that all sorts of bargains were being made by the guilty to be let off, and one of the supervisors assured us that some of the most guilty were let off where there was no necessity whatever. The District Attorny Mr Hasleton wrote me that agreements had been made without his knowledge & that the letter was sent most timely (He can send you a copy of the letter) Indeed the District Attornies at Chicago & Milwaukie seemd to have no definite knowledge of what bargains (by special) counsel) were made.—very alarming statements were made about the way some of the greatest criminals were to be let off. I believed the statements were exagerated as my circular letter shows, but I believed what we now know to be true, that there was enough, not only to justify the letter but to make it a great necessity. you knew better than I how much reliance could be placed upon the information and time has proved & Mr Bangs & Mr Hazeltons letters confirmed that your apprehensions of the threatend injustice, which were stronger than mine, were the more correct. The letter was an official letter, confidential of course, as such letters always are; intended only as a caution to the District attornies and to warn them of the complaints which were made—(*See the circular letter*) It was never supposed that it could be public or influence a human beings' testimony, but only make the District attornies careful in the discharge of their delicate duties. I had been District Attorney in Newyork and I knew full well that when combinations of men are discovered in a fraud, how ready they all are to turn, not only upon their associates in crime, but upon the *innocent*, in order to cover their own guilt. you were urgent that a letter should be written, but you did not dictate it or examine a draft of it or approve or disapprove. I neither showed you a draft or copy before it was sent & I have never so stated to any one—I stated directly the contrary under oath & it was public through the Journls The letter seemd timely, & subsequent events have proved that it was timely—The mischief came of the publication. The letter was seized upon in the excited state of the public mind as intened to aid Gen. Babcok, whereas he was never thought of in issuing the letter. The only person to whom I showed the letter was Major Bluford Wilson (before it was made public) & if he made a word of unfavorable criticism upon it I certainly never heard it. Never until it was taken up by the NewsPapers & the cry raised that the Presidnt & the Attorny General were trying to shield Gen. Babcock. Any one of the slightest fairness of judgment can see (*if they will read the letter*) that if it had gone to the officials, *for whom alone it was intended*, it could by no possibility have 'discouraged witnesses' It was intended for *no witness*, no witness was expected to see it no witness had a right to see it" ALS, USG 3; ADf, CtY. USG endorsed this letter. "Give this to Mr. Sniffin when he reaches Washington to be filed with the letter to which this is an answer." AE (initialed, undated), USG 3.

On Jan. 26, Pierrepont had written a circular letter to U.S. attorneys. "My attention has to-day been called to many newspaper reports, stating that in Saint Louis, Chicago, and Milwaukee large numbers of guilty men who confess their guilt are to be let off from prosecution and punishment. I cannot suppose that this is true, but my attention being called to it, I direct a letter to each of those places, that the district attorneys may know that suggestions have been made that quite too many guilty men are to go unpunished. I am aware that in the excitement many unfounded rumors will gain credence, and I repose in your good judgment to prevent any possible scandal from anything that would *even look like* favoritism toward those who have defrauded the Government. It is the President's reiterated desire that 'no guilty man shall escape.' I do not know that there is any intention on the part of any one charged with the administration of the laws to favor any person, and the *appearance* of any such favoritism should be very carefully avoided. I write this by way of abundant caution, for I am determined, so far as lies in my power, to have these prosecutions so conducted that when they are over the honest judgment of the honest men of the country—which is sure in the main to be just—will say that no one has been prosecuted from malice, and that no guilty one has been let off through favoritism, and that no guilty one who has been proved guilty, or confessed himself guilty, has been suffered to escape punishment." HMD, 44-1-186, 7–8, 497–98. On Feb. 1 and March 7, Secretary of State Hamilton Fish recorded in his diary. "The President speaks with a great deal of feeling about the conviction of McKee of St Louis for conspiracy in connection with the Whiskey Frauds, and says he has read all the testimony published and not a word is charged against him by any person who is not himself confessedly a purjerer and a felon; while every respectable person who testified did so in his behalf. He said he had supposed there would have been a divided Jury in-as-much as whatever might be the evidence of his innocense the state of feeling was such that there was sure to be some who would try to convict. Pierrepont asked him ~~why~~ where he had read the evidence, that he himself had only seen an abstract of it as published in the Eastern papers The President said it was that which he had read and remarks that he thinks the conduct of our prosecuting officers in the Chicago cases was perfectly attrocious; that their stipulating to let clear the confessed rogues with the hope of being able to convict a few prominent persons he thinks outrageous Pierrepont disclaims the knowledge of any such proceedings—The President says—he repeats what has been told him by Dutton [*Tutton*] (Supervisor of Internal Revenue) Bristow subsequently mentioned that Dutton, (who had left the Presidents Office after the hour of Cabinet Meeting), was desirous of some other appointment. The Presi-

dent says Yes! he had been speaking with him about it The President seems to think that
the Solicitor General is responsible for the line of conduct pursued which he condemns.
Bristow says he saw the letters of Wilson the Solicitor and they do not authorize the
course attributed to the prosecuting officers and he does not think they are pursuing the
course attributed to them. The Attorney General is instructed to write to the District Attorney at Chicago to ascertain what assurance the Counsel associated with him in the
prosecution may have given to any of the indicted parties who are being used as witnesses
in the prosecution" "The President then spoke of Dyer with a great deal of bitterness
which led to a reference to the Attorney Generals letter to the District Attorney in the
west which ~~which~~ has been the cause of much comment and criticism. Pierrepont remarked that General Babcock had told him that he had procured and furnished a copy of
the letter that it was no matter how he got it but he got it, that they were trying to drown
him, and that he had a right to use every effort in his power for his own protection. The
President said he had never seen the letter and asked the Attorney General whether he had
ever sent him a copy, Pierrepont replied Yes! and that he understood was the copy which
Genl Babcock had forwarded to St Louis. The President, repeated that he had never seen
or heard of it and seemed some-what surprised. Pierrepont emphatically repeated that he
had sent it addressed to him to the White House. It is apparent from this that Babcock intercepted the letter and did not allow it to come to the Presidents knowledge, but pur-
loined it for his own purposes. In speaking of Dyer the President said he was a black-guard
that he had obtruded himself repeatedly upon the Grand Jury urging the indictment of
Babcock; that finally one of the Jurors had addressed the foreman saying that if Mr Dyer
wanted the indictment of Genl Babcock he insisted he be sworn as a witness, that he was
thereupon sworn and, upon his evidence the indictment found. I asked the President how
he obtained this information he said the grand juror who had insisted, had told him of the
proceedings; I remarked that in that case the grand juror was a perjurer and should be indicted and convicted, that the oath of the Grand Juror was one of the most solemn, to observe the secrets of the body. Bristow Pierrepont and Robeson united in the expression of
the same opinion, Robeson quoting the words of the oath. The President seemed surprised
but still is inclined to accept the statement of the Grand Juror in question (whom I have
reason to believe is Fox father of the man nominated yesterday as Consul at Brunswick) I
remarked that the man who would for-swear the oath taken as a grand juror could not be
accepted for any purpose whatever." DLC-Hamilton Fish. See Nevins, *Fish,* pp. 792–97.
On March 23, Pierrepont was questioned concerning the circular letter. "Do you recollect
what newspapers those reports were in?—A. I do not recollect them all. They were newspaper slips which the President had in large numbers. They were at his office. I know that
some of them were from the Inter-Ocean. The others I do not know. . . . Q. Your attention
was called to those newspaper slips by the President at the time?—A. Yes. . . . Q. I see that
in your official letter to Mr. Lord, dated 4th March, 1876, you state that 'about the middle
of January, and subsequent thereto, various newspaper slips, private letters, and personal
statements came to the President, and in a lesser degree to the Attorney-General, that
bargains were being made, or were about to be made, with criminals, whose testimony was
not in the slightest degree needed, by which a large number of criminals were to be let off
from any kind of punishment, and to be relieved of prosecution in a manner likely to bring
scandal upon the administration of justice,' &c. . . . Do you know by whom those statements were made personally to the President?—A. He told me of two or three. I remember one of them very distinctly, on account of his being an official. That was Supervisor
Tutton. I remember him the more distinctly from his subsequently having made the same

statement to me, and with a great degree of vigor. . . . The thing which was particularly impressed on me when he came to see me (which was subsequent to his seeing the President) was, that he said that the very counsel whom I had employed, and who were responsible to me, were making bargains of this kind with a large number of important criminals; and he added that it would cause a heavy scandal before this business was over, particularly in Chicago. . . . Q. Did he not tell you who were in danger of being indicted and punished if such bargains were made?—A. No; he did not go into it with anything like minuteness to me. He did to the President, according to the President's statement to me. All this conversation with Tutton was after what the President had told me and was not before I wrote the circular-letter. I saw him after I wrote the letter. . . . Q. Did you believe that your district attorneys and special counsel whom you had employed were entering into such bargains as represented to you?—A. I did not to the degree stated. . . . It seemed to me, that this thing which was pressed upon the President so much, and which he told me, was exaggerated, and the whole tone of my letter shows that I thought so. As I told them, I sent the letter by way of 'abundant caution.' Q. At whose suggestion was the letter written?—A. At the President's. . . . Of course I should not have written the letter at all had it not been for the President having so many things pressed upon him, which induced him to believe that some caution ought to be given. . . . Q. What purports to be a copy of this letter seems to have been published on the 1st of February in the Chicago papers. Do you know how it got into the possession of the publishers of these papers?—A. . . . I ascertained it from General Babcock. . . . I sent for him and squarely asked him if that letter did not get out through that office. He said, 'Yes; I suppose it did.' He said, 'I was drowning. They were trying to destroy me, and I had a right to anything that I could get hold of.'. . . Q. Can you recollect how many interviews you had with the President in regard to the writing of that letter before it was finally written?—A. No; I cannot undertake to tell the number of interviews; but he spoke to me about it several times, and called my attention to those things that were being pressed upon him. . . . He was very much disturbed, and he was quite earnest. . . . I never knew any case before in which he had any personal part, except in the trial of Joyce and McDonald. He seemed to be quite interested in those trials. He took a very strong interest in them. This phrase, which has gained so much notoriety, 'Let no guilty man escape,' he indorsed upon a paper making a charge or suggestion against General Babcock. . . . I ought to say here that I heard the President say, five or six times in the progress of that case, 'If Babcock is guilty, there is no man who wants him so much proven guilty as I do, for it is the greatest piece of traitorism to me that a man could possibly practice.'. . . Q. Is it not a fact that the publication of that letter at that time produced a perfect panic among the witnesses by whom the prosecuting attorneys expected to fix guilt on Babcock?—A. I do not understand that it affected any witness in his testimony at all. . . . Q. What did the President say about it?—A. He did not say anything. . . . He treated it as he frequently treats things, with entire silence. Q. He said nothing?—A. No; and nobody could tell what he thought." *HMD,* 44-1-186, 8–12, 22. See *ibid.,* pp. 26–28; *Chicago Inter-Ocean,* Jan. 8, 18, 1876. On April 1, David P. Dyer, U.S. attorney, St. Louis, testified that he sealed and hid the circular letter upon receipt. "I thought it would have a tendency to alarm the witnesses who were to be used, or expected to be used, by the Government in other prosecutions, by telling them that whatever they might testify to, whatever services they might render the Government by way of developing these frauds, it would in the end go as hard with them as with those who did not confess. . . ." *HMD,* 44-1-186, 43. On Jan. 27, 12:15 P.M., Levi P. Luckey had written to Bluford Wilson, solicitor of the treasury. "The President says to drop you a note and ask you to come over and see him." *Ibid.*, p. 366. On July 28, Wilson testified: "I went over to see the President promptly, and learned that he was dissatisfied with the course of the Secretary and myself with reference to the conduct of the prosecutions at Milwaukee, Chicago, and Saint Louis. He objected specifically and earnestly to our permitting persons who pleaded guilty to be used as witnesses to convict others; . . . He said to me, 'Major, when I said let no guilty man escape, I meant it, and not that nine men should escape, and one be convicted.' I said to him, 'Pardon me, Mr. President, we are not in this battle counting heads. We are trying to break up the unlawful conspiracies and combinations which we all know exist, . . .' Secretary Chandler sat just back at the farther end of the Cabinet room, and I said to the President, 'Mr. President, I notice the presence of a member of the Cabinet. If you give me time to go into this matter, I think I could satisfy you that you are laboring under a misapprehension.' 'O,' said he, 'it is not worth while; it is not worth while. I simply wanted to call your attention to the fact that, in my judgment, there is too much of this going on.'" *Ibid.* Wilson returned to the White House with Bristow later that day. ". . . After the Secretary and myself had concluded our statement and the explanation of our position, the President expressed himself wholly satisfied therewith, and referred with great kindness to General Webster, and then ensued a very kind and friendly interview touching other matters . . ." *Ibid.*, p. 367. Wilson testified that on or about Jan. 29, Pierrepont read to him the circular letter. ". . . He said, 'You note, Wilson, that I do not go so far as the President wanted me to.' I took a draught of that letter over to the President, and read it to him, and he was not satisfied with it, and wanted me to say in specific terms that the testimony of no man who entered a plea of guilty should be used in any prosecution, but that the parties should be given to understand that they should be brought to punishment.'. . ." *Ibid.* See *New York Herald*, Feb. 17, 1876.

On Aug. 11, Asa C. Matthews, former supervisor of Internal Revenue, testified that in Dec., 1875, prosecutors in Chicago had agreed to offer immunity to certain distillers in exchange for information implicating Anton C. Hesing and Jacob Rehm. "It resulted immediately in the seizure of property as to which condemnations followed in most cases— property to the value of about four or five hundred thousand dollars—and the arrest of some twelve or fifteen persons, and among them Buffalo Miller, who was a very prominent politician, as also Hesing and Rehm, and their conviction, and the utter destruction of anything like a whisky organization in the city of Chicago. . . ." *HMD*, 44-1-186, 526. On Dec. 18, Joseph D. Webster, collector of Internal Revenue, Chicago, wrote to Matthews supporting the immunity proposal. *Ibid.*, pp. 526–27. On the same day, Matthews left Chicago for Washington, D. C. "I handed the letter to Secretary Bristow, and he took it to the Cabinet. . . . When he came back he told me that the President read the letter, I think, twice, and remarked that the proposition was broad, (the proposition was, at that time, to give criminal and civil immunity to these men;) but while it was pretty large, according to his idea, yet no price was too high to pay for that kind of men. . . . He gave me that as the substance of the President's language—that no price was too large to pay for that kind of 'ringsters,' I think his expression was." *Ibid.*, p. 527. On Dec. 30 and 31, Matthews, Chicago, telegraphed to Wilson. "The bottom is out here and I am looking after the dead. Seized seven houses yesterday—grand jury meets on fourt Januay" "Hessing and Rhem both arrested and each held to bail in the sum of fifty thousand dollars. Also seized the Illinois Distilling Company evidence seems certain" Copies, DLC-USG, IB. On Dec. 30, Wilson telegraphed to Matthews. "Keep the facts under your feet, your legal advisers well informed, and in full accord, and fight hard for unconditional surrender all round." Copy, *ibid.*

On May 22, 1876, Culver C. Sniffen wrote to Commissioner of Internal Revenue

Daniel D. Pratt. "The President directs me to request, that, you will inform him whether there was any investigation of Supervisor Tuttons official acts while he was Assessor at Reading, Penna, or at any other time, which effected his standing—" Copy, *ibid.*, II, 3. On May 31, USG nominated Alexander P. Tutton as collector of customs, Philadelphia. See letter to Seth J. Comly, May 16, 1876. On July 29, Tutton, Philadelphia, wrote to USG. "Enclosed please find slip from 'Phila. Evening Bulletin' of yesterday taken from 'New York Daily Graphic', which seem to give a fair outline of the Whiskey prosecutions in Chicago, but as the Editor seems to incline to doubt Bristows knowledge of these facts, I will merely say for your information, that there should be on file in the Treasury Departmt a telegram from me dated January 13th, 1875 [*1876*] giving him full notice of what it was proposed to do the next day, viz: to have these thieves plead guilty on one count with the understanding there was never to be any motion for sentence, and the telegram from Mr Bristow to me, given in Wilson's testimony is the answer thereto. Chief Washburn telegraphed Wilson on the same day and to the same effect, and on the 15th January I made a full report to the Secretary of the corrupt bargain and sale which had been made. These telegrams and my report will show that he (Bristow) was fully informed on the subject. I also enclose you a slip from the 'Phila Evening Bulletin' of today with reference to the same subject, especially Wilson's testimony" ALS, DNA, RG 206, Miscellaneous Letters Received; clipping, *ibid.* On July 26, a correspondent had reported from Washington D. C. that ". . . certain facts have been brought out in affidavits filed within a few days with the Attorney-General in connection with the application for a commutation of the sentence of A. C. Hesing, of the Chicago Whiskey Ring, which place Mr. Bristow and Mr. Wilson in a very disagreeable position for honorable men to occupy." *New York Daily Graphic*, July 27, 1876. On Jan. 13, [*1876*], Tutton, then supervisor of Internal Revenue, Chicago, had telegraphed to Secretary of the Treasury Benjamin H. Bristow. "By agreement of counsel, Golsen, Eastman, Mason, Miller, and Fredricks, of Lake Shore, Roelle, Junker, Russell, Furlong, and perhaps others, are to plead guilty tomorrow morning, with the understanding that they are never to be sentenced, in consideration of information given, or to be given by them, against Rehm, Hesing, and the houses recently seized. I have only got down to this bargain this evening, and have protested against this immunity being granted, but to no purpose. If you do not approve of this arrangement or bargain, telegraph the district attorney at once." *HMD*, 44-1-186, 444–45. On Jan. 14, Bristow telegraphed to Tutton. "As we have not directed any arrangement with indicted parties, so we decline to interfere with any that has been entered into by the district attorney with approval of his associates and the local revenue officers. Having confidence in their judgment and fidelity, we leave the prosecutions in their hands, not doubting that they will do what will best subserve the interest of the Government." *Ibid.*, p. 445. On Aug. 2, Tutton testified that on or about Jan. 20 he had met with USG "and stated to the President substantially what had taken place there, and that all these people whose places I had seized, together with a large number of gaugers and store-keepers, as well as distillers, were in this agreement. I said to the President that it might be good policy, though I doubted it very much, and at any rate if that policy was to be carried out, of letting thieves who had stolen hundreds of thousands of dollars, which we could prove against them, to go free and be relieved from punishment, no man in the revenue-service was safe; that these men who had been committing perjury right along, both distillers and gaugers, month after month, would swear anybody into the penitentiary in order to escape it themselves. I did not want to have anything to do with matters of that kind. . . . The President said that he thought something ought to be done to stop that wholesale bargain and sale business, . . ." *Ibid.*, p. 448. See *ibid.*, pp. 407–19, 504–15; *Chicago Inter-Ocean*, Feb. 8, 10, 1876.

On Feb. 13, Emery A. Storrs, defense counsel for Orville E. Babcock, St. Louis, had telegraphed to William A. Cook, Washington, D. C., also representing Babcock. "Dyer yesterday rec'd letter from Bristow stating that pierreponts letter to dis't atty's here and at chicago & milwaukee was written without consultation with him & directing Dyer to go ahead with & perfect his arrangements without reference to Pierreponts letter Bristow's letter has been Exhibited to government witnesses by Dyer two of whom are to be called tomorrow one of these witnesses is to be recalled after having had this letter shewn to him washburn of Secret Service is now here by Bristows order as letter states my information comes from a direct Source and is unquestionable. show this to president tonight and answer." Telegram received (at 8:30 P.M.), USG 3.

On May 12, Charles L. Wilson, *Chicago Evening Journal,* and Joseph Medill, *Chicago Tribune,* telegraphed to USG. "charley hall has gone to Washn to be appointed marshall vice campbell it would be most unfortunate selection whiskey ring would rejoice but all good citizens grieve we all protest" Telegram received (at 6:40 P.M.), DNA, RG 60, Records Relating to Appointments. Benjamin H. Campbell continued as marshal, Northern Ill.

On May 27, Storrs, Chicago, wrote to USG. "A series of Government cases, known as the 'Whiskey Cases,' which has excited so much feeling, and aroused such general interest, in this city, is about drawing to a close. The end has thus far been, and will finally, I think, be, precisely that which I predicted months ago in conversation with you—an end not at all anticipated or wished for, I am quite certain, by yourself, or by any one who earnestly desired the prosecution of the real offenders and the prevention of frauds against the revenue. There have so far been in this city two trials, namely, the case against Rush & Pahlman, who were distillers, who had always stood high, and who to-day stand well, but who, refusing to turn States' evidence, were placed upon trial, and the whole strength of the first band seized in this city, brought against them. It was really a case where Rush & Pahlman were compelled to expose the frauds practiced upon the revenue, and the Government officials were compelled to defend the integrity of those who had been most largely engaged in the perpetration of such frauds. Yet it was with the greatest difficulty that a conviction could be secured even in this case, although there were about seventeen witnesses against the defendants, the jury absolutely refusing to credit the uncorroborated testimony of these accomplices, and reaching their conclusion simply upon the testimony of two witnesses who had not turned states' evidence, and who were not active participants in the frauds concerning which they testified. The next case, that of Mr. Daniel Munn, formerly Supervisor of Internal Revenue, has just closed, and has resulted, as the entire community expected and wished, in an almost immediate verdict of acquittal. The leading witness against Mr. Munn was Jacob Rehm, who has, for the last fifteen years, been most potential in the local politics of this city and county. The whole public were astonished when Jacob Rehm, who was the organizer of this scheme of fraud against the Government in this city, and who has been prominent in every scheme of political plunder in the county of Cook for the last fifteen or twenty years, joined hands with the Government and seemed at least to be acting in co-operation with it and under its protection. His testimony and that of the other witnesses in the Munn Case demonstrated the fact that Rehm was the fountain-head of these frauds, that he absolutely dominated and controlled the appointment of all the subordinate officers here, that they held their positions subject to his will, and that it has been utterly impossible, since the Spring of 1872, for any one engaged in the business of distilling, to prosecute it without paying contributions to Mr. Jacob Rehm. The fact is, that he has received by this course of plunder from the distilling interests in this city, since the spring of 1872, it is safe to say, at least four hundred thousand dollars. The shallow pretence he made, that he was seduced by Mr. Hessing into this business, and that he had himself retained none of the money which he had thus extorted from the distillers, met, when the pretence was first made, with universal derision and contempt, and was totally overthrown during the progress of the trial. The entire community felt that the conviction of any man upon the testimony of Mr. Rehm would be such an outrage upon the rights of the citizen, that it could not for an instant be tolerated; and although the Government officials put forward the case of Mr. Munn first as being doubtless the strongest one, yet his acquittal meets with universal approval, and the course which Mr. Rehm has pursued, and the protection which he seems to be receiving from the Government, meet with as universal condemnation. The present District Attorney, Judge Bangs, is a most faithful, efficient, and, without doubt, honest officer. He apprehends, as clearly as I do, the unfortunate position in which the Government is placed whenever it seeks the conviction of any man upon the testimony of such a witness. He understands, as clearly as I understand, that every effort now made in that direction, is a discredit to any administration which makes it. From the prosecutions of any officials based upon the testimony of Mr. Rehm, is withdrawn every element of moral support in this community. I venture to say, that in this entire State not one intelligent, honest-minded citizen, can be found who would not deplore any further efforts in that direction, believing that a continuance of these prosecutions would result in the most serious discredit to the Government itself, and believing also, so thoroughly aroused is the public feeling against this man, that a conviction is an utter impossibility. There still remain upon the docket undisposed of two cases: one against the former Collector, Mr. Wadsworth, and the other against the former District Attorney, Mr. Ward. I think it is safe to say that in this community where Mr. Wadsworth is known, not one man in a thousand to-day believes he is guilty, not one in a thousand ever believed it. The case against him is weaker than the case against Munn, and it practically rests upon the unsupported testimony of Jacob Rehm. There is practically no case against Mr. Ward except such as Mr. Rehm may see fit to swear to. But the difficulty has been that up to the present time at least, Rehm has held the distillers in such complete subjection as, by threats and otherwise, led them to believe that, if they told the truth against him, severer punishment would be inflicted upon them for it; so that it has been impossible to expose the full extent and measure of his iniquities. I have represented to Judge Bangs this condition of affairs and the terrorism under which the distillers have rested, and he assured me that he was not aware of it, and I do not believe that he was. I think, however, he now credits my statement, and I do not believe that, if left to his own judgment, he would deem it wise or just or decent to go one step further in the prosecution of the cases against either Wadsworth or Ward. From a personal interview with Judge Drummond, I know very well what his views are, and am entirely satisfied that, if left to him, he would be very free to state that no conviction should be had or asked for upon the testimony of Mr. Rehm. I have nothing to say now as to this business of immunity, although it is a matter upon which I have very positive opinions that will probably be a subject for future investigation; but I desire to state to you that my profound conviction is, that the league which, unwittingly or otherwise, the government, through its representatives in this city, has made with the worst men engaged in the whiskey business, does more damage, and inflicts an infinitely greater injury upon public morals and the substantial public interests, than all the robbing of the revenues since we had a national existence. The Government has demonstrated that it is sufficiently powerful to protect itself against frauds upon its revenue. The Whiskey Ring in this city, of which Jacob Rehm was the au-

thor, is crushed out of existence. The members of that ring are to-day bankrupt without a
single exception. And it is not only my opinion, but the opinion, I believe, of every fair-
minded man in this community that the time has now come when the government should
stay its hand, and declare that through no self-proclaimed thieves and perjurers will it seek
the conviction of any one. Regarded merely from the low stand-point of political expediency, it is perfectly clear that a continuance of the methods which have been employed in
these prosecutions, would be most unwise. The fact is, that in the prosecutions in this city
the Government itself has been in league with the Whiskey Ring, and Rush and Pahlman
in their case, and Munn in his, have been, and Wadsworth in his case will be, compelled to
attack that ring and the members of it. The earliest sinners and the worst have stood the
highest in the favor of the Government. Such men as Goleson, Parker R. Mason, and Jacob Rehm, who have always been utterly disreputable and characterless, seem at least to
have had the control of the prosecutions, and to have dictated the methods in which the
prosecution should be carried on. They have had the confidence and the ear of the officers
of the Government. This condition of affairs, Judge Bangs is beginning to understand. I
do not believe that he relishes the position in which he finds himself placed. He has, I understand, written to the Attorney General with reference to the cases of Wadsworth and
Ward, and he declares to me that, left to himself, he should have no hesitancy, in directing
the dismissal of these cases. I have troubled you upon this subject for the reason that I felt
desirous you should understand what the general feeling of the public is, and I assure you
nothing could be done which would meet with more unanimous and cordial approval of
our entire community, and the more thorough endorsement of our best public sentiment,
than the discountenancing of the employment of such men as Jacob Rehm, by the dismissal
of the cases in which he figures as the principal witness. I am anxious that you should understand what this feeling is, and that the Attorney General should understand it; and,
were he inquired of, I have not the slightest doubt that Judge Drummond and every friend
that you have in this city would thoroughly endorse what I have said. Among the many
distillers who have been indicted and pleaded guilty, there are a few who have always stood
well. H. B. Miller, Mr. Powell, Dickinson, Leach & Company, and Rush & Pahlman are men
who went into the distillation of illicit spirits when it became evident that the Government
would not assist them in the prevention of frauds in other cities, and that they must either
themselves engage in the manufacture of illicit spirits or quit the business. These men have
already been most severely punished; they are all bankrupt; they are useful men, and, in
the main, good citizens. They are entitled to belief; they have not sought their own escape
by the ruin of their associates and competitors in business. Their course has been manly
and straightforward; and yet the curious result seems to be reached that they are specially
to be made to suffer, while the infinitely guiltier ones are to escape. It is through them,
and through the exposure which Mr. Hessing has made, that the full extent and measure
of Mr. Jacob Rehm's long-continued frauds upon revenue have been discovered. Upon
Mr. Hessing, Mr. Rehm, taking advantage of his position as a Government witness, attempted to unload. Of course such an effort was ridiculous upon the face of it, and encountered utter and shameful failure. Whatever Mr. Hessing's political errors may have
been, he is a truthful man, and, at the risk of added years of imprisonment with which he
was threatened, he took the stand, and, as far as he was permitted to do so, told the truth
of Mr. Jacob Rehm. These, however, are matters to be considered in the future. It will be
well and wise, I think, at some future period for the Administration to understand precisely the facts—the truth, the whole truth, and nothing but the truth. I am certain as I
am of anything in this world, that if you ever come to know the truth, justice will be

done—not such justice as seems to have been arranged for in these prosecutions, but such as an intelligent, honest public sentiment will approve. As to the disposition of the Wadsworth and Ward Cases, there can be, as I have said, no doubt upon that question as I understand immediate action is to be taken, and I do trust that it will be such as is in the interests of justice and as the better sense of the public will approve." ALS, *ibid.*, Letters from the President. Storrs represented Philip Wadsworth, former collector of Internal Revenue, and others charged with conspiracy in the Chicago whiskey frauds. On June 13, prosecutors dropped charges against Wadsworth and Jasper D. Ward, former U.S. attorney. See *Chicago Inter-Ocean*, May 25, June 14, July 11, Aug. 17, 1876; *HMD*, 44-1-186, 380–88. On June 24, Judge Henry W. Blodgett sentenced Anton C. Hesing, editor, *Illinois Staats Zeitung*, to two years in prison and a $5,000 fine. On July 25 and 26, a correspondent reported from Washington, D. C. "Mr. Storrs, the attorney for A. C. Hesing, has been in consultation with the President and Attorney General to-day, and feels very much encouraged. The matter of a commutation of Hesing's sentence was considered at Cabinet meeting, the facts having been fully explained by Attorney General Taft, . . ." "Mr. Storrs has had another interview with the President and Attorney General, to-day, in reference to the pardons of the Chicago whisky convicts, and has made arrangements for a final hearing before Judge Taft to-morrow, at which he has requested District Attorney Bangs to be present. Mr. Storrs is armed with a formidable array of documents—petitions with lists of names dozens of feet long, affidavits without end, and an argument which he describes as being 'powerful enough to convince the most obstinate, instruct the most ignorant, and refresh the most weary.' Mr. Storrs will ask that the sentences pronounced by the court be reduced to three months, that being the same as the sentences of the squealing distillers . . ." *Chicago Inter-Ocean*, July 26, 27, 1876. On Sept. 21, USG commuted the sentences of Hesing and three others to three months in prison and a $1,000 fine. Copy, DNA, RG 59, General Records. See *Chicago Inter-Ocean*, June 26, 28, Sept. 5, 21, 23, 25, 1876.

On Aug. 25, William F. Coolbaugh, Chicago, had written to USG. "I enclose herewith a note from Mr D. W. Munn in whose recommendation of Mr Doolittle as an able & efficient Atty I fully and cordially concur. Should it be deemed advisable to employ assistant counsel in a civil suit against Rhem to recover a portion of the sum stolen from the Governmt there are good reasons why Judge Doolittle might render very efficient service" ALS, DNA, RG 60, Letters from the President. On Aug. 24, Daniel W. Munn, Chicago, had written to Coolbaugh. "[I] learn that Mr E. A. Storrs is employed, and directed, [by] the Governmt to bring suit vs *Jacob Rehm* for ¼ million or so. I commend the Govt for its course. I occurs to me however that in a case so important, that at least one able assistant should be employed to aid Mr Storrs. In my judgment no Lawyer would so completely fill the bill, as Hon J. R. Doolittle of our city As a jurist he stands as you know at the head of the profession—and being of council in my late trial he is perfectly familiar with the case vs Rehm.—the law of such cases he thoroughly understands; his legal argument to the Court & Jury in my case was universally commended as unsurpassed; Col Ingersoll his associate said it was one of finest ablest & most effective argumnts he ever heard." ALS, *ibid.* On Oct. 6, USG commuted Jacob Rehm's sentence from six to three months in prison, and reduced the fine from $10,000 to $1,000. Copy, *ibid.*, RG 59, General Records.

1. On June 5, Thomas C. Fletcher, St. Louis, had written to USG. "Dyer intends to resign his office of Dist Atty. E Dist of Mo' You may remember that at the time his predecessor, Patrick, was appointed, I wrote you, saying that I would accept the place and 'could do the Govt'. some good service in that place.' I had at that time only suspicions of rev-

enue frauds. I am now through with all the cases in which I have been engaged for the defence in the U. S. Dist' Court and the place of U. S. Dist Atty being in the line of my profession I am willing to perform its duties and if entrusted to do so will justify by my course
& action your confidence in me." ALS, *ibid.*, RG 60, Records Relating to Appointments. See
PUSG, 26, 115.

On June 6, Carman A. Newcomb, St. Louis, wrote to USG. "It has been announced in
the Public press of this City, and on authority as I understand, that, Col D. P. Dyer is about
to resign the office of U. S. Atty for this Dist. Wm H Bliss Esqr now first Assist U. S. Atty
who has held the position since 1872. desires to be appointed to the successorship. I have
known Mr Bliss intimately ever since his connection with the Dist Attys office. He is a son
of Hon Philemon Bliss, formerly a Member of Congress from the Ashtabula Dist State of
Ohio, more recently a Judge of the Supreme court of this State. During the recent prosecutions against the Whiskey ring here, Mr Bliss has earned great credit by his earnestness
and ability he has displayed in the preparation and presentation of the cases. In my opinion Mr Bliss will make a capable, and efficient officer, and will reflect credit upon your
administration. I most cordially reccommend him to your favorable consideration." ALS,
DNA, RG 60, Records Relating to Appointments. On June 19, John M. Krum, St. Louis,
wrote to USG recommending William H. Bliss. ". . . He is a *friend*—unflinching friend &
supporter of your Administration—While the party Col. Dyer desires as his successor is
a Henderson attaché & of course opposed to you & to your Administration—" ALS, *ibid.*
Favorable recommendations from James B. Eads, William H. Benton, John F. Long, Hiram
W. Leffingwell, and others are *ibid.* On June 23, James E. Yeatman, Isaac H. Sturgeon, and
Henry C. Wright, St. Louis, telegraphed to USG on the same subject. Telegram received
(at 9:19 P.M.), DLC-USG, IB. On June 24, Sturgeon wrote to USG. "Mr. Wm H. Bliss applied to me to recommend him for the position of United States District attorney and
knowing from his own lips that he had never sympathized in the attacks made upon you
and regarding him as a pure good man I recommended him—Last evening your personal
and political friend and mine the Hon D. T. Jewett called upon me to say that he was thinking of applying for the position and would let me know this morning—I explained to him
that I had recommended Mr Bliss and that whilst that would have to stand I could and
would write saying that if you should not see proper to appoint Mr Bliss that his appointment would be an excellent one & most acceptable to the Republicans of this District—
. . ." ALS, DNA, RG 60, Records Relating to Appointments. See *PUSG*, 26, 375–85. On
July 8, USG nominated Bliss as U.S. attorney, Eastern District, Mo.

To Senate

To The Senate of the United States

In response to the resolution of the Senate, of July 20th 1876,
calling upon the President to communicate to the Senate; if in his
opinion not incompatible with the public interest, ~~any~~ [any] information in regard to the slaughter of American citizens at Hamburg,
South Carolina, I have the honor to submit the following enclosures:
towit:

No 1   Letter of the 22d of July /76 from Gov. D. H. Chamberlain of South Carolina to me.
No 2   My reply thereto.
No 3   Report of Hon. Wm Stone, Atty. Gen. of South Carolina.[1]
    4   Report of Gen. H. W. Purvis Adj. & Inspector Gen. of South Carolina[2]
    5   Copy of evidence taken before a Coroners Jury investigating facts relating to the Hamburg Massacre[3]
No 6   Printed Copy of Statement by M. C. Butler, of South Carolina[4]
    7   Printed letter from the same to the Editor of the Journal of Commerce.[5]
    8   [Copy of] Letter from Gov. Chamberlain ~~of South Carolina~~ to the Hon. T. J. Robertson[6]
    9   An address to the American people by the Colored ~~people~~ [citizens] of Charleston, South Carolina.[7]
   10   An Address by a committee appointed at a convention of leading representatives of Columbia South Carolina.[8]
   11   [Copy of] Letter of July 15th 1876 from the Dist. Atty. of Miss. to the Atty. Gen. of the United States
   12   Letter from same to same
   13   Copy of report of a Grand Jury lately in session in Oxford, Miss.[9]

These enclosures embrace all the information in my possession touching the late disgraceful and brutal slaughter of unoffending men, at the town of Hamburg, ~~Miss.~~ [S. C] My letter to Governor Chamberlain contains all the comments I wish to make on the subject. As allusion is made in that letter to the condition of other States, and particularly to La. & Miss. I have added to the enclosures letters and testimony in regard to the lawless condition of a portion of the people of the latter state. In regard to La. affairs, murders & massacres of innocent men, for opinions sake, or on account of color, have been of too recent date and of too frequent occurrence to require recapitulation or testimony here.[10] All are familiar with their horrible details, the [only] wonder ~~only~~ being that so many justify them or apologize [for] ~~doing~~ them.

But recently a Committee of the Senate of the United States ~~have~~ visited the State of Mississipp~~yi~~ to take testimony on the subject of frauds and violence in elections. Their report has not yet been made public, [~~but all I have said to the testimony they present touching Mississippi affairs I submit as relevant to affairs in South Carolina~~ —but] I ~~submit all I have said touching Mississippi affairs to the testimony they may give~~ [present], ~~on this subject.~~ [await its forthcoming with a feeling of confidence that it will fully sustain all that I have stated relating to fraud and violence in the State of Mississippi [11]

U. S. Grant

Executive Mansion July 31st 1876]

ADf (bracketed text not in USG's hand; tabular material expanded), DLC-USG, III. *SED,* 44-1-85. See letter to Daniel H. Chamberlain, July 26, 1876; *New York Herald,* Aug. 2, 1876.

    On Aug. 3, Noah Thomas, London, Ohio, wrote to USG. "Having long been one of your steadfast friends, and Supporters and not being personally acquainted with you, I have greatly desired to communicate to you my very high regard and esteem for you, but a sense of propriety has restrained me from doing so, knowing how much you must have been perplexed with various manners of correspondants since your induction into office, and having read in yesterday's and today's Cincinnati Gazette your recent message to the house relative to appropriations &c and of that to the Senate concerning the Hamburg massacre, my convictions of your high moral, and political character, your fidelity to the principles of a free government, and your avowed purpose while in office, to do to the extent of your ability what you deem for the best interests of the whole people, remains unimpaired, and I have this morning assumed the responsibility, and taken the privilege to thus communicate to you my friendship, and admiration for you, and I do so now with greater freedom, for the reason that your Second term of office is nearing its close, and you will not feel that I am applying for a position. I have often been urged by my friends and associates to apply for a place in the employ of the government, but for reasons above stated have never done so. In my judgment, many of the investigations had in, and about, Washington have aimed at your character, and I thank God that they have all failed to identify you with any of the frauds purpetrated upon the government. I have always felt sure they would fail in this I saw you for the first time, May 5 1864, as you crossed the Rapidan. River passing the head quarters of the Sixth Army Corps, of which I was a member. You will remember, that the old 6th was a fighting Corps. I was a member of the 110 O. V. I. Gen J Warren Keifer's Regt., who by the way, we have nominated as our candidate for congress from this (8th) Dist who will succeed f William Lawrance, present incumbent. I lost my left arm at the battle of Cole Harbor June 2nd 1864 Having no other object in this than to communicate to you my high regard, and unwavoring friendship for you as a Soldier, and your great efficiency as cheif Executive of the Nation, I hope you will pardon me, for thus presuming to address you in this familiar mode, in your dignified position, and ask that you recognize in me a true friend with a very earnest desire that you may live to *yet,* realize, and enjoy in the fullest sense, what you fought for during the late war, and what you have labored so arduously for in your Executive capacity since, a full and complete return of peace, and prosperity to every Section of the country, North and South, and that it may be my good fortune in the future to enjoy your personal acquaintance." ALS, USG 3.

1. Born in 1842, William Stone, former capt., 19th Mass., served as 1st lt., 45th Inf. (1866–70), and later practiced law in Charleston. On Wednesday, July 12, 1876, Stone, S. C. attorney gen., wrote to Governor Daniel H. Chamberlain of S. C. "According to your request of Monday last, I have visited Hamburgh for the purpose of ascertaining the facts connected with the killing of several men there on the night of the 8th of July. My information has been derived chiefly from Trial-Justice Rivers and from the testimony of persons who have been examined before the coroner's jury now in session, and from those who received wounds from the armed body of white men who had taken them prisoners. . . . It may be possible that a careful judicial investigation may show some slight errors in some of the minor details stated in this report. But making due allowance for such errors, the facts show the demand on the militia to give up their arms was made by persons without lawful authority to enforce such demand or to receive the arms had they been surrendered; that the attack on the militia to compel a compliance with this demand was without lawful excuse or justification; and that after there had been some twenty or twenty-five prisoners captured and completely in the power of their captors, and without means of making further resistance, five of them were deliberately shot to death and three more severely wounded. It further appears that not content with thus satisfying their vengeance, many of the crowd added to their guilt the crime of robbery of defenseless people, and were only prevented from arson by the efforts of their own leaders." *SED*, 44-1-85, 6, 9–10.

2. Born in Philadelphia, Henry W. Purvis, son of black abolitionist Robert Purvis, studied at Oberlin (1863–66) and settled in S. C., where he served as state representative (1868–70) and later as AG and inspector gen. On July 12, 1876, Henry Purvis wrote to Chamberlain. ". . . The town of Hamburgh presented just such an appearance as one would that was, after being raided upon by a hostile army, with but this difference, that the latter would not descend to robbery and plunder, as well as murder. Nearly every colored man's house in the town (and Louis Schiller's, white) was broken into, and plundered, furniture broken, bedding and clothing stolen, and a general scene of devastation prevailing everywhere. From all I could ascertain, as well as from the testimony taken before the coroner's jury, (copy herewith transmitted,) General M. C. Butler is charged with being the sole cause of the trouble, and from conversation held with many citizens in Hamburgh, all agreed that had he, Butler, been so disposed, one word from him would have stopped the scene of carnage that ensued. . . ." *Ibid.*, p. 10. For related testimony by Purvis, see *SMD*, 44-2-48, II, 401–6.

3. See *SED*, 44-1-85, 11–33.

4. Matthew C. Butler, attorney and former maj. gen., C.S. Army, wrote an undated letter to "*Editors Columbia Register*" claiming that he was in Hamburg to represent clients involved in a complaint with a black militia co. "Certain newspaper editors and reporters have done me so much injustice by false reports in reference to the recent disturbance in Hamburgh, that it is due to myself to make to the public a statement of my connection with it. . . . This collision was the culmination of the system of insulting and outraging of white people which the negroes had adopted there for several years. Many things were done on this terrible night which, of course, cannot be justified, but the negroes 'sowed the wind and reaped the whirlwind.' I did not attempt to accomplish by force what I could not accomplish by peaceful means. I was not the leader of this body of infuriated men. I was there in the line of my profession. The collision was a sort of spontaneous combustion. I thought I saw it approaching, and did all that any human being could be expected to do to prevent it. I have no objection to being saddled with whatever responsibility fairly attaches to my conduct, but I have no idea of permitting newspaper reporters, for the sake of a sensation or any other purpose, presenting me as the leader of a mob, when I was no more the leader, and no more responsible, than any other person who might have been there in the line of

his duty." *Ibid.*, pp. 33, 35–36. On Jan. 2, 1877, Butler, Columbia, S. C., testified before a Senate investigating committee on the same subject. *SMD*, 44-2-48, II, 237–46. See *PUSG*, 20, 248–49; *SRC*, 42-2-41, part 4, pp. 1185–218.

5. On July 16, 1876, Butler, Edgefield, S. C., had written to the editors, *Journal of Commerce*. "The high joint commission, consisting of William Stone, carpet-bag attorney-general, and the mulatto adjutant-general of the State, Purvis, have lately visited Hamburgh to investigate the 'horror,' and the former has made his 'report.' Why Governor Chamberlain should have subjected the State to the expense, and these two dignitaries to the trouble of going to Hamburgh, is somewhat surprising. When we read the 'report,' and consider the data from which it is made, the *ex-parte* statements of lying negroes, and the partial, partisan, and false conclusions of its facile author, the suggestion arises, why the affidavits were not written out in Columbia, made to order there, and sent by express to be executed without limit by the dusky affiants of that rendezvous, Hamburgh. This plan would have answered the purpose of the outrage-manufacturers and their hireling newspaper champions just as well. If this so-called attorney-general had been in the pursuit of truth, why did he confine his inquiries to the besotted negroes and a few perjured white men who had instigated them into an armed insurrection against the laws of the country, the rights and property of its citizens, and the safety and peace of that community?... The town had a negro intendant, negro aldermen, negro marshals. It was almost a terror to every white man whose business required him to pass through it. They had harbored thieves and criminals from every direction. They had arrested and fined some of the best and most peaceable citizens for the most trivial offenses against their ordinances—... The negroes had assembled riotously; were in a state of armed resistance to the laws, and any citizen or number of citizens had the right to disperse the rioters and suppress the riot, and to use just so much force as was necessary to accomplish it, and if every negro engaged in the riot had been killed in the suppression, it would have been excusable, if not justifiable.... I am indifferent to the opinion of those howling hypocrites, and ask no favors at their hands, and shall grant none. Their threats of United States soldiers have no terrors for me or the people of Edgefield. We have had these soldiers with us and have no objection to their coming again. We have found the officers gentlemen as a general thing, and the men orderly and law-abiding, and they will do no more than execute their orders and enforce the laws. I invite a judicial investigation, and am prepared to submit to the abritrament of the law, and such is the feeling, as far as I have been able to learn, of every white man who is in any degree connected with the affair. The white men of this country have some rights which the negroes are bound to respect. They have no other feeling for them than kindness and pity. Kindness for their loyalty to our families during the war, and pity that they will permit themselves to be made the tools of bad, mischievous, designing white men and mulattoes. So long as they obey the laws, every honorable man of the country will feel bound to protect and encourage them in happiness and prosperity." *SED*, 44-1-85, 36–39.

6. On July 13, Chamberlain had written to U.S. Senator Thomas J. Robertson of S. C. concerning the Hamburg massacre. "... If you can find words to characterize its atrocity and barbarism, the triviality of the causes, the murderous and inhuman spirit which marked it in all its stages, your power of language exceeds mine. It presents a darker picture of human cruelty than the slaughter of Custer and his soldiers, for they were shot in open battle. The victims at Hamburgh were murdered in cold blood after they had surrendered and were utterly defenseless. No occasion existed for causing the presence of a single armed citizen in Hamburgh on the day of the massacre. No violence was offered or threatened to any one. It is indeed said, as usual, that 'the niggers were impudent,' but the evidence shows that all the actual physical aggression was on the part of the whites; ... I

am glad to testify to the horror which this event has excited among many here who have not been wont to heartily condemn many of the past bloody occurrences at the South. Nothing, however, short of condign and ample punishment can discharge the obligation of society and our State toward the authors of such a causeless and cruel massacre." *Ibid.*, pp. 39–41.

7. On July 10, Richard H. Cain, chairman, J. L. Graves, secretary, and fifteen others, "colored citizens of Charleston," had issued a protest. ". . . The late unwarrantable slaughter of our brethren at Hamburgh, by the order of General M. C. Butler, of Edgefield County, was an unmitigated and foul murder, premeditated and predetermined, and a sought-for opportunity, by a band of lawless men in that county, known as regulators, who are the enemies of the colored race in that county, composed of ex-confederate soldiers, banded together for the purpose of intimidating the colored laborers and voters at elections, and keeping the 'negroes in their place,' as they say. . . . These men have sworn to carry these upper counties this election, and this *unarming of the colored militia* is the precursor of their work of blood and murder which they propose to inaugurate this fall, in order to carry the election. We cannot contemplate this state of affairs without feelings of horror at its existence. Were we brought face to face with men of honor, with men who could and would observe the rules of honorable warfare, we could feel some degree of satisfaction in knowing that we ha[d] honorable foemen to contend with; but when midnight riders, and ungovernable and unprincipled murderers rush from behind bushes and by-paths and shoot unarmed men, and *burn the houses over the heads of unoffending women and children*, as has been done in Edgefield, and plunder the homes of men whom they have just slain and chopped their flesh into mince-meat, and exhibited it to the *by-standers, and taunting the children of the murdered with offers of their parents'* flesh to eat, as was done on the 8th of July in Hamburgh by South Carolinians, there is no language in the English vocabulary sufficiently strong to characterize such a people and such conduct. . . . The negro in this country will not always be docile—he will not always be restrained by his law-abiding character—the rising generation are as brave and daring as are white men; already that spirit is taking deep root in the minds of thousands who have nothing to lose in the contest, and who would rejoice in an opportunity to sacrifice their lives for their liberty." *Ibid.*, pp. 41–44. Related resolutions are *ibid.*, pp. 44–47.

8. On July 21, S. C. Representative Robert B. Elliott and fifty-nine others, "colored citizens of South Carolina," wrote about the Hamburg massacre. "In view of the many gross misrepresentations of the origin and cause of the outrage and the circumstances connected with its perpetration, we deem it to be highly essential to truth and to justice, and eminently due as well to the memories of those who were murdered by the participants in that massacre as to the characters of their surviving associates, that a calm, dispassionate, and truthful exposition of that terrible affair should be presented for the information and consideration of the American people. . . . In view of the foregoing detailed statement of the facts and circumstances immediately connected with the recent disgraceful occurence, as well as the circumstances which usually attend similar occurrences in our section of the country, we cannot avoid the irresistible conclusion which is thereby forced upon our minds, that they have their origin in a settled and well-defined purpose to influence and control political elections. . . . Since our emancipation we have, as a class, been peaceable and law-abiding, docile and forbearing; forbearing to such a degree that in the presence of stupendous wrongs and gross outrages daily and hourly inflicted upon our persons and committed against our property, although conscious of our rights, we have manifested a spirit of patience and endurance unheard of and unknown in the history of the most servile population. We ask that we be not cruelly goaded on to madness and desperation by such unholy burdens as are imposed upon us. We ask that, constituting as we

do a large producing class in our State, contributing what bone and sinew we possess to the development of its industries, we be not hindered by violence in our endeavors to increase the prosperity and material wealth of our commonwealth, and in our efforts to advance the commercial interests of our country. . . . We would also call upon his excellency the governor of the State to invoke every constitutional agency and legal method for the enforcement of the laws and the arrest and punishment of those, whoever they are, that may be shown to have been principals or accessories, or aiders and abettors in the recent murders committed at Hamburgh. We do most earnestly call upon his excellency to see that the law in this Hamburgh outrage, as well as in all other cases of infraction and violation of the public peace and general security, be most faithfully executed. . . . We would likewise appeal to his Excellency the President of the United States to enforce the constitutional guarantee by affording the national protection to the citizens of the United States domiciled in South Carolina, against domestic armed violence, and to aid the chief executive of this State in all proper efforts on his part to arrest and bring to punishment the perpetrators of the bloody crime at Hamburgh. . . ." *Ibid.*, pp. 47, 52–54. For Elliott's related testimony, see *SMD*, 44-2-48, II, 447–76.

9. On July 8, William D. Frazee, foreman, and W. H. Dodson, clerk, "United States grand jury for the northern district of Mississippi," Oxford, had written to Judge Robert A. Hill. ". . . Although we have had a protracted session, we have only made a partial and cursory examination of the innumerable cases of violations of the election-laws that have come to our knowledge. We regret to report that from the examination had, we must say that the fraud, intimidation, and violence perpetrated at the late election is without a parallel in the annals of history, and that time would fail us to take the testimony that could be easily introduced, demonstrating the fact that there is sufficient grounds for the finding of thousands of indictments against persons who are grossly guilty of the above-mentioned violations of the election-laws. From the facts elicited during this grand inquest, and from our own knowledge of the reign of terror that was inaugurated during the late election campaign, we can only recommend to the citizens of Mississippi to make an earnest appeal to the strong arm of the United States Government to give them that protection that is guaranteed to every American citizen—that is, protection in freedom of speech, in their person and property, and the right of suffrage. We do assert that all of these rights were openly violated and trampled in the dust during the late election, and that there is no redress for these grievances under the present State government, and unless the United States Government enforces that shield of protection that is guaranteed by the Constitution to every citizen, however humble and obscure, then may the citizens of Mississippi exclaim farewell to liberty, farewell to the freedom of the ballot-box. . . ." *SED*, 44-1-85, 56. On July 15, Thomas Walton, U.S. attorney, Oxford, wrote to Attorney Gen. Alphonso Taft. "I have the honor to submit herewith the report of the grand jury lately in session here, together with the evidence on which it is based. This evidence, you will see, plainly required the jury to indict a great many persons for violations of the election-laws; but, out of eighteen jurors, seven were found who refused to concur in any such indictment. I learn, however, that all but one of the jurors voted for this report. All but this one professed to belong to the republican party; and some of those who finally voted against the eleven who were for the indictments were throughout the whole session apparently the most reliable men we had to sustain the indictments, and the most zealous in investigating the cases. This was particularly true of the man who wrote this report, yet he finally went against all prosecutions, though we had conceived him to be the most earnest, as he had certainly been the most active, man among us, in bringing to justice, or at least in investigating the election cases. I can only lament the shameful failure of justice which has taken place, and I have little doubt that it must and will give a most unbridled license to

lawlessness at the next State, if not at the next Federal, election." *Ibid.*, p. 55. On July 16, Walton wrote to Taft on the same subject. *Ibid.*, pp. 55–56; *HED*, 44-2-30, 112. Born in Ga. and raised in Miss., Walton, lawyer and planter, had been nominated as U.S. attorney, Northern District, Miss., in April. On July 21, Taft wrote to USG. "Inclosed i[s] a copy of the report of the Grand Jury of the Northern Dis. of Miss'ppi, and of the letters of the Dis. Atty. I do not think that the use of the report, or of the general statements of the Dis. Atty as to the frauds, would be any breach of confidence. If they had found bills, it might be necessary to keep their proceedings secret in order to effect the arrests. Whether this report is valuable to publish may be a question. How the grand jury came all but one, to be republicans I do not know, but suppose it was fair. But they came to an impotent conclusion. . . . P. S. Still the report is an authentic statement of the frauds and the grossness of them." ALS, CSmH. See *HED*, 44-2-30, 115–20.

On Sept. 9, U.S. Senator Blanche K. Bruce of Miss. wrote to USG. "I have the honor to enclose herewith, a letter this day received by me calling my attention to the recent course of Hon. Thomas Walton, U. S. Attorney for the Northern district of Mississppi. I have information from sources which leaves me no room to doubt the truth of the statement contained in the letter I enclose to you. The acceptance of a nomination to Congress will, it seems to me, prevent that attention to the duties of his office, which will be necessary to a faithful performance of them. I can only say to your Excellency: in conclusion, that the course pursued by Walton is a surprise to me and that I have been grossly deceived and misled in regard to his character as a Republican. He stood high in our party in that state as an open and fearless advocate of the principles of the Republican party, was a gentleman whose character was without stain or blemish and held the confidence of Republicans generally. I regret that his late course has made it necessary for me no longer to support or defend him in public office and I respectfully ask his removal and the appointment of Judge Orlando Davis of Miss. as his successor, Judge Davis is a lawyer of large experience, a staunch Republican, a man of high character whose appointment will be entirely satisfactory to the country." LS, DNA, RG 60, Letters Received, Senate. On Sept. 8, Jonathan Tarbell, president, Miss. Republican Association, and three others, Washington, D. C., had written to Bruce. ". . . It is evident that no one holding the views expressed by Judge Walton can be relied upon for efficiency and thoroughness in prosecuting violators of those laws which secure to the late slaves their rights as freemen and voters. His acceptance of the nomination for Congress, were he disposed to do so zealously and thoroughly, precludes a proper attention to the duties of his office." LS, *ibid.* A clipping quoted Walton, in a campaign speech, as promising to defend Jefferson Davis in Congress. *Ibid.* (from *New York Times*, Sept. 7, 1876). On Sept. 15, Abraham Doss, Carrollton, Miss., wrote to USG. "I herewith enclose you an extract from a speech made by Judge Thos Walton who is now U. S. District Atty for the Northern District of Missi I am a republican and have battled for the cause for years past, and I submit to you if a man ought to hold a government office who will make such a speech as this. Comment is unnecessary." ALS, DNA, RG 60, Letters from the President. A clipping of the same speech is *ibid.* Walton lost the election but continued as U.S. attorney. See *HED*, 44-2-30, 123–29.

10. See *PUSG*, 24, 121–26; *ibid.*, 25, 213–28; *ibid.*, 26, 3–35.

On Jan. 15, 1876, Stephen B. Packard, U.S. marshal, La., Washington, D. C., had written to USG. "I deem it my duty to call your attention to the condition of lawlessness that prevails in some parts of the state of Louisiana. Armed bands of men are continually perpetrating deeds of violence, extending to the taking of life, the eviction from office of the duly elected representatives of the people, and the banishment from localities of others. I will not now enter into details, thinking it sufficient to call your attention to the fact in general terms. The evil seems to be rather increasing than otherwise, and I am fearful that unless some remedial measures should be applied at an early day it will so spread as to create a condition of anarchy in that State, and set at naught both federal and State authorities. Many lives have been sacrificed, more are endangered, and indeed such a condition of lawlessness prevails as to disgrace the very name of free government. In two noted instances men have been rescued from the Sheriff's hands by these armed bands, and have been deprived of life without any process of law, and the fact that such deeds are perpetrated without punishment attending them at the hands of the State authorities implies their powerlessness to give due protection, or to vindicate the law. My statement will be corroborated by Louisiana citizens generally and by members of the delegation in Congress here present, and I appeal to you, as the Chief Executive of the Nation to direct that the protection of the laws be afforded to those who suffer from these outrages, and that those who perpetrate them may be brought to justice." LS, DNA, RG 60, Letters Received, La.

On Feb. 17, Grenville N. Peirce, Wilderness Plantation near Baton Rouge, wrote to USG. "The undersigned a citizen of Louisiana respectfully represents to the General Government that a State of lawlessness exists in this section of the State which renders life & property very unsafe. That a band of marauders are riding roughshod over the country at the dead hour of the night committing murder, arson, and other crimes with perfect impunity. Colored men are taken out, and shot, whipped, and sometimes burnt. Last night a colored man on my Plantation was taken from his house at about midnight, dragged with a slip nooze around his neck for more than a quarter of a mile, and then hung;—no mock trial, and not even a notice given him. The perpetrators of these acts have in no instance been arrested. The county Officers can do nothing;—The State Government does nothing. A reign of terror exists worse than during the late civil war. We have no county or Parish Judge no Sheriff,—and if we had them they would not dare go outside the limits of the Town of Baton Rouge. In the name of common humanity, for myself and familly, and more than thirty colored famillies I respectfully ask can not some protection be given us?. . . P. S. A large majority of the colored people are compelled for safety to sleep in the woods at night for safety, and my Plantation with six hundred acres of land about being put in cultivation will be abandoned by the entire force of laborers, and their famillies— as they are afraid to return to the home where they have lived for the past twenty years.— I am satisfied if an investigation were to take place a state of affairs would be exhibited that would shock the feelings of every law abiding citizen throughout the country" ALS, *ibid.*, RG 94, Letters Received, 1344 1876. On Feb. 22, Lt. Col. Henry A. Morrow, Baton Rouge, reported to AG, Dept. of the Gulf, New Orleans, supporting Peirce's charges. ALS, *ibid.* On March 1, Col. Christopher C. Auger, New Orleans, endorsed these and related papers. ". . . Although U. S. Troops can do very little in the way of suppressing these outrages, their presence is felt as a moral support to the good citizen in their vicinity, and their post becomes a place of refuge to the parties driven from their homes. I have already ordered a company to Bayou Sara in hopes their presence may have a beneficial effect in stopping the outrages committed in that vicinity." ES, *ibid.*

On May 15, 11:00 P.M., Act. Governor Caesar C. Antoine of La. telegraphed to Governor William P. Kellogg of La., Washington, D. C. "Despatches from all quarters agree that a most serious condition of things prevails in west Feliciana and all along the mississippi line much blood has already been shed and much more will be shed unless prompt action is taken the sheriff officially calls upon me for military aid the last Legislature made no appropriation for militia purposes I have laid the whole matter before Gen Augur but his instructions do not authorize his interference unless a US officer is attacked there are united States troops Stationed in the town of Bayou Sara an authorization to them to

preserve Peace would avert all further bloodshed" Telegram received (on May 16), *ibid.*,
307 1876. On May 16, Gen. William T. Sherman wrote to Lt. Gen. Philip H. Sheridan,
Chicago. "Please instruct by telegraph General Augur as follows:—Upon the request of
the Governor of Louisiana, and it appearing that the State authorities are unable to maintain order, he General Augur is authorized at his discretion to interfere to the extent
of aiding the State authorities, to prevent bloodshed and lawless violence. The above is in
the exact language of the Secretary of War, who is just from the President." Copy, *ibid.*
Related papers are *ibid.* On May 31, Kellogg, New Orleans, wrote to Sheridan. "*Personal*
. . . General Augur informs me that he proposes leaving for Chicago to night   I presume
he will submit some suggestions for your consideration regarding the disposition of
troops and the policy to be adopted by the military authorities during the pending campaign. After I saw you at Phila I visited Washington on my way home and saw the President   He gave me every possible assurance I could or did ask   Both he and the Attorney
Genl stated to me that every possible assistance should be furnished us to keep the peace
and enforce the laws and secure a fair election   I think Genl Augur understands the situation fully, and I am confident you have the inclination if you can consistently do so to afford him all the assistance you can   The republicans of this state depend greatly upon you"
ALS, DLC-Philip H. Sheridan.

On May 29, Matthew Evans and four others, New Orleans, had written to USG. "We
are true republicans in the state of Louisiana Situated in Parish of West Feliciana and
seems imposible for the poor people to get along in this State of affairs   Our men in this
Parish are Strung and Hung and assasined in their beds like a parcell of sheep. I am here
now in New Orlean[s]   I had ~~had~~ to run from my own land and property and I have not
seen any steps that governer has taken to avoid   what are we poor Colored population are
to do   they runed us from our own homes and nothing to live on and no work do   I know
that You are impowred to do something for us   Please for God sake in this state of affairs
try." L, DNA, RG 60, Letters from the President.

On July 24, a correspondent reported from Washington, D. C. "Secretary Robeson
and General T. Morris Chester, the colored Assistant State Superintendent of Education
of Louisiana, had an interview with the President to-day, the conversation being about
Southern political affairs. The President told him he had given up all hope of carrying any
of the Southern States except the Carolinas and Louisiana, but that, as to Louisiana, troops
would be furnished and measures would be adopted to bring out the colored vote, and
money would be supplied for campaign purposes and to execute the plans made for carrying the State. Chester returns to New Orleans with a letter from the President to Marshal
Packard telling him not to be in a hurry to resign the marshalship as he wishes him to put
in operation the plans he has formed for carrying the State." *New York Herald*, July 25,
1876. See *ibid.*, July 31, 1876.

11. On Aug. 7, the Senate's "Select Committee to Inquire into Alleged Frauds in the
Recent Election in Mississippi" submitted majority and minority reports, accompanied by
voluminous testimony. See *SRC*, 44-1-527; *PUSG*, 26, 312–26.

On June 3 and July 27, William F. Simonton, Shannon, Miss., had written to USG. "I
have determined to try to reach you with a letter, though I have little hope of success. If I
succeed in my effort you may consider it presumptuous impudence. Do as you think best
about that. Can't something be done to stop the massacres and assassinations of Republicans in the Southern states? The lives of white and colored Republicans, are taken here
with impunity, by our savage Regulators, who have no regard for anything except the
strong arm of the government. Many of us prefer risking our lives a while longer, to voting the Democratic ticket; but if the government cannot and will not afford any relief, we

ought to be authoritatively informed to that effect, and then we will make the best terms with the Regulators we can. I am a Southron by birth education &c. I have lived where I now live twenty five years, and here I expect to be burried. I was the Presidential Elector of the 1st congressional dist this state in 1872. I have never been a Rebel voluntarily nor involuntarily. Now Sir, I am not preparing to ask you for an office; I simply wish to urge my humanity plea, by giving you some reasons to believe my statements. I thought you a great and good man in 1872, and I still entertain that opinion; though I think you have been led astray on this southern question. I believe it is in your power to give us justice, and I still hope you will do it. We can have a sort of peace and protection here, by voting with the Democrats, and accepting a moral and political serfdom. In a short time Republicans will be curiosities here, if this Democratic guerrilla warfare is permitted to go on. Doubtless you think this a plain letter. I think you a plain man and the more sensible for it. Of course I don't expect an answer; but I hope you will properly weigh this mite of testimony." "Inaugurate at once a pollicy that will guarantee a full free and fair vote in this state, or say to Republicans here that the government cannot afford us the protection we need. If troops are not sent here right away there will be absolutely no votes cast for Republicans. We should by all means have a company in this county as speedily as possible. There is no freedom here. Republicans cannot hold meetings nor make any effort to organize the party without eminent danger of being massacred. We have been neglected in this portion of the state when protection to some extent at least has been afforded elsewhere until we are well nigh crushed out. I have little hope of this reaching you, but feel it my duty to write anyhow. I was Presidential Elector here in 1872." ALS, DNA, RG 60, Letters from the President. *HED*, 44-2-30, 112–13. On June 27, Simonton, Jackson, testified on political violence in Miss. *SRC*, 44-1-527, I, 781–89.

To House of Representatives

To The House of Representatives.

The act making appropriations for sundry civil expenses of the government infor the fiscal year ending June 30th 1877,[1] is so defective in what it omits to provide for that I cannot announce its approval without, at the same time, pointing out what seems to me to be its defects. It makes but inadequate provision for the service at best, and in some instances fails to make any provisions whatever. (Insert)

[Notably among the first class is the reduction in the ordinary annual appropriations for the revenue cutter service, to the prejudice of the customs revenue.

The same may be said of the signal service; as also the failure to provide for the increased expenses devolved upon the mints and assay offices by recent legislation, and thus tending to defeat the objects of that legislation.

Of this class also are public buildings, for the protection, preservation and completion of which there is no adequate appropriation, while the sum of one hundred thousand dollars only is appropriated for the repairs of the different navy yards and stations and the preservation of the same, the ordinary and customary appropriations for which are not less than one million dollars.

A similar reduction is made in the expenses for armories and arsenals.

The provision for the ordinary judicial expenses is much less than the estimated amount for that important service, the actual expenditures of the last fiscal year and the certain demands of the current year.

The provision for the expenses of the surveys of public lands is less than one-half of the usual appropriation for that service, and what are understood to be its actual demands.

Reduction in the expenditures for light-houses, beacons and fog stations is also made in similar proportion.

Of the class for which no appropriation is made, among the most noticeable, perhaps, is that portion of the general expenses of the District of Columbia on behalf of the United States, as appropriated in former years, and the judgments of the Court of Claims. The failure to make a reasonable contribution to the expenses of the nation's capital is an apparent dereliction on the part of the United States, and rank injustice to the people here who bear the burdens, while to refuse or neglect to provide for the payment of solemn judgments of its own courts is apparently to repudiate. Of a different character, but as prejudicial to the Treasury is the omission to make provision to enable the Secretary of the Treasury to have the rebel archives, and records of captured and abandoned property examined and information furnished therefrom for the use of the Government.

Finally, without further specification of detail, it may be said, that the act which in its title purports to make provision for a diverse and greatly extended civil service, unhappily, appropriates an amount not more than sixty-five per cent. of its ordinary demands.

The legislative department establishes and defines the service, and devolves upon the Executive departments the obligation of submitting annually the needful estimates of expenses of such service. Congress properly exacts implicit obedience to the requirements of the law in the administration of the public service, and rigid accountability in the expenditures therefor. It is submitted that a corresponding responsibility and obligation rests upon it to make the adequate appropriations to render possible such administration, and tolerable, such exaction. Anything short of an ample provision for a specified service is necessarily fraught with disaster to the public interests, and is a positive injustice to those charged with its execution. The demand for brick without adequate straw has never been regarded as anything but an unreasonable exaction.[2]

To appropriate and to execute are corresponding obligations and duties, and the adequacy of the former is the necessary measure of the efficiency of the execution][3]

In this ~~ninth~~ [Eighth] month of the present session of ~~the present~~ Congress— ~~more than~~ near[ly] one month of the fiscal year ~~having passed~~ to which this appropriation applies having passed—I do not feel warranted in vetoing an absolutely necessary appropriation bill; but in signing it I deem it a duty to show where the responsibility belongs for whatever embarrassments may arise in the execution of the trust confided to me.

[U. S. GRANT

EX MAN. JULY 31ST 1876]

ADf (bracketed material not in USG's hand), DLC-USG, III. *HED*, 44-1-187. See *CR*, 44–1, 5031–32, 5604–5.

On July 21 and 25, the cabinet discussed appropriation bills and proposals to reduce government staff, particularly in the State Dept. Hamilton Fish diary, DLC-Hamilton Fish. On Aug. 15, USG transmitted "to the Senate in answer to its resolution of the 24th ultimo, a report from the Secretary of State with its accompanying statement—" Copies, DNA, RG 59, Reports to the President and Congress; *ibid.*, RG 130, Messages to Congress. *SED*, 44-1-92. On the same day, Fish had written to USG furnishing "the aggregate number of civil officers in, or connected with the Department of State (not including laborers, or mechanics employed by the day, or contractors)" for every second year between 1859 and 1875. Copy, DNA, RG 59, Reports to the President and Congress. A table is *ibid. SED*, 44-1-92.

1. See *U.S. Statutes at Large*, XIX, 102–22.
2. The final version of this message omits this sentence.

3. This block of bracketed text is drawn from a letter of July 28 from Secretary of the Treasury Lot M. Morrill to USG. LS, DLC-USG, III.

Proclamation

Whereas the Congress of the United States did, by an Act approved on the third day of March, one thousand eight hundred and seventy-five authorize the inhabitants of the Territory of Colorado to form for themselves out of said Territory a State Government with the name of the State of Colorado, and for the admission of such State into the Union, on an equal footing with the original States upon certain conditions in said Act specified.

And whereas it was provided by said Act of Congress that the Convention elected by the people of said Territory to frame a State Constitution should when assembled for that purpose and after organization declare on behalf of the people that they adopt the Constitution of the United States, and should also provide by an ordinance irrevocable without the consent of the United States and the people of said State, That perfect toleration of religious sentiment shall be secured, and that no inhabitant of said State shall ever be molested in person or property on account of his or her mode of religious worship, and that the people inhabiting said Territory do agree and declare that they forever disclaim all right and title to the unappropriated public lands lying within said Territory and that the same shall be and remain at the sole and entire disposition of the United States, and that the lands belonging to citizens of the United States residing without the said State shall never be taxed higher than the lands belonging to residents thereof, and that no taxes shall be imposed by the State on lands or property therein belonging to or which may hereafter be purchased by the United States, and

Whereas it was further provided by said Act that the constitution thus formed for the people of the Territory of Colorado should by an ordinance of the Convention forming the same be submitted to the people of said Territory for ratification or rejection at an election to be held in the month of July eighteen hundred and seventy-six at which election the lawful voters of said new State should vote directly for or against the proposed Constitution, and the returns of said election should be made to the acting Governor of the Territory, who with the Chief Justice and United States Attorney of said Territory or any two of them should canvass the same, and if a majority of legal votes should be cast for said Constitution in said proposed State, the said acting Governor should certify the same to the President of the United States together with a copy of said Constitution and ordinances; whereupon it should be the duty of the President of the United States to issue his Proclamation declaring the State admitted into the Union on an equal footing with the original States without any further action whatever on the part of Congress:

And whereas it has been certified to me by the acting Governor of said Territory of Colorado, that within the time prescribed by said Act of Congress a Constitution for said proposed State has been adopted, and the same ratified by a majority of the legal voters of said proposed new State in accordance with the conditions prescribed by said Act of Congress, and whereas a duly authenticated copy of said Constitution and of the declaration and ordinance required by said Act has been received by me,

Now, Therefore, I, Ulysses S. Grant, President of the United States of America, do, in accordance with the provisions of the Act of Congress aforesaid, declare and proclaim the fact that the fundamental conditions imposed by Congress on the State of Colorado to entitle that State to admission to the Union have been ratified and accepted and that the admission of the said State into the Union is now complete.

In testimony whereof I have hereunto set my hand and have caused the seal of the United States to be affixed.

Done at the city of Washington this first day of August, in the year of our Lord one thousand eight hundred and seventy-six, and of the Independence of the United States of America the one hundred and first.

U. S. GRANT

DS, DNA, RG 130, Presidential Proclamations. See *CR*, 43–1, 4691–92, 43–2, 1671–90; *U.S. Statutes at Large*, XVIII, part 3, pp. 474–76; *HRC*, 42-3-8.

On [*July 31, 1876*], USG wrote to Culver C. Sniffen. "Send word to Atty. Gn. that the proclamation giving notice that Colordo is a state will be issued to-day. It will then be necessary to re-appoint the Marshal & Dist. Atty. If he will send over the nominations I will send them in" AN, OHi. Also on July 31, USG nominated Charles C. Tompkins as marshal and Thomas G. Putnam as U.S. attorney, Colo.; on Aug. 14, USG withdrew Putnam's nomination. See *PUSG*, 26, 78–84.

Endorsement

Refered to the Sec. of State. This gives in more detail the transactions of N. C. officials in the matter of "Blockade cotton funds" than the memorandum given to the Sec. of State on Friday last.

U. S. GRANT

Aug. 7th /76

AES, DNA, RG 59, Miscellaneous Letters. Written on a letter of Saturday, Aug. 5, 1876, from Thomas B. Keogh, chairman, N. C. Republican Executive Committee, Washington, D. C., to USG. "Since my conversation with you on Friday last, I have received a letter from the Adjutant General of North Carolina, advising me that he has found a book in his office which gives many particulars concerning the 'Blockade Business,' and covering cotton transactions of John Deveraux Major and A. Q. M. from November 1863 to Feby. 28 1865. It appears that business was done with Theo. Andrea, Power, Low & Co; and Alexander Collie & Co, all of London. The name which I gave you as Collier is Collie. I am told that a balance of $60.000 in gold, due North Carolina on account of blockade cotton, was in the hands of one or all of the above parties at the time of the surrender of the confederate Army. Gov. Vance controlled the fund during the existence of the confederacy: and, if I am correctly informed, drew a portion of it in 1865 and 1866. One Joseph Flanner, who now lives in Paris, was Vance's agent in London—After the war he disposed of the state fund by appropriating a part to his own use and placing the balance to the credit of Gov. Vance—I am anxious to get a statement of the cotton account in detail; and as the money belonged to the United States after the surrender of the Confederacy I presume it is the duty of the proper Treasury officers to look it up." ALS, *ibid.* On Aug. 14, John H. Haswell, chief, Bureau of Indexes and Archives, State Dept., reported. "There is no information, to my knowledge, on file in this Department, in regard to the cotton transactions of John Deveraux. In order to speak with certainty however, it would necessitate the examination of all the Miscellaneous Indexes in the Department covering the period referred to in the letter of Mr Keogh. This would involve considerable time, without I think meeting with any success. As the Treasury Department has charge of captured and abandoned property, that Department may be the proper one to obtain the information desired." ADS, *ibid.* See Joseph H. Flanner to Zebulon B. Vance, April 15, May 2, 14, June 11, 29, 1864, North Carolina Division of Archives and History, Raleigh, N. C.; Frontis W. Johnston *et al.*, eds., *The Papers of Zebulon Baird Vance* (Raleigh, 1963–), I, 354–55, II, 161–62, 310–12, 335, 337; Glenn Tucker, *Zeb Vance: Champion of Personal Freedom* (Indianapolis, 1965), pp. 219–23.

On Oct. 6, Keogh, Raleigh, wrote to USG. "I presume you have by this time had some return from the London Vance matter, if it is possible to get anything. I am anxious to hear from it if there is anything, because November is not far off. I have sufficient information upon which to start the discussion of the matter, but do not want to start off with anything I cannot substantiate. Our campaign so far has been satisfactory to us. Judge Settle says he has seen no reason to change his mind about the result. He expects to be elected by a large majority. I am a little fearful of the influence 'Hampton's Cavalry' will have on our people on the southern border. Some raids have been made into our state by the 'Critter Companies', as they call them, for the purpose of showing our democrats how the South Carolinians expect to purify their state government—" ALS, DNA, RG 59, Miscellaneous Letters. On Oct. 20, a State Dept. clerk endorsed this letter. "reply that the investigations in London and Paris have not produced anything" E, *ibid.* See *New York Times*, Oct. 22, 1876. On Nov. 7, Zebulon B. Vance defeated Thomas Settle for N. C. governor.

On Aug. 3, Philip Walter, court clerk, Jacksonville, Fla., had written to USG. "It is with feelings of much regret that I have to announce to you the death of the Hon Philip Fraser, U. S. Dist Judge for the Northern District of Florida on the 26th day of July A. D. 1876 at Montrose Penna where he had gone in search of health." ALS, DNA, RG 60, Letters from the President. On Jan. 16, 1877, U.S. Senators Aaron A. Sargent of Calif. and Henry M. Teller of Colo. telegraphed to USG. "Judge J. W. Archibald State circuit Judge at Jacksonville Fla, should be appointed to the vacant U. S. Judgeship—We were earnestly requested by leading colored men Republican lawyers and citizens to solicit his appointment as a measure of safety, now that all state judicial power is in hands bitterly hostile to them, he is a good lawyer firm republican and generally respected—we have papers in the case that we will lay before you tomorrow at eleven oclock" Telegram received, *ibid.*, RG 107, Telegrams Collected (Bound). On Jan. 24, Sargent wrote to USG. "Mr Conover informs me that you think well of a recommendation of his in favor of Judge Settle of North Carolina as Judge, Florida. I am satisfied with such action." ALS, CSmH. On Jan. 26, USG nominated Settle as judge, Northern District, Fla. On the same day, U.S. Senator Simon B. Conover of Fla. telegraphed to USG. "The nomination of Judge Settle reads for the District of Florida should read northern District of Florida Can it be Corrected today," Telegram received, DNA, RG 107, Telegrams Collected (Bound). See Jerrell H. Shofner, *Nor Is It Over Yet: Florida in the Era of Reconstruction 1863–1877* (Gainesville, 1974), p. 335.

On March 4, Samuel Bard, Pensacola, telegraphed to USG. "Cant you induce prest Hayes to appoint Judge Thomas Settle to a Cabinet position It would fully meet the demand of wisdom justice & moderation in the entire south. you know him well—" Telegram received (at 8:55 P.M.), OFH.

Note

[*Aug. 9, 1876*]

Ask the Sec. of the Treas if he will send the name of Mr. Wilkins for Collector of the Port of Balt. vice Booth resigned. I believe the full name of W. is before the Sec.

AN, Wayde Chrismer, Bel Air, Md. On Aug. 9, 1876, Culver C. Sniffen wrote to Secretary of the Treasury Lot M. Morrill. "The President directs me to request that you will have the nomination of Mr Wilkins for Collector—Port of Baltimore—vice Booth, resigned, prepared and sent to him—The President understands that you know Wilkins full name—" Copy, DLC-USG, II, 3. Edward Wilkins, former col., 2nd Eastern Shore Md., was a noted agriculturist, known especially for fruit cultivation. Washington Booth's extensive business interests included insurance, mining, and transportation. See *New York Times*, Dec. 29, 31, 1878, April 5, 1892; *PUSG*, 23, 428–31. On Aug. 11, a correspondent reported from Washington, D. C. "Colonel Edward Wilkins, the new Collector of the port of Baltimore, to-day waited upon President Grant, accompanied by Hon. J. A. J. Creswell and C. C. Fulton, Esq., to return thanks for the unsolicited honor conferred upon him. This was the first time for several years that Colonel Wilkins had seen the President. The President received him cordially, and expressed the hope that his appointment would tend to the restoration of harmony and good feeling. He thought that by a cordial union of the Republicans and Reformers on the Congressional nominations two or three districts might be carried, and if a fair election could be had that the electoral vote of the State might be cast for Hayes and Wheeler. . . ." *Baltimore American and Commercial Advertiser*, Aug. 12, 1876. See *New York Times*, Aug. 11, 1876.

On March 16, 1875, H. B. Beymer, Baltimore, had written to USG. "While the Controversy is going on in regard to the Colector of this port, I wish to Call your attention to the fact that while the late Union orphans Fair was in operation in this City that not a Booth or Dennison ever darkend the door, in fact none of the Republicans here high in power was there, I am not interested in this Collector fight in any way. Came here some Eight years ago from Ohio, dont meddle in polatics & dont want any position but do think men like those in power in this city should show more Charity for the orphans whose dead Fathers gave them the positions they occupy, or should resign in favor of men who will not forget the debt they owe them" ALS, DNA, RG 56, Letters Received From the President. In two petitions docketed April 10, "Importers, Merchants and Citizens of Baltimore" communicated to USG their support for Booth's retention as collector of customs, Baltimore. DS (undated), *ibid.*, Collector of Customs Applications. See *New York Times*, April 9, 1875. On Monday, Jan. 17, 1876, Levi P. Luckey wrote to Booth. "The President wishes me to ask you if you will not come over on either Wednesday, Thursday or Saturday of this week, so as to call upon him about noon of the day you come" Copy, DLC-USG, II, 3. On July 12, Sniffen wrote to Booth. "I am directed by the President to say that he has, this afternoon had an interview—and a very pleasant one—with a delegation of republicans from Maryland—The result of it all is that they think your present Deputy should be requested to resign—The President is satisfied that that much should be conceded—You can then make selection of a man for the place.—(he has none to suggest—) who will be satisfactory to all parties—The President does not know Dr Reese well enough to judge whether the opposition to him is well founded or not—But there is great opposition to him among republicans—and a great many of them, and heed should be given to it—The Doctor being, as the President believes he is, a good republican, will, without doubt, make the sacrifice, if it is one for the general good—" Copy, *ibid.* Sniffen added a note. "The President requests that this envelope be opened by no body but Collector Booth—" Copy, *ibid.* On the same day, a correspondent reported from Washington, D. C. "A delegation of thirty-five, representing the Republican element of the State of Maryland, headed by Mr. T. S. Hodson, called upon the President this afternoon and advanced some very substantial reasons why the removal of United States Marshal Goldsborough and Deputy Collector Reese would materially contribute to the advancement of the political interests of the State. . . ." *Baltimore American and Commercial Advertiser*, July 13, 1876. See *Baltimore Sun*, July 13, 1876. On July 16, Booth, Long Branch, wrote to USG. "I have the honor to acknowledge the receipt of your letter of 12th inst. in reference to my Deputy Dr Wm S. Reese. In reply I cannot but express my surprise that any republican in Maryland should intimate that the discensions existing in the party have been produced by him, or could be healed by his removal. from the position which I am proud to say he has filled with so much ability, and with such entire satisfaction to myself. Mr Hodson Collector of Customs at Crisfield Eastern Shore Md. who headed the delegation to visit you, up to a very recent date has been the warm personal and political friend of Dr Reese, and I cannot account for his hostility now, for any other reason than his failure to secure an appointment for his county. In this con[ne]xion I desire to say that every removal and appointment made in my office to the lowest subordinate is made by my direction and at my instance for causes which I deem sufficient. Dr Reese is in no way responsible for my action, and it is a gross injustice to him to allege that he is. During my sickness all the removals and appointments made in my office have been submitted to the Secretary over my own Signature, or that of my Special Deputy Mr. Gray by my order. How the Doctors removal can in any way benefit the republican party I am at a loss to know, on the contrary it would be a positive injury. He is a gentleman of respectability and position in the State, and probably has as large an acquaintance, and as many warm personal friends as any other gentleman in our community. Politically I can say from my personal knowledge that no man has a more consistent record from 1860 down to the present time, nor has served his party more faithfully and effectively. No one in Maryland understands his character and ability better than our mutual friend Mr. Creswell, with whom he served in the first Union Legislature of this State in 1861 & 1862. He was also actively engaged with Col. Creswell then Adjt. General of the State in organizing, and sending forward to the Army the drafted men of Maryland, and in 1863 was the Elector from his District for Mr Lincoln. Mr Creswell I am sure will endorse all I say of him, and indeed if it were necessary a delegation of any number of the most respectable republicans of Maryland will call upon you and oppose the injustice of the attempt to prejudice your mind against this faithful officer of the Government. Since I assumed charge of the Custom House I do know that no one republican in Maryland has done as much good work for the party as the Doctor. For three years past he has been a member of the State Central Committee and for two years its Secretary, during which time he was in constant correspondence with the leading men of the State, and with Mr Askew arranged and managed all the campaigns of the party, during these three years. Most of this work was done outside of office hours, and involved a great deal of labor. What the present Committee lacks in making a vigorous campaign now, is the absence of this kind of material. This recent attack on Dr Reese, after they have exhausted their efforts on me, I cannot account for unless they desire to embarass me in the administration of the business of my office during my temporary absence, as the duties I have assigned him, are the general management of the official business pertaining thereto; and how efficiently and faithfully he discharges these duties, all the Chiefs of the various bureaux of the Treasury Dept. can testify. If necessary Dr Reese will visit you with such friends as you *know*, and have confidence in here, who will corroborate all that I have said. In conclusion permit me to say that it is always my pleasure to carry out your views, but I am satisfied that any impression made upon your mind by the ex-parte statements made to you by the parties visiting you on the ocassion referred to, can be removed. I therefore earnestly appeal to you to suspend any furthur action in this matter till I am able to see you and explain more fully the embarassing position I would be placed in if I am compelled to loose the services of Dr Reese at this time. I am happy to say that my sojourn here has been of great benefit to my health. I am daily growing stronger and hope in a couple of weeks to resume my duties, when it will give me great pleasure to make my respects to you in person. Thanking you for your many kindnesses, may I ask you to drop me a line here on receipt of this letter furthur expressive of your desire." LS, USG 3. On July 28, Sniffen wrote to George Small, Baltimore. "The President directs me to say that he is satisfied that if your and his friend,

Booth, would resign his position as Collector of the Port, to make place for some good active republican—like Ed Wilkins of Chesterfield, for instance—it would probably have a beneficial effect—The President retains his former confidence in the present Collector's superior qualifications for his position—but his health, unfortunately, is not such as to enable him to perform the duties of the office himself—and with the present divisions in the State, he does not believe that a Deputy—not so fully responsible as he would be if holding the chief position—can heal dissensions—" Copy, DLC-USG, II, 3. On Aug. 3, Booth wrote to USG. "In consequences of my continued indisposition, and consequent inability to discharge my duty as collector of Customs of Baltimore, I herewith tender my resignation of said position. In doing so, allow me to tender you, my sincere gratitude for the kindness you have always manifested to me upon all occasions, which will be ever remembered, and most kindly appreciated." LS, DNA, RG 56, Collector of Customs Applications. See *Baltimore American and Commercial Advertiser*, Aug. 7, 1876.

On Aug. 7, Henry T. Gover, Baltimore, wrote to USG. "I observe from the public prints that Collector Booth of this City has resigned his position, I hereby apply for the same—Believing I could perform the duties about as well as those who have been appointed If necessary I could furnish as many recommendations from Merchants and other business men as would satisfy of my fitness If the appointment is to be made *purely* from political services and *wire pulling*, perhaps some others might make heavier claims—As all I could say in that line is that my three sons and myself are reliable republicans, But when we take the history of the republican party in our state into consideration for the past ten years,—Its contentions its splits, and quarrelings it would seem time that in such appointments politics were ignored and business men appointed to places of trust, until the party could unite and harmonize in feeling Believing I have as good a right to hold the position as any other good Citizen, I make free to solicit the appointment and if made would be ever gratful therefor" ALS, DNA, RG 56, Collector of Customs Applications.

On Aug. 9, Thomas R. Rich, Baltimore, wrote to USG. "As Mr Booth has resigned the Collectorship at this Port & his successor is about to be appointed I would most respectfully call your attention to the immense petition, filed with you sometime since, endorsing Mr Robt Turner for the position. Mr Turner's appointment would meet with general approbation & would unite the entire party in our State. . . ." ALS, *ibid.* A related letter is *ibid.*

On Oct. 6, J. C. Hall, Laurel, Md., wrote to USG. "As your term of services as President, is about expiring as one of the first Lincoln Republicans in Baltimore, and been treated badly by the party, I, write to you to know whether you could not, appoint me to some position under the Goverment, at this late day of you term, I. have been before you a year or two ago to ask for a appointment, If you could endorse Me to the Collector of Baltimore Md, or the Departments at Washington, or something connected with the Navy, Paymaster or puser, It will be all the Same to you and Me in hundred Years from Now" ALS, *ibid.*, Applications.

To Congress

To the Senate and House of Representatives:

I transmit herewith a telegram of the 5th of August instant from Lieutenant-General Sheridan to General Sherman; a letter of the

11th of the present month from General Sherman to the Secretary of War; and a letter from the latter of the same date to me—all setting forth the possible needs of the Army in consequence of existing hostilities.

I would strongly urge upon Congress the necessity for making some provision for a contingency which may arise during the vacation, for more troops in the Indian country than it is now possible to send.

It would seem to me to be much more economical and better to authorize an increase of the present cavalry force, by twenty-five hundred privates; but, if this is not deemed advisable, then, that the President be authorized to call out not exceeding five regiments, one thousand strong, each, of volunteers, to serve for a period not exceeding six months.

Should this latter authority be given, I would not order out any volunteers unless, in my opinion, based upon reports from the scene of war, I deemed it absolutely necessary, and then only the smallest number considered sufficient to meet the emergency.

U. S. GRANT.

EXECUTIVE MANSION, *August* 11, 1876.

SED, 44-1-90. See message to Senate, July 8, 1876. On Aug. 5, 1876, Lt. Gen. Philip H. Sheridan, Chicago, telegraphed to Gen. William T. Sherman. "I have not yet been able to re-enforce the garrison at Red Cloud or Spotted Tail's or at Standing Rock, to be strong enough to attempt to count the Indians or to arrest and disarm those coming in. I beg of you to see the military committee of the House, and urge on it the necessity of increasing the cavalry regiments to one hundred to each company. General Crook's total strength is seventeen hundred and seventy-four; Terry's, eighteen hundred and seventy-three; and to give this force to them I have stripped every post from the line of Manitoba to Texas. We want more mounted men; we have not exceeded the law in enlisting Indian scouts; in fact, have not as many as the law allows; the whole number in this division is only one hundred and fourteen. The Indians with General Crook are not enlisted, or even paid. They are not worth paying; they are with him only to gratify their desire for a fight and their thirst for revenge on the Sioux." *SED*, 44-1-90, 2–3. See Sherman to Sheridan, Aug. 8, 1876, DLC-Philip H. Sheridan. On Aug. 9, Sherman wrote to Secretary of War James D. Cameron transmitting Sheridan's telegram. ". . . Inasmuch as Congress may soon adjourn prudence dictates that we should be prepared for any possible contingency, and if it is not possible to obtain the increase of 2500 men asked for our Cavalry Regiments I would most respectfully advise that the President be requested to ask authority to accept the services of five thousand volunteers for the period of six months or during hostilities, these volunteers to be accepted and mustered in from the states and Territories most convenient to the Theatre of operations." Copy, DNA, RG 108, Letters Sent. *SED*, 44-1-90, 2. On

Aug. 11, Cameron wrote to USG. "I have the honor to transmit herewith the copy of a despatch from Lieut. Gen. P. H. Sheridan, dated the 5th instant, with a letter of this date from General Sherman, transmitting the same. I desire to renew the expression of my opinion that the best way to reinforce the troops now operating against the Indians will be to add the 2500 privates to the Regiments already in existence; but if Congress should not do this, then I advise that the President be authorized, in his discretion, to call for volunteers not to exceed five thousand in number. I trust that Generals Terry and Crook may be able to deal such a blow to the hostile Indians that even this may not be necessary, yet prudence dictates that measures should be taken to meet all possible contingencies" LS (press), DNA, RG 94, Letters Received, 4409 1876. *SED*, 44-1-90, 2. A provision in the army appropriation bill signed by USG on July 24 had increased the authorized size of cav. cos. to one hundred men. See *CR*, 44−1, 3874; *U.S. Statutes at Large*, XIX, 98. On Aug. 12, USG signed a bill enabling the army to employ up to 1,000 Indian scouts. See *ibid.*, XIX, 131; *CR*, 44−1, 5138, 5463; *New York Herald*, Aug. 13, 1876. On the same day, Sherman wrote to Sheridan on measures to enlarge the army. ". . . The President seems inclined to remove all the Peaceful Sioux to the Indian Territory south—especially the families of the bucks who are out on the War Path. Im afraid if they get down there, they will excite the Cheyennes, Arapahos, Kioways, & Comanches to break out again. . . ." ALS, DLC-Philip H. Sheridan. On Aug. 15, USG signed a conference committee bill to "increase the cavalry force of the United States, to aid in suppressing Indian hostilities" that appropriated $1,634,700 and empowered USG to add up to 2,500 enlisted men temporarily. *U.S. Statutes at Large*, XIX, 204. The House of Representatives favored temporary vol. enlistments while the Senate desired permanent recruits for existing cav. cos. See *CR*, 44−1, 5596−99, 5678−79, 5694−96.

On Sept. 1, during an interview at Long Branch, USG commented on Lt. Col. George A. Custer. "I regard Custer's massacre as a sacrifice of troops, brought on by Custer himself, that was wholly unnecessary—wholly unnecessary. . . . He was not to have made the attack before effecting the junction with Terry and Gibbon. He was notified to meet them on the 26th, but instead of marching slowly, as his orders required in order to effect the junction on the 26th, he enters upon a forced march of eighty-three miles in twenty-four hours, and thus has to meet the Indians alone on the 25th. . . . General Crook is the best, wiliest Indian fighter in this country. He has had vast experience in Indian fighting. His campaign against the Idahos and many other tribes show his brilliant talent as an Indian fighter. . . . He is as wily as Sitting Bull in this respect, that when he finds himself outnumbered and taken at a disadvantage he prudently retreats. In Custer's case Sitting Bull had ten men to every one of Custer. . . . It is our present intention to cut off the supplies from the Sioux by removing all the Indians from the reservations down to the Indian Territory, or, if they will not consent to that by treaty, down to the Missouri River. Then a military barrier is to be placed between all these Indians and the hostile Sioux, so that all communication and all supplies will be cut off. Hitherto these hostile Indians have gone on the warpath, but when they can't get any food they come back, get fed and take ponies and recruits along with them when they leave again for the warpath. All this play is to be stopped. We are taking up now all the hostile Indians that come to the reservations and disarming them." *New York Herald*, Sept. 2, 1876.

On Aug. 10, John Worthington, Chelsea, Wis., had written to USG. "having Served 3 years in the rebellion and being acquainted with Indian character and the Ojibways in perticular and being a Hunter & trapper myself being versed in the Language character and Habites of the Aforesaid tribe of Ojibways they being the natural Enemise of the Sioux I propose to raise 200, Warriors of the Ojibway tribe said Warriors to be armed and enlisted in the, U. S Service I have every possible facility of raising the aforesaid troops & if this meets your approbation send me a commission at once" ALS, DNA, RG 94, Letters Received, 3830 1876.

On Aug. 12, L. D. Miller, Baltimore, wrote to USG. "Having read your Message in this Morning Sun Paper, in regard the Indian War, I take pleasure of introducing myself to your Excellency as an Ex. Lieut. of the Late War, I am in readiness and can ~~furnish~~ form a Company of One Hundred Men, in a short time, and if such should be the case, of the Bill passing in Congress to raise such Regiments, I am prepared at any moment, and think that I can enlist as many men as any man in Baltimore and also think that I could raise one Company in One Week, providing your Excellency will Commission me as Captain of the Volunteer Service for the time mentioned in your Message, hoping to hear from you soon . . ." ALS, *ibid.* On the same day, I. Hart Stout, St. Louis, wrote to USG. "In event of the calling out of Volunteer for service on the frontier would respectfully file an application for authority to raise a Battalion of cavalry, of say Ten or more squadrons, not doubting of my ability to select material that would be of service— . . ." ALS, *ibid.*

On Aug. 14, Governor John S. Pillsbury of Minn. telegraphed to USG. "I desire to tender you two or more regiments of volunteers in case congress authorizes such aid for suppressing Indian hostilities" Telegram received (at 3:00 P.M.), *ibid.* On the same day, U.S. Representative William Terry of Va., former brig. gen., C.S. Army, wrote to USG. "I have the honor to forward to you the tender of a battalion for Indian service by capt Thos S. Gibson—In forwarding this tender of service, I desire to say it is in good faith and evinces the fidelity of the people of Lee County Virginia—Should their services be needed their deeds in the field will be their highest endorsement." ALS, *ibid.*

On Aug. 15, Governor Thomas A. Osborn of Kan. telegraphed to USG. "If you have occasion to call for Volunteers I hope you will permit me to furnish at least one regiment" Telegram received (at 1:36 P.M.), *ibid.*

On Sept. 1, Romeyn B. Fish, Rolfe, Iowa, wrote to USG. "Some time ago I wrote to the War Department Concerning the raising of a Company of Cavelry to be recruited for 6 months or 1 year just as they saw fit. I received a reply from them referring me to the recruiting office in Chicago I then wrote them sending my letter from the Department with it & they sent me a Circular of men suited for the regular service to enlist for the term of 3, 4, & 5 years but no married men taken this let me out, I now see by the Inter Ocean of Aug 17th that there is 5,000 volunteers wanted to serve 6 months now if this is the case I can raise 150 or 200 men heare & they are mostly old Soldiers some of whom have served under you I have served over two years in the late war & am willing to go again if needed. I am a married man 29 years old, We can furnish our own Horses if we go the Goverment of course paying us a fair price for same I can raise this ammount of men in two weeks time & all Stout hearty men that can stand Considerable Grief My Wife is perfectly willing I should go & I am willing to leave my bussiness to go any time after fair warning I want no office private is good enough for me, If you would like to have us please send me a recruiting Commission & if you do not need us please write us . . . If you need us send along Instructions &c" ALS, *ibid.*

On Sept. 18, Joseph H. Blackburn, Liberty, Tenn., wrote to USG. "I have ventured to address you a short letter, hoping that you will do me the honor of giving it a careful and considerate perusal. Its mission is, to ask of you a favor. Through the daily and hebdomadal papers of the day, I have kept myself pretty well 'posted' as to the present Indian war now going on in the West. The crimes and depredations of the blood-thirsty savages, and their cruelty toward the helpless and suffering whites, have aroused my hatred of both the Indians and the white renegades who uphold them in, and urge them on to, thir hellish deeds, and my sympathy for those who are strugling to clear the track for the car of Civalization. So I have resolved, through your aid and by your consent, to give my country a helping hand; have resolved to 'make up' a company and go West as soon as I have a favorable reply from your excellency. I have never gone through my four years at West Point, but I fought all through the Rebellion in the service of the Union, and was promoted to the rank of Colonel. Not boasting, I may here say that I have done as much good for my country in protecting it from the 'bushwhackers,' guerillas, &c., infesting it, as any one. As to my ability as a soldier, I would refer you to Hon. C. C. Dibrel, W. B. Brownlow, Hon. Horace H. Harrison, and Hon. John Trimbol, of Nashville. Please favor me with a reply as soon as possible." ALS, *ibid.* See *PUSG*, 20, 355–56.

On Oct. 20, Milo Leaften, Lesueur, Minn., wrote to USG. "alow me to drop A fiew lines to you in re gard of the Great Indian war of the west of the present time Mr President Grant While you chief Magistrate of the chief supreme ruleing Power i be long to one of tribes of the west Known as the sisetons i have not a proper education to write to you in a proper way so your Excenency i hope will for give me for my Poor writeing sinc that the Government turend a Gainst us on account of the Black hills I have come among my white Frends and have Found thousands of warm sympathisers among Now President Grant Say Di[d] your honor not sanction the Bill or the treaty of the Black Hills to belong to Us and also the representitives of the United Stats of America have signd and Granted to us this reservation where the Black Hills are in cluded You folks of washington Know that we are a powerless indian you take A way from us our right by force after You Greate Father have Granted us the right of that Reservation but Mr President let me tell You it only the Greate speculators that are The cause of this present Indian war in The far west such as the Brakeing of a bargain By the whites of the reservation of the black Hills President i beg to you to hold fast to our Dear and beloved cause du not Consent to a new treaty som of the chiefs Have signd the new treaty bill but how Can such a vile treaty be solid when The tripe is not in particular satisfied Our Greate heavenly Father knows it is a Wrong thing to take a way from us our Land and give it in to the hands of rich Speculators Mr President it is in your Power only to save us From starvation and Famine also after the Greate Congress of the United States have Granted to us the Recervation of the Black Hills and now it is on The way of being broking up on account of of i being a read man you must not throw a side my note of mercy to you Why Such as brakeing a bargain of the Black Hills of the Indians after the President of the United States and Congress too Such is a shock and will be to all civiliced Nations of the Earth i beg From all civil-iced christians If it is not a fire Sham of the U United Stats Government to do so with its subjects to cheat them of there right of home and land and what wors than all to drive us In the baren rigeon of the Rocky mountains Most Humble Frend Useless Grant i say Had we Frend that could talk for us or had We the strong influence of a good atorney I a sure thing in the Black hills would be difrent to what the are now Mr President the U. S Government can sub due us to eny thin they Want us you know it too 40 000 000 of a people should Be able to combat with a fiew helpless indians But let me tell you if it comes rite to the point to cheat us out of our right meny and Meny a drob of Blood have to be spild before It can be accomplished—also in minnesota in 1863 the war between the whites and indians was caused by they Rascalish swindeling of the agent of the Yelow medicine Agency Give us our right of the Black Hills and the war is over if not it will cost The U. S government mor than what they oferd Us by the laws of the U. s Government you cannot take our lan a way from us more trouble will come yet Some of relations are Britis subjects and they are Driven a way from there homes President du you think the British Goverment will alow the United stats to do so no never i shall soon writ to the British

Minister in regard of her subjects being treated so   Greate Father of Us state youse your most powerful Influence of us powerless People   rite Soon to me" ALS, DNA, RG 75, Letters Received, Dakota Superintendency.

On Nov. 22, Secretary of the Interior Zachariah Chandler wrote to USG transmitting an order to prohibit "the supply of special metallic cartridges to hostile Indians," based on a congressional joint resolution. LS, *ibid.*, Letters Received, Miscellaneous. On Nov. 23, USG signed this order applying to "all Indian country or country occupied by Indians, or subject to their visits lying within the Territories of Montana Dakota and Wyoming and the States of Nebraska and Colorado." DS, *ibid.* See *CR*, 44–1, 4864, 5011.

On Nov. 28, USG ordered a tract of land in Dakota Territory east of the Missouri River added to the existing Sioux reservation. DS, DNA, RG 75, Orders. *HED*, 45-2-1, part 5, I, 637, 45-3-1, part 5, I, 744, 47-2-1, part 5, II, 323, 49-2-1, part 5, I, 540; *SD*, 57-1-452, 884. On Sept. 30, Sheridan had written to Sherman opposing transfer of any Sioux to Indian Territory and arguing "for dismounting and disarming and putting them all on the Missouri river." Copy (press), DLC-Philip H. Sheridan.

On July 4, from "Camp near Big Horn on Yellowstone River . . . We the enlisted men the survivors of the battle on the Hights of Little Horn River, on the 25th and 26th of June 1876, of the 7th Regiment of Cavalry who subscribe our names to this petition, most earnestly solicit the President and Representatives of our country, that the vacancies among the Commissioned Officers of our Regiment, made by the slaughter of our brave, heroic now lamented Lieutenant Colonel George A. Custer, and the other noble dead Commissioned Officers of our Regiment who fell close by him on the bloody field, daring the savage demons to the last, be filled by the Officers of the Regiment only. That Major M. A. Reno, be our Lieutenant Colonel vice Custer, Killed; Captain F. W. Benteen, our Major vice Reno, promoted. The other vacancies to be filled by Officers of the Regiment by senority. Your petitioners know this to be contrary to the established rule of promotion, but prayerfully solicit a deviation from the usual rule in this case, as it will be conferring a bravely fought for and a justly merited promotion on Officers who by their bravery, coolness and decision on the 25th and 26th of June 1876, saved the lives of every man now living of the 7th Cavalry who participated in the battle, one of the most bloody on record and one that would have ended with the loss of life of every Officer and enlisted man on the field; only for the position taken by Major Reno, which we held with bitter tenacity against fearful odds to the last. To support this assertion—had our position been taken 100 yards back from the brink of the hights overlooking the river we would have been entirely cutt off from water; and from behind those hights the Indian demons would have swarmed in hundreds picking off our men by detail, and before midday June 26th not an Officer or enlisted man of our Regiment would have been left to tell of our dreadful fate as we then would have been completely surrounded. With the prayerful hope that our petition be granted, we have the honor to forward it through our Commanding Officer." DS, DNA, RG 94, ACP, 3984 1876; facsimile in W. A. Graham, *The Story of the Little Big Horn: Custer's Last Fight* (Harrisburg, 1945), between pp. 158–59. On Aug. 5, Sherman endorsed this petition. "The judicious and skilful conduct of Major Reno, and Capt Benteen is appreciated, but the promotions caused by Genl Custers death, have been made by the President, and Confirmed by the Senate, therefore this petition cannot be granted. . . ." AES, DNA, RG 94, ACP, 3984 1876. For USG's nominations to fill vacancies in the 7th Cav., see *Senate Executive Journal*, XX, 282–83, 285.

On July 8, Lea Febiger, Washington, D. C., had written to USG. "Having seen in the newspapers the account of the disaster to the 7th Cavalry, it has occurred to me that perhaps it may be your pleasure to order me before the board of officers for examination for appointment of 2d Lieutenant in the Army, earlier than you anticipated when I had the interview with you a few days since. . . ." ALS, DNA, RG 94, ACP, 3809 1876. Related papers are *ibid.* On Aug. 11, USG nominated Febiger as 2nd lt., 23rd Inf.

On July 8, Robert H. Anderson, former brig. gen., C.S. Army, Savannah, had written to USG. "I have the honor very respectfully to request that you will confer upon me the appointment of Captain in the 7th U. S. Cavalry to fill one of the many vacancies occasioned in that Regiment, by the massacre of its gallant officers, and men by the Sioux Indians on the 25th ulto. I am a graduate of West Point of the class of 1857, and served in Oregon and Washington Territory until 1861 as a second Lieutenant of the 9th Infantry, where I had some experience in Indian service with my own Regiment, as well as with the 1st Cavalry, then 1st Dragoons. . . . My political disabilities having been removed by Congress I will be under many obligations if your Excellency will kindly give me an appointment in the Army. In making special mention of the 7th Cavalry, I do so, as I desire active service, and in consequence of the recent terrible casualties in that Regiment I thought an opportunity might be offered your Excellency of appointing me without conflict and detriment to the surviving officers, or any one in the service. Trusting that my application may receive your favorable consideration . . ." ALS, *ibid.*, Applications for Positions in War Dept. On July 20, AG Edward D. Townsend wrote to Anderson "that there is no law under which appointment in the line of the Army, from civil life, can be made save in the grade of 2nd Lieutenant." Copy, *ibid.*

On July 11, Brig. Gen. Oliver O. Howard, Portland, Ore., telegraphed to Sherman. "Please ask the President to appoint Guy Howard my son to Lieutenancy in Seventh Cavalry" Telegram sent, MeB; telegram received, DNA, RG 94, ACP, 4569 1876. On Dec. 4, USG nominated Guy Howard as 2nd lt., 12th Inf.

On July 11, Patrick H. Rooney, New Orleans, had written to USG. "The recent catastrophy on the western plains to five companies of 7th, U: S. Cavalry, my old regiment, and when discharged, 1st Sergeant Company "H," that regiment, calls to mind that recently thro' the Hon G. L. Fort, of Ill, I had the pleasure of transmiting to your Excellency the recommendations among others that of the late General Geo. A. Custer, . . . I feel that I have experience, and am anxious to join my old Comrads in the field—I am but 30 years of age 13 of which has been spent in the U. S. Cavalry— . . . I have taken the liberty to enclose you my photograph that you may have some idea of the man who has taken the liberty of applying to you personaley for his appointment as 2d Lieut. U. S. A. Mr President: I beg of you do not consign my papers hitherto sent you or the enclosed to the waste basket. . . ." ALS, *ibid.*, 3247 1875. Two photographs and related papers are *ibid.*

On July 14, George R. Nugent, Camp Douglas, Utah Territory, telegraphed to USG. "The undersigned son of major Nugent united states Army begs leave to invite attention to applications & recommendations long on file for appointment as second Lieut & solicits favorable consideration many vacancies at present" Telegram received (on July 15, at 11:56 A.M.), *ibid.*, 3798 1876. On July 29, Brig. Gen. Andrew A. Humphreys, Washington, D. C., endorsed to USG a related letter from the applicant's father, Maj. Robert Nugent. "I would say not only a good word but many good words, in behalf of Col. Nugent, who in the closing operations of the war commanded a brigade, known as the Irish brigade, in the 1st Div. of the 2d Corps, and was a most gallant and excellent officer in every respect." AES, *ibid.*, Applications for Positions in War Dept. Related papers are *ibid.*; *ibid.*, ACP, 788 1876. See *New York Times*, June 21, 1901.

On July 23, Georgiana M. Adams, St. Louis Arsenal, had written to USG. "Knowing the kindly interest you have ever shown, (where admissible) to women who have sought favors at your hand, I have presumed to ask for an appointment for my son, John Adams in the 7th Cavalry; my husband, Genl. John Adams, was a rebel and died gallantly, for the cause he believed right. I must be candid & state this fact. Hoping to receive a favorable reply at an early day, . . ." ALS, DNA, RG 94, Applications for Positions in War Dept. On Nov. 6, Brig. Gen. John Pope, Fort Leavenworth, Kan., wrote to USG concerning the appointment of John Adams as 2nd lt. ". . . It does not seem to me that this request would be fitting until after the sons of those who died in the Country's service have been cared for. . . ." ALS, *ibid.* A related letter is *ibid.*

On July 27, Sherman wrote to Maj. Gen. John M. Schofield. "I have yours of July 25 but as the President took the precaution to reduce to writing his decision as to Professor Weir & his successor (Lieut Larned), and as the orders have been made, I think it would do no good & might do harm to show ~~him~~ your letter to the President. . . . His estimate of Young Larned is extravagant, but as it is based on personal acquaintance it is hard to combat—Larned was in the 7th Cavalry—promoted by the deaths in Custers fight—was by me ordered to his Regt, came here, staid at the Presidents, and I received orders from him personally to repeal the order—Still it is said young Larned had the Soldierly instinct to join his Regt but was dissuaded by his mother & the President— . . ." ALS, CSmH. On July 13, USG had nominated 2nd Lt. Charles W. Larned, USMA 1870, for promotion to 1st lt.; on July 25, USG nominated Larned to be professor of drawing, USMA, to replace Robert W. Weir. Larned had served as asst. professor of drawing since Aug. 30, 1874. See *PUSG*, 24, 482.

On July 28, 1876, Joseph B. Kiddoo, New York City, had written to USG. "I beg leave to invite your attention to the enclosed letter of Eaton A. Edwards—He was the Hospital Steward under Surg John Moore U. S. Army here in New York for three years, and is still serving in that capacity. Dr Moore Gen Ingalls and myself have been trying for a long time to have him appointed a 2nd Lt in the Army, but thus far without success. I venture now to ask you to sufficiently interest yourself in him to order his appointment as there no doubt are some vacancies since the late disasters on the Plains— . . ." ALS, DNA, RG 94, Applications for Positions in War Dept. The enclosure is a letter of July 27 from Eaton A. Edwards, New York City, to Kiddoo. ". . . I entered the Army as a volunteer in 1861 at the age of fifteen, and having served continuously to the present time, can only look to the Army for any further advancement, my age now—thirty years, being almost too much to commence anew in civil life, . . ." ALS, *ibid.*

On July 29, U.S. Representative Alexander H. Stephens of Ga., Crawfordville, wrote to USG. "Mr. Joseph A. Twiggs, a young gentleman, constituent of mine, resident of Augusta, in view of the present Indian war in the West, is anxious to join the U. S. Cavalry service as Leiutenant. He is of a most respectable family, and I vouch for his gallantry as an officer if he should be appointed I, therefore, earnestly recommend him to your favorable consideration" LS, *ibid.*

On the same day, Lt. Col. Rufus Saxton, deputy q. m. gen., Fort Leavenworth, wrote to USG. "I venture to request at your hands the appointment of Charles B. Thompson of Pennsylvania to the position of Second Lieutenant in the Second Cavalry U. S. Army. This vacancy in the 2nd Cavalry was caused on the 19th of July, 1876, by the death, at his camp on the Yellow Stone River, of Mr Thompson's elder brother, Brevet Major Lewis Thompson Captain of Company "F" 2nd Cavalry. Major Thompson served with credit throughout the war of the rebellion At the battle of Gettysburg his served on the staff of Genl W. Merritt; on the second day of the battle while bearer of dispatches for that officer, was captured and confined for twelve months in Libby Prison, and four months in Charleston Prison. Since the war he has been on duty with his company in Montana. He was the first to march to the relief of Reno after the Custer massacre, and was as brave and gallant an officer as ever died in the discharge of duty. His mother is a widow and has now lost her main stay. Mr Thompson for whom I ask this appointment is now employed as a clerk in the Quartermaster De'pt at this place, and is a most excellant young man, as every officer here will bear witness, and should you be pleased to appoint him will I know do honor to the app[oi]ntment and to the service. In the hope that it may seem to you a proper recognition of the gallant services of his dead brother to grant this request— . . ." ALS, *ibid.*, ACP, 6694 1876. USG endorsed the docket. "Some time during the coming Winter I would li[ke] to make this appoint[ment.]" AES (undated), *ibid.* On Sept. 11, Charles B. Thompson, Fort Leavenworth, wrote to Cameron changing his request for appointment from the 2nd Cav. to an art. regt. ALS, *ibid.* On Dec. 21, USG again endorsed the docket. "Make this appointment now." E (initialed), *ibid.* On Dec. 22, USG nominated Thompson as 2nd lt., 17th Inf.

On Aug. 3, Daniel L. Baker, Deadwood, Dakota Territory, had written to USG. "I have the honor very Respectfully to make application for a commission in the united states Army—I will state for your information that I entered the service when 16 years old on May 25th 1861 in 14th Ills Infty Vols I served in latter Regt until the close of the war being wounded at Shilo and Atlanta—I was on duty at Head qr's Army of the Tenn, at time of Genl McPhersons death & helped to bring the latter off the field—at the Close of the war I entered the 18th Inf & was discharged after 3 years service as 1st Sergeant— . . . I have lost every thing I possess this summer by Indians—& have concluded to soldier the remainder of my existence—as I am contented while in the army & shall only be too happy to give my life in defence of my country against the Sioux— . . ." ALS, *ibid.*, Applications for Positions in War Dept.

On Aug. 13 and 16, George Templeton Strong, Jr., New York City, wrote to USG. "Remembering most distinctly being introduced to you when dining at our house, & knowing that my father (late Geo. Templeton Strong,) was a friend of yours, when he was treasurer of the Sanitary Commission, I have taken the liberty of addressing you with regard to my getting a position in one of the forts or posts near the Yellowstone River, or in fact any where 'far West.' I should prefer a 'non military' position or in other words, I should like to be employed in one of the forts or trading-posts. . . . P. S. I cannot help mentioning to you how keenly aware we all are of the compliment you paid my poor father's memory plast year, by attending the funeral at 'old Trinity'—" "Should no position be left, such as I called for in my letter of the 13th inst, I will be happy to take any low military position, if only a private & furthermore, I shall be happy to 'wrestle' with the Sioux. I have belonged to the Seventh Regiment of this city for two years and am familiar with the manual but I confess entire ignorance of the duties in Camp. *Please* answer this abrupt epistle at your earliest convenience—" ALS, *ibid.*, ACP, 4699 1876. See *New York Times*, June 29, 1948.

On Aug. 21, Madeleine Vinton Dahlgren, "Near Boonsboro," Md., wrote to USG. "My brother-in-law, Mr. Charles BC. Goddard of Zanesville Ohio, desires an appointment in the new cavalry force about to be organized, and I would esteem it as a favor if a commission could be given him—He served as a Captain in the 17th Infantry, from 20. Sep. '61 to 26. May '64, when he consented to resign, although with great reluctance. . . ." L (incomplete, writer's name on docket), DNA, RG 94, Applications for Positions in War Dept.

On Aug. 23, John M. Cooke, Washington, D. C., wrote to USG. "Allow me to introduce myself as John M. Cooke a brother of the late Col Cooke Adjutant of the 7th Cavalry, who fell with Gen'l Custer on the 25th of June last The object of this letter Mr President is to ask you for an appointment in the Army for myself—I do not know if I am taking the regular course in addressing this letter to you but I adopt it, as the quickest way, and should it be out of order, I trust you will not consider my request unfavorably, on that account—My present position is, as clerk in the Quartermaster General's Office, in this city. I have just returned from General Terry's Camp on the Yellowstone River at the mouth of the Rosebud, which place I started for as soon as I heard of my brother's death, and I should have remained with the expedition during the remainder of the campaign, but seeing how impracticable it would be for me to do so without an appointment, I hastened back here, and now take this means of communicating my desire to you hoping that should you consider my application favorably I may yet be in time to get in some work in the Big Horn Country. In reference to myself I would say to you (aside from the fact of my being Col Cooke's brother) that General Rufus Ingalls knows me personally and well   I was with him in New York City before I came into the Quartermaster General's Office here—I am anxious that our name shall not die out of the Army—Should you see fit to give me an appointment (which I sincerely trust you will), I would hope my assignment to be in the Department of Dakota, as it would be some satisfaction for me to feel that I was continuing the Campaign that my brother started on, and should occasion require, I would show to you, and the world, that, I would give my life, as freely as he did his, to sustain the Government of our Country." ALS, *ibid.* Other letters to USG concerning army commissions, prompted by Sioux hostilities, are *ibid.*

On Aug. 29, Grant Marsh, capt., "Steamboat 'Far West,' At Junction of Yellowstone & Powder Rivers," Montana Territory, to USG. "Although personally unknown to you, I feel that I owe my escape from capture during the late war to you, having been on board the boat with you on the morning of the battle of Shiloh, and I have always believed that I owed my escape on that occasion (as did your whole command,) to your ability and generalship. This is a debt in partial payment of which you have received my deepest gratitude and heartiest support ever since, and it is only in consideration of the past, and of the fact that you have always been quick to recognize and reward bravery and ability whenever brought to your attention, that I now presume to take the liberty of addressing you in behalf of one who, I believe, merits a higher recognition of his services in a critical moment than he has yet received. I refer to Col. Benteen of the 7th Cavalry. In Gen. Custer's fight on the 25th of June he had command of the detachment guarding the pack-train and but for his timely arrival Major Reno, who was almost surrounded by an overwhelming force, would have shared the fate of his commander. My boat was but fourteen miles from the scene of action; had the Indians been successful in their attack upon Reno, their next move would have been upon this boat, which they could have destroyed without difficulty at that time and place with all on board, this to be followed, in all probability, by an attack, with every chance of success, upon Gen. Terry's advancing command. This train of disasters was prevented, as already stated, by Col. Benteen's rapid movements and the courage and ability he displayed on that most critical occasion—a fact to which every officer out here is willing to certify. I call your attention to these facts as a simple act of gratitude on my part to Col. Benteen for saving, as I sincerely believe, me, my boat and all under my command, from destruction, as well as to secure, if possible, some official recognition of the services of one to whom the whole command owes so much—having yourself gained your high military distinction by similar acts in the field. I have the honor of intimate personal acquaintance ̶y̶with your son, Col. F. D., and with nearly all the officers out here at present, any of whom will be pleased to satisfy you as to my personal character. Begging pardon for thus imposing upon your time and attention, and hoping that this letter will receive your favorable consideration, . . ." ALS, *ibid.*, ACP, 5142 1876.

On Jan. 10, 1877, Col. Samuel D. Sturgis, Fort Abraham Lincoln, Dakota Territory, wrote to USG. "When I had the honor in 1869 to ask you to appoint my son as Cadet to

West-Point, you very kindly assured me that he should have the appointment, and you did not forget it when the time came: so he went to the academy—graduated with credit and was in every respect a most promising young officer; but his life was cruelly sacrificed on the 25th of last June. Now my dear General we have but one boy left, out of five,— Saml D. Sturgis Jr.—and his Mother having set her heart upon his going to West-Point, is urging me daily to write to 'Genl Grant'—and this is my apology for taking the liberty of addressing you as an old friend. . . ." ALS, *ibid.*, Correspondence, USMA. Samuel D. Sturgis, Jr., graduated USMA in 1884.

To Edward Y. Goldsborough

[8/11 76]

E. Y. GOLDSBOROUGH
U. S. MARSHAL
DEAR SIR:

As I informed you in a recent interview that if your resignation of the office of U. S. Marshal was desirable, in the interest of republican success, I would inform you first, and that you need not heed what might be said by the press or public rumor on the subject. Since that a number of delegations have called to see me on the subject. Not one has yet ventured a reflection upon your character or official integrity, but the great majority do say that the think a change is necessary to draw out the republican vote. Many of the colored men, after their former experience, declare that they can not risk themselves out on the day of election without a change. I have concluded therefore to ask your resignation in order that I may comply with what seems to me to be the ~~better~~ popular judgement of the republicans.

In making this request allow me to assure you of my continued confidence and esteem.

[Very truly yours
U. S. GRANT]

ADf (bracketed material not in USG's hand), DLC-John Russell Young; LS, Stephen V. Feeley, Alexandria, Va. On Aug. 14, 1876, Edward Y. Goldsborough, U.S. marshal, Baltimore, wrote to USG. "I received your letter of the 11th Inst. requesting my resignation, and regret not being able to see you at the White House this morning, having learned from Mr. Crook that you were at the Capitol. I am and always have been ready to comply with your wishes as far as I can, and sincerely hope you will not construe this request, to be allowed to present for your consideration, the facts in my case, as a desire to oppose you in any way. Dismissing all personal considerations and self interest, I am willing to resign at any time that I can do so without being placed in the false position in which I am now put, by the efforts of those opposed to me here, as you will see by the enclosed copies of resolutions cut from the columns of the 'Baltimore [A]merican,' and of the truth of which statements my resignation would be accepted as an admission. These resolutions have been prepared and sent to the clubs and put before them when only a moderate number of persons were present. At a large meeting of one of the strongest clubs in the City, similar resolutions against me were laid on the table and other clubs now say they are prepared to pass resolutions favorable to me. You very justly say in your letter, 'not one has ventured a reflection upon your character or official integrity,' yet here they attempt, by falsely charging me with neglect of duty, to create the impression that they would not venture before you. I have always discharged my duty. Have given protection at the polls so fully, that there has never been a complaint that any man, by the neglect of duty of any Special deputy Marshal, was deprived of an opportunity to cast his ballot at any election, where deputy Marshals were authorized to serve. The election in November 1875, as you are aware was entirely a state election, and of course an election at which the enforcement law did not apply as to Deputy Marshals, and where there was no law authorising interference at the Polls by the national authorities, and this fact coupled with the outrages at that election form part of the blame cast upon me by unthinking people, when really I had no power to act. Over the Supervisors I have no control and yet I am charged with the resposibility of their acts. The deputy Marshals have always been appointed from the lists furnished by the authorised committees of the Republican Party in the city, and if bad men have been among them, it was their fault, not mine, as I always reserved and exercised the right to reject such as I found unfit for the position, as will appear by the records in my office. I am convinced that this opposition is being made under the direction of a few men from motives not connected with the enforcement of the laws, and will stop if you request it or refuse to take any further notice of it, as appears by the statement of committees that have recently called to see me. The better element of the party, especially in Western Maryland, the only portion of the State that can be relied on for a Republican majority, is opposed to this change. Leading Republicans say that my removal from the office, under existing circumstances, would be injurious to the success of the party in the state, and insist that I ought to remain if possible. My friendship for you, a sense of duty to the community and to myself compel me to say, that under the circumstances, a transfer to the indiscreet, rash men who are endeavoring to obtain it, of the power vested in the Marshal, to be used by them in the manner indicated by their public utterances, would be a direct challenge to the rough element of the city to a bloody contest, that would cause an immense amount of trouble, by destroying the peace at the polls that the law is intended to secure, and reflect discreditably on your administration, because by executing the law with firmness and discretion and not in a vindictive spirit, I am convinced that a fair election can be had and trouble avoided. The fears that some colored men have expressed are dictated by bad men who are either using or misleading them, as I am sure they have no ground for such fears, which will be allayed by the assurance of the protection of good men as deputies, such as I propose to secure if permitted, and the declaration that I had intended to make at the proper time, of arming a large force to keep peace at the Polls. I shall be glad by your permission to see you and tell you much more than I feel at liberty to tire you with in a letter, that I may have a better opportunity to refute these false charges and put myself in a just position. I hope Sir, I have not said anything offensive, and if anything herein seems objectionable I assure you it is not so intended. Hoping that I may continue to be honoured with your confidence and esteem, [a]nd with assurances of my highest regard and friendship, . . ." ALS, DNA, RG 60, Records Relating to Appointments. On Aug. 10, Thursday, a correspondent had reported from Washington, D. C., concerning Goldsborough. "It can be positively stated, as coming from the President's own lips, that he to-day, in conversation with a friend, said that he should for the present decline to remove him. He considers him an efficient and painstaking officer, and he believes that the service and the party will receive no benefit from his removal. To again quote his words, the President said: 'He has as much influence in his favor as against him.' Last Monday Marshal Goldsborough was in Washington. His coming at that time was brought about by a Washington telegram to the Baltimore *Sun*, which, though not directly indicating that the President had concluded to appoint a new Marshal, strongly intimated that a change was possible. Mr. Goldsborough had an audience with the President, and told him that his resignation was at his disposal at any time that he gave a suggestion to him that it was desired. The President then and there at that interview told Mr. Goldsborough that he had not decided to make a change, and that when he did so decide he would not carry it into effect without first notifying him. He appeared considerably vexed about the telegram printed in the *Sun*, and gave the Marshal the assurance that he need not be further troubled concerning his office by any statement which might be made public in the columns of that paper, . . ." *Baltimore American and Commercial Advertiser*, Aug. 11, 1876.

On Aug. 15, William J. Albert, Baltimore, wrote to USG. "From the persistent efforts made to you to consent to the removal of my friend Edwd Y. Goldsborough from the office of Marshal of the District I feel it my duty to write you a word in his behalf. You know enough of Committees and resolutions passed at meetings that, as a general thing, they are valueless as an expression of public opinion. The meetings and resolutions in this City in reference to Goldsborough are of that character, and dont represent either party or public opinion and are manufactured to order and eminate from one source. The pretext that under another man as Marshal, that the State of Maryland can be carried for the Reform and Republican ticket at the ensuing Presidential election is simply absurd. There is no more prospect of Hays and Wheeler carrying Maryland than Kentucky. The reaction in Baltimore county in which I live is something fearful to contemplate against the so called reform party, and will culminate in giving the County to the Democratic party by a large majority. There is some hope of electing our candidate for Congress in the Sixth District and even that hope will be imperilled by the removal of the Marshal who has a large following of friends and supporters in the District. The Republican prospects in the other Districts of the State are gloomy in the extreme. Goldsborough has discharged the duties of the office with so much efficiency and fidelity to principle and his character is so good and unimpeachable that all good and wise men would be shocked by his removal from office without cause and in my judgement you could not do a more unwise and unpopular act" ALS, DNA, RG 60, Records Relating to Appointments. On Aug. 18, Judge Hugh L. Bond, 4th Circuit, Baltimore, wrote to USG. "I wish to say to you before you leave Washington in opposition to what I think has been stated to you that the Marshal of this Dist is the best we have had here since I was at the Bar or on the Bench I have seen in the newspapers that a number of persons who have no knowledge of the conduct of Courts or of what is required of a Marshal in the execution of his duties have asked you to remove the present incumbent and to appoint a successor. I hope you will do no such thing. No good citizen here has any fear that the laws of the United States will not be executed by the present incumbent fearlessly I think the Dist Judge will agree with me that not only has the present Marshal been active and efficient in the discharge of his official duty but that he has elevated the office by his conduct of it, from the disgraceful condition in which it was when he took it into one of dignity trustworthines & efficency I think & I therefore say to you that ~~I think~~ the removal of the present Marshal no matter whom you appoint in his place would serve no useful purpose and it would be a matter of regret to both of us Judges and to all parties representing litigants in causes depending in both U S courts I do not on ordinary occasions have any thing to say upon matters purely political but as this matter in my judgment relates to the efficiency of the Courts themselves I have had less scruple" ALS, *ibid.* Related papers are *ibid.* On Aug. 17, a correspondent had reported from Washington, D. C., that "the President sent for Mr. Goldsborough, and gave him an audience, lasting probably twenty minutes. He came out looking very cheerful, and stated that he had sent some days ago to the President a statement in writing which he (the President) had not received, and that he had given the original to the President at the interview he had just had with him." *Baltimore American and Commercial Advertiser*, Aug. 18, 1876. On the same day, USG met a Baltimore delegation. "At twenty minutes of three o'clock President Grant sent word to the delegation that he would see them. Mr. C. K. Brewer advanced to the head of the table at which the President was sitting and said: 'Mr. President, I, with others now in the room, represent all the Hayes and Wheeler clubs in the city of Baltimore, by whom we have been delegated to advise you that it is for the best interests of the Republican party in the State of Maryland to remove Marshal Goldsborough from office.' Mr. Brewer then stated that he had a copy of a series of resolutions adopted by all the Hayes and Wheeler clubs in Baltimore, which he begged the President would seriously consider. The President took the roll of manuscript and said substantially that he did not propose to make any more removals in Maryland until the Republicans of their State healed their own disaffections. He said that he understood that many good Republicans were denied representation on the State Central Committee. He advised the delegation to go home and unite the disturbed elements within the party, and then he would do all in his power to help them." *Ibid.* See *ibid.*, Aug. 17, 1876.

On Aug. 11, Alfred D. Evans, Baltimore, had written to USG. "The writer of this has never held a federel office of profit, but has performed important duties and Services for the Goverment, for which I have never been Compensated, . . . I do desire that: Democratic Ruffians and Murderres Shall *not be made Election Supervisors and Marshalls.* I do know that Marshall Gouldsboro—has been imposed upon or he certainly would not have appointed Some whom I Speak of—I believe him to be a true man but he does not kno the Democratic elements in our City. he must be *instructed,* as if the Same kind of Supervisors are appointed as were appontd two years Since it will be no use to make a fight in Maryland. Our State has been most miserably butcherd—by the two wretched *factions* now *infesting* the State, neither of which are worthy of consideration, being time Servers and ploders. I would like to have about One hours talk when I could tell your Excelency Some thing that would Startle you—The State of Maryland could have been carried for you at the last Election by a proper arrangement which was Sugested to Hon J A J Creswell who Seemed not to care for any body but himself—" ALS (incomplete), DNA, RG 60, Letters from the President. On Aug. 15, Theodore F. Lang, Baltimore, wrote to USG. "I have the honor to enclose further reports of proceedings of meetings held in this city Also of a meeting of Colored Republicans of Balto. County. I am convinced more and more each day of the importance and necessity of a change in the Marshalship of this state. will forward further proceedins as they are reported to the press of the City." ALS, *ibid.*, Records Relating to Appointments. On Aug. 16, Thomas S. Hodson, Baltimore, wrote to USG. "In my recent interview as chairman of a delegation of the Maryland State Central Committee the name of Major E. Y. Goldsbough, Marshall, was mentioned. In that interview, I stated that as a practitioner in the U. S. Court I had been brought into personal and official relations with Marshal Goldsbough and I had found him courteous as a gentleman and faithful and efficient as an officer. That, however, citizens of Baltimore City had informed me that he had failed, on election days, to carry out the wise and salutary provisions of the Enforcement act, so as to preserve the purity of the ballot box, in the way the law designed. That, not being a resident of the City, I knew nothing of this, of my own personal knowledge, but that there were men, from the city, present, from whom, you could obtain information, on that point. . . ." ALS, *ibid.*

In a letter dated "Saturday," William H. Wiegel, Baltimore, wrote to USG. "PERSONAL . . . When I wrote to you some days since, tendering you my *personal services*, I did not do so, in the expectation of securing any office—but because I wanted to serve you, honestly, truly and squarely—Every 'THIEF' in the Country, who had some kind of control or influence, over and with a newspaper, undertook to abuse you, and I did not like it, because I had 4 years ago, *unjustly* and *under undue influence* said some untruthful things against you, and for 4 years, I have been endeavoring to undo that mistake and atone for my folly—for folly it was, and not spite or vindictiveness— . . . I do not desire to say one word against any one—but beware of the men from this City and State, who pretend or did pretend to you, that they were in favor of yourself for a 3rd term & then came on here & laughed at you—God help them—Beware also, of the leading(?) Republicans here, who say they can carry the State &c—*a meaner, more contemptible* and *selfishly, cowardly* and *thoroughly lying and unprincipled set* of men, never were known. There are some few exceptions of course. I will name the exceptions—Archibald Sterling, U. S. Marshal Goldsborough, . . ." ALS, USG 3.

On Oct. 15, R. A. McAllister, Baltimore, wrote to USG. "Cant you give us a Marshal in the place of Goldsborrough   If you send a wooden man he will suit fully as well as he we will loose Maryland and you and Goldsborrough can have the credit (men kept in by influance of women make bad politicians" ALS, DNA, RG 60, Letters from the President. On Oct. 23, "A One Armed Soldier of the old Sixth Army Corps," Baltimore, wrote to USG. "I am only an old Soldier but please permit one who followed ~~of~~ Sedghwick brave and true as you know he Sedghwick was, to ask of You one favor, Genl Grant retain Mr Goldsborough as U. S. Marshall at Balto. remember it was the boys who Carried Musket that done the work." L, *ibid.* On Oct. 25, George W. Thompson, Baltimore, wrote to USG. "As one of your old soldiers who served under you. I feel it my duty to make known to you the true state of affairs in this state and at the sametime make some suggestions. the Republican Party is in a demoralized condition in this state. while it is divided into factions the Republicans have very little confidence in the present Marshal. . . ." ALS, *ibid.* Goldsborough continued as marshal.

On Feb. 5, William Jones, Baltimore, had written to USG. "I see there is a prospect of some change in the U S Marshalship in this city which will have the effect of reassuring the respectable people of this place, while the moral effect upon the ruffians of the Ring will be incalcuable, but in view of the serious condition of affairs it would be well to select a man whose force of Character will give them to understand that your determination is to see that every man is protected in his rights as an American citizen. we have several men whose appointment would carry that weight with it, while it would carry terror into the hearts of that religious bigot and fraud Gov J Lee Carrol and his minions. there is Col Marsh ~~an~~ Col Hill and last though not least Major Joe Carter, who hails from Carroll's own county. all three of these gentlemen occupy positions under Mr Booth. ~~either one~~ any one of ~~which~~ whom would have the desired effect upon the riotous element this man Carter although occupying position under Mr Booth ~~wh~~ has refuesed to pay his taxes in support

of Catholic schools which the Jesuits have succeded in placing upon the county: this he announced in the papers of his county in 1874: and now defyies them to collect them: showing that spirit of independence which is seldom exhibited by an officeholder under a man
of the ~~religious~~ church which is now making an attempt to destroy that cherished institution surely you ought to encourage the spirit he has displayed as he lives in a county in
which the Jesuits have their headquarters and the chief of their order in this county resides
namely at St Charles College at Woodstock Md—it would be well to inquire into the character of the man from men who have no prejudice in the matter for he has some enemies in
his own politcal party. whom his natural determined character has perhaps interfered with
their little selfish programme" ALS, *ibid.*, Records Relating to Appointments. On Feb. 26,
Md. Senator S. Taylor Suit wrote to USG. "I desire to say, when by the advice, of my political Friends. I consented to the use of my name, for the position of U S Marshal, I felt
quite sure, that the whole of the Republican party, of the state. with the exception of the
so called 'Custom House Ring' would advocate my appointment. In that, I am not mistaken. I have keept at least one dozen delegations from bothering you, and I now have at
least fifty letters, to you on the subject. I called on my friends the Messr Jas A. Garey, and
C. C. Fulton—they declined calling on, or writing you, on the subject, but said, they would
be *very much pleased* to see me get the appointment. . . . Something will have to be done, to
harmonize the opposition to the Custom House Ring, OR THE STATE WILL BE LOST. In my
judgement, the 'Ring,' cannot controle the state another day, *if it ever did. . . .*" ALS (incomplete), *ibid.* Related papers are *ibid.*

On Aug. 1, Samuel Edmond *et al.*, Baltimore, petitioned USG. "The undersigned, a
Committee of Republicans of Baltimore City, who had the honor of an interview with your
Excellency a few days since, in reference to the U. S. Marshalship for the District of Maryland, would again most respectfully invite your attention to the importance of having that
office administered, in view of the approaching Presidential election, in such manner as
that the laws shall be executed to the fullest extent, so that *every citizen* shall be protected
in his right to vote, and that violators of the law shall be brought to a speedy and certain
punishment. To give full and complete protection to *all voters*, we believe that a change in
the Marshalship is essential; and if your Excellency should see the necessity of removing
the present incumbent, we would then recommend *Mr. Wm Thomson*, of *Baltimore City*, as
a gentleman in every respect qualified to fill that position in an acceptable manner to the
Government, and with great satisfaction to the Republicans of Maryland. Mr. Thomson is
an old citizen of Baltimore, who has a thorough knowledge of our people, and from his
long experience we think he would be invaluable to the Republican Party at this time." DS
(6 signatures), *ibid.* A related petition is *ibid.*

On Aug. 10, Thursday, Cadmus M. Wilcox, USMA 1846 and former maj. gen., C.S.
Army, Washington, D. C., wrote to USG. "Some two months ago, I was induced to believe
that, the present US Marshal for the State of Maryland would be removed. This opinion
was formed from what I had Seen in the Baltimore papers. I wrote at the time to Genl
Maxey, Senator from Texas and, requested him to See you & Say in the event of removal I
was an applicant for the position; he replied that he had Seen you and you had not then determined to make any change, and expressed the opinion that, if a vacancy was made it
would be filled by a political appointment. May last, a a year ago, I was thrown out of employment, by what I claim to have been bad faith on the part of those contracting with me.
I had recourse to the Courts, and the 'laws delay', and inability to contend with a corpora-
tion, after ten months litigation, forced me to compromise for about one fourth of what was
due me. There was a double wrong, witholding money & throwing me out of business. In
a few months, unless I get Something to do, my Small funds will have disappeared. I made
the request that I did, for the reason that I was already in Baltimore, & was acquainted with

and liked the people & it was near Washington, in easy reach, of my nearest kindred. I can understand, how you may decline to do what I ask, even with a desire to help me; and I don't know that is right, to ask, when if you Should grant my request, you render yourself liable to abuse and Sharp criticisms. I was in Washington last Saturday, called between one & two o'clock and did the Same yesterday but failed to See you, and regret that I have to return to Baltimore without Seeing you for, I wanted to thank you for the appointment promised my nephew." ALS, *ibid.* See letter to Mary E. Wilcox, April 12, 1882.

On Aug. 9, a correspondent had reported from Washington, D. C. "Messrs. J. H. Butler, Simon Smith and James A. Handy, representing the colored element of the Republican party of Maryland, had an interview, covering twenty minutes, with the President to-day. They came representing the interests of General Tyler for the appointment of the Marshalship, to succeed Marshal Goldsborough if that officer is removed. The President heard the delegation patiently, treated their representations with deliberation, and entered into quite a conversation with the delegation concerning what in their judgment would best tend to promote harmony in the party and place it in a position to present a solid front to the common enemy. . . ." *Baltimore American and Commercial Advertiser*, Aug. 10, 1876. On Aug. 12, Saturday, John Franklin, Baltimore, wrote to USG. "Enclosed you will find a copy of Resolutions offered at the residence of one J. B McNeal a friend of Genl Tyler. who is going around to the various Hayes & Wheeler Clubs with a steryeotype set of resolutions in behalf of Tyler—the said McNeal—informed me that he had placed a copy of the American containing the same in the hands of Dr Cox your family physican whom he assured me had shown them to you—they are getting up a delegation to come down on Wednesday to call upon you in his behalf—they do not represent over 5, wards out of 20 as they have not elected delegates from more than that number—As to the resolutions they were written in Tyler or Fulton's office and put before these 5 clubs who adopted them as they would if any other name had been presented instead of Tyler—I only wish you to be posted as to the fraudulent character of the proposed delegation" ALS, DNA, RG 60, Records Relating to Appointments. On Sept. 9, Joseph F. Carter wrote to USG. "Enclosed you will find resolutions purporting to be adopted in behalf of Genl. Tyler for the position of Marshal—this explanation is due you. there are parties here in Baltimore who have been working up Genl Tyler's case. the reason Fulton takes such an interest in Tyler is that he claims to be a personal friend of Genl Hayes. by putting him up as a prominent man Fulton thinks to make a catspaw of Tyler to work upon Hayes that accounts for the free use of the American that Tyler has for every little puff that in this case emenated from a meeting of a few negroes called together by one white man who is making application for position in the Custom House. for my place to which Genl Tyler is urging him as for the reason that I withdrew in Goldsborough's interest. . . ." ALS, *ibid.* Letters advocating Isaac Ranney and Richard W. McMahon as marshal, Md., are *ibid.*

To J. Russell Jones

August 13th, 1876—

DEAR JONES—

I have authorized the Secretary of the Treasury this a. m to ask your resignation—on the request of the two Senators from the state—I yield to this because, I think, it is right that they should be heard—Both are men who served during the war; have been elevated to the senate, one of them has been twice elected Governor of the state, while you have held civil office, by appointment, from the inauguration of Mr Lincoln in 61. to date, without the recommendation of elected officers—This, the Senators feel, I think not, without justice—Were you in their place you would have much to say about the appointees in the State.—

My confidence in your fitness for the place you now hold, or for almost any place under the Government is not, in the least shaken, but I yield to what I believe to be due to two senators who have not failed the Republican party in any emergency—

Yours Truly

U. S. GRANT—

HON: J. RUSSELL JONES

COLLECTOR—CUSTOMS—CHICAGO—ILLS—

Copies, DLC-USG, II, 3; DLC-Elihu B. Washburne. On Aug. 16 and 17, 1876, J. Russell Jones, collector of customs, Chicago, wrote to USG. "Yours of the 13th instant is this moment to hand. I regret that the matter could not have been managed without the intervention of the Secretary. That however would not have satisfied Logan, who wants me to go on the records as having been turned out. You are aware that I was appointed Collector without my solicitation, and that I accepted the position at the earnest request of the Secretary of the Treasury. I have for some time known that Logan would not be happy so long as I occupied any public position in this State, I have never thought however that you would be a party to such an act of injustice as to remove me, just at the close of your administration from an office, the duties of which I am faithfully discharging, merely to gratify him. If the interests of the public or of the party were to be subserved by my resignation I should cheerfully tender it, but you know perfectly well that those considerations cut no figure in the demand made upon you by General Logan. I have at all times been loyal to the party and to you, and faithful to the interests confided to me." "I was nearly blind when I wrote & telegraphed you yesterday, with one of my worst headaches. I have had a night to think of your letter of the 13th, and the more I think of it the more cruel it seems to me. I did not ask you for the mission to Belgium. It cost me $75.000. more to hold it than I recd from the Govt I did not ask for this position, nor for the Scty'sp of the Interior tendered me by you in Sept last. Oglesby & Logan knew me & my qualifications just as well when they both voted for my confirmation as now. I refused advantageous offers of business engagements to enable me to take this office, and took Ben, my boy out of a Bank to make him my cashr here. Being turned out now leaves us both in a very awkward fix— at a time like this, when it is so difficult to find an opening. Since my return to Chicago a year ago, the Repn party has been rescued from a most deplorable condition & has been twice successful at important elections. No one will pretend that I am lacking in loyalty or devotion to the Party, or that the duties of this office are not being faithfully & efficiently [dis]charged. All that can be urged against me is that I am not a Logan man. Oglesby really cares nothing about the matter—but is drawn into this by Logan & Hurlbut. I dont believe that you can afford to permit those men to require you to turn your back on me after these long years of friendship, and kick me out, just at the close of your administration. I have not deserved this at your hands, and there is nothing in the demand now made upon you to warrant you in in thus disgracing me, under the circumstances I beg you to think seriously of the position this action of yours places me in, and I shall not be without hope that you will conclude to let me serve out my present term, not that I care particularly about the emoluments of the office, (though they are quite an important item to me, as I am now situated) but *I cant afford to be thus publicly disgraced by you*, simply to oblige Logan." ALS, USG 3. See *PUSG*, 26, 284–90.

On Aug. 20, Jones wrote to [*Elihu B. Washburne*]. "I sent you a copy of the Presidents & Sectys letters & now give you copies of mine On the 16th I telegd the Prest; 'I hope no action will be had until you get my letter' & on the same day wrote the old man him. . . . My letter to the Secretary was as follows. I have the honor to acknowledge the receipt of your letter of the 16th instant informing me that you are instructed by the President to advise me that the Senators from Illinois recommend a change in the Collectorship which youI hold and that my resignation will be acceptable. . . . I have written the President, and, before taking any action in regard to your letter shall take the liberty of waiting a few days in order to hear further from him. It is evident that this request is not made because the public interests, or those of the party require a change, but simply to gratify the Senators from Illinois. I was appointed to this position in Septr last, without my Solicitation and without my knowledge. The first intimation I had of it was a telegram from your predecessor informing me of my appointment & begging me to accept it. Both of the Ills Senators voted for my confirmation. It is not pretended that I am not loyal to the Repn party or that the duties of this office are not being faithfully & efficiently discharged, but I am asked to resign, Simply because the Illinois Senators prefer that some other person shall occupy the position. I beg to call your attention to the 5th declaration of principles adopted by the National Repn Convention at Cincti in June last . . . I w'd give a stern-wheel boat for five minutes with you. I dont want to make a mistake by refusing to resign but it dont seem to me that I can afford to resign, to oblige Logan. I'snt it funny that the matter has not leaked out?" AD, DLC-Elihu B. Washburne.

On Sept. 11, Jones wrote to USG. "It is nearly a month since I wrote you in regard to Logan & Ogleby's demand for my removal, and as I hear nothing from you, am inclined to hope that you are not disposed to kick me out. My position is a very embarrassing one. There has never been a time when I would not do anything to oblige or serve you, but I am under no obligation to either L. or O, and I see no good reason why I should voluntarily permit them to place such an indignity upon me. I dont believe the interests of the party or the public service would be subserved by turning me out, and I hope soon to hear that you have decided to let me serve out my term. With kind regards to Mrs Grant & the children, . . ." ALS, USG 3. Jones continued as collector. See George R. Jones, *Joseph Russell Jones* (Chicago, 1964), pp. 75–77; *New York Herald*, Sept. 5, 1877.

To House of Representatives

To the House of Representatives.—

In affixing my signature to the River and Harbor bill. (bill No 3022. I deem it my duty to announce to the House of Representatives my objection to some features of the bill, and the reason why I sign it—If it was obligatory upon the Executive to expend all the money appropriated by Congress, I should return the River and Harbor bill, with my objections, notwithstanding the great inconvenience to the Public interests resulting therefrom, and loss of expenditures from previous congresses upon incompleted works—

Without enumerating, many appropriations are made for work of purely a private or local interest, in no sense national—I cannot give my sanction to these and will take care that during my term of office, no public money shall be expended upon them.—

There is very great necessity for economy of expenditures at this time growing out of the loss of revenue likely to arise from a deficiency of appropriation to insure a thorough collection of the same—The reduction of revenue districts, diminution of special agents and total abolition of Supervisors, may result in great falling off of the revenues.—It may be a question to consider whether any expenditure can well be authorized under the River and Harbor appropriation further than to protect work already done and paid for. —Under no circumstances will I allow expenditures upon works not clearly National.—

U. S. Grant.

Executive Mansion—August 14—1876

Copy, DNA, RG 130, Messages to Congress. *HED,* 44-1-190; *SMD,* 49-2-53, 399–400. See *U.S. Statutes at Large,* XIX, 132–39. On Aug. 14, 1876, U.S. Representative John H. Reagan of Tex. spoke about USG's message. ". . . It is essentially an assumption by the President of the right to exercise an act of personal government, instead of obedience to the laws. . . . I desire simply to call attention to this matter, because it seems to me that a document so remarkable in its character, with all respect to the President, announcing so great a departure from the Constitution, and containing so singular an avowal in advance that he will not obey the law of the land, should not be permitted by the Representatives of the people to go before the country without at least calling attention to it and expressing some dissent. . . ." *CR,* 44–1, 5628. U.S. Representative Henry L. Pierce of Mass. also spoke. ". . . When I consider how this bill was made up, how the committee was importuned by members of the House to make appropriations for this little river and that little harbor, I feel that it is of the utmost importance to sustain the President in the position he has assumed, which is simply the position the Engineer Department has always held and acted upon, that if there are any appropriations useless and extravagant, and which will accomplish no good whatever, he will not authorize the expenditure of the public money for that purpose, but will allow it to remain in the Treasury so that Congress may review their action at the next session. . . ." *Ibid.*, p. 5632. See *New York Times*, Aug. 15, 1876.

On Aug. 11, U.S. Representative Samuel J. Randall of Pa. had written to USG. "The enclosed is respectfully referred" ALS, DNA, RG 77, Rivers and Harbors Div., Letters Received. The enclosure is a letter of Aug. 10 from Daniel Young, Rondout, N. Y. "I see the conference committe have appropreated to Rondout $30.000 for navigation purposes this is all wrong a large amount of money has been spent already for this purpose. and benefits no one accept Thos Cornell & Co they are the cause of the obstuction to navigation by hawling their fires after entering the creek from some thirty five boats therby filling the channel this amount will keep a lot of Republicans to squander the money. I have an interest in property here and protest against this fraud to spend the peoples money" ALS, *ibid.* See James D. Cameron to Randall, Jan. 23, 1877, *ibid.*

On Aug. 19, Robert P. Lewis, New Ulm, Minn., wrote to USG. "In traveling through the State, at this point I find in the St Paul Dispatch the inclosed paragraph, to which I wish to call your attention The fact is, as stated. The Government is expending $100,000 a year to keep up a Mill Dam for the owners,—which *they* kept up till they succeeded in getting the Government to shoulder it. There is no navigation above the Falls & never will be. . . ." ALS, *ibid.* See *HED*, 44-2-23, 12–13.

On Sept. 4, Secretary of War James D. Cameron telegraphed to USG, Long Branch. "The Engineer Department have sent in their reports on the River and Harbor Bill and recommend to expend within five hundred thousand dollars of the entire appropriation. I propose to expend say two millions ($2.000.000) in all and let Gen. Humphreys make the selection of work to be done. If however you would prefer to make the selection yourself I will send Lieut. Greene down with the papers and recommendations. Please answer soon as I would like to leave town this evening" Telegram sent, DNA, RG 107, Telegrams Collected (Bound). *HED*, 44-2-23, 37. On the same day, USG telegraphed to Cameron. "I WOULD LIMIT THE ENGINEERS TO TWO MILLIONS EXPENDITURES ON THE RIVER AND HARBOR APPROP." Telegram received, DNA, RG 77, Rivers and Harbors Div., Letters Received. *HED*, 44-2-23, 37.

On Sept. 16, U.S. Senator John H. Mitchell of Ore., Ogden, Utah Territory, telegraphed to William H. Crook. "Please say to President that order preventing expenditure appropriated at Cascades columbia river will ruin us politically in Oregon, people are paying twelve cts per ton per mile freight on that river after earnest effort we got appropriated—If suspended by executive, result is ~~ruin~~ disastrous in extreme present my appeal that work may go on answer me jacksonville Oregon" Telegram received (at 10:45 P.M.), DLC-USG, IB. See *SRC*, 44-1-251; *SED*, 44-2-33, 2; *HED*, 44-2-23, 38.

In [*Sept.*], Mayor Henry Winter and City Clerk James W. Howard of Cairo, Ill., petitioned USG. "The undersigned your memorialists, The Mayor and City Council of the City of Cairo in behalf of its citizens would respectfully call your attention to the dangerous condition of our City, caused by the rapid cutting away of the Mississippi river banks adjoining our City from the foot of Dickeys Island to the mouth of the Ohio. The channel of the river being out of its proper course is cutting off the piers and stone dykes attached to the banks for their protection leaving them in the middle of the channel, dangerous to navigation and an injury to the commerce of the Mississippi Valley. The rapid abrasion of the banks is making sad inroads into the City fully one fourth of a mile in depth of embankments. Levees and lots have gone into the river. Last year the City built a new levee for its protection at a large outlay as a temporary relief, till we might interest the general government in our behalf, which assistance we were in hopes would have reached us ere this. The people being heavily taxed to the amount of seven per cent on their taxable property, and having suffered greatly since the war by prostration of business, causing great depreciation of property, are entirely unable to build new levees or cope with the 'father of Waters.' Besides this, even if we had the means we have no authority to go into the river and change its channel   All we can do in our present condition is to try to stop the cutting, and prevent an abrasion of the river banks, as far as we can until the government renders us the relief Congress in its wisdom has seen fit to appropriate for the improvement of the river between the points named. If the abrasion continues at its present rate, by the first of the year it will have cut fully one half mile more into the City. The danger is not only to the old levees but to the new one and its destruction is a foregone conclusion and the City will be deluged with water, causing great distress and loss of property, among which would be the injury to the Govt Custom House and Post office   We are therefore on account of your decision in regard to local improvements led to fear that we shall be at the mercy of the water of the river this winter, and would earnestly appeal to you to investigate the report of General J H Simpson of the Engineer Corps, upon the condition of the river at this point, and if in your judgment and kindness you could change your views, and order through Genl Humphreys Chief Engineer that the work of changing the channel of the river be proceeded with, without delay, by the expenditure of the appropriation made by Congress for that purpose your petitioners in behalf of the citizens of Cairo would forever feel grateful to your excellency for your kindness" DS (undated), DNA, RG 77, Rivers and Harbors Div., Letters Received. On Sept. 17, U.S. Senator John A. Logan of Ill. endorsed this petition to Brig. Gen. Andrew A. Humphreys, chief of engineers. "I have read this memorial carefully and endorse every word of it. I deem it of the greatest importance that work be done on the Mississippi river near Cairo Ills at once. . . ." AES, *ibid.* A related letter is *ibid.* See *HED*, 44-1-126, 44-2-23, 10–11, 45-2-1, part 2, II, 511–13.

On Oct. 23, 1st Lt. Francis V. Greene wrote to Humphreys. "The President wishes to see the Secretary and yourself at the White House at two o'clock to day on the subject of the distribution of the $2,000,000, for rivers and harbors. The Secretary desires you to go with him from here, and to take with you such papers or memoranda as are necessary to fully discuss the subject." Copy, DNA, RG 107, Letters Sent, Military Affairs.

The river and harbor bill had appropriated $8,000 to repair the east pier at Cleveland, contingent on negotiations with the Pittsburgh and Cleveland Railroad Co. concerning use and occupancy of the pier. See *U.S. Statutes at Large*, XIX, 133. On Oct. 30, USG named a commission to draft an agreement. DS, DNA, RG 77, Rivers and Harbors Div., Letters Received. The co. subsequently agreed to pay for future maintenance on the pier. See *HED*, 45-2-1, part 2, II, 965.

In [*Nov.*], U.S. Senator Algernon S. Paddock of Neb. wrote to USG. "I beg to call your attention to the clause in the River & Harbor appropriation act of the last session of Congress authorizing an expenditure for the improvement of the Missouri River opposite Nebraska City Nebraska. It will be found on page 137 of the published statutes at paragraph nineteen. This improvement is absolutely necessary to save the port of Nebraska City— the second Town in importance in our state; it can be best made at this season of the year— It is the only appropriation of this kind asked for during the existence of the state and I urgently request that it may be used as is imperatively demanded by great commercial interests at once. Will you not instruct the Secretary of War to have immediate action taken in the case" ALS (undated), DNA, RG 77, Rivers and Harbors Div., Letters Received. On Nov. 29, Greene endorsed this letter. "Approved by the President. The Secretary of War directs that $15000 be allotted for the purpose mentioned within" AES, *ibid. HED*, 44-2-23, 43.

On Dec. 9, Culver C. Sniffen wrote to Humphreys. "The President directs me to inform you that the whole of the appropriation for Oakland Harbor, California may be expended." ALS, DNA, RG 77, Rivers and Harbors Div., Letters Received. *HED*, 44-2-23, 45.

In his Dec. 5 annual message to Congress, USG noted that $2,000,000, later increased to $2,237,600, had been allocated from the $5,015,000 appropriated by the river and harbor bill. On Jan. 12, 1877, USG wrote to the House of Representatives. "In reply to the Resolution of inquiry, dated December 23d, 1876. of the House of Representatives, respecting the expenditure of certain moneys appropriated by the Act of August 14— 1876. for River and Harbor improvements, I have the honor to transmit herewith, for your information, a report and accompanying papers received from the Secretary of War, to whom the Resolution was referred—" Copy, DNA, RG 130, Messages to Congress. *HED*, 44-2-23. On Jan. 11, Cameron had written to USG. ". . . Immediately after receiving the bill, the Chief of Engineers was directed to ask for statements from the Engineers in charge of works. as to what works could be postponed for the present. The replies from these officers recommended the expenditure of about $4.500.000 of the appropriation. This reduction was so slight, as practically to amount to nothing, and therefore, on the 4th of September. having obtained your approval, I directed the Chief of Engineers whose knowledge of this subject is more extended than that of any other officer of the Government, to make allotments from the sums appropriated for the various works, according to the best of his judgment, and in such manner that the total amount should not exceed $2.000.000 only providing that no new works should be begun, and none continued that were not national in character. In making these allotments it was found that the amount designated, two millions of dollars, was not quite sufficient for the purpose of carrying on the works absolutely necessary, and, therefore, the Chief of Engineers, after an extended interview with the President, was authorized, in October, to increase the amount to $2.237.600. . . ." Copy, DNA, RG 107, Letters Sent, Military Affairs. *HED*, 44-2-23, 1–3. On Jan. 12, Reagan attacked Cameron's report and charged USG with "unlawful and arbitrary action." *CR*, 44–2, 610.

On March 1, U.S. Representative Horace F. Page of Calif. wrote to USG. "I have the honor to hand you herewith a petition of citizens of Stockton, California, asking that the appropriation of $20.000# for the improvement of the San Joaquin River, be applied to that purpose. And I very respectfully ask that the Secretary of War be directed to expend said appropriation forthwith at the points indicated by the petition." ALS, DNA, RG 77, Rivers and Harbors Div., Letters Received. Related papers are *ibid.* On March 2, USG endorsed these papers. "Referred to the Sec. of War. I have no objection to the expenditure of this appropriation." AES, *ibid.*

Veto

To the House of Representatives—

I herewith return House bill No 4085, without my approval— The repeal of the clause in the original bill for paving Pennsylvania

Avenue, fixing the time for the completion of the work by December 1st. 1876. is objectionable in this, that it fixes no date when the work is to be completed—

Experience shows that where contractors have unlimited time to complete any given work they consult their own convenience and not the public good—should Congress deem it proper to amend the present bill in such manner as to fix the date for the completion of the work to be done by any date between December 1st and close of my official term it will receive my approval—

U. S. GRANT.

EXECUTIVE MANSION—AUGUST 15TH 1876

Copy, DNA, RG 130, Messages to Congress. *HED*, 44-1-193; *SMD*, 49-2-53, 401–2. On July 19, 1876, USG signed a bill to repave Pennsylvania Avenue in Washington, D. C. See *U.S. Statutes at Large*, XIX, 92–94. On Aug. 15, Congress passed, and USG signed, a bill that established Jan. 15, 1877, as a completion date. See *ibid.*, p. 207; *CR*, 44–1, 5388–89, 5453, 5482, 5663–64, 5689.

On Dec. 22, 1876, USG wrote to Congress transmitting the report of a commission appointed to oversee the repaving work. Copy, DNA, RG 130, Messages to Congress. *SED*, 44-2-8.

To Senate

To THE SENATE OF THE UNITED STATES—

Upon further investigation, I am convinced that my Message of this date, with holding my signature from Senate bill No 779. entitled "An Act to provide for the sale of a portion of the reservation of the confederated Otoe and Missouria and the Sac and Fox of the Missouri Tribes of Indians in the States of Kansas and Nebraska,"— was premature, and request therefore that the bill may be returned in order that I may affix my signature to it—

U. S. GRANT—

EXECUTIVE MANSION AUGUST 15TH 1876

Copy, DNA, RG 130, Messages to Congress. *SMD*, 49-2-53, 403. An undated clerical note is appended to the copy of USG's message. "Bill not returned—but passed over Presidents Veto—owing to this message having been submitted to the Senate—" Copy, DNA, RG 130, Messages to Congress. On Aug. 15, 1876, USG had vetoed the proposed reservation sale upon information received from the act. secretary of the interior. Copy, *ibid. SMD*, 49-

2-53, 403. See *ibid.*, pp. 403–4; *CR*, 44–1, 3447, 4517–18, 4772–73, 5336, 5664–65, 5696–97; *U.S. Statutes at Large*, XIX, 208–9; *HED*, 44-2-1, part 5, I, 500, 502–3.

To House of Representatives

To the House of Representatives.

In announcing, as I do, that I have attached my signature of official approval to the "Act making appropriations for the Consular and Diplomatic service of the Government, for the Year ending June 30, 1877. and for other purposes," it is my duty to call attention to a provision in the Act directing that notice be sent to certain of the Diplomatic and Consular Officers of the Government "to close their offices.—" [1]

In the literal sense of this direction, it would be an invasion of the Constitutional prerogative and duty of the Executive.—

By the Constitution, the President "shall have power by, and with the advice and consent of the Senate, to make treaties, provided two thirds of the Senators present, consent, and he shall nominate, and by and with the advice and consent of the Senate, shall appoint ambassadors, other public ministers and Consuls &c. &c.

It is within the power of Congress to grant, or with hold appropriation of money for the payment of salaries and expenses of the Foreign Representatives of the Government.—

In the early days of the government, a sum in gross was appropriated leaving it to the Executive to determine the grade of the officers, and the Countries to which they should be sent—

Latterly, for very many years, specific sums have been appropriated for designated missions or employments, and, as a rule, the omission by Congress to make an appropriation for any specific post, has heretofore been accepted as an indication of a wish on the part of Congress, which the Executive branch of the Government respected, and complied with.—

In calling attention to the passage which I have indicated, I assume that the intention of the provision is only to exercise the constitutional prerogative of Congress over the expenditures of the

Government, and to fix a time at which the compensation of certain
Diplomatic and Consular Officers shall cease; and not to invade the
Constitutional rights of the Executive, which I should be compelled
to resist—and my present object is not to discuss or dispute the wisdom of failing to appropriate for several offices, but to guard against
the construction that might possibly be placed on the language used
as implying a right in the Legislative Branch to direct the closing, or
discontinuing of any of the Diplomatic or Consular Offices of the
Government.—

U. S. GRANT.—

WASHINGTON—AUGUST 15TH, 1876.—

Copy, DNA, RG 130, Messages to Congress; Df, *ibid.* *HED*, 44-1-192; *SMD*, 49-2-53,
402–3. See *U.S. Statutes at Large*, XIX, 170–75; *CR*, 44–1, 5684–89.

1. On Oct. 16, 1876, George H. Stuart, Philadelphia, wrote to USG. "You will doubtless be able to recall *Mrs Dr Harris*, who went as an angel of mercy among the Soldiers,
whom you gallantly led to victory. I enclose you an extract from one of her recent letters,
which speaks for itself, and which I have taken the liberty of endorsing to the State Department, who I hope will be able to meet her wishes, by giving the appointment asked, to
her honored husband, whom I have personally known for many years   Trusting the application will meet your approval, . . ." LS, DNA, RG 59, Letters of Application and Recommendation. On March 25, 1870, USG had nominated John Harris as consul, Venice.
After Congress discontinued this consulate in the 1876 appropriations bill, Ellen M. O.
Harris wrote to Stuart for help in obtaining a new appointment for her husband. Copy,
ibid. Related papers are *ibid.* See Frank Moore, *Women of the War; Their Heroism and Self-
Sacrifice* (Hartford, 1866), pp. 176–212.
    The appropriations bill also eliminated the post of minister to Colombia, ousting
William L. Scruggs. On Jan. 5 and 19, 1877, Scruggs wrote to USG. "The diplomatic and
consular bill, reported by the House Committe yesterday, fails to restore any one of the
suspended Legations. It however, provides for the distribution of the appropriations for
Consular service *at the discretion of the Executive.* Should therefore the bill pass in this
shape—as it probably will—might not a Consul General be named to the U. S. of Colombia, with residence at such point therein as may be deemed expedient?" "I wrote Mr Fish
yesterday to say that, upon condition my past services should be deemed satisfactory, I
should like to continue in the diplomatic or consular service. As both parties claiming the
Presidential succession, no less than the respective candidates themselves, are pledged
to civil 'service reform,' and to make honesty, experience and efficiency,—rather than
supposed party influence—the only test, it seems to me the usual objections to appointments by an outgoing administration loose much of their force. To place this matter beyond embarrassment however, my resignation, should you favor my application, will be
tendered to your successor—whomsoever he may be—when he is regularly inaugurated;
and in case the new incumbent should be Mr Tilden, its immediate acceptance requested.
I have spoken to no member of Congress on this matter, and shall not do so." ALS, DNA,
RG 59, Applications and Recommendations, Hayes-Arthur. Related papers are *ibid.*
Scruggs regained the post of minister to Colombia in 1882. See *PUSG*, 23, 206; *ibid.*, 26,
195, 247.

In a petition dated Feb. 12, Alberto Keller and many others, Milan, wrote to USG. "We, the under-signed merchants, proprietors, residents and land-owners in Milan have heard with regret that, for reasons of financial economy, the praiseworthy Government of the United States of America have suspended, among others, also this Consulate, whose functions have now with great diligence, distinguished equity and justice been performed for nearly six years by the well-known and esteemed gentleman Mr Henry William Trimble. . . ." DS (in Italian), DNA, RG 59, Applications and Recommendations, Hayes-Arthur; translation, *ibid.* On April 6, 1874, U.S. Representative Marcus L. Ward of N.J. had written to Secretary of State Hamilton Fish requesting Henry W. Trimble's promotion from commercial agent to consul, Milan. ALS, *ibid.*, Letters of Application and Recommendation.

To Rutherford B. Hayes

Aug. 16th 1876,

MY DEAR GOVERNOR;

Congress has adjourned and I leave for Long Branch on Saturday.[1] Mrs. Grant and I will be pleased to see Mrs. Hayes and daughter[2] there when they come East, and very much hope you will change your mind and come too. I should like very much to meet you before the Campaign advances far, though I do not know of any special advantage to arise from it. You will have my hearty support in any event, and I hope—and fully believe—the result in November will designate you as my successor.

I received your second letter[3] in due time. I am not aware of any feeling personal to myself on account of your allusion to your determination not to be a candidate, under any circumstances, for a second term. Whether it was wise to allude to the subject in a letter of acceptance is a question about which people might differ. But in this you have largely the advantage of your competitor. You say distinctly what course you will take, without condemning what the people have done on seven distinct occasions—re-elect the incumbent. Your opponent, condemns the system and thinks no true reform can be effective until the President is disqualified for re-election by constitutional provision, without a pledge as to whether he would accept the office for a second term.[4] Possibly Mr. Tilden feels that he has promised more than he can deliver—*if elected*—and is hedging, as his friend and supporter, John Morrissey,[5] would say.

I hope Governor you will conclude to accompany Mrs. Hays and pay us a visit if it is but for a few days.

Very Truly Yours
U. S. GRANT

GEN. R. B. HAYS

ALS, OFH. Governor Rutherford B. Hayes of Ohio did not visit Long Branch. See letter to Rutherford B. Hayes, July 4, 1876.

On Sept. 18, 1876, a correspondent in Long Branch reported USG's response to "Carl Schurz's alleged muzzling by Zach Chandler, the chairman of the Republican National Committee, for remarks in his speeches offensive to the President." "I never thought or heard of such a thing until I saw it in the newspapers. . . . I never even thought of such a thing. . . . It would be a most absurd thing for me to do. The campaign isn't run in my interest, but in that of another candidate, whom I want to help along as much as I can, and I certainly would not be doing so by interfering with any speaker for Hayes and Wheeler. . . . As I understand it, Mr. Schurz's engagement is not with the National Committee, but with the State Committee, so that Mr. Chandler has nothing whatever to do with Mr. Schurz. . . ." *New York Herald*, Sept. 19, 1876. See Hans L. Trefousse, *Carl Schurz: A Biography* (Knoxville, 1982), pp. 230–31.

1. On Aug. 19, USG, Julia Dent Grant, and Ulysses S. Grant, Jr., left on the 9:00 A.M. train for Long Branch. See *Washington Evening Star*, Aug. 19, 21, 1876.

2. Fanny Hayes, the only daughter, born in 1867.

3. On July 8, 1876, Hayes wrote in his letter accepting the Republican presidential nomination. ". . . The declaration of principles by the Cincinnati Convention makes no announcement in favor of a single Presidential term. I do not assume to add to that declaration, but believing that the restoration of the civil service to the system established by Washington and followed by the early Presidents can be best accomplished by an Executive who is under no temptation to use the patronage of his office to promote his own re-election, I desire to perform what I regard as a duty in stating now my inflexible purpose, if elected, not to be a candidate for election to a second term. . . ." *New York Times*, July 10, 1876. On July 14, Hayes wrote to USG. "I learned from Mr Platt of New York in a recent conversation with him here that at least one person has mis[co]nstrued the paragraph in my letter of acceptance as to a second term as a reflection on you. Nothing I assure you is further from the fact. In addition to the reason given in the letter there was another which had much weight with me. I was not a prominent candidate outside of my own State. There were at least four gentlemen who in this respect were in advance of me. The five leading candidates are all younger men than I am. Four years hence, I think, they will all be younger than I am now. At any rate they may all reasonably expect to be candidates in future if they desire to be. It seemed to me therefore that nominated as I was, it would tend to unite and harmonise their friends if it were certainly known that I would not be in their way four years from now. If elected, it will surely strengthen my administration. I need hardly assure you that I would not say anything to reflect on you, but under the circumstances this much seems proper." ADfS, OFH. On the same day, a correspondent reported from Washington, D. C. "The President one day last week gave an audience to an Ohio private citizen in no way connected with public life, and voluntarily conversed very freely with him upon the public situation. Among other things, the President criticised very severely Mr. Hayes's letter. He said he considered it in extremely bad taste, and thought that

it reflected upon the present Administration. The President further said to this gentleman that he hoped the time would come when the American people would be permitted to elect a President for as long a time as they chose. The inference left upon this gentleman's mind was very strong that the President was grievously annoyed that any consideration whatever had been given to the question of the third term. The President's entire manner indicated complete dissatisfaction with the political situation, and much personal anger." *New York Tribune*, July 15, 1876. See Keith Ian Polakoff, *The Politics of Inertia: The Election of 1876 and the End of Reconstruction* (Baton Rouge, 1973), pp. 105–7; Ari Hoogenboom, *Rutherford B. Hayes: Warrior & President* (Lawrence, Kan., 1995), pp. 266–67.

4. On July 31, Governor Samuel J. Tilden of N. Y., in his lengthy letter accepting the Democratic presidential nomination, wrote "that no reform of the civil service in this country will be complete and permanent until its Chief Magistrate is constitutionally disqualified for re-election, experience having repeatedly exposed the futility of self-imposed restrictions by candidates or incumbents. Through this solemnity only can he be effectually delivered from his greatest temptation to misuse the power and patronage with which the Executive is necessarily charged." *New York Times*, Aug. 5, 1876. A lifelong Democrat and wealthy New York City lawyer, Tilden campaigned on his record of successful opposition to corruption in government. See *New York Herald*, July 29, 1876; Polakoff, *Politics of Inertia*, pp. 71–77.

5. On May 26, N. Y. Senator John Morrissey, gambling house owner, former heavyweight boxing champion, and Democratic U.S. Representative (1867–71), "Fifth Ave Hotel," had written to USG. "Allow me to express my full appreciation of the manner that you have adopted ever since your occupancy of the highest office that a generous and grateful people can bestow upon any private citizen, namely the withholding on every occasion, of any views or ideas that may have suggested themselves to your mind upon the subject of a nations affairs. I for one, and I believe my influence is not wholly departed ~~upon~~ from the masses, will and have been for the last 2 months, endeavoring to show my constituents the folly of nominating a new man to the office of President. We know what your policy is and we can act accordingly but not so if you refuse another term." ALS, USG 3. See Simon Wolf, *The Presidents I Have Known from 1860–1918* (Washington, 1918), pp. 77–78.

To James N. Tyner

—————

Long Branch, N. J.
Aug, 20th 76

DEAR SIR:

Before leaving Washington I intended speaking specially in favor of the appointment of Maj. Griswold, of Balt. to some position in the P. O. dept. if possible. The Major's circumstances are very necessitous, no doubt largely due to the political stand taken by him a few years since, and continued to the present.

If you should meet the Sec. of the Treas, I wish you would speak to him in behalf of the Major if you should not be able to do any thing for him yourself.

Very Truly

U. S. GRANT

Copy, USGA. USG also enclosed a note dated July 18, 1876. "I wi[sh] the Postmaster General would see Mr. Griswold, of Md., the gentleman of whom I spoke to him." Copy, *ibid.* Elias Griswold, former asst. AG and maj., C.S. Army, lost an 1872 congressional election to Democratic U.S. Representative Thomas Swann of Md. On Jan. 10, 1877, Culver C. Sniffen wrote to Attorney Gen. Alphonso Taft. "The President directs me to say that he desires to have Elias Griswold nominated to the vacant Dist. Judgeship in Florida unless you know of some good reason to the contrary. We will prepare the nomination here if you will be kind enough to send over the datea" ALS, DNA, RG 60, Letters from the President. On Jan. 11 and 18, USG nominated Griswold as judge, Northern District, Fla., only to withdraw both nominations. On Jan. 20 and 23, Sniffen wrote to Taft. "The President directs me to enquire whether there is a vacant judgeship in New Mexico, and if so, has any one been designated for, or promised the appointment.?" Copy, DLC-USG, II, 3. "I am directed by the President to prepare a nomination for Elias Griswold—(recently nominated as U. S. Dist. Judge in Florida) to the vacant Judgeship in New Mexico. As our records do not show what vacancies exist, will you please send me the necessary information to prepare the nomination correctly." LS, DNA, RG 60, Letters from the President. On the same day, USG nominated Griswold as associate justice, New Mexico Territory; the Senate did not confirm this nomination. As of Sept. 30, Griswold clerked in the Justice Dept.

Proclamation

———

It is with extreme pain that the President announces to the people of the United States, the death of the Speaker of the House of Representatives, the Honorable Michael C. Kerr, of Indiana.

A man of great intellectual endowments, large culture, great probity and earnestness in his devotion to the public interests, has passed from the position, power, and usefulness to which he had been recently called.

The body over which he had been selected to preside, not being in session to render its tribute of affection and respect to the memory of the deceased, the President invites the people of the United States, to a solemn recognition of the public and private worth and the services of a pure and eminent character.

U. S. GRANT

WASHINGTON, AUGUST 21ST 1876.

DS, DLC-Executive Orders. After illness had limited his attendance in Congress, Speaker of the House Michael C. Kerr died on Aug. 19, 1876. Born in 1827, Kerr had practiced law in New Albany, Ind., served as a Democratic U.S. Representative (1865–73), and regained his seat in 1875. An investigation into charges that Kerr had accepted $450 to procure an army appointment troubled his final months. See *HRC*, 44-1-654. On Aug. 20, 1876, Secretary of State Hamilton Fish, Garrison, N. Y., telegraphed to USG, Long Branch. "If you think proper to issue a notice of Mr Kerr's death, please telegraph immediately to Mr Cadwalader at Washington. I have telegraphed, to him, ~~to be issued~~ a notice to be issued if you deem it proper" ADfS (press, telegram sent), DLC-Hamilton Fish. On the same day, USG telegraphed to "Sec of state," Washington, D. C. "Please issue usual notice of the decease of the speaker of the House of Representatives" Telegram received, DNA, RG 59, Miscellaneous Letters.

Endorsement

Referred to the Sec. of the Navy. I am clearly of the opinion that the Adm.l & Vice Adm.l [1] of the Navy occupy honorable positions that should not be touched by any order of the department in a way to reduce their pay or to detract from the dignity of those positions. I do not suppose any order has been published having such an object. But if any injustice has been done, inadvertently or otherwise I think it should be corrected.

U. S. Grant

Aug. 21st /76

AES, DNA, RG 45, Letters Received from the President. Written on a letter of Aug. 18, 1876, from Admiral David D. Porter, Narragansett, R. I., to USG. "In 1870 I received an order from the Secretary of the Navy to take charge of the 'Inspection duty of the Navy', report upon its efficiency from time to time, visit the Naval Stations and make an annual report to the Secretary of the Navy, and the regulations of the Navy recognize me as at all times on duty—On the 11th inst I received an order from the Secretary of the Navy detaching me from those duties and placing me on 'waiting orders', I think I have a right to complain of the manner in which this has been done stripping me of all authority for as Admiral of the Navy I certainly am entitled to the same [cou]rtesy as General of the Army and I have the honor to request that you will do me the justice to have the order revoked and have me placed in the same position I lately occupied— . . . I dislike very much to trouble you just at the time when you are enjoying a little rest after your arduos duties at the Capital, but you are the only one I can appeal to, and I do so now with perfect faith that you will leave me no cause to complain of injustice from any quarter—I am sure that you have not forgotten that I am one of your Colaborers in the great cause and in the great war, which you brought to a successful termination for which the nation recognized your services by bestowing its highest honors upon you—Ours are minor positions, but we value them highly and should cease to do so if they were shorn of a tythe of the dignity and honor which rightly belongs to them—" LS, *ibid.* See *Washington Evening Star*, Aug. 15, 1876. On

Aug. 14 and 18, Porter had written to Gen. William T. Sherman expressing outrage over Secretary of the Navy George M. Robeson's actions. ALS, DLC-William T. Sherman.

On Aug. 27, Robeson, North Hampton, N. H., wrote to USG. "I have received the letter of Admiral Porter to you, bearing date the 18th. instant, and complaining that I have relieved him from the duty to which I assigned him in 1870, and further complaining, that this may have the effect, under the general order placing all unemployed officers on furlough, of reducing his pay at the same time that it reduces the pay of other officers of the Navy. He seems also to think, or at least to suggest, that it is a want of courtesy or consideration for his rank, on the part of the Navy Department, to relieve him from the performance of certain special duties to which it had previously assigned him, and suggests, also, that he has a right to complain of the manner in which it has been done; and this, perhaps, is his excuse for making this complaint and sendin[g] it directly to yourself without making any complaint to the Department or sending it through it. Upon neither of the points suggested, however, has he, in my opinion, any reason to complain. The inspection duty from which he has been relieved was invented by myself for the purpose of giving him some nominal duty, and also, of giving him the opportunity of writing a report to the Secretary of the Navy, which I, at the time thought might contain some valuable information and suggestions. In this last regard I have been thoroughly disappointed. His reports have been of no real value to the Department or to anybody else. They have, from the first shown a lamentable ignorance or disregard of the real condition of the Naval service. They have been full of complaints concerning defects which have grown inevitably out of the condition in which our Navy was, and the character of the service itself, to the producing of which defects he had himself contributed as much as, if not more than, anyone else. The suggestions of the reports were almost always utterly impracticable, without consideration of the means at the command of the Department, and reckless of the provisions and limitations of existing laws; and the reports themselves were little else than elaborate attacks upon the policy of the Department, and covert suggestions of how much better it could be carried on if the Admiral of the Navy were given control of the Naval Establishment. . . . I can see very readily, since he has made this request of you, why you should not wish to refuse it, and as no great harm will result to the service by giving him the additional money for which he has appealed to your magnanimity, I shall be perfectly ready, and indeed, rather desirous, if you say so, to issue an order exempting him, by your directions, from the operation of the general order putting the other unemployed officers on furlough. With this explanation I am ready to make the order I suggest, upon the receipt of any intimation that you would like it to be made." Copy, DNA, RG 45, Letters Received from the President. On Sept. 1, Robeson issued an order exempting Porter from the pay reduction. See *HMD*, 44-1-170, part 5, pp. 404–42; *HED*, 44-2-1, part 4, pp. 24–26.

On Aug. 23, Robeson, North Hampton, had written to USG. "I received yesterday, a letter from Com. Ammen, written in compliance with your ~~suggestion~~ direction, about your suggestion of the removal of Mr Hanscom, chief of the bureau of Construction and Repair in the Navy Department, and requesting that I should communicate to you my views on the subject—As the Commodore did not give me (and perhaps did not himself know) the *particular reasons*, which influenced your judgment, I cannot now speak of them in particular—but, on general principles I beg of you that you will not act affirmatively in this matter till all sides of it can be looked at & considered carefully & until I can myself see & talk with you on the subject—I am at present detained here by a continuance of the same malarial attack which drove me so suddenly from Washington & which has taken the form of a severe *lumbago*, but I *must* go to Washington by about the 1st of the month & will go to Long Branch at that time & see you on this subject—I am the more anxious about

it, because the position, is in a mechanical and service point of view, of the greatest importance to the Navy, & particularly at this time, when so many of our ships are actually in
the process of reconstruction, and that under plans, specifications and directions made and
carried on by Mr. H. himself—He is a constructor of first rate ability, almost, if not in fact,
the only one of the ~~best~~ first class now left in the corps—a mechanic who worked himself
up from the bench till he has built the finest & most efficient ships of our navy—Thus, in
a mechanical & service point of view he is a very good chief of bureau—of course with little
of legal ideas & less of an accountant, but I am very loath to believe that he would *inten-
tially* do any thing that was really wrong; and if he has only made mistakes, I have made so
many myself (of which I am conscious) that I cannot find it in my heart to be very severe
on him, ~~since he has~~—Of course if he has done any intentional wrong, he ought not to stay
under any circumstances, but I have always thought him an honest, though an uncultivated
man, with first rate ideas, but slow of speech & expression and very awkward in explaining & making himself understood. And I confess, I feel the more kindly towards him because he has (next to myself) been the special target of the devils who spent so many
months in raking over the dead bones of the navy department & particularly of Burleigh,
who bargained to join the democrats on every thing if they would attack & destroy
Hanscom, and also because the only officers in the line of succession, who would be eliga-
ble for his place under the law were sent for by members of the committee, (Burleigh &
others) & encouraged to attack him—*with a view to get his place*—Besides I cannot but feel,
if he has made mistakes, that I am not unlikely to be largely in fault myself for submitting
to him questions with which he was not familiar, & acting on his reports without sufficient
consideration and review—again, if he is removed, the question of his successor at once
arises, and this is a most difficult one: there are but two constructeors, who can be appointed under the law (which limits the choice to those of the rank of captain) and both of
these are most objectionable—one, Mr. Hart, is a loud mouthed, drunken cross grained
blackguard, who is reccommended for ct. martial himself—the other, Mr Webb, is a fair
ship carpenter, but utterly ~~illiterate~~ illiterate & can hardly write his name—& though so-
ber & quiet, is a bitter & virulent democratic partizan—he was hanging round the committee all winter & specially employed to work up things against Hanscom—I state all
these things to you, my dear Mr President, because they enter into the question if it is one
of *fitness* only—If it is a question of intention[al] wrong I can only repeat, if he is guilty, he
ought not to stay—but I think that ought to be fully investigated—But I will go to Long
Branch & see you personally about this matter, as I have said by the 1st of the month or as
soon as I am able to travel if not by that time & I beg that nothing affirmative may be done
in the mean time—will you let Buck write me a line acknowledging the receipt of this—
Hoping you are all well at the cottage—..." ALS, PHi. Isaiah Hanscom continued as chief,
Bureau of Construction and Repair, Navy Dept. See *PUSG,* 21, 413; letter to George M.
Robeson, March 2, 1876; *HMD,* 44-1-170, part 5, pp. 45–57, 643–61, 669–76, 729–33.

1. Stephen C. Rowan. See *PUSG,* 21, 67.

To James N. Tyner

Long Branch, N. J.
Aug. 30th, 1876.

DEAR SIR:

Your letter of yesterday in relation to the Hot Springs, Ark: post-office is received. Since yesterday I have had a number of dispatches from there indicating a very general—in fact almost unanimous—preference for Mrs. Ida Walsh for the office. I have also seen Senator Dorsey this morning. He says that all republicans are for Mrs. W. Her husband is in prison now for defending himself against a body of rowdies who were attempting to drive him from the place. He has therefore the sympathy of all Union men in the county and state. For this reason they desire the office retained in the family, at least until after his trial.

Casey is represented to be a very good man, though not a resident of the county in which the office is located. He is, I believe, postal clerk in a line of road leading into Hot Springs.

On the whole I am inclined to believe it better to appoint Mrs. Walsh.

Yours Truly
U. S. GRANT

Copy, USGA. On Dec. 12, 1876, USG nominated Ida Walsh as postmaster, Hot Springs, Ark., in place of David C. Casey. On Dec. 8, 1874, USG had nominated William P. Walsh as postmaster.

To Alphonso Taft

LONG BRANCH N. J. AUG. XXXIST. [*1876*]
ATTY. GENL. WASHINGTON D. C.
PLEASE SEND APPOINTMENT OF MARSHAL FOR KY. FOR SIGNATURE. I HAVE NO CHOICE AMONG CANDIDATES BUT IF THE REPUBLICAN MEMBER OF CONGRESS FROM THAT STATE [1] HAS A CANDIDATE WHO THE ATTY. GENL.

BELIEVES WELL QUALIFIED I WOULD GIVE HIM THE
PREFERENCE.

U. S. GRANT.

Telegram received (at 10:40 A.M.), DNA, RG 60, Letters from the President. On Aug. 31,
1876, Attorney Gen. Alphonso Taft telegraphed to USG, Long Branch. "I am waiting for
answer from White and for some further information to come in a day or two, See letter."
Copy, *ibid.*, Letters Sent to Executive Officers. On Aug. 25, U.S. Representative John D.
White of Ky., Lexington, had written to Taft. "According to promise I now write you concerning the appointment of a successor *vice* Eli H. Murray late U. S. Marshal for Kentucky.
Maj. A. T. Wood of Mt. Sterling Ky. of whom I spoke so favorably refuses to accept should
he be appointed since he desires to perform the duties assigned him as elector for Hayes &
Wheeler in my district (9th Ky.). The Mr. Tarleton of whom we spoke, I fear is not just the
man for the place. There is a deserving gentleman however living in the extreme south-
eastern portion of Ky. whom the President appointed Consul to Port Said, Egypt but who
resigned, after some months waiting for the Consular & Dip. App. bill to pass, in consequence of sickness in his family and a belief (subsequently confirmed by fact) that there
would be no appropriation for Port Said. This gentleman is Cap't. A. E. Adams of Piketon,
Pike Co. Ky. . . ." ALS, *ibid.*, Records Relating to Appointments. On Sept. 2, USG endorsed
this letter. "Returned to the Atty. Gen. I know of no reason for declining to make this apt."
AES, *ibid.* On Aug. 31, L. P. Tarlton, Jr., Washington, D. C., had written to USG. "Owing
to my absence from home I did not know of the vacancy, caused by the resignation of General E. H. Murray, in the office of Marshal Kentucky District, until some ten days after it
had been tendered. At the suggestion and solicitation of many Republican friends of my
state I have applied for the appointment as his successor. When I reached Washington
yesterday I learned from your Attorney General that my name had been presented to
yours and his consideration by kind friends without my knowledge and the appointment
had been asked for me. Mr President as a personal interview is impossible before you decide this matter without my intruding upon the privacy and disturbing the rest you have
sought away from here ~~after~~ I take this means of stating to you as briefly as possible the
grounds upon which I base my application and ask for them your kind consideration. Since
I reached manhood I have been allied with the Republican party and have been an active
and working member of that party, always openly advocating its principles, part of the
time to my pecuniary loss, as Editor of the only Republican paper in Central Kentucky. I
have never before been an applicant for any appointment nor have I ever held any office under the U. S. Government. . . ." ALS, *ibid.* A related letter is *ibid.* See letter to Alphonso
Taft, Sept. 4, 1876.

On June 22 and July 31, White had written to USG. "I take pleasure in presenting for
appointment, to a Territorial judgeship or its equivalent in some of the departments, the
name of Maj. A. T. Wood of Mt. Sterling, Ky. He was a good soldier; is a true Republican;
is qualified for a high position; and, is an honest and honorable gentleman. He canvassed
in 1872, the 9th Cong. Dist., Ky. as the Repub. candidate for Congress. . . ." "It now appears
that I was not mistaken in the qualifications of Maj. A. T. Wood of Mt. Sterling, Ky. for the
position of U. S. Dist. Att. for Ky. (see his letter enclosed herewith) But I think that as the
abilities of Hon H. F. Finley are better known his appointment will receive more universal
approval. If, however, a change is determined on in the office of U. S. Marshal I can-not
recommend Maj. Wood too highly for the place." ALS, DNA, RG 60, Records Relating to
Appointments.

On July 17, "J. R.," Louisville, wrote to USG. "I have the honor to enclose herewith various articles taken from the Louisville Sunday Argus of the 9th and 16th inst. relative to practices of the offices of United States Marshal and District Attorney in this District, which demand investigation, It will hardly be admitted by even the close friends of the Dist. Atty Mr G̶Wharton that he is qualified for the duties of his high position. Personally he is a clever gentleman but could such practices be carried on so boldly for a series of years without his knowledge. True he has recently made an effort at reform in matters of fees &c. but it is believed that he has acted mainly with a view of holding his own position. It is well known here that in the late contest between aspirants for the Presidential nomination, Dist Atty Wharton and Marshal Murray made efforts to barter away public positions to men who would consent to support Mr Bristow, and in other instances threatened Government officers with dismissal if they continued to oppose Mr Bristow's nomination. Let an investigation be made of the management of these offices by an officer sent from abroad. I do not sign this letter for the same reasons advanced in my letter of this date on another subject. . . . P. S. Let the officer confer with O. H. Rothacker, Managing Editor Louisville Sunday Argus and also Louisville Evening Ledger." L, *ibid.*, Letters from the President. The enclosures are *ibid.* See *Louisville Courier-Journal,* July 20, 1876. On July 16, "J. R." had telegraphed to USG. "Await letter mailed tonight before signing collector Buckners relief bill" Telegram received, DLC-USG, IB. On July 22, Secretary of the Treasury Lot M. Morrill wrote to USG after a review raised no objections to a bill settling the accounts of James F. Buckner, collector of Internal Revenue, 5th District, Ky. Copy, DNA, RG 56, Letters Sent to the President. On July 29, this bill became law without USG's signature. See *U.S. Statutes at Large (Private Laws),* XIX, 56–57; *HRC,* 44-1-511; *SRC,* 44-1-443; *CR,* 44–1, 3763–65.

On July 27, John M. Harlan, Louisville, telegraphed to Taft. "It is rumored that a movement is on foot to Remove Dist atty Wharton & U. S. marshal murray of this state. my daily observation of the manner in which they discharge their duties enables me to say that they have been faithful & efficient officers and that there is no stain whatever upon them either as offices or citizens I know where complaints against them originate & I know such complaints to be utterly without foundation I beg to assure you that their removal would be unfortunate in many respects and is in no sense demanded by the public interests I earnestly hope it will not be done they were gallant officers in the union army and deserve the full confidence of the government if there is any purpose to remove them I respectfully ask that they have an opportunity to be heard" Telegram received, DNA, RG 60, Letters from the President. On July 28, USG wrote a note to have Hugh F. Finley nominated as U.S. attorney, Ky., to replace Gabriel C. Wharton. Cohasco, Catalogue No. 30, Oct. 26, 1989, no. 115. See *PUSG,* 20, 94–95; *CR,* 47–1, 2911–12; *Louisville Courier-Journal,* July 28, 29, Aug. 1, 1876.

On Aug. 7, Lucy M. Porter, postmaster, Louisville, wrote to USG. "The note you did me the honor to write me was duly received and gave me infinite satisfaction. I had so long been humiliated and tortured by the clique I wrote of, that the hope of being delivered from their snares and persecutions was a relief to my mind and heart greater than I can express. I thank you Mr. President for your patient hearing of the long recital of my troubles. Since the receipt of your note I have been made happy by the decapitation of some of the conspirators who were *pledged* (I am informed a secret society of Bristow men existed with one C. C. Adams of the Treasury at the head) to defeat your nomination for a third term at any sacrifice and by any means. This Jesuitical order was composed largely I suppose of appointees of Col. Bristow or men recommended by him. Gov. Jewell's removal and the dismissal of of Col. Bristow's most suppliant tools, Col. Wharton and the perfidious Brown caused a panic among the guilty Government officials here which I confess I was highly delighted to see. Genl Murray was selected by the clique to visit Washington, not only in his own interest but to gloss over the defects of the rest of the followers of the ex-Secretary and make their paths straight, before them. Like a flock of birds without a leader the clique of disconcerted Bristow men are clutching at every one whom they suppose can help them. Capt. Sherley is violently besieged by them and Gov. Morton of Indiana also. Mr. President, could you have a request sent to Col. Buckner to drop from his rolls the names of G. H. Irwin and W. M. Collins store keepers in the Revenue service? These men were very active in disseminating slanders against you and were insulting to me; and still hang round the post-office to the injury of the service. As I wrote you, the above mentioned parties were clerks in the post office and were given offices by Col. Bristow as a reward for their opposition to you and their persecution of me. I wish Mr. President I could tell you all I know of the deception and the corruption of the Bristow politicians of this city. My office is in the Custom House where I see their actions and hear of their caucusing. one of them, said to me a few days since—'Genl Grant is making this a personal Government.' No one has so good a right to do so, (I replied) for it is due to General Grant that we have a Government. The man then proceeded to say something about the dishonesty of your friends. I said to him, did you ever hear of Col. Bristow's only brother Frank—who was Commissioner of Bankruptcy in Bowling Green and who absconded, a defaulter to a considerable amount? Please Mr. President excuse me; I did not intend to impose so long a letter upon you." ALS, USG 3.

On Aug. 12, Jonathan D. Hearne, president, Covington City National Bank, wrote to USG. "Herewith find two slips cut from newspapers of date as indicated on each—I have no knowledge as to the contemplated change spoken of but desire to express my unqualified disapproval of the appointment of Col (?) Weden O'Neal to any office whatever—as to his appointment receiving the approval of the Republicans of this ~~district~~ section it is not true. I regard his appointment as one that would scandalize the administration wherever he is known—" ALS, DNA, RG 60, Letters from the President. The enclosures reported the likely removal of Eli H. Murray, marshal, Ky., and suggested Weden Oneal, former lt. col., 55th Ky., as his replacement. *Ibid.* On Aug. 14, Judge Bland Ballard, U.S. District Court, Ky., Oakland, Md., wrote to USG. "I learn from Gen E. S. Murray U. S. Marshal in the District of Ky that the Attorney Gen. informs you desire him to resign his office. I do not know what considerations have prompted this desire; but justice to a gallant soldier, an honorable gentleman and a faithful officer, and justice to you demand that I should ask your Excellency to reconsider this matter. . . . Gen Murray entered the service of the U. S. during the war of the Rebellion when he was, I believe, only seventeen years old. For his gallantry and service he was promoted to the rank of Brig. Gen. and, I have often heard, that he was the youngest Brig Gen. in the army. He was a true friend of the Country during the Rebellion and he has ever been its true friend since. Whilst some of his comrades in arms returned home and then surrendered to to the Rebels, he remained faithful—a true patriot and a zealous Republican. . . ." ALS, *ibid.* On Aug. 15, Murray, Louisville, wrote to USG tendering his resignation. ALS, *ibid.,* Letters Received, Ky. See *Louisville Courier-Journal,* Aug. 18, 1876.

On July 27, 1870, Benjamin H. Bristow, Louisville, had written to USG. "Genl Eli H. Murray is active, & efficient in the office of U. S. Marshal and as a member of the Republican Executive Committee for this state is rendering valuable service for the party. He is entirely acceptable to the party and the interests of the public service are safe in his hands. His removal would effect injuriously the prospects of the party as well as the public business entrusted to him. The rumor that his removal is contemplated creates surprise here and, were it deemed necessary, he could furnish a remonstrance from almost every Republican of this state. I sincerely hope he will not be disturbed" ALS, DNA, RG 60, Records Relating to Appointments. Related papers are *ibid.*

On Aug. 17, 1876, Fred Van Seggern, Louisville, wrote to USG. "having seen in the papers that Genrl Eli Murry has tenderd his resignation as United States Marshal of Kentucky I appeal to you to give my name a consideration I have been a citizen of Louisville for Thirty years and a Republican from its Birth having worked hard for the party when their was but few here I appeal to you to give me a chance I was unfortunate and lost all I had & am in nead of a place . . ." ALS, *ibid.* On Aug. 19, John J. Speed, Louisville, telegraphed to USG. "I have the honor to apply for office of united States marshal Kentucky, as to fitness I refer to Bankers & Business men of Louisville as to politics to Local Republicans—I can also refer to General sherman Genl Benj Harrison & Genl John Coburn all of whom know me as assistant adjutant Genl Third Division twentieth Corps will apply by mail—" Telegram received (at 9:25 P.M.), *ibid.* Related papers are *ibid.* On Aug. 21, James H. Ashcraft, Paducah, wrote to USG. "I see that Genl E. H. Murray has tendered his resignation as U. S. Marshal of this District. Mr J. R. Puryear of this place is an applicant for the position I take great pleasure in recomending him to your consideration. he is a high toned gentleman a thorough and working Republican and I think his appointment would give satisfaction to the Republicans generally of the District and I am certain would not injure our cause in this state" ALS, *ibid.* On Aug. 25, James D. Shortell, Owensboro, Ky., telegraphed to USG. "The appointment of General Hobson as marshall of Kentucky would gratify your friends and republicans Petition Sent you today" Telegram received (at 11:10 P.M.), *ibid.* On Aug. 29, Theodore S. Bell wrote to USG. "In case the resignation of General Murray is accepted, to which I am opposed, I take great pleasure in commending Col. R. M. Mosby for the place. He is one of the most faithful of the Union Men of Kentucky, & his qualifications eminently fit ~~him~~ him for the duties of this Marshalship. His appointment will command the confidence of the Union men of Kentucky, or wherever Col. Mosby is known." ALS, *ibid.*

1. Born in 1849 near Manchester, Ky., White studied law and medicine at the University of Michigan. In 1875, he was admitted to the Ky. bar and entered the House of Representatives as the only Republican in his state's congressional delegation.

On March 30, 1876, White wrote to USG. "It lies in your power to help me out of a political difficulty. Some time ago I was notified by the Sec. of War that I was expected to appoint a cadet to West Point to fill a vacancy in the Military Academy. He also recommended that I select that cadet by holding a competitive examination This plan was adopted by me although it was an unheard of precedent in my district. The first effort was a failure. The second time, the examining board met, and after an animated contest the result was that the Board decided to recommend for me to secure the appointment of a young man whose father is a bitter democrat and was a bad rebel. If the Board has acted fairly, and I suppose it has, I can-not do otherwise than fill the vacancy with this successful candidate who secured the recommendation of the Board of Examiners. But now I earnestly recommend that you appoint Mr. M. J. Treadway, of Booneville, Owsley co. Ky., as cadet at large. He passed quite as creditable an examination as the successful candidate did, and he is in other respects far more worthy of a favor. Mr. Treadway is a son of Maj. Treadway who did excellent service in the Mexican War and in the late war he was one of the first to enter service, was wounded, more than once in battle, and came out with a bright record. Both young Treadway & father are republicans of the staunchest kind. . . ." ALS, *ibid.*, RG 94, Correspondence, USMA. Morgan J. Treadway did not attend USMA.

On July 7, White wrote to USG. "In an interview with you the other day in regard to the appointment of *F. C. Anderson*, of Montgomery county Kentucky, to his former position in the Navy I failed to give his proper initials which are as written above. I shall be very glad if you will reappoint him to the Navy. His father is a most uncompromising republican; and while he is gloomy over Bristow's defeat at Cincinnati, and thinks Kentucky irretrievably lost, yet he is firm in his devotion to the principles of the Republican party and is hopeful of a National triumph. I have thought it not improper to say this much on Mr. J. J. Anderson's account since I gave you a portion of his letter which might bear an unfavorable interpretation; but which the writer meant should be confined to Kentucky. Again in regard to Mr. F. C. Anderson, the applicant for reappointment to the Navy I merely wish to say that he is a true Republican, and is put to this necessity on account of his untimely resignation, and his present ill-health. Hoping that you will reinstate, or reappoint him at an early day, . . ." ALS, *ibid.*, RG 45, Letters Received from the President. On Jan. 18, 1875, William T. Dowdall, *Peoria National Democrat*, had written to USG. "as an old Illinois friend I write to ask a favor Mr Jno Jay Anderson of Kentucky is an applicant for the mission to Ecuador and knowing him to be a gentleman of culture ability and a thorough radical I feel and know you will find in him one in every way worthy your trust and confidence and hope you will weigh well his claims. At the breaking out of the war he was a large land & negro owner and though surrounded by a real hot set of rebels he at the earliest approach of war allied himself on the side of the Union and ever stood firm for which he was driven from his home and lost heavily pecuniarily by so doing. I hope you will give him the place" ALS, *ibid.*, RG 59, Letters of Application and Recommendation. Related papers are *ibid.* No appointment followed.

On Aug. 8, 1876, Culver C. Sniffen wrote to White. "The President directs me to say that you need not select a name for Collector of Internal Revenue for Kentucky— Under the appropriation bill before Congress about one third of those already in will have to go out—This will drop two if not three from those now in Kentucky—" Copy, DLC-USG, II, 3.

To Alphonso Taft

———

Long Branch, N. J.
Sept. 4th /76

HON. ALPHONZO TAFT:
ATTY. GEN.
DEAR SIR:

I have returned to you by to-day's mail all the papers relating to the Ky. Marshalship, without remark. Any nomination you will send to me, after investigation, I will approve. Hon. J. D. White having been invited to nominate a man however I think he should be advised if his selection is not concurred in.

The gentleman about whom I telegraphed to-day makes the

point that Mr. White's district has had two state apts recently—
the Pension Agency and the Dist. Atty.ship—while his—a district
largely loyal during the rebellion—has not had a federal appointment during the sixteen years of republican rule.—You may regard
these arguments as you believe for the best interests of the public
service.

Very Truly

U. S. GRANT

ALS, DNA, RG 60, Letters from the President. On Sept. 4, [*1876*], USG, Long Branch,
telegraphed to Attorney Gen. Alphonso Taft. "IF YOU THINK IN VIEW OF THE
FACT THAT THE TWO RECENT APPOINTMENTS DIST. ATTY. AND PENSIONS
AGENTS WERE MADE FROM MR. WHITES DIST. IN KENTUCKY THAT THE
MARSHALSHIP SHOULD COME FROM ANOTHER DIST. I HAVE NO OBJEC-
TION TO MR. WHITE BEING SO INFORMED AND THE APPOINTMENT
GIVEN TO MR. TARLTON IF YOU FEEL SATISFIED WITH HIS CREDENTIALS."
Telegram received, *ibid.* See telegram to Alphonso Taft, Aug. 31, 1876.
   On Sept. 4, U.S. Representative John D. White of Ky., Lexington, wrote to Taft.
"*Confidential* . . . As I have to leave here to-morrow, I shall answer your communication of
the 30th ulto. now. I have consulted with Mr. Finley. He thinks it unwise to take the Mar-
shal from our district (9th). Therefore I withdraw the name of Capt. A. E. Adams. Please
write him such a letter as will explain this to him: for he may expect the appointment from
what I wrote him. He is a good man, and since he lost his property and health for the Union
I shall thank you to remember him when another vacancy occurs. The County in which he
lives is now democratic by a large majority. During the war it was strong for the Union.
Some attention to such true & worthy men as Adams would help us in that part of the Big
Sandy Valley. As to Tarleton I am clearly of the opinion that he is not the man that you
need. For several reasons I must say that Bradley should not be appointed. I am reliably
informed that he is a disorganizer, and has more than once played fugleman to democratic
politicians in Louisville. That he is the fast friend and daily associate of E. D. Standeford
ex-member of Cong. (Dem)   The appointment of Bradley will not strengthen the party in
the State. It will not meet with the approval of the friends of the Administration living in
Louisville. If I could remain till to-morrow I might tell you something definite concerning Gen. S. S. Fry and Mr. Thos. E. Burns both of whom I learn to be fine gentlemen of
high character. At present I am inclined to the opinion that it would be a wise thing to appoint Gen. S. S. Fry. He is not from my district nor from Louisville; and so far as I can learn
is probably the best man of those named for the place. Besides he lives in the 8th Cong.
Dist.—the only one besides the 9th (my dist.) which we hope to carry this fall. The appointment of Fry would probably strengthen us in that section. Mr. Finley promisesd to
write you fully and make a recommendation. I shall defer to his opinion. He is all right,
and will prove himself worthy of the position which he has accepted." ALS, DNA, RG 60,
Records Relating to Appointments. On Sept. 7, USG endorsed this letter. "Atty. Gn. I will
approve the recommendation of — made by—Mr. Finley." AES, *ibid.* On the same day,
Taft wrote to USG. "I inclose the letter and inclosures from Mr Finley. I am satisfied that
General S. S. Fry Speed S. Fry is the best nomination, taking everything into consideration. This nomination comes from the right part of the state, (which is not very important)
has the recommendation of both White and Finley, and I also received a letter from Col.

Finnell of Covington; with whom I am well acquainted, and whose statement gives a good opinion of the man. It seems, that he was the man who killed Zollifcoffer in battle. Musgrove from Miss. has been here and complaining that Lake was removed and urging that he be now appointed postmaster of Jackson, turning out the old one. I believe that we did right, and that there is no occasion to recant. Senator Bruce, and Shaugnessy, the candidate for congress and Hill the secretary of State for Mississippi have been in this morning. They think there is no occasion to be concerned, about Lake, or his paper. They say that both Lake and Musgrove (who are partners in the paper) have voted with the democrats quite as much as with the republicans, & that the paper has done the the republicans more harm than good. I give you this as a sample of the charity these Mississippians have for each other. I presume that ~~they~~ some of them have called on you, or will call." ALS, *ibid.*

On Aug. 31, W. B. Belknap, Louisville, had written to USG. "I learn that Mr Thos Bradley is an applicant for the office of Marshall in the place of Genl Murray resigned. I do not hesitate to express the opinion that his appointment will be a mistake." ALS, *ibid.* On Sept. 5, James L. Wheat, Louisville, wrote to Taft. "(Confidential) . . . I am requested by Hon H. F. Finley U. S. Dist Atty to give my opinion in writing, to be submitted to you, as to the propriety of Thomas Bradley Esqr of this City being made U. S. Marshal for the Dist of Kentucky. . . . As a republican, most earnestly desiring the success of the party, having no personal friend seeking the place, and enjoying scarcely a speaking acquaintance, with either of the more prominent applicants for the position, except Mr B, I am compelled to say that I would deem it most unfortunate for the Administration as well as for the success of our party in this city and state, for this gentleman to be appointed Marshal. . . ." ALS, *ibid.* On Sept. [8], Hugh F. Finley, U.S. attorney, Louisville, telegraphed to Taft. "Please defer action on Marshalship until you receive my letter of yesterday" Telegram received (at 9:00 A.M.), *ibid.*

On Sept. 9, Horace Scott, general superintendent, Jeffersonville, Madison & Indianapolis Railroad, Louisville, wrote to USG. "enclosed find letter from Hon O. P. Morton I had hoped to have found time to make a flying visit East for the purpose of a personal interview with you, relative to the vacancy of U. S. Marshall for Kentucky Caused by the Resignation of Genl Eli Murray. But to my surprise I read in the ~~Morning~~ Cincinnati Morning papers that Speed S Frye of Danville Ky is to be appointed to the place. I have together with a large number of Republicans of this district been strong advocates of your administration and was strongly in favor of Hon O. P. Morton as Candidate before the Cincinati Convention We were ostracised and shamefully treated by Genl Harlan and Genl Wharton Eli Murray and most of the other Government officials and at the Ward Primary Meetings ~~for the purpose of nominating~~ for the purpose of nominating delegates to the State Convention that elected delegates to the Cincinnati Convention, they were guilty of most infamous Conduct, such as distributing Goverment Patronage and Packing Meetings with Irish and democrats wherever they could be hired; in fact guilty of such conduct as would disgrace any party, and all for the purpose of disgracing the Administration and Riding Mr Bristow throug on the great Moral Reform platform; the position which Mr Tilden now occupies We had hoped that after this was all over and their infamous movements had been gloriously defeated, that we would be able to secure the appointment to some of the various offices, a citizen of Louisville who would assist us in Building up a Republican party here, and to that end had put forward Mr Thos Bradley for US Marshall (who is a native of Louisville and commenced voting the Republican ticket when John C. Freemont was Candidate for President in 1856, and has been a consistant republican ever since). But it seems that we are doomed to disapointment and one Speed S. Fry who was a strong Bristow Man is to have the Place Loyalty to Bristow and denunciation of the Administration seems to be the test for a good Kentucky Republican . . ." ALS, *ibid.* On

Sept. 14, Robert M. Kelly, *Louisville Commercial*, wrote to USG. "Some time ago at the request of Col. T. E. Burns, who was an applicant for the position of U. S. Marshal for this Dist. I addressed a letter to the Attorney General stating that he had been a gallant officer, an active Republican and a firm supporter of your administration and that in my opinion if he were appointed it would be generally acceptable to the Republicans of the District. In regard to Gen S. S. Fry who is also an applicant I desire to make the same statement. Gen Fry has the respect of everybody and the warmest regards of all Republicans for his services in behalf of the Country & the party, and the news recently disseminated that he would receive the appointment was heard with general approval. I do not wish to withdraw anything I said of Col. Burns but it is suggested that in justice to Gen. Fry who has my highest esteem that I should make this statement." ALS, *ibid.* On the same day, James Speed, Louisville, wrote to USG recommending Speed S. Fry as marshal, Ky. ALS, *ibid.*

Also on Sept. 14, Finley wrote to USG. "*Confidential* . . . I see a statement in this days papers that Col T. E. Burns has been appointed Marshall for Kentucky and with others telegraphed you requesting that no action be taken in this matter until we could write— when it was announced some days since that Genl Fry was appointed marshall the Republicans were highly gratified all agreeing he was the man of all the aspirants that should have been appointed—that report proved as I have since heard to be untrue and I hope this last is also untrue   Genl. Fry is so well known as a man of the strictest honor integrity and good ability and will if appointed give more general satisfaction than any applicant for the position. . . ." ALS, *ibid.* On Sept. 23, L. H. Noble, Louisville, wrote to USG. "A friend of Col. Thomas E. Burns, and a constand friend of your administration, has just informed me that a late applicant for the office of United States Marshall for Kentucky, has within the past two or three days written your Excellency a letter, containing an article or the substance of an article that lately appeared in the Cincinnati Enquirer, and which was copied into one of our evening papers, but refused insertion by other papers here, reflecting on the character and habits of Col. Burns. That article was seen by the Colonel, and being advised that the source was of a character that forbid his taking public notice of, it, he refrained from doing so, although smarting under its charges. He knows nothing of the above-mentioned letter, & is at his home in Marion County completing his preparation to enter on the duties of his office, therefor, as his father-in-law, knowing his high character, and the character of said article I take the liberty, in justice to him, and to truth, to address your Excellency this note, pronouncing said article false from beginning to end, unsupported by one particle of truth. . . ." ALS, *ibid.*

On Sept. 21, William C. Morton, Hartford, Ky., had written to USG. "The enclosed clipped from the Daily papers will indicate to you the situation of some matters in this District, One is from the Republican Journal published at Evansville Ind. and the other from the Bristow organ Louisville The orgaization life and Sucess of the Republican Party in this section depends upon having true Republicans in Office under the Genl Government and not men who denounce your Adminestration and the Republican Party and who aim only to serve their own ends" ALS, DNA, RG 60, Letters from the President. The enclosures are *ibid.*

On Sept. 22, William O. Watts, former capt., 37th Ky., Louisville, wrote to USG. "I desire very respectfully, to suggest, that if it is your intention to make any further removals, in this state, that you can, in my opinion do the Republican party great good by appointing persons who served in the late war *in the ranks*, of the Federal Army. There is a general complaint among those who belonged to the ranks that they have been overlooked & ignored and that Gov't patronage has been divided out among their *officers*. Now, while I do not endorse that complaint, and think that ability to fill civil offices would more likely be found among the officers than among the private soldiers, yet there are numerous gentlemen in this state who served the government during the late war, faithfully from its beginning to its close, in the privates uniform, whose ability would, and does guarantee efficiency in any civil office to which they may be appointed. Notably among these is Mr Edwin M Clark of this city, who has recently applied to you for appointment to the place given to Col Burns. He would give satisfaction generally to the people, and his appointment would shut the mouth of the complaints mentioned, and give a new viger to the energies of our party, among the soldiers. I have taken the liberty to write you thus Mr President, because I have no axe to grind myself, and for what I deem the good of the Republican party. I believe you will recollect me. I have been your staunch *personal* as well as political friend, ever since an interview I had with you at Cairo when you were commanding there, when you gave me a pass & transportation for troops that I had recruited there for Camp Joe Holt, and through thick & thin I have been steadfast in my friendship. I have also had great friendship for Col Bristow, who has been my personal friend, but I have never had one impulse of sympathy with any person or party that would sink or even effect injuriously your administration in the adulations of any single individual. I consider your letters to Blackburn & Chamberlain, as par excellence the best tests of fealty to the *Republican party*, to the rights of the Executive, & to the rights of the people, which have ever been put upon record I say this that you may believe me your friend." ALS, *ibid.* On Nov. 3, USG suspended Thomas E. Burns as marshal, Ky. On Nov. 11, Edwin M. Clarke, Louisville, wrote to USG. "Understanding that dissatisfaction exists, and that remonstrances had been sent to you regarding the appointment of Col Weden ONeal of Covington to the Marshalship of this State, I ask again the appointment to that position. Col. ONeal has not qualified and has telegraphed that he will be here on Monday 13th. It may turn out from the present state of affairs that the Marshals of this and the different states should posses firmness and courage, and with due modesty, I think that I may be allowd to claim a sufficient quantity of both. I am Sir, with great respect—and with more additional respect since your action yesterday, in regard to the counting of the Southern Vote— . . ." ALS, *ibid.*, Records Relating to Appointments. Related papers are *ibid.* On Dec. 16, Clarke wrote to USG. "I most respectfully ask at you hands, the appointment to the position of 'Appraiser of Merchandise' in this city now held by a Mr Howlet. The times demand that all of the Office holders, especially those who obtained their places at your hands should be strong 'Administration' men, through grattitude if nothing else, and from *appearances, and from past actions* I think that our *Custom House* is not filled up with your supporters. As to myself you know me, both through a personal interview which I had with you at Long Branch last September and since then by letters, from which you can judge as to my loyalty to you. Your course since Nov 6th I endorse heartily, and am willing if it becomes necessary to take my gun again and support the Government. I again give you Mrs L M. Porter as reference. Col Weden Oneal, U. S. Marshal told me a few hours ago 'that I was at liberty to use his name as an endorsement, and if you think it necessary, you can correspond, or refer to him upon the subject in regard to me. His reasons for not giveing me a written endorsement to send with this, were, that you might consider him as officious, and he gave me leave to mention what I have' I am certain that if you give me this appointment I will have to fight all of the 'Bristow element' here, who will do all they can to make my confirmation by the Senate impossible. . . ." ALS, *ibid.*, RG 56, Appraiser of Customs Applications. On Feb. 27, 1877, Clarke telegraphed to USG. "Give me appointment vacated by the removal of C Adams" Telegram received, OFH. No appointment followed.

On Nov. 22, 1876, Weden Oneal, Louisville, had written to Taft returning his commission as marshal, Ky. ALS, DNA, RG 60, Letters Received, Ky. On Dec. 14, USG nominated Oneal as marshal, Ky. On Feb. 5, 1877, USG withdrew Oneal and nominated Fry.

See *Louisville Courier-Journal*, Feb. 7, 1877. On Feb. 17, Oneal wrote to USG. "Since you, did me, the kindness to appoint me, U S Marshal, for the Dist of Ky. I think I can, say without fear of contradiction that I have discharged the duties promptly, faithfully and efficiently And, that no act of mine has ever been inconsistent with true friendship to you, and your Administration, it is certainly well known all over Ky. that I have always been a true staunch and ardent supporter of your administration. And, it is just as well known, that all the opposition that has been urged against me, comes from those who were supporters of or in sympathy with, what I have, always characterized as the Bristow Conspiracy against your administration—..." ALS, DNA, RG 60, Letters from the President. On Feb. 27, USG withdrew Fry and again nominated Oneal as marshal, Ky.

On Jan. 19, USG had nominated John E. Hamilton as U.S. attorney, Ky., to replace Finley. On Jan. 22, White wrote to USG. "You will please allow me to say that, in my opinion, the effort made to remove H. F. Finley U. S. Dist. Atty. for Kentucky is one for the sole purpose of securing the appointment of a Mr. Hamilton in his stead. I am sure there is no good cause for Finley's removal, and I think I know whereof I speak. Finley is an honest, noble gentleman a faithful republican and ever has been a friend to the Administration. It will be approved by all your friends in south-eastern Kentucky if it shall please you to with-draw the name of Hamilton and allow Finley to remain." ALS, *ibid.* See Walter Evans to White, Dec. 24, 1876, *ibid.* On Feb. 2, 1877, White telegraphed to USG. "I learn that complaint is made because Finley did not let a telegram from me to him remain at the attorney general's Office. The following is a copy of it—which was by accident left with Finley's papers for atty general to get an abstract—to wit: Hon S F Finley Louisville Ky. Confirmation a trick the President has locked up commission till you are heard, signed J. D. White January 25th noon 1877. You will remember Mr President that confirmation was to be delayed if you requested it in writing you did so—but the confirmation was not delayed. You then promised to withhold commission till Finley should be heard. I sincerely thank you for so doing for I feel that Mr Finley has fully vindicated himself." Telegram received, *ibid.*, RG 107, Telegrams Collected (Bound).

To James N. Tyner

Long Branch, N. J.
Sept. 4th /76

Hon. J. N. Tyner;
Postmaster Gen.,
Dear Sir:

Before leaving Washington I intended to speak to you in behalf of a young man running on the cars between—I think—Cleveland and Sandusky, Ohio, as postal clerk, by the name of Jones. He is a brother of Senator Jones, and is doing probably the first work of his life to earn a cent. He is much younger than any other member of the family, and has therefore been petted all his life, and has scarcely any thought of providing for himself. The salary of his position is no object to his family, but the education to do some thing is of value, and his brothers, particularly the Senator, will esteem it a great favor if you will advance him if his record will justify such a course.

I wish you would look into

Copy (incomplete), USGA. Frederick K. Jones continued as railway post office clerk.

On Sept. 9, 1876, a correspondent spoke with Jesse Root Grant, Jr., and Julia Dent Grant at their Long Branch residence before discussing politics, Indian hostilities, and future plans with USG, who said that Republican defeats in Ohio and Ind. would mean Democratic presidential nominee Samuel J. Tilden was "as good as elected. . . . The great danger of allowing the democratic party to obtain control in all the branches of the government that I see is that they would temporarily bankrupt the country. . . . By allowing Southern war claims and damages for property destroyed during the war amounting to millions and millions, and by pensioning off the Confederate soldiers. . . . On what possible plea? Because they will claim that these men fought honestly as American citizens for an honest purpose and in as good a spirit as the Northern soldiers who have been pensioned, and that they were provoked and driven into the war by the North. There would even be danger that the claims for the value of slaves would be considered and paid. . . . Crook is undoubtedly our best Indian fighter, and I feel convinced that he will finally settle the Sioux as he did the Idahos. We had no more trouble with the Idahos after he whipped them, and so we shall have no more trouble with the Sioux after the present campaign. . . . Crook is not going to put himself into a position where he can be whipped. He is a prudent man. But now that the cold weather will soon begin the Indians will find it impossible to find sustenance for their ponies, and will have to sue for terms. Crook is going to do with the Indians as I did with Lee. when I got after him, and when I did not give him time to repair damages. . . . The only danger I see now is that the Sioux may turn upon the miners in the Black Hills and destroy them. I don't know whether they are strong enough for that, but they may be. . . . There is no doubt that a vast quantity of gold exists. A few days before I left Washington Governor Edmunds, of Dakota, who is a brother of Senator Edmunds, of Vermont, showed me specimens of the gold found, and from what he said I became convinced that gold exists in the Black Hills in large quantities. According to Governor Edmunds' reports there is not so much placer gold as there is quartz gold. When the mines shall have been thoroughly explored as much gold will be found there as in California. . . . I should advise people to stay away until the present troubles are over and until we have extinguished the titles of the Indians to the lands which they sold by treaty. This treaty was not a wise one. We shall regain the title to the land by treating with the friendly Indians and taking no notice of the hostile savages. . . . I shall go to Europe, but I shall have no set programme and go just where I like. When I go to a place I shall stay there just as long as I like and take my time leisurely. . . . I shall be very glad to travel quietly. . . ." The correspondent asked USG where he would live upon his return from overseas. "If I had my free choice I suppose I would say in Washington. I have lived longer in Washington and been more identified with it than with any other city. I have lived there since 1865—eleven years. . . . I have never felt identified with Galena—I only lived there a year. As to New York, my means would not allow me to live there, even if I preferred it. . . . The rent of a first rate house in New York, in the best locality, would be as much as I could live for in Washington. In Washington the only item of great expensiveness consists of entertainments, and these a man can limit according to his means and pleasure. I suppose I shall settle in Washington. I feel at home there. I feel more identified with it than any other city. . . ." Asked what prompted the removal of Marshall Jewell as postmaster gen., USG replied. "There are a great many things of which no exact explanation could be given. I don't know that I could give precisely an explanation of his removal. You select a Cabinet. Well, after a while, you find that you do not like a member's way of doing business: why should you not get rid of him? Not that he does anything wrong, but simply that you don't like his way of doing the business intrusted to him; that's all. I got very tired of Mr. Jewell generally at the Cabinet meetings. I have nothing in the world against Governor Jewell, but I got very tired of him. That's all. . . ." *New York Herald*, Sept. 12, 1876.

To Hamilton Fish

Long Branch, N. J.
Sept. 7th 1876.

DEAR GOVERNOR:

Should not a proclamation be issued declaring the ratification of the Sandwith Islands treaty? and establishing rules thereunder for the receipt of their products? I believe no such proclamation has been issued.

Has any thing been heard from Tweed[1] since his arrival in Spain? If the Spanish Govt. returns him to Cuba, as promised, a Naval vessel should be on the spot to return him to Mr. Tilden who must be very anxious to see him.

Very Truly Yours
U. S. GRANT

HON. HAMILTON FISH, SEC. OF STATE

ALS, DLC-Hamilton Fish. On Sept. 9, 1876, Secretary of State Hamilton Fish, Garrison, N. Y., wrote to USG. "The Proclamation to put the Hawaiian treaty into operation, has been prepared for some time—it must be preceded by a *protocol* signed by the Hawaiian Minister & Secretary of State—this also has been in readiness: awaiting Mr Allen's signature—He left Washington for Maine, immediately on the adjournment of Congress, & was to be in Washington *yesterday*—the protocol may be signed by Mr Hunter as Acting Sec: unless he & Mr Allen prefer to send it to me. The first of October was suggested as the date to be named in the protocol, to allow time for the instructions from the Treasury (which were prepared before I left Washington) to reach the several Collectors, and that the Hawaiian Authorities might also be prepared to admit articles from the U S—under the Treaty—So soon as the Protocol, (which is recited, in words, in the Proclamation) is signed, the Proclamation will be sent to you for signature—your letter of 7th reached me last Evening—About one hour previous to its reception, I received a telegram, announcing from Madrid, the arrest in Spain of 'Secor,' & his companion, and had telegraphed requesting their return &c—& had also written to advise you of the fact—I hope that we shall succeed in delivering the precious rogue to his friend Govr Tilden. Genl Cushing has returned 'on leave'—He came up here yesterday, & speaking of 'Secor,' said that the Spanish Govt would act in good faith if he reached Spain, but doubted whether he would go there—About an hour after Cushing had left: the telegram arrived—Cushing, is a wonderful man for his age—he looks remarkably well, & as young & active as he did fifteen years ago. He talks of going back, on the expiration of his leave, says that the *present* Government of Spain is very kindly affected to the United States—that it expects by the efforts now making to suppress the insurrection in Cuba, during the coming winter, but the question of *finance* makes it doubtful in his judgment, & that if the present efforts fail, & the present administration remains in power, he thinks that they will make overtures to our Government, for a solution of the difficulties—The opposition to the present Government is strong and active—Cushing thinks, however, that the Government will sustain itself in power—But the instability of Spanish politics, is such, that the future, even the future of a single month, or week, is uncertain—I have nothing further from Thornton, on the Extradition question—but as the Cabinet Meetings in London, are held on Saturday it is not improbable that he may receive instructions, to day or tomorrow—I will act upon the authority & approval given in your telegram— . . . P S. A letter, this moment received, from R. M. Douglas, speaks very hopefully of the result in North Carolina—" ALS, USG 3; press, DLC-Hamilton Fish. For negotiations with Great Britain concerning extradition, see message to Congress, Dec. 23, 1876. On July 13 and Aug. 2, Fish had recorded in his diary. "I call the Presidents attention to the non action by the Senate, on the Bill to carry into effect the Hawaiian Treaty and urge him to write to Sen Cameron requesting him to have the bill passed He says he thinks Cameron does not take much interest in it, that he has spoken to him about it and also to Sen Howe who says it will pass but he must not ask his vote for it. I endeavor to impress on the President the importance of getting it through a measure on which the Administration is committed." "The President requested, and I complied, that I should go up to the Senate this morning to endeavor to get some legislation passed for the carrying into effect of the Hawaiian Treaty." DLC-Hamilton Fish. On Aug. 15, USG signed legislation listing allowable imports under a commercial treaty with Hawaii, signed Jan. 30, 1875. See *U.S. Statutes at Large*, XIX, 200; *PUSG*, 26, 42–43. On Sept. 9, 1876, USG proclaimed the treaty in effect. DS, DNA, RG 130, Presidential Proclamations. *Foreign Relations, 1876*, pp. 3–5.

On Feb. 16, 1877, William N. Grier (USMA 1835), Col. Rufus Ingalls, and Maj. William Myers, San Francisco, wrote to USG. "The undersigned having recently made an unofficial visit to the Sandwich Islands, had full opportunities to become acquainted with the principal people there, and to learn their sentiments touching the interests of the Islands as connected with the United States. The present condition of things seems satisfactory; and quite all, from the King down, hope that our present admirable and courteous Minister Resident, the Hon. Henry A. Peirce may long be continued in his present office. Knowing his entire fitness for the place, we take the liberty to address you on the subject, and to suggest that this paper be referred to your successor. We do this without regard to party politics." LS, DNA, RG 59, Applications and Recommendations, Hayes-Arthur. Related papers are *ibid.* President Rutherford B. Hayes replaced Henry A. Peirce as minister to Hawaii with James M. Comly.

1. Born in 1823 in New York City, William M. Tweed served one term as Democratic U.S. Representative from N. Y. (1853–55) before building the prototypical political machine, the notorious "Tweed Ring." Convicted on corruption charges, "Boss" Tweed escaped from a New York City jail in Dec., 1875, and eventually fled to Spain, via Cuba, using the alias John Secor. On Aug. 2 and 7, 1876, Fish recorded in his diary. "I showed the President the telegram received from Hall last night to the effect that Secor had started from Santiago on a Spanish Vessel on the 27th July for Vigo Spain, that Jovallar proposed

telegraphing requesting his return to Cuba if he cannot be Extradited from Spain. The President advises communication with General Cushing on the subject." "Called on the President and showed him telegram from Cushing of 5 August relative to the return of Tweed to Cuba and suggesting that no mention be made in Cabinet except to the Secretary of the Navy which he approved." DLC-Hamilton Fish. On Sept. 8, 11, and 12, Fish wrote to USG. "A telegram from Madrid just now received, announces the arrival, and arrest of 'Secor'—I have telegraphed instructions as to his return, and will communicate with the Navy as soon as I receive definite information." "I have nothing further from Madrid, but the Herald of yesterday had much of the 'Secor' case which must have been obtained from there. Watson Webb is busy in his denunciations and abuse, & falsehood. His trial was, I think, mismanaged, & under the same direction, I fear the same result. Allow me to suggest that a letter from you to the Attorney General, impressing upon him the importance of an *efficient* prosecution of the case may lead to a more thorough prosecution of the case. I have frequently spoken to the Attorney General, but fear that his numerous engagements have prevented an interview between him & the Counsel retained to assist the District Attorney. I understand that the case may be called in October, but it would be better to continue it, for another term of the Court, than allow the trial to be brought on before the Attorney General shall have had a full conference with the Associate Counsel." "The Chargé at Madrid, telegraphs that the fugitives will be returned, & will probably be sent by mail boat to sail on the twentieth from Santander (the cipher is not quite clear as to that name, but I understand it to mean Santander). He says 'it is hinted to me that they would be delivered to a United States vessel, if desired.' He does not say whether this means in Spain, or in Cuba. To send a vessel from the U S. to Spain, at this season, would involve a long passage & delay, unless Mr Robeson has some vessel in the Mediterranean or in the neighbourhood of Spain, to which instructions might be sent by Cable. There would probably be less risk of escape, or of collusion, in case he be delivered to a National vessel in Spain. It is however only Mr Adee's interpretation of a supposed 'hint.' I can, however, if you think it adviseable, ascertain from Secretary of the Navy if he has a vessel available for the purpose of receiving Tweed in Spain & can also instruct Adee to ascertain the real willingness & purpose of the Spanish Government—I shall go to Was[hin]gton in a few days to complete arrangements in this matter—" ALS (press), *ibid.* See letter to Hamilton Fish, Sept. 13, 1876; Nevins, *Fish*, pp. 840–41; Leo Hershkowitz, *Tweed's New York: Another Look* (Garden City, N. Y., 1977), pp. 286–96.

On Jan. 27, 1877, USG wrote to Culver C. Sniffen. "Write a note to the Atty. Gen. asking him to instruct the new Dist. Atty. in New York City—if he has not done so—to push the Webb Case." AN, Wayde Chrismer, Bel Air, Md. On the same day, Fish recorded in his diary. "I spoke to the President of Judge Taft's continual failure, or forgetfulness of business, and instanced the Webb case, which I told him had better be discontinued under his administration, if not brought to trial. . . ." DLC-Hamilton Fish. James Watson Webb, former minister to Brazil, had been accused of bribery and theft stemming from his involvement in the *Caroline* claim. See *PUSG*, 25, 387; Nevins, *Fish*, pp. 642–46; James L. Crouthamel, *James Watson Webb: A Biography* (Middletown, Conn., 1969), pp. 191–93.

Endorsement

Atty. Gn. Rely on the troops now in La. for the present. It may be possible later to send some Colored troops from the plains to that state. Gen. Sherman might be seen about this matter at once if he has not left the city. If he has a telegram might reach him & the Sec. of War.

U. S. GRANT

SEPT. 7TH /76

AES, DNA, RG 60, Letters from the President. *HED*, 44-2-30, 151. Written on a telegram of Sept. 5, 1876, from Stephen B. Packard, U.S. marshal, New Orleans, to James R. Beckwith, U.S. attorney, La., Washington, D. C. "Violence increasing   Ask the Attorney General if the Governor should make call on the President or rely on Attorney General's order troops   Don't fail as to the White or Colored troops" Copy, DNA, RG 60, Letters from the President. *HED*, 44-2-30, 150.

On the same day, Attorney Gen. Alphonso Taft wrote to USG. "Mr S. B. Packard U. S. Marshal for Dis. of La. has sent in his resignation. Senator West, United States Dis. Atty Beckwith, Mr Packard himself and Mr Morey Ex. M. c. join in recommending John Robert Graham Pitkin to be appointed to the vacancy. I cannot doubt but that it is the right thing to do. I send you the recommendation & the resignation. Mr Beckwith who is now here will go to LongBranch Thursday. B. is likely to prove efficient in enforcing law against the election rioters. He appears to be a man of vigor, and a lawyer. I have your letter of yesterday and shall hope to be able to answer to-morrow. I am waiting to hear from White in answer to my letter, and from Finley who telegraphs me that he has written, and that White has also written. Mr Beckwith has just come in with a despatch received from Packard a copy of which I enclose. B. thinks that regiment of colored cavalry, or a portion of it which is on the Indian frontier wd help them through in Louisiana. I sent him and Senator Wells over to talk with General Sherman about it." ALS, CSmH.

Also on Sept. 5, Governor William P. Kellogg of La., Chicago, telegraphed to USG. "I respectfully request the appointment of Whoever Marshal S. B. Packard recommends as his successor" Telegram received, DNA, RG 60, Letters from the President. On Sept. 14, U.S. Senator J. Rodman West of La. wrote to USG, Long Branch. "The General Appraisership of Louisiana, made vacant by the recent appointment of Mr Pitkin as Marshal, could be very worthily and properly bestowed upon Hon: Frank Morey—Permit me to recommend you to appoint Mr Morey; I would prefer that you should do so through a private note to Secretary Morrill with whom I will confer as to the time of making the announcement public." ALS, *ibid.*, RG 56, Appraiser of Customs Applications. USG endorsed this letter. "Approved but suggest that no apt. be made until after the Oct. elections." AE (undated), *ibid.* No appointment followed.

On Sept. 12, Henry T. Crosby, chief clerk, War Dept., had telegraphed to Secretary of War James D. Cameron, Denver. "Following received from the President. If it is possible to spare Colonel Grierson from where he is I wish he with as many companies of his regiment as can be spared be sent to Shreveport, Louisiana, the troops to be distributed afterwards as circumstances may demand. U. S. GRANT. Please telegraph instructions." LS (telegram sent), *ibid.*, RG 107, Telegrams Collected (Bound). On Sept. 13, Crosby telegraphed to USG. "Orders as to disposition of Colonel Grierson's regiment and appointment of Robert Wasson Paymaster were communicated to Secretary of War by telegraph on receipt. He will probably be at Denver by noon to-day. A telegram to Cheyenne would reach him to-morrow." LS (telegram sent), *ibid.* See letter to James D. Cameron, Sept. 12, 1876. Also on Sept. 13, Wednesday, Cameron telegraphed to USG. "Your dispatch to war Dept about moving grierson is just received here   I had a very full talk with sheridan at st Louis on this general subject & have telegraphed him to write you his views about affairs in that region   After hearing from him it is possible you may change your views as to the propriety of making this move just at present   I will delay further action until I hear from you. I am going up in the mountains tomorrow morning return here friday & start for Cheyenne & Ogden saturday morning." Telegram received, DLC-USG, IB.

On Sept. 14, West wrote to USG. "*Personal* . . . Being unable to pay you a visit I beg leave to submit the following for your consideration—1st The electoral vote of Louisiana may decide the Presidential Contest. 2d There are two U S Senators to be elected. 3d Up to this time the fight has been maintained by our own people without any assistance whatever. 4th The 5th Congressional district, of which Monroe, the scene of the recent murder of Dr Dinkgrave, is the centre contains a voting majority of 9,000 colored men. 5th The White League is more violent and designedly so in that District than any other. It's loss to the Republican party, loses the State. 6th With military protection there of the proper character we can maintain peace, protect our people and carry the State. 7th Grierson, himself a host, with such of his regiment as can be spared from Texas, with head quarters at Monroe, (Augur perhaps giving Grierson a district of No La as a district command) would accomplish all that is desired   8th Genl Sherman's letter with stations of 10th Cavalry is transmitted herewith—Genl S. said that the transfer could be made in two weeks   9th The Adjt Genl could issue the necessary orders on your order to him. 10th It is imagined that any movement of troops to La would damage the Republican campaign in the North. I do not think there is any point in this—this aid is needed now. I am announced to speak early in October throughout North Louisiana, including this district, and feel the great necessity of the aid asked to give confidence to the Republican voters that they will not be interfered with during the canvass. I beg to refer you to Hon. Frank Morey for details and explanations— . . . P. S. It is my opinion that we will fail without Grierson's aid." ALS, USG 3. On the same day, Secretary of the Interior Zachariah Chandler wrote to USG. "Senator West and Representative Frank Morey of Louisana represent such a state of affairs existing in Northern Louisiana that it seems to me necessary that some speedy action be taken to protect unionists and show the rebels of that locality that they cannot ride rough shod over the peaceful law abiding citizens, with impunity, because they happen to have a colored skin, or are identified with the Republican party. The gentlemen above named are desirous that Griersons Regiment of Cavalry—or such portion of it as can be spared be sent to that portion of Louisana and I heartily concur with them in this proposition" LS, *ibid.*

On Sept. 15, Lt. Gen. Philip H. Sheridan, "Phillips' Ranch, Chugwater River," Wyoming Territory, wrote to USG. "While en route to Fort Laramie, I received a despatch from Hon. J. D. Cameron, Secretary of War, desiring me to write to you on the subject of the transfer of Col. Grierson and a portion of the Tenth Cavalry from Texas to Shreveport, Louisiana. At a conference which Mr. Cameron and myself had at St. Louis, his views and mine seemed to coincide on this subject, and we were of the impression that the movement of the six companies of this regiment to Louisiana would not be effectual to secure a fair election there next November, if the white people of that state had made up their minds to carry the state by intimidation and violence. It is my belief that this small force of cavalry—and it is all that can well be sent—would not, by its influence nor by any positions it might occupy, secure fair voting throughout the state. It has been my belief that since the Congresses of 1874 and 1875 weakened, and the decision on the Grant Parish Massacre took place, it is extremely doubtful if any fair election can be had in Louisiana. I therefore thought that no good result could be obtained, unless by the honest action of the Returning Board, whose duty it is to correct fraud when the returns are brought in. These are my views and are probably not worth much, but Mr. Cameron seemed to agree with me. If a change of troops is desired, Gen. Ord, I think, can spare Col. Grierson and six companies of the Tenth Cavalry from Texas to report to Gen. Augur at Shreveport, and the latter can bring into Louisiana three or four companies of infantry from Alabama; and any directions given on the subject will be cheerfully obeyed." Copy, DLC-Philip H. Sheridan. On the same day, Cameron telegraphed to USG. "sheridan telegraphs from cheyenne That six companies of Griersons regiment can be spared if deemed advisable & that he has written to you. I shall do nothing further until I hear from you again   leave here tomorrow saturday for California Via cheyenne" Telegram received (on Sept. 16), DNA, RG 60, Letters from the President.

On Sept. 20, D. G. Aber, Arrow Rock, Mo., wrote to USG. "Will you listin a moment to an humble citizen who is no politician & no partisan? Some wise & forseeing intelligence seems to have placed you at the head of our nation to meet the present critical juncture of affairs. All lovers of our government are called upon to thank God that we have no Buchannon in the Presidential chair now. I am an old citizen of North Louisiana & was acquainted for more than 15 years with judge Crawford, who was assassinnated in 1874, *in* & *for* his efforts to maintain law and order. I also had a son—a youth of only 18 years of age assassinnated by the same Klan in 1868—Aug—in order to control the negro vote at the presidential election & make it all go one way. I state these things that you may see from what stand-point I write. What are we to do when our dearest friends are murdered for political purposes & their murderers must go, not only ~~go~~ untried & unpunished, but be Eulogized & defended? Is not such a government a failure? My dear President, our government at present occupies a criminal position in relation to the negro. But the Southern White Liners & the Bourbon Democracy of the north are more criminal. The only innocent party concerned is the negro. Where, however, the government is in error, the 'White Liner' is correct in *principle*, & *that it is*, which gives them such immense vantage power. Now in order to expose to the world their hypocracy of character, & the true Enormity of their guilt & their selfish ambition, the Republican or governmental party must utter a policy that will test the integrity of their professions of being so white & pure—a policy, on a higher plane, that is more white & pure than they have dreamed of. This will effectually disarm them, & take all animus out of their claims. Then, *they* will be black & the blacks ~~will be~~ white, according to their own definition. I hope my dear sir, that you will give the policy which I have outlined and which I enclose you a thoughtful consideration. I have another article in contemplation which I think will greatly strengthen & enforce this policy upon attention. But the great trouble is I am unknown & my name will give no weight to it. Could you not secure some statesman of acknouledged ability to take hold of the subject & discuss it from a different stand-point? Another Congress will assemble before your term expires. Much might be done before you retire. Will you have the kindness to acknouledge the receipt of this communication?" ALS, *ibid.* Aber enclosed a clipping of his article, "The African Race: Its Nationalization Within the United States" (*St. Louis Republican*, Aug. 17, 1876), which argued that the races were incompatible and advocated the resettlement of blacks in Mexico and Africa.

On Oct. 3, West, Delta, La., wrote to USG. "Permit me to submit to you briefly my convictions of the prospect of political affairs in this state   Every colored man in the State will vote the Republican ticket and sincerely desires to do so, if he shall be permitted to ~~do so~~ by the White Line Democracy. This Democracy is organized with as much method and discipline as were the armies of the Confederacy—is animated with as much hatred of Republicanism and is determi'd to succeed by violence—The Republican vote cannot be brought out unless some military forces are sent into this region, upon whom the colored people can rely for protection. Unless Grierson and his command reach the northern part of the state by the 20th of this month, you may give up Louia to Tilden   I am on a stumping tour all through the northern parishes—my hearers believe, but their faith will be of

little avail unless they can manifest it by their votes" ALS, DNA, RG 60, Records Relating
to Appointments. *HED,* 44-2-30, 151.

On Oct. 17, John R. G. Pitkin, U.S. marshal, New Orleans, wrote to USG. "I venture
to communicate my earnest conviction that a critical juncture is imminent in Louisiana.
The temper of the aggressive element in her Democracy is sullen and portends mischief.
The original Democratic plan of the Campaign, (Document 1) revealed in a confidential
circular which came surreptitiously to my hands, was after several murders of Republicans, modified by instructions from the Democratic State Committee, as will appear by
Document 2. It was apparent upon the issue of the latter circular that the intemperate element of the Democracy was premature in its atrocities, and it is equally apparent now that
the violent purpose simply stands adjourned till on or just before the day of election, when
troops may not be forewarned to be within reach to interpose in troublous sections. I conceive that an increase of military force, to be apportioned in detachments in different parts
of the state, is absolutely vital to discourage attempts at violence not only just before and
on election-day, but also for a period after election-day, during which period the violent elements, chagrined at the defeat of their party by a fair election, will be almost certain to
quicken anew the old vicious tumult, and repeat their 14th of September 1874 *coup d'etat.*
It is but just to add that there is a large conservative element in the anti-Republican organization, but it is so far subject to the same despotism from which Republicans suffer,
that it dare not openly condemn violence, from which in the recoil that element suffers in
its every material interest. Many of this element—and as a native here I am thoroughly
familiar with the shades of public sentiment—will quietly vote for Mr Packard in the hope
of his election, but they dare not imperil their status by overtly denouncing Democratic
murders and intimidation. The seeming moment of Louisiana to the National interests,
whether considered with reference to the electoral college, to the two U. S. Senators to be
elected by her Assembly in January next, to the members of the lower house of Congress
or with reference to the policy (and local desire) to present our full honest figure of a majority as a final piece of testimony as to the exact justice of the course of the Administration in reference to the Kellogg-McEnery issue,—impels me to address you this communication, which will be handed you by Hon. J. R. West." ALS, DNA, RG 60, Letters from
the President. *HED,* 44-2-30, 151. The enclosures are *ibid.,* pp. 152–54.

On Oct. 23, Pitkin telegraphed to USG. "Entrance effected in State House at midnight important election records stolen but recaptured custodian gagged two policemen
dangerously wounded evidence Points direct to Democratic Committee two Prominent
democrats Caught Secreted in Corrider & Now in durance being baffled Democratic leaders & Prints Charge radical trick." Telegram received (at 6:10 P.M.), DNA, RG 60, Letters
from the President. *HED,* 44-2-30, 154.

On Oct. 27, Pitkin telegraphed to Chandler. "Unless attorney General allows my requisition for seventy five hundred dolls for special deputies Impossible to preserve peace &
purity of ballot in this turbulent city. acting atty Genl Smith in absence of atty Genl declines to honor my requisition answer" Telegram received (at 2:34 P.M.), DNA, RG 60,
Letters from the President. On Oct. 28, USG endorsed this telegram. "Referred to Act.
Atty. Gen. with the suggestion that a dispatch be forwarded to Atty. Gen. to ascertain
whether it would be legal to grant the requisition referred to and if he would approve it.
Notify U. S. Marshal of La. of the reply." AES, *ibid.*

On Oct. 31, Cameron wrote to Sheridan. "There are grave reasons for anticipating
that owing to the excitement incident to the coming election, the Board of Canvassers or
Legal Returning Board in Louisiana may be prevented by force or intimidation from performing their proper functions. The President therefore directs that you advise yourself
thoroughly of the facts in the premises, and that you be prepared to protect this Board, if

necessary, in the proper exercise of their legal duties, by the Officers and soldiers under your command." Copy, *ibid.*, RG 107, Letters Sent, Military Affairs. See Joseph G. Dawson III, *Army Generals and Reconstruction: Louisiana, 1862–1877* (Baton Rouge, 1982), pp. 227–34.

Endorsement

Will the Postmaster Gn. please examine the charge that Massey is not a supporter or friend of republican administration, and if true appoint Mr. McLean [1] to his place.

U. S. GRANT

SEPTR 7TH /76

AES, DNA, RG 56, Applications. Written on an undated letter from Wilmer McLean to USG. "I understood your endorsement of my application for a position in the Treasury Mailing Room, made the day before you left Washington, as peremptory upon the Department. They however do not so construe it, and I am still without the place, my application having been placed *on file*, and *no disposition* being shown to advance it, I have therefore withdrawn it, that I might send it to you, for you to make it peremptory, if such was your intention, as I clearly understood it to be. You know my position, and how I have sustained your administration" ALS, *ibid.* In [*Aug., 1876*], McLean had written to USG. "I respectfully request the appointment to the position in the Mailing Room of the Treasury Department now held by E. W Massey." ALS (undated), *ibid.* On Aug. 18, USG endorsed this letter. "I endorse this application understanding that the present occupant is not entitled to recognition under this administration." AES, *ibid.* On Aug. 19, John S. Mosby, Washington, D. C., wrote to USG. "I would be greatly obliged if you would ORDER our friend Major McLean to be appointed in the Treasury. He has always been a faithful friend of yours & is very destitute. There are a number in the Treasury appointed by influences hostile to you & who are personally unfit to hold their places. Major McLean is perfectly competent to fill any one of them—" ALS, *ibid.* On the same day, USG wrote. "I endorse this application understanding that Mr Massey has no calims to consideration under this administration" Copy, *ibid.* A clerk endorsed the docket. "Employed in Printing Bu. from Sept. 20 /76" E, *ibid.* As of Sept. 30, 1877, McLean and E. W. Massey served as customs inspectors at Alexandria and Old Point, Va., respectively.

1. Born in 1814 in Alexandria, Wilmer McLean was a merchant in 1853 when he married Virginia H. Mason, a widow, and settled on her plantation near Manassas. Forced to move after the First Battle of Bull Run, the McLeans eventually settled in Appomattox Court House, where their home was used for the surrender on April 9, 1865. See Frank P. Cauble, *Biography of Wilmer McLean* (Lynchburg, Va., 1987).

On April 6, 1871, James Longstreet, surveyor of customs, New Orleans, wrote to USG. "I take great pleasure in recommending my friend Wilmer McLean of Va for the Office of Marshall of his State. I have known Mr McLean many years and believe that I can recommend him with entire safety as reliable gentleman and well suited to the duties of the office; and worthy of your entire confidence as a friend." ALS, DNA, RG 60, Records

Relating to Appointments. On Jan. 6, 1872, Jeremiah Morton, Mitchell's Station, Culpeper County, Va., wrote to USG. "Major W. McLean is desirous to obtain the appointment of Marshall of the Eastern District of Virginia. He is a gentleman of good sense, high integrity, urbane manners and fine address. Think he would make a valuable and popular officer. Few man in the state, have *more* or *warmer friends*. He was an old whig, and is 'to the manor born'. The expulsion of 'carpet baggers', and the giving appointments to *native citizens*, would be *justice* & *sound policy*" ALS, *ibid.* On Jan. 23, McLean, Manassas, wrote to Orville E. Babcock. "In leaving you on Friday last, I omitted to hand you the enclosed letter from the Hon. Senator Lewis, which you will do me the favour of placeing with those left with you. Seeing you so much pressed, I thought it best to defer my conversation to some future day, when I shall be most happy to confer with you on the subject. (with your approbation.) In makeing this application, I hope that you will understand that it not with the desire to transplant the present occupant, but supposeing that the President would elivate him to a higher position, as he is a worthy Gentleman, and a good Officer. The object is to build up the Administrations power in the State, which would be done by appointing to office, Old line Whigs, to the manor born, within her borders. I am confidant, and am assured by the most prominent Gentlemen in the State, that if General Grant will addopt this course, he can gather around him, a party that will carry the State in the next election, and would have done so in the last, if he had of carried out this plan in the beginning. I do hope, My Dear Friend, (do not consider it arrogance) will do all in his power, to aid me in my claim before His Excellency, the Presidnt. who has made me Historical, and now if he will make me more comfortable, it will make a worthy family happy. . . . Please pardon me, if I have asked too much of you." ALS, *ibid.* U.S. Senator John F. Lewis of Va. had written to USG. "Mr McLean has shown me an application for the position of Marshall, for the Eastern Dist of Virginia, which he intends to submit to Your Excellency—I am *sure*, that the policy of appointing natives, (such as have maintained their allegiance to the Govt) to fill the offices in the State of Virginia, would have resulted in giving us, (the republicans) the control of the state by a very large majority. Where we have gained one vote by the appointment of an officer, coming from another State, we have repelled five, or six, and I have almost despaired of success, in Virginia. But allow me to say that, I am not of the number who believe that a *majority* of the old Whigs will unite with us, some of the most bitter rebels in Va were old Union whigs, and are rebels still. I do not write this in opposition to Mr Parker, who is, as I believe, a good Officer, & a gentleman. And if all the appointments, of men from other States, had been as accommodating, & honest as he, there would have been less reason for complaint, on the part of our people—When I say I have almost despaired of making Va a Republican State, I do not mean to intimate, that I have the *least* idea, of ceasing to war upon the rebel democracy, this I will continue to my lifes end." ALS (undated), *ibid.* On May 22, McLean wrote to Lewis. "With unfeigned reluctance I again write, to try and enlist your influance for me, with the President. He has seen my papers ere this, as Gen. Babcock kindly promised me to hand them to him. If you would only interest yourself a little in my behalf, I am confidant much will be accomplished. I am sure I can do more for the Administration than the present Marshall. . . . I have entertained at my House at Appomattox, and Manassas, over three hundred Northern Gentlemen and strange to say, almost without an exception, they were much in favour of the President giving me an appointment. He has handed my name down to posterity, but forgotten to send a little prosperity with it. If you please, say to the President, (for me) he knows the value of a good Recruiting Officer, and when I buckle on my Armour, he will say well done. . . ." ALS, *ibid.* Related papers are *ibid.* In 1873, McLean was appointed Internal Revenue gauger, Manassas.

To James D. Cameron

Long Branch, N. J.
Sept. 12th 1876.

Dear Sir:

The papers this a. m. announce the death of Maj. Seward,[1] of the pay Department. To prevent pressure for applicants for the vacant place you may appoint—and announce it, Robt. Wasson, of Iowa, but at this time in Japan.

Yours &c.

U. S. Grant

The Sec. of War.

ALS, DNA, RG 94, ACP, 2871 1871. On Sept. 13, 1876, Secretary of War James D. Cameron telegraphed to Henry T. Crosby, chief clerk, War Dept. ". . . Make out Wasson's appointment as Paymaster. Will send instructions about Grierson after communicating with the President." Copy, *ibid.* See letter to Edward D. Townsend, Sept. 14, 1876.

On June 21, James R. Wasson, Tokyo, had written to USG. "I have the honor to enclose herewith a copy of a letter which I have just received from the office of the 2nd Auditor, by which I am informed of a charge against me on the books of that office of $187 50 on account of an alleged overpayment made to me as 2nd Lieutenant in the 4th Cavalry for the months of October, November and December 1871. during which time it is stated that I was only entitled to half pay, being on leave of absence. Your Excellency will perhaps remember the circumstances of the case; and that, while I was absent in Japan during those months, I was under the orders of Genl Schofield during that period, as will appear from the orders of which I enclose copies—and that, also, I was on duty for the Navy Department during that time—And that on my return I was informed by your Excellency and likewise by the Secretary of War that it would be considered that I that I was on duty for the whole of that time, and that I would be entitled therefore to full pay. In accordance with these verbal instructions I drew the pay—but owing to some apparent informality the above charge appears—A word from Your Excellency to the Adjutant General would cause the record to be corrected, and would relieve me from the appearance of having attempted to defraud the Government out of a petty sum of money. If it is not too much to ask, I would beg of your Excellency to have the kindness to do me this favor—I am emboldened to ask you to take this trouble in my behalf by the many acts of kindness for which I have to thank your Excellency in the past, and hoping you will pardon the liberty . . ." ALS, DNA, RG 94, ACP, 2871 1871.

1. Maj. Augustus H. Seward (USMA 1847), son of William H. Seward, died Sept. 11. On the same day, Brig. Gen. Benjamin Alvord, paymaster gen., wrote to USG. "*Personal* . . . I have received the very painful news of the death of Paymaster *A. H. Seward* at Montrose, Westchester Co. N. Y. Pray allow me to express a hope that you will at once fill the vacancy.—I want very much to send another Paymaster to St Paul where Col Seward was stationed. You will excuse me for re-iterating that I shall also be pleased to have another

vacancy made by the retirement of Major V. C. Hanna Paymaster. If you shall be willing to hear my own recommendation, I ~~will~~ recommend that Mr. *Robert Swartwout* of Santa Fe N. M. now there as Paymaster's Clerk, be appointed to one of these vacancies— . . ." ALS, *ibid.*, Applications for Positions in War Dept. Related papers are *ibid.* Robert Swartwout continued as paymaster's clerk, Santa Fé. On June 21, Alvord had written to USG. "I recommend the retirement of *Major V. C. Hanna* Paymaster who was 62 years of age last September. He has been at Detroit sick since Sept. 1874 having had a partial stroke of paralysis at Santa Fé—He has done very good service, but ought now to be retired." ALS, *ibid.*, ACP, 4889 1873. On Jan. 11, 1877, USG nominated Alexander Sharp as paymaster in place of Maj. Valentine C. Hanna, retired. On Jan. 26, U.S. Senator Simon Cameron of Pa. telegraphed to USG. "Doctor Sharp is confirmed:" Telegram received, *ibid.*, RG 107, Telegrams Collected (Bound). On Feb. 26, USG signed a surety bond for Sharp. DS, *ibid.*, RG 39, Surety Bonds of Officials.

Endorsement

Returned to the Sec. of State. I have no one in mind for the place spoken of within. I will approve the apt. of either of the three gentlemen mentioned in the letter which inclosed this

U. S. GRANT

SEPT. 12TH /76

AES, DLC-Hamilton Fish. Written on a letter of Aug. 11, 1876, from Elbert E. Farman, consul gen., Cairo, to Secretary of State Hamilton Fish. ALS, *ibid.* On Sept. 7, Fish, Garrison, N. Y., wrote to USG, Long Branch. "I enclose a letter from Mr Farman, our Consul General & Agent in Egypt, on the subject of the appointment of another Judge, for the Courts in that Country—It is desireable that we should be fully represented in those Courts—but it may be difficult to find the person who will combine the requisites of high personal character & integrity—of professional capacity—& of competent familiarity with either the French or Italian languages—I am not quite sure what is the Compensation which the Egyptian Governmt allows. I think however, that it is six thousand dollars. I know of no person whom I can suggest for the appointment—unless possibly it be Mr Farman himself, & with regard to him, I do not know that his familiarity with the languages is sufficient—Unless you have some one in view, I submit whether it would be well to telegraph to Farman to enquire whether he feels himself competent to undertake the duties—I think that he would answer conscienciously—Henry Vignaud, now Second Secretary of Legation in Paris, has, I think, *all the qualifications required*—whether he would be willing to leave Paris for Egypt may be doubtful. Benjamin Gerrish now Consul at Bordeaux is a very intelligent man, thoroughly familiar with the French language, but I do not know how much of a Lawyer he may be—this can be ascertained by enquiry of some parties in New Hampshire. Will you be kind enough to give me your instructions on this point, & to return Mr Farmans letter—The appointment must be made, if at all, before the 15th of October—" ALS, USG 3; press, DLC-Hamilton Fish. No appointment followed. See *Foreign Relations, 1877*, pp. 614–23.

On March 23, 1874, USG had signed an act "to authorize the President to accept for citizens of the United States the jurisdiction of certain tribunals in the Ottoman dominions, and Egypt, . . ." *U.S. Statutes at Large*, XVIII, part 3, p. 23. In [*July*], U.S. Representative Charles R. Thomas of N. C. *et al.* petitioned USG. "The undersigned respectfully reccommend Victor C. Barringer Esqr of North Carolina, as a fit person to be designated, on behalf of the United States, for the judicial appointment by the Government of the Sublime Porte, or that of Egypt, . . . Mr Barringer held the appointment of Attorney General of No. Ca. in 1869; & more recently has served on a Commission to Revise & Codify the U. S. Statutes." LS (6 signatures; docketed July 30), DNA, RG 59, Letters of Application and Recommendation. Established in 1875 to replace the judicial functions of ministers and consuls in cases involving foreigners in Egypt, the so-called mixed courts, staffed by foreign and Egyptian judges, consisted of an upper appeals court at Alexandria and three lower district courts. Victor C. Barringer represented the U.S. on the upper court; George S. Batcheller served on the district court at Cairo. See Jasper Yeates Brinton, *The Mixed Courts of Egypt* (New Haven, 1930), pp. 71–73, 392–95.

On Oct. 29, 1874, USG had issued a proclamation pursuant to section 2 of the March 23 act, "to accept the recent law of the Ottoman Porte ceding the right of foreigners possessing immovable property in said dominions." DS, DNA, RG 130, Presidential Proclamations. On March 27, 1876, USG issued a proclamation in accordance with the first section of the act, recognizing the jurisdiction of the mixed courts and suspending the judicial powers of U.S. diplomats. DS, *ibid. Foreign Relations, 1876*, pp. 1–2.

To Hamilton Fish

Long Branch, N. J.
Sept. 13th /76

DEAR GOVERNOR:

I think it will be advisable to ascertain if the Spanish authorities propose to give "Secor" up in Spain, and if so if there is a Naval Vessel handy to take charge of him.—The Sec. of the Navy has not yet come to the Branch and probably will not until the last of this week. Otherwise I would ascertain myself whether a vessel is convenient to take charge of the prisoner.

The Herald is very anxious to learn whether it is true that Tweed is to be used as a witness against Tilden in a suit to recover funds due the Govt.[1]

Very Truly Yours
U. S. GRANT

HON. HAMILTON FISH, SEC. OF STATE

ALS, DLC-Hamilton Fish. See letter to Hamilton Fish, Sept. 7, 1876. On Sept. 16, 1876, Secretary of State Hamilton Fish, Garrison, N. Y., telegraphed to USG. "I go to Washington tonight—Have telegraphed and written in accordance with your letter of thirteenth, and will carry out your views—" ALS (press), DLC-Hamilton Fish. On Sept. 20, Fish wrote to USG, care of Anthony J. Drexel, Philadelphia. "I enclose a copy of a despatch from Mr Washburne (marked 'confidential' by him) in reply to an enquiry wh you desired to have made, for Mr Keogh, respecting certain cotton transactions of Govr Vance. A telegram from Mr Adee received last night states that arrangements for delivery of Secor were formally completed yesterdy. He is to be delivered at Vigo. I have seen Commodore Howell, this morning, and arranged with him that orders be telegraphed to the Franklin, (which is expected to arrive to day, at Gibraltar,) to proceed to Vigo, and receive the illustrious American traveller—" ALS (press), *ibid.* See Endorsement, Aug. 7, 1876. Also on Sept. 20, Fish wrote to Commodore John C. Howell, act. secretary of the navy. ". . . On arrival of the vessel at New York it is desirable that no communication with the ship, or those on board be allowed until orders shall have been recd as to the disposition to be made of Secor. . . ." ADf, DLC-Hamilton Fish.

On Oct. 6, Fish, Garrison, wrote to USG. "Tweed may arrive in New York any time about the latter part of this month, & the question arises, 'what will we do with him'? We may either I deliver him to the Sheriff of New York, from whose custody he escaped, while held under a *Civil* suit—II. deliver him to the District Attorney of New York, on a Bench Warrant, under the Criminal charges pending against him—III. place him at the disposal of the Governor of New York—My own judgment, is that the last, is the proper and best course to pursue—It is in accordance with the general practice of the Federal Government, to deal with the Authorities of the States, rather than with local or Municipal Authorities—then too,—it is a New York question; & the Head of the Government of that State should decide it—or at least, have the opportunity to decide it, if he chooses so to do—if he decides, then the responsibility as to what becomes of Tweed is removed from the President—if he refuse or omit to decide then you may be obliged to assume the decision, but will be relieved of criticism in your decision, by having made the offer to the Governor—I have conferred with Mr Phelps, the District Attorney of New York, and he is decidedly of opinion that the most adviseable course, is to place Tweed, on his arrival, at the disposal of the Governor of New York—I have drafted a letter to the Governor, for submission, in case you approve this course: and have written to Mr Cadwalader, requesting him to submit it to you. Should you however think either of the other courses preferable, instructions will be prepared accordingly." ALS, DNA, RG 59, Miscellaneous Letters; press, DLC-Hamilton Fish. On Oct. 7, USG endorsed this letter. "The surrender of Tweed to the Gov.r of nNew York—the 3d suggestion—is approved." AES, DNA, RG 59, Miscellaneous Letters. See John L. Cadwalader to Fish, Oct. 7, 1876, Fish to Thurlow Weed, Oct. 20, 1876, DLC-Hamilton Fish. On Oct. 17, Fish recorded in his diary. "General Sharpe Surveyor of the Port of New York called on me this morning at Glenclyffe as he said by request of the President to speak with reference to the expected arrival of Tweed in N. Y. He dwelt on the importance of the Federal Officials having an opportunity to examine his papers before they might be passed into the hands of the State Authorities That Geo Bliss had told him that there was a Statute of the United States, under which the federal government might make complaint for the misrepresentation of citizenship. I told him what instructions had been issued which embrace the exclusion of all persons from on board ship until Tweed should be surrendered in accordance with the Presidents instruction and in pursuance of a request from the Governor of New York into the hands of the Sheriff that his personal effects alone were to be given up to him that, that they were to be examined by the U S District Attorney (Bliss) the District Attorney of New York (Phelps) and an officer of the customs whose inspection would be confined to seeing that no dutiable articles were intoduced, that it was understood that certain packages had been seized by the Spanish Authorities and sealed and delivered on board the Franklin which were supposed might contain papers of importance that these would be retained for examination within the Federal Jurisdiction of the District Attorney of the United States and the District Attorney of NewYork. . . . As to the Presidents having suggested his coming I do not believe a word of it but that Mr Bliss, who is good for nothing as a lawyer but simply goods as a detective and general mischief maker had wished to have his fingers in the pie and had induced Sharpe to see the President and suggest Bliss' great discovery and propose an interview with me that between them they might flatter themselves or persuade the public of their importaneet services in the matter. Sharpe who I think is a good fellow evidently seemed mortified that he had been made use of on a bootless errand professing to make suggestions on a subject of which they really knew but little." DLC-Hamilton Fish. On Oct. 24, John L. Cadwalader, act. secretary of state, recorded in Fish's diary. "Mr Robeson asked, by President's direction for a copy of Tilden's letter, as to Tweed, evidently for political purposes—I asked the President and he said, yes, but he had told him not to publish it until the Secretary of State made correspondence public.—I ordered it sent." *Ibid.* See Fish to Governor Samuel J. Tilden of N. Y., ADf (press, undated) and copy, Oct. 9, 1876, Fish to Cadwalader, Oct. 9, 14, 1876, Cadwalader to Fish, Oct. 19, 1876, Fish to George M. Robeson, [*Oct.-Nov., 1876*], *ibid.*

On Nov. 1 and 3, Fish recorded in his diary. "I also read a letter from A. M. Young Consul at St Diago de Cuba dated Higginsport 29 October tendering his resignation to take effect after the time of its receipt and requesting that the President be notified as he is one of his bondsmen. The President expressed great surprise at this statement saying he had not conciously signed any such instrument, that if his name appears on it it had been put there without his knowledge of its nature. He says Mr Cadwalader had explained to him the charges against Young and had read Mr Halls 2 letters to him on the subject. I tell him Young has been requested to come to the Department it being our intention to interrogate him upon his supposed connection with Tweed at San Diago, that I supposed that it was this notice which has excited his suspicion and induced his resignation, that before accepting it I thought it would be advisable to await the arrival of Tweed and possibly his passport might show whether it had been visaed by the Consul and if so I thought he should be dismissed instead of his resignation being accepted, in which the President concurred." "Reverting to the tender of the resignation of A. R. Young Consul at San Diago de Cuba and who stated the President was one of his bondsmen I told him as he had supposed J R. Grant was on the bond but not himself he replied then the man lies, it is an additional reason for removing him and not accepting his resignation." *Ibid.* On Nov. 29, Fish wrote to USG. "I send herewith for signature the suspension of Mr A. N. Young, Consul at Santiago de Cuba. Mr Young called upon me this morning and during the interview his complicity in the escape of Tweed was fully established. Among other things it was ascertained that he applied to and obtained from the Spanish authorities in Cuba a passport for Tweed under a false name previous to his escape from the Island." Copy, DNA, RG 59, Reports to the President and Congress. Fish's interview with Alfred N. Young is described in an undated memorandum, DLC-Hamilton Fish. See *PUSG*, 20, 273.

On Nov. 28, USG authorized Caleb Cushing, U.S. minister, Madrid, to negotiate an extradition treaty. LS, DNA, RG 84, Spain, Instructions. A draft treaty is *ibid.* On Jan. 25, 1877, USG wrote to the Senate transmitting a treaty for ratification. Copies, *ibid.*, RG 130, Messages to Congress; (dated Jan. 26), *ibid.*, RG 59, Reports to the President and Congress. On Feb. 9, the Senate ratified this treaty. On Feb. 19, USG authorized Fish to exchange ratifications, proclaimed on Feb. 21. DS, DLC-Hamilton Fish.

1. On Sept. 13, 1876, a correspondent had reported from Long Branch that USG's "attention being called to the story in this morning's HERALD regarding rumors that Tweed was to be used by the government as a witness against Governor Tilden, the President, with considerable earnestness of tone and manner, said:—'I have not even heard such an idea suggested,' and he gave these reports an emphatic denial." *New York Herald,* Sept. 14, 1876.

On Oct. 27, Fish recorded in his diary concerning Secretary of the Treasury Lot M. Morrill. "Before the other Members of the Cabinet had appeared he read to the President and myself confidentially a letter from Geo Bliss U. S Attorney for New York addressed to the Commissioner of Internal Revenue with relation to Gov Tildens Income Tax stating generally that he had satisfactory evidence of the receipt of Tilden of various large fees greatly in excess of the amount on which he had paid tax during the years in which those fees had respectively been received. He thinks the letter had been written for the purpose of publication that it could only be published in Washington by his authority. The President and myself both think that he should not be called on to assume the responsibility of its. Mr Morrill added that Mr Bliss might allow it to be published in New York if he saw fit to do so." DLC-Hamilton Fish. See *New York Times,* Oct. 28, 30, 1876.

To Alphonso Taft

Dated LONG BRANCH N. J. SEPT 13TH *1876*
To ATTY. GENERAL WASHN D. C.
I think it advisable to notify W. B. Redman that his appointment as marshal Southern district of Mississippi is suspended & Mr Lake that he will be continued unless he is otherwise advised.

U. S. GRANT

Telegram received, DNA, RG 60, Letters from the President. On Sept. 13, 1876, Attorney Gen. Alphonso Taft wrote to USG, Long Branch. "I enclose herewith an order suspending W. B. Redmond, U. S. Marshal for the Southern District of Missi[s]sippi. On receiving notice that the order has been signed I will inform Mr. Redmond of his suspension and cause the commission of Mr. Lake to be forwarded for your signature." Copy, *ibid.,* Letters Sent to Executive Officers. On Sept. 18, H. R. Ware, Jackson, Miss., telegraphed to USG. "Redmond is the Choice of Republicans of the state for marshal of this District with him they are active & hopeful of success while the Reinstatement of Lake would paralyze the party throughout the state" Telegram received (on Sept. 19), *ibid.,* Records Relating to Appointments. Born in New Orleans, William B. Redmond had served as private, C.S. Army, and deputy revenue collector. In June, 1876, Redmond and Ware, Jackson, testified on political unrest in Miss. See *SRC,* 44-1-527, I, 73–86, II, 1215–43.

On Jan. 28, 1875, Miss. Representative M. B. Sullivan had written to USG. "I transmit herewith a copy of Resolutions adopted in the Joint Republican caucus of the Mississippi Legislature, in relation to the office of U. S. Marshal for the Southern Dist. of Mississippi" LS, DNA, RG 60, Records Relating to Appointments. Enclosed are resolutions adopted on Jan. 27 endorsing Redmond for marshal. DS, *ibid.* On Aug. 18, 1876, USG endorsed an undated memorandum urging the removal of John L. Lake, Jr., as marshal and Redmond's appointment. "Referred to the Atty. Gn. approved." AES, *ibid.* On Aug. 19, William M. Hancock, chairman, Republican State Executive Committee, Jackson, wrote to USG. "I write to you in regard to the suspension of Mr. J. L. Lake Jr, as Marshal of the Southern District of Mississippi. In my opinion, it will have a very damaging effect upon our party in this State at the present juncture of the Canvass. He is a Staunch Republican, and worthy gentleman, and I believe can fill the position with as much satisfaction to the Government, and credit to himself as any one in the State. He is the editor and publisher of the 'Times,' published at Jackson, Miss., the only daily Republican paper in this State, and which exercises a vast and controlling influence. His suspension from the office of Marshal will almost certainly cause the suspension of this paper, and at this time would prove very calamitous to our party   The political affairs in this State are in such trepidation, and in such a critical condition, that I am fearful of the bad results of the suspension of Mr. Lake, and I write to you to urge upon you the necessity for the interest of our party for the revocation of the order of suspension, and the reinstatement of Mr. Lake to the position of Marshal. I am confident it will tend much to the success of our party. I think I am as well advised of the condition of this State as any one in it; and of the necessities of our party, and have written to you promptly and frankly. Trusting you may give this a favorable consideration . . ." ALS, *ibid.*, Letters from the President. See *PUSG*, 25, 309; *ibid.*, 26, 315, 325–26.

To AG Edward D. Townsend

Sept. 14th 1876.

DEAR SIR:

Notice may be sent to Mr. Robt. Wasson of his appointment as Maj. in the Pay Dept. U. S. A. without communicating with the Sec. of War. Mr. Wasson is now in Japan, but a communication directed to him, in care of Judge Bingham, U. S. Minister to that country will reach him.

Respectfully &c.

U. S. GRANT

GEN. E. D. TOWNSEND, ADJ. GEN.

ALS, DNA, RG 94, ACP, 2871 1871. Written on the letterhead of "Darling, Griswold & Co., Fifth Avenue Hotel New York." On Sept. 14, 1876, AG Edward D. Townsend telegraphed to USG, Long Branch. "Does your order to appoint Robert Wasson Paymaster refer to James R. Wasson of the class of seventy-one?" LS (telegram sent), DNA, RG 107, Telegrams Collected (Bound); copy, *ibid.*, RG 94, ACP, 2871 1871. On Sept. 15, USG, Long Branch, telegraphed to Townsend. "JAS. R. WASSON HEAD OF CLASS OF EIGHTEEN HUNDRED AND [S]EVENTY ONE IS THE PERSON NAMED AS PAYMASTER." Telegram received, *ibid.* On Sept. 16, Townsend wrote to USG. "I have the honor to ack the receipt of your note of the 14th instant, ~~wit~~and telegram of the 15th instant, relative to the appointment of J. R. Wasson as paymaster, and to inform you that the appointment ~~was~~ will be mailed to him ~~yesterday~~ to-day, Care of ~~the~~ Hon. J. A. Bingham Minister to Japan The Secretary of War left some blank appt~~s~~ointments *signed;* so that all has been done in due form." ADf, *ibid.* See *PUSG,* 22, 37–38.

On Nov. 13, 1876, John A. Bingham, U.S. minister, Tokyo, wrote to USG. "Be pleased I pray you to accept my grateful thanks for the appointment of James R. Wasson to be Paymaster in the Military Service of the United States with the rank of Major. Mr Wasson sends by this mail his letter of acknowledgment to you and also his letter of acceptance &c. As Mr Wasson was instructed by the Secretary of War to report *by letter* to the Adjutant General, I infer that it is intended that he shall await further orders here. I hope this may be the fact, as it would be a loss to him to leave at once and thereby be deprived of the necessary time to close his business with this government and dispose of his property. He will start however, immediately on receipt of notice to report in person. I am not yet advised of the result of the Presidential election, but hope to receive a telegram in a few days acquainting me that the people have elected General Hayes and have thereby fittingly rebuked the bold attempt to crown the chiefs of the rebellion with the honors of the Republic. Whatever may be the result, I shall not dispair of the final triumph of the right and the ultimate success of the great experiment of free representative government. In anticipation of the approaching new year, I beg leave to tender to Mrs Grant and yourself my best wishes for the health & happiness of each of you and of your children." ALS, DNA, RG 94, ACP, 2871 1871. On Dec. 29, 1st Lt. Francis V. Greene wrote to Townsend. "The President directs that Major Wasson be telegraphed at once (American Legation, Tokio Japan) authorizing him to remain in Japan until his successor—Chaplin—arrives. Chaplin sails from San Francisco in steamer of 15th January." ALS, *ibid.*

On Oct. 31 and Nov. 16, 1882, Secretary of War Robert T. Lincoln wrote to USG. "*Personal . . .* I have your letter of yesterday. We have no difficulty in finding enough paymasters to perform all the duties now required of them; and I do not suppose that there would be any serious trouble in the way of Major Wasson's having the leave which you suggest. But before inquiring of the Paymaster General on the subject, it occurs to me that it would be well to invite your attention to the last clause of section nine (9), of the first article of the Constitution, which would seem to prevent Major Wasson's accepting any emolument or office from the Japanese Government, without the consent of Congress. I infer from your letter that it is contemplated by him to receive pay. Has this been considered by him?" "I have your letter of November 11th instant, recommending Master John Hains, son of Major P. C. Hains, for appointment to the existing vacancy as a cadet-at-large at the Military Academy. I have seen the young gentleman, and am very much pleased with his appearance, and am sure he would be an excellent cadet. I will, with pleasure, submit your letter and other papers on his behalf to the President within a few days. The only candidate I now have in mind who is very strongly pressed for the same place is a son of Gen. Henry F. Clarke, assistant Commissary General of Subsistence. I know that a number of persons are strongly urging him for appointment. Not having received any reply to my letter of October 31st last, on the subject of Major Wasson's leave, it has occurred to me that possibly you did not receive it." LS (press), Robert T. Lincoln Letterbooks, IHi. John P. Hains graduated USMA in 1889.

On May 22, 1883, Wasson, San Antonio, wrote to USG, New York City. "I am in receipt of your telegram of today and I cannot express to you the depth of sorrow it gives me—I think I did not properly explain to you the purpose I had in view in asking permission of you to use in my statement to the court your letters. If you will be so kind as to read this letter I will tell you what that purpose was—and I wish to explain to you without reserve my situation and what lead to it—then you may judge me, and I know you will do so fairly—I am, I confess, guilty of great wrong; but I am fully conscious of my wrong doing and realize the terrible results of my folly and sin; yet I feel that I should not give myself up as lost and that the honor which I have maintained through my life has not died within me, and that I am not incapable of leading a life yet which shall wipe the disgrace of my fall—Read my story and ask yourself if I need be wholly lost and if I am worthy, through my determination to lead a useful life and to live down the disgrace which I have brought upon myself, of a word of counsel and encouragement from you who have been my greatest friend—If not, let me go my way—but if you can believe in my strength of purpose and my ability to commence anew and with patient industry, a blameless life and such training as I have to build up a reputation upon the wreck of my life and hopes, I pray you to give me some word of cheer—for no man needs it more and from no man living can I derive such courage as from you—Until last January my official career was above all reproach, I truly believe, and I would have scorned the thought that I could have been brought to my present situation by such means—cards, and that alone, brought me down—I had never before been a gambler though I had often played cards for small or nominal stakes—but never where I would lose or win a sum of importance and always among friends either officers or other gentlemen in private parties—this I considered no great wrong though I can now trace to it my ultimate ruin—Last January I was playing among a party of gentlemen and as the game progressed the stakes (for they were men of ample means) were increased—but I did not, as I should have done, quit the game when I saw it become serious, being restrained from doing so by a sense of false pride—I lost what was for me a large sum—but I was satisfied that I had simply had unusually bad luck and that I could easily regain all I had lost—so I played again and again, but always this 'bad luck' pursued me, until in a few days I had lost something near two thousand dollars—I then determined to stop and did stop for the time—I had not at the time the money to pay these losses but knew where I could obtain it soon and to settle up this gambling debt I drew upon my public funds but with the certainty, as I thought, of being able in a few days to replace the money—I was just starting away on a pay trip and made my arrangements to have this money ready to deposit on my return—When I came back I found to my dismay that the money I had depended upon was not forth coming—I yeilded to the hope of now having better luck and the fascinations of the game and again lost—in a few days, as much as before—Every hope I had of getting money at once to replace what I had withdrawn from my official account was disappointed and I knew that soon the quarterly inspection of my accounts would reveal my shortage—I made one more desperate effort to recover my loss, only to lose again and it was then, a month ago that I formed the mad design, not to rob the government, but to hide my deficiency by what I now see was as great a wrong as the first—but I will ask you to remember that I was oppressed with a maddening fear, which haunted me continually, drove sleep from my eyes and almost crazed me by the thought of the ruin which menaced me, brought upon myself by such blind and needless folly, and I was not in possession of my mental faculties or ordinary reasoning powers—And here I would say that I am not trying to *defend* my conduct to you, but rather to explain how it became possible for a man such as you have known me to be to so forget himself—My desperate plan was to cause it to appear that I had been robbed—I left in a place of security $18500. and then caused the belief that I had been robbed of $24000—It was my intention as soon as possible after fully establishing this be-

lief to go home on a leave to arrange with my bondsmen—They would I knew enable me
to raise there $5500.—the amount I was short—and then I would let them understand
that if they would show their confidence in me to this extent I could do the rest myself and
replace to the government the entire 24000 purported to have been lost; I apparently taking upon myself the loss and all chance of recovery—and really the government would not
lose a cent and I at the cost of about two years pay would have learned a lesson to last my
lifetime—I thought in this way I would hide my fault and save my credit, never to endan-
ger it again, for I had made a most solemn vow never to touch a card again, a vow which
after this horror I knew I would keep—I had no sooner embarked upon this mad scheme
beyond retreat than I saw its fatal defects—i. e. that the critical examination of my accounts which the authorities would make so as to aid in relieving me of blame in the matter if I was not to blame, would not fail to show what I was so anxious to hide—my shortage before I left Galveston—and all the terrible results which must follow—But I was
compelled to keep up the deception for a few days, until I could get to San Antonio for if I
did not I was in fear of being arrested by civil authorities—and so with a heart sick with
the full sense of my crime for I now recognized it as such, I was forced still to dissemble
my true fear and appear to be actively striving to obtain some clue to the robbery and to
place in operation all the machinery proper for the discovery of the perpetrators, who, as
I knew did not exist—In these days I suffered the torments of the damned, for I was not a
hardened criminal and my sense of honor had only been smothered and not killed and
it now fully avenged itself upon me—As soon as it was possible I came here with a full
knowledge that I must confess all and take the consequences—And you will observe here
that had my intention been at any time *theft* there was nothing to prevent my escape with
the eventual possession of the money I had left behind and what I still had with me
($5000)—But, as I hope for God's mercy, this thought, though with a thousand others it
crossed my mind, was never entertained for a moment even—I preferred to it my complete destruction—for I thought I would die, if by my own hand and meant in this way to
pay my debt—but after all that is a cowards way of meeting trouble—and God in His
mercy put that thought from my mind and I have resolved with all my strength and aided
by Him who does not refuse his help to them who confess their wrong and implore His
pardon, to show that I am not debased and that I may yet live an honorable life—which I
shall do if it is only that of a common laborer—but I have been brought to believe that the
work of half a life time—for it is now nearly 20 years since I became a soldier—need not
be all overthrown even by so great an error as I have committed—I am still young and
strong and have had a training and a career that fit me for useful and important work—
the fall I have had will give me new strength for it has pointed out to me my own weakness, a knowledge of which is strength—this is something which in the past I have not
paid sufficient heed to—I had been too successful and had grown to overestimate my self
and my powers—It is not my intention to make any defense, properly speaking before the
court but to confess my fault and explain it there as frankly as I do to you—But I did hope
that by making my past reputation and recor services a matter of record in the trial to influence the reviewing authority to commute my sentence to merely dismissal at the worst
and perhaps, especially as I shall have paid up the full amount of my defalcation before my
trial, which I think will be postponed till June 6th—, to accept my resignation instead—
I have already sufferred a terrible punishment, to which so far as *I* am concerned nothing
can add, in the sense of the disgrace I have brought upon my self and family and the wrong
I have done you and all who trusted me—none can appreciate this better than you who
have known my hopes and ambition—Now, sir, I have told you all and it is a pitiful story—
As soon as I am permitted to do so I shall seek employment, probably on some rail road

and shall be willing to begin at the bottom and go up as I show myself competent and trustworthy which I have hopes of doing in due time—I know myself and can say that I am a better man for all this trouble than ever before and I am capable of a greater effort than ever in my life—I have now a greater incentive than most men—for besides having my debts to pay, which I shall do in time, I have as well a reputation not to make but to *retrieve*—And now having opened my heart to you as I have done to God, for after Him I owe it most to you, I will add but little—of course without your consent I would not think of using your letters—I crave your pardon most earnestly and sincerely for the betrayal of that confidence which you placed in me and I only ask leave to work to regain your respect—I would be glad to be assured of your pardon and shall ask you not to forget me, but to watch the struggle I shall make with as friendly an eye as is possible— . . ." ALS, USG 3.

On June 11, Bingham, Tokyo, wrote to USG. "Relying upon your generous nature and your uniform kindness to me and not forgetful that you recommended Major James R. Wasson to this government and afterwards kindly appointed him to be Paymaster in our Army I venture to pray your good offices in his behalf not only for his sake but also for the sake of his wife & little son, both of whom are with me and have been for the past four years and have been supported by me in order as I supposed to relieve the Major from his assumed liabilities for his father. We had hoped that Major Wasson after his visit to us last year and his return to duty, would be permitted to come to us again on leave of absence for a year or two, but alas! this privilege was denied him and now comes to us a sad and crushing report concerning him thro' the San Francisco Chronicle and the Natl. Republican, slips cut from each of which papers I beg leave to enclose. These telegrams dated 8 & 14 of May from San Antonio & Galveston we have kept from the knowledge of our dear daughter Mrs Wasson & her son lest the knowledge of this great calamity might prove too much for them & deprive them of life. We are grateful that they are with us, and humbly trust it may please the Good Being to spare them to us in our Sorrow. I have no knowledge whatever of the truth of these reports as published in the enclosed slips. You will observe that in his reported confession Major Wasson says that his shortage was occasioned in an endeavor to help his embarrassed father (who lives in Iowa) that he intended to reimburse the money, that his bondsmen in Iowa, are good for his indebtedness to the gov'mt, and finally that he designated the places where $18.500—of the money can be found; to obtain which it is added, officers have been sent. Should it be (assuming these telegrams to be true) that Major Wasson and his bondsmen do make full reparation to the government for the missing money, may I invoke your kind offices to secure to him by the favor of the President a release from imprisonment though he may be cashiered, and dishonorably discharged from the service of his country in which he has heretofore acquitted himself honorably even in the peril of battle when but a youth. I seek this great favor to the end, that he may be free to live in the sweet light, of home, to regain his family & friends, and may not be denied the privilege by good conduct to make up in the future for his Shortcomings in the past, and above all that his young manhood ~~may~~ so full heretofore of promise may not perish in the gloom of a prison. Whatever may be the sentence of the Court-Martial, it is as you know in the power of the President to commute so much thereof, upon due consideration of all the facts in the case as may appear to him to be just and advisable. The violated law should be vindicated, but its justice may and sometimes is wisely tempered with mercy, by the President in the exercise of the pardoning power with which the Constitution has so wisely & humanely clothed him. In sending you this my humble Petition I am sure I address one who will not mock at my calamity." ALS, DNA, RG 94, Letters Received, 1746 1883. The enclosures are *ibid.* On July 18, USG endorsed this letter.

"Respectfully forwarded to the President of the United States." AES, *ibid.* On June 26, President Chester A. Arthur had confirmed Wasson's court-martial sentence of dismissal and hard labor for eighteen months. Copy (printed), *ibid.*, RG 153, Court-Martial Case QQ 3901, James R. Wasson. See *New York Times*, June 25, 1883.

Endorsement

Referred to the Atty. Gen. for such action and instructions as he deems judicious.

The writer of this letter, S. G. French, was a class mate of mine at West Point; served a number of years in the regular Army— through the Mexican War—resigned and settled in Miss. During the rebellion he was a rebel General and can, no doubt, see attrocities committed by blacks in a very different light from what he would see them if colored peopl[e] alone were the sufferers. But it is our duty to protect white & black, democrat & republican alike, and if justice is to be reached by the course recommended by Gen. French—who always bore an honorable character so long as I knew him—let him be instructed accordingly.

U. S. GRANT

SEPT. 16TH /76

AES, DNA, RG 60, Letters from the President. Written on a letter of Sept. 13, 1876, from Samuel G. French, Woodbury, N. J., to USG. "The information given in April last to the Grand Jury of Washington County Mississippi disclosed the existence of a society of desperate characters banded together by a common oath and called 'Brothers & Sisters' and having between fifty & sixty members. They lived chiefly in the town of Greenville and the object of their organization was murder arson and robbery. They have committed—by their own testimony—four murders, three times have burned the town, and broken into stores again and again. I think about thirty of this band have been apprehended and are awaiting trial. A few were tried by the last court and convicted. Now it is in evidence, given by some of the prisoners, that a man named R. H. Brentlinger is or was a member of the gang. Brentlinger was the Postmaster in Greenville. One of the fires destroyed the Post-office He was I believe a defaulter—at least on some charge he was tried at Jackson by the U. S. court convicted, sentenced to imprisonment and is now in the Penitentiary in Albany N. Y. The presumption from the testimony is that he knows the persons who committed all the murders, and most of them who were engaged in the different cases of arson, robberiesy &c and that could he be procured as a witness it would further the ends of justice and enable the courts to mete out such punishments as their evil deeds deserve: and to this end I have been written to, and been requested to see Brentlinger, ascertain what he knows; and, if his testimony would be important learn if he, be willing to turn 'state's evidence'. I would, therefore, most respectfully request you will cause *instructions to be given me,* to enable me to have an interview with Brentlinger. And then should he prove to be an important witness could I hold out to him a reasonable expectation of executive pardon to enable him to testify? I presume he could not be a witness unless pardoned. I will here state to you that so far as I am aware there is no object whatever in view, directly or indirectly in this matter except to endeavor to bring to justice these desperate men and to rid the community of them by process of law. The organization was composed chiefly of blacks. Brentlinger was one ~~and true~~ of the members and a true bill has been found against him. Being a member of the Grand Jury I know what testimony was given by the witnesses." ALS, *ibid.* On Aug. 24, 1867, Robert H. Brentlinger, former capt., 6th Ky. Cav., Louisville, had written to USG, secretary of war *ad interim,* seeking an army commission. ALS, *ibid.*, RG 94, ACP, B337 CB 1867. Related papers are *ibid.* No appointment followed. On Jan. 6, 1873, USG nominated Brentlinger to continue as postmaster, Greenville.

To Alphonso Taft

Long Branch, N. J.
Sept. 16th 1876

HON. A. TAFT:
ATTY. GEN.
DEAR SIR:

I have your letter of the 14th inst. in relation to the employment of Mr. Riddle as Asst. Consul in the Safe burglary cases. I am aware of no objection to Mr. Riddle in that connection. I agree with you that there should be good counsil employed so that the public should be satisfied, after the trial, that the verdict of the Court was a fair and impartial one. My acquaintance with the bar of the District is not sufficient for me to suggest any name for that place.

Very Truly Yours,
U. S. GRANT

ALS, DLC-William H. Taft. On Sept. 18, 1876, USG, Long Branch, telegraphed to Attorney Gen. Alphonso Taft. "In Selecting assistant counsel in the Safe burglary cases might be well to consider the ridiculous CORRESPONDER of Riddle in the Blain matter before Selecting him but to avoid any charge of favoritism I would Select the very best Counsel" Telegram received (at 10:25 P.M.), DNA, RG 60, Letters from the President. In 1874, Albert G. Riddle had served as government counsel in the so-called safe burglary case, in which a D. C. official allegedly had his own safe robbed to discredit opponents. The ensuing trial ended in a hung jury. See James H. Whyte, *The Uncivil War: Washington During the*

Reconstruction 1865–1878 (New York, 1958), pp. 227–28, 263–67; *HRC*, 43-1-785; *PUSG*, 18, 85–86. In May, 1876, Riddle and U.S. Representative James G. Blaine of Maine corresponded concerning Riddle's late son-in-law, James W. Knowlton, and railroad bonds Blaine allegedly received. See *New York Times*, May 4, 5, 15, 1876.

On April 15, a D. C. grand jury had indicted Orville E. Babcock and others on charges of conspiracy in the reopened safe burglary case. On April 18, William A. Cook, Washington, D. C., wrote to Attorney Gen. Edwards Pierrepont. "Allow me as Atty. for Gen: O. E. Babcock, to request if you deem it proper, a copy of the pardon, or paper in nature of a pardon, delivered to the Investigating Committee of the House of Representatives, or a member of it, for Col. Whitley?" ALS, DNA, RG 60, Letters Received, D. C. Former secret service chief Hiram C. Whiteley had implicated Babcock after receiving immunity. See *PUSG*, 22, 400.

On June 12, Fred. A. Lehmann, patent attorney, Washington, D. C., wrote to "Sir," probably either USG or Taft. "Although a stranger to you, I ask you in the name of decency, honor, & justice, to interpose your powerful influence to prevent the Babcock trial from being a farce. In God's name don't let justice become a mockery. Don't let a man be tried by his own confederates. I neither know, nor care, in one sense of the word, whether Babcock is guilty or innocent, ~~or~~ but in the name of decency, interpose your influence, & keep him from being tried by those for whom it is said he plotted." ALS, DNA, RG 60, Letters Received, D. C. Riddle again served as government counsel at the Sept. trial, which resulted in Babcock's acquittal.

To Abel R. Corbin

Long Branch, N. J.
Sept. 16th /76

Dear Sir.

While in Elizabeth Jennie told Julia that she would take care of some books & trinkets which we wish to remove from here as we do not expect to occupy the house again for at least a couple of years Accordingly we are now packing up about a ton of articles to be shipped to you, by Ex. on Monday next.[1] We expect Nellie here tomorrow and to leave permanently on the Thursday following   We go to Phila. for a few days, and from there to Ithaca, N. Y. then to Washington, Pa reaching the Capitol about the 10th of October.[2]

Family are all well

Yours Truly
U. S. Grant

A R. Corbin, Esq.

ALS (facsimile), *New York World*, May 2, 1897. See following letter.

On Jan. 21, 1876, Abel R. Corbin, Elizabeth, N. J., had written to Secretary of the Treasury Benjamin H. Bristow. "Dr. E. Lyon Corbin has been a $1.200 Clerk in the Second Auditor's Office for several years. Being an educated man, and of good habits, he *ought* to be a valuable clerk; having a family to support, and not having applied for promotion during all these years, ought not to count against him. His promotion would greatly benefit him and please me; and yet I fear to ask it for the young man. I have not been inside of the Custom House since Gen. Grant has been President; nor have I asked for an appointment from him, nor from any government officer, for any person whatsoever. I do not propose, during the short period of service remaining to the President, to change my policy in this regard. But in view of the merits & needs of the young man I have thought it might not be considered immodest, in this single instance, to express a hope that you would *inquire into the merits of his case.*" ALS, DNA, RG 56, Applications. On May 31, 1869, Corbin had written to Secretary of the Treasury George S. Boutwell recommending Eliakim L. Corbin for appointment. ALS (on White House stationery), *ibid.* As of Sept. 30, 1877, Eliakim Corbin earned $1,400 yearly as a Treasury Dept. clerk.

1. Sept. 18.
2. USG and Julia Dent Grant arrived at Washington, D. C., on Oct. 6.

To William H. Crook

———

Long Branch, N. J.
Sept 16th /76

DEAR SIR:

You need not send me any Mails to this place after Tuesday next.[1] Please so inform all the Depts. From Wednesday to Saturday, inclusive, they may be sent to me, care A. J. Drexel, West Phila[2] After that I shall go to Ithaca,[3] thence to Washington Pa[4] It will not be necessary to send me anything after Saturday, by ~~m~~Mail, except to Washington, Pa. Dispatches will reach me any place on the road between my leaving Washington, Pa a period of four or five days.

Yours &c.
U. S GRANT

WM H. CROOKE, ESQ. ACT. SEC

ALS (facsimile), Henry Rood, ed., *Memories of the White House: The Home Life of Our Presidents From Lincoln to Roosevelt, Being Personal Recollections of Colonel W. H. Crook . . .* (Boston, 1911), p. 102. On Sept. 18, 1876, William H. Crook, act. secretary to USG, wrote to Commodore Daniel Ammen, act. secretary of the navy, concerning USG's itinerary. ALS, DNA, RG 45, Letters Received from the President. Crook wrote similar letters to other cabinet officers.

On Sept. 11, Crook had written to USG, Long Branch. "I learn from Mr. Conant to day, that the Secretary of the Treasury will probable not return to Washington before the last of this week or the first of next. The papers in regard to the First Auditorship are retained in this Office since the 4th inst., as you directed that they be presented in person, must I keep them until he returns or hand them over to Mr. Conant to be forwarded to him." Copy, DLC-USG, II, 3. David W. Mahon continued as 1st auditor.

1. Sept. 19.
2. On Sept. 4, USG had written to George W. Childs. "Mrs. Grant and I will go directly to the Exposition Grounds . . . take breakfast there and when we leave the grounds in the evening go to the Continental . . . There has been so much Typhoid fever from the amount of breaking up of ground around the park this season that we think this course the best . . ." Charles Hamilton Auction No. 53, Oct. 21, 1971, no. 173. On Sept. 19, USG telegraphed to Crook. "I leave for Phila tomorrow mails may ᴛᴏ be sent to Corner thirty ninth (39th) & Locust Streets" Telegram received (at 5:44 ᴘ.ᴍ.), DLC-USG, IB. On Sept. 21, Anthony J. Drexel, Philadelphia, twice telegraphed to Crook. "Two trunks of presidents baggage missing one belonging to Mrs Grant one to Mrs Sartoris please see whether they arrive in Washington with other baggage & if so send to me at once by express directed thirty ninth & Walnut" "Baggage recovered before reaching Washn" Telegrams received (at 1:42 and 6:49 ᴘ.ᴍ.), *ibid.* See *Philadelphia Public Ledger*, Sept. 22–23, 25, 1876.
3. USG and Julia Dent Grant spent Sept. 26–28 at Ithaca, N. Y., visiting their son Jesse, a junior at Cornell University. See *New York Times*, Sept. 27, 28, 1876.
4. On Sept. 27, Wednesday, USG, Ithaca, telegraphed to William W. Smith, Washington, Pa. "Mrs. Grant and I alone will reach Pitts. friday morning" Telegram received (at 10:55 ᴀ.ᴍ.), Washington County Historical Society, Washington, Pa. On Sept. 30, a "colored men's marching club" serenaded USG at Smith's home. "The President in response thanked the club for the honor done him, and expressed his gratification at the assurance given in their behalf, that in common with the people of their race, they were faithful to the Union on the basis of freedom and equality of political privileges for all men. He said that it was feared that in some sections of the country colored men would not be left as free to exercise the rights of citizenship as they were here; but to the extent of the power vested in him, it was his purpose to see that every man of every race and condition should have the privilege of voting his sentiments without violation or intimidation. When this was secured we would then, and only then, deserve to be called a free Republic." *Pittsburgh Telegraph*, Oct. 3, 1876.

Addressee Unknown

Long Branch, N. J.
Sept. 17th /76

Dᴇᴀʀ Gᴇɴ.

The day is so bad that I will not be able to go over to see you as I wanted to do to-day to ask if you can, without inconvenience, make arrangements for sending our servants and traps to Washington on

Wednesday next.[1] There are eight horses, one large carriage & three buggies, and about the usual amt of other plunder.

Mrs. Grant & I will go the same day—afternoon train—as far as Phila

Yours Truly
U. S. GRANT

ALS, ICarbS.

    1. Sept. 20, 1876.

Endorsement

I think the system of counting demerit proposed within a decided improvement on the regulations now in vouge on that subject. In directing the present system, I gave but little thought to the subject further than to correct what I believed to be a very defective & unfair one.

The change proposed by you I think an improvement and it has my approval.

U. S. GRANT.

SEPT. 19. 1876.

Copy, DNA, RG 94, Correspondence, USMA. Written on a letter of Sept. 18, 1876, from Maj. Gen. John M. Schofield, superintendent, USMA, to USG, Long Branch. "I beg leave to submit for your consideration a proposed modification of the demerit system, having for its object to more perfectly carry out your excellent idea of giving credit for more than ordinary good conduct, by wiping out a corresponding portion of the cadet's previous bad record. As the regulations now stand it is only the Cadet who succeeds in getting *absolutely no* demerit for a whole month, who receives any benefit from the credit system. We all know how hard that is to do. Even justice requires that earnest efforts to improve in conduct be rewarded in *proportion to their success*; and the question of *relative* justice to members of the same class, striving for class standing is largely involved in the system. . . . I want to propose to the Secretary of War some changes in the Regulations when he returns from California, but upon this subject of demerit I desire first to consult you, because of the interest you have heretofore taken in the subject, and because my suggestions are in some respects different from the views which I understand you to have expressed on the subject. Will you have the kindness to indicate your approval or disapproval of these views, so that I may be governed accordingly in submitting regulations for the action of the Secretary of War." Copies, *ibid.*; DLC-John M. Schofield. See William T. Sherman to Schofield, Dec. 20, 1876 (2), CSmH; *HED*, 45-2-1, part 2, I, 149–57.

Endorsement

Referred to the Sec. of War. The troops now in Miss.—three companies of them—may be stationed in the Counties of Mississippi indicated within, if they can be spared from their present location.

U. S. GRANT

SEPT. 22D /76

AES, DNA, RG 94, Letters Received, 4788 1876. Written on a letter of Sept. 13, 1876, from James H. Pierce, U.S. marshal, Oxford, Miss., to Attorney Gen. Alphonso Taft concerning preparations for the Nov. 7 election. ". . . In the counties of Monroe, Lowndes and Noxubee, where so much intimidation was practised at last election, there seems to be a perfect reign of terror, and unless quick, and positive action is taken to suppress it, there will be no election held in those counties, I don't think it is so bad in Monroe; but in the other two, I am satisfied it would be difficult to one not having an idea of the state of affairs, to comprehend the real situation. In Noxubee there are quite a number of white republicans of the best courage, and they have met, and addressed me a letter asking me not to appoint any of them deputies to act in their own county; that they will go anywhere else and act, but in their own county such terrorism is exercised over them that it is worth their lives to act, I have promised to visit them soon, and give them all the encouragement I can. From the earnest solicitations made by all the leading Republicans living in the three counties mentioned, I am induced to believe that the presence of the military in those counties is absolutely requisite for the public peace and good of that section. And I most earnestly request and recommend that you advise the sending of one company of Infantry to each of those counties. I am advised that good and comfortable quarters can be had at Macon, Columbus and Aberdeen for the troops. From my knowledge of affairs in this state I am warranted in saying that unless the most active and strenuous measures are taken and at once, by the Federal officials, that a fair and free election cannot be had, and that unless steps are soon taken the canvass will be virtually abandoned by the Republicans, and they will refuse to go to the polls. I shall feel it to be my duty to call upon the Government to furnish me with at least ten companies of U. S. Troops With my force of deputies then in active service, and the troops to act if necessary, I can insure a quiet and fair election." Copies (2), *ibid.* *HED*, 44-2-30, 122–23. On Sept. 19, Taft wrote to Secretary of War James D. Cameron transmitting a copy of Pierce's letter. ". . . I desire to invite your attention especially to his statements relative to the amount of military force necessary in his District, and the places where he thinks they should be stationed." LS, DNA, RG 94, Letters Received, 4788 1876. On Sept. 23, USG endorsed this letter. "Returned to the Sec. of War. The number of troops called for it will be impossible to give under any circumstances. No further action need be taken until the return of the Sec. of War, and myself, to Washington." AES, *ibid.*

On Aug. 10, U.S. Representative Scott Lord of N. Y., a Democrat, had introduced a resolution calling for the protection of voting rights under the Fifteenth Amendment. *CR*, 44–1, 5419. On Aug. 15, Cameron wrote to Gen. William T. Sherman. "The House of Representatives of the United States, on the 10th inst., passed the following preamble and resolution; . . . The President directs that in accordance with the spirit of the above, you are to hold all the available force under your command (not now engaged in subduing the savages of the Western Frontier) in readiness to be used upon the call or requisition of the proper legal authorities, for protecting all citizens, without distinction of race, color, or political opinion, in the exercise of the right to vote as guaranteed by the Fifteenth Amendment: and to assist in the enforcement of 'certain, condign and effectual punishment' upon all persons who shall 'attempt by force, fraud, terror, intimidation or otherwise, to prevent the free exercise of the right of suffrage' as provided by the law of the United States; and have such force so distributed and stationed as to be able t[o] render prompt assistance in the enforcement of the law. Such additional orders as may be necessary to carry out the purpose of t[hese] instructions will be given you from time to time, after consultation with the law officers of the Government" Copy, DNA, RG 107, Letters Sent, Military Affairs. *HED*, 44-2-30, 5.

On Sept. 1, Henry B. Whitfield, Columbus, Miss., wrote to USG, Long Branch. "*Private:* . . . Enclosed you will find a copy of 'The Columbus Index,' the leading Democratic paper published in this section of Mississippi, of this date, with marked articles, to which I desire to call your attention. The resolutions adopted by the Democratic Club express the real sentiments of a certain class of people in this part of the country. Freedom of speech and personal liberty are mere mockeries. Republican government in Mississippi is worse than a farce. It has been generally supposed that American citizens in the South had some rights, which Democrats, even, were bound to respect. We are not able to decide, from our surroundings here, whether this is a myth, or a reality. It is alleged, in these resolutions, that I made an incendiary speech to the negroes. I only told them, and there was but a small crowd, some thirty of the leading men of that race in the county, who had urgently requested me to give them information and advice, in as simple language as I could command, what was the condition of affairs in the Country, reading them the 'Lord resolution,' Secretary Cameron's order, and giving some general advice as to their rights and duty in the present canvass. This is deemed '*treason to the State,*' as you will perceive. I only wish to add, that I was born and raised in this part of the country; my father was once Governor of the State; I have been a practicing lawyer for over eighteen years; was Dist. Atty. for the State four years past; was a eConfederate soldier for nearly four years; lost a handsome fortune by the war; and *dared to presume*, from this record, that I had a right to speak my honest sentiments." ALS, DNA, RG 60, Letters from the President. *HED*, 44-2-30, 121. See *ibid.*, pp. 115–17.

Also on Sept. 1, Hugh M. Foley, Natchez, wrote to USG. "This will inform you of the condition of affairs in Wilkinson County. I was compelled to leave my home in that County for fear of violence to me offered by the armed men of that County for my sentiments and principals as a republican. I was summoned before Mr Boutwells Committee to testify of the late State Election held in this State and riot in that County. by reference to the Evidence taken by the Committee you will see what I and others testified. I have been away from my family for some considerable time here in this City awaiting for some protection, that I might return home, also Mr Peter Crout from that County who testified before that Committee have been threatened with death should he return he is a man of considerable property Mr N B Earheart, John J Foley, and Abram Scott, all received each thier coffin to leave within fifteen days or else they must prepare themselves to suffer the consequences. the late named jentlemen is the County Assessor, the others are not officers, but are leading republicans and old residents of the County, and own both real & personal property in the town of Woodville. The republicans are not permitted to assemble peaceably in thier meeting for fear violence and these so called armed Regulators say publicly that we shall not exercise our political opinion or preferences I have to the best of my ability in a brief maner to lay before you our troubles and grievances in that County. I therefore ask you in the name of God and the suffering republicans of that County to send us troops that we may be protected and saved from personal destruction I request you to please keep this secret for fear that our enemies might destroy my property in thier immediate midst, as I am engaged in farming and have agood many hands employed and all that I am worth is there invested. I sincerely hope this may receive your most favorable consideration and reply at your earliest convenience all of which I shall humbly pray." ALS, DNA, RG 60, Letters from the President. *HED*, 44-2-30, 120–21. See *SRC*, 44-1-527, part 2, II, 1533–43, 1624–29.

On Oct. 19, George A. Place, "Formerly of the 75th New York Vols—and for 3 Months a member of Co I. 1st R. I. Vols 'when Burnside was its Colonel," Macon, Miss., wrote to USG. "*'Strictly Private'* . . . It may seem to be presumptious on my part to address your excellency upon any subject—but sir my condition is such that I hope you will pardon me for this audacity—What I want to know isof you is of vital interest to me as well as many others in this state. We are here from different states of the north—and have been for several years have become acclimated—have families and are in no condition financialy to move back north. The Political pressure is so strong upon us by the Democrats that we live in fear all the time—are forced to keep our mouths shut—and the truth is our lives are in danger of midnight assasinations &c—Now I ask you to please drop me a few lines giveing me your own opinions of the result of the Nov-Elections My reasons for asking this are these if you should say that you thought Tilden had any chance of election I shall leave this state with in twenty four hours after receiving your letter—for I know that if he is elected we will all be killed—it is the boasts of these people and I know them well enough to believe that they will carry out their threats—I dont want to be caught as many a northern man was in 1861—here and was not permitted to leave this time it will be as much as a mans life is worth to be known as a native of New York state—I dont write to you sir for any political purpose I am not a politician, I simply writing for advice or rather your opinions of the result of the elections that I may know what course to take to save my life, no man can picture the state of affairs in the south with his pen it is a panorama that must be seen to be fully understood—I am sir no sore headed carpet Bagger. I am not a politician hold no office never did, nor do not want any. I only want to keep posted and to be able to save my neck from the rope of the white leaguers of this country—I ask you to please write to me a few words of your own opinions I will not use it politcialy or even publically—The truth is I am frightened and nervous and want to get something to give me an Idea how to prescribe for the relief of My self—By complying you will greatly oblige . . ." ALS, DNA, RG 60, Letters from the President.

On Oct. 20, William R. Moore, dry goods merchant, Memphis, wrote to USG. "*Strictly* CONFIDENTIAL. . . . Allow me to say *all honor* to you for sending troops to S. C. to see that American Citizens *vote for whom they please.* The same necessity *equally exists in Miss.* Intimidation and proscription are *the rule* also in that state; and only yesterday an old country merchant customer and *life long* citizen from there told me that the report of Seanator Boutwell *did not tell* HALF the political enormities of the state; and that *no man,* even if he was never outside the state in his life,—could safely stay in Miss if his name was known in even publicly acknowledging the truth. In the name of patriotism, of country, of civilization, of Christianity, of God!! is this thing to be allowed to go on in this Country. The danger of rebel success seems to me to be greater today than ever; and if they are elected, may God protect the friends of the Nation. UNDER NO CIRCUMSTANCES use my name publicly. . . . P. S. I am not a 'carpetbagger,' and can have no possible motive but the promotion of the *material interests* of our *whole* country. *I only want every citizen equally protected.*" ALS, *ibid. HED*, 44-2-30, 129–30.

On Oct. 22, Sunday, Henry W. Henley, West Point, Miss., wrote to USG. "I have been thinking of writing you a Small note for Several Reasons first that your Birth day and mine are in the Same year day and date April 27, 1822, thare may be maney cases of the Same,

But thare ma not be know other man But my Self Born on the Same day and year as your Self, and a Live union man in Mississippi Born in N. Carolina and lived through the war without taking up arms a gainst my Goverment. I Excepted office under Ames the first in Lounds County and I have been Abused As a union man all the time I Still Live and, I Entend die with my Republican Principals in the next place I wish to State Breaflay Some things that are going on down here. I was at Columbus when the Solders arived thare in a fiew hours the men that would cut your throt and Evry other union man, was going to head quarters with invitations come to certan places and get evrry thing that is good &c, to get the good Side of the officers and Beat us in the count, as they did Last fall. men are know telling the freedman if you do not vote the Democratic tickett you Shall leave my place and if needs be we will kill a fiew of and we Entend what we Say. the freedman come to me and Say what Shall we do. they thretan them with Death after the Soldiers are gon. Thirsday at Mayhew Station M & O. R John Connell Told the Negros they had as much to have meetings as whites and for that he was wated on by a croude and told his life was in danger if he advised the Negros aney moore that the Democraceys intendid to Rule this contrey didnot care a d.m.d for Grant and his Soldiers we have as good men here union men as aney in the Land and for feare have to hold thare tonges our candate for Congress is to Speak here and Pal Alto Friday and Saturday next I Learn this morning that the Democrcy Says that Lee Shall not Speak he is a good man lives in Aberdean I Expect we will have a hot time they are taking the canon and Shooting and abusing the Negroes and we are going to care the Election or Bust the canon and kill Some of you and have them Badley frighten. they are going all over the county to Evrry plantation with all kinds of threts to the freedmen So they tell me and I am certan Such is the fact, thare is know doubt tha[t] our State would go for Hayes By a Large vote if all can have a fear chance I hope you will See that we Shall have a free and honest Election let me tell you that they are worse to [d]ay than they ware in 1861. If they are Such union men how is it that they abuse us as union men, if they are Such good union Loving men and want to be Bered in the old flage when they die god deliver us from Such men, I hope that you and your Sucksesar will meat out to those hell deserving Secsion democracys that are Still at work to Brak up this union at all hasards that is thare intent they are Shoing the cloven foot, and Say we would not give Gef Davis for a car Loads of Grants. if you can Stand them much Longer you will certanlay have moore paticence than Job, had of Old times . . . Whites had a speaking in the day Just as the Whites 20, in number go to the door Some one in the white croud Said fire it Being darke all the Negros was all in the house and the Speeker was up and Speaking and he was amonge the killd. the Negros had no guns So Says the Irashman to me I understand that the Democracey are dertemind to kill and Scare them out of the county you know Last fall Octibha went Republican By a Large vote I could go on all day and State facts and then not get through If you had lived here as I have Since the war and throught the war, Sean and heard and felt what I have, you, would think it was time we war thind out you of corse are aware of the people down South how they are talking about you and the goverment If we can get ride of those Scondreles we can get along the Negros are working well and have quitt Steeling hogs and cows &c and are trying to make a good Living and are making Better men than a great maney of thare old master are for the Last two years I have Sean a desided change in them as to thare deportment kindness and Politness to the whites. anny man can See the change, and now they claim a right to Vote for Hayes as they say you are going to Vote for him and we must Stick to our friend and think you would not Vote for a man that would ronge them all the freedmen thinks the Sun rises and Sets in you and the Republican party you will pleas pardon all mistakes as you find them what I have Said are facts hoping we may never live to See an other Democratice president in this our nation" ALS, DNA, RG 60, Letters from the President.

On Oct. 26, Edwin B. Smith, act. attorney gen., wrote to USG. "I have the honor to enclose herewith a letter of the 19th inst., addressed to the Attorney General by J. L. Lake., Jr., Esq., U. S. Marshal for the Southern District of Mississippi, in which is enclosed a communication of the 27th ult., addressed to him by Hon. John R. Lynch; also a letter of the 20th inst., addressed to the Attorney General by J. H. Pierce, Esq., U. S. Marshal for the Northern District of Mississippi; also a letter of the 21st inst., from the same to the same, enclosing resolutions of the Republican Executive Committee of Clay County, Miss. The subject of all these communications is the furnishing of military protection to the people of Mississippi in view of the approaching Presidential Election, and the places where such force is needed. Having myself little practical knowledge concerning these matters, in the absence of the Attorney General I have the honor to refer these documents to you for your consideration." LS, *ibid.*, RG 94, Letters Received, 4788 1876. The enclosures are *ibid.* On the same day, Sherman wrote to Lt. Gen. Philip H. Sheridan, Chicago. "The enclosed papers were received from the President today. The Secretary of War is absent, and I have seen the President himself, have explained that every man in the Division of the Atlantic is now at the South, and the best I can do is to send these papers to you, with discretion to order to Mississipi any troops that you may deem necessary, that can be spared Elsewhere. I am now endeavoring to fill up the 8th & 10th Cavalry, in Texas, to the limit of law. Please return enclosures when used." ALS, *ibid.* On Oct. 28, Sheridan telegraphed to Brig. Gen. Christopher C. Augur, New Orleans, conveying instructions from USG and Sherman that troops be distributed among Okolona, Hernando, Fayette, and West Point, Miss. ADfS (telegram sent), DLC-Philip H. Sheridan; LS (telegram sent), *ibid.*

To Lot M. Morrill

Oct. 6th 1876.

Hon. Lot M. Morrill;
Sec. of the Treas.
Dear Sir:

This will introduce Mr. Gratiot Washburne, of Galena, Ill. son of Hon. E. B. Washburne now Minister to France. Mr. Washburne is anxious to obtain a position in the New York City Custom House which he understands is about to be vacated, and asks an interview on that subject.

Will you please see him.

Very Truly Yours,
U. S. Grant

ALS, NNP. Gratiot Washburne secured a clerkship in the New York City Customhouse and earned a $1,600 salary as of Sept., 1877.

On Aug. 6, 1875, Washburne, 2nd secretary of legation, Paris, had written to USG. "Pardon the liberty I take in addressing you on a subject of much interest to myself, and in which I ask your good offices. The new Tribunals which the Egyptian Government has lately organized, with the concurrence of the Great Powers, meet in October next, and all the positions had not as yet been filled. By the order of the Khedive, Cherif Pacha, Minister of Justice wrote to Mr. Beardsley, U. S. Consul General at Cairo, under date of November 19th 1874, requesting him to ask his Government to designate two officers for the lower court as Judge and pro-Attorney General. I enclose you a copy of the translated despatch. Mr George S. Batcheller, of New York, was duly appointed judge by yourself and Mr Fish, and has been regularly installed. The position of Attorney General remains unfilled, and Mr. Batcheller has asked me if I would accept it. I have assented and he will write Mr. Fish to day requesting his good offices in my behalf. The place is one that would be agreeable to me, as I have acquired, during my residence abroad, a knowledge of the languges most required in the incumbent, and such acquaintance with European usages and laws as would facilitate the discharge of the duties. I shall be deeply grateful if you find it consistent with your sense of duty to name me for the position to Mr Fish. Our family are all very well, and join me in kind regards to you and yours." ALS, DNA, RG 59, Letters of Application and Recommendation. The enclosure is *ibid.* On Aug. 11, Elihu B. Washburne, Paris, wrote to USG. "I learned yesterday for the first time that Gratiot had written you in regard to some appointment connected with the new tribunals in Egypt. He understands that Genl Batchelder, who has recently been sent out as one of the Judges, has expressed a wish to Mr. Fish that he may be appointed to one of the under places in the Court as a sort of adviser or attorney, but I do not know whether such be the case or not. If not, of course, that is the end of the matter, because it is not likely that an appointment of that kind would be made without his recommendation. I have not seen the Genl since his return from Egypt. What I wish to say in the matter is that I have no connection with it and that I should very much regret to lose Gratiot from the Legation. He thinks, however, that I ought not to interfere to prevent an appointment, which he considers so much to his advantage, and which he imagines he is qualified for, from the experience he has gained in diplomatic and other matters here, and from his knowledge of French and Italian, languages necessary in the country. Should it be possible for the appointment to be made, I would beg leave to ask that his place might be filled by *Henry Vignaud, of Louisiana,* but now in Paris, not only for the reason that his appointment would be gratifying to me personally, but on the higher ground that it would be eminently advantageous to the public interest. Mr. V. is a man of rare intelligence and high character and distinguished as a *publicist.* He is thoroughly acquainted with diplomatic affairs and well known in diplomatic circles. He has been much about the Legation and is somewhat familiar with the duties of a Secretary. He was of great service to the Alabama Commission and he has recently assisted me very much in the negotiation of the Metrical Treaty. I can assure you that if an appointment of a Second Secretary of this Legation is to be made his would be eminently a fit one. I should not have troubled you in this business had not Gratiot told me he had written you. His having done so, I deemed it proper to let you know my relation to the affair." ALS, DLC-Hamilton Fish. On Aug. 24, Secretary of State Hamilton Fish, Garrison, N. Y., wrote to USG, Long Branch. "No letter of Gratiot Washburnes in relation to the Egyptian appointment has been received—Genl Batchelder has written to me, that Gratiot Washburne had expressed to him a desire for the appointment, & Batchelder endorses the application—I think however that we have advised the Egyptian Government that we would not make a nomination for this place, which I understand to be something like a prosecuting Attorney—he holds this office wholly at the pleasure of the Egyptian Govt & when this place was first suggested, it was thought not advisable to send a person on such an uncertain tenure, & hence (as I think) we renounced the ap- right of appointment. I expect to return to Washington before long & will then examine—Gratiot Washburne, no doubt, has the requirements of familiarity of languages—what professional acquirements he has I am uninformed. Mr Vignaud whom Mr W. recommends in Gratiots place, is an exceedingly accomplished & intelligent man. He was an ultra rebel: but is I believe very thoroughly reconstructed—that is, he accepts the situation, & has rendered *most valuable* service to us, on the Alabama & other questions. He finally has no idea of ever returning to the United States, prefers living in Paris, but is an *American* against every thing except the allurements of Paris—" ALS (press), *ibid.* On Oct. 29, Fish recorded in his diary. "I mention to the President the vacancy of the Consul Generalship in Constantinople; and the names of several applications therefore He said he thought we had concluded to give the appointment to Eugene Schuyler. I suggest to him that in that case there will be a vacancy in the Secretaryship of Legation at St Petersburg He says I can appoint any clever young fellow I see fit I remind him of the application of E. B Washburne for the appointment of his son Gratiot, to a position in Egypt; & suggest that that was a professional appointment and I was not sure that Gratiot Washburne was a lawyer I further stated that we had informally intimated to the Khedive that we should not fill the place but should we do so I was decidedly of opinion that it ought to be filled by a lawyer of some experience" *Ibid.* On Dec. 7, Fish recorded in his diary a discussion with Gratiot Washburne on the same subject. *Ibid.* On Dec. 8, USG nominated Gratiot Washburne as secretary of legation, St. Petersburg, Henry Vignaud as 2nd secretary of legation, Paris, and Eugene Schuyler as consul gen., Constantinople.

On Sept. 16, Alphonso Taft, Cincinnati, had written to Fish. "I learn from Col A. H. Waters of Massachusetts, who is now on the Bosphorus near Constantinople, Turkey, that the consulship there is vacant, and that he wants the place. . . ." ALS, DNA, RG 59, Letters of Application and Recommendation. Related papers are *ibid.* On Sept. 21, Postmaster Gen. Marshall Jewell wrote to Fish reiterating his support for Schuyler as consul gen., Constantinople. LS, *ibid.* Related papers are *ibid.* On Sept. 30, Lewis Seasongood *et al.*, Cincinnati, petitioned USG. "The undersigned citizens, knowing the worth, integrity, honor & ability of Mr *Benjamin F. Peixotto*, now U. S. Consul at Bucharest Roumania, respectfully request his appointment as Consul General of the U. S. to Constantinople, feeling confident, that Mr Peixotto will represent the interests of the United States most creditably in Said position,—and that his past Services deserve Promotion." DS (47 signatures), *ibid.*, Applications and Recommendations, Hayes-Arthur. Related papers are *ibid.* For Benjamin F. Peixotto, see *PUSG*, 21, 74, 77; *ibid.*, 23, 115–17.

On Jan. 31, 1876, Fish wrote to Elihu Washburne. "Private . . . You have doubtless seen articles in several newspapers commenting, with great severity, upon an advertisement said to have been published with the name of Mr Gratiot Washburne subscribed. Both the President and I, as well as others of his friends here, believe the advertisement to have been a hoax and forgery, where-in his name was improperly used, without his knowledge, and that he is suffering unjustly in the public estimation. This article has however caused much comment and inquiry and the President has directed a letter to be written to him to obtain a denial of the authenticity of the advertisement, which letter the President requests me to forward open, under cover to you, not knowing whether Mr Gratiot Washburne has yet left Paris for St Petersburg. Should he have left he requests that you will seal and forward the letter to him, giving it the proper address, and should he be still in Paris, that you will hand it to him." LS, DLC-Elihu B. Washburne. The advertisement in question initially "appeared in the *Clipper*, the well-known sporting paper of New York city, on Oct. 30 last: WANTED—For J. W. Myers' Great American Circus, Paris, France, the palace circus of the world, containing eighty-two luxuriously furnished private boxes, and a seating capacity of seven thousand five hundred—a first class bareback male and female rider. Address, stating lowest terms and business, GROTIOT WASHBURNE, No. 14 East Fifteenth street., N. Y., Up to Nov. 25. . . ." *Illinois State Register*, Jan. 21, 1876. On Feb. 15, Fish recorded in his diary. "I read a telegram received from J. W. Myers London stating that Gratiot Washburne was never agent for his circus in any way and any advertisement inserted in American papers has no reference to him (Mr Myers) the substance of which the President thinks had better be given to the press." DLC-Hamilton Fish. See *Washington Evening Star*, Feb. 16, 1876. On Feb. 29, Fish recorded in his diary that he read to USG a letter "from Gratiot Washburne admitting that he had inserted the advertisement with regard to the Circus Company which had been commented upon by the Press. The President expresses much surprise." DLC-Hamilton Fish. On March 4, Fish again recorded in his diary. "Called upon the President and read him a very manly note from E. B. Washburne about his son Gratiot, lamenting his indiscretion in the matter of the advertisement and stating that he had directed him not to leave Berlin for his post until he had heard from me by telegraph,   he referred to a letter from his son stating that if I, and the President, so desired not to hesitate a moment but to let him know and he would resign. The President says that under ordinary circumstances he would overlook Gratiot's mistake but that now there are so many scandals about Belknap Babcock Schenck & now Washburne that it is better that he should resign. He requested me so to telegraph and to write a kind letter to his father by the first mail informing him of the reason" *Ibid.* On March 6, Fish wrote to Elihu Washburne, Paris. "Your letter of 15. Feb reached me on Saturday (4th) & was immediately read to the President, who expressed himself warmly, as to its frank and generous tone—I had received on 1st inst a letter from Mr Gratiot Washburne, in reply to one which I had forwarded to him through you,—in which he mentioned the fact of having authorized the advertisement which was the subject of inquiry in my letter to him— . . . When your letter was received (three days later) the President felt that were the case of Mr Gratiot Washburne presented alone & without the attendant circumstances with regard to several other public Officers whose conduct had attracted a large amount of public criticism & censure, he would be inclined to pass it by, as a thoughtless indiscretion, which as a solitary & individual act of imprudence, might be overlooked—but amid the many complaints which are attaching to numerous public Officers, & the necessity of his not ignoring any of the acts which are brought to his notice, & which reflect improperly on the public service, he directed me to telegraph to Mr Gratiot Washburne, not to proceed to his post, & that his resignation would be required—He does not regard the act of the young gentleman as involving any moral wrong—it is the peculiarity of the service to which he was appointed, that demands prudence, and discretion as among its chiefest requisites, that gave to the act, a character of entire incompatibility with the position to which he was named—The President desires me to express to you, his high appreciation of your very frank & generous letter & at the same time to express the personal regret which attends the course, which he has felt it his duty, under the circumstances, to adopt—He does not doubt that you will appreciate the friendship which he entertains for you, & for your son, & that you will understand how severe a strain upon that friendship, his sense of public duty has imposed upon him— . . ." ALS, DLC-Elihu B. Washburne. See Gratiot Washburne to Hamilton Fish, Feb. 22, 1876, DLC-Hamilton Fish; Fish diary, March 7, 1876, *ibid.*; *New York Times*, March 10, 1876.

On March 21, James H. Wilson, New York City, wrote to USG. "Having seen it announced that Gratiot Washburne has resigned his position as Secretary of Legation at St Petersburg, I venture to suggest the name of Colonel Hoffman Atkinson, of this city, late capt and assistant Adjutant General of Volunteers on the Staff of Gen'l Wm Sooy Smith, as that of a person entirely competent to fill the place with credit to himself and the Country. He is an accomplished linguist, a gentleman of character, ability and standing, and withall one of unexceptionable morals, and a large acquaintence with affairs throughout the world. His appointment could not fail to give satisfaction & I am sure it would add to the consideration of the country abroad." ALS, DNA, RG 59, Letters of Application and Recommendation. USG wrote an undated note attached to this letter. "Gen. S. Smith says A. speaks fluently French, Italian and Japanese, is a good German scholar and may speak the language, but of this is not certain." AN, *ibid.* On March 24, USG nominated Hoffman Atkinson as secretary of legation, St. Petersburg. See Fish diary, March 24, 1876, DLC-Hamilton Fish.

Endorsement

Referred to the Atty. Gen. Mr. Hester[1] was formerly employed by the Dept. of Law to ferret out the KuKlux in N. & S. C. and it was through his exertions and fearlessness that so many were brought to justice. I hope his services can be continued.

U. S. GRANT

OCT. 14TH /76

AES, DNA, RG 60, Letters from the President. Written on a letter of Sept. 30, 1876, from Joseph G. Hester, Washington, D. C., to USG. "*Personal* . . . While in the midst of my operation's in North Carolina a few day's ago, where I was obtaining information of the plans of 'the Ku Klux,' and their intended operation's, to be inaugurated after the October elections, and while preparing to foil them; I received a letter from the Attorney General, (who did not know the circumstances under which I was appointed,) informing me that in order to reduce the expenses of the Department, my services would be discontinued to-day. Judge Settle is in a remote part of the State canvassing; For this reason I take the liberty of stating the above fact's, and of suggesting the importance of my remaining in North Carolina for the present." ALS, *ibid.* On Aug. 4, 1876, Attorney Gen. Alphonso Taft had written to Hester, special agent, Reidsville, N. C., ending his employment. Copy, *ibid.* On Oct. 7, USG endorsed this letter. "I regret that it has been found necessary, in the reduction of force—to suspend Mr. Hester, and hope the Atty. Gn. may be able to restore him to his past service." AES, *ibid.*

On Oct. 23, David T. Corbin, U.S. attorney, Aiken, S. C., wrote to Taft requesting Hester's employment as a detective. ALS, *ibid.*, Letters Received, S. C.

1. See *PUSG*, 22, 11–12. On Aug. 5, 1872, Hester, Raleigh, had telegraphed to Frederick T. Dent. "We have carried the state beyond all doubt by Eleven hundred republican majority. Gains are coming in favorably—" Telegram received (at 6:59 P.M.), USGA.

On Feb. 1, 1873, Hester reclaimed from the State Dept. papers recommending him for marshal, Constantinople. ANS, DNA, RG 59, Letters of Application and Recommendation. On Feb. 18, USG nominated Hester as consul, Santiago, Cape Verde. In March, Hester resigned as consul to represent U.S. manufacturing interests at the Vienna Exposition. See *New York Times*, March 27, 1873.

On Jan. 21, 1874, U.S. Representative William A. Smith of N. C. wrote to USG. "I take great pleasure in recommending Captain Joseph G. Hester, one of my constituents, for a position in the public service. The country and our State owe him a debt of gratitude for his brilliant achievements and valuable services during the Ku-Klux reign of terror at

the South. To him we owe the tranquillity we now enjoy. Mr. Hester is a courageous, dash-
ing, energetic man, quick-witted, ever on the alert, and possesses all the qualifications to
fit him for the position he seeks. Morally, he has not a blemish; strictly temperate; in every
respect reliable. He has had the best home-training possible, being the son of the Rev.
B. B. Hester, of North Carolina." *HRC*, 43-2-262, 1044. Other recommendations are
ibid., pp. 1044–45. For Hester as special agent, Post Office Dept., Sept.-Nov., see *HMD*,
44-1-187, 60–75; *HRC*, 43-2-262, 1007–17, 1022–40. For Hester's testimony on his past,
including service in the C.S. Navy and assignment as special agent, Justice Dept. (as of
Dec. 1, 1874), see *ibid.*, pp. 1017–22. See also *O.R.* (Navy), I, i, 508–9, 688–90, xv, 563–64,
II, iii, 806, 857.

On July 29, 1875, Hester, Washington, D. C., wrote to USG. "Your Excellency may
perhaps remember my name in connection with service rendered in the Southern States,
within the last few years. An opportunity now presents itself, in my humble opinion, for
the rendition of important service to the country in the same locality; as there are at present unlawful combinations more powerful than ever since the war; being organized of
which I do not know whether your Administration is informed or not." ALS, DNA, RG 60,
Letters from the President.

On July 3, 1876, Culver C. Sniffen wrote to Henry T. Crosby, chief clerk, War Dept.
"The President directs me to say that if not against precedent, the bearer—Mr J. G. Hester, may be allowed to take copies of letters of Governor Vance to Jeff Davis, and of the orders from Vance to his Conscript officers.—" Copy, DLC-USG, II, 3. See Endorsement,
Aug. 7, 1876.

Proclamation

Whereas it has been satisfactorily shown to me that insurrection and
domestic violence exist in several counties of the State of South Carolina, and that certain combinations of men against law exist in
many counties of said State known as "Rifle Clubs," who ride up and
down by day and night in arms, murdering some peaceable citizens
and intimidating others, which combinations, though forbidden by
the laws of the State, cannot be controlled or suppressed by the ordinary course of justice;
And Whereas it is provided in the Constitution of the United States
that the United States shall protect every State in this Union, on application of the legislature, or of the executive when the legislature
cannot be convened, against domestic violence; and Whereas by laws
in pursuance of the above it is provided (in the laws of the United
States) that, in all cases of insurrection in any State (or of obstruc-
tion to the laws thereof,) it shall be lawful for the President of the
United States, on application of the legislature of such State, or of

the executive when the legislature cannot be convened, to call forth the militia of any other State or States, or to employ such part of the land and naval forces as shall be judged necessary for the purpose of suppressing such insurrection or causing the laws to be duly executed; and Whereas the legislature of said State is not now in session and cannot be convened in time to meet the present emergency, and the executive of said State, under Section 4 of Article IV of the Constitution of the United States and the laws passed in pursuance thereof, has therefore made due application to me in the premises for such part of the military force of the United States as may be necessary and adequate to protect said State and the citizens thereof against domestic violence, and to enforce the due execution of the laws; And Whereas it is required that, whenever it may be necessary, in the judgment of the President, to use the military force for the purpose aforesaid, he shall forthwith, by proclamation, command such insurgents to disperse and retire peaceably to their respective homes within a limited time: Now, therefore, I, Ulysses S. Grant, President of the United States, do hereby make proclamation, and command all persons engaged in said unlawful and insurrectionary proceedings to disperse and retire peaceably to their respective abodes within three days from this date, and hereafter abandon said combinations and submit themselves to the laws and constituted authorities of said state.

And I invoke the aid and co-operation of all good citizens thereof to uphold the laws and preserve the public peace.

In witness whereof I have hereunto set my hand, and cause the seal of the United States to be affixed.

Done at the City of Washington this seventeenth day of October, in the year of our Lord eighteen hundred and seventy-six; and of the Independence of the United States One hundred and One.

U. S. GRANT.

DS, DNA, RG 130, Presidential Proclamations. *SMD*, 44-2-48, III, 450, 537; *HED*, 44-2-30, 16; *HRC*, 44-2-175, part 2, pp. 32–33, 45-2-806, 33; *HMD*, 45-1-7, 12–13; *SD*, 57-2-209, 183–84. On Oct. 11, 1876, Governor Daniel H. Chamberlain of S. C. wrote to USG. "I have to inform you that insurrection and domestic violence exist in various portions of this State, especially in the Counties of Aiken, Barnwell and Edgefield, against the peace and government of this State, to such an extent that I am unable with any means at my command to suppress the same: . . ." DS, DNA, RG 60, Letters Received, S. C. *SMD*, 44-

2-48, III, 95; *HED*, 44-2-30, 102. See Hamilton Fish diary, Oct. 12, 17, 1876, DLC-Hamilton Fish; Nevins, *Fish*, pp. 842–43. On Oct. 17, Secretary of War James D. Cameron wrote to Gen. William T. Sherman. "In view of the existing condition of affairs in South Carolina there is a possibility that the Proclamation of the President of this date may be disregarded. To provide against such a contingency you will immediately order all the available force in the Military Division of the Atlantic to report to Gen. Ruger, commanding at Columbia S. C.; and instruct that officer to station his troops in such localities that they may be most speedily and effectually used in case of resistance to the authority of the United States. It is hoped that a collision may thus be avoided, but you will instruct Gen. Ruger to let it be known that it is the fixed purpose of the Government to carry out fully the spirit of the Proclamation and to sustain it by the military force of the general government supplemented if necessary by the militia of the various States" LS, DNA, RG 94, Letters Received, 4788 1876. *SMD*, 44-2-48, III, 538; *HED*, 44-2-30, 17; *HRC*, 45-2-806, 33–34; *HMD*, 45-1-7, 13; *SD*, 57-2-209, 184.

On Sept. 20, Wednesday, L. Cass Carpenter, collector of Internal Revenue, 3rd District, S. C., Columbia, had written to USG. "*Private . . .* I am to day in receipt of reliable information, through a mail agent named Julius Moyer, who runs on the Port Royal Rail Road, which is startling in the extreme. Permit me to say, that I beleive all that Moyer tells me, as I have known him for several years, and know he has no reason to tell anything but the simple truth. There has been a report for two days of a disturbance at Ellenton, in Barnwell County, on the rail road where Moyer runs, but this is the first direct information yet received. This man is a sworn officer of the government, and only tells what he saw with his *own eyes.* I give his story as he gave it to me and I take occasion again to say, I beleive it from begining to end: 'I left Augusta for Beaufort on my regular trip Tuesday morning at 8.30. A. M. we proceeded as far as Ellenton when Capt M M Hudson conductor of the train refused to proceed further, as reports had reached him of a proposed collision at "Roberts" a few miles below. while waiting at Ellenton probably not more than half an hour, I saw S. P. Coker walking with several white men with guns on their shoulders, I do not think he felt that he was in any danger, He went over to a store near the station and in plain sight, but a few yards away and sat down on a bench and talked with the white men After a few minuets they all got up and walked about 30 or 40 yards into a field under a large oak tree, all talking together, The white men then left Coker about 30 paces off, and shot him, Two men shot him after he fell. I saw all this while sitting in the cars, I also saw two other men dead by the side of the rail road, one with his head blown almost entirely off, When I went down on m̶Monday, I never saw a single colored man, except those in the cars, A colored man named Morrison was on the train, I think he was once a member of the Genl Assembly from Beaufort; A. P. Butler I think is his name: (I mean the man with one arm) and while on the train, was elected to command the company of white men then on the train: He went up to Morrison, and drawing his pistol was going to shoot him at once, and would have done so, if the conductor had not told him that Morrison was in his charge, and should not be hurt, He (the conductor) finally put Morrison in the baggage car, and told him to lock himself in, and stay there until he told him to come out. Morrison went to Augusta from there, Butler was very drunk. Most of the men I saw there, were from Columbia County Georgia, they said they had killed every nigger that they had seen, and I beleive they had, I saw two lying by the side of the rail road dead, one with his head shot almost entirely off, and the other shot in several places.' Is there nothing that can be done to stop this slaughter of innocent men? What is done, must be done at *once.* I have written the Attorney General on the same subject: Under no circumstances should the name of this agent be divulged, as his life would not be worth a farthing after it was found out that he had communicated the intelligence:" LS, DNA,

RG 60, Letters from the President. *SMD,* 44-2-48, III, 92; *HED,* 44-2-30, 99–100. See Richard Zuczek, *State of Rebellion: Reconstruction in South Carolina* (Columbia, 1996), p. 176. Julius Mayer, former slave and S. C. representative (1868–70), continued as route agent, Port Royal, S. C., to Augusta, Ga.

On Sept. 25, James Majar *et al.,* Aiken, S. C., petitioned USG. "I We write to tell you that our people are being shot down like dogs, and no matter what democrats may say; unless you help us our folks will not dare go to the polls we are confident who are the sufferers The democratic whites are going about bush whacking the people of color for our political opinion and throwing there threats around saying that they will kill the last one of us before the day of election we the undersigned wish that you will see to having a Deputy U. S. Marshal appointed forthwith as we believe that it will be the means of saving a many lives we desire further to call Your Excellency's attention that we the undersigned desire to have Dr F. A. Palmer appointed as deputy United States marshall a gentleman who have been lately recomend by all the leading republicans of this county to United States Marshal Wallace for the position. Dr F. A. Palmer is well known to us all to be a gentleman and a true and good republican and fully qualified to discharge the duty of deputy marshal if appointed he is a northern gentleman born and raised in the State of New York he has purchased lands here among us for this four years. we the undersig[ned] knows your Excellency can do a great de[al] in having the deputy appointed fort[h]with. now to support what we ha[ve] said about our troubles let us state some of the late circumstances on Friday Sept 15th a colored man was dragged out of his sick bed and killed by the white democrats in order to get up a riot after which time the Georgians came over in S. [C.] and murdered the Republicans like dogs the U. S. troop went to the scene and queled the riot, but since that the whites democrats are going through the country in squads murdering the colored and white republicans. therefore we the undersigned pray your Excellency to take the matter into your immediate consideration and save our lives which are being taken every moment and we will greatfully Pray" DS (15 signatures), DNA, RG 60, Letters from the President. *SMD,* 44-2-48, III, 93; *HED,* 44-2-30, 100–101.

On Oct. 4, Anonymous, Boston, wrote to USG. "I have been in South Carolina and I believe the enclose letter is true, and if the Colo Men of the South are not protected in their rights it will be a dis grace to our nation and the Administation for they have the constitunatn right so to do if it should take ten Thousand troops, we profess to be a Christian nation and yet I beleive" L (incomplete), DNA, RG 60, Letters Received, Mass. The writer enclosed a clipping from the *New York Times,* Oct. 3, 1876.

On Oct. 13, John Binny, New York City, wrote to USG. "I am very sorry national troops, in sufficient number, have not been sent to South Carolina before this. We have only three weeks to Canvas South Carolina North Carolina, Louisiana & Florida. and While you send a sufficient number to overawe South Carolina, you should send a proper number to the other States to protect the Canvas & the elections, in the event of any attempt being made to intimidate the people.—Not an hour is to be lost. You will see from the Copy of the Times N. Y. I send you, how desperate is the State of South Carolina.—The Governor has no military forces able to cope with the Ex-rebels.—Boldness now is wisdom & safety. So soon as Governor Chamberlain has a sufficient body of national troops to protect the Republicans & support the Administration, he ought to arrest General M C Butler & the other leaders of the Hamburg Massacre & his brother the one armed Butler who has been guilty of the murder of coloured men since.—This should have been done a month ago. The arrest of Butler & his brother & their accomplices will strike terror into the hearts of the Ex rebels. If these states are not properly protected, you surrender the elections into the hands of the Democrats, and cast the nation under Rebel rule." ALS, DNA, RG 60, Letters from the President.

On Oct. 14, John C. Winsmith, Spartanburg, S. C., wrote to USG. "Confidential . . . It is with some hesitation that I again address you in reference to the condition of affairs in S. C., as I fear my former communications may have annoyed you; but I am impelled to write to you now from a high sense of duty to my country. Nothing but the declaration of martial law speedily by Gov. Chamberlain, and the exhibition of the power and authority of the National Government can save South Carolina from a bloody revolution and the domination of Hampton and Gary and Butler. These conspirators, by means of their rifle, sabre, pistol and artillery clubs have control of the State. They have impressed the citizens of the dark class with an exhibition of their power, and have declared to them that the U. S. government has forsaken them, and that their only hope for safety is in voting the Democratic Party into power. The articles from the newspapers, enclosed herein, will disclose to you the condition of affairs here. Hampton's main reliance for a military force to install himself and his co-conspirators in power is in the up-country, beginning with Anderson Co, and taking the other counties above Columbia. He also relies upon a force from Georgia. Hill, Toombs and Gordon have been with him in the upper counties, and have scattered the seeds of sedition and rebellion broadcast. To put down this new rebellion in S. C. will require more nerve in the National executive than was ever displayed by President Jackson. The appearance of some military officer, *high in command*, at Atlanta or in S. C., is indispensably necessary. Gov. Chamberlain has told the entire truth, but unless he is aided at once, Republican government in S. C. will be forced to yield to the revolutionists. He can furnish Five Thousand armed soldiers, the U. S. government will from necessity have to furnish Five Thousand, which together with the presence of war vessels in Charleston Harbor will preserve the integrity of the State government and that of the U. S.; for if left unchecked the rebellious Traitors will go to any lengths. Troops should at once be sent to Anderson and the other upper counties to enable Gov. Chamberlain to disband the revolutionary clubs, and to prevent the wholesale slaughter of the friends of the National Government. Hampton has declared openly that he favors the hanging of leading Republicans, and he and Gary and Butler have breathed nothing but rebellion since this campaign opened. It is in every sense a military campaign which they have been conducting. The charges made by the treacherous Judges, Mackey and Cooke, against Gov. Chamberlain are all false. They have been intimidated and employed by the conspirators to do their hellish work. Act, Mr. President—act speedily and all will be well." ALS, *ibid.* HED, 44-2-30, 103–4. See *PUSG,* 25, 339–41.

On Oct. 16, Auguste H. Girard and five others, Washington, D. C., wrote to USG. "At a regular meeting of the South Carolina Republican Club, an address to the people of the United States, adopted at a conference of colored citizens held at Columbia, South Carolina, July 20 and 21, 1876, submitting a statement of facts relating to their condition as citizens of the United States, and more especially in connection with the massacre of peaceable and law-abiding citizens of the State, at Hamburg, on the 8th day of July 1876, having, by Major Wm F. De Knight, been formally laid before the Club, on his motion the following resolutions were unanimously adopted: Resolved, That profoundly realizing the lamentable condition of affairs at present existing in the State which could render such outrages, as have recently been occurring there, possible—barbarities that shock the sensibilities of a civilized world—most sincerely do we condole with and extend our heartfelt sympathy to our bereaved, persecuted and still patiently enduring fellow-citizens in South Carolina, Resolved, That being deeply alive to the vital issues involved in the grave questions of the day, which can alone be fairly determined by a free and full exercise of the elective franchise, we tender, not merely our commiseration, but we also stand ready, individually and collectively, and here pledge ourselves to devote our utmost endeavors, in whatever manner we best can, honorably and lawfully to insure our common interests by securing protection for all alike at the polls at the approaching election in November. Resolved, That to this end—the mean while not being unmindful of his eminent patriotism and of the inestimable services which he had already rendered to our State and the nation, we most earnestly urge upon the Chief Executive of our great Republic the absolute necessity for forcibly stretching out the strong arm of the General Government to shield from actual destruction at the blood-stained hands of traitors the only truly loyal masses of citizens in the Southern country. Resolved, That, further, we solemnly invoke the countenance and moral—and provisionally the material support of all loyal and good citizens everywhere to aid in frowning down, and if needs must, to effectually crush out this horrible condition of affairs that, pressing like a hideous nightmare on its fair bosom, threatens to bring withering blight on the face of the land. . . ." DS, DNA, RG 60, Letters from the President. On May 6, Girard, Treasury Dept. clerk, had written to Secretary of State Hamilton Fish seeking a consular appointment. ALS, *ibid.*, RG 59, Letters of Application and Recommendation. On Oct. 19, U.S. Senator Oliver P. Morton of Ind., San Francisco, telegraphed to USG. "I Congratulate you on your proclamation in regard to South Carolina. Republicans Confident of California—" Telegram received (at 5:35 P.M.), *ibid.*, RG 60, Letters from the President.

On Oct. 21, William Stone, S. C. attorney gen., wrote to Attorney Gen. Alphonso Taft. ". . . You will be glad to know that the result of the prompt action taken by the President has been very beneficial here. In many cases the Rifle Clubs have formally disbanded and several large Republican meetings have been held at which no attempt to 'divide time' or disturb speakers was made . . ." ALS, *ibid.*, Letters Received, S. C.

On Oct. 22, Edward C. Stewart, "for the People," Bennettsville, S. C., wrote to USG. "In this County there are three thousand voters fourteen hundred white & Sixteen hundred Colored voters the present prospect is that the fourteen hundred whites and about four hundred Colored will vote the Democratic Ticket If they are not intimidated by the Radicals in power here who are making every effort to prevent them from voting for Hayes & Hampton which is the popular ticket in this County   these Radicals caught a colored man on the 17th Inst and beat him nearly to death   they Curse us both white & Colored as we pass on the high way   if we appeal to the authorities they say a man's mouth is his own & he can say what he pleases   Yet if we resent any of their abuse by words they have us arrested & put in prison by *your* Troops under the *marshals* who are the vilest men on earth We find the Troops very Civil & Courteous but they are obliged to obey orders from the marshals who if a man says hurrah for Hampton will have him arrested & put in jail. Now Honored Sir We have no desire to resist the powers of the Uninted States and we do deprecate any disloyalty on the part of any citizen and we do all in our power to keep peace by submitting to every indignity abuse & insult imaginable but Dear Sir you can probably imagine an end to human endurance and if things go on as they have for the past week this People will become desperate & will decide to die trying to protect themselves instead of dying submisively, of course if we should resist such a thing as happened yesterday (a white man being taken from his horse in the street for no offence the Colored men being put up to it by their leaders) the troops would be called on to arrest us every one. Now in Gods name what are we to do die like cowardly dogs or die resisting it? For God's Sake advise us what to do or in the last agony of desperation we may do some thing that will be construed resistance to the uninted States Allow me to assure you the Union is Safer now so for as the South is Concerned than it ever was In mercy Condecend to reply to an oppressed people . . . This county is only one of many in the same condition" ALS, *ibid.*, Letters from the President.

On Oct. 25, William Quirk, secretary, Democratic Club, Florence, S. C., twice telegraphed to USG. "The following dispatch has been sent to Govr Chamberlain but has evoked no response. To D H CHAMBERLAIN Columbia S. C. Armed men all black with muskets & bayonets under officers are parading here in the republican procession intimidating White Voters Signed by me. please proclamate by telegraph Will you not issue a proclamation & send down U S Navy" "Gov Chamberlain has since noticed my despatch and ordered the armed men to disband but the President of the Republican meeting told them they were State militia and had a right to carry arms where they pleased In former despatch read the word troops instead of Navy" Telegrams received (at 1:12 and 5:25 P.M.), DLC-USG, IB, and DNA, RG 60, Letters from the President.

On Oct. 30, Thomas H. Clyburn, Lancaster Court House, S. C., wrote to USG. "Enclosed you will please find a certified copy of the Report and Presentment of the Grand Jury of Lancaster County, made and filed in this Office on the 24th inst, which is herewith forwarded, by Order of his Honor T J Mackey Presiding Judge," ALS, *ibid.* John B. Erwin, foreman, and thirteen other grand jurors had addressed Judge Thomas J. Mackey and reported relative calm in Lancaster County. ". . . It is true that we are passing through a political crisis warmly contested in the whole State, and our people are earnestly striving for better times: but at the same time; they mean no insurrection no resistence to lawful authority and no domestic Violence, . . ." Copy, *ibid.*

On Nov. 2, "Detective," Charleston, wrote to USG. "Please let this be strictly private for god's sake & my sake as I believe my life to be already in danger Read & neither publish or show to any one but destroy & act at once I am your friend, do as I tell you. . . . In haste I Write you relative to the present state of affairs here & the coming election, I believe that one of the grandest frauds that ever was enacted in this city will take place if the election is allowed to be held & which in my opinion will end in blood shed & the destruction of the city by fire I am taking no part in politics but if I should I would go Republican, but I write you this for the sake of humanity & if possible to preserve life, & for this cause to have the election postponed untill about the 15th January or untill investigations can be made & arrangements made to have a fair & honest election, do you know that I may say hundreds of poor deluded Cold Men have been bribed &c to vote for Hampton & many have been forced for fear of loosing situations & many have been discharged also white men for not going democratic, it is my Opinion that the democrats intend to carry the election here either by the ballot or bullet (*mind what I say*) I have good reason to believe that at least one regiment will be here from alabama to vote & fight if necessary, also some from florida, I am told that when the govr ordered extra police the order was over ruled by a general here in command of Rifle clubs some of which I believe to be Ku-Klux these bands patroled the streets Until very recently, some of them called Butler Guards have a hall or an old carriage shop in spring st near Rutledge avenue, where they meet near every night in the week Speech making & howling & yelling & when broken up some go home but others congregate to do develment in the upper wards, I do not consider any Republicans safe in his bed. I believe that sevl Cold & White Men have been slyly done away with, firing of guns & pistols are continualy heard throughout the upper wards, I have reason to believe that myself & at least 50 Republicans are marked for the dagger or to be mobbed, While there are some good police the majority are worthless & in case of mobbing I believe would give way or hide, almost daily may be seen a crowd of Idle boys at Ku Klux Hall in Spring street I give it this name for I believe many who visit it belong to this band & believe some of them give it this name themselves, I I consider every man's life in danger who does not belong to the democratic party the hellish work goes on so slyly that it would hardly be thought of here by many but I believe many to be knowing to it but afraid to say anything, but to the point & I write you to have the Humbug postponed for the sake of non politicians, non combatants Women & children, you can see their end in case of a street or city fight & fire which I beleive to be inevitable if the election is allowed to take place, I believe the bought & imported voters with other mixe[d] affairs will cause it, the Colored people are generally quiete, but start them & I believe they will lay the city in ashes & I fear will butcher many inocent people together with women & children who never owned a slave & care nothing for politics. I have no interest in writing further than peace making & the prevention of blood shed I believe I have done my duty in giving you this information & it seems I could not rest untill I did so which I believe to be evidence that something awful is ahead without this election is postponed & investigations made if you doubt I say be on the safe side & investigate for yourself, it is hardly supposeable that you know not your duty then I say be wide awake & so sure that you permit this election to take place & there be a slaughter, I believe that almighty God will hold you *accountable* for the blood of every human being killed, e[xc]use writing &c it is done in great haste hoping you will immediately act in this case . . . P. S. I could tell you more but believe this to be sufficient I believe some want to have things the old way as before the war & say be wide awake a word to the wise is sufficient, this may be the starting point for the South since I believe the alabaman, & floridans will be here" L, *ibid.* See letter to James D. Cameron, Nov. 26, 1876.

Note

——

[*Oct. 17, 1876*]

Say to the Members of Parliament, in a note that it is a universal custom in this Country that when any foreigner has an Address to th deliver to the Govt. it should be delivered to the State Dept. and, if proper the Sec. of State will fix the time and place for its delivery. If improper to receive it the Address will then be returned to the party having it in charge with reasons, if necessary for its non reception

AN, Mr. and Mrs. Philip D. Sang, River Forest, Ill. On Oct. 17, 1876, Culver C. Sniffen wrote to Charles Stewart Parnell and John O'Connor Power, members of Parliament. "Referring to the Address of Congratulation from Ireland which it is understood it was your purpose to deliver to the President of the United States, I am directed by the President to say that it is the uniform custom of this country to require that a copy of papers of such or of a similar character be presented at the Department of State and the Secretary of State, after examination, consults with the President as to a time and place for the delivery of the original. It is also the usual custom in such cases to ascertain that the presentation in question is acceptable to the foreign representative accredited to this government." Copy, DLC-USG, II, 3. On the same day, Parnell and Power, Arlington Hotel, Washington, D. C., wrote to Secretary of State Hamilton Fish. "We have been deputed to present to the President of the United States an address from the people of Ireland congratulating the people of America upon the Centenary of American Independence; and in obedience to the commands of the President we arrived in Washington this morning for the purpose of presenting it. We have however learned that it is requisite to forward to you copies of such documents for your examination, and we now beg to enclose herewith a copy of the address with which we have been entrusted." LS, DNA, RG 59, Miscellaneous Letters.

Patrick Egan, James Kavanagh, and Robert J. Dunne had addressed USG at length. "While the mighty republic over which you preside commemorates the centenary of its deliverance, the Irish nation, universally moved by kindred sympathy, desires to mingle its accents of congratulation with the exultant jubilation of a victorious, a great, and a free people. America has now enjoyed one hundred years of freedom, preserving with unremitting fidelity the sacred trust confided to her care; Ireland has borne seven centuries of oppression without having for a single instant forfeited her fervent love of liberty. . . ." Copy (undated), *ibid.* See Fish diary, Oct. 16–19, 1876, DLC-Hamilton Fish; John L. Cadwalader to Fish, Oct. 13, 1876, Fish to Cadwalader, Oct. 16, 1876, *ibid.* On Oct. 23, Parnell and Power wrote to Sniffen. "The Acting Secretary of State having definitely expressed his inability to make arrangements for the reception by the President of the Centennial address of congratulation from the people of Ireland; may we ask you to be good enough to deliver the address, which we left at the Executive Mansion, to the bearer of this note?" LS, Gallery of History, Las Vegas, Nev. See *CR*, 44–2, 321, 2237; Fish to Thomas Swann, Dec. 29, 1876, DNA, RG 59, Reports to the President and Congress; F. S. L. Lyons, *Charles Stewart Parnell* (London, 1977), pp. 55–57.

Speech

[*Oct. 18, 1876*]

GENTLEMEN OF THE SOCIETY OF THE ARMY OF THE TENNESSEE:— I could scarcely tell how your worthy President knew that I was going to speak. I am sure I gave no indication of such an intention, and my previous practice has shown no signs of fondness for public speaking. I am glad to meet with the army which I first commanded. I hope, after me, you will call upon your other commanders to speak in the order that they appear upon the platform, and they will perform the duty that they have attempted to force upon me, knowing my inability in that way.

Report of the Proceedings of the Society of the Army of the Tennessee, at the Tenth Annual Meeting, . . . (Cincinnati, 1877), p. 519. USG spoke at a banquet, Gen. William T. Sherman presiding. The Society of the Army of the Tennessee met Oct. 18 and 19, 1876, at Washington, D. C., where on Oct. 18 the society unveiled a statue to James B. McPherson.

On June 8, a correspondent had reported from Washington, D. C. "The mother of the late Gen. McPherson lately telegraphed to Gen. Grant placing the remains of her son at his disposal for final sepulture. The President thereupon gave the necessary instructions for their removal from Clyde, Ohio, to this city, where it is proposed to inter them beneath the McPherson statue. . . ." *New York Times,* June 9, 1876. McPherson's body remained at Clyde after local officials blocked its removal. See *Proceedings of the Society of the Army of the*

Tennessee, . . . (ninth and tenth annual meetings), pp. 320–21, 475–76; letter to George S. Canfield, June 30, 1881.

On Oct. 6, Culver C. Sniffen wrote to Admiral David D. Porter, chairman, committee on arrangements for the McPherson statue. "The President directs me to say that it will give him great pleasure to meet again and take by the hand any of his old associates of the Army of the Tennessee, who may be pleased to call on him at 9 oclock on the evening of the 19th instant" Copy, DLC-USG, II, 3.

On Oct. 9, Ulysses S. Grant, Jr., wrote twice to Secretary of the Navy George M. Robeson. "The President directs me say that the several departments of the government will be closed at 12 o'clock M, on Wednesday the 18th inst., to enable the employés to attend the unveiling of the Statue of Genl. McPherson." "The President directs me to request you to hold the Marine Band at the service of the McPherson Monument Association for the 18th and 19th instant." LS, DNA, RG 45, Letters Received from the President.

Speech

[*Oct. 31, 1876*]

Mr. Cardenas,

I welcome you as the Diplomatic Representative of the Republic of Nicaragua. In doing this, I cannot omit to thank you for your flattering reference to the progress of this country under republican institutions; a progress which, here at least, leaves no reason to distrust their efficiency for all the great purposes of government and for the freedom of individuals.

The motives for special sympathy between the United States and Nicaragua, to which you are pleased to allude, are candidly and cordially acknowledged by me. It is to be hoped that, during your mission, these may be illustrated by some signal international measure, the effect of which would be to combine the interests and to strengthen those cordial relations between the two Republics, which I hope will always continue.

D, DNA, RG 59, Notes from Foreign Legations, Central America. On Oct. 31, 1876, Adan Cárdenas, Nicaraguan minister, presented his credentials and addressed USG. ". . . Being animated by the most earnest desires to see the great work of the inter-oceanic Canal through the Central American isthmus realized as speedily as possible, and feeling convinced that it will be accomplished, unless the decided support of the American Government and people be wanting, it has seen with the highest satisfaction (regarding these as an earnest of future progress for Nicaragua and Central America) the reiterated efforts of your Government to insure the speedy commencement and accomplishment of an enterprise of such transcendent importance to the nations of this continent and to the world at large. And now that, thanks to those efforts, science has designated the isthmus of Nicaragua as the most suitable point for the union of the two oceans, my Government is ready to facilitate and protect the execution of the work by all the means in its power, and in any way that may be consistent with its own safety. Having this object in view, it desires to obviate, in concert with Your Excellency's Government, all obstacles to its realization which may arise now or hereafter. Confiding in the good will of which Your Excellency has given unequivocal proofs to the Government and people of Nicaragua, and in the special interest shown by Your Excellency in the work alluded to, I entertain the most sanguine hopes that the important mission confided to me will be as successful as my Government desires." DS (in Spanish), *ibid.*; translation, *ibid.* See Speech, [*March 21, 1876*].

On Oct. 9, Monday, USG had telegraphed to Secretary of State Hamilton Fish, Garrison, N. Y. "Please Meet Me at Fifth Ave. Hotel Wednesday or Thursday Noon—" Telegram received, DLC-Hamilton Fish. On the same day, Fish telegraphed to USG. "Will meet you at Fifth Avenue Hotel, either Wednesday or Thursday as shall be most convenient to you—Unless I hear to the contrary, I will be there on Thursday noon—" ALS (press, telegram sent), *ibid.* Fish described the Oct. 12 meeting in his diary. "He showed me a letter from Mr Benard late Minister to this country from Nicaragua addressed to Com. Ammen mentioned the appointment of Mr Cardenas as Minister from Nicaragua to the United States that he came hoping to negotiate a Treaty for Inter Oceanic Communication, he mentions that Cardenas was in New York staying at the same hotel & he had seen him. The President expressed much interest for the completion of the Canal and the negotiation of a Treaty—Ammen who seems to have taken the matter under his especial charge has been talking with the President. I mention to the President what Peralta had told me of the combinations being make Chevallie and others and of the want of sympathy in the project on the part of the powers of Europe and the unfriendly relations between Nicaragua and Costa-Rica that I would see the Minister and if possible come to some arrangement. While we were conversing Mr Cardenas card was sent in and he was introduced. He brought me a letter of introduction from Ammen and told me he had called twice at my house in New York and wished to be presented to the President, which of course I could not do but told him Mr Cadwalader would present him at any time should I not be in Washington. He said he should be detained in New York until after the 17th awaiting his mail. He appears to be a gentlemanly man without much knowledge of Diplomatic ceremonies." *Ibid.* See Fish diary, Oct. 8, 1876, *ibid.* On Nov. 2, Fish recorded in his diary. "Nicaraguan Minister Dr Cardenas is anxious to open the subject of his mission for the negotiation of a Treaty for the construction of the Inter Oceanic Canal. I assure him of the earnest desire of the President to effect this result, that I presume an agreement will also be necessary with Costa Rica in order to obtain the entire security and neutrality of the Canal. He says that there are questions of boundary between Costa Rica and Nicaragua which are not admitted by the latter, and draws a rough sketch of the lake and the course of the river, but still stating that the admitted boundary of Costa Rica touched a part of the San Juan River where it will be necessary to erect dams to create a slack water, the abutments of which dams must be on the Costa Rica side of the River. I explain to him that to secure the neutrality of the Canal and a contiguous belt of territory in case of war we will require the neutralization of the water at either terminus for a radius of possibly forty leagues to prevent any blockade. I call his attention to the recent concession of Columbia to Mr Gogorza of a route of the River Atrato and show him the reports and maps which accompanied Mr Washburnes #1369. He asked whether this route should appear practicable it would interfere with the negotiation of an arrangement with Nicaragua—I think that we might proceed with the negotiation although should the other appear practicable it would probably prevent the construction of the one by the Lakes— . . ." *Ibid.* On the same day, Fish met with Francisque de Vaugelas, French chargé d'affaires. "He says he has been instructed to ask whether we have done anything with reference to the Nicaraguan Canal. I explain to him that the views of this government to be generally that we desire a Canal constructed in whatever way may prove to be the most practicable route. That the United States will seek no advantages to itself over any other nation that will unite in the neutralization of the Canal and its approaches that from the report of the Commission sent out by the Government we had been induced to suppose that the Nicaraguan Route presented the greater advantages but I had recently learned that the International Geographical Congress assembled in Paris last year raised doubts on that point and represented the practacability of a Canal without locks by the way of the Atrata River and was of opinion that Captain Selfridge had been lead into an exploration of a wrong branch of the Atrato, that we were disposed to unite with other governments in investigating the present proposed route, that the President would prefer that no concession be given to any individual until the route be possevety determined and the arrangements toward neutralization be perfected." *Ibid.* On Nov. 3, Fish briefed the cabinet. "I stated the purport of my conversation of yesterday with the Nicaraguan Minister and submitted Mr Washburnes 1369 on the Inter Oceanic Canal and the maps attached to the accompanying reports also Kossouth's letter to him and that of Gorgoza & General Turr. The President thinks that if properly applied to it would be well to appoint an Engineer to join in the survey of the route by the Atrato does not think it necessary to answer Kossouth's letter." *Ibid.* On Sept. 3, Louis Kossuth, Collegno, Italy, had written at length to USG. ". . . On the 28th of May last a Concession has been granted by the Columbian government for the construction of an interoceanic Canal *without either sluices or tunnels* across the Isthmus of Darien, between the gulf of Uraba on the Atlantic, and that of San Miguel on the Pacific Ocean The concessioneers are a Syndicate established at Paris and presided over by a distinguished Countryman of mine the General Türr wellknown from the prominent part he took under Garibaldi in the emancipation of Italy and allied by marriage to the Bonaparte family   Said concession is framed in the most liberal spirit, with a particular care to assure to the undertaking a truly international character, free from either partiality or exclusiveness. It is expressly stipulated therein, that the ports at the two extremities, and the waters of the Canal shall be free for all the Nations of the earth and *shall be considered neutral even in the case of a war with Columbia.* And is has further been stipulated that to render even more evident the FUNDAMENTAL CHARACTER OF INTERNATIONALITY: the tracings and plans which are to serve as a basis for the definitive constitution of the executive company, must be the work of Engineers and other competent scientific men, not of any one single country whatever, but chosen from different countries so that their verdict might present the highest possible guaranty. . . ." ALS, DNA, RG 59, Miscellaneous Letters. On Sept. 7, Anthoine de Gogorza, Paris, wrote to USG. "I have been introduced to you some ten years ago by general Comstock, on particular recommendation of general J. H. Wilson your devoted friend, to submit to you my scheme of an Interoceanic canal; and I have had the honour to speak about it with you in different interviews. But I was then strongly opposed by influential people of the Panama R. R. Co—and when the official survey of the Isthmus took place, Commander Selfridge was either made nervous by the intense sufferings he endured in crossing the swamps of Cacarica,—or misled by his guides. The fact is that he disregarded my route, to adopt a more southern one, and left therefore the ground fairly open to a new verification; inasmuch as every time that the work of his efficient staff came across my own line of levels, they confirmed its accuracy. Now, providentially, Colonel

Farrand late U. S. Consul at Callao, went over the place, so much as to demonstrate, by his unbiased testimony, that I am right in my statement of two distinct cordille[ras] separated by a valley which has been,—and is yet accidentally—a natural water communication between the tw[o] oceans; showing thereby the feasibility of opening a Canal without neither locks nor tunnel. Colonel Farrand expressed further th[e] intention to obtain a hearing, to impr[ess] upon your mind the convenience that our government should now recognize and encourage my scheme as a nearly accomplished fact. . . ." ALS, *ibid.* On Sept. 15, Stephen Türr, Budapest, wrote to USG. "Mr Kossuth late Governor of Hungary has brought to the knowledge of your Excellency that I have obtained from the respective authorities a Concession for a navigable Canal across the Isthmus of Darien . . . I therefore take the liberty to petition your Excellency that you may kindly nominate in an official or semi-official form Colonel Farran[d] late United States Consul at Calao (Peru), who but lately has been person[ally] across the very line we propose to re-explore, and pronounced his opinion as to the perfect feasability of the scheme and if I might ask a further favor, it would be that the United United States Government would during the time that our re-exploring expedition will be out at work, station a U. S. Frigate with a steam embarkation in the Gulf of Duraba at the Delta of the Attrato from November 28th of this year." LS, *ibid.* On Nov. 13, Fish wrote confidentially and at length to Elihu B. Washburne, Paris. ". . . I am informed that some years since Mr. de Gogorza sought an introduction to General Grant (possibly before his inauguration as President) professing a desire to submit the results of his explorations for consideration, with a view to some aid, either of moral or of material support, or of the endorsement of his project. That a highly accomplished officer of the Engineer service was detailed for the examination, whereupon Mr. de Gogorza declined to submit the results of his exploration on the alleged ground that they would become public, and he be deprived of the advantages which might be derived from them. . . ." Copy, *ibid.*, Diplomatic Instructions, France. See *Foreign Relations, 1876*, pp. 87–93; *ibid., 1877*, pp. 125–26.

Fish drafted a canal treaty with Nicaragua in early Dec., but negotiations stalled over proposed amendments. See Fish diary, Dec. 7, 8, 1876, Jan. 5, 25, 1877, DLC-Hamilton Fish; Cárdenas to Fish, Dec. 8, 1876, DNA, RG 59, Notes from Foreign Legations, Central America. On Feb. 1, 1877, Fish recorded in his diary. "Costa Rican Minister Mr Peralta calls and says he has been consulted by Dr. Cardenas with regard to the proposed Treaty We discuss several points of it. I tell him the impossibility of our attempting to negotiate on the basis proposed by Nicaragua; that nearly all the engagements were on the part of the United States, and the benefits to Nicaragua; that it is illogically drawn; and in language vague and indefinite; that, for instance, it refers to obligations contracted by France or Spain, which are not stated or named, and which would have to be assumed by the United States; also to a Treaty of Managua of 1860 which is not known. It refers to a Treaty of Washington of April 11th 1864; there is no such Treaty; and various other provisions in the Treaty, which are wholly objectionable, and I express to him, the fear that there is not time during the present session of Congress, and the Administration, to reconsider such entirely extraordinary propositions; I also mention that while these negotiations have been pending, Nicaragua has made a concession of a Canal to Henry Meigs & Son. He expresses great surprise, thinking I must be mistaken, and that it must be a Rail Road. I showed him a certified copy of the concession; and he shrugged his shoulders saying, that is the way Nicaragua always does I told him it would be useless to negotiate any treaty with Costa Rica, until the terms of one with Nicaragua could be agreed to, and I feared in present prospects that would not be likely to be agreed to" DLC-Hamilton Fish. See Fish diary, Feb. 2, 8, 15, 1877, *ibid.*

On Feb. 23, Commodore Daniel Ammen wrote to Ulysses S. Grant, Jr. "The President was good enough to ask from the State Department the loan of the paper of the commission of what it supposed should form the basis of a Treaty with Nicaragua to secure the construction of an Interoceanic canal. You too, kindly promised to secure it but owing to your many occupations may have not been able to do so. Please pardon this reminder.—I will at once return the paper." ALS, DNA, RG 59, Miscellaneous Letters. On the same day, Grant, Jr., wrote to Fish conveying this request. ALS, *ibid.* On Feb. 28, Fish wrote to members of the diplomatic corps enclosing copies of treaty drafts and his correspondence with Cárdenas. DS, USG 3. See *SED*, 46-2-112, 132–49; *Young*, II, 156–57.

Calendar

1876, JAN. 1. Clinton B. Fisk, chairman, and six other members of the Board of Indian Commissioners, Washington, D. C., to USG. "During the past year there has been no organized act of hostility by any tribe or band of Indians, the most of them having remained quietly on their reservations, and having manifested a disposition to comply with the requirements of the Government. This is the more noteworthy, from the fact that two years ago all the bands of Sioux threatened to wage war upon any individuals or parties who might visit the Black Hills, and that the Cheyennes, Arapahoes, Kiowas, and Comanches, of the Indian Territory, and the Apaches, of Arizona, until within the last year were the terror of the white settlers, and in a condition bordering on hostility. The improvement in these respects, especially among the wilder tribes, is as conspicuous as it is gratifying, and denotes that the polic[y] which has been pursued has been generally satisfactory to the Indians, and salutary in its influences upon them. The Sioux, relinquishing their threatening attitude, have permitted many parties to visit the Black Hills during the year without molestation, whether with or without military escort; and, for a consideration which until recently they would have scouted as totally inadequate, have voluntarily relinquished their right to hunt outside their reservation. . . . An interesting illustration of the progress of the Indians in habits of industry, education, and religious and moral ideas, is furnished by the statistics bearing upon these and related subjects which have been collected by the board, and a random selection from them will afford a view of the comparative condition of the Indians in several years, and of the advance that has been made by them generally in intelligence and self support. . . . Undoubtedly the progress of the Indians in education, industry, and other kindred elements of civilization has been such as to encourage the philanthropist, and to fully justify the wisdom of the Government in the method which it has adopted of dealing with these helpless children of the forest. The information derived from these and other sources proves beyond question that the results of the present humane policy are highly satisfactory; and it is the opinion of this board that the peace and safety of our frontier settlements, the public economy, the welfare of the Indians, as well as the interests of morals and religion, demand a steady adherence to this policy until the Indians shall no longer need to be treated as a separate and peculiar race. We are also of the opinion that the facts which have been cited, and the evidence to which we have referred, conclusively prove the capacity of the Indian for civilization, and the duties and privileges of citizenship. . . . At the present time the proposition to turn the government of the Indians over from the Department of the Interior to the War Department is gravely discussed, and finds many adherents among those who have heretofore given but little thought to the solution of what is called the 'Indian problem.' The opinion of the board on this important subject having been sought, officially and otherwise, we present the following as representing our views: It should be remembered that the Indians once owned this broad continent from the Atlantic to the Pacific Ocean, and that our ancestors and ourselves have acknowledged their original ownership, and have purchased and acquired by treaty and by force all the lands we now possess. On the discovery of this continent, it is estimated that it was occupied by about three millions of Indians. Now there are less than two hundred and eighty thousand remaining within the limits of the United States. We have removed them, by treaties and otherwise, before the tide of white population, until they are confined within a comparatively narrow space. Now, the conscience of the very large majority of our fellow-citizens insists that we should be both just and generous with them, as they are rapidly dwindling away under the adverse influences to which they are greatly exposed by vicious and greedy white men, with whom they are surrounded. The only hope of saving this remnant of a noble race lies in their education, civilization, and Christianization. During the last seven years, under many difficulties of administration, there has been a set purpose to improve their condition, which has borne good fruit, and has succeeded beyond any reasonable expectation, as can be established by indubitable evidence. During this time, however, there have been those who have cruelly asserted that these Indians should be exterminated to make room for white men. Such advocates are found plentifully on the borders of Indian reservations and on the march to the Black Hills. Indeed, wherever the Indian has desirable lands, men of this class can be found looking eagerly for an opportunity to enter in and possess them. These men to-day are all of the opinion that the Indians should be handed over to the care of the military. There is another and more respectable class who think it the 'manifest destiny' of the white race to wipe out the aborigines, and that their extinction is only a question of time. Therefore, they, too, are quite in favor of putting them under military control. But the vast majority of the American people, when their attention is directed to the subject, will, under a conscientious impulse, oppose any such measure. . . . We cannot see any benefit whatever that is likely, or even possible, to result from relegating the care of the Indian to the Army. The Army is admirable in its place, but its function is not that of civil government in a republic like ours. . . ."—*Seventh Annual Report of the Board of Indian Commissioners,* . . . (Washington, 1876), pp. 3, 5–6, 14–15.

On Dec. 21, 1875, Col. James A. Hardie, inspector gen., Philadelphia, had written to USG. "I think there is a fair chance of the Indian Department being turned over to the War Department this Session. In case it should, please consider me a candidate for Commissioner of Indian Affairs; if Army officers are to be detailed. Some few years ago, you may remember the same proposition was up and I was then spoken of as a fit candidate, but then I did not care for it. Now, I would like it. I feel entirely confident that I could satisfy your administration in this place. I have lived among Indians and know them and their management; and I think within the last ten years I have seen as many Indians on the frontier as most Army officers—And besides, I have spent years in my earlier life, as you know, in frontier service. My wife and myself when you were here did our best to pay our respects to Mrs. Grant and yourself. We failed to have the pleasure and the honor of seeing you. But if we had known that you were not to leave the city until the next day, we should have gone to see you again."—LS, DNA, RG 94, ACP, 22 1877.

On Jan. 12, 1876, a correspondent reported from Washington, D. C. "To-day a delegation of Cherokees, Choctaws, Creeks, and Seminoles called upon President Grant to pay their respects, and to talk of affairs in the Indian Territory, which they represented to be in a good and prosperous condition, with abundant crops. They took occasion to express their opposition to the proposed territorial government in their country, when the President informed them that no bill passed by Congress for that purpose would receive his approval without the consent of the Indians."—*Chicago Tribune,* Jan. 13, 1876.

On June 1, George Whipple, secretary, American Missionary Association, New York City, wrote to USG. "It has been reported to us that there is a vacancy in the Board of Indian Peace Commissioners, which it may be agreeable to you to fill by the appointment of a suitable person from the Congregational body of Christians. If so, allow me to request your favorable consideration of the name of Rev. E. Whittlesey, now holding some connection with the Board. If you desire testimonials of his fitness for this position, I shall be happy to furnish you such from Gen. C. B. Fisk, John D. Lang, A. C. Barstow and others of the present Board."—LS, DNA, RG 48, Appointment Div., Letters Received. On March 11, 1869, Brig. Gen. Oliver O. Howard had written to USG. "I wish to ask a special favor in behalf of one who has served with me as Gen. Rawlings & Maj Bowers did with you.—Gen. Eliphalet Whittlesey. He was judge advocate on my staff, as Maj. then Lt. Colonel. Then he became Colonel of a Regiment, at the close of the war brevetted a Brigadier General.—He sufferred Mr Johnson's displeasure, because in a N. Carolina report he spoke of the disastrous effect of his 1st veto. . . ."—ALS, *ibid.,* RG 59, Letters of Application and Recommendation. On March 17, Eliphalet Whittlesey, Washington, D. C., wrote to USG seeking a consulship.—ALS, *ibid.* No appointment followed.

1876, JAN. 1. Lyman M. Kellogg, USMA 1852, Key West, Fla., to USG. "From the 1st to the 23rd of Decr 1875, I almost daily, by exerting all my physical strength, managed to crawl up the stairs of the Executive Mansion in order to personally present my case to you, but, I failed to see you; finally, with Death staring me in the face, I yeilded to the entreaties of my Wife and the advice of Dr Basil Norris, Surgn U S A, Army Dispensary &c, and left for Key-West, Florida. Weak and crippled as I am from wounds, of course my Wife had to come with me—My *full* Captains pension ($20 monthly) will *not support* us, and our little means are *rapidly dwindling*—I have been from 6 to 8 months yearly confined to room & bed at my home in Ohio—I refer you especially to Dr Norris U S A, and I *implore* you, in the name of *humanity* and *justice,* to *read* the enclosed 'Brief' & 'Application' of a Graduate of the Mil Acady & Ex Officer of many years service, crippled from wounds in battle when commanding his Regiment—"—ALS, DNA, RG 94, Applications for Positions in War Dept. Among the enclosures and related papers is a letter of Dec. 20, 1875, from Kellogg, Washington, D. C., to USG requesting appointment as 2nd lt.—ALS, *ibid.* No appointment followed. See *PUSG,* 17, 384–86; *SRC,* 48-1-256.

1876, JAN. 2. Corodon O. Hewitt, Ward's Corners, Iowa, to USG. "as I was under your command at the battle fought at Port Gibson recieved a wound threw the wright foot disableing me for farming haveing a large family. we have 3 at one birth as you may see by there picture three little girls the 8 dollars per mounth pension which I get seems in Sufficient for the dissebility I recieved in the Sirvice I thought I would lay the case befour you and See if there could be

eny thing more done pleas excuse the rongs if there be eny in writeing to
you"—ALS, DNA, RG 48, Miscellaneous Div., Letters Received. No increase
followed.

1876, JAN. 4.   USG note. "Desires a place as counter in the Treas. The husband
was a badly wounded soldier and died recently from the effects of his wounds.
He was one of the Messengers at the Ex. Mansion at the time of his death, and
had been for more than six years, a sufferer all that time from his previous
wounds."—ANS, DNA, RG 56, Applications. On Jan. 15, Ellen A. Joice received
appointment as a counter.—N, *ibid.* On June 21, USG wrote another note. "I
would be pleased to have Mrs. Joyice retained in the reduction about to take
plac[e.] She is the widow of a worthy soldier who died from the effect of wounds
rec'd in service"—ANS, *ibid.* Related papers are *ibid.*

1876, JAN. 5.   USG order. "Upon the recommendation of the Secretary of the
Interior, and for the convenience of pensioners, it is ordered that the Agency for
paying pensions at Macon City, in the State of Missouri, be removed to and located at St. Joseph in said State."—DS, DNA, RG 48, Miscellaneous Div., Letters Received. On Jan. 14, USG ordered the pension agency moved from St. Joseph to Hannibal, Mo.—DS, *ibid.* On Jan. 19, USG issued an order returning
the pension office to St. Joseph.—DS, *ibid.* See *PUSG*, 24, 295–98; *HMD*, 44-
1-183, 33–35.

1876, JAN. 5.   USG endorsement. "Refered to the Sec. of War. Let special attention be invited."—AES, DNA, RG 94, Correspondence, USMA. Written on
a letter of the same day from Maj. Henry C. Hodges, q. m., USMA 1851, Washington, D. C., to USG. "Thinking that perhaps the application I made to you
some time since, for an appointment to the Military Academy at West Point for
my son, may have been mislaid I venture to renew the application. . . ."—ALS,
ibid. On March 28, 1874, Hodges, New Orleans, had written to USG on the
same subject.—ALS, *ibid.* For Hodges's reminiscences of USG, including a
conversation with USG on this matter, see typescript, DLC-William Conant
Church. Henry C. Hodges, Jr., graduated USMA in 1881.
    On [*Feb. 2, 1877*], USG wrote concerning Hodges, Sr. "Enquire into the
cause of reprimand in /71. A[sks] removal of censure. Papers were seized while
his child was laying at point of death, and the investigtion occurred in Washington while the investigated was in Phila and not heard in his own defence"—
AN (undated), DNA, RG 94, ACP, 469 1872.

1876, JAN. 5.   Levi P. Luckey to Attorney Gen. Edwards Pierrepont. "The
President directs me to say that in reply to your note in relation to Mr Waldo
to be Chief Justice of New Mexico, that he agrees with you and to make the
nomination. He, also, suggests that at the same time you have prepared a nomination of an Associate Justice in Arizona [*Idaho*] and he thinks you better take
the recommendation of the former Governor and now the Delegate in Congress
Mr Bennett"—Copy, DLC-USG, II, 3. In a petition docketed Dec. 28, 1875, Pedro Sanchez, president, New Mexico Territory Legislative Council, *et al.* had

written to USG. "We the undersigned members of the Legislative Assembly of the Territory of New Mexico, having learned with the deepest regret of the death of the Hon Joseph G Palen late Chief Justice of the Supreme Court of the Territory of New Mexico; And having full and entire confidence in the ability, integrity and legal capacity of our fellow citizen Henry L Waldo, who has been a resident of this Territory for the last two years and a half during which time he has been engaged in the practice of his profession, believe that Mr Waldo's knowledge of the people of this Territory and the laws, and rulings of the courts as also his knowledge of the Spanish language eminently qualify and fit him as a proper person to be appointed to the office of Chief Justice of the Territory of New Mexico, . . ."—DS (39 signatures, undated), DNA, RG 60, Records Relating to Appointments. On Jan. 6, 1876, Giles A. Smith, Santa Fé, telegraphed to USG. "Appointment of Waldo Chief Justice here is very desirable He is entirely competent and capable, will give satisfaction,"—Telegram received, DLC-USG, IB. On Jan. 6, USG nominated Henry L. Waldo as chief justice, New Mexico Territory; on Jan. 13, USG nominated Henry E. Prickett as associate justice, Idaho Territory, to replace William C. Whitson, deceased.

On Dec. 23, 1875, U.S. Senators Thomas W. Ferry and Isaac P. Christiancy of Mich. had written to USG. "We respectfully recommend Judge Charles R. Brown of Michigan for the position of Chief Justice for the Territory of New Mexico, made vacant by the recent death of the late incumbent."—LS, DNA, RG 60, Records Relating to Appointments. On Dec. 25, R. Holland Duell, commissioner of patents, wrote to USG. "I earnestly recommend the appointment of F. A. Durkee Esq of Binghamton N. Y. as Chief Justice of New Mexico. Mr. Durkee is well qualified by learning and experience for the position, and is an active earnest Republican."—ALS, *ibid.* Papers recommending Larkin A. Byron, William D. Lee, Ezekiel Y. Bell, and George H. Young, other unsuccessful applicants for chief justice, New Mexico Territory, are *ibid.*

1876, JAN. 5. Mary E. T. Cone, Oil City, Pa., to USG. "Pardon the liberty I take in addressing you, a stranger, though I had the honor to be appointed one of a committee to receive your gracious lady in Oil-City. I have no influential friends in Washington, but remembering your kind lady, your sweet-faced daughter, and your august but unostentatious self, so kind, and so indulgent even to the children, I thought I might venture to appeal directly to you. I had seen you, our Country's Savior, before at the graves of our buried heroes Mt. Arlington, and since at Mayville, but you will have no recollection of your correspondent, for in the words of the beautiful Persian proverd 'The moon looks on many flowers, the flowers see but *one* moon.' Mr. Andrew Cone, my husband, a good man in word and deed, is suffering from a bronchial affection, and physicians have ordered him to some warm dry climate, consequently, I am very anxious to obtain a consulate for him, and I thought as changes were being made, and some of the consuls would attend the Centennial and not return, there might be a chance for him. We would be willing to go anywhere that your Excellency might indicate, even Turkey, Spain, or Cuba, having already traveled in foreign lands, and being not entirely ignorant of other languages, especially French. I do not know what to say to influence your Excellency favorably towards us, but

I do believe, if you understood all the circumstances, there would be no hesitation on your part, in speaking a kind word for us, and whose word in Washington is so potent as ~~that of~~ your own? With great respect and admiration, . . ."—ALS, DNA, RG 59, Letters of Application and Recommendation. On Feb. 3, Governor John F. Hartranft of Pa. wrote to USG. "I have the honor to commend Mr. Andrew Cone of Oil City, Pa. to your Excellency for appointment to a Consulate at some European or Asiatic post. Mr. Cone has the necessary qualifications, is a gentleman of character and excellent habits, and his appointment would be gratifying to a large circle of friends in this State, and place me under great personal obligations as I am indebted to the family of Mr. Cone for many acts of kindness."—LS, *ibid.* Probably soon after, USG wrote a note. "Will the Sec. of State please see Mrs. Cone, of Oil City, Pa. Mr Cole—the husband—is an applicant for a Consulate, strongly endorsed by Gov. Hartranft."—AN (undated), Columbia University, New York, N. Y. On Feb. 22, Mary Cone, West Conshohocken, Pa., wrote to Julia Dent Grant. "I would not venture to address you if this could reach the eye of the President, but I am told he cannot begin to read the flood of letters that arrive daily. When your card went into the President I was admitted, and his Excellency was MOST KIND—indeed I found no one in Washington more benignant than the great head of the nation. He wrote on his card, which I myself delivered to Secretary Fish these words: 'I will be pleased if you can confer an appointment.' Mr. Sec. Fish gave me the choice of one in Brazil, Argentine Republic, Hayti, Mexico & St Paul de Loando, Africa. I assented to the latter, because I understood there was neither salary nor perquisites to any of the others, and we couldn't live on nothing. But my friends in Phila. assure me it is so unhealthy on the West coast of Africa, *it means death*, and they also assure me that the President is too courteous too chivalrous a gentleman to permit any other than a good appointment given a lady on *his* recommendation. Besides, they say that as Gov. Hartranft, *who rarely solicits a consulate*, requested it as a personal favor to himself, for service rendered to himself, the favor conferred upon Mr. Cone would be worthy of the President and of the Governor. Mr. Cone only stipulated for a warm, healthy climate, and would be willing to go anywhere on the *Northern* coast of Africa, Chili, Brazil, Mexico, Sandwich Islands, anywhere that there was enough salary for the necessities of life, though we should prefer a European or Asiatic port: If in Sicily even, or Egypt. . . ."—ALS, DNA, RG 59, Letters of Application and Recommendation. Related papers are *ibid.* On Feb. 21, USG had nominated Andrew Cone as consul, St. Paul de Loando; on March 14, USG withdrew this nomination and nominated Cone as consul, Pará.

On Feb. 25, 1875, Frederick Pond, vice consul, Pará, had telegraphed to USG. "The American residents at Para have the honor to congratulate the president on the completion of telegraph Communication betwen north and south America"—Telegram received, DLC-USG, IB.

1876, JAN. 5. Katie Wehe, Cincinnati, to USG seeking a pension for her mother because of her brother's death from a lung wound received while serving with the 11th Ohio. "If you read those lines you will think, who is this from! it is from a poor person who sets ~~all~~ her last hope in you, thinking, perhaps you have feelings enough to help where is need is it is in this case. I have a sister in Toledo Ohio where got married to a man who treats her dreadfully, she writes me, that if she would not get soon help, she would not wkow what to do; she dont even feel her child save with him. If I only could get money enough to have them to come here and to furnish a Room so we could work here together, we would pai every cent back again. It is not h[er] herself who suffer so I have a poor mother who is with her who suffers with her to. . . ."—ALS, DNA, RG 48, Miscellaneous Div., Letters Received.

1876, JAN. 6.   USG endorsement. "Refered to the Sec. of War for special attention when appointments are made to West Point."—AES, DNA, RG 94, Correspondence, USMA. Written on a letter of the same day from Mary A. Johnson, Washington, D. C., to USG. "Knowing how hard it is to see you, owing to your important duties, I thought it best to send you my application for an appointment for my son. Last summer you kindly promised to give him one, at the same time telling me I could remind you of it. He does not want it before June 1877, so I hope I may be in time, & that you will be able to grant me this favor. With continued thanks for your past kindnesses, . . ."—ALS, *ibid.* Also on Jan. 6, and Feb. 21, Johnson wrote to USG. "I have the honor to apply to you for an appointment for my son—Howard Johnson to West Point for June 1877. His Father Henry D. Johnson was for many years a Government Officer, & died on his way to Constantinople, as Consul Genl. to that place. His Grandfather Col. J. J. Abert was chief of the Topographical Corps, for many years." "I must ask you, if you will give my son an alternate appointment for West Point— . . . I have been working in the Treasury for twelve years, the most I have been paid is $75 per month—I am thankful to do so—if I can only see my two sons making a living. I know that my family have been faithful servants to the Government, & am sure you will not regret the help you only, can give. . . ."—ALS, *ibid.* Howard Johnson did not attend USMA.

[*1876, Jan. 7*].   USG note. "D. C. Cameron expresses great anxiety to have Jos. T. Mason, of Va aptd. Consul at Dresden or at some equally good place," —AN (undated), DLC-Hamilton Fish. See Rudolph Lexow to Hamilton Fish, April 28, 1876, *ibid.*; *PUSG*, 24, 80–81, 433.

1876, JAN. 8.   H. I. Chapman, Washington, D. C., to USG. "I desire to make known to you some of the facts in regard to the peculations in office of Wm McMicken, Surveyor General of Washington Territory. Mr. McMicken was appointed to office at the instance of Senator Windham in July 1873, and at the time of his nomination it was charged against McMicken that he was a traitor to the Republican party having worked and voted for the Democratic nominee for Congress against Mr. Garfield the Republican Candidate, and that he was guilty of other charges which should prevent his appointment. Upon these charges being made (in 1873) the Secretary of the Interior sent a special Agent, Mr. Pierson, (now employed in the Interior Departmnt) to investigate the charges against Mr. McMicken. Mr. Pierson on his arrival at Olympia, Washington Territory satisfied himself that Mr. McMicken was guilty of all the charges and reported by telegraph to the Secretary of the Interior as follows: 'Charges all sustained.' But on leaving Olympia the next day he proceeded to Kalama where he was met by Col. John R. Wheat, a friend of Mr. McMicken's, who induced Mr. Pierson ~~to change his~~ by the use of money and the promise that the Brother of Mr Pierson should have the chief clerkship under Mr. McMicken, to change his report and to exhonerate said McMicken. This Mr. Pierson did do as can be seen by his *two* reports now on file in the Departmt of the Interior, . . . Mr. McMicken is now, and has been every since his appointment, paying a money consideration to Senator Windham for keeping him in ~~his~~ office. . . ."—ALS, DNA, RG 48, Appointment Div., Letters Received. On Dec. 2, 1873, USG had nominated William McMicken as surveyor gen., Washington Territory. On Sept. 7, 1876, Byron Barlow, Steilacoom, Washington Territory, wrote to USG with allegations against McMicken. ". . . 3d That his Chief Clerk, Geo- L Pearson has been intoxicated time and again on the public streets of Olympia during business hours in the Surveyors Generals office being entirely unable to transact any business, and the said McMicken positively refuses to dismiss him from the public service. 4th That the said McMicken has industriously worked with the Democratic party useing all means in his power in 1872 to elect the Democratic Delegate to Congress, and he has declard openly if the Republicans did not keep him in his office he would burst the party in Washington Territory; Finally I am in agreement with the mass of Republicans in the Territory who believe that the said McMicken is a very corrupt man in office useing his position for gain, and other corrupt practices and unworthy to occupy the position of Surveyor General of Washington Territory." —ALS, *ibid.*, Appointment Papers, Wyoming Territory. A related letter is *ibid.* McMicken continued in office.

1876, JAN. 10.   USG note. "Will Com. Patterson please see Mr. Plumsel with the view of giving him some position which he may be able to fill."—ANS (facsimile), USGA.

On March 10 and Oct. 10, 1869, petitioners had written to USG recommending Thomas Plumsill as D. C. justice of the peace.—DS, DNA, RG 60, Records Relating to Appointments. No appointment followed.

1876, JAN. 10.   Maj. Gen. John M. Schofield, San Francisco, to USG. "I have the honor to solicit your kind consideration of the application of Charles C. Morgan for an appointment at large to the Military Academy. He is the oldest son of the late Major C. H. Morgan, 4th Artillery who recently died at Alcatraz. Major Morgan was one of the most excellent officers of his age in the Army. His record, both in peace and war, was one of which any officer might be proud. He died at his post of duty, leaving his family, a widow and six children, with very limited means of support. Young Morgan is a bright lad of excellent character, well worthy of a Cadet appointment, the receipt of which would be extremely gratifying to all Major Morgan's old comrads in the Army."—ALS, DNA, RG 94, Correspondence, USMA. On Jan. 20, Gen. William T. Sherman, St. Louis, endorsed this letter. "I heartily approve and endorse the within letter of Genl Schofield. Maj Morgan was an officer well known to the President, so that any thing I might add to what is herein given would be superfluous."—AES, *ibid.*

Letters from Charles C. Morgan, Maj. Gen. Winfield S. Hancock, and Lt. Gen. Philip H. Sheridan on the same subject are *ibid.* Probably in late May, USG ordered Morgan's appointment "to fill the vacancy in Cadetships at Large in place of Wm B Le Duc of Minnesota Def Rejected by Acad Bd April Examn 76."—D (docketed May 31), *ibid.* Morgan failed the entrance examination.

1876, JAN. 12.   USG note. "Will the Sec. of the Treas. please place Mr. F. A. Wordell,—a soldier for four years, recently discharged from the Capitol—in a position in the re-organization of the Comptrollers or Auditors office."—ANS, DNA, RG 56, Applications. On Jan. 24 and 27, Benjamin R. Cowen, asst. secretary of the interior, telegraphed to Charles F. Conant, asst. secretary of the treasury, to appoint Leicester King as a treasury clerk in exchange for the appointment of Francis A. Wordell as a pension clerk.—ALS (telegrams sent), *ibid.* Related papers are *ibid.*

1876, JAN. 13.   Luman Case, "a Poor old Survivor of the War of 1812," Reading, Mich., to USG requesting "a few crums that may fall from his Masters Table . . . if nothing better I would like a Special Act in my favour."—ALS, DNA, RG 48, Miscellaneous Div., Letters Received. A law of March 3, 1881, authorized a pension for Case.—*U.S. Statutes at Large,* XXI, 650. See *SRC,* 46-2-664.

1876, JAN. 14.   U.S. Representative Harris M. Plaisted of Maine to USG. "I desire to state in reference to the Houlton Postmaster that so far as I have any second choice I prefer Mr Boyd a soldier to Mr Hussey, & by letters from Houlton just recd, I am authorized to say that Mr Boyd prefers the appointment of my friend Mr Pearce as a third man I am satisfied no good can come to the party or public by evading the friendly issue between two capital soldiers—I stand squarely for Pearce."—Telegram received, DNA, RG 107, Telegrams Collected (Bound). On the same day, Culver C. Sniffen wrote to Postmaster Gen. Marshall Jewell. "At the request of Senator Hamlin, the President directs me to say, that he would like you to bring the Holton Post Office papers before him to day"— Copy, DLC-USG, II, 3. On Jan. 19, USG nominated William L. Boyd as postmaster, Houlton, Maine.

1876, JAN. 17.   USG endorsement. "Refered to Hds. of Depts for such consideration as they may be able to give these recommendations."—AES, DNA, RG 56, Applications. Written on a letter of the same day from Judge Alexander Rives, Washington, D. C., to USG. "Mrs. Garrett is from my county and is a lady of good connections and character. She is without means; and has a family dependent on her for support. . . ."—ALS, *ibid.* Related papers include an undated statement by Mary G. Garrett. ". . . For the last ten years I have been supporting myself by *dress makeing* but the constant use of the sewing machine has so injured my health as to render frurther use of it fatal. . . ."—ADS, *ibid.* No appointment followed.

[*1876*], JAN. 19.   Benjamin M. Harney, "Nephew of Gen W. S. Harney," Louisville, to USG. "I was a soldier in the Mexican war, in Company "A" '4th Ky infantry volunteers,' under Captain Timothy Keating. I was captain of Co A 9th

Ky Cavalry in the last little unpleasantness between the north & south, I am a son of John H. Harney, formerly editor of the Louisville Democrat. I have some reputation as a mathematican & civil engineer & am out of work   I only ask for employment which I can fill to your or any bodies satisfaction, If you can give me any position in the army or civil life which will pay expeses, please look at the the the thing   My Wife is Mag Draffin, Some *awful long way off kin-folks of yours*   My father was editor of the Louisville Democrat. I was Captain of Comany "A" 9th Ky Cavalry. I was Colonel in Caraballo's revolution in Mexico, Col in the Crittenden expedition to Cuba & in short there has never been one damned fool place I have not been   Help me to a place if you can or are willing to do so. I refer you to Gen B. H. Bristow, E Y. Parsons James B B. Beck or any body else from Kentucky Phil Speed, Eli Murray or *any nobody*   Read this letter yourself. I was with you in Mexico & believe I have a right to ask you to read at least"—ALS (docketed Jan. 22, 1876), DNA, RG 56, Applications. No appointment followed. Harney later taught school in Louisville.

1876, JAN. 20.   Augustus N. Lowry, Washington, D. C., to USG. "There is a Son of Mr M. Bailey Jamestown NY (Charles Justin Bailey) who is an applicant for an appointment to West Point—Mr Bailey is a very prominent Methodist and Republican of that district (33d) who could but ignore Mr Norton with thousands of others in that district at the last election—Young Bailey is 17 years of age, (lost his only brother in the War) . . ."—ALS, DNA, RG 94, Correspondence, USMA. Lowry unsuccessfully contested the election of U.S. Representative Nelson I. Norton of N. Y. See *New York Times*, Dec. 1, 1875. On Feb. 2, John H. Vincent, Methodist Book Rooms, New York City, wrote to USG. "The bearer Milton Bailey Esq. is a warm personal friend of mine, and is in every way worthy of your confidence. If you can regard his present application I shall be as grateful as if the service were rendered to a brother of mine."—ALS, DNA, RG 94, Correspondence, USMA. On Feb. 10, Milton Bailey, Jamestown, N. Y., endorsed this letter to USG. "Inadvertently I took up this letter from your table with other papers when I was in the Presidential chamber on the 4th inst and take this opportunity to return it to you"—AES, *ibid.* Related papers are *ibid.* Appointed from N. Y., Charles J. Bailey graduated USMA in 1880.

1876, JAN. 21.   Alberta Barnes, Georgetown, D. C., to USG. "I take the liberty of enclosing an application to the Secretary of War, which I beg you will endorse, also a proof of the loyalty of my family during the war, which I hope you will do me the great kindness to read. I am the daughter of the Alexander Poland named in the accompanying paper, and the Sister of Alexander Poland Jr that you told last summer to call on you after your return to Washington, and you would do something for him, he obtained the place of street car Conductor, and last September was killed on the cars, leaving My Mother and family entirely destitute. We now have my Mother and young sister to support, beside our immediate family. My husband has been out of employment for sometime without any prospects, and we are indeed in very destitute circumstances. I believe you to be charitable and kind, believe me this case deserves your attention. I earnestly beseech you, to assist us by reccommending my husband to the Sec of War as Messenger, Doorkeeper, or Watchman."—ALS, DNA, RG 107, Appointment Papers. On Jan. 29, Secretary of War William W. Belknap wrote to Barnes "that it will be impossible to gratify your wish, as there is no vacancy existing to which he could be assigned. The name of Mr Barnes has, however, been placed upon the list of applicants—and they are numerous—for consideration when a vacancy occurs."—LS (press), *ibid.* On May 1, Barnes, Washington, D. C., again wrote to USG. ". . . I am the daughter of Alexander Poland of Leesburg Va., who was murdered by a portion of Mosbys men while at his table feeding the Union Soldiers, leaving my Mother and nine children, perfectly destitute as his stocks and provisions had all been appropriated. . . . I beseech you to help us, by giving my husband G. R. Barnes. a letter to the Sec. of War, for a position of any kind that will enable him to obtain bread for his family."—ALS, *ibid.*

1876, JAN. 21.   Josiah Gorgas, Sewanee, Tenn., to USG. "I beg to submit this application for the appointment of my son William C. Gorgas, as Cadet at West Point   The accompanying letters of Gen. C. C. Augur, Gen. Jno. B. Hood, Judge Jno. A Campbell, & Bishop J. P. B. Wilmer, of La. will assure you of his fitness for the appointment. You will perhaps recall me as a member of the class of '41, at West Point; and should it be in your power to grant this application, I shall be deeply grateful to you."—ALS, DNA, RG 94, Correspondence, USMA. On Jan. 17, Brig. Gen. Christopher C. Augur, New Orleans, had written to USG. "I write this letter in behalf of a son of our old friend Gorgas, of the Ordnanc formerly. Gorgas is entirely above and without the scope of politics. He is the head of the University of the South, and is devoting his whole mind to the good work of organizing and building up the institution under his charge. His son is a young man of about twenty—clever and well educated, and with fine physique. All his life he has been earnest and determined to get to West Point. . . ."—ALS, *ibid.* On Jan. 20, John B. Hood, New Orleans, wrote to USG. "Having served for a Short period with you in the same regiment in California, I have assumed the privilege of addressing you in the interests of an old brother officer, a graduate of West Point. I am informed that Mr W. C. Gorgas, Son of Genl J. Gorgas, is an applicant for an appointment as Cadet at WestPoint. He is well qualified for the position, as he has been educated & trained by his Father, who is President of the University of the South, at Sewanee Tennessee. I feel certain that you could not make an appointment which would be more highly appreciated by the recipient, as well as by the friends of his Father who belonged to the old Army."—ALS, *ibid.* The two other enclosures and a related letter are *ibid.* On Jan. 24, Brig. Gen. Stephen V. Benét, chief of ordnance, endorsed these papers. "In submitting these papers for the consideration of the President, I beg to say that the appointment of the son of my old friend Gorgas will gratify all of his old friends in the Ordnance."—AES, *ibid.* William C. Gorgas did not attend USMA but entered the U.S. Army as asst. surgeon as of June 16, 1880. See Frank E. Vandiver, *Ploughshares Into Swords: Josiah Gorgas and Confederate Ord-*

nance (Austin, 1952), pp. 300–302; Sarah Woolfolk Wiggins, ed., *The Journals of Josiah Gorgas 1857–1878* (Tuscaloosa, 1995), p. 248; John M. Gibson, *Physician to the World: The Life of General William C. Gorgas* (Durham, N. C., 1950).

1876, JAN. 22.   Governor Samuel B. Axtell of New Mexico Territory to USG. "It becomes my duty to address you Officially in relation to the disturbed condition of Colfax County in this Territory and to ask you for assistance to enable me to enforce the laws. The following Statement of facts has been carefully prepared. Colfax is a new County and altho of very large extent is sparsely settled—Cimarron, the County seat numbering probably not over a hundred men, and the other settlements all being small. The population is largely American—but there is also considerable number of Mexicans as a class poor and unarmed, along the Vermejo some 10 or 15 miles from Cimarron, there is a band of Texas cattle men about 40 in number organized and led by a man known as Capt Allison This man is a noted desparda, his band are all perfectly armed and well mounted On their raids they carry a Winchester rifle two Colt's revolvers and a knife. They have committed many acts of violence in Cimarron, within three months have murdered five men publicly—have destroyed the printing Office and thrown the material into the river, have run out of the County the Probate Judge the Justice of the Peace at Cimarron, some of the merchants and other peaceable citizens, and created such a terror in the minds of the people that no one will voluntarily appear to prosecute them before the Courts, nor even make an affidavit on which to found a warrant for their arrest. Allison however is known to have killed several men, and we are now collecting affidavits to this end. Considering the condition of terror into which the County was thrown The Territorial Legislature acting under the advice of the Governor The Chief Justice and the U. S. Dist Attorny passed an Act annexing Colfax County to the adjoining County of Toas for Judicial purposes—in order that a Grand Jury might be obtained which should impartially and without fear examine into this condition of affairs Their delegate to the Legislature is afrid to return. The Sheriff of the County has informed me that he cannot enforce the Law. Threats have been made that the Court will be attacked when it meets in Toas—and its Officers killed. under all the circumstances as I have no millitia, and our people are very poorly armed, I am reluctantly compelled to ~~give you~~ to give you this information and to ask you to place at my disposal a company of U. S. Cavalry to assist me in making arrests, in protecting the Court and its Officers, and in guarding the prisoners, as our jails are insecure. I have requested our Delegate Hon S B Elkins to lay this communication before you as his perfect familiarity with the locality and persons will aid your Excellency in obtaining a fuller understanding of the situation than I have been able to convey. The Legislature empowered the Governor to restore the Terms of Court to Colfax after two terms held in Toas, provided that in his judgment it should then be safe to do so. I am fully persuaded that order can be restored as soone as the leaders of the mob are arrested and punished. I ask for assistance simply to enable me to enforce the laws of the Territory"—ALS, DNA, RG 94, Letters Received, 640 1876. On Feb. 3, U.S. Delegate Stephen B. Elkins of New Mexico Territory wrote to USG. "The enclosed telegram is from Gov. Axtell & is a reference to the matter to which I called your attention this morning & refered to in his letter to you. I earnestly hope troops may be placed at the disposal of the Governor—because unless it is done the authorities in Colfax Co. will be unable to mantain order & protect the lives of the citizens. If the order could be made to Genl Pope by telegram I would be glad"—ALS, *ibid.* Related papers are *ibid.* See Jim Berry Pearson, *The Maxwell Land Grant* (Norman, 1961), pp. 66–71; Howard Roberts Lamar, *The Far Southwest 1846–1912: A Territorial History* (New Haven, 1966), pp. 152–55.

1876, Jan. 25. USG note. "Examine case of Capt. Owen, formerly 9th Inf.y with view of permitting withdrawel of charges—were sent in after resignation had been accepted."—AN, DNA, RG 94, ACP, 4856 1873. Drunken episodes in 1873 prompted charges against Capt. Philip A. Owen and his resignation as of Dec. 31. See *SRC*, 45-2-245. On April 30, 1874, U.S. Senator George Goldthwaite of Ala. wrote to USG requesting Owen's reinstatement.—ALS, DNA, RG 94, Applications for Positions in War Dept. Related papers are *ibid.* No reinstatement followed. See *ibid.*, ACP, J315 CB 1867.

1876, Jan. 25. Governor John F. Hartranft of Pa. to USG. "In selecting the gentlemen to be visitors at West Point I shall be gratified if your Excellency can find it consistent with your views of the public service to designate Rev. G. D. Carrow of Stroudsburg, Pennsylvania, as one of the visitors. . . ."—LS, DNA, RG 94, USMA, Board of Visitors. On Feb. 2, Levi P. Luckey wrote to Secretary of War William W. Belknap. "The President directs me to say that he desires that Mr. G. D. Carrow, of Stroudsburg, Monroe Co. Pa. be appointed a member of the Board of Visitors at West Point."—Copy, DLC-USG, II, 3. USG also appointed Charles Devens, Matthew H. Buckham, Henry C. Cameron, Richard P. Hammond (USMA 1841), John W. Sterling, and Abner N. Ogden to the board of visitors, USMA, for June, 1876.—D (docketed Jan. 27), DNA, RG 94, USMA, Correspondence. See *HED*, 44-1-2, part 2, I, 349–58.

In Dec., 1875, U.S. Senators Phineas W. Hitchcock of Neb. and John J. Ingalls of Kan. wrote to USG. "We respectfully recommend the appointment of the Rev. D. J. Holmes, Pastor of the Methodist Episcopal Church of Topeka Kansas, as one of the Board of Visitors at the West Point Military Academy."—LS, DNA, RG 94, USMA, Board of Visitors. On Jan. 19, 1876, U.S. Senators Robert E. Withers and John W. Johnston of Va. wrote to USG. "We have the honour to bring to your attention the name of Rev: George Woodbridge of Richmond Virginia, in connection with the appointment of Board of Visitors of the Military Academy at West Point—He was a member of the Class of 1826, and is very solicitous to meet the surviving members of the class who may attend the annual re-union in June next"—LS, *ibid.* On Feb. 8, U.S. Representative Alpheus S. Williams of Mich., and two others, wrote to USG. "The undersigned respectfully request the appointment of Colonel T. B. W. Stockton of Flint Michigan as one of the Board of Visitors at the next annual ~~Election~~ Examination of the Cadets at West Point Academy Col Stockton is a graduate of West Point—He served in the Mexican War as Colonel of 1st Michigan Infantry & with gallantry in the late civil war In his advanced years he would like once again to visit his *Alma Mater* and the pleasant scenes of his early life—We regard him as eminently qualified for the appointment"—LS, *ibid.* On March 10, U.S. Senator Frederick T. Frelinghuysen of N. J. wrote to USG recommending Nathaniel Niles for the board of visitors. ". . . He has been a leading member of the Legislature of N. J. and is an influential and public-spirited man—Many of our friends would be gratified by his appointment"—LS, *ibid.* No appointment followed.

1876, JAN. 25.   James E. Johnson, Natchez, to USG. "You will please find enclosed a 'petition' of the *prominent republican* voters of this city, asking the appointment of myself as 'Collector of Customs' and I hope you will give the 'petition' a consideration. If you desire further information *you* can see our Representative (Hon Jno R Lynch) that is relative to my reputation. Hon Sir, my petioners have placed themselves in the attitude of the poor man, at the rich mans door asking for the crumbs, from the table of the rich. I can assure you sir, that you have no warmer friends for the 'third term'—than my 'petitioners'"— ALS, DNA, RG 56, Collector of Customs Applications. The enclosure with twelve signatures is *ibid.* No appointment followed.

1876, JAN. 26.   USG endorsement. "Refered to the Sec. of the Treas. with the hope that he may be provided a place equal to the one lost."—Typed copy, DNA, RG 56, Applications. Filed with papers concerning Charles P. Bundick, appointed Treasury Dept. messenger as of Feb. 23.

1876, JAN. 26.   A. Y. Estees, Big Sandy, Tenn., to USG. "I hope your honor will parden my boldness, in writing you, a total stranger as I am to you, but you are not to me, nor to any of us down here who observe and try to obey the laws of god and man, when I tell you I am in distitute Circumstances and what I have done for this Country in time of need & peril. I am the individual who piloted your troops through the Counties of Benton and Henry, Tenn, from Fort Henry to Paris Tenn, for which work I recied the tortures of seviere unpleasentness. They never permitted to live in Benton any more after that up to last summer, my health was ruined by lying out through all manner of weather, and when discovered would have to go away to some Other place. I have tried every thing I could honorable to make a living. Even tried teaching a Colored school and the KuKlux, Came to my house One night and tuck me out into the woods, thats been three year ago now, and beat me almost to death. They thot they left me dead but I acted that out to save my life. Then I left there, that was in Weakly County. They twice visited me since I have been back to my old home, but Only took me out & cursed me & threatened me in case I had any thing to do with a damned nigger as they choose to call the words. There is some who will swear to certain parties we *know* to be members. You know nothing of Condition the poor are in in this Country, because there is no news papers published here, and them that is nearest here are run by KuKlux frinds who will never say a word about thier doings save to make the Governmt belive there is no such thing in existance. I am afraid now to put my true name to this but if you answer this,

you can have it, for our Post Masters are nearly all of that Confederate Centi-
mnts to a man. My health is such now that prevents me doing manual labor any
more. if Consistant I would be thankfull would the Govermt help me a little, to
feet my little Ones, until somthing else can be done. The blacks have nearly all
left the County and gone into Arkansas to live. Would the Goverment pay any
thing for the identy of the KuKlux now. A man would have to leave Tenessee for
ever, for they would kill him sure if remained after reporting any of their members. When they want a good man to leave they tell him to obey their laws.
They nail a copy of thier laws to his door in the night, and if he fails to obey that
notice, he Catches fury. Some hold their written orders, and the hand writing is
well known. Justice Graham remarked on seeing one of these notices, 'why he
couldnot get around owning up to that, its his writing sure. This my dear sir &
frind is not for any One save Your self, & burn this letter after you read it. If you
should answer me please direct letter to . . . and much oblige a true frind."—
ALS, DNA, RG 60, Letters from the President.

1876, JAN. 27.   George M. Johnston, Maineville, Ohio, to USG. "I this day mail
you copies of the Cincinnati 'Commercial' of the 19th and 24th inst. containing articles on the third term question written by the undersigned. I take this
further means of informing you that the third term sentiment is wide spread in
this district and with a little encouragement can be made of great use. A third
term newspaper established at some convenient point in the district would
strengthen the weak-kneed and give the bolder courage to openly advocate
their sentiments. As it is, with no advocate, they will let the movement die. I am
an experienced journalist, but much as I desire the success of the third term
cause, my circumstances are such that I can not afford to establish a newspaper
advocating it, unless I could secure some support from the government. I was
engaged for two years in journalism in the South, and thoroughly understand
the Southern question, through which the success of the third term movement
must come. If you design to become a candidate, you might find it to your advantage to communicate, in some manner, with me. The fact of my being unknown to your Excellency need be no bar to friendly intercourse, as the refer-
ences which I give can satisfy you that I can be depended upon. You will readily
understand all allusions to other prospective candidates in my articles. Said allusions are merely guards or foils to the enemy. The way must be blazed before
it can be entered upon."—ALS, USG 3.

In a letter received on Jan. 25, Anonymous had written to USG. "I have good
reasons to think you are going to *run* for the third (3d) term as the president
of this United States—Sir I am one of Her Sons (the United States) And now I
take An Oath from here to Heaven and upon the Honer of a Gentelman of Heigh
Standing 'If you do run for the third term (3d term as president of the U S)
'*I Kill You*' 'if it cost my own Life' I Hope Sir you will 'think of this & bear it in
mind' if you are elected as president again *I kill* you while you Hold the Office—
I will act as that man who is Loved So by a Southerner His name is Booth my
name is __ __ _____ of Richmond Va I Have four Brothers and Love my Country that *you* cannot do as you are expected to"—L (undated), *ibid.*

On Feb. 23, John A. Bingham, U.S. minister, Tokyo, wrote to USG offering constitutional support for a third term.—William J. Novick, *Heirlooms of History*, III, no. 68.

James M. Comly, *Ohio State Journal*, recalled USG's remarks on the presidency. "There is nothing I so much desire, personally, as to rest from the cares of this office. If it could be possible in any way for me to make a sacrifice for the American people, I would like to repay them by some sacrifice for the great honors they have conferred on me. *I have never been able to make a sacrifice for them. I have tried several times, but every sacrifice I have attempted has turned out to be an additional reward.* The Presidency of the United States, conferred as it is by the choice of the people themselves, is the highest and most honorable place among all the nations of earth. I have only done my duty to the best of my [ab]ility, and they have rewarded me with this."—D, Comly Papers, OHi. Comly commented on his recollection. "This is an exact report of what General Grant said to me in March 1876, when I talked with him at the Executive Mansion about the 'Third Term' hullaballoo in the newspapers. We were alone, in the Cabinet Room of the Executive Mansion. The President lit a cigar, handing one also to me, and we talked the whole matter over together. Also talked about Sheridan, &c."—ADS, *ibid.*

1876, JAN. 28. USG speech. "I receive with reluctance the letter which recalls you from your mission. . . . It is gratifying to learn that during your stay in this country you have received favorable impressions of the working of a free Government which has jurisdiction over so wide a territory. . . ."—*New York Times*, Jan. 29, 1876. On the same day, Manuel Freyre, Peruvian minister, had addressed USG.—*Ibid.* See *PUSG*, 19, 185–86.

On [*Oct. 27*], Freyre presented new credentials as Peruvian minister.—Copy (undated), DNA, RG 59, Notes from Foreign Legations, Peru. Freyre also presented a letter dated Aug. 5 from Mariano Ignacio Prado, Peruvian president, to USG. "Having been called to the Presidency of the Republic by the free suffrages of my fellow-citizens, and having been proclaimed by the National Congress, I have the honor to announce to Your Excellency that, on the 2d instant, I took the oath prescribed by the constitution, and assumed the supreme command. . . ."—LS (in Spanish), *ibid.*; translation, *ibid.* On Nov. 14, USG wrote to Prado sending congratulations.—LS (partial facsimile), eBay, May 10, 1999. See *Foreign Relations, 1876*, pp. 426–28.

1876, JAN. 31. USG endorsement. "Refered to the Sec. of the Treas."—AES, DNA, RG 56, Applications. Written on a letter of Jan. 10 from Annie Harding, Washington, D. C., to USG. "I have the honor to ask your favorable consideration of the accompany application and request if not inconsistent with your public duties, your endorsement thereion. Mr. Harding, you will remember, was, at the time of his death, holding the position of Sec'y. of the North-western Boundary Survey Commission, you having honored him by recommending him to the Senate for that position, and I would be extremely grateful if you would extend to me the same courtesies you so kindly extended to him during his life-time,"—ALS, *ibid.* On Jan. 8, Harding had applied to Secretary of the

Treasury Benjamin H. Bristow for a clerkship.—ALS, *ibid.* As of Sept. 30, 1877, Harding worked as copyist, Q. M. Dept.; her husband, Josiah F., had served as private, 14th Maine.

[*1876, Jan.*].   USG endorsement. "Ask Gov. Wells to call to-morrow morning if not engaged—Retain this letter"—AE (undated), USG 3. Written on a letter of Jan. 27 from Bluford Wilson, solicitor of the treasury, to USG. "Since returning to the Treasury Department I learn on further inquiry that Govr Wells was shewn a letter from you to Gen. Rhoddy endorsing him in general terms as worthy of belief and reliable. I have no doubt it is the same letter referred to by you as having been written with reference to Rhoddy's patent. It seems also to have been shewn in the Treasury Department at the time of the allowance of the $53.000 to Brooks in February '74. I respectfully suggest that you send for Governor Wells and find out from him just what the facts are. Undoubtedly the letter is being used in a manner never contemplated by you."—LS, *ibid.* In March, Congress investigated naval contracts involving Frank W. Brooks and Philip D. Roddey. See *HMD*, 44-1-170, part 5, pp. 198–205, 331–35; *New York Times*, Jan. 9, 1873.

[*1876, Jan.*].   USG note. "Will the Postmaster Genl. please bring up re-appointment of ____ [W. M.] Morrison at Cedar Falls, Iowa."—AN (initials not in USG's hand), OHi. On April 20 and Dec. 6, 1869, and Dec. 17, 1873, USG had nominated William M. Morrison as postmaster, Cedar Falls; on Jan. 12, 1876, USG nominated Charles W. Snyder to replace Morrison.

[*1876, Jan.*].   USG note. "Senator How recommends Conrad Moser, Jr. for vacancy under 2d Comp, or 3d Auditor. Is a lawyer and a very competant man. Place next in rank [in] the Dept."—AN (undated), DNA, RG 56, Applications. On Oct. 13, 1876, Conrad Moser, Jr., wrote to Secretary of the Treasury Lot M. Morrill resigning "as chief of division in the Second Comptroller's office."— ALS, *ibid.* Related papers are *ibid.* See *PUSG*, 26, 466–67.

1876, JAN.   U.S. Senator William W. Eaton of Conn. *et al.* to USG. "We respectfully suggest as an appropriate appointment for *Cadet at Large* to the *U. S. Military Academy,* on the list for 1876, Master WARREN PUTNAM NEWCOMB of *East Hartford, Conn.,* the great great grandson of both the revolutionary generals whose names he bears, and the only living male descendant of Gen'l. Joseph Warren. In this connection attention is respectfully invited to the annexed genealogical table and to the certificate of Gen'l Franklin's Examining Board."— LS (6 signatures), DNA, RG 94, Correspondence, USMA. The enclosures are *ibid.* Warren P. Newcomb graduated USMA in 1882.

[*1876, Jan.-Feb.*].   William Jeffers and four others to USG. "We, the undersigned citizens of Chicago in the State of Illinois, do hereby respectfully present, for your consideration, a sett of resolutions adopted at a mass meeting held in this city on the Twenty Sixth Day of December last—in company with printed copies of letters from exiles in New Caledonia including a copy (accompanied by a translation) of the official order relative to the labor of exiles and the discontinuance of their customary rations. The harsh treatment of these unfortunate sufferers has been a subject of comment for the press of this entire nation and of Europe, and, considering that it has been customary with all civilized nations, from time immemorial, to extend amnesty to all vanquished enemies, especially to those within their own borders, even when fighting for an unjust cause—calculated to threaten the existence of the nations involved in the struggles—as an example we refer to our late civil war, the insurgent participants in which, were promptly granted amnesty after their defeat, and the leader of whom is now at liberty and demanding full and unconditional forgiveness for his past offences. Considering these facts, we believe that the continuance of the persecution of these unhappy men who are in exile for the crime of having defended a municipal government regularly and legally adopted by a popular vote of the city of Paris, at a time when anarchy reigned supreme throughout France—the Empire having fallen and the people being literally without a government—(The municipal officers of Paris having deserted their charge and left the city to its fate)—is an unnecessary severity and an outrage on Humanity. We therefore respectfully request Your Excellency to have the truth of these statements investigated and the entire matter laid before Congress for action thereon—We believe that a request, forwarded to the French Government, for an extension of amnesty to these suffering thousands would be proper and humane, and we therefore beseech you to grant us your attention and sympathy in this matter—"—DS (docketed Feb. 3, 1876), DNA, RG 59, Miscellaneous Letters. Among the enclosures are a preamble and resolutions adopted on Dec. 26, 1875. "Whereas The colonial government of New Caledonia in its treatment of the transported Parisian defenders of Communism, exhibit the most inhuman and merciless persecution, contrary to all rules of humanity and civilization— . . . In shooting them down without trial on the most shallow pretexts, and, to the dishonor of all modern civilization, reviving the most barbarous tortures practised by the Inquisition in the Middle Ages— and Whereas We believe these outrages are committed with the full knowledge and consent of the French government—indeed, of its political head—for the deliberate purpose of exterminating these unfortunate thousands—and Whereas—Such horrible treatment of human beings, or even of dumb animals, is contrary to the commonest principles of humanity and civilization—contrary even, to the the laws of the French nation itself, relating to transported convicts; therefore be it Resolved That with all the intensity of the highest indignation, we raise a solemn protest against the commission of these fiendish outrages— . . ."—DS, *ibid.* See *Chicago Tribune,* Dec. 27, 1875.

1876, Feb. 1.   James W. Flanagan, Jr., Henderson, Tex., to USG. "Permit me to write you once in life knowing that you and Father are particular friends . . . While my Father acted Senator, I would not ask a position. But now say that I will accept of any Position that you may see propper to give me. I can give the best of *Refferences.* I will make a good Revenue Officer or would make a better Detective. I understand the Business perfectly well, having been State Police under Davis ex Govenor, & I must say that I love the *business.* . . ."—ALS, DNA,

RG 56, Applications. As of Sept. 30, 1877, Flanagan, Jr., managed two mail routes in Tex. See Flanagan, Jr., to Benjamin Harrison, Aug. 23, 1888, DLC-Benjamin Harrison.

1876, FEB. 1.   Edward S. Tobey and four others, New York City, to USG. "At the late Annual Meeting of the American Missionary Association, the Rev. Mr. Howard of Chicago offered a resolution which was afterwards amended and adopted as follows: 'Whereas, we gratefully recognize the endeavors of the Government of Egypt to abolish the traffic in human beings, and the hearty and effective co-operation of the people of Great Britain to promote the same end, therefore, *Resolved,* that a Committee of this body be appointed to memorialize the Government of the United States and urge it to exercise its influence to encourage and sustain the Khedive of Egypt in all efforts to suppress the slave trade in Africa. *Resolved,* That the Hon. E. S. Tobey, of Boston; Rev. Cyrus Hamlin, D. D., of Constantinople; Rev. Edward Hawes, of New Haven; Rev. Theodore D. Woolsey, D. D., of New Haven, and Rev. Geo. Whipple of New York, constitute this Committee.' This Committee beg leave respectfully to submit to you the following very brief statement of reasons for asking the Government of the United States to use its influence in any way that you may deem expedient, to encourage the Viceroy of Egypt in this work of reform. The Khedive is engaged in a work, your Committee believe, which contravenes some of the most cherished principles of Islamism. It is known that slavery is sanctioned both by the 'Koran' and by the 'Sunnah,' or tradition, and that both these authorities are equally sacred to the Moslem. The slave-trade, or more exactly, the capturing and enslaving of men, women and children, of enemies in war, and of idolaters, at all times, have, in their opinion, the highest and most sacred religious sanctions. To subdue and enslave idolaters is a work of religious merit as well as financial profit in the Moslem system. It is assumed by that system that the persons thus enslaved are *property* by the most sacred tenure, 'possessions of the right-hand,' as won in battle. Moslem laws soften slavery, but guard, perpetuate and sanctify it. No Moslem power ever existed without it. For this reason the Khedive is regarded as, and called, by all 'true believers' a 'Giaour,' or infidel. Since he has assumed a position on the great subject of slavery in harmony with modern Christian civilization, but against his own Moslem faith, kith and kin, he should have the moral support, and the strongest approbation of the civilized world. This committee assume that it is eminently within the sphere of the moral influence of the Government of the United States, to assure the Khedive that in his great contest with slavery, he has the warmest sympathy of the people of the United States. In behalf of the Association we represent and soliciting your favorable attention to this memorial . . ."—LS, DNA, RG 59, Miscellaneous Letters.

1876, FEB. 2.   To Secretary of the Treasury Benjamin H. Bristow. "Pursuant to the provisions of Section 48 of the Coinage Act of 1873, I have this day designated as a Commissioner to examine and test the coins reserved by the several Mints during the year 1875, Professor Robert Peter of Lexington Ky in place of Dr T. S Bell of Louisville Ky declined."—Copy, DNA, RG 56, Miscellaneous Appointments, Series QE. On Feb. 8, USG designated Joseph Wharton, Philadelphia, as another commissioner.—Copy, *ibid.* See *U.S. Statutes at Large,* XVII, 432.

On Feb. 11, John Cadwalader, chairman, Philadelphia, wrote to USG. "In the course of the proceedings of the Commissioners to examine and test the fineness and weight of the coins reserved by the several mints of the United States in the year 1875 it appeared that there was one dime of short weight in the delivery of the Carson Mint. . . ."—ALS, DNA, RG 56, Letters Received from the President.

1876, FEB. 3.   USG veto. "I have the honor to return herewith, without my approval, House bill No. 1561 Entitled 'an act transferring the custody of certain Indian trust funds from the Secretary of the Interior to the Treasurer of the United States' for the reasons set forth in the accompanying communication of the Secretary of the Interior"—Copy, DNA, RG 130, Messages to Congress. *HED,* 44-1-118; *SMD,* 49-2-53, 391. On Feb. 2, Secretary of the Interior Zachariah Chandler had written to USG. ". . . I am fearful that the act is not sufficiently definite in terms to accomplish the end desired, namely, the mere transfer of the custody of said trust-funds, enabling this Department to receive the interest from the custodian and apply it as heretofore without the intervention of Congress. The nature of the guardianship and control over the Indians, exercised by me as Secretary and trustee, is such as to require this Department to keep an account of the funds to their credit or held in trust for them, and to receive the interest on their trust-funds promptly when due. I am fearful that this bill may not allow me to do so, and to guard against any danger of embarrassment in the transaction of this business, I inclose a draught of a bill which, if substituted for the one already passed, will, it is believed, obviate the difficulties which may arise if the present bill should become a law."—*Ibid.* On June 10, USG signed the bill that Chandler drafted.—*U.S. Statutes at Large,* XIX, 58. See *CR,* 44–1, 617, 638, 881, 1394.

1876, FEB. 3.   To House of Representatives. "In answer to the resolution of the 6 of January instant of the House of Reps., requesting to be informed 'of the number of Indian Agents, regular and special clerks and other employees in the Indian Service, except those on duty in the office of the Secy. of the Interior and the amounts paid to each as salaries & expenses'—I have the honor to transmit herewith a copy of the report dated the 31st ultimo from the Commissioner of Indian Affairs, together with the statement therein referred to"—Copy, DNA, RG 130, Messages to Congress. *HED,* 44-1-128. The report is *ibid.* On March 27, USG wrote to the House of Representatives submitting "a supplemental report received from the Secretary of the Interior, respecting and explaining a clerical error to be found in that portion of the statement of the Indian Office which relates to expenditures of the Board of Indian Commissioners."—Copy, DNA, RG 130, Messages to Congress. *HED,* 44-1-150. The report is *ibid.*

1876, FEB. 3.   George G. Smith, Santa Fé, to USG. "As the pastor of the Presbyterian Church in this town I am deeply interested in the efforts of the Missionary Boards of our denomination for the improvement of the tribes of Indians assigned to their care. Many mistakes have been made, and numbers of bad men have held positions as Agents, but I am persuaded that the management of Indian affairs in New Mexico at present is in the hands of men (in most cases) exceptionally competent and trustworthy. Having learnt of a plan to take the most interesting and numerous of all the tribes (the Pueblo Indians) from under Presbyterian care to put it under Roman Catholic domination I am impelled to address a brief letter to you personally concerning this matter. I am afraid to write to any of your subordinates lest my letter should fall into the hands of a Romanist. Moreover you are the source of power appealed to by those who seek a change, and you are, I am assured, deeply interested in the welfare of the Indians. The accompanying copy of a letter received by Agent B. M. Thomas from the Indians of *San Ildefonso* will at once make clear to you the aims, and the under-handed and deceitful procedures, of the Roman Catholic Authorities of New Mexico. In a few words let me comment upon their plan. I. They design to get rid of all schools which really afford instruction to the Indians. The faithful Roman Catholics here regard Education as worse than the small-pox. If they are forced to have any degree of it among the people they vaccinate with the minutest possible particle of the poison. II. They have had three-hundred years in which to educate these Indians: they have taught them nothing but superstition. III. They fear the effects of such enlightenment as the present system of 'Pueblo Schools' will promote. IV. Their fear of the results of such work as Dr. Thomas is having done is a compliment which acknowledges his efficiency and wisdom. V. They want a *tool*—a brainless, cringing Mexican agent. I do not believe your Excellency will step back three hundred years to gratify them. I could give much information regarding the present condition of affairs among the Pueblos, and the encouraging prospects opening before them under the supervision and control of Agent Thomas, but I will not encroach longer upon your time and patience. . . . P. S. Should Congress pass an 'Enabling Act,' with a view to the admission of New Mexico to the Union, I hope you will not sign it. I will soon give in some eastern news-paper (probably the *New York Evangelist* or the *Evening Post*) enough reasons why such a bill should be rejected."—ALS, DNA, RG 48, Appointment Papers, New Mexico Territory. The enclosure is a letter of Jan. 30 from Lucas Peña, governor, and six chiefs of the Pueblo of San Ildefonso, to Benjamin M. Thomas, agent, Pueblo Agency. ". . . on the 28th inst. we were called to the Priest's house. As we were there assembled he showed us a letter which was brought by another Priest from the Bishop; at the same time telling us to sign a petition that was enclosed in the letter. That said petition was to be sent to the President of the United States, stating that we (all of the Pueblo Indians) desire to have in our Pueblos, Catholic Schools, and that our children be taught the Spanish language, and that we also desire to have a mMexican Agent. This Priest did not read us the petition nor the letter saying it was written in the English language. We told him that we had a Teacher who could read it for us, but he would not let us have it. He (the Priest) also said that all the Pueblos from below had signed it, also the Pueblo of San Juan. Now as we are under the flag of the U. S. Government, which is protecting us and has sent us an Agent to defend us, therefore we obey our Agent with great pleasure. We did not sign the petition. After having a meeting to-day we have resolved to send word to our Agent, and await his instructions before signing any thing of the kind. We are doubtful whether our agent knows any thing of the matter. . . ."—Copy, *ibid.* On Aug. 24, Thomas, Santa Fé, wrote to John Q. Smith, commissioner of Indian Affairs, reporting favorable reaction to a Presbyterian mission at the Pueblo of Laguna.—*HED,* 44-2-1, part 5, I, 515.

1876, FEB. 4.   Paul Strobach, Montgomery, Ala., to USG. "Yesterday's call for *two* Republican States-Conventions, for the purpose of electing *two* sets of Delegates to Cincinnati, satisfies me, that,—if the Republican Party shall not be ruined for ever in Ala.,—a change must be made in the most prominent offices, now held by, either incapable, or treacherous men, and I take the liberty to remind Your Excellency the services for the Party, of Your ever devoted and obedient servant"—ALS, DNA, RG 60, Letters from the President. On Feb. 7, U.S. Senator George E. Spencer of Ala. wrote to USG. "*Personal* . . . I respectfully ask your attention to the unfortunate condition of the Republican Party in Alabama and the causes that have effected it. The Republican State Convention created a State Executive Committee, consisting of twelve members, to hold until thier powers should be taken from them by a succeeding State Convention. This Committee elected a Chairman, Mr Charles Mayer, and he, in conjunction with the members of the Committee, has conducted three political campaigns, viz: The election for members of Congress and State Officers in November 1874; (in which we polled 8000 more votes than ever before) for the Constitutional Convention; and for the rejection or adoption of the Constitution. During all this time the authority of the Committee and its Chairman was acknowledged by evry Republican in Alabama. On the 28th day of December last the Chairman of the Committee published a call for a meeting of the Committee at Montgomery Alabama on 2nd day of Feby inst. Mr Mayer gave notice, by publication in the Montgomery State Journal, that the meeting would be held in a certain place, viz: in the Exchange Hotel. But to his surprise and without having given him any information thereof, N. S. McAfee District Attorney for the Northern and Middle Districts of Alabama, published a notice that 'the reorganised Committee would meet at the same hour at which Mr Mayer had called the Committee, but at another place. The result was that two bodies pretending to be the State Executive Committee, met at the same hour, and two State Conventions have now been called to meet at different times in the month of May next, for the nomination of candidates for State Officers to be voted for at the election in August next, and the election of delegates to National Convention. The movement to divide the Republican Party in Alabama, and set up a new State Executive Committee in defiance of the action of the Convention which created the Committee is without precedent in the history of American Politics; as far as I have been able to learn. No attempt had been made to create another Committee during three political campaigns through which the Party has passed, since the genuine Committee was created by the Convention. But now when the only thing remaining for the Committee to do, is to call a Convention, this new Committee is created. What is the object of it? What is the cause of it? I shall answer these questions. It is well known Mr President, that I am one of your supporters. It is further well known, that I do not favor the

Calendar: FEBRUARY 4, 1876 *367*

election of Mr Bristow a member of your Cabinet to succeed you as President of the United States. This is the cause of the movement in Alabama. It was instigated from the Treasury Department, and Mr Bluford Wilson Solicitor of the Treasury was the adviser of those who organised this split, and it was upon this advice that they acted. Wilson has acted through R. W. Healey United States Marshal for the Middle and Southern Districts of Alabama, and Healey being assured by Wilson, that the Conspirators should have all the support they wanted from the Treasury and Post Office Departments, so advised his co-conspirators. In accordance with these instructions the new Committee has sent a delegation of Eight men to Washington and they will soon be here, to present their claims for support, having been previously assured that they would be heartily welcomed, and be given all that they desired by the Secretary of the Treasury and the Post Master General. The object of the movement is to break me down and to secure a Bristow delegation from Alabama to the National Convention. I recently recommended Mr William Dougherty, a citizen of Alabama, for appointment to a clerkship in the Treasury Department, he passed a creditable examination, was duly appointed and assigned to the 2nd Auditor's Office. Dougherty was then refused the place on the plea that he could not take the 'iron clad oath' although it was made known that his disabilities, if he ever had any, had been removed by a special act of Congress. On Mr Healey's arrival here he informed Dougherty, that he was confident he could get the place for him. And after Mr Healey had seen Solicitor Buford Wilson on the subject, the latter informed Dougherty, that Mr Bristow had consented to his appointment, and that it should be made. Doubtless it will be. You will admit Mr President that from the day on which I first took my seat in the Senate until the present hour, I have not only been unwavering in my fidelity to the Republican Party, but the constant friend and supporter of your administration. I have the right then to expect and to ask that the members of your Cabinet shall not use the power of their offices to strengthen my enemies and destroy my influence. Throughout Alabama the belief has been instilled in the minds of my constituents, that I have no influence with your Administration; that those holding Federal Offices in the State can only retain their positions by opposing me and sustaining the new movement to make Bristow President. My Friends are in dispair; my Enemies rejoicing. Never would this movement have been commenced or the new Committee formed or delegates sent to Washington in opposition to me had the Conspirators not been assured before hand that they would be sustained by your administration. Shall they be, or shall they continue to be? M. D. Wickersham Post Master at Mobile; R. W. Healey United States Marshal for the Middle and Southern Districts of Alabama; and J. J. Martin Post Master at Montgomery are among the principal office holders engaged in this war upon me. I respectfully ask thier immediate removal, and that Mr George Turner of Mobile shall be made United States Marshal vice R. W. Healey, James Gillette Esq of Mobile Post Master at Mobile vice Wickersham, and Honorable James T Rapier of Montgomery Post Master at Montgomery vice Martin These persons whom I recommend are men of the highest respectability and will fill the respective offices with ability and integrity. Unless these appointments are made and made at once, I shall be forced to confess the

truth to be what my enemies claim—that in my position as Senator of the
United States and a constant friend of your administration I am utterly powerless to exert any influence therewith, while my enemies are all powerful."—LS,
ibid., Letters Received, Senate. On Feb. 16, 1875, Judge William B. Woods, 5th
U.S. Circuit, Galveston, Tex., had written to USG. "I beg leave to say that in my
judgment the public interests would be subserved by the re-appointment of
General Robert S. Healy as U. S. Marshal for the Southern and Middle Districts
of Alabama. Gen. Healy has proved a faithful efficient and honest public officer
and I am satisfied his continuance in office would give great satisfaction to the
bar and the people of all classes"—ALS, NIC. On March 14, 1876, USG nominated George Turner as marshal, Middle and Southern Districts, Ala., to replace Robert W. Healy; on Aug. 15, USG nominated Thomas C. Bingham as
postmaster, Mobile, to replace Morris D. Wickersham. John J. Martin continued as postmaster, Montgomery. On Aug. 10, Thursday, George E. Yarrington
and six others, Mobile, had telegraphed to Spencer. "By a systematic Course
of frauds in this city over one thousand Colored men were prevented from voting on monday last. Prosecuting against the ring leaders has and will be commenced in the united states Courts Under section fifty five hundred & ten of
revised statutes unless prosecuted vigorously & successfully it will be useless
for for colored men to go to the polls in November . . ."—Telegram received (at
8:48 A.M.), DLC-USG, IB. See *Washington Evening Star*, Feb. 8, 10, 1876; *SRC*,
44-1-331; Sarah Woolfolk Wiggins, *The Scalawag in Alabama Politics, 1865–
1881* (University, Ala., 1977), pp. 108–16.

1876, FEB. 7, Monday.   Lt. Gen. Philip H. Sheridan, Chicago, to USG. "Thanks
for your kind invitation, Mrs Sheridan is obliged to send regrets, if you have
a nook for me, without deranging plans I will accept and will be in Washington Saturday Morning,"—Telegram received, DLC-USG, IB. In Washington,
D. C., Sheridan testified before a congressional committee against any reduction of the army and for transfer of Indian affairs from the Interior Dept. to the
War Dept. See *Washington Evening Star*, Feb. 17, 1876.

1876, FEB. 8.   Byron S. Barrett, Nice, France, to USG. "I beg you will pardon
the liberty I take in addressing you, but, seeing by the public Journals that you
now have under consideration the matter of a Treaty of Commerce between
France and America, I feel it a duty to urge the consummation of so important
a measure, at the earliest date I have been in France but a short time, but I find
that the absence of a treaty between our country (United States) and France
puts us at a very great disadvantage as compared with other nations. . . ."—
ALS, DNA, RG 59, Miscellaneous Letters.

1876, FEB. 8.   William Thomas and J. H. Clayton, Marietta, Ga., to USG. "I
Seat myself to drop you a few lines to let you know the condition of the colord
people of Georgia our Suffering is great. and it Seems that all hopes of free
privilidge has passed and we as a people do apply to you the Said president of
the united States for help in time of need. also in our suffering condition. this
makes the 2. or 3. letter that we have writen you. but we have not recd any an-

swer as yet. We would be very glad to hear form you as soon as we can. Mr president we are deturmened to get a hearing from you. before the next presidental campaign 1876. if we have to send a delage to see you. we are interested and troubled on ever Side And as the thing now Stand and is Still coming, time of liberty, & prospirity is dead with us. as a colord peope. we as citizens of the united States want the protection and the right of these laws as much So as any other citizens of the united States   we have tried it longer enough to know that we cant live hear under the present administrators of the law any longer without a change & that a big one. we now Stand as the fox in the den of the mountian. we know that our Spelling & writing is bad but but we hope that you can under Stand it with careful Examination   As we doubt you geting our letter, we will ~~just~~ close by Saying that the hole is not told as yet—please answer"—ALS, DNA, RG 60, Letters from the President.

1876, FEB. 9.   W. Penniman Clarke and John B. Sanborn to USG. "We called this evening to present the enclosed letter of Gen. Crook, indorsed by Gen. Macfeeley in favor of Master H. G. Squies, a young friend of ours, who desires an appointment to West Point, and as we learn that the appointments have been made for 1877, we respectfully request that he may be appointed one of the Alternates. This boy is a natural born soldier, who we doubt not will confer honor upon the service, and whose success we have much at heart. He called upon you last winter, and is endorsed by the Minesota delegation, from which State he hails. Gen. Crook also spoke to you in his favor, and his ambition is such, and he is so much in earnest, that we fear his dis~~pappointment~~ will ~~prove~~ impair his usefulness for life."—ES, DNA, RG 94, ACP, 2925 1877. Written on a letter of Jan. 21 from Brig. Gen. George Crook, Omaha, to Secretary of War William W. Belknap recommending Herbert G. Squiers for an appointment to USMA.—ALS, *ibid.* Related papers are *ibid.*; *ibid.*, Unsuccessful Cadet Applications. See *New York Tribune*, Oct. 21, 1911.

1876, FEB. 9.   William Stickney, secretary, Board of Indian Commissioners, Washington, D. C., to USG. "There seems to be strong opposition to the confirmation of W. P. Ross as Agent for the consolidated tribes of the Indian Territory arising from his antecedents, he having been a rebel officer during the rebellion, still maintaining he owes no allegiance to the United States Government. If the Senate should decline to confirm his nomination, the Baptist denomination will nominate a man whom they deem in all respects competent for the position, one who will bend all his energies to carry forward the humane policy already inauguerated. I need not say that our denomination feels a deep interest in this matter and have but one object. viz the welfare of the Indians. They would doubtless feel aggrieved if deprived of this privilege which has already been accorded to them by the Secretary of the Interior."—ALS, DNA, RG 48, Appointment Div., Indian Territory. On Feb. 1, USG had withdrawn the nomination of Sylvester W. Marston, a Baptist, as agent, Union Agency of Cherokees, Creeks, Choctaws, Chickasaws, and Seminoles, Indian Territory, and nominated William P. Ross; on Feb. 29, USG withdrew Ross and nominated Marston. For Ross, see *SRC*, 41-2-113; *HMD*, 43-1-276; *HED*,

44-1-132, 44-1-134; Gary E. Moulton, ed., *The Papers of Chief John Ross* (Norman, 1985), II, 735.

On Sept. 1, 1869, Ross, Fort Gibson, Indian Territory, had written to USG. "The undersigned very respectfully asks for the appointment of Lewis Albert Ross as a Cadet in the U. S. Military Academy at West Point in the class to enter in the year 1870. Mr. Ross is a native of the Cherokee Nation and no disqualification is known to exist in his case. If the appointment sought shall be conferred by you, it will be esteemed by us a high honor bestowed not only upon him but also upon the Cherokee Nation—"—ALS, DNA, RG 94, Correspondence, USMA. On Jan. 26, 1870, William A. Phillips, Washington, D. C., wrote to USG. "I have received the enclosed communication from one of the most distinguished citizens of the Cherokee Nation The application is for the appointment of a cherokee of mixed blood of a respectable and highly educated family, to a cadetship at West Point. The family were Union refugees during the War, the boy having been, until recently educated in Pensylvania. It gives me pleasure to join the others who endorse it, in asking this recognition from you I learn that young educated indians have formerly received such recognition, and there are special reasons at this time that seem to urge an appointment from the Cherokee nation"—ALS, *ibid.* On March 7, Gen. William T. Sherman endorsed this letter. "Inasmuch as the Cherokees have no representative in Congress this appointmt would have to be 'at large' I have no personal knowledge of the applicant but the case seems worthy the consideration of the President."—AES, *ibid.* Lewis A. Ross did not attend USMA.

1876, FEB. 11.   U.S. Senators John H. Mitchell of Ore. and Aaron A. Sargent of Calif. to USG. "We earnestly and for special and important reasons recommend the appointment of Hon Saml K. Johnson as Indian Agent at Malheur Agency Oregon"—Telegram received, DNA, RG 48, Appointment Papers, Ore.; *ibid.*, RG 107, Telegrams Collected (Bound). On Feb. 25, Mitchell wrote to USG. "The Secretary of the Interior informed me some time ago that a change must be made in the Indian Agent at Malheur Agency— . . ."—ALS, *ibid.*, RG 48, Appointment Papers, Ore. On April 19, USG nominated William V. Rinehart as agent, Malheur Agency, to replace Samuel B. Parrish. See *HED*, 44-2-1, part 5, I, 525–26.

On May 15, 1875, and Jan. 28, 1876, USG had signed orders adjusting the boundaries of the Malheur reservation.—*Ibid.*, 45-2-1, part 5, I, 640, 45-3-1, part 5, I, 763–64, 47-2-1, part 5, II, 347, 49-2-1, part 5, I, 573–74; *SED*, 48-2-95, 600; *SD*, 57-1-452, 888–89.

1876, FEB. 14.   Maj. John C. Tidball, USMA 1848, Fort Monroe, Va., to USG. "A few weeks ago I made official application for a Cadet appointmt to the Mil. Academy, for my son Walton C. Tidball. I trust that you remember me, in the Army of the Potomac, sufficiently well to give my application a favorable consideration."—ALS, DNA, RG 94, Correspondence, USMA. Walton C. Tidball did not attend USMA.

1876, FEB. 15.   William H. Newell, St. Louis, to USG. "I allow myself to inform Your Excellency that certain Claims of Court of Allabama have been sold by the loosers for almost nothing at the time when there was little prospect of recovery, Some Widows are not aware while others by power of Attorney are for the claims, therefore I beleave it would be of great benefit to the U. States if your Excellency order the payments to me made *personally* to the claimants who realy sustain[ed] the losses; those who did can easely afford to go there, *or their legitimat[e] heirs.*"—ALS, DNA, RG 59, Miscellaneous Letters.

1876, FEB. 16.   USG note. "Rob.t. S. Chew desires a position in one of the Territorie[s] or to travel. Is now in Riggs bank.—Son of the late Chief Clerk, State Dept. If there is a vacancy which can be given to Mr Cew I will be pleased to confer it."—ANS, Columbia University, New York, N. Y. No appointment followed.

1876, FEB. 21.   Joseph Giorda, Catholic priest and missionary, St. Ignatius, Montana Territory, to USG. "From informations which I cannot altogether disregard, I learn that the Flathead indians in Bitter Root, Montana, are restless,—and may, if driven to the wall, go and join the hostile tribes on the plains—Two are the grounds of dissatisfaction. First, few years ago a Treaty was made by which they, Flatheads, are bound to leave their homes, and migrate to Joko Reservation etc; which Treaty has been signed by no real chief, and has been protested against by the Mass of Flatheads; The Treaty makers having made a non-Flathead Chief for the sole purpose that he was willing to Sign it. Secondly, in consequence of that Treaty now the Sheriff of Missoula County wants to compel them to pay taxes. I doubt it not that Your Excellency with an insignificant trouble and outlay can keep the Flatheads at rest and friendly, *as there is no indian tribe so peaceable and friendly to the whites*; and that on the contrary much greater trouble and expense would follow, should the Flatheads ever break loose. This I had brought before Hon. Brown years ago, but latest advices seem to point to a culmination, and call for immediate preventive action of the Executive. The well known indian caracter does not permit me to be more informed on such matters."—ALS, Marquette University, Milwaukee, Wis. See *PUSG,* 22, 224–28; *HED,* 44-1-1, part 5, I, 807; Robert Ignatius Burns, *The Jesuits and the Indian Wars of the Northwest* (New Haven, 1966), pp. 385–86, 429–30.

1876, FEB. 22.   Henry W. Bellows, New York City, to USG. "I beg to ask your personal attention to the claims of Mrs. Eliza H. Powers, of New Jersey, to some place in the gift of the Government. During our late unhappy but glorious war Mrs. Powers, then in comfortable circumstances, raised, by her indefatigable exertions, $10,000 and twenty thousand articles of clothing for the relief of our sick and wounded soldiers. She wore out her health in the unpaid service then rendered to the country. A woman of education, a lady in breeding and of unimpeached character, she is reduced to poverty by misfortune, and has to earn her daily bread, at seventy-three years of age, by her personal labor. If such a patriotic and venerable woman has not claims to a clerkship, which her superior knowledge, accomplishment in languages, and extraordinary energy fit her to occupy with advantage to the Government, who can have a claim worthy the attention of the Government or its Chief Magistrate? As I had charge of the Sanitary Commission during the war, I was a special witness of Mrs. Powers's sacrifice and advantageous labors for our soldiers. I have felt specially called to testify in her case, and have felt that her age made it not improper to bring the subject directly to the President's notice."—*SRC,* 48-1-95; *HRC,* 48-1-1945. See *U.S. Statutes at Large,* XXIII, 611.

1876, Feb. 23.   U.S. Senator John H. Mitchell of Ore. to USG requesting that Thomas M. Patton replace Medorem Crawford as appraiser, Portland.—ALS, DNA, RG 56, Collector of Customs Applications. On Feb. 29, Mitchell wrote to USG. "It is of *vital* importance that the changes I have recommended in the offices of Collector of Customs—Appraiser & Marshall in Oregon—be made at once,—any other course will in my judgment be disastrous to the Republican Party in that state. Delay but adds to the difficulty—"—ALS, *ibid.* On March 3, Mitchell telegraphed to USG. "*Personal,* The nomination of Hannah Collector of Customs at Portland Oregon vice Scott came to senate yesterday, The same reasons exist for *immediate* change in Marshal and Appraiser of Customs as per my letters on file. Early action is very important,"—Telegram received, *ibid.,* RG 60, Records Relating to Appointments. On March 1, USG had nominated Samuel Hannah as collector of customs, District of Willamette, to replace Harvey W. Scott; on March 4, USG nominated Patton to replace Crawford. For Scott, see *DAB,* XVI, 491.

On Feb. 29, Mitchell had written to USG. "Referring to my personal interview with you on the 18th instant, and to a letter I then presented to you bearing upon the question of a change in certain officials in the State of Oregon, I now respectfully, and in obedience to what I understand to be the almost universal and emphatic wish of Oregon Republicans, in so far a change is concerned ask that Capt. Abner W. Waters, of Oregon, be appointed United States Marshal for the District of Oregon, vice Mr. Melarky. to take Effect April 1st 1876. As I stated to you in that conversation it is charged by Republicans generally throughout Oregon that Mr. Melarky, at present United States Marshal, together with certain other Federal officials in that State, shortly prior to the last election, conspired for certain reasons to cause the suspension of the publication of the Bulletin, the only leading Republican paper in our State and to throw all its patronage to the 'Oregonian,' which for the past three years has been the uncompromising enemy of your administration and of the Republican party generally—National and State. This charge, whether true or false, as I say, has come to be generally believed throughout the State, the result of which is that Republicans have lost confidence in Mr. Melarky, and for that reason earnestly and emphatically demand a change. Therefore, believing as I do that the interests of the Republican party are paramount to those of any one man, whether friend or foe, I feel impelled to make this recommendation. Mr. Melarky is and has been my personal friend, and never in my life have I taken any course in politics that I so much regret, on account of personal friendship, as I do this step."—LS, DNA, RG 60, Records Relating to Appointments. On March 9, USG nominated Abner W. Waters as marshal to replace Daniel J. Malarky.

1876, FEB. 23.   Bishop Alexander W. Wayman, African Methodist Episcopal Church, Baltimore, to USG. "Having understood that there is a probability of a vacancy occuring in the mission to the Republic of Liberia Africa If So I take great pleasure in recommending to your favourable consideration William Willyams a Gentleman who is in every respect well qualified for the position. He was educated in Europe and speaks the Italian and French languages fluently and is also recognized as being a Gentleman and one that the Republican party of Maryland indorses for his honesty and integrity And Should there be a vacancey in the mission above named and Should your Excellency appoint Mr Williams—I feel assured that he will reflect great Credit upon the Country he represent and the race with which he is identified"—ALS, DNA, RG 59, Applications and Recommendations, Hayes-Arthur. Related papers are *ibid.* No appointment followed for William A. Willyams, who had trained for the Catholic priesthood.

1876, FEB. 24.   Mrs. L. J. Wasson, Atlanta, to USG. "I beg your attention to a late bill passed by the Legislature of Georgia, to let out convicts to private individuals Such as *R R* Companies who place Overseers over them who use them most brutally under the lash, and starvation.   those men pay nothing to the State, for there Services, they pretend to clothe them and board them.   this they do not do, and when one of them ask for food he is Striped of his clothes and lashed till the blood trickles to his feet.   now I beg of you to Send and have this thougerly investigated and in the name of humanity and Christianity for god Sake put a stop to this Human Cruelty, and Murder.   it has not been long Since one poor fellow was whipped until he fell exausted.   they then drenched his body with water, then had two Other prison convicts Rub his back with Salt and turpentine and next morning repeated the same treatment until he fell and died in the most agonizing groans. . . ."—ALS, DNA, RG 60, Letters from the President. *SMD*, 44-1-76. See Matthew J. Mancini, *One Dies, Get Another: Convict Leasing in the American South, 1866–1928* (Columbia, S. C., 1996), pp. 82–88.

1876, FEB. 25.   Lt. Gen. Philip H. Sheridan, Chicago, to USG. "Miss Sheridan—born this morng sends respects to the President & Mrs Grant."—ADfS (telegram sent), DLC-Philip H. Sheridan.

1876, FEB. 25.   Rowland G. Hill, Washington, D. C., to USG. "I have the honor to request of you an appointment as a cadet at large in the United States Military Academy. My name is Rowland G. Hill. I was born at Muscatine, State of Iowa, on the sixth day of July, 1857, and am now eighteen years and seven months old. My father, Col. Sylvester G. Hill, was colonel of the 35th Iowa Volunteer Infantry, and commanded that regiment, (except when in brigade command) from its organization, until the 15th of December, 1864, on which day he was killed at the battle of Nashville, while in command of a brigade in Gen. Smiths corps. My father, at his death, left nine children, five being older, and three younger than myself. My oldest brother, Ed., served three years and a half, in the Seventh Iowa Volunteer Infantry, enlisting at the age of seventeen. My second brother, Fred, also enlisted, at the same age, in my fathers regiment, and was killed at the battle of Yellow Bayou, Louisiana, on the eighteenth day of May 1864. My mother is desirous that one of her sons should hold a position in the regular army of the United States, and in accordance with that desire, as well as my own inclination and ambition, I respectfully, but most earnestly, ask for this appointment at your hands, Mr. President. I respectfully call your attention to the accompanying letters from the Senators and Representatives in Congress, from the State of Iowa."—ALS, DNA, RG 94, Correspondence, USMA. A related letter is *ibid.* Hill graduated USMA in 1881.

[*1876, Feb.*].   USG endorsement. "Asks to be restored. Is less than twenty-one years of age; his father was a loyal man during the rebellion and a republican ever since."—AE (undated), DNA, RG 56, Applications. Written on a testimonial from Edward O. Graves, superintendent, National Bank Redemption Agency, Treasury Dept., Feb. 18, 1876. "Mr Allen M. Howison was employed as an assorter of national-bank notes in this Agency from soon after its organization until the 15th instant, and became one of the very best assorters in the Office. He is a young man of good habits, exemplary in all respects, expert in the handling of money, accurate, faithful and honest, and as such I cheerfully commend him."—ADS, *ibid.* Related papers are *ibid.*

1876, MARCH 3.   To House of Representatives. "In answer to the Resolution of the House of Representatives of the 21st ultimo, I transmit herewith a Report from the Secretary of State and accompanying papers, together with a report from the Secretary of the Treasury."—Copies, DNA, RG 59, Reports to the President and Congress; *ibid.*, RG 130, Messages to Congress. *HED,* 44-1-140. Reports and enclosures related to payment of the $15,500,000 awarded to satisfy the *Alabama* Claims are *ibid.*
      On Feb. 8, 1874, Samuel F. Miller, U.S. Supreme Court, had written to USG. "Understanding that there is a vacancy in the Board for distribution of Alabama claims I wish to recommend my friend Hon Wm Penn Clark as eminently suited for the place Mr Clark has had a very successful practice for several years in this District and in our court and I have known him for many years as a practitioner in other courts and I feel safe in endorsing his capability and integrity. I should also be personally obliged by his appointment."—ALS, DNA, RG 59, Applications and Recommendations, Hayes-Arthur. On Feb. 6, 1875, U.S. Delegate Norton P. Chipman of D. C. wrote to USG. "Learning that it is probable a vacancy may occur in the Court of Alabama Claims I beg to recommend for appointment Col Wm Penn Clarke, . . ."—ALS, *ibid.* No appointment followed. See *PUSG*, 26, 447–48; *Washington Post*, Feb. 8, 1903.

1876, MARCH 4.   Mary E. C. Butler, Brooklyn, to USG. "I again appeal to your honor, trusting that you will not forget, to reply, and do not deny me my request. My husband is now Stationed at Fort Totten D. T. and as it is all in your honors power, I sincerely beg of you to send me his discharge, or if not do please give him again his office, or former position, which was Post Commissary, Sergeant, at some nice Post, that I could live at & be with him . . ."—ALS, DNA,

RG 94, ACP, 1249 1875. On June 25, 1st Sgt. James Butler was killed in action at the Little Big Horn. See Edgar I. Stewart, *Custer's Luck* (Norman, 1955), pp. 489–90.

1876, March 6.   To Senate. "In answer to the Resolution of the Senate of the 7th of January last, requesting a 'statement of the number of military arrests made in the Territory of Alaska during the past five years together with the date of each, the charge on which made in each case, the names of the persons arrested, and the period and character of the imprisonment of each in that Territory before trial or surrender to the civil authorities for trial'—I have the honor to submit herewith the report of the Acting Secretary of War."—Copy, DNA, RG 130, Messages to Congress. *SED,* 44-1-33. On March 24 and April 6, USG wrote to the Senate transmitting further reports on the same subject.— Copies, DNA, RG 130, Messages to Congress. *SED,* 44-1-33, parts 2 and 3. On March 1, Brig. Gen. Oliver O. Howard, Dept. of the Columbia, Portland, Ore., had written to AG Edward D. Townsend defending military authorities and attributing delays in prisoner transfer to "irregularity of the voyages of the steamship and uncertainty on the part of the judicial authorities upon the question of jurisdiction."—*Ibid.* (part 3), p. 2.

1876, March 6.   To ministers and consuls. "This will introduce to you Mr. F. B. Thurber of New York City, who visits Europe for pleasure, and for the benefit of his health. Mr Thurber is commended to you as a gentleman worthy of such courtesies as you may be able to extend to him while he remains in your vicinity."—Copy, DLC-USG, II, 3. See *New York Times,* July 5, 1907. USG wrote similar letters of introduction for Beulah Dickey, wife of T. Lyle Dickey (May 23), Charles W. Eliot (June 26), Robert C. Fox (Aug. 15), Bishop Gilbert Haven (Oct. 18), and George W. Williams (Nov. 13, addressed to Edwards Pierrepont).—Copies, DLC-USG, II, 3. On July 25, USG, Long Branch, had written to [*Ayres P. Merrill, Jr.*] introducing a man "who I am pleased to have as a neighbor and esteem as a personal friend. While he is in Brussels I hope it may be your pleasure to show him some attention."—Christie's Sale No. 7086, June, 1990, no. 132.

1876, March 6.   William W. Nevin, *Philadelphia Press,* to USG. "Revd Joseph S Travelli of Pittsburg visits Washington in the hope of restoring to the rolls of the army the name of Lieut. Adair a faithful and brave ~~and~~ officer who bears severe wounds received in service—His errand is one of mercy and I trust that in this case mercy may be also found to be justice . . ."—ALS, DNA, RG 94, ACP, 4540 1871. On March 10, Joseph S. Travelli, Washington, D. C., wrote to Julia Dent Grant that he had secured "admission to the National Insane Asylum of Capt. John I. Adair—who is my nephew. . . . His insanity was caused by his fourth wound recd in Georgia; injuring a portion of the base of the brain. The aberration of mind was at first apparently slight but has gradually & steadily grown worse & is likely to continue we fear & may sooner or later lead to some act of violence, tho he at present is harmless. . . ."—ALS, *ibid.* Related papers are *ibid.*

1876, MARCH 7.   Lizzie Cottingham, Jersey City, to USG. "Doubtless you will be somewhat surprised to receive a Letter from a young lady but when you have read it, and understand my object, if I have unconsciously taken an unwise course, I know you will excuse me for it. Yesterday I wrote a letter at my father's request to the Hon. Senator Carpenter applying for the position as Detective on the secret service. Now President Grant, what I want to ask of you is, if there is anything you can do for my father wont you please take an interest in his behalf. He is an old soldier and was one of the principal men in the capture of the conspirators of our martyred President Lincoln. I have tried to condense my letter so as not to trespass too long upon your valuable time. Trusting you will favor me with a speedy reply, . . ."—ALS, DNA, RG 56, Applications. No appointment followed. See Benn Pitman, comp., *The Assassination of President Lincoln and the Trial of the Conspirators* (1865; reprinted, New York, 1954), pp. 124–25; *U.S. Statutes at Large,* XIV, 341.

1876, MARCH 8.   U.S. Representative Horatio C. Burchard of Ill. to USG. "I respectfully recommend for appointment as Consul General to Egypt Mr. Chancellor Martin formerly of Illinois now a resident at Alexandria Egypt. Mr. Martin is a graduate of the West Point Military Academy, has honorably served as an Officer in the United States regular Army from which he resigned to engage in Mercantile business at his home in Illinois. His *military, literary* and *business* education give him *special* qualifications for this position, as in addition to other acquirements he is conversant with both the *French* and *Arabic* languages I can unhesitatingly recommend him for honesty and integrity as well as ability and should be pleased to learn of his appointment"—ALS, DNA, RG 59, Letters of Application and Recommendation. No appointment followed for Chancellor Martin, USMA 1868, who had served in the Egyptian army since 1874.

1876, MARCH 8.   Henry J. Tutson, Jacksonville, Fla., to USG. "I tak pleasuar in writing you a feu lines and I hope these feu lines Will find you Well as the leave me at present and Thange god for it. I rite to you to see if you cante do sumten for the poor Freed man. We are here in the south and we have a hard time to Get sumten to live on. the Democratic Will note pay aus what we are Worth for our labor. they give aus $1 a day and we have to feede our self oute of it. & thy sel aus ~~Baco~~ Bacorn from 15 to 19¢ a pound. if we coud Get pay for our labor we would soon be come a nation of people and if you can do sumten for the Poor Freed man god will bless you for it. because we are republican is the reasen they Wonte Pay aus for our labor. there is a nomber of collar men sente from here to penetentuel for steal sumten to eate. and if there cood have Gote work to do thy Wouldent ben in state Prisentemente to day. I am a poor Cold man, and the first of the mansipation I never noud the firste letter in the alfebeate. and please Write to me soon as you can."—ALS, DNA, RG 59, Miscellaneous Letters.

1876, MARCH 9.   John Smith, agent, Warm Springs Agency, Ore., to USG. "I have the honor to present herewith a report of the declarations of the Indians at Warm Springs Indian Agency Oregon, Made Jan. 19th & 20th 1876, in regard to removing to Some other Agency They have rendered signal service to the government in assisting to subdue hostile Indians, notably so in the famous Modoc War. They are becoming industrious, intelligent and prosperous under the present management, and are in a fair way to be self sustaining by the time their treaty expires. Any such change could hardly be otherwise than injurious, and I cannot but feel that you will not willing consent to any change that will have any tendency to undo the work that has been the result of your humane policy here, . . ."—LS, DNA, RG 75, Letters Received, Oregon Superintendency.

1876, MARCH 10.   To Senate. "I transmit to the Senate for consideration with a view to ratification a Metric Convention between the United States and certain foreign governments signed at Paris on the 20th of May 1875 by Mr E. B. Washburne the Minister of the United States at that capital acting on behalf of this Government and by the representatives acting on behalf of the foreign powers therein mentioned. A copy of certain papers on the subject mentioned in the subjoined list, is also transmitted for the information of the Senate."— Copy, DNA, RG 130, Messages to Congress. *HRC*, 45-3-53, 36, 46-1-14, part 1, p. 43. No action followed.

On May 4, 1875, Joseph Henry, Smithsonian Institution, had written to USG. "I have the honor to transmit to you herewith in conformity with a resolution of the National Academy of Sciences, adopted at its session April 22d 1875, the expression of their opinion on the usefulness of an International bureau of weights and measures which is now the subject of a diplomatic conference at Paris, and of their solicitude that this Government should ratify the Convention which has been prepared to that effect; and to ask your favorable consideration of the same."—LS, DNA, RG 59, Miscellaneous Letters. The enclosure is *ibid.*

1876, MARCH 13.   Secretary of the Interior Zachariah Chandler to USG requesting that he detail an army officer to oversee the distribution of annuity goods to the Cheyenne and Arapahoe Indians.—LS, DNA, RG 94, Letters Received, 1438 1876. Related papers are *ibid.* See *HED*, 44-2-1, part 5, p. 454.

1876, MARCH 13.   Culver C. Sniffen to Augustine J. H. Duganne, New York City. "The President is in receipt of your favor of the 9th inst. and directs me to say in reply to your inquiry that though it will be impossible to set the hour, he will endeavor to see you should you be in this city within a few days."—Copy, DLC-USG, II, 3. Duganne, a labor advocate who had served as lt. col., 176th N. Y., wrote *Camps and Prisons: Twenty Months in the Department of the Gulf* (New York, 1865) and numerous works of poetry, fiction, criticism, and journalism.

On June 6, the "Central Grant Club," Duganne, president, adopted an address to the Republican National Convention in Cincinnati, urging delegates to set aside regional differences and nominate USG for a third term. ". . . He is the only Presidential opponent feared by a Democracy that will gather *all its forces*, North and South, for the coming contest. With Grant as our Republican candidate, Republicans in Southern States can neither be intimidated nor cajoled. A Republican Presidential Ticket, *other than a National one* such as his name and position guaranty respect for, *will not bring out the Republican strength in Southern States.* Vindicate President Grant! It is your duty, as Republicans, to tender this faithful President of our whole People, a renewal of your confidence in him. He seeks not the office, which so many are seeking, as it was never sought before. It is *you* who should seek the man for that office, this Centennial year, if you would retain the Republican authority and influence, at home and abroad, which his consistently Republican Administration has secured . . ."—DS (2 signatures), USG 3.

1876, March 13.   Charles M. Howard, Detroit, to USG. "Knowing the friendship that existed between yourself and my father, the late Senator Howard, I am emboldened to ask from you the [a]ppointment to some office in Colorado. I desire the position of Register or Receiver of some U. S. Land office in that Territory. During the whole term of my father's service in the U. S. Senate he never procured or tried to procure any office for any relative. He died poor. My health is such that I have been advised to go to Colorado, and pecuniarily I am unable to go without the assurance in advance of some office, and Mr President, I beg this appointment in consideration of my father's services to the Republican party and the Country."—ALS, DNA, RG 48, Appointment Papers, New Mexico Territory. On March 6, Howard had written to Secretary of the Interior Zachariah Chandler on the same subject. ". . . Through a limited knowledge of business and unfortunate investments I have exhausted the little patrimony left me by my Father, some $7000, . . ."—ALS, *ibid.* On April 25, USG nominated Howard as land office register, Beaver, Utah Territory.

1876, March 14.   Ben: Perley Poore, clerk, U.S. Senate, to USG. "A dispatch from the Boston Journal office dated three fourteen says that they are receiving the first votes from New Hampshire and they are very cheering,   Rollins says so many towns have been gained that they can stand a heavy back fire,"— Telegram received (at 3:35 p.m.), DNA, RG 107, Telegrams Collected (Bound).

1876, March 15.   Arthur Shepherd, Washington, D. C., to USG. "I respectfully ask the appointment of U. S. Consul at Demerara British Guiana, to fill the position now held by Phillip Figyelmesy. I base my application upon the following facts.—Heretofore in attempting to obtain employment at the hands of the United States Government I have been met with the objection, to being placed in official position, that I was a citizen of the District of Columbia; and to put me in place would be against the interests of citizens of some one of the States. The present incumbent of the Consulate applied for is a naturalized Hungarian, is accredited to the District of Columbia and has held the position now for more than eleven years, having been appointed thereto by President Lincoln January 30th 1865. I therefore claim that having been in place for such a length of time; I am justified in asking that I may be appointed in his stead— . . ."—Copy, DNA, RG 59, Applications and Recommendations, Hayes-Arthur. On March 24, Shepherd again wrote to USG. "I have the honor to apply for appointment as Consul to La Guayra Venezuela and hereby withdraw my application previously made for appointment to Demerara."—Copy, *ibid.* Related papers are *ibid.* No appointment followed. See *PUSG,* 26, 537–38.

1876, MARCH 15.   U.S. Representative Charles G. Williams of Wis. *et al.* to USG. "The undersigned respectfully represent that Leonard Paul Bradshaw, is the youngest son of Henry Bradshaw of Gloucester County, New Jersey; that the said Leonard Paul Bradshaw is a brother of Henry Bradshaw, Jr., who was one of the gallant soldiers who assaulted Fort Sumpter, S. Ca. on the night of Sept. 7, 18763, and who was captured on the failure of the attack and died at Andersonville, Ga. July 14, 1864, after passing through the various rebel prisons in Charleston, Columbia, Richmond & Macon, on the day he became twenty one years of age. The parents of this young gentleman whom we wish to bring to your notice are Quakers but no family suffered greater sacrifices in the late war for the Union than this: Gettysburg, Fredricksburg, Chancellorsville, Cold Harbor and Petersburg each mark the resting place of one of its members—a family history of which Leonard is justly proud, and one which we deem highly fitting for bringing the young man to your attention for an appointment to West Point or the Naval Academy:"—LS (8 signatures), DNA, RG 94, Correspondence, USMA. On March 24, U.S. Representative Stephen A. Hurlbut of Ill. wrote to USG presenting this letter.—ALS, *ibid.* Leonard P. Bradshaw did not attend either academy. See *O.R.* (Navy), I, xiv, 622–24.

1876, MARCH 16.   U.S. Representative James A. Garfield of Ohio to USG. "The invitation for this Evening Seven P, m, is received and accepted with pleasure,"—Telegram received (at 1:55 P.M.), DNA, RG 107, Telegrams Collected (Bound).

1876, MARCH 16.   Mrs. Hettie K. Painter, Lincoln, Neb., to USG "in regard to John Harrison Blair who was kidnaped from this country by two Englishmen on Nov. 13th 1875 . . . Mr. Blair was taken to Manchester put in prison, then taken to Liverpool for trial, . . . Mr. Blair had no witness, the case was hurried thro', & he sentenced on the 13.th of Dec. to 18 mos imprisonment at hard labor; . . . You may perhaps remember Mrs. H. K. Painter an agt. from Pa. & N. J. for relief of sick & wounded, & to whom you so kindly gave a [g]eneral pass, . . . Now I come [to] you with an ernest prayer that you may give attention to this [s]ad case, & that you may hasten the day when Mr. Blair may [r]eturn to his family, now so striken with grief. . . ."—ALS, DNA, RG 59, Miscellaneous Letters. Related clippings are *ibid.* U.S. Senator Algernon S. Paddock of Neb. endorsed these items to USG. "Numerous papers in this case have been filed with the Hon. Sec'y of state who notified me some time since that he had communicated with the then Minister to Great Britain, but no result seems to have been reached. It is certainly a case that demands attention"—AES (undated), *ibid.* John H. Blair, supposedly a forger and perjurer, allegedly procured silks from a British co. upon false pretense. See Hamilton Fish to Robert Schenck,

Jan. 4, 18, 1876, *ibid.*, Diplomatic Instructions, Great Britain; *New York Times,* Jan. 16, 1876.

1876, March 18.   Robert S. Todd, auditor's office, Baltimore & Ohio Railroad Co., Baltimore, to USG. *"Personal,* . . . Can you give me no encouragement, in reply to my letter to you of some days ago? My expenses far exceed the salary paid me by this Co! & I must seek other employment to enable me to meet them. You told me, in December last, that you could probably send me abroad as 'Secretary of Legation,'—My education fully qualifies me to fill such a position, & I wou[l]d gratefully accept one of that, or any other kind. Your early attention will greatly oblige one, who would endeavor, stronly to deserve your good will and favor."—ALS, DNA, RG 59, Letters of Application and Recommendation. Related papers are *ibid.* As of Sept. 30, 1877, Todd, who claimed Abraham Lincoln as his uncle, clerked in the Third Auditor's Office for a $1,200 annual salary.

1876, March 20.   Postmaster Gen. Marshall Jewell to USG. "General Price of Lexington arrested & convicted a man for robbing the Post Office at Lexington. His barn with its contents was burned the day after the conviction he thinks by the parties convicted which together with the prosecution has entailed large loss upon him. He thinks he can convince you that misrepresentations to say the least have been made in regard to the wishes of the Republicans at Lexington & desires an interview to explain matters."—Telegram received, DNA, RG 107, Telegrams Collected (Bound). On the same day, Ulysses S. Grant, Jr., telegraphed to Jewell. "All interviews with the President on the P. O. at Lexington subject will have to cease. Genl Price may submit anything in writing to him he chooses"—ALS (telegram sent), *ibid.* On Jan. 22, Jewell had written to Samuel W. Price, Lexington, Ky., concerning USG's decision to remove him as postmaster. Price then visited Washington, D. C., in an effort to retain his office.—*Louisville Courier-Journal,* March 9, 1876. On Feb. 28, Jewell again wrote to Price. "I am directed by the president to say that, after having had considerable conversation with parties from Kentucky who are interested in the affairs of that State, and after taking time to examine the case with more care, and in view of the fact that you have held the office for seven years, he desires your resignation. It is hardly necessary to enter into details, as the matter has been fully discussed; and I do not need to assure you that it is not on account of anything that the president or this Department may have against you that a change is desired, but only for the purpose of giving the office to another gentleman whose claims have been very urgently pressed upon the president by many influential friends."—*Ibid.* On March 7, USG nominated Hubbard K. Milward as postmaster, Lexington.

   In March, 1869, William O. Goodloe, Price, and twenty-six others, Lexington, had petitioned USG. "The undersigned Republicans and citizens of Kentucky cordially recommend to you the bearer of this Col H K. Milward of Lexington Ky late of the 18th Ky Vet Inft. for any proper official appointment under the Government. He seeks the *Consulship to Honolulu Hawaiian Islands,* and for that position knowing his ability and probity we specially commend him. . . ."—

DS, DNA, RG 59, Letters of Application and Recommendation. Related papers are *ibid.* No appointment followed.

1876, March 20. William A. Darling, Washington, D. C., to USG. *"Personal . . .* In order to releive you & the Secretary of the Treasury from any embarrassment growing out of the accusations made against me & which will at some time be shewn to be unjust and cruel, I propose to forward you to-morrow my formal resignation as appraiser of the Port of New York"—ALS, DNA, RG 56, Appraiser of Customs Applications. On the same day, Thomas Murphy, New York City, telegraphed to USG. "my decided conviction is that it would be wise to make no selection of appraiser until early next week"—Telegram received, *ibid.,* Letters Received From the President. On March 24 and 29, Hugh J. Hastings, John Hoey, and William B. Dinsmore, New York City, wrote and telegraphed to USG. "If you have not settled upon a successor to Mr W. Darling late General Appraiser for the city the undersigned join in recommending Mr Geo M Van Nort of this city as a suitable person for the office. . . ." "If the party we recommend for the office of appraiser is agreeable we can send the best commercial endorsement the undersigned will esteem his success a personal compliment"—LS and telegram received, *ibid.,* Appraiser of Customs Applications. On March 28, USG nominated Murphy's friend, Stephen B. French, as appraiser. See *New York Times,* March 8, 1876, Feb. 4, 1896; *New York Tribune,* March 21, 29, 1876.

On Jan. 20 and March 9, John Dolan, Third Avenue Savings Bank, New York City, had written to USG. ". . . I ask you Sir what Claim has Wm A Darling. on this Govt who never Shouldered A musket, who holds the office of an appraiser & who is Supposed to be one of the Robbers, of this, Bank If that is the Class of men you Select for prominent places, it is, manifest no Irish need apply You Shall Certainly get a good account of me in the next Campaign, by that time your Friend Darling may be in States Prison. So much, for Conklin & Buckingham I could get you more votes in one hour than Darling, Arthur or James Could get In a year. . . ." "Permit me, to address you & Say you have been Led into bad Company. by Selecting Such men for to fill prominent positions, here is a Sample of your Black Hearted Methodists, that Comprised the directors of this unfortunate Bank, and the Cause of more misery than you Can Imagine, for the Sake of your own name get rid of all those theives who never Shouldered a Musket. get rid of this black hearted villian Darling . . ."—ALS, DNA, RG 56, Applications. A clipping headed "The Plundering of the Third Avenue Bank" is *ibid.* On March 15, James Walker, New York City, wrote to USG condemning Darling as "infinitely worse than Belknap, for he has fleeced the widows, and, orphans."—ALS, *ibid.,* Letters Received From the President. A related clipping is *ibid.*

In a letter dated "Wednesday," probably March 22, Anonymous wrote to USG. "You have done a most meretorious thing in removving Darling the Appraiser for which act you will be thanked by thousands of the Third Avenue Savings Bank depositors. Besides it was just in time Darling has done things which it would be very unpleasant to have had revealed by a committee of investigation. I see by the news papers that Senator Conklin is to name Darlings

successor Now President have you not some merchant friend a man of honor
whom you could request to name some merchant an honorable man to fill the
pPost of Appraiser. only a few months ago A T Stewart went to a friend of his
on the United States Grand Jury to try and have Darling indicted. But nothing
can be done while you have Bliss the present Dictrict Attorney in Office President Grant did you read Bliss's telegram to Babcock after his acquital at St
Louis Let me suggest that you ask Mr B. B. Sherman president of the Mechanics Bank one of our *most respectable* citizen's to name a new appraiser and a
new district attorney. President you have honored yourself and the country by
your nomination of Mr Dana now nominate good men for appraiser and district
attorney"—L (docketed March 27), *ibid.* On Jan. 10, 1877, U.S. Senator Algernon S. Paddock of Neb. telegraphed to USG. "May I request that the New York
matter may not be concluded today"—Telegram received, DLC-USG, IB; DNA,
RG 107, Telegrams Collected (Bound). On Jan. 11, USG nominated Stewart L.
Woodford as attorney, Southern District, N. Y., to replace George Bliss, Jr.
Franklin A. Paddock, the senator's brother, had contended for this nomination.
See *New York Times*, Jan. 12, 1877.

On Jan. 10, 10:30 A.M., William Blaikie, New York City, had written to USG.
"Personal. . . . If you want to make 'a man after your own heart' U. S. Attorney
for this District, try Hon. Thomas Simons your present Asst. Atty. General in
charge of the government cases in the Court of Claims. For over seven years he
was a subordinate in the U. S. Atty's office here, gradually working up from the
lowest clerkship to be the head assistant of Noah Davis and George Bliss Jr. and
then called by Judge Pierrepont, who had found his worth, to his present post.
He is a regular wheel-horse, always doing the heaviest work and never talking
about it, indeed is one of the most modest men I ever knew. Judge Donohue of
the N. Y. Supreme Bench says he has the best legal mind of any man he ever saw,
while his strict and entire integrity, great fidelity, and exceptionally large acquaintance with the very duties he would undertake, would cause him to fill the
place as any man not so experienced could not. He is almost universally known
to the members of the bar who practise in the U. S. Courts, and would be welcomed from sheer merit, as well as his uniform courtesy Ask Judge Taft—or
telegraph Judge Davis or G. Bliss Jr—what they think of him— . . . Talk to him
and measure him yourself. I was Atty. Genl Hoar's pardon clk. & introduced by
him to you. Wd. refer to Messrs. Douglas, Luckey or Sniffen of your office"—
ALS, NHi.

1876, MARCH 20.   Charles Robertson and many others, Rusk, Tex., to USG
concerning Democratic intimidation of Republicans. ". . . they wants to turn you
and flanagan out . . ."—L, DNA, RG 60, Letters from the President.

1876, MARCH 21.   James W. Taylor, consul, Winnipeg, to USG. "A year ago,
during absence on leave, I published a communication and [su]pplemented it
with an editorial in a St Paul paper on the currency question which I beg leave
to enclose for your perusal. The memorial referred to in these articles was
drawn by me, as my instructions to the National Board of Trade, at Richmond
Va., and which I presented and advocated during its session in December 1869.

Pardon a further personal reference. I believe I could be of service to the country at this juncture, if the appointment which you kindly favored in the winter of 1869–70, as Special Agent of the State Department on the relations of the United States and Northwest British America, commercial and political, was renewed. As this Consulate will probably be abolished, please consider whether I cannot be of service to your administration in such a position."—ALS, DNA, RG 59, Letters of Application and Recommendation. The enclosures and related papers are *ibid.* Taylor remained consul.

1876, MARCH 22. Angelica Haynes, Washington, D. C., to USG. "I have the honer to request the favor of an appointment for my son Lenny Haynes to the first vacancy—either at the Military Acadamy at West Point—or the Naval Acadamy at Annapolis—I make this application for the reason that I think that I have some claim to consideration—My husband left Texas in the begining of the war and raised a regiment for the Union service— . . ."—ALS, DNA, RG 94, Correspondence, USMA. Related papers are *ibid.* Lenny Haynes did not attend either academy. On March 8, USG had renominated John L. Haynes as collector of customs, Brownsville. See Carl H. Moneyhon, *Republicanism in Reconstruction Texas* (Austin, 1980), pp. 67, 115–16, 169.

1876, MARCH 24. George T. Jones, Port Matilda, Pa., to USG. ". . . I now have a family of fore Children the first Sone that we had is a bout 9 years old now and a very fine Sone he is I Gave him the name U. S. Grant in fool and I thot I would rite to you and inform you of the fact I was allso a Solgdier in the wore I receved a Gun Shot threw the right leg which ingers me very much from labor I received my wound at the Battel of Chanclers ville on the third day of May I belonged to Co H 148 Reg Penna voulenteers 2 Army Cor . . . I have Got a very hard way to Get a long since I have went through the wore and I wood ask you to Doo in your Grait wisdom Some thing fore me if you will Pleas Do Sou fore the name Sake ore fore my Sake it would bee receved with meny thankes let it Bee what ever it will I Get 8 Dollars Pension I onely Got a increas of 2 00 Dollar Per month lately I onley Got 6 Dollars before but I am very thankful fore it I love my Country and love the man that Saved it ore in other words that laid the Planes that Did Save it . . . I have howled long and loud fore you and Collfax I have Shook my old hat till midnight and Cherd fore you I have been at the Election Poles Erly and late fore you both Elections . . . Since the Panic Set in work is hard to Get and wages is very low I Get $1 30 Per day fore working on a Saw mill and I have to work every day and days that I am not hardly abel to fore my leg but I am Com Peld to Do Sou fore the montanance of my famly this is a Solum fact now your honor Pleas read this if you Can which I hope you may and Dont fore get to make Plenty of a lowance fore my inability in Cholar Ship I am Poor in that as well as in Pocket . . ."—ALS, DNA, RG 48, Miscellaneous Div., Letters Received.

1876, MARCH 24. Cyrus K. Osgood, Washington, D. C., to USG applying "for the Collectorship of the Port of Savannah."—ALS, DNA, RG 56, Collector of Customs Applications. On March 30, U.S. Senators John Sherman of Ohio,

Henry L. Dawes of Mass., and Thomas J. Robertson of S. C. wrote to USG. "Understanding that the Office of Collector of the Customs for the Port of Savannah may become vacant and having solely in consideration the best interest of the public service; the undersigned beg leave respectfully to present the claims of the *Honorable Joshua Hill* of Georgia, as one who in the discharge of the duties of said office would reflect honorably upon your administration and subserve the highest interest of the government"—LS, *ibid.* U.S. Senators Oliver P. Morton of Ind. and John A. Logan of Ill. favorably endorsed this letter.—AES (undated), *ibid.* On March 14, USG had nominated incumbent James Atkins as collector of customs, Savannah. See *PUSG*, 20, 437; *ibid.*, 23, 31–32.

1876, MARCH 27. USG veto. "I have the honor to return herewith without my approval House Bill number 83 entitled 'An act for the relief of James A. Hill of Lewis County Missouri' for the reasons set forth in the accompanying communication of the Secretary of War."—Copy, DNA, RG 130, Messages to Congress. *HED*, 44-1-149; *SRC*, 45-3-571; *SMD*, 49-2-53, 392. On March 25, Secretary of War Alphonso Taft had written to USG concerning a bill to provide lost pay and bounty to James A. Hile, former private, 21st Mo. ". . . On the muster out roll of company dated April 19. 1866. he is reported deserted March 1. 1866 at Bladen Springs Alabama. This man in his application to this office for discharge, stated under oath (affidavit dated July 27. 1870) that he left his command without leave and returned to his home, February 28. 1866. having previously applied for a furlough which was refused. 'This man according to his own statement under oath did desert as reported, and if this bill becomes a law, it will be an injustice to every soldier who served honorably with his command until his services were no longer required by the government, in addition to falsifying the record, as the bill directs the record shall be made to show he is no deserter This is only one of many similar cases.' The remarks of the Adjutant General, adverse to the passage of the bill are concurred in."—Copy, DNA, RG 107, Letters Sent, Military Affairs. *HED*, 44-1-149; *SRC*, 45-3-571; *SMD*, 49-2-53, 392. A bill benefiting Hile passed in 1879.—*U.S. Statutes at Large*, XX, 618.

1876, MARCH 30. U.S. Senator Roscoe Conkling of N. Y. to Ulysses S. Grant, Jr. "I am distressed to hear that your father is really ill Please telegraph me how he is."—Telegram received, DNA, RG 107, Telegrams Collected (Bound). A report the next day stated that USG had recovered sufficiently "from his indisposition to attend to his official duties. His sickness has not been as serious as reported, merely being an unusually severe attack of sick headache to which he is subject."—*Washington Evening Star*, March 31, 1876.

1876, MARCH 31. USG veto. "For the reasons set forth in the accompanying communication from the Secretary of the Treasury, I have the honor to return herewith, without my approval, Senate Bill, No 489 entitled 'An Act for the relief of G. B. Tyler and E. H. Luckett, assignees of William T. Cheatham'—"—Copy, DNA, RG 130, Messages to Congress. *HED*, 44-1-44; *SRC*, 44-1-278, 2; *SMD*, 49-2-53, 393. On March 30, Secretary of the Treasury Benjamin H. Bristow had written to USG "that there are no data on file in the Department, so far as I can learn, which indicate that the amount it is proposed by this bill to refund to the assignees of Mr. Cheatham, was wrongfully collected, or that the amount should be refunded."—Copy, DNA, RG 56, Letters Sent to the President. *HED,* 44-1-44; *SRC,* 44-1-278, 2; *SMD,* 49-2-53, 393. G. B. Tyler and Edward H. Luckett sought $164 in disputed bonded warehouse fees that William T. Cheatham, former whiskey distiller, had paid to the collector of Internal Revenue, Second District, Ky. On April 4, U.S. Senator Thomas C. McCreery of Ky. criticized USG's veto as "a hasty and ill-advised act."—*CR,* 44–1, 2180. On May 26, Congress overrode USG's veto. See *U.S. Statutes at Large (Private Laws),* XIX, 21.

1876, APRIL 1.   James Long, Cincinnati, to USG complaining of persecution by Ky. authorities. ". . . at the last Election of President Lincoln I was the only Irishman that Voted for him Except one that Belonged to the Eighteenth Ky and I can assure you it took Nerve that day, to do so, . . . My treatment Such as I Received is Not Recorded in the annals of History this partty Says I am a Lunatic   if I am how is I am a *Odd fellow* in good Standing . . ."—ALS, DNA, RG 60, Letters from the President.

1876, APRIL 3.   Philip Henry, National Soldiers' Home, Dayton, to USG seeking employment as messenger or watchman. ". . . In the year, 1872, I, with more than a hundred of my comrades, through patriotism, went to Pittsburgh, to ratify your nomination, and to make the numbers there, larger,   It cost each of us, not less than $50, and now I am laid up high and dry, in the soldiers home, not through any falt of mine, but through the failure of J, Cook, &Cs' bank. Before the late war broke out, I had to honor to serve my country, on board of the U. S. Frigates, Colorado, and Roanoke, commanded respectively, Commodores, Mc'Cluney, and Mc'Intosh. I helpt to bring the Japanese to this country in, 1860, and joined the Infantry, soon after the war broke out, by which I lost an arm below the elbow. I have been an inmate of the soldiers home since the 18th day, of Octber 73, and have not been brought before the Governor, for censure, under any circumstances whotsoever, . . ."—ALS, DNA, RG 56, Applications. See *HRC,* 45-2-342; *SRC,* 45-2-398.

1876, APRIL 10.   Henry A. Pemberton, Princeton, Minn., to USG. "I Am requested to rite to you for information, and I Should like to have you answor, to the Best of your knoledge, as it is of a grate consequnce to ower comunity and more So to ower frendley Indians, of Said Mille lac County, a grate Deal of hard feelings amongs them, in regard to there rite of the reservation, as there is a grate manny men teelling them that it is not theres only to live on, others Saying theres no use of them trying to hold the land. there is a pine ring trying to get this land all in there hands So as not to let actuel Setters have a chance to get any chance to home Sted it. I have been taulking with the Indians aboute the matter and I told them that ~~them~~ I would rite you a letter and Explain it to you, So that you would give them or me a corect Statement of the affair. those are the qustions 1st can any man homested that land 2 or can any man Scrip that land 3 or can any Partys club to gather and hold Said land in anny Shape So as to get the land if So Please answor to the best of your knolage. this is a cincear matter with us on the frontier Dear Sir I am married to one of those Indian wimen and have been for ninteene years, and the Indians have a grate deal of confidence in me, as to there little matters and afairs when they get in dispute with those Partys that is all the time Bothering the Indians telling them that the goverment is going to move them, others telling them that they will help them, to Stay, this helping them is Some party that is trying a kind of an under mining, So as to get Some favor, or Some clew on Some peices of that land as some is better timberd with pine than others. Dear Sir Please answor Soon So I can answor the chieves there qustions corectly in regard to this matter And I will put your answor in ower paper in print to the wone that was put in of late . . . I have a qustion to ask you of my owne. why cant you let me get the Names of the half Breedes of this county on purtishen for them to have Scrips Ishued to them as I have been with them for the last twenty five years and if you can do this and apoint me for agent I will atend to gettin there names this Sumer Dear Sir you under Stand how this matter Should be handled better Down wheare your are than I Do up heare to get the Scrip Bill through,"—ALS (tabular material expanded), DNA, RG 75, Letters Received, La Pointe Agency.

On May 22, Clara Moore, Upper Sandusky, Ohio, wrote to USG. "I write to you for imformation my mother was an Indin woman belonging to the Chipaways tribe. She gave me away when I was about three years old to a family rase. She was kild by a drun king Indin a few days afterwords I under stood that each one was intitled so much from the govermunt every year I think I ought to have what was coming to my mother ~~and~~ as I was the only child my mother had please writ and let me know what part of Wesconcen I will haf to go to get what coming to me from my mother estate or if I can git it without going I am a girl now about 15 years old the lady that raised me was very kind to me and sent me to school and always taught me I was an Indian girl belong to the Chipaway tribe. please ancer as soon as poseble. . . . P. S. the lady that raised me I go by her name Moore."—ALS, *ibid.*

On May 23, Alexander Laurance, Brooklyn, wrote to USG. "I have been advised to write to you to let you know how I am Setu ated. I am an Indian of Rain[y] lake. I was to be Chief of the Otchebway tribe. the tribe that I belong we was all at Fort William Lake Superior on a vessile where we meet with plenty other tribes of Indians. Some belong to the United States. And Some belong to the British the Chief of the British Indians. had a fine Red Coat and pants Black and vest and a hat that was give to him by the British Government. a flag and a larg Salver meddle. for we american Indians we Could Not Show nothing In regard of been Chief of American thearfor. I left the tribe to Come to the City of new york I told the tribe that I was going to the father of Ower Contry U. S. of A—for a Sout of Close as a preasant to Sartefy that I was the Chief of the american Indians. Dear Sir please to Send me a uneform A Coat and Vest and pants and Hat or Cap. Ornemented like a Navey Officer. I Beg you to Send me these as A preasant I shall be here. on till the forth of July. And I will return to my Own tribe A gain. at red river. please write to me. And Let me know what to do. please and write Soon. If you Send me the Close please to get them Black or Blue the will last longer. for I whant them Once every year My Size Is. five feet. ten Inches. 180. lbs weght Dear Sir. please to Send them to me you will Oblige me Very much . . . My Indian name is—Megese Egel"— ALS, *ibid.* Me-gee-see, or the Eagle, had signed an 1854 treaty as second chief of the Lac du Flambeau band of Chippewa.

[*1876, April 12*].   USG note. "Capt. Chas. E. Jewett 10th Inf. asks 6 mos. lave for the purpose of going into business: at the end of that time to join Company or to tender resignation at the end of further six months leave. Grant it"—AN (undated), DNA, RG 94, ACP, 1476 1876. 1st Lt. Charles E. Jewett resigned as of April 25, 1877.

1876, April 13.   Joseph Henry, Smithsonian Institution, to USG. "The letter of Mr. *J. H. Cadenhead* referred to this Institution by your order, and herewith respectfully returned, was at once transmitted to our Collaborator in Numismatics, Mr. *W. E. Dubois, U. S. Mint, Phila*—The following is his communication with reference to the Copper coin refered to by your Correspondent; 'The impression of the medal which forms the subject of Mr Cadenheads letter is too feeble to decipher, and it will be necessary, to do that, to see the actual piece It is evident, however, that he is quite mistaken as to its age and character, and that it is a medal of French execution, about A. D., 1752. We have nothing similar "Senatus Consulto" is an inscription of both ancient and modern times, implying a Senatorial authority in the case, which I am not able to understand in our Colonial history.' With the assurance that it will give us pleasure to have the matter in question further examined into on receipt of the medal, or coin, itself, . . ."—LS (press), Smithsonian Institution Archives. On May 16, Henry wrote to USG and quoted from a report on the medal. ". . . It possesses almost no value, and that for two reasons. First the Count Mazzuchelli, in whose honor it was struck, although he achieved a fame in his own country as a literary biographer (as you are aware,) is not much known out of Italy; and then the medal is so defaced, that no collector would give it a place in his cabinet. The fact of its being found in Texas is curious, but adds nothing to its interest . . ."—LS (press), *ibid.*

1876, April 15.   USG pardon for Samuel B. Murdock, convicted in D. C. of "sending a threatening letter," recommended "by the Hon: Fernando Wood, the person to whom the threatening letter was sent."—Copy, DNA, RG 59, General Records. Murdock had served eighteen months of a two-year sentence. In June, 1874, Murdock (or Murdoch) had written to U.S. Representative Fernando Wood of N. Y. "I am satisfied as to your guilt. I have one reason for not shooting you. I will settle for $50,000, you to take the woman and keep her. The alternative—I will empty seven chambers of a Colt's revolver into you on the first opportunity. Answer immediately in writing to messenger. . . . If you do not comply with these terms I will publish you in all the New-York papers, and write to your wife."—*New York Times,* Sept. 25, 1874.

1876, April 15. Marie Giovanni, Philadelphia, to USG. ". . . My public or travelling name is simply the first of my two names—Madame Giovanni. Years back, the name was rendered célebre on the old Continent from the fact that A. Dumas had reviewed and published my notes of travels around the World. at this very time I am on my way to Paris again to publish a highly interesting book of notes on the Republics of Mexico—U. States and America Central. I have been an eye witness in the Southern part of the Civil war in the U. S. (was at Manasas, and at Corrinth day after the terrible battle) was present at the taking of New Orleans.—was equally present every where during the whole time of the French Intervention in Mexico—I am owner of a large landed property situated in the Ithsmus of Tehuantepec, have been twice Special bearer of Despatches from the French Legation at Mexico, to prime Minister at Paris Mr Drouyn de lhuys before the intervention, at the time Monsieur Sartige was french Minister at Washington, and one of my best friend Marquis de Montholon was Consul General in New york. in short I am a perfect honorable person, and should Mr Captain Shufeldt Commanding the Expedition that came to study the local capacities of the Ithsmus for the construction of a canal—or any of his officers be near at hand, to them your Excellency might refer to, as they all, during their stay had several times the pleasure of enjoying my hospitality at my property of 'La Puerta' situated in the beautiful virgin forest of Tehuantepec— . . . The Notes in my manuscrit treating to give a correct account of U. S. american Society on the Ithsmus—on the Gulf and on the Pacific Coasts, are certainly of a very unfavorable caractere—but to tell the truth the notes concerning all other foreigners, are not a bit better. It is a sad scandalous Mixture of would be called civilysed nations—But unfortunately in connection with this bad population of Strangers—and even at *the head of it,* I have been compelled to place and Note *apart* the U. S. American Consuls of the Pacific side, at the City of Tehuantepec Mr J. A Wolf and Gulf side R C. M. Hoyt Minatitlan—It was my facilities for years to be made acquainted with a great number of néferious transactions made by them undercover, but early in the year 1870 Mr Hoyt appeared to suddenly move about briskly as if under the influence of some news of importance—he took his departure for the city of Tehuantepec wherein arriving he created a A J Wolf Agent Consul for the purpose of examining and forwarding American claims against Mexico and there and then under the protection of the spangled banner they established a Company composed of A. J Wolf—R. C. M. Hoyt, a young rascal named Parker, and *Thomas Woolrich* (of Mexican wide notoriety as a schémer and adventurous Speculator—he is canadian English, and no doubt, Mr Thornton must know him) The company once established, they applied themselves with great zèle to the Manufacture of *imaginary Claims* and *fabrication* of *Citizenship* Some poor american men whom they persuaded to let them manufacture a reclamation under their names for considerable sums of money, were not in reality worth the cloths on their back. . . . Notes that approach official personnality always command attention, give value to a publication, but all this long letter has been written to say to your Excellency if you wish me to cancel that part of the Notes which has regard to the American Consuls and the Claim forgeries, *I will do* it for the sake of *avoiding* your Excellency the sorrows of seeing official scandal reach Europe under a the name and the plume of a traveler who certainly will be believed. Simply hoping that under the form of a gratification left to your Excellency' discretion, it will simply remunerate, the interesting matter lost to the publication In whatever way your Excellency may be pleased to regard this communication I beseech him, to allow the feeling which prompted it to be pure et honest and to a high degree disinterested."—ALS, DNA, RG 59, Miscellaneous Letters. On May 16, 1871, USG had nominated Hermon Bronson as consul, Minatitlan, in place of Rollin C. M. Hoyt, deceased. Alexandre Dumas had published Giovanni's travel journals in 1856, prefaced by a note. "I shall not disclose my true name; certain family considerations prevent me from making this public. Such publicity, furthermore, given to the name of a woman, a mother, might perhaps at times prevent me from being as frank as I might wish to be. . . ."—Alexandre Dumas, *The Journal of Madame Giovanni* (New York, 1944), p. xxxi. See Honore Forster, "Voyaging Through Strange Seas: Four Women Travellers in the Pacific," *National Library of Australia News*, X, 4 (Jan., 2000), 3–6; Patrick O'Reilly and Édouard Reitman, *Bibliographie de Tahiti et de la Polynésie française* (Paris, 1967), pp. 140–41.

1876, APRIL 17.   USG endorsement. "The within request is approved and the reservation is made accordingly. The Secretary of the Interior will cause the same to be noted in the General Land Office."—Copy, DNA, RG 94, Military Reservation Div.; *ibid.*, RG 107, Letters Sent, Military Affairs. Written on a letter of April 13 from Secretary of War Alphonso Taft to USG recommending a military reservation at Camp Grant, Arizona Territory.—Copies as listed above. Also in 1876, USG ordered land set aside for military reservations in Neb. (Camps Robinson and Sheridan) and to enlarge Camp Verde, Arizona Territory.—Copies, *ibid.* In 1877, USG approved military reservations in Tampa (Fort Brooke), Arizona Territory (Camp Apache), and Montana Territory (Fort Missoula); returned part of the military reservation at Fort Sully, Dakota Territory, to the Sioux; and reserved two square miles of timberland for use at Fort Fetterman, Wyoming Territory.—Copies, *ibid.*

[*1876, April 17*].   USG note. "Address note to the Postmaster Gn. saying that he may if he pleases bring up nomination of Mr. Beach for postmaster, St. Joe, Mo"—AN, OHi. On April 18, USG nominated James T. Beach as postmaster, St. Joseph, Mo. On May 25, after the Senate failed to act, USG nominated Robert P. Richardson. On Dec. 12, USG renominated Beach.

1876, APRIL 17.   William Strong, U.S. Supreme Court, to USG. "I concur heartily with Judge McKennan in commending to you Hon James A. Logan as a fit person to fill the expected vacancy in the District Judgeship of Western Pennsylvania. . . ."—ALS, Betts Collection, CtY. On June 7, USG nominated Winthrop W. Ketchum as judge, Western District, Pa., to replace Wilson McCandless, retired.

1876, APRIL 18.   Luther S. Fish, "1st Ohio, V. H. A during the war and Brother in law to the Prisoner," Cleveland, to USG. "This is in behalf of Edward, A

Phalen, of Salem Mass. who was Captain in the Union Army, and now enrolled upon the pension list of disabled soldiers. While acting in the capacity as chief clerk on the postal route between Boston and Bangor, the following circumstances occurred, which caused him to be incarcerated in the Essex County jail of Mass, for the period of three years from December 1875. Here are the facts. Having a very important engagement one night at 8 P. M. he picked up a package of letters on leaving his Car at the Boston end of the route, and placed it in his pocket as a reminder of his engagement. The relieving clerk saw him put the bundle in his pocket, and gave a sign to the detective, who at once invited him up to the office. Arriving there, he was declared under arrest for robbing the Mails. . . . The G. A. R. are administering to the wants of his wife & child who live at No. 13 Pickman st. Salem Mass. He has a great desire to learn the Phonetic or short hand system of writing, but the jailor emphatically refuses the privilege—not a very wise course for a reformatory institution to pursue. . . ."—ALS, DNA, RG 60, Letters from the President. See *O.R.*, I, xlvii, part 1, 641.

1876, APRIL 18.   U.S. Senator Frederick T. Frelinghuysen of N. J. to USG requesting an autograph for the cornerstone of the First German Dutch Reformed Church of Newark.—William J. Novick, *Heirlooms of History*, III, no. 72.

1876, APRIL 19.   USG endorsement. "Refered to the Sec. of War. I have no objection to this apt. being made."—AES, DNA, RG 94, ACP, 3625 1873. Written on a letter of April 17 from U.S. Senator James M. Harvey of Kan. to USG. "I had the honor some months ago to request the appointment of Lieut. S. K. Thompson to a position in the regular army. Since that time a law has been passed by Congress authorizing his appointment, and I respectfully renew the application, referring in support of my request to the papers in his case on file in the office of the Secretary of War"—LS, *ibid.* U.S. Senators John J. Ingalls of Kan. and Powell Clayton of Ark. favorably endorsed this letter.—AES, *ibid.* On April 21, USG nominated Samuel K. Thompson as 2nd lt. See *U.S. Statutes at Large (Private Laws)*, XIX, 2–3; *CR*, 44–1, 572–73, 1303.

On Feb. 27, 1875, Thompson, Washington, D. C., had written to USG. "I have the honor to respectfully ask to be appointed Second Lieutenant in the U. S. Army, with date of commission and relative rank in the Army as held by me prior to the 10th day of August 1874.—The facts in my case are as follows: I was cashiered in August last, on a charge, with one specification, of 'Violation of the 45th Article of War.' My defense was badly conducted by my counsel, some of the witnesses for the defense were not in the Department, others could not be found, and still others were not called before the Court. . . . As to habitual use of intoxicating liquor, the testimony of the Captain of my company, and my testimonials go to prove quite the reverse. Asst. Surg. Steinmetz in his testimony dated Feb. 8th 1875—(on file with the Senate Mil. Committee,) says, that at the time of my arrest and for some days after, I was under his medical treatment for tonsilitis, and that from that cause I articulated with difficulty, . . ."—ALS, DNA, RG 94, ACP, 3625 1873. On April 12, Secretary of War William W. Belknap endorsed papers in this case. "Upon the recommendation of the Judge Advocate General, the President directs that Mr. Saml K. Thompson be appointed Second Lieutenant—"—AE (initialed), *ibid.* Related papers are *ibid.* Senate adjournment delayed Thompson's efforts at reinstatement.

1876, April 19.   To James F. Fagan, U.S. marshal, Western District, Ark., concerning Osi (or Osey) Sanders, a Cherokee convicted of murdering Thomas S. Carlyle near Tahlequah, Indian Territory. ". . . *Whereas,* it is alleged that doubts have arisen as to the guilt of the said Sanders, and a delay of the execution of the said sentence is prayed for that time may be had for an investigation of the facts of the case; You are, therefore, hereby informed that the execution of the said sentence has been, by me, *respited* and *delayed* until Friday, the second day of June, . . ."—Copy, DNA, RG 59, General Records. On June 1, USG ordered Fagan to delay the execution to Sept. 8, as recommended by Judge Isaac C. Parker.—Copy, *ibid.* Sanders was hanged on Sept. 8. See Glenn Shirley, *Law West of Fort Smith: A History of Frontier Justice in the Indian Territory, 1834–1896* (New York, 1957), p. 213.

1876, April 26.   USG endorsement approving a recommendation that the agent for the Osages act as agent for the Kaws without additional pay.—Copy, DNA, RG 75, Letters Received, Osage Agency.

1876, April 26.   James H. Ellinger, Philadelphia, to USG claiming a $50 reward for informing on an illegal distillery.—ALS, DNA, RG 60, Letters from the President.

1876, April 27.   USG endorsement. "Refered to the Sec. of the Treasury. I am satisfied from conversation, and testemonials that this is a case worthy of the most favorable concideration. I hope it will be practicable not only to restore Mr. Bailey but to advance him to a permanent Clerkship."—AES, DNA, RG 56, Applications. Written on a letter of April 26 from William T. Bailey, Washington, D. C., to Secretary of the Treasury Benjamin H. Bristow. "I have the honor to request that you will direct the revocation of Department letter of the 4th instant, dispensing with my services from and after the 15th instant, and promote me to a first-class clerkship to take effect from and including the 16th instant." —ALS, *ibid.* On July 26, 1875, Samuel F. Maddox, chairman, Republican congressional committee, Richmond, had written to Bristow urging Bailey's promotion, citing his record as a Unionist and "sufferings in the Rebel prisons."— LS, *ibid.*

1876, April 27.   USG endorsement. "Will the Supt. of the Bureau of Printing & Engraving, Treas. Dept. please see the bearer, Miss Burch?"—AES, DNA, RG 56, Applications. Written on an undated letter from Alice G. Burch, Washington, D. C., to USG. "I have called in behalf of a family whose only support has been taken from them by the bureau of Engraving and Printing being closed. The family consists of three persons, mother daughter and son, the son held the office until furloughed, they are now in most destitute circumstances, being obliged to move from their present place, because they cannot pay the rent, now at this time every thing is in utter confusion, the mother is a confirmed invalid, the daughter is lying in spasms, and what they will do, I cannot tell I beg of you Mr President to give me a letter for Mr Lochry so that he can get his place back"—ALS, *ibid.* Charles H. Lochrey was appointed laborer, Bureau of Printing and Engraving.

1876, *April* 27.   USG authorization for Secretary of State Hamilton Fish to negotiate with Mexico.—DS, DLC-Hamilton Fish. On April 29, Fish recorded in his diary. "Mexican Minister Mr Mariscal calls by request at 2 o'clock and we sign in Triplicate the convention for extending the time for the Umpire to conclude the business on the Mexican Claims Commission I keep one copy and Mr Mariscal takes the other two to send to his government by different routes as the Mails are now often obstructed in Mexico owing to the Revolution there."—*Ibid.* On May 1, USG transmitted this convention to the Senate, which ratified it on May 24.—Copies, DNA, RG 59, Reports to the President and Congress; *ibid.*, RG 130, Messages to Congress. On June 29, USG authorized Fish to exchange ratifications with Mexico.—DS, DLC-Hamilton Fish.

On Feb. 2, 1877, USG transmitted to the Senate a report on the claims commission.—Copies, DNA, RG 59, Reports to the President and Congess; *ibid.*, RG 130, Messages to Congress. *SED*, 44-2-31.

[*1876, April 28*].   USG note. "Lovel H. Webb of Kan. late Cadet at Naval Academy may be pardoned if no legal inability to granting it exists."—AN, Columbia University, New York, N. Y. On April 28, Secretary of State Hamilton Fish recorded in his diary. "The President handed me a card with the name of J. S. Rutan; remarking that Genl Hartranft could fill all the Consulates, also; one asking for the pardon of Cadet L. H. Webb. of the Naval Academy—I remind him that the Attorney General has given an opinion that a pardon cannot be granted in this case and that I am unable to make out a pardon without requisition in the proper form. The President asked if I had seen the opinion—I said no I had not received it from the Secretary of the Navy, who then says it is misslayed and the Attorney General is requested to send him a copy."—DLC-Hamilton Fish. On March 14, Fish had recorded in his diary. "I read a letter addressed to me by the Secretary of the Navy requesting a warrant of pardon from Lowell H Webb a cadet midshipman who had been convicted of hazing and had been dismissed under act of 23rd June 1874 Sen Harvey had been to see me in reference to this case, saying that the pardon was wanted in order to renominate and have him appointed to a Cadetship. I told Sen Harvey I would bring the matter up before the Cabinet. . . ."—*Ibid.* See Fish diary, March 17, 1876, *ibid.* No pardon followed for Lovell H. Webb.

On March 31, Governor John F. Hartranft of Pa. wrote to USG. "I beg leave to earnestly ask your Excellency to appoint Hon. James S. Rutan of Pennsylvania to a Consulate in Europe, or to one of the Judgeships in the Territories. . . ."—LS, DNA, RG 59, Letters of Application and Recommendation. Related papers are *ibid.* On [*April 28*], USG wrote a note. "[Hon. J. S. Rutan Consulate] Recommended by Gov. Hartranft"—AN (bracketed material not in

USG's hand), Columbia University, New York, N. Y. On May 5, USG nominated James S. Rutan as consul, Cardiff.

On May 1 and 24, Fish recorded in his diary, the first after a conversation with USG. "He tells me of the death of the Consul General at Florence and says he wishes to make a nomination immediately to avoid the importunities and asks if I know Wirt Sykes—whose name I have never heard—He says he is the husband of Olive Logan and his wishes to appoint him—he sends his name on a card to his son directing the nomination to be made." "I mention to the President that Sen Cameron last evening at the Secretary of Interior's had called attention to the nomination of Wirt Sykes as Consul at Florence, several Senators have also spoken to me and likewise to the President—Cameron says he wants a gentleman appointed, that it is but a show place, and suggests without apparently much interest the name of Mr Routan recently appointed Consul at Cardiff. The President requests me to send a message withdrawing Sykes and nominating Routan and says I may nominate any one I please for Cardiff"—DLC-Hamilton Fish. On May 25, USG nominated Rutan as consul, Florence, in place of William Wirt Sykes; Rutan later declined. On May 26, Fish reported a conversation with USG. "He asked if any appointment had been made to Cardiff he says that Mr Wales of Miss desires the appointment of McAllister. Wirt Sykes and wife have called on the President; as they did on me this morning, but neither of us saw them; the President states that when the message withdrawing Sykes nomination was sent in yesterday that the Committee had just reported favorably on Sykes confirmation—he says the Committee have not treated him rightly—that two Senators one on the Committee and the other not (meaning Cameron & Conkling) had called on him and myslf remonstrating against the appointment and requesting its withdrawal and he says that as such was the case he would probably re-nominate him, but eventually authorizes me to offer him the nomination to Cardiff should he call upon me."—*Ibid.* On June 1, U.S. Senator Roscoe Conkling of N. Y., chairman, Committee on Commerce, wrote to USG. "I have the honor to state that I am directed by this Committee to inform you, that in considering the nomination of Mr. Wirt Sykes, as Consul of the United States at Florence, Italy, the Committee examined fully into the various reports and rumors in circulation derogatory to his character, and found unanimously that they were without foundation. The Committee think it just to make this expression because of information that Mr. Sykes has been or may be presented for the position of Consul of the United States at Cardiff Wales."—LS, DNA, RG 59, Miscellaneous Letters. On June 6, USG nominated Sykes as consul, Cardiff. On Aug. 23, 1897, Olive Logan, Washington, D. C., wrote to John Russell Young. "I have been trying to find, among my old letters to the newspapers years ago, a copy of the interview I had in Paris with General Grant, in which he spoke so highly of the literary work you had done in connection with his travels. 'John Russell Young's is emphatically the best account' he said, with every evidence of admiration of your work; and he added, 'Young's is far better than Badeau's.'. . ."—ALS, DLC-John Russell Young.

On May 1, 1876, Richard McAllister, Jr., Washington, D. C., had written to USG. "The place in Utah which you suggested to Col Wells and my wife for me has been filled. I understand that the 'Consulship' at *Florence, Italy* is vacant. Will you not appoint me to this place? My application, and recommendations, are on file in the state Department."—ALS, DNA, RG 59, Letters of Application and Recommendation. Related papers are *ibid.* On [*June 6*], USG wrote a note. "Richd McAlister, Jr. Miss. A territorial apt. or consulate."—AN, Columbia University, New York, N. Y. On the same day, Fish recorded in his diary. "The President handed me a card with the name of Mc Allister upon it for a Consulate. I told him there were only two vacant Laguayra ($1500) and Guayaquil ($1000). He desired me to nominate him to Guayaquil adding that if he did not accept it at any rate it would relieve him of the pressure."—DLC-Hamilton Fish. On June 9, USG nominated McAllister as consul, Guayaquil.

On Dec. 6, USG nominated Rutan as surveyor of customs, Pittsburgh, to replace Thomas Steel. On Feb. 26, Postmaster Gen. Marshall Jewell had telegraphed to USG. "I am in receipt of the following telegrapm from Genl. James S. Negley 'Please ask President to delay action in case of Thomas Steele collector of customs. the efforts to remove him emanate from base motives'"—Telegram received, DNA, RG 107, Telegrams Collected (Bound).

1876, M AY 1. Governor Benjamin F. Potts of Montana Territory to USG. "I have the honor to enclose the petition of Members of the Bar of this city asking the reappointment of Merritt C. Page as U. S. Attorney for Montana Territory. I have the honor to say that I fully endorse said petition and I may also add that Mr. Page has been the most active and successful Attorney that has ever represented the government in Montana. He has been blamed by some persons for not instituting certain proceedings in Indian Cases, but as to such cases he has fully obeyed the wise instructions of the Honorable Attorney General. I earnestly recommend his reappointment"—LS, DNA, RG 60, Records Relating to Appointments. The enclosure is *ibid.* On May 19, USG nominated Merritt C. Page to continue as U.S. attorney, Montana Territory.

On [*Oct. 25*], USG wrote a note. "Remove Dist. Atty. Page of Montana"—AN, OHi. On Nov. 13, Page, Helena, wrote to USG. "I have received from the Attorney General a copy of your Order dated Oct 25th suspending me from office—I have reason to believe that this is due to the efforts of Indian Inspector E. C. Kemble who recently visited this Territory and on his departure threatened to have me removed from office because I refused to institute criminal prosecutions against D. E. Clapp late Agent of the Crows. My course in this matter would be, as my previous course with reference to the Crow Agency has been, endorsed by Governor Potts and every other respectable lawyer in this Territory. If Mr. Kemble has discovered any matter which is properly the subject of a criminal prosecution he has not made it known to me—I beg leave to refer you to the correspondence between Inspector Kemble and myself in his possession and to my letter to the Attorney General on the subject dated Oct. 24th My office is not worth a contest, but I protest against your being misled by charges the nature of which I am not apprised of but which certainly have no foundation in fact—"—ALS, DNA, RG 60, Records Relating to Appointments. On Aug. 4, USG had nominated Lewis H. Carpenter as agent, Crow Agency, in place of Dexter E. Clapp. See *PUSG,* 24, 412.

On June 7, Andrew J. Smith, surveyor gen., Montana Territory, wrote to USG. "I enclose Gov. Potts letter to you which will explain my reasons for troubling you. The affair was one that could not be avoided, loyalty to yourself and my own Self respect alike demanded the course I pursued. I send this with enclosure to be handed to you in the event that Wilbur F. Sanders attempts to injure me in your good opinion. I hope you will pardon me for troubling you with my private affairs—"—ALS, USG 3. On the same day, Potts wrote to USG. "Genl. Andrew J. Smith Surveyor General of this Territory has always conducted himself gentlemanly in his official and personal intercourse with our citizens and has secured their respect and confidence. Recently he was driven to an encounter with one W. F. Sanders of this place who never looses an opportunity to abuse the President of the United States and other official of the government. This man Sanders is one of the most abusive men I have any knowledge of, and merits a personal castigation daily. Genl. Smith's castigation of Sanders has increased the respect our best citizens entertained for him heretofore. If Sanders should prefer charges against Genl. S. before the Department I respectfully request that he be fully heard before any adverse action is taken"—ALS, *ibid.* Smith continued as surveyor gen. On March 1, 1872, USG had nominated Wilbur F. Sanders as U.S. attorney, Montana Territory; Sanders declined. On May 13, USG nominated Page.

On Sept. 16, 1876, Potts wrote to USG. *"Personal . . .* I regret to learn that one Charles Rumley of this place has been appointed Assayer for the New U S. Assay office at this place. This man Rumley is a Democrat of the bitter school, is now and always has been, and as he has the employment of the Workmen none but democrats will be employed. Mr Rumley is totally unfitted to manage any kind of business and has been a total failure through life—in the management of his own private affairs. His endorsers here are generally Democrats and Such men as the Fisks & W F. Sanders who are trying to hang on to the Skirts of the Republican party for spoils but who Supported Greely and villified you and your administration. . . ."—ALS, DNA, RG 56, Asst. Treasurers and Mint Officials, Letters Received. Charles Rumley continued as assayer, Helena.

1876, May 2.   USG endorsement. "Refered to the Sec. of the Treas. I see no objection to the change asked for."—AES, DNA, RG 56, Naval Officer Applications. Written on a letter of April 13 from U.S. Representative Chester B. Darrall of La. and three others to USG. "We hereby present the recommendation of a number of the leading colored men in our State for the appointment of A. F. Riard as Naval Officer of the Port of New Orleans. We can entirely endorse all that is said of Mr Riards capacity and integrity and feel confident he will if appointed conduct the business of the office to the entire satisfaction of the Department. We think this appointment would be wise at this time from the fact that no colored man holds any Govt. position of any considerable importance in the State."—LS, *ibid.* A related petition is *ibid.* On May 3, USG nominated Alexander F. Riard as naval officer, New Orleans.

On Feb. 5, Lionel A. Sheldon, New Orleans, had written to USG. "I have been informed that a movement is on foot to procure the removal of Charles Dillingham the Naval Officer at this Port, and to secure the appointment of a

colored man in his place. The issue in this state has practically become one of
color so far as the organization of political parties ~~are~~ is concerned, an issue
brought about by the action of both races. The result is unfortunate for the state
and especially the colored people, They are now so demoralized that it is
doubtful if many of them will vote at the next election. I regard every act as unfortunate that tends to increase the race conflict. The republicans cannot maintain their ascendancy unless there is considerable support from the whites. In
this aspect I think the rumored change would be unwise. Beyond this Col Dillingham is a good republican—a gentleman—and a very efficient and popular
officer. It seems to me that there can be no public reason for his removal. If the
change suggested were made it would strike the business community especially
unpleasantly."—ALS, *ibid.* Related papers are *ibid.* and include a letter of Feb. 7
from James F. Casey to USG. On May 13, Stephen B. Packard, U.S. marshal,
New Orleans, telegraphed to Matthew H. Carpenter, Washington, D. C. "Informed my letter february Seventh remonstrating against removal Col Dillingham has not been Seen by President I still believe he should be retained & request you to lay my letter before President"—Telegram received (at 9:10 P.M.),
DLC-USG, IB. On May 22, Culver C. Sniffen wrote to Secretary of the Treasury Benjamin H. Bristow. "The President directs me to request that you will
to-day forward to the Chairman of the Senate Committee on Commerce all the
papers in your Department relative to the charges against, and the retention of,
the Naval officer at New Orleans."—ALS, DNA, RG 56, Letters Received from
the President.

1876, M AY 4.   USG note. "Will the Sec. of State please see Mrs. Gassaway,
daughter of Judge Paschal of Texas who desires a position in the Dept. which it
is underst[ood] will be vacant soon"—ANS, Columbia University, New York,
N. Y. On Feb. 25, U.S. Senator Samuel B. Maxey of Tex. and seven others had
written to USG. "We the undersigned Senators and Representatives of the
State of Texas respectfully ask Your Excellency to exert your influence to obtain the appointment of Mrs. Bessie Paschal Gassaway to a Clerkship in one of
the Departments of the Government."—LS, DNA, RG 56, Applications. No appointment followed.

1876, M AY 4.   Secretary of the Treasury Benjamin H. Bristow to USG. "I hand
you a letter this moment received from Honble B. G. Caulfield Chmn &c. Will
you please indicate by pencil memorandum what answer you think should be
made to this request. Do you think it would be well to furnish the copies?"—
ALS, CSmH. On April 25, Secretary of State Hamilton Fish had recorded in his
diary. "Bristow has been before one of the Committees which asked him to send
some original papers from his Department (accounts of extra expenses of the
Marshal and Supervisor of New York from 1871 to the present time) but that in
pursuance of the instruction of the President he had declined furnishing the
originals but had offered either to furnish copies or a room in the Treasury Department where the originals might be inspected, by any member of the Committee, under the charge of some clerk who would be able to explain them. Some
conversation had passed between Mr Caulfield the Chairman of the Committee

and the Secretary which would seem to indicate an intention on the part of the Committee to make an issue on the question. The importance of being quite right in the position to be assumed was felt and much discussion was held, resulting without much doubt as to the propriety, not to give up the papers. In compliance with a request from the President the Members of the Cabinet consider the question in its legal aspect and in the mean time Bristow will write a cautious letter avoiding an immediate assent or refusal."—DLC-Hamilton Fish. On the same day, Bristow wrote to U.S. Representative Bernard G. Caulfield of Ill. ". . . I have submitted your communication of yesterday to the President, who directs me to say that, while there is no purpose to obstruct by any means the investigations of your committee, he has not felt that it is consistent with the duties imposed by law upon the Executive Department of the Government to permit original records, called for by the various committees of the House, to be removed from Department. Of course you do not fail to perceive that the right to call for any particular original papers in any one of the Departments implies the right to call for all the papers in all the Departments, and thus stop completely the entire machinery of the Executive Department of the Government. . . ."—Clipping, *ibid.* On May 2, Fish recorded in his diary. "The President read a letter from the Attorney General on the question of the right of Congress to call for original papers, the same as he read to me yesterday. The question was considered in various aspects and with an entire concurrence of opinion that papers were not subject to be called for, or inspected unless by the approval of the President. The President requested the Members of the Cabinet not to allow any individual members of Congress to have access to papers without special knowledge of for what purpose their inspection was desired and he authorizes Members of the Cabinet under his authority to refuse whenever they saw fit so to do."—*Ibid.*

[*1876, May 8*]. USG note. "Lt. H. R. Lemly, 3d Cav.y, asks to be detailed at the Artillery school. If it can be consistently done I would like to have the detail made. Will the Sec. of War please consult with Gen. Sherman about the propriety of it."—AN, OHi. On the same day, Gen. William T. Sherman endorsed papers in this case. "The Artillery School is a special school for Artillery. When an officer of Infantry or Cavalry can be spared, an exception has been made. But in this particular case the 3rd Cavalry is on the point of taking the Field—Lt Lemley is actually under orders to take out a detachment of recruits and he ought on every possible rule of service to go at once to his Regiment. If the discretion rest with me I must ad[vise] against this detail"—AES, DNA, RG 94, ACP, 2397 1876. On sick leave until May 16, 2nd Lt. Henry R. Lemly participated in action against the Sioux on June 9 and 17.

1876, MAY 10. Susan B. Fiske, Quincy, Ill., to USG. "I wish to make application for a *Chaplaincy* in the Army or Navy for my husband, the Rev. Wm Allen Fiske. My Father was Col. John Bradley, an old army officer. My brother was a Midshipman & fell on board the U. S. S. Richmond as she was passing the Forts, St Philip, & Jackson I cite this, not as claiming any reward for their services, but that you may know who I am. I remember yourself & Mrs Grant, pleasantly, as visiting at my Father's house in Brownville when you were stationed at Sacketts Harbor. . . . I can refer to the Secretary of War Judge Taft, & to Judge Bartley, who both knew my husband, when he officiated in Cincinnati."—ALS, DNA, RG 94, Applications for Positions in War Dept. See *PUSG*, 1, 221. On Sept. 30, Sarah M. Bradley, Trenton, N. J., wrote to USG on the same subject. ". . . You knew my husband well I believe as an old officer of the Army & you may of heard that I lost my only son at the battle of New Orleans"—ALS, DNA, RG 94, Applications for Positions in War Dept. No appointment followed. On Dec. 12, USG nominated Bradley A. Fiske, son of Susan and William A. Fiske, as ensign.

1876, MAY 11.   John Montgomery, Winona, Minn., to USG complaining of a reduction in his pension. ". . . My hernia gets larger and worse all the time and i am broke down in harte from hardships endured in the army   I am very much troubled with the asthma hoping you will be a friend to the Poor Soldier and see that the mistake is rectified and made all right by the next Payment . . ."— ALS, DNA, RG 48, Miscellaneous Div., Letters Received. On June 23, Montgomery wrote to USG on the same subject.—ALS, *ibid.* On Sept. 12, Montgomery, Elba, Minn., wrote to USG. "I wish just to let you know the Condition that we are in we are nakekd and bare footed we nothing to eat but Dry bread & water and all the flour we have in the house is 25 lbs and no means of buying more I have already notified you i was sick all last winter and consequently i Could not do anything with the team the grain and hay to keep the team all winter & Medic- Medicine and docter bills amounted to 200 dollers I had not all the team paid for and they threatned to foreclose on the team so i was oblidge to sell the team we realised nothing out of them so i had neither team nor seed nor feed to put in any Crop in the Spring and what farming tools i had to sell in order to live through the summer and we moved to Winona in hopes that i could get some light work i could do but i could not get nothing that i was able to do I tried working on a small boat at 30 dollers amonth if i had been a sound man and could have stood it till the latter part of september i would have had 180 dollers when i jump ashore to tie the line instead of tyeing the line i would have to lay down on my back and work my rupture back so i had to quit. so you see what the army has done for me. . . ."—ALS, *ibid.*

1876, MAY 15.   USG order confirming the boundaries of a reservation along the Colorado River in Arizona Territory and Calif.—*HED*, 45-2-1, part 5, I, 632, 45-3-1, part 5, I, 727, 47-2-1, part 5, II, 304, 49-2-1, part 5, I, 511–12; *SED*, 48-2-95, 200; *SD*, 57-1-452, 803–4. On June 23, USG ordered 89,572 acres along the Trinity River in Calif. set aside for the Hoopa Valley Reservation.—DS, DNA, RG 75, Orders. Printed in the last five sources listed above. On Aug. 31, USG ordered land near the Gila River in Arizona Territory added to a reservation for the Pima and Maricopa Indians.—DS, DNA, RG 75, Orders. Printed in the sources listed above.

1876, MAY 15.   To House of Representatives concerning claims of U.S. citizens against Venezuela.—Copies, DNA, RG 59, Reports to the President and Congress; *ibid.*, RG 130, Messages to Congress. *HRC,* 44-1-787, 6. USG wrote to the House of Representatives (May 16) and to the Senate (May 19) transmitting further information on the subject.—Copies as above. *HRC,* 44-1-787, 52, 56; *SED,* 44-1-66. See *PUSG,* 22, 278–79; *ibid.,* 26, 258–59.

On Jan. 8, 1877, USG responded to a resolution of the House of Representatives by transmitting official correspondence (since May 15, 1876) related to Venezuelan claims.—Copies, DNA, RG 59, Reports to the President and Congress; *ibid.,* RG 130, Messages to Congress.

1876, MAY 15.   U.S. Senator Phineas W. Hitchcock of Neb. to USG. "I respectfully recommend Hon. John J. Redick of Nebraska for appointment to the vacant Judge-ship in New Mexico—Mr. Redick is an able lawyer, prominent citizen and an active Republican—He is endorsed by Judges Dillon and Dundy, U. S. Circuit and District Judges for our U. S. Circuit and District. His appointment will give general satisfaction."—LS, DNA, RG 60, Records Relating to Appointments. Related papers are *ibid.* On May 16, USG nominated John J. Redick as associate justice, New Mexico Territory.

On May 6, U.S. Representative A. Herr Smith of Pa. and six others had written to USG. "It affords us pleasure to bear testimony to the integrity and judicial capacity of J. B. Amwake, Esq, of Lancaster, Penna. If appointed to fill the vacancy occasioned by the death of Judge Johnson late of the 2nd Judicial District of New Mexico, we have no hesitation in saying that he will give entire satisfaction to the Government and the public."—LS, *ibid.* Related papers are *ibid.* On May 23, U.S. Senator Simon Cameron of Pa. wrote to USG. "I am forced both from the desire of his friends, and my own high esteem for him, to present to you the name of B F. Fleniken of Waynesburg Pa for consideration as a fit man for Judge in New Mexico. He is a most excellent man, a good lawyer, and a most excellent republican. I do not know a more deserving one"—ALS, *ibid.*

1876, MAY 16.   Alfred L. S. Leighs, Portsmouth, England, to USG promoting his invention of a covering "wherby Any ship can be rendered Ball Proof & so that no Torpedo can Damage it."—ALS, DNA, RG 45, Letters Received from the President.

1876, MAY 18.   USG endorsement. "This will introduce to the American representative at Copenhagen, Capt Kenneworth, an American Citizen by adoption, who visits his native land. He will appreciate any attention he may receive as I will also."—AES, DNA, RG 59, Applications and Recommendations, Hayes-Arthur. Written on a letter of May 17 from U.S. Representative Burwell B. Lewis of Ala. *et al.* to Michael J. Cramer, U.S. minister, Copenhagen, introducing Herman Kenneworth, former capt., C.S. Army.—LS (6 signatures), *ibid.* Related papers are *ibid.* On July 29, Kenneworth, Copenhagen, wrote to USG. "It is due to you that I send you my hearty thanks for your kindness in introducing me to our honored representative at Copenhagen. I was received by him and his estimable wife with the kindness and hospitality characteristic of the *American lady* and *gentleman.* Your good sister, whose birthday on yesterday, we had the pleasure of honoring, is quite well and happy, and so are also, her husband, Miss Clara and little Jessee Grant; the *prettiest* boy in Europe."—ALS, USG 3.

1876, MAY 18.   USG endorsement. "Refered to the Chief of Bureau of Printing & Engraving, Treas. with the hope that this lad may be given an opportunity to learn a trade and make himself useful."—AES, DNA, RG 56, Applications. Written on a letter of the same day from Mrs. William H. Goddard, Washington, D. C., to USG. "I have called to see you this morning, bringing with me, Master John Carnes, the son of a union soldier who gave his life in our late struggle for his county's defence, this little boy was raised in the Sailors, and orphans, home in this City, at the age of sixteen they are expected to start out in the world for themselves, . . ."—ALS, *ibid.*

[*1876, May 19*].   USG note. "Drop a note to Fred Douglass asking him if he will be kind enough to call on me between 11 & 12 some day early next week"— AN, OHi. On the same day, Friday, Frederick Douglass, Washington, D. C., wrote to Culver C. Sniffen. "In answer to your note of to day I have to say that it will be convenient for me to call at the Executive Mansion on Monday Morning, and if I learn nothing from you meanwhile requesting otherwise I will call on Monday at Eleven O.clock a. m—"—ALS, Gilder Lehrman Collection, NNP.

1876, MAY 20.   USG endorsement. "Refered to the Sec. of the Int. I wish the sec. would see Mr. Havens, who will call to-day, and if satisfied, nominate him for the vacant Commissionership to the Land Office."—AES, DNA, RG 48, Appointment Div., Letters Received. Written on a letter of May 19, from U.S. Representative William P. Frye of Maine *et al.* to Secretary of the Interior Zachariah Chandler. "The undersigned members of the House of Representatives most respectfully recommend and request the appointment of Hon. Harrison E. Havens of Springfield, Missouri, as Commissioner of the General Land Office. Mr. H. served in the 42nd and 43rd Congresses, and is known to us as deserving, competent and worthy." LS (24 signatures), *ibid.* On June 3, Walter D. Hubbard, Springfield, Mo., wrote to USG that he had investigated homestead frauds in southwest Mo. ". . . I therefore certify and State now as a Commissioner of the U. S. Circuit Court that Mr Havens name never was to my knowledge even mentioned as that of a party by any possibility connected with those land swindlers . . . During the time the frauds were being perpetrated (the time afterwards being ascertained) Mr Havens was to my knowledge attending to his own private business being part of the time interested in the proposed Kansas City & Memphis Rail Road Compay—and later being engaged in his office in Springfield as editor of the Missouri Patriot. . . ."—ALS, *ibid.* Related papers are *ibid.*

On May 13, Samuel S. Burdett, New York City, had written to USG. "I have the honor to hereby tender to you my resignation of the office of 'Commissioner of the General Land Office' and in so doing beg to be permitted to express to you my sincere appreciation of the confidence reposed in me thus far, and my unfeigned regret, that my administration of the trust confided to me has in any manner failed of the most perfect realisation"—ALS, *ibid.* Burdett reportedly disappeared after resigning. ". . . He left Washington for Philadelphia in May, 1876, to see about the Centennial; thence he proceeded to New York, and was last seen at the Astor House. Three months ago his family heard that he was in Australia, and sent him money to come home. In April, 1876, Burdett was in St. Louis, and was then suffering from some disease of the stomach, and was very much depressed in spirits. He spoke of resigning his office and going on a stock farm for the benefit of his health. . . ."—*St. Louis Globe-Democrat,* Sept. 3, 1877.

On May 16, U.S. Senator Thomas W. Ferry of Mich. *et al.* wrote to USG. "Should a vacancy occur in the Office of Commissioner of the General Land Office, we respectfully recommend the appointment of U. J. Baxter of Michigan; now employed in that Office. Mr Baxter entered as a first class clerk, and advanced on his merit, step by step, to the head of a division & has recently been acting Commissioner in the absence of Commissioner Burdett. His experience as well as his ability for the place isare his best commendation, and we earnestly commend him for such position"—LS (8 signatures), DNA, RG 48, Appointment Div., Letters Received. Related papers are *ibid.* Uri J. Baxter continued as chief clerk, General Land Office.

On May 20, Llewellyn Davis, Ironton, Mo., wrote to USG. "In view of the announcement a day or two ago in the daily StLouis papers of the resignation of Hon. S. S. Burdett as Com. Gen. Land Office I have the honor to ask of you the favor of the appointment of myself as his successor should the appointment be made from this State and respectfully refer you to my earnest efforts to discharge my duty faithfully as Receiver of the Land office at this place also to such well known republicans as Ex Gov. McClurg, Ex Congressman Ira B Hyde and others if desired"—ALS, *ibid.* Davis continued as land office receiver, Ironton.

Also on May 20, Bishop Gilbert Haven *et al.*, Baltimore, wrote to USG recommending "Judge R. F. Crowell of St Paul Minnesota" to replace Burdett.— LS (8 signatures), *ibid.*

On May 25, U.S. Representative John A. Kasson of Iowa and eight others wrote to USG. "Col G. L Godfrey of Des Moines Iowa has been recommended by several prominent gentlemen of that state, for appointment as Commissioner of the General Land Office. Col Godfrey is about 38 years of age, a lawyer by profession, has been a member of the Iowa Legislature, has an honorable record as an officer in the late war, has been for several years Receiver at the consolidated Land Office at Des Moines and is well informed of the Land Laws of the United States. He is a gentleman of integrity and ability and the undersigned cordially recommend him for appointment"—LS, *ibid.* A related letter is *ibid.*

On May 29, U.S. Senators Phineas W. Hitchcock and Algernon S. Paddock of Neb. and four others wrote to USG. "We beg respectfully to recommend Mr. O. H. Irish for appointment as Commissioner of the General Land Office— Mr. Irish is a sound lawyer, has had great experience in the land system of this country, has good executive ability, strict integrity, and is a steady and consistent Republican."—LS, *ibid.*, RG 56, Applications. USG wrote a note. "Have the Sec. of the Int. investigate the record of Mr. Irish while in the Indian Bureau"— AN (undated), *ibid.* Related papers are *ibid.* Orsamus H. Irish later served as asst. chief, Bureau of Printing and Engraving. See *PUSG,* 26, 439.

On June 12, Hoyt Sherman, Des Moines, wrote to [Gen. William T. Sherman]. "General Williamson wishes me to write to you in his behalf, to help him secure an appointment under the Government—that of Commissioner of General Land Office. He is now in a peculiarly unfortunate condition as to his business affairs. He has always followed the real estate business—had no other profession—and now that the whole bottom has fallen out of that, he has nothing to fall back upon. He has a very interesting family, but his children are all young and girls, and in raising and educating them he has become very poor. He recently made a strong canvass for nomination as member of Congress from this District and failed by only a few votes. If you can help him I sincerely hope you will. All are well and wish to be remembered to you."—ALS, DNA, RG 48, Appointment Div., Letters Received. Gen. Sherman endorsed this letter to USG. "Genl Williamson Commanded one of my Brigades at Vicksburg—He is a man of inteligence and force. I think you must know him. The writer of this is my brother."—AES (undated), *ibid.* On June 20, USG nominated James A. Williamson to replace Burdett.

On Feb. 10, 1877, U.S. Senator Oliver P. Morton of Ind. wrote to USG. "Learning that the friends of Senator Clayton are urging his appointment as Commissioner of Public Lands, I desire to add my earnest recommendation. He was a gallant soldier, has always been a faithful republican and friend of your administration, is an honest man, and beyond all dispute highly qualified for the position. His appointment would give great satisfaction to his Republican colleagues in the Senate and would be to me personally gratifying"—ALS, *ibid.* On Feb. 24, U.S. Senator James G. Blaine of Maine wrote to USG on the same subject.—ALS, *ibid.* Related papers are *ibid.*

On Feb. 26, U.S. Senator William Windom of Minn. wrote to USG. "I respectfully recommend Hon J. M. Waldron of Minnesota for the position of Comr of Genl Land office made vacant by resignation of Mr Williamson. Mr Waldron is at present a member of the Minnesota State Senate and I have no doubt would make a good Commissioner, should he be favored with the appointment. . . . At the time I signed the recommendation for another gentleman, I was not advised of Mr Waldron's wishes on the subject."—ALS, *ibid.* Williamson retained the position.

1876, MAY 20. USG pardon for Hope H. Slatter, serving four years for manslaughter in D. C., as recommended by more than twenty-five senators and congressmen.—Copy, DNA, RG 59, General Records. On the same day, William H. Crook wrote to Secretary of State Hamilton Fish. "The President directs me to say,—there is no objection to Mrs Slatter being the bearer of the pardon of her husband—"—Copy, DLC-USG, II, 3. On April 14, 1875, Orville E. Babcock had written to Attorney Gen. George H. Williams. "The President directs me to ask if you are ready to report on the Slatter application for pardon and if not cannot you with propriety delay his departure for the Penitentiary until decision is reached."—Copy, *ibid.*, II, 2. See *Washington Evening Star*, March 31, 1875.

1876, MAY 20. William de Rohan, Washington, D. C., to USG. "Permit me to state briefly *why* I consider I have a claim upon the action of my Government—

1st I served with Col Crockett for a brief while in Texas in 1835; 2d I served under Lieut McLaughlin in the Seminole War:—3d I was a Boatswain's Mate in the Texas Navy, and in April or May 1845 hauled down the Texas flag for the last time afloat and handed the wrecks of the Navy over to the U S. S. Porpoise:—4th I volunteered into the 3d Artillery and served through the Mexican Campaign, ending as Captain in the 1st Michigan Volunteers 5th—The records of the State Department will show how I served the flag during the Rebellion, in England, France and Italy, though Mr Chas F Adams appropriated to himself the merit of my acts—These Mr President are the grounds on which I found my claim to your kindly intervention to obtain for m[e] from Italy what a civilized nation would never have compelled me to sue for—"—ALS, DNA, RG 59, Miscellaneous Letters. USG endorsed this letter. "State"—AE, *ibid.* Born William Dahlgren, de Rohan changed his name after a dispute with his brother, Admiral John A. Dahlgren. During the struggle to unify Italy, de Rohan lent money for a fledgling navy, which he helped to command. See *New York Daily Graphic,* Dec. 16, 1887; *Wm. de Rohan vs. the Italian Government* (n. p., [*1876*]). On May 23, Secretary of State Hamilton Fish recorded in his diary. "Captain de Rohan has been to see the President about his claim against the Italian Government. I explain its nature to the President and say it it̶s doubtful whether the Italian Government will recognize it but that Mr Marsh has been authorized to use his good offices. de Rohan wishes to have it made a Diplomatic Claim which this government cannot accept to."—DLC-Hamilton Fish. On April 29, Fish had written to U.S. Representative Charles J. Faulkner of Va. on this subject.—Copy, DNA, RG 59, Reports to the President and Congress. See de Rohan to Fish, Sept. 10, 1873, *ibid.,* Miscellaneous Letters. On Dec. 15, 1874, de Rohan had written to Fish seeking a consulship. ". . . I found my claim to the position chiefly on having from 1861 to 1865 watched narrowly the movements of traitors in England, France, Italy and elsewhere in Europe and kept the US. Minister in England and the Sec'y of State constantly advised of all their movements, for which service I received the formal thanks of Mr Seward at the close of the war—also that I have frequently been called upon in different parts of the world to perform temporarily consular duties or give advice—"—ALS, *ibid.,* Letters of Application and Recommendation. On Jan. 12, 1877, de Rohan wrote privately to Fish, complained of inaction on his claim, and sought a consulship in Samoa, "having been there first in 1842, and passed years of my life among the South Pacific Islands."—ALS, *ibid.* Related papers are *ibid.* No appointment followed.

1876, MAY 21. Albert Fritsch, Cincinnati, to USG. "You took the oath to protect the citizens and the constitution of the United States You are aware that poison and crime flourishes in Ohio unheeded by the proper officials You are vested with the power to declare martial law if you do not stop this crime you stand before the civilized world as a perjurer"—Telegram received, DLC-USG, IB.

1876, MAY 23. Frederick A. P. Barnard, New York City, to USG. "In compliance with the duty imposed upon me in one of the resolutions herewith submitted, adopted by the American Metrological Society at their recent semi-

annual meeting in this city, I have the honor herewith to transmit to you copies of the resolutions referred to, and to solicit your favorable consideration of
the same."—LS, DNA, RG 59, Miscellaneous Letters. The enclosed resolutions, adopted May 17, asserted "that the recent large depreciation in the value
of silver brings prominently to view the disadvantage of a double standard of
coinage, and especially the danger to public and private credit," and that "any
legislation which proposes to make silver coin a legal tender to indefinite
amounts, would be disastrous in its consequences to the business interests of
the country."—DS, *ibid.* On April 17 and July 22, USG approved legislation
regulating the issue of silver coin. See *U.S. Statutes at Large,* XIX, 33–34, 215.

1876, MAY 23.   Charles H. Chapin, Chicago, to USG. "I wish to learn the
whereabouts of Major French who served on your Staff at Vicksburg in the year
1863 I was a Lieutenant in the 4th Ill. Cav Vol & was hurt while out with a forage train in the rear of Port Gibson on the 10th day of October 1863 I think
Major French was the Surgeon that attended me by giveing me his address you
will cofer a great favor."—ALS, DNA, RG 94, ACP, 2756 1876. See *O.R.,* I, xxx,
part 2, 799.

1876, MAY 24.   USG note. "Will the apt. Clerk of the Treas. see John Cro-
nin, an old soldier of my old regt. of thirty years ago."—ANS, DNA, RG 56,
Applications.

1876, MAY 25.   Judge Robert W. Hughes, Eastern District, Va., Norfolk, to
USG. "I have been asked by prominent citizens from the principal officials of
this city to forward to you the enclosed paper soliciting the continuance at this
station of commodore T. H. Stevens. The paper is addressed to Secretary Robeson, but those who have signed it desire that your personal & official attention
be called to it. . . ."—ALS, DNA, RG 45, Letters Received from the President.
The enclosure is *ibid.* In June, Commodore Thomas H. Stevens was reassigned
from commandant, Norfolk Navy Yard, to chairman, Norfolk harbor board. See
PUSG, 19, 92.

[*1876, May 26*].   USG note. "Gov. Alcorn asks the apt of Toby W. Johnson, of
Mis, as consul to Belge, vice _____ Pierson who intends to resign. Johnson
was college class-mate of Pierson; has been vice consul, and is in good circumstances as wel as familiar with the duties"—AN, Columbia University, New
York, N. Y. On May 26, Toby W. Johnston, Washington, D. C., wrote to Secretary of State Hamilton Fish on the same subject.—ALS, DNA, RG 59, Letters of Application and Recommendation. U.S. Senators James L. Alcorn and
Blanche K. Bruce of Miss. favorably endorsed this letter.—ES (undated), *ibid.*
Richmond Pearson continued as consul, Verviers and Liège.

1876, MAY 26.   Flavel B. Tiffany, Medford, Minn., to USG. "Please excuse the
liberty I take in addressing you. I wish to ask a favor of you—should it be yours
to grant—viz an appointment from our government to Europe where I can
serve the government and at the same time improve myself by attending Lec-
tures in the Europine Hospitals. I am very desirous of taking a special course

that I may make my self more proficient and competent to practis Surgery. . . ."
—ALS, DNA, RG 59, Letters of Application and Recommendation. No appointment followed. See Irving A. Watson, ed., *Physicians and Surgeons of America. A Collection of Biographical Sketches of the Regular Medical Profession* (Concord, N. H., 1896), pp. 383–84.

1876, MAY 27. John R. Cushman, Indianapolis, to USG seeking a diplomatic appointment. ". . . When Thomas L. Hamer came to the neighborhood of Batavia, Ohio, in the days of his youth, to teach school, he boarded at my grandfathers, which he also did when he studied law under some one, Judge Morris, I beleive it was, or Judge Fishback. My father afterward studied under General Hamer and Judge Morris, and I have often heard my grandfather, John Reiley, who is yet living, at the age of of 86, has often told me of those men and of your father, with all of whom he was well acquainted many years ago. My prayer for a situation is an earnest one, as it seems I have nothing in the world to do. May I look for a kind reply?"—ALS, DNA, RG 59, Letters of Application and Recommendation. No appointment followed.

1876, MAY 28. Susan Stout, Pottsville, Pa., to USG. "I would like to know how it is that I do not get an answer to my claim. I need it very bad now. You would oblige me very much if you would see about it, as I am the widow of William. R. Stout. I am broken down very much, by hard labor, trying to keep my children to-gether. I have furnished all the papers you have asked for, with satisfaction, and now I do not hear any thing more about it. And you shall please attend to it, and give me an answer. All others get it and why is it that I can't have mine."—ALS, DNA, RG 48, Miscellaneous Div., Letters Received. On July 27, Stout wrote to USG on the same subject. ". . . I don't want to go to the Poor house as long as the Government owes me a pension, . . ."—ALS, *ibid.* Stout received $8 monthly beginning in March, 1877.

1876, MAY 29. USG endorsement. "Refered to the Sec. of State. Dr. Harrison served as a Surgeon in our Navy for a number of years. He is now an applicant for a consulate."—AES, DNA, RG 59, Letters of Application and Recommendation. Written on a note dated May 1 from John S. Mosby. "I am very well acquainted with Dr Harrison who was a citizen of Loudon Co: Va—& take great pleasure in recommending him to the President."—ANS, *ibid.* On June 6, Secretary of State Hamilton Fish discussed this endorsement with USG. "I enquire whether he wishes any thing done—He replies O, no!"—Fish diary, DLC-Hamilton Fish. No appointment followed. See *O.R.* (Navy), II, ii, 559.

1876, MAY 30. USG endorsement. "War. Please call special attention to this application when apts are made to the Army."—AES, DNA, RG 94, ACP, 4354 1876. Written on a letter of May 23 from Annie J. Van Leer, Philadelphia, to Adolph E. Borie. ". . . When I last had the pleasure of seeing Genl Grant, in March, he told me he would Appoint my Son 2nd Lieut from Civil life, . . ."—ALS, *ibid.* William J. Van Leer failed arithmetic in his examination for appointment as 2nd lt.—N, *ibid.* Related papers are *ibid.*
On July 2, 1875, Annie Van Leer had written to USG. "On Feby 10th of this

year You generously answered my petition by appointing my Son W. J. Van Leer to a cadetship at West Point   he was examined last month but failed   the short time between his appointment and his examination (about three months) gave him hardly time to prepare for such a rigid examination, and I feel certain that if you will give him another chance in September, he will be Successful, . . ."— ALS, *ibid.*, Correspondence, USMA. Related papers are *ibid.*

1876, May 31.   To House of Representatives transmitting a report on steps taken to protect Americans from anti-Christian violence in Turkish-controlled Macedonia.—Copies (the first misdated May 29), DNA, RG 59, Reports to the President and Congress; *ibid.*, RG 130, Messages to Congress. *HED*, 44-1-170.

[*1876, May*].   USG note. "Geo. H. Scidmore applies for Consular Clerkship. See Sec. of State in regard to it."—AN, Columbia University, New York, N. Y. On May 6, George H. Scidmore was appointed consular clerk, Liverpool.

[*1876, May*].   John H. Vincent, Baltimore, to USG. "On my own account allow me to speak a word in behalf of my friend Mrs. Havener who has been removed from position on the ground that 'she is a wealthy rebel.' So I am told you have been informed   Now, Mr. President, let me assure you that these two statements are untrue. 1. She is *not* a rebel. I have known her for ten years. I believe her to be loyal. 2. She is not wealthy but *poor* and in need of the support which the office yielded her. Excuse my boldness of speech, but I know your goodness of heart and I know the worthiness of my friend Mrs. Havener."—ALS (docketed May 31, 1876), DNA, RG 56, Applications. In 1875, Mary C. Havenner had clerked in the Pension Office for $1,200 annually; she later clerked in the Census Office for $1,000. For Vincent, see *PUSG*, 5, 132–33.

1876, June 1.   Daniel J. Hogan, New York City, to USG. "Allow me to renew my application for an appointment under the federal government. In a former application I stated that I had served in the Volunteer Army during the war entering the service as a private in the 5th New Jersey Battery and being discharged as 1st Lieutenant in the 43d U. S. Colored Infantry. I was a supporter of yours in the campaign of 1868, having been then Vice President of the Soldiers and Sailors Campaign club of the County of New York. I have been much persecuted as I believe by religious zealots, who made use of a system apparently mesmeric in its nature by means of which they have given me great trouble, greatly reducing my bodily strength and destroying my business. *In defence of my home from these attacks* I have both tried personal effort and sought the protection of the authorities, but the transgressors have either been so secret in their operations or have had such influential backers that my efforts have been of little avail. In this strait, sir, I make bold to apply to you, hoping that the *American Soldiers* heart will not be closed against the appeal of a persecuted and suffering comrade."—ALS, DNA, RG 56, Applications. Related papers are *ibid.* On April 10 and June 4, 1869, Hogan had written to Secretary of State Hamilton Fish seeking appointment as consul, Matamoros.—ALS, *ibid.*, RG 59, Letters of Application and Recommendation. Never appointed, Hogan blamed "air telegraphing and electro-magnetism" for his problems. See Hogan to Benjamin Harrison, Aug. 4, 1888, Dec. 9, 1892, Hogan to Elijah W. Halford, May 17, 1892, DLC-Benjamin Harrison.

1876, June 2. USG order. "The within recommendation of the Secretary of the Interior is hereby approved, and he is authorized to take such measures as may be necessary to carry it into effect."—ES, DNA, RG 48, Appointment Div., Letters Received. On June 1, Secretary of the Interior Zachariah Chandler had written to USG recommending that the Northern Superintendency be discontinued after June 30.—LS, *ibid.* On April 3, USG had issued an order. "For the reasons given by the Commissioner of Indian affairs, in his letter of March 30th 1876. funds for the several agencies of the Northern Superintendency, will, until otherwise ordered, be remitted directly from the Treasury to the several agents thereof."—Copy, DNA, RG 75, Letters Received, Northern Superintendency.

1876, June 5. USG endorsement. "Refered to the Sec. of War. If a vacancy exists such as Dr. Dews asks for I hope it may be confered on him."—AES, DNA, RG 107, Appointment Papers. Written on a letter of June 2 from John P. Newman, Washington, D. C., to USG. "I feel so much interest in my friend Dr Crews & as the first application, addressed to the Interior Department, has failed, I take the liberty to write again. If any man in the country deserves an appointment it is Dr Dreus. He is an estimable Christian, an excellent physician, & sacrificed a good practice to serve the country during the war. He now applies for a clerkship in the War Department, which I hope he will get without delay." — ALS, *ibid.* U.S. Senator Oliver P. Morton and U.S. Representative Morton C. Hunter of Ind. favorably endorsed this letter.—AES, *ibid.* Samuel B. Crew, former surgeon, 89th Ohio, served as watchman, Post Office Dept.

1876, June 5. USG endorsement. "Refered to the Sec. of State. The present incumbent to the Glasgow Consulate being from Iowa, and the delegation being unanimous for this chang, I approve the same."—AES, DNA, RG 59, Letters of Application and Recommendation. Written on an undated letter from U.S. Senator George G. Wright *et al.* to USG. "The Iowa delegation respectfully ask you to appoint Samuel F Cooper of Grinnell Iowa United States Consul to Glasgow in Great Britain"—LS (9 signatures), *ibid.* On June 6, Secretary of State Hamilton Fish discussed this endorsement with USG. "He says Wilson of Iowa is very anxious, he concludes that should the Iowa Delegation obtain the resignation of Glasgow now then all right but that he wished them told that he did not wish to make any removals until after the pending election."—Fish diary, DLC-Hamilton Fish. On July 21, USG nominated Samuel F. Cooper as consul, Glasgow, to replace Samuel L. Glasgow. See *PUSG*, 19, 432–33.

1876, June 5. James Ruddock, Attica, Mich., to USG concerning his application for a pension. ". . . I received a reply may 4th 1876 that the office would not reopen my rejected claim for the reason that the disability from which I was suffering was the result of Syphilis now my Dear Sir that is a desease that I never had neither in the army nor out of it in fact I did not know the meaning of the word untill I inquired of my family Physician and I can assure you I was justely indiginent at his explanation . . ."—ALS, DNA, RG 48, Miscellaneous Div., Letters Received. Ruddock did not receive a pension.

1876, June 6.   Senate resolution. "That the President be requested, if not in his opinion inconsistent with the public interests, to furnish the Senate with a *fac simile* copy of the original draft of the letter of the Secretary of State to the Minister of the United States at the Court of St. James in May, 1861, in relation to the Proclamation of Her Majesty the Queen of Great Britain recognizing the belligerent character of the Confederate States."—DS (by George C. Gorham, secretary), DNA, RG 59, Miscellaneous Letters. On June 14, Secretary of State Hamilton Fish recorded in his diary. ". . . Some years since when Gov Boutwell was Secretary of the Treasury and pending the discussion in the Alabama Claims this paper was brought before the Cabinet and the remarkable nature of Mr Lincolns amendments led to its being photographed confidentially at the Treasury Department and 8 or 9 copies made one of which was furnished to the President and to each Member of the Cabinet. Robeson suggested that that might deprive it of its secrecy, but it was thought that being distributed in Cabinet & to Cabinet Members it was of Cabinet confidence."—DLC-Hamilton Fish. Facsimiles included in "A Famous Diplomatic Dispatch," *North American Review,* CXLII, CCCLIII (April, 1886), 402–10; Allen Thorndike Rice, ed., *Reminiscences of Abraham Lincoln By Distinguished Men of His Time* (New York, 1888), pp. liv–lxix. See Lincoln, *Works,* IV, 376–80.

1876, June 8.   U.S. Representative John A. Kasson of Iowa to USG. "I beg to call your attention to some extracts from 'The Record' of today, touching the land bill of which I spoke to you this morning. The following is the bill as it come from the Senate:. . . When it was first up before the House it was so strenuously opposed that it was sent back to the Committee for the purpose of excluding agricultural lands from its operation, leaving these subject to the homestead principle exclusively. The Committee then agreed upon amendments as follows to accomplish that end: . . . It seems they were subsequently persuaded to withdraw that amendment, and apply the previous question to the bill without amendment; and it thus passed the House by the small majority of eleven votes. You will observe, that while our public policy has abandoned the offering of public lands at public sale, in order to preserve lands for actual settlers, this bill *compels* the public sale, and prohibits private entries until they shall have been so offered, thus giving preference to speculative ownership. In this respect the bill is reactionary and establishes in the other direction an exceptional rule for public lands in the five states named, and to the prejudice of the homestead settler. Knowing the devotion of our Western people to the homestead principle, you will pardon me for calling your special attention to the measure."— ALS, OFH. Senate Bill No. 2, repealing homestead provisions for public lands in Ala., Miss., La., Ark., and Fla., became law without USG's signature. See *CR,* 44–1, 3654–55; *U.S. Statutes at Large,* XIX, 73–74.

1876, June 9.   USG veto. "I return herewith, without my approval, Senate Bill, No 165—entitled 'an Act for the relief of Michael W. Brock, of Meigs County, Tennessee, late a private in Company D, Tenth Tennessee Volunteers—The objection to affixing my signature to this bill may be found in the endorsement (which accompanies this message.) by the Adjutant General of the Army.—"—Copy, DNA, RG 130, Messages to Congress. *SED,* 44-1-73; *SMD,* 49-2-53, 395. Charged with deserting in Nov., 1864, and taking a horse and other government property, Michael W. Brock had been cleared of desertion and sought relief from the property charge. See *SRC,* 44-1-53.

1876, June 9.   Adolph E. Borie, Philadelphia, to Julia Dent Grant. "Your wellcome telegram of yesterday was received by me this morning (we being now in the country) and I beg leave in my wife's name as well as my own, to offer you all our sincere congratulations and heartiest wishes for the little stranger Our niece Mrs Lewis has not been so fortunate, having been confined a week ago, and losing her fine boy in the birth, but now doing well And now my dear Mrs Grant, do tell us if what we have seen in the newspapers, and see affirmed about Nellie's boy is true? I hope yet against hope almost, that it is not true. With love to the General . . ."—ALS, USG 3. Julia Grant, daughter of Frederick Dent and Ida H. Grant, was born June 7 at the White House. Grant Sartoris died May 21 in England.

1876, June 10.   Pattie A. Guild, Tuscaloosa, to USG. "I don't know why I write to you, except for the sake of the dear 'old Army' to which you belonged, and my dear husband, and I heard of you in those happy days, of my early married life, at Fort Humboldt, where you had been, before the dreadful war—and because you are powerful to help me if you will, and I think you will—My Husband—Dr L. Guild—was Medical Director of our dear Gen. R. E. Lee's Army —during the war. He is dead now—and I am left dependent. I want to support myself—and I beg of you to give me some place where I can do it—Some clerkship that ladies fill—and I will do my part faithfully—I know Gen Barnes— your Surgeon General, and others—who knew us in the old Army—but I apply to you—knowing you are all powerful—and I pray the Holy Spirit may incline you to help me—and bless you for it—If you are not in your present high position long, still one of your last acts will be one of kindness to a helpless woman—if you will place me in a position to support myself—My address is Mrs L. Guild Tuscaloosa Alabama—Hoping you may read this letter—"— ALS, DNA, RG 56, Applications. No appointment followed.

1876, June 13.   USG endorsement. "Refered to the Sec. of the Treas. hoping that something may be done for Mr. Boutwell."—AES, DNA, RG 56, Applications. Written on papers that include a letter of May 4 from Edward B. Boutwell, Washington, D. C., to USG. "Nothing but dire necessity compels me to trouble you with this communication. I therefore beg of you to give me your attention for a few moments and my case shall be briefly stated; it is as follows. The greater part of the fortune of my grand mother and her sister, was in money, and was placed in the hands of Governor Nelson of Virginia, who paid it to the scotch merchants to redeem the continental bonds, issued during the Revolutionary war. That money has never been returned to the heirs. I served forty two years in the Navy of the United States, and did not leave the service from choice, but was driven out of it by the treatment I received at the hands of Secretaries Toucey, and Welles. I served three months in prison in the city of Richmond in 1861 for being a union man. I was appointed a clerk in the Second Auditors office, Treasury Department, in 1871 by Secretary Boutwell, at the request of Mrs General Sherman, and was dismissed in June 1874, when the reduction of the appropriation by congress made it necessary to reduce the number of clerks in that Department. Since that period I have been a beggar, and have frequently passed a day and a night without eating a meal. Thus, honored sir, I have been as brief as possible in the relation of my story, and conclude by begging that I may receive some employment by which starvation may be avoided."—ALS, *ibid.* On July 27, Boutwell again wrote to USG. ". . . In 1874, when the reduction took place in the Treasury Department I was discharged from office and although I appealed to Secretary Bristow to reappoint me when a vacancy occurred, I was unable to persuade him to do so, because he desired to give all the vacancies to his own friends. Since my dismissal from the Treasury Department I have been unemployed and in a state bordering on starvation. I have taken the liberty of appealing once more to your justice and mercy, and pray that you will interpose your authority to save me from starvation. This appeal would have been made in person, but for the fact that I have not decent apparel to appear in the presence of the chief magistrate of the Nation."—ALS, *ibid.* See *SRC*, 35-2-340; *HRC*, 44-1-750; Boutwell to "Editor Freemans Journal," Feb. 22, 1864, InNd.

1876, JUNE 13.   USG pardon for Daniel Pratt, convicted in Mich. of "sending through the mails, indecent postal cards," after one year of a two and one-half year sentence.—Copy, DNA, RG 59, General Records.

1876, JUNE 14.   To Senate. "In answer to the Resolution of the Senate of the 26th, April, ultimo, I herewith transmit a report from the Secretary of State, with accompanying documents."—Copies, DNA, RG 59, Reports to the President and Congress; *ibid.*, RG 130, Messages to Congress. *SED*, 44-1-74. On the same day, Secretary of State Hamilton Fish wrote to USG forwarding correspondence related to claims "arising from captures by the rebel cruiser 'Shenandoah.'"—Copy, DNA, RG 59, Reports to the President and Congress. *SED*, 44-1-74.

1876, JUNE 15.   USG endorsement. "Refered to the Sec. of the Navy who may— if he thinks proper to do so on on examination of the case—remit the unexpired part of the sentence, and discharge the prisoner."—AES, DNA, RG 45, Letters Received from the President. Written on an undated letter from Mary O'Brian *et al.* to USG. "The petitioner, an aged and helpless widow prays for a pardon for her son, her only support, and respectfully presents for consideration the following facts:—That, in the month of March last, at the port of HongKong,

China, Patrick O'Brien of Boston, Mass. a seaman on the United States Steamship Tenneessee, was tried before a Naval Court Martial on the charge of using disrespectful language to an officer; was convicted and sentenced to three years confinement. That the offense was not a willful breach of discipline but was committed while ashore and under the influence of liquor and against an offercer belonging to another vessel and that by reason of his short experience in the service the offender was not aware that in using disrespectful language to an officer of another vessel he was committing a criminal breach of discipline. . . ."—DS (11 signatures), *ibid.*

1876, JUNE 15. USG endorsement. "Mr. A. C. Sharpe may be appointed with his class, without further examination."—AES, DNA, RG 94, ACP, 3364 1876. Written on papers including a letter of March 29 from Governor Rutherford B. Hayes of Ohio to Secretary of War Alphonso Taft. "I am personally acquainted with Mr Alfred C Sharpe. He is a young gentleman of education and talents, and I am confident that he will, if restored to the Army, be an honor to his profession. The circumstances of his withdrawal entitle him to special consideration. I therefore *earnestly* and *specially* recommend favorable action in his case—" —ALS, *ibid.* On July 27, 1875, Hugh L. Scott *et al.* had petitioned USG. "We, the undersigned, being all of the members of the *First class* of the *United States Military Academy*, would respectfully request that *Mr. Alfred C. Sharpe.* of *Iowa*, who was for three years our esteemed comrade and class-mate, be appointed a 2d Lieutenant in the United States Army to fill any one of the vacancies now existing—"—DS (50 signatures), *ibid.* On the same day, Orville E. Babcock wrote to Elliott W. Rice, Washington, D. C. "I have your letter relative to young Sharps appt. as a Lieut. I have submitted it to the President and he says he cannot do it—before his class graduates. He has followed this rule, and has within a month declined in two similar cases—and to now make an exception would be not only a violation of the rule but an injustice to those who have been refused."—Copies, DLC-USG, II, 2, 3. On June 22, 1876, USG nominated Alfred C. Sharpe as 2nd lt., 10th Cav. On June 27, U.S. Senator William B. Allison of Iowa wrote to Secretary of War James D. Cameron. "I take the liberty of enclosing to you *unofficially* letter just recd from my young friend A. C. Sharpe and beg to request that you will comply with his wishes. He spent 3 yrs at West Point, and was run into in some way by some other Cadet while exercising in the Cavalry & so disabled that he could not complete his course You were kind enough to appoint with his class. If it is practicable to assign to infantry I would be glad to have it done—sorry that I am compelled to trouble you so often"— ALS, DNA, RG 94, ACP, 3364 1876. The enclosure and related papers are *ibid.* On July 28, USG nominated Sharpe for transfer to the 22nd Inf.

1876, JUNE 15. Clara B. Jordan, Cincinnati, to USG. "When I was at the Executive Mansion, a few weeks ago, you very kindly offered, at the request of my uncle Gen. James Loudon of Georgetown Ohio, to speak to the Secretary of the Navy, concerning a claim of ours for Prize Money. Unfortunately Secretary Robeson was not present at the Cabinet meeting that day. Hence, this communication. Our claim is for the capture of cotton by the 'Juliet,' one of the vessels of the 'Mississippi Squadron' during the late war. . . ."—ALS, DNA, RG 45, Letters Received from the President.

[*1876, June 17*].   USG note. "Send word to Sec. of the Int. to notify Minnesota delegation that they must send a name for Surveyor Gen. of their state." —AN, OHi. On March 17, 1875, USG had nominated James H. Baker as surveyor gen., Minn. Baker continued in office.

1876, JUNE 17.   U.S. Senator David M. Key of Tenn. to USG. "I have the honor to enclose herewith the application of Dr Thos. W. Humes, Prest East Tenn. University at Knoxville Tenn, for the detail of a Military Professor for that College, under section 1225, of the Revised Statutes of the United States. . . ." —ALS, DNA, RG 94, ACP, 3162 1876. A letter of June 15 from Thomas W. Humes, Knoxville, to USG is *ibid.* On June 18, 1875, Humes had written to USG. "A. H. Nave, 2d Lieut. 7th U. S. Cavalry, has been elected Professor of Military Science and Tactics in this institution by its Board of Trustees, and he has consented, by and with your approval, to accept the position. I respectfully request that you will detail him to that office, under the provisions of the Act of Congress allowing Officers of the U. S. Army to be assigned to such duty in Colleges & Universities. This Institution during the Collegiate Year just closed, has numbered 315 Students, and its influence in the South-Western States is continually growing. I trust therefore that this request will be granted, at the earliest opportunity."—ALS, *ibid.*, 3377 1874. Related papers are *ibid.* On July 5, 1876, USG signed a bill increasing from twenty to thirty the number of army officers authorized for such detail. See *CR*, 44–1, 3770–75. On July 13, USG promoted Andrew Humes Nave, USMA 1871, to 1st lt., 7th Cav., to date from June 25. Nave joined his regt. as of Sept. 22.

On June 22, 1875, Governor William P. Kellogg of La. had written to USG requesting assignment of 2nd Lt. Samuel N. Holmes, 13th Inf., to "the Agricultural and Mechanical College of the State of La."—LS, DNA, RG 94, ACP, 3237 1873. On July 10, Maj. Thomas M. Vincent, asst. AG, endorsed this letter to Secretary of War William W. Belknap. "There are now no vacancies to be filled—all being filled by a detail or the promise of one. One request— from the East Tenn. University, thro' the Hon. H. Maynard—has, by the Secretary of War, been made contingent on an opportunity; and of Course that has precedence over the present application."—AES, *ibid.* Holmes, USMA 1873, was later court-martialed for gambling at cards after pledging to abstain. On May 23, 1876, USG mitigated his sentence from dismissal "to '*a suspension from rank and command, with forfeiture of half pay for six months.*'"—D (printed), *ibid.*

On April 29, U.S. Senators Phineas W. Hitchcock and Algernon S. Paddock of Neb. had written to USG. "In behalf of the University of the State of Nebraska we respectfully request the detail of an Officer of the Army as instructor at said institution . . ."—LS, *ibid.*, 2211 1876.

In [*May*], U.S. Representative George A. Jenks of Pa. *et al.* petitioned USG. "The Undersigned, Members of the House of Representatives of the 44th Congress, respectfully ask that an officer of the Army may be detailed to act as Professor in Allegheny College, located in the city of Meadville, State of Pennsylvania, under the authority and in accordance with the law approved July 28, 1866, the said College having the capacity to educate not less than one hundred and fifty Students at one time, as required by the law aforesaid."—DS (17 signatures, stamped May 20), *ibid.*, 2655 1876.

On Sept. 25, 1st Lt. Charles A. L. Totten wrote to USG. "I have the honor to transmit, here with, a copy of the proceedings of the Convention of Army Officers on College duty lately called at Chester Pa. Trusting that its proceedings will interest your Excellency, . . ."—ALS, *ibid.*, 5570 1876. The Sept. 20 convention, held at the Pennsylvania Military Academy, Chester, recommended guidelines for military instructors, such as detailing officers "for four years— the usual period of a college course."—Copy, *ibid.* See *ibid.*, 5762 1876.

On Dec. 13, George Fuller *et al.*, trustees, Houghton High School, Houghton, Mich., wrote to USG requesting that 2nd Lt. George LeRoy Brown be assigned as military instructor, noting "that there is in the upper Peninsula of Michigan, no Military School, and no place where young lads can obtain military training."—LS (5 signatures), *ibid.*, 3800 1876. No appointment followed.

1876, JUNE 18.   Col. Joseph J. Reynolds, Washington, D. C., to USG. "I would respectfully recommend. *1st Lieut. H. W. Lawton,* 4th Cavalry, for the position of *Captain A. Q. M. . . .*"—Copy, DLC-Henry W. Lawton. No promotion followed.

1876, JUNE 21.   J. E. Amos, Washington, D. C., to USG. ". . . My information through the Baptist 'confessional' will be worth much to you. A year ago I was informed by the most influential man in political and religious circles in Ga. that Genl Gordon is to be made President not by election but by a coup de etat then your Excellency will be impeached either before or after the expiration of ~~his~~ your term of office. A careful observer of events in the senate will notice he is gradually growing in influence over the senate. Physicians are cooperating with him in both houses and ere long by declaring some insane and 'ousting' or unseating others he will be President of the Senate. *Mark these words for future reference.* You can now have him unseated for buying his senatorship (as the proof is abundant) of the Ga. legislature: soon it will be too late and *you* with many others will be at *his mercy* and he knows not the mercy described by Shakespeare. In Ga. which he has the assurance to say is a law abiding state I was at three different times thrown in prison (in a Lunatic Asylum) on the recommendation of three physicians, *without a trial* or any defence. . . . Who of us is safe if three persons may deprive you of your liberty? Are physicians more infallible than others, especially the distinguished gentlemen who gave me hearty commendation *after* I had been in the Asylum twice among them Bishop Simpson? It is on *record* in the files of the *daily* papers of the country that prominent physicians have *hinted* in unmistakable language that your Excellencys penchant for horses and sea side resorts is evidence of insanity. I declared I had been chased by a self appointed *armed* vigilance committee in one of the Southern states and had seen Colored citizens knocked down and their attempted murder in New Orleans. They were afraid I would communicate this, and also use my influence for your administration. . . . As I am an exile from home and property can not your excellency direct one of the departments to employ me for my board at least . . . I have suffered much in a business point of view. My credit has been prostrated by this false accusation & imprisonment without a defence: have a piano that appeals to the nasal organs, as the ordinary piano does to the organs of hearing. In other words it makes music by odors or perfumes. You know how powerfully some odors or scents affect the nervous system. I have not been able to bring this before the public for the want of funds or credit. Ga has several millions of property. I purpose prosecuting the state for damages to my business credit. If I recover I can repair the injury to some extent. P. S. As they were taking me by *force* to the Asylum the officer asked 'what is your politics *now?*—you were once a Grant man.'"—ALS, DNA, RG 60, Letters from the President. On June 23, a clerk noted on the docket: "Not answered, there being grave doubts as to the sanity of Mr Amos"—E, *ibid.*

1876, June 22.   Jacques Boisset, Freissinières, France, to USG. "I beg you, permit a french citizen to come, very humbly but with liberty and an entire confidence to lay before you the pressing necessities of the whole valley of the Upper Alps. Under Louis Fourteenth, during the cruel religious persecutions our fathers, not shamefully to abjure their faith and sell their conscience, freely abandoned their property, their wealth and the luxuries of life, and driven at the point of the bayonets of the dragoons of him whom they called—the great king—they took refuge with their wives and children upon the heights of the Alps where their persecutors abandoned them. Since that deplorable time, many generations have succeeded in France skilful & hardy husbandmen have toiled in vain and spent their strength in these barren mountains where there is but little good earth upheld by wall and surrounded on all sides by rocks and precipices which seen near make one dizzy. Our winters are interminable and often we are reduced to the most frightful suffering. . . . Already, several families of our Valley two years ago left for your vast country. We ardently wish to follow their example. Possessing no resources and having no means of procuring any it will be absolutely impossible without your benevolent assistance to emigrate to the immense possessions of Your Excellency. . . ."—ALS (in French), DNA, RG 59, Miscellaneous Letters; translation, *ibid.*

1876, June 25.   Jerry Lee, Lebanon, Conn., to USG. "I was a Slave and Enlisted in 1861 in Washington on the Ship Brooklyn at the Navy Yard Capt Bell was Commander I was a Sawer and Carpenter and So I (was) put in their Class when we got to Pensacola we found things in a bad way in the Navy yard the Adramal Faragut Said theire was no Sawers to get the lumber in shape to mend or get the Ships in order so thay put me on shore in the yard to work thay had offerd men $5.00 per day but thay did not know how to do such work so I had to go I was hear one year and half I was one day while lifting and laying lumber rupturd in the side I told the Surgon of the Ship Brooklyn of he said that theire was no truss on bord so I had to take an iron hoop and make one the best I could . . . I work hard in that Navy yard. After the rebols deserters came in theire thay paid theme $3.00 per day for doing the Same work which thay made me do for $10 per month . . . P. S. The agents name at Washington who is trying to get me a pension is George. E. Lemon Lock. Box. 47"—ALS, DNA, RG 45, Letters Received from the President.

[*1876, June 26*].   USG note. "Forward to Sec. of the Int. at once to be sent to-day to the Committee having the nomination in charge"—AN, OHi. A clerk noted on the reverse. "Papers in the matter of the Reg L. O. at Yankton D. T. In favor of Bayliss & agst apptmt of Ellerman"—N, *ibid.* On May 24, USG had nominated Lott S. Bayless to continue as land office receiver, Yankton; on June 6, USG withdrew this nomination in favor of Herman Ellerman. On June 30, USG renominated Bayless.

1876, JUNE 26.   U.S. Senator Simon Cameron of Pa. to USG. "The bearer Mr Leisenring now Post Master at Charlestown—W. Va has been supplanted by the nomination of Mr Turner Schley. Mr L is a good man and a good republican, as I know, and he thinks he can offer some good reasons against the contemplated change. I will be much obliged if you will give him a hearing"—ALS, ViU. On June 27, USG withdrew the nomination of Towner Schley as postmaster, Charlestown, West Va.

1876, JUNE 26.   George P. Ihrie, New York City, to USG. "I am reliably informed that 'Mr. __ Kearney, lately appointed and confirmed U. S. Vice Consul-General at ~~Hayti~~ Port-au-Prince, Hayti, is appointed Consul-General of Hayti for the Port of New York, and will arrive here in two or three days.' If so, the office of U. S. Vice Consul-General at Port-au-Prince, Hayti, is, or soon will be, vacant. If agreeable to you, Mr. President, do me the favor to appoint me to fill said vacancy, and oblige your old friend—"—ALS, DNA, RG 59, Letters of Application and Recommendation. Related papers are *ibid.* No appointment followed.
   On May 3, 1884, Ihrie, Washington, D. C., wrote to Brig. Gen. William B. Rochester, paymaster gen. "I herewith enclose original Certificate of Genrl. U. S. Grant, certifying that I 'joined his Staff as A. D. C. on or about the 7th May, 1862,' and request that a certified copy of it be placed on file in your office, and the original returned to me."—ALS, DNA, RG 99, Letters Received.

[*1876, June 28*].   USG note. "Wm P. Titcomb. Mass Asst. Register of the Treas. [vice Graham resg—from 1-July-76.]"—AN (dated "6/28," bracketed material not in USG's hand), Wayde Chrismer, Bel Air, Md.

1876, JUNE 28.   Secretary of the Interior Zachariah Chandler to USG. "Have consulted both New Hampshire senators they will report to you in the morning."—Telegram received, DNA, RG 107, Telegrams Collected (Bound). On June 21, Edward H. Rollins, Boston, had written to Chandler. "I propose to write you about New Hampshire politics. I learned, late in the evening of our Senatorial caucus, that the President had, at the request of—Ex. Gov. Stearns —directed the appointment of Mr. Whitford as Pension Agent at Concord. This, I am sure he did under a misapprehension, . . . It was arranged by Senator Cragin and others that the position of Pension Agent at Concord should be given to Daniel Hall, Chairman of our Committee to enable him to devote sufficient of his time to do the work necessary to ensure Republican success in our State. . . ."—LS, DLC-Zachariah Chandler. On July 1, USG nominated Edward L. Whitford as pension agent, Concord.

1876, June 28. Col. Rufus Ingalls, New York City, to USG. "Personal . . . This will be handed to you by one of my oldest and truest of friends—*Mr. Emil Justh*—of this city. I have spoken to you in his behalf on three occasions to induce you to give him a Consulate in Europe, say at *Havre*, France—He is a naturalized citizen, supported your election—is of good standing—is an accomplished gentleman—is conversant with the manners, customs and languages of most all Christian nations. I most earnestly ask your recognition of his great fitness for a Consulship, and trust you will find yourself able to offer him one— There are very many of the Army & Navy, as well as gentlemen in civil life, who will bear testimony to his thorough uprightness—"—ALS, DNA, RG 59, Letters of Application and Recommendation. Retired Rear Admiral James Alden favorably endorsed this letter.—AES (undated), *ibid.* No appointment followed. See *New York Times,* Dec. 18, 1883.

1876, June 28. Alfred L. Carlow, Nîmes, France, to USG. ". . . In 1871 I was first mate aboard the American Steamer 'Lausanne,' plying betwing Hong-Kong, Singapore and Saïgon. I unfortunately formed connection with an Italian woman, to whom I subsequently intrusted the greater portion of my savings. This money, which I had destined to bettering my position, was used by her, without my knowledge, for her own purposes. When I heard of this breach of confidence, which involved such a heavy sacrifice for me, I lost entirely control over myself, and drawing my revolver, I fired at the woman and slightly wounded her. For this act, which was certainly most reprehensible, and which I have never ceased to regret, I was condemned, in February 1872, by the French Court of Saïgon to six years reclusion, and conveyed to France, to undergo my sentence. I have been now four years in this House, and my conduct has won the approbation of the Administration, who has interested itself very much to obtain my pardon, but, the fact of my being a foreigner unprotected by my own Government, has prevented success. . . . May I not hope that my Country, of whom I think daily with tears in my eyes, will aid a suffering son to extricate himself from misery; that she will give him an opportunity of returning home to close his parents eyes, and receive their last embrace; that she will, by giving back the husband and father, bring joy to the desolate wife and Child who, since so long a time have been watching for him in vain. In this hope, I have the honour to be, . . ."—ALS, DNA, RG 59, Miscellaneous Letters. On Oct. 25, Elihu B. Washburne, Paris, wrote to Secretary of State Hamilton Fish concerning Carlow. ". . . I have the honor to state that the application I had made for the remission of the unexpired term of his sentence has been granted. . . ."—LS, *ibid.*, Diplomatic Despatches, France.

1876, June 28. Daniel O'Neill, Pittsburgh, to USG. "Understanding that efforts are being made for the recalling of Mr. McCormacks appointment as U S. District attorney for western District of Penna ‡The undersigned Editor of the Daily Despatch would respectfully urge upon your Excellency the fitness and wisdom of Said appointment and earnestly hope that no change will be made therein It is an appointment that is only exceeded in the thoroughness of the Satisfaction it gives the party the public and the Bar by the gratification felt in

the removal of the present incumbent and if the efforts being made to retain
the latter in office Should prove Successful it would create deep dissatisfaction
without accomplishing any possible good either for the party or outside of
it The move in Mr Reeds favor is confined wholly to a clique inimical alike to
your administration and Mr. Camerons friends and it needs only a little familiarity with the Status of affairs here to feel assured that you could not in his connection commit a graver mistake than to recall Mr. McCormacks appointment
or keep Mr Reed longer in position that̶n̶t̶ is necessary to be closing up of th̶i̶s̶e̶
business of his office all of which is respectfully Submitted"—Telegram received, DNA, RG 60, Letters from the President. On the same day, S. A. Neal
et al., Pittsburgh, telegraphed to USG. "In behalf of the Colored Citizens of
Pittsburg & Allegheny we earnestly protest against the removal of Hon David
Reed from the position of District Attorney for the western District of Penna &
pray you to revoke the order—"—Telegram received (at 10:08 A.M.), *ibid.* Similar telegrams on both sides are *ibid.* On June 29, Ulysses S. Grant, Jr., wrote to
Attorney Gen. Alphonso Taft. "The President suggests that all the telegrams
and papers concerning the U. S. Attorney for Western District of Penna in your
hands be sent to the Judiciary e̶Committee of the Senate to assist them in their
action on the new nomination to that position"—ALS, *ibid.* On the same day, the
Senate confirmed Henry H. McCormick, nominated June 23 as U.S. attorney,
Western District, Pa.

In [*March, 1874*], USG had written a note. "Ask Atty. Gn. to send nomination of David Reed, of Pittsburgh, for Dist. Atty. for Western district of Pa
Would like to get it so that it may be sent to the Senate this afternoon or tomorrow. m̶o̶r̶n̶i̶n̶g̶"—AN (facsimile), eBay, July 12, 2001. See *PUSG*, 20, 333.

1876, JUNE 28.   Henry Sherman to USG. "It seems to me that the bare statement of this case might enlist your sympathy in behalf of the Applicant, without any words from me. Nevertheless, I earnestly advocate his application."—
AES, DNA, RG 94, ACP, 5116 1876. Written on an undated letter from Edward
Quinn to USG. "having Served 35 years, in the army of the United States, Honorably & faithfully, and having Served at the Post of Fort Gibson, when you
joined the 4th U S. Infantry also in the mexican War, I would most Respectfully
request Some Situation to enable me to Support my family in my old days, as I
am without any means at the present as I am considered not capable of being
Reenlisted   you could not confer a greater favor on an old faithful Soldir this
Centennial year of the Nations Independance, than to promote me to a Second
Lieutenant and to be placed on the Retired List, and afford me the means, of
Supporting my poor young family, I make this appeal to you not only as the
chief Executive of a great nation but as a kind Father of a family."—ALS, *ibid.*
No appointment followed.

1876, JUNE 28.   John P. Taggart, Salt Lake City, to USG. "When you took command of the military forces at Cairo Illinois in the beginning of the war and
publicly announced your staff you assigned me a member of that Staff as Medical Purveyor. The order was lost among other papers during the high water in
that city in the Spring of 1862 or 63. May I ask that you will furnish me an

official copy of the same at your earliest convenience I ask this favor because
of the fact that at this writing if my memory serves correctly I am the sole
surviving member of that Staff"—ALS, DNA, RG 94, Letters Received, 4054
1876. See *PUSG*, 3, 331.

[*1876, June 29*].   USG note. "Make nomination of Jas. Gilfillen, [of Conn.]—
Cashier of Treas.—Asst. Treas. of the U. S. at Washington vice Albert U.
Wyman aptd. Treas."—AN (bracketed material not in USG's hand), OHi.

1876, JUNE 29.   P. H. Kinney, Hanceville, Ala., to USG. "The Griffith, familey,
has a very large estate in Wails. & the heirs are all in this country. it is the estate of William Griffith, & has been there ever sence before the war, & when the
war come up it stoped every thing of the kind; & we have never made any efort,
sence   The estate is a very large one. & we can make all necessary proof: if
I mistake not William Griffith was King of Wails at his death   will your excellency please inform me how to proceed to get it. I would have writen to Wails,
but do not know who to address & I knew you could tell me how to proceed.   your early attention will very much oblige . . ."—ALS, DNA, RG 59,
Miscellaneous Letters.

1876, JUNE 30.   USG veto. "I return herewith without my approval, Senate
Bill, No 692, entitled 'An Act to amend chapter one hundred and sixty six of
the laws of the Second Session of the Fortythird Congress—The objections
to affixing my signature to this bill may be found in the report, which accompanies this message, of the Chief of Engineers of the Army, to the Secretary
of War—"—Copy, DNA, RG 130, Messages to Congress. Objection to the bill
centered on responsibility for flood damage during improvements on the Fox
and Wisconsin rivers in Wis. See *CR*, 44–1, 2149, 4339.

1876, JUNE 30.   James F. Casey, collector of customs, New Orleans, to USG. "I
desire to recommend for assistant Secretary of Treasury E. P. Champlin formerly of Michigan but for a long time my deputy collector. He was a soldier and
is one of the most competent men I know of. Secretary Chandler knows him
well & will urge him for any place requiring ability"—Telegram received (at
11:20 P.M.), DNA, RG 56, Applications. On the same day, Casey telegraphed to
Secretary of the Interior Zachariah Chandler on the same subject.—Telegram
received, *ibid.* No appointment followed.

1876, JUNE 30.   Samuel Robbins, Salisbury, N. H., to USG seeking aid in obtaining a pension as a War of 1812 veteran. ". . . Dear President it is most
strange that they are so slow to let a Man languish and Die before being attended to—I know it is said they are sure—but long neglect to a Man slowly
dying is terrible. . . ."—L, DNA, RG 48, Miscellaneous Div., Letters Received.

1876, JUNE 30.   U.S. Senator J. Rodman West of La. to USG. "I take the liberty
of presenting to you Mrs. Hitt, a lady from Louisiana, bearing letters from estimable citizens, friends of ours in that State, highly commending her to your

favorable consideration. Be so kind as to grant her an interview."—LS, Ford Collection, NN.

1876, JULY 1. USG note. "Will the Atty. Gen. please examine the application for pardon of ~~JGeo~~. Young, confined ~~in~~ in Phila penetentiary—I think—for sending obscene literature through the mails. My impression is that there are circumstances attending his case which would justify a pardon at this time."—ANS, DLC-USG, VIII. On the same day, Robert W. Mackey, Philadelphia, telegraphed to Secretary of War James D. Cameron. "Please see the President and urge him to pardon Young so that he can join his family on the fourth answer,"—Telegram received, DNA, RG 107, Telegrams Collected (Bound). Also on July 1, Cameron telegraphed to Mackey. "The President has ordered his release"—ALS (press, telegram sent), *ibid.* On July 3, Mackey telegraphed to USG. "Has geo. young pardon been made out yet? his family are very anxious about it"—Telegram received, DLC-USG, IB. On July 4, Cameron telegraphed to Mackey. "The Attorney General says he will attend to Youngs case today"—ALS (press, telegram sent), DNA, RG 107, Telegrams Collected (Bound). On July 8, USG pardoned "George W. Young, *alias* William Young," after he had served seven months of a one-year prison sentence for "depositing unlawful matter in the mail," upon recommendations "by the jurors by whom he was tried, as well as by Bishop Simpson of the Methodist Episcopal Church, and other citizens of Pennsylvania."—Copy, *ibid.*, RG 59, General Records. See *Philadelphia Public Ledger*, Dec. 20, 1875.

1876, JULY 5. To Lt. Gen. Philip H. Sheridan, Philadelphia. "The condition of legislation and necessary department changes will render it impossible for me to attend the Army meeting in Philadelphia, or to absent myself from this city during this week. I regret my inability to meet the *Society of the Army of the Cumberland.*"—*Society of the Army of the Cumberland, Tenth Reunion, Philadelphia, 1876* (Cincinnati, 1876), p. 26. On the same day, Wednesday, Sheridan had telegraphed to USG. "The society of the Army of the Cumberland beg you to honor its meeting ~~on fo~~ Wednesday Evening ~~your~~ at the Academy of Music"—ADf (telegram sent), DLC-Philip H. Sheridan. The annual meeting officially commenced on July 6.

On June 5, Sheridan, Pittsburgh, had telegraphed to USG. "I am sorry I cannot accept the detail on board on visitors to naval academy a thousand thanks for your kind considration hope to meet you in Philadelphia at army meeting tomorrow"—Telegram received (at 1:25 P.M.), DLC-USG, IB. USG did not attend the Army of the Potomac reunion at Philadelphia.

1876, JULY 6. USG endorsement. "Refered to the Sec. of the Navy to be by him refered to the Atty. Gen. for opinion as to the validity of the claim of Comdr Bohrer for pay from date of dismissal to date of restoration."—AES, DNA, RG 45, Letters Received from the President. Written on papers that include a memorandum of July 3 from Cyrus C. Carpenter, second comptroller, rejecting retired Master Julius S. Bohrer's claim for back pay from Dec. 30, 1865, to June 5, 1876, after a court-martial found him innocent of charges that had led to his dismissal. ". . . The accounting officers cannot allow the claim (except the six months leave pay) however just and well supported it may appear to them. It must have been the intention of the Congress to reserve this class of claims to another tribunal than the Treasury Department, to which the organic Act entrusted the settlement of 'all claims and demands whatever by or against the U. S.' The accounting officers have no powers except those conferred by the Acts of Congress; and they have no authority to question the propriety or constitutionality of these acts."—DS, *ibid.* On March 3, 1877, USG signed a bill authorizing payment of Bohrer's back pay.—*U.S. Statutes at Large (Private Laws),* XIX, 102. See *SRC,* 44-1-27; *HRC,* 44-2-98; *CR,* 44−2, 1976−77, 2141−42.

On June 12, 1876, Mrs. John T. M. Orendorf, Washington, D. C., had written to USG. "I have the honor to thank you for your kindness in having my father, Mr. Julius S. Bohrer, restored to the Naval service as Master on the retired list; and his dismissal of Dec 30th 1865 declared void. I beg you will allow me to submit to you the grounds for his promotion, . . . I therefore most respectfully ask of you to nominate him for promotion on *active* list, as he feels himself able to do any duty, save sea service, and still has nearly nine years before he reaches the age of sixty two. For all of which your petitioner will ever pray."—ALS, DNA, RG 45, Letters Received from the President. No action followed.

1876, JULY 7.   USG pardon for John H. Nichols, convicted on May 6 of mail robbery in D. C. and sentenced to one year in the federal prison at Albany, N. Y., "*on condition* that he be imprisoned and confined in the Jail in the District of Columbia," until May 6, 1877.—Copy, DNA, RG 59, General Records. On May 25, 1876, Culver C. Sniffen had written to Attorney Gen. Edwards Pierrepont. "The President directs me to request that you will have the prisoner J. H. Nichols detained here in the District Jail until papers now in course of preparation are received."—ALS, *ibid.,* RG 60, Letters from the President. On June 15, Ulysses S. Grant, Jr., wrote to Attorney Gen. Alphonso Taft. "The President says that he has no objection to the detention of John H. Nich[ol]s in the prison here until Wednesday next if you have not."—ALS, DLC-William H. Taft.

1876, JULY 8.   USG note. "Will the Sec. of the Treas. please see Chas. Davis who is desirous of procuring a place as Messenger if changes take place to create such a vacancy. Mr. D. will explain his claims upon the govt. for position."—ANS, DNA, RG 56, Applications. On July 12, U.S. Representatives Clement H. Sinnickson and Samuel A. Dobbins of N. J. wrote to Secretary of the Treasury Lot M. Morrill recommending an appointment for Charles Davis, who "served with honor in the volunteer service during the late war and is unable to perform manual labor by reason of wounds received in action."—LS, *ibid.* Related papers are *ibid.* As of Sept. 30, 1877, Davis worked as a Treasury Dept. watchman.

1876, JULY 10.   USG endorsement. "Refered to the Sec. of the Treas. hoping that he may be able to restore Miss Boyd to her position in the Int. Rev. and on the permanent roll."—AES, DNA, RG 56, Applications. Written on a letter of July 1 from Leonard Myers, Philadelphia, to USG. "Miss A. P. Boyd, Int. Rev. whom I presented to you yesterday, & whom you kindly promised to appoint when the new Secy of the Treasury should take his place, is the daughter of a *seaman of the War of 1812* who was for many months *confined by the British in the Dartmoor prison.* Secy Bristow promised her a permanent Clerkship, yet she has been kept on a temporary roll for a year & now discharged. . . ."—ALS, *ibid.* Related papers are *ibid.*

1876, JULY 10.   Culver C. Sniffen to Secretary of War James D. Cameron. "The President directs me to say that he will be pleased if you will cause inquiry to be made as to the condition of Lt John G. Kyle, now confined in the Government Insane Asylum.—"—Copy, DLC-USG, II, 3. Wounded during the Modoc War, 2nd Lt. John G. Kyle (USMA 1870) secured sick leave as of Nov. 19 and died at Xenia, Ohio, on March 30, 1877.

1876, JULY 10.   Culver C. Sniffen to George S. Koontz, general agent, Baltimore and Ohio Railroad. "The President directs me to say that he will be glad to accept the offer of a car on Friday morning next, which he would like attached to any train arriving at Deer Park before, or by 10, Oclock at night.—"—Copy, DLC-USG, II, 3. Secretary of State Hamilton Fish accompanied USG to Deer Park, Md. See Fish diary, July 13, 17, 1876, DLC-Hamilton Fish; John F. Stover, *History of The Baltimore and Ohio Railroad* (West Lafayette, Ind., 1987), p. 156.

1876, JULY 10.   Middleton Braddock, New Comerstown, Ohio, to USG. "Al tho Comparitively A. Stranger to your honer Circunstances Compells me to Appeal to your honer for Justice and Equity for it seems verry Singular to me how it is that Stout harty Able bodied men Who are Able to Live on the interist of their money Can and do obtain A suport from the Government While A poor Afflicted sickley and Disolate person Who has Entirley lost his health in the service and has sacrifised his home and last Dollars Worth to live on may Die or Go to the poor house   Now the facts are simpely this   I have not since my Discharge from the US. A bin Able to do manuel Labour and the result has bin I have had to Live on What I had and Now I have sunk About fifteen hundred Dollars by the vileny of my first Atturney Who retained my papers till in Aug. /75 and sinc that time All Nessesary Evidance has bin furnished and Now I Wold be glad to Know Why it is that I am kept Suffering and in want Just on the virge of Starvasion and Suffering onable to do anything Scaircely Able to get out of the house and have to Depend on What little A poor Woman Can make over the Wash tub   Now if this is Justice to brace up the ricth and tramp the poor and Disolate under foot then I have Naught to say but I Cannot think that it is the intention of the Government to do an injustice but it is verry plain to be seen that thare is hundreds of Welthey persons Getting A pension that dos not Need it or shold not have it some few of Who I Cold Easely Name While hundreds of Widows and poor men Who are Justley intitle to A help that do not Get it and Why it is becaus they arenot Able to pay A large fee . . ."—ALS, DNA, RG 48, Miscellaneous Div., Letters Received. On Sept. 23, Braddock wrote to USG and cabinet after learning that his pension application had been denied.—ALS, *ibid.*

1876, JULY 11.   USG veto. "For the reasons set forth in the accompanying report of the Secretary of War, I have the honor to return herewith without my approval, House bill No 1337, entitled 'An act for the relief of Nelson Tiffany'.—"—Copy, DNA, RG 130, Messages to Congress. *HED,* 44-1-182; *SMD,* 49-2-53, 396. On July 7, Secretary of War James D. Cameron had written to USG. "I have the honor to return House Bill 1337 'for the relief of Nelson Tiffany.' The Adjutant General, to whom the bill was referred reports as follows: 'Nelson Tiffany, private Company "A" 25th Massachusetts Volunteers, deserted October 10. 1864. and remained absent until April. 25, 1865. when he surrendered under the Presidents proclamation thereby acknowledging his desertion.' If this bill becomes a law, it will not only falsify the records of this Department but be an injustice to every man who served honorably during the war of the rebellion.' I enclose the report (No. 402) of the Senate Committee on Military Affairs in the case."—Copy, DNA, RG 107, Letters Sent, Military Affairs. *HED,* 44-1-182; *SMD,* 49-2-53, 396. Arguing that Nelson Tiffany was recovering from a wound and not deserting, supporters overrode USG's veto on July 31. See *CR,* 44–1, 4773–74, 4939–40, 5011–12; *U.S. Statutes at Large (Private Laws),* XIX, 58–59.

1876, JULY 12.   Culver C. Sniffen to G. Peabody Russell, New York City. "The President directs me to say in reply to your note of the 3d inst, that he will attend the annual meeting of the Peabody Education Trust, at the White Sulphur Springs Va, on the 3d of August next—"—Copy, DLC-USG, II, 3. USG, a Peabody trustee, did not attend this meeting.

1876, JULY 13.   USG veto. "For the reasons stated in the accompanying report by the Commissioner of Pensions, to the Secretary of the Interior, I have the honor to return without my approval House Bill No 11. entitled 'An act granting a pension to Eliza Jane Blumer'.—"—Copy, DNA, RG 130, Messages to Congress. *HED,* 44-1-183; *SMD,* 49-2-53, 397. On July 8, Charles T. Gorham, act. secretary of the interior, had written to USG. ". . . In the opinion of this Department the misdescription of the soldier in the bill is of such a character as would render it difficult, if not impossible, to carry the provisions of the bill into effect should it become a law."—*HED,* 44-1-183; *SMD,* 49-2-53, 398. On Aug. 12, U.S. Representative John C. Bagby of Ill. introduced a new bill that correctly described Eliza Jane Blumer's husband Henry A., former private, 47th Pa., "as having belonged to Company A, instead of Company B."—*CR,* 44–1, 5553. On Aug. 15, USG signed this revised bill.—*U.S. Statutes at Large (Private Laws),* XIX, 82. See *HRC,* 44-1-145.

1876, JULY 13.   To House of Representatives. "I transmit herewith in answer to a Resolution of the House of Representatives of the First ultimo, a Report from the Secretary of State upon the subject—"—Copies, DNA, RG 59, Reports to the President and Congress; *ibid.,* RG 130, Messages to Congress. *HED,* 44-1-181; *HRC,* 48-1-1543, 13; *SRC,* 49-2-1736, 23; *SMD,* 52-1-167, 127. On the same day, Secretary of State Hamilton Fish had written to USG. ". . . No correspondence has taken place between the Department of State and the government of Great Britain in relation to the sequestration of the lands and property in New Zealand claimed by William Webster, an American citizen. In the years 1841 to 1844 certain correspondence was had between the Legation in London, and the Foreign Office of Great Britain, in reference to the general question of land titles held in New Zealand by American citizens, but no correspondence has taken place in regard to the particular claim of Mr Webster."—Copy, DNA, RG 59, Reports to the President and Congress. *HED,* 44-1-181; *HRC,* 48-1-1543, 13–14; *SRC,* 49-2-1736, 23; *SMD,* 52-1-167, 127–28.

1876, July 13.   J. Russell Jones, Chicago, to USG. "This mornings Washington Despatches say there is talk of appointing Sam Felker Chief of the Treasury Secret-Service. I have no idea there is anything in it, but will say that F. is regarded by everybody here who knows anything about him as *a very bad lot*"— ALS, DNA, RG 56, Applications. On Oct. 7, Isaac S. Stewart, Washington, D. C., wrote to USG. "I have been requested to say a word to you in behalf of Samuel M Felker of Chicago Ill, who is an applicant for the office designated as chief of the Secret Service Treasury Department I have reluctantly consented, (not because I hesitate to indorse Mr Felker for the position he seeks for I desire to be understood as indorseing him as a man eminently fitted to discharge the duties incident to the office) but in view of of the fact that so many false representations had heretofore been made to you touching my presumption in claiming your friendship, I questioned myself as to the propriety of indorseing any one,   I concluded that the purpose of my Kentucky enemies who invented all kinds of falsehoods regarding me was pretty well understood and that when your mind reverted to me, your judgment would say that I correctly represented the facts as to Bristow and his gang, . . ."—ALS, *ibid.* A related letter is *ibid.* No appointment followed.

1876, July 15.   John L. Smithmeyer, Washington, D. C., to USG concerning William A. Potter, supervising architect of the U.S. Treasury. ". . . As is well known he is a member of the architectural firm of Potter & Robertson in New York, and when he was appointed, his choice was severely criticised on account of this connection which under the law ought to have disqualified him for that position, but the public whispers were silenced by the presumption that his partnership had been dissolved at least for the time during which he should hold the office so nearly involving his personal interests. However recent developements display quite the contrary in this that he certainly used his position indirectly to favor the said firm in the case of the designs &c of the contemplated Congressional Library. Congress had authorized and the Committee on the Library had invited a public competition of all architects for plans for that purpose and having awarded prices to the most successful competitors, I received the highest premium in the contest, and it was to be presumed that the victorious architect, having thus given evidence of his professional ability would have either the honor of seeing his design executed, or be at least consulted in the preparation of any new design. Such is not the case & the architect of the Treasury not only prepared & submitted designs of his own for the building mentioned but actually solicited from the Committee having charge of this matter, that he (his firm) be intrusted with the execution of said public edifice. Such action on his part, if not directly illegal, is certainly grossly improper, and should he be successful, the construction of the new Library building would be a breach of faith to all architects who have honestly & faithfully done their best to comply with the wishes of the Government and unquestionably would result to the disadvantage of the public interest. . . ."—ALS, DNA, RG 56, Letters Received from the President. On July 17, Alexander R. Shepherd, Washington, D. C., wrote to Culver C. Sniffen requesting that Smithmeyer's letter be conveyed to USG.—ALS, *ibid.* See *Washington Post*, March 13, 1908; Helen-Anne Hilker, *Ten First Street, Southeast: Congress Builds A Library, 1886–1897* (Washington, 1980).

On Aug. 11, correspondents reported from Washington, D. C. "Secretary Morrill to-day appointed Mr. James G. Hill Supervising Architect of the Treasury Department, in place of Mr. Potter. Mr. Hill has been several years in the Architect's office, and has been for some time Assistant Architect. . . ."—*New York Times*, Aug. 12, 1876. "Notwithstanding the 'satanic' press have been endeavoring to create the impression that the President contemplated the reappointment of A. B. Mullett as Supervising Architect of the Treasury contrary to the wishes of Secretary Morrill, it is not believed the President ever indicated a desire to have him appointed. He has left the matter in the hands of Secretary Morrill, . . ."—*Baltimore American and Commercial Advertiser*, Aug. 12, 1876. See *PUSG*, 26, 114.

1876, JULY 18.   John S. Mosby, Washington, D. C., to USG. "The bearer—Mr Baylor—of Va—was a Confederate soldier who served under me during the War—He is a member of one of the most respectable families of Va—& a gentleman in whom the most implicit confidence may be placed. He desires a commission in the U. S. Army & I take great pleasure in recommending him as a gallant gentleman."—ALS, DNA, RG 94, Applications for Positions in War Dept. On July 14, Maj. Thomas G. Baylor (USMA 1857), New York City, had written to Gen. William T. Sherman concerning his brother Robert W. Baylor.—ALS, *ibid.* No appointment followed.

1876, JULY 19.   USG endorsement. "Mr. Hays, as is shown by his discharges, was a Union Soldier during the rebellion."—AES, DNA, RG 56, Applications. Written on a letter of July 18 from William Hayes, Washington, D. C., to Postmaster Gen. James N. Tyner seeking reinstatement as a laborer in the Post Office Dept. after he incurred "the displeasure of a high official & was summarily dismissed."—ALS, *ibid.* Related papers are *ibid.* A veteran of the 10th and 181st Ohio, Hayes later worked in the Internal Revenue Bureau.

1876, JULY 19.   To House of Representatives. "I transmit a Report from the Secretary of State in answer to the Resolution of the House of Representatives of the 1st of April last, on the subject of commercial intercourse with Mexico and Central America.—"—Copies, DNA, RG 59, Reports to the President and Congress; *ibid.*, RG 130, Messages to Congress. *HED*, 44-1-185. On the same day, Secretary of State Hamilton Fish wrote to USG that providing the requested diplomatic correspondence "at this time would be adverse to the public interests."—Copy, DNA, RG 59, Reports to the President and Congress. *HED*, 44-1-185.

1876, JULY 20. USG veto. "I have the honor to return herewith, without my approval, House Bill, No 2684., entitled. 'An Act to amend sections 3946. 3951: and 3954. of the Revised Statutes'—It is the judgment of the Postmaster General, whose report accompanies this Message. that if the accompanying bill should become a law in its present form, it would fail to give effect to its provisions—The remedial suggestions in his report are respectfully recommended to your attention.—"—Copy, DNA, RG 130, Messages to Congress. *HED*, 44-1-186; *SMD*, 49-2-53, 398. On July 19, Postmaster Gen. James N. Tyner had written to USG concerning this measure to revise bidding on mail-route contracts. ". . . The bill is a very important one for the service of the Post-Office Department. Efforts have been made for four or five years past to induce Congress to pass just such a law. To break up the vicious system of straw-bidding, this bill would be very valuable, and I regret exceedingly that a mistake should have been made in the title and enacting clause which will render its provisions inoperative. . . ."—*HED*, 44-1-186, 2; *SMD*, 49-2-53, 399. The House of Representatives referred this bill to committee and took no further action. See *CR*, 44-1, 3689–90, 4376, 4549.

1876, JULY 20. Lt. Gen. Philip H. Sheridan, Chicago, to USG. "This note will introduce to you Mrs. James Harrison, widow of the late Col Harrison of the 5th Cavalry. She is desirous of a personal interview with you and I would be much gratified if you could grant it."—Copy, DLC-Philip H. Sheridan. Bvt. Lt. Col. James E. Harrison had died on Nov. 4, 1867.

1876, JULY 21. USG note. "J. W. Gilges having served several years in the regular Army may be appointed without examination and the fact of his now being over thirty years of age overlooked."—ANS, DNA, RG 94, ACP, 3681 1876. On July 29, a clerk endorsed papers in this case. "The President has been misled as to the Applicant serving in the regular Army. He did not so serve either as an officer or enlisted man. He ought to be examined else a precedent—a bad one—will be established which will overturn the regulations. Shall he be ordered before the Board?"—E, *ibid.* On Aug. 1, 1st Lt. Francis V. Greene endorsed these papers. "The President directs that J. W. Gilges, be *not* appointed 2d Lieut."—Copy, *ibid.* Related papers are *ibid.* No appointment followed for James W. Gilges, who had served in the 12th Kan. and as 1st lt. and capt., 11th and 113th U.S. Colored Troops.

1876, JULY 26. Secretary of the Navy George M. Robeson to USG. "I have the honor to return herewith the Act (Senate Bill 123) for the relief of Medical Director Philip S. Wales, which provided that his name be placed on the prize list of the U. S. S Pensacola, to share in the proceeds of prize money, awarded to the Fleet under Admiral Farragut at New Orleans, to the approval of which you ask if there is any objection. The name of Dr. Wales was borne in the books of the

Colorado, a ship which was not in action at New Orleans, and was not included
in the share of distribution. The Department had no authority to place his name
on the rolls of the Pensacola one of the sharing vessels as he was not on board
during the action, nor borne on the books thereof. Congress alone has the
power to grant the relief asked for, and has passed a bill accordingly. While the
Department is of the opinion that the prize Act, which limits those who are
entitled to share in proceeds of capture, to such as are on board the vessel in
action and are presumed to be exposed to danger, is wise; it is indisposed to
offer any obstacle to Dr. Wales receiving relief, considering the peculiar service in which he was engaged, administering to the sick, and those wounded in
action. It would feel it a duty to interpose an objection in case of officers not
of the Medical Corps. A copy of the report of the Naval Committee of the Senate, in the case is herewith enclosed."—Copy, DNA, RG 45, Letters Sent to
the President. On July 29, this bill became law without USG's signature. See
SRC, 44-1-41; *U.S. Statutes at Large (Private Laws)*, XIX, 58; *New York Times*,
Feb. 26, 1896.

1876, JULY 27.   George Rydill, Dewsbury, England, to USG. "Please to pardon
the liberty I take in saying that as the Sanitary question has become a matter of
great importance in all Countries on account of the difficulty to treat Sewage
economically, I beg to say that should your Government be desirous of having a System to purify the Sewage of Towns in America I would undertake for
the Sum of £500,000 to introduce a System the most perfect and economical
known also one that would certainly enrich Your Country . . . I have done what
lays in my power for years to induce the English Government to take notice of
my improvements but England is now So rich as to make her careless of Ge-
nious which has alone made her so famous . . ."—ALS, DNA, RG 48, Miscellaneous Div., Letters Received.

1876, JULY 28.   Charles Randolph, secretary and treasurer, National Board of
Trade, Chicago, to USG transmitting a board resolution seeking diplomatic
negotiations "to secure, if possible, immunity, at least for the shipping of the
United States from the further payment of Light-dues in the ports of the United
Kingdom."—ALS and copy, DNA, RG 59, Miscellaneous Letters. See *PUSG*,
23, 369.

1876, JULY 31.   U.S. Senator John P. Jones of Nev. *et al.* to USG. "We most
earnestly recommend Charles. F. Powell of Nevada for Consul at Trinadad-de-
Cuba. Mr Powell is a well known Republican and an active worker in the Party
a Gentleman of probity and diligence. We trust that you may deem it fit to
appoint him to this vacancy."—LS (6 signatures), DNA, RG 59, Letters of Application and Recommendation. On Jan. 25, 1877, Thomas Settle, Washington,
D. C., wrote to Secretary of State Hamilton Fish recommending Charles F.
Powell, former vice consul, Callao, Peru, as "Commercial Agent, or Consul at
Iquique—Peru."—ALS, *ibid.* Related papers are *ibid.* On Feb. 16, USG nominated Powell as consul, Iquique, a new post intended to promote the guano and
nitrate trade.

1876, JULY 31.   John S. Mosby, Washington, D. C., to USG. "I have mentioned to you the fact that Mr *Robert Frazer* of Va—whom you appointed Consul at Palermo Italy—is now at home on furlough & for domestic reasons desires to exchange his position for one in the civil service at home. During the administration of his predecessor at Palermo the Consulate's expenses exceeded its receipts by $1000 annually: under Frazer the government realized annually a profit of about $4000—The records of the State Department show these facts. I think he is peculiarly adapted to a position as Special Agent in the Internal Revenue service and accordingly request that he be allowed to resign his Consulate for such a place. He is a finely educated, high toned & conscientious gentleman. If it is your desire to do something for Mr Bayly I wo[u]ld respectfully recommend him for [t]he Palermo Consulate. These gentlemen are not only your political but *personal* friends."—ALS, DNA, RG 59, Letters of Application and Recommendation. On Aug. 18, USG wrote a note. "The Sec. of State may apt. S. P. Bayly Jr consul to palermo vice Frazer who resigns."—ANS, DLC-Hamilton Fish. On Aug. 24, John L. Cadwalader, asst. secretary of state, wrote to Secretary of State Hamilton Fish. ". . . Robt Frazer Consul at Palermo has resigned to take Effect the 26th—Mosby brought me the resignation—and with it the Enclosed card— . . ."—ALS, *ibid.* On Dec. 7, USG nominated Sampson P. Bayly, Jr., as consul, Palermo.

On May 18, Sampson P. Bayly, Delaplane, Va., had written to USG. "Mr J. E. Blackwell who will hand you this has been removed from the Architect department I have been informed upon the charge that he is a Democrat, I know that such is not the fact, Mr Blackwell was not of age at the last election and has never voted, *his Father* and Uncle were earnest active supporters of yours, and will support the Republican Candidate for President. Mr Blackwell has held the office about two years and given Satisfaction, he is a young man of good moral character and industry, Col Mosby procured the appointment for him and would now give the matter some attention, was it not for the fact that he lost his wife last week, she died suddenly and he is in great distress,"—ALS, DNA, RG 56, Applications. On May 26, Secretary of the Treasury Benjamin H. Bristow endorsed papers related to James E. Blackwell, computer, supervising architect's office, Treasury Dept. "The President directs the restoration of Mr Blackwell"—AE (initialed), *ibid.*

[*1876, July*].   USG note. "Will the Sec. of State please see Mr. Cuthburt Jones, of La. the young gentleman of whom I spoke yesterday as desiring a Consulate."—ANS (undated), Columbia University, New York, N. Y. USG had written another undated note. "Cuthburt Jones, La. Consulate. Is one of a ~~U~~Native Union family who have ~~served~~ been exterminated or driven out."—AN, *ibid.* On July 28, USG nominated Cuthbert B. Jones as consul, Tripoli. See Hamilton Fish diary, July 25, 1876, DLC-Hamilton Fish; *New York Times*, June 1, 1885.

1876, AUG. 2.   U.S. Representative Charles O'Neill of Pa. to USG. "My constituent Mr Alexander S. Zelensky desires to withdraw some papers from the Executive Office which recommended him for appointment. I will be much obliged if you will send them to me. I will forward them to Mr Zelensky."—

ALS, DNA, RG 59, Letters of Application and Recommendation. USG endorsed this letter. "Return the papers asked."—AE (undated), *ibid.* On July 31, Alexander S. Zelenski, Philadelphia, had written to O'Neill that he desired "particularly the Recommandation from late Genl *George Gordon Meade.*"— ALS, *ibid.*

1876, AUG. 3.   Mary R. Hayward, Canterbury, N. H., to USG concerning the legality of her second marriage. ". . . in. 1844, I Marrid had 2 Children 1849 he Runaway & stold the oldest a Boy. wich I Not sean nor heard from him sence. No Not Wether they are Dead or alive. My Daughter Dide 24 years of age. . . . have you Not the Power to Grant Me a Divorce from My fomer husband in 1849 if Posable. it seams as tho I Could Not bare the Reproch aGin. I think Enofe of him he of Me he is Most 70 years I am 50 years. . . . I Never told them I Never hade No Bill from My first Nor I Wont till they prove it. . . . I Begg you take Notis it is My thoughts Day & Night. Exkuse poor writan & spelin I am so Nervest I hardly know"—ALS, DNA, RG 60, Letters from the President.

1876, AUG. 4.   U.S. Senators Phineas W. Hitchcock and Algernon S. Paddock of Neb., and three others, to USG recommending Henry W. Hawes as appraiser, Louisville. ". . . Mr Hawes is one of the oldest Republicans in Kentucky and his two sons, (all he had), served through the war in the Union Army. We join them in asking the appointment of their Father to this office, as a recognition of his consistency and steadfastness to the Republican Party"—LS, DNA, RG 56, Appraiser of Customs Applications. USG wrote an undated note. "Henry W. Hawes for Appraiser of Merchandise, Louisville, Ky vice Howlett to be removed."—AN, *ibid.* On Dec. 8, 1875, USG had nominated Luther S. Howlett as appraiser, Louisville; he continued in office.

1876, AUG. 4.   U.S. Delegate Jefferson P. Kidder of Dakota Territory and John A. Burbank, Washington, D. C., to USG. "Please send in the name of Gustavus A Wetter as register of the Land Office Yankton Dakota to harmonize matters"—Telegram received, DNA, RG 107, Telegrams Collected (Bound). On the same day, USG nominated Gustavus A. Wetter as land office register, Yankton, Dakota Territory, to replace Oscar Whitney. On Aug. 9, Augustine S. Gaylord, asst. attorney gen., telegraphed to Ulysses S. Grant, Jr. "The secretary wishes to know what place is intended for Oscar Whitney of Yankton"—Telegrams received (2), *ibid.* Grant, Jr., replied. "Any place you can give him the President would be glad for him to have"—ANS (undated), *ibid.* Whitney served as div. chief, Indian Affairs, as of Sept. 30, 1877.

[*1876, Aug. 5*].   USG endorsement. "Referred to the Sec. of War. The writer is the brother of Maj. Ringgold, killed early in the Mexican War, and the founder of the Light Artillery System of the Army. I hope the old gentleman may be continued."—Paul C. Richards, Catalogue No. 19 (1968), no. 506. Written on a letter from Frederick Ringgold to USG complaining that his clerkship was threatened by efforts of the "so-called Democratic Congress" to cut staff.—*Ibid.* On Aug. 29, Ringgold wrote to Secretary of War James D. Cameron on the same subject. ". . . I am a Clerk in the Office of the Chief of Engineers to which position I was appointed by the President of the United States in 1870, he having served on the battlefield of Palo Alto, Mexico, alongside of my late brother Major Ringgold [U.] S. Army, who lost his life in the service of his Country, in 1846. . . ."—ALS, DNA, RG 107, Appointment Papers. Ringgold retained his position.

On May 11, 1875, Ringgold, Washington, D. C., had written to USG. "Pardon me for annoying you again, but during my interview with you on yesterday, I neglected to say, that, if the Secty. of War were to advance me to a higher grade it would be to a $1400.00 Clerkship which would only give me an increase of $16.00 per month—unless you were to particularly request him to give me a $1600. clerkship. My object in calling upon you was principally to urge you to give me a position by which I could save something for my family in the event of my death—I suggested at the time a position as Special Agent of the Post Office Department, which, you seemed to think, at the time, would not suit me on account of my age, as they generally confer those appointments on young men who are more active than I am; . . ."—ALS, *ibid.* On the same day, Secretary of War William W. Belknap endorsed this letter. "The President desires that Mr. Ringgold be promoted to the next $1600. clerkship in which there is a vacancy, provided he is deemed competent to perform its duties—"—AE (initialed), *ibid.* On May 31, Ringgold wrote to USG on the same subject.—ALS, *ibid.* As of Sept. 30, Ringgold served as War Dept. clerk at $1,200 per year.

1876, AUG. 5.   John B. Blake, secretary, Washington National Monument Society, Washington, D. C., to USG transmitting a resolution concerning "the act of Congress providing for the construction of the Monument."—LS, DNA, RG 59, Miscellaneous Letters. The resolution is *ibid.* On Aug. 6, Ulysses S. Grant, Jr., wrote to Secretary of State Hamilton Fish. "The President asks that you will please examine the law making appropriation for the Washington monument and advise him what steps are necessary to organize so the work may go on. He would like to have this matter attended to before Congress adjourns"—ALS, *ibid.* See *PUSG*, 24, 86–88.

1876, AUG. 7.   USG endorsement. "Refered to the Sec. of War. This is an appointment I would like to make some time. during the coming fall or winter."—AES, DNA, RG 94, ACP, 6226 1876. Written on a letter of Aug. 1 from Charles Byrne, San Antonio, to USG. "I have the honor hereby to apply for an Appointment as 2nd Lieutenant in the Army of the United States. I am the son of Dr B. M. Byrne, late Surgeon U. S. Army, and grand son of Colonel J. J. Abert, late Chief of The Topographical Engineers U. S. Army. I was born at Fort Vancouver, W. T., in the year 1855, and was educated at Columbian College, D. C. I served as Clerk with the United States Scouting Expedition, under Lieut. Col. Shafter, U. S. A., on the Frontiers of Texas, during the Summer and Fall of 1875, and since, have been connected with the Government, as a Clerk in the Chief Quartermaster's Office, Department of Texas, under Lieut Col. A. J. Perry, Deputy Qr. Mr. Genl. U. S. A., at San Antonio, Texas."—ALS, *ibid.* On Dec. 13, USG nominated Byrne as 2nd lt., 6th Inf.

1876, Aug. 7.   USG note. "The Sec. of War may order Allen Dyer before the present Board of Examiners for Army apt. to await vacancy if he passes a satisfactory examination."—ANS, DNA, RG 94, ACP, 4200 1876. On Dec. 4, USG nominated S. Allen Dyer as 2nd lt., 23rd Inf., to date from Aug. 31.

1876, Aug. 10.   William D. W. Barnard, Springfield, Mo., to USG. "Enclosing a partial copy of the charges and specifications wh' I learn have been forwarded by ex state Senator Lewis Benecke of Mo, against U S Dist Atty Botsford of the Western District, I can say from personal knowledge, after passing through the District that his removal would be hailed as an act of justice by the bar, irrespective of politics and by your true friends, who have had almost single handed to fight your local battles here, would be regarded with special favor—the daily encounters with men who carry in their pockets commissions signed by you, is not pleasant and we feel as though we had a right to ask such changes—Col Van Horn expects to have the pleasure of an early personal interview and will explain fully the matter and its bearings—May I not ask you to give the subject your favorable action. H. M. Pollard of Chillicothe and John K Cravens of K/C have been favorably mentioned by our friends for the position—Mr P having resently been nominated in his Dist for Congress—Mr Cravens would make an excellent officer and I believe from what I hear said, is the man for the place"—ALS, DNA, RG 60, Letters from the President. The enclosure is *ibid.* On Aug. 22, Ulysses S. Grant, Jr., Long Branch, wrote to Attorney Gen. Alphonso Taft. "The President directs me to ask if there have been any complaints made against the U. S. District Attorney for Western Missouri (they are made by a man named Brinnecke from Brunswick) If you think there ought to be a change the President would like to suggest the name of John K. Cravens Kansas City—Missouri as one very highly recommended to him."—ALS, *ibid.* On Aug. 30, Robert T. Van Horn, collector of Internal Revenue, 6th District, Mo., Pittsburgh, telegraphed to USG, Long Branch. "If Change is made of District attorney Western Missouri it should be at once   have not seen anything   hope it has been as a change is much needed"—Telegram received, *ibid.* See *PUSG,* 21, 406–7.

On Jan. 5, 1877, John P. Usher, Kansas Pacific Railway Co., Lawrence, wrote to USG. "Understanding that the friends of Mr. L. C. Slavens of Kansas City are about to unite in a request for his appointment as District Attorney for the Western District of Missouri. I beg leave to be considered as uniting in such application. . . ."—LS, DNA, RG 60, Letters from the President. Related papers are *ibid.* On Feb. 7, USG nominated Luther C. Slavens to replace James S. Botsford. On Feb. 8, Botsford, Jefferson City, telegraphed to USG. "I respectfully ask that the nomination of mr. Slavens be withdrawn until I can reach Washn in justice to myself so that if misrepresentations have been made I may be able to meet them"—Telegram received (at 11:45 a.m.), *ibid.* A related telegram is *ibid.* On Feb. 20, USG withdrew Slavens and nominated Alexander W. Mullins as U.S. attorney, Western District, Mo.

On July 15, 1876, George Smith, U.S. marshal, Western District, Mo., Cameron, had written to USG. "I have been credibly informed that there is a movement on foot to have me removed from the position I hold by your appointment. I know nothing of the nature of the charges or reasons for such removal. If any charges should be presented to you that would warrant investigation, I will be thankful to have a notification thereof. I regret very much to trouble you with a letter of this kind, annoyed as you certainly must be by the treachery of pretended friends, but having held several official positions during the last forty years without a charge of intentional wrong doing, it would be a sad close in old age to be cut down through false charges prompted by the malice of bad men. Relying upon my integrity of purpose in my official acts as U. S. Marshal, I will cheerfully acquiesce in any course your sense of justice may indicate."—ALS, *ibid.* Smith continued as marshal.

1876, AUG. 10.   John E. Bryant, Savannah, to USG. "I was today nominated for Congress Unanimously on first ballot"—Telegram received (at 11:20 P.M.), DLC-USG, IB. On Aug. 31, Postmaster Gen. James N. Tyner wrote to USG, Long Branch. "I have had a call today from J. E. Bryant, Esq., chairman of the Republican State Central Committee of Georgia, and candidate for Congress in the Savannah district. From him I learn that he had a conversation with you concerning the removal of John G. Clark, postmaster at Savannah. I requested that the substance of our conversation here should be presented to me in writing, which request he has complied with. I hand you herewith his letter, in connection with other papers referring to the same subject. I presume from the tenor of his conversation, as well as from what I see in his letter, that he had your approval to some extent for the proposed change. I have no doubt Mr. Clark is acting very badly, and that probably some action ought to be taken. Mr. Bryant informs me that you have a personal acquaintance with General Mc Laws, whom he recommends for appointment; if so, you will be able to determine for yourself whether or not the general is a proper person to succeed Clark. I have no hesitation whatever in saying that in my judgment Mr. Clark ought to go out at once, if it were not for the fact that the Republicans in all the southern states are torn into factions, and entertain towards each other the bitterest hostility—a feeling which seems to pervade the Republican atmosphere in and about Savannah. Will you be kind enough to look over all these papers, and indicate to me any instructions you may have to give."—TLS, *ibid.* On Sept. 7, James Atkins, collector of customs, Savannah, wrote to USG. "I have heard with regret that Gen'l Lafayette McLaws, Collector of Internal Revenue for the first district of Georgia; has been dropped in the consolidation of the districts. From the course the matter has taken I am led to suspect that some misrepresentations have been made to you in regard to Gen'l McLaws. I have conferred with him freely, and can speak advisedly of his political views and purposes. He is fully in accord with the principles & candidates of the National Republican party, including a hearty endorsement of the idea of the national character of our government as against the pernicious doctrine of what is sometimes called 'states-rights,' sometimes 'state-sovereignty,' and, latterly, more frequently, 'local self-government.' He is, on all the questions that separate the two parties, fully on the side of the Republican party. . . . Gen'l McLaws did not support Col. J. E. Bryant in this district for Congress, giving as his reason his utter want of confidence in the man. Over sixteen hundred colored Republicans of the district went much further and openly ran a candidate of their own and gave their votes for him. . . . P. S. Col. Bryant, who is supposed to be interesting himself to have Gen'l McLaws removed, is claiming that this should be done for his benefit as a candidate for Congress in the first district. I would say if such is the fact, that Col Bryant has been the means of dividing the party until he has no possible chance either to be elected or to make a respectable race."— ALS, *ibid.* On the same day, Atkins again wrote to USG concerning Lafayette McLaws. ". . . If you cannot consistently with your sense of duty restore him to the place from which he has been deposed, I trust you will give him the post-office at Augusta, the position for which you originally designed him as you doubtless remember. . . ."—ALS, *ibid.* On Sept. 8, Alexander N. Wilson, appraiser, and John G. Clark, Savannah, both wrote to USG in support of McLaws. —ALS, *ibid.* On Dec. 12, USG nominated McLaws as postmaster, Savannah, replacing Clark. See *PUSG*, 24, 76–79.

On Oct. 29, Bryant, Jesup, Ga., had telegraphed to USG. "Am in midst of my Canvass Mr Prince of Augusta is Chairman of Committee Conducting Campaign. A necessary Supporter I beg you to retain him until after Election"— Telegram received (at 8:50 P.M.), DLC-USG, IB. Charles H. Prince continued as postmaster, Augusta. On Nov. 7, Bryant lost to Democrat Julian Hartridge. See Ruth Currie-McDaniel, *Carpetbagger of Conscience: A Biography of John Emory Bryant* (Athens, Ga., 1987), pp. 137–42.

1876, AUG. 10. U.S. Representative Thomas J. Henderson of Ill. to USG. "Since I spoke to you sometime ago in reference to the appointment of a friend of mine, as One of the Board of Visitors to the Military Academy at West Point, next year, I have examined the Statutes, and am of the opinion that the Members of the Board appointed by the President, as well as those appointed by the President of the Senate and the Speaker of the House of Representatives, should be appointed at the Session of Congress next preceding the Examination: And I again recommend my friend Mr Stephen G Paddock of Princeton, Bureau County, Illinois, as a suitable person to be appointed One of the Board of Visitors to be appointed by you for the Examination of 1877. . . ."—ALS, DNA, RG 94, USMA, Board of Visitors. Related papers are *ibid.* On Jan. 3, 1877, U.S. Senator Oliver P. Morton of Ind. wrote to USG. "Major W. A. Brown, of Greencastle, Indiana, one of the leading lawyers at that bar, desires an appointment as visitor at West Point. . . ."—LS, *ibid.*, Correspondence, USMA. On Jan. 9, Secretary of War James D. Cameron wrote to USG. "I find that the records of the Department show that the Board of Visitors in 1869 was selected by yourself on the 23d of April of that year."—Copy, *ibid.*, RG 107, Letters Sent, Military Affairs. On Jan. 12, Edward D. Neill, president, Macalester College, Minneapolis, wrote to USG. "By your courtesy, last year, I was appointed a visitor to the U. S. Naval Academy, and my inspection of the operations of that Institution, has been of service to me, as the President of a College now being organized. If there are no obstacles in the way, I ~~should~~ would be gratified to be appointed one of the Board of Visitors to the West Point Military Academy, the present year."—ALS, *ibid.*, RG 94, Correspondence, USMA. On Jan. 16, Cameron wrote to Neill that USG "will not select this new Board of Visitors. They will not be appointed until April, next."—LS (press), *ibid.* On Jan. 17, Cameron wrote similarly to George Pattison, Jacksonville, Fla.—LS (press), *ibid.* See Pattison to Simon Cameron, Jan. 10, 1877, *ibid.* On Feb. 10, Nathan Goff, Jr., U.S. attorney, Clarksburg, West Va., wrote to USG recommending Henry Haymond, who "served about eight years in the regular army," for USMA visitor.—ALS, *ibid.* On Feb. 17, Cameron wrote to Goff as he had to Neill and Pattison.—Copy, *ibid.*, Letters Sent. For unsuccessful efforts to secure Haymond an appointment as army paymaster, see *ibid.*, ACP, H242 CB 1870.

1876, AUG. 12. USG note. "Will the Sec. of the Treas. please hear Mrs. Mc-Gunnigle, the widow of a gallant Naval officer, in her appeal for a months leave from her place as a clerk?"—ANS, DNA, RG 56, Applications. Isabella R. Mc-Gunnegle worked for the Light-House Board.

Probably in March, 1875, McGunnegle had written to Postmaster Gen. Marshall Jewell. "I respectfully make application for a clerkship in your Department. I am the daughter of the late Surgeon Hyde Ray U. S. Navy, and widow of the late Lieut. Commdr. Wilson McGunnegle U. S. N. My husband died during the war, from disease contracted in the service The little means I had have been expended in the education of my children, and I now find myself unable to support my daughter and Son, upon the small pension allowed. Hoping that my application may meet with your favorable consideration, . . ." —ALS (undated), *ibid.* USG endorsed this letter. "I have known the husband of Mrs. McGunnegle, and his family in St. Louis, since he was a boy. He served many years in the Navy, and died in the service. His widow comes under the class that should be favored by the Govt. when it can be done without prejudice to the service."—AES (undated), *ibid.* Related papers are *ibid.* See *PUSG*, 19, 541.

1876, AUG. 12. Rear Admiral Christopher R. P. Rodgers, Annapolis, to Ulysses S. Grant, Jr. "May I beg you to ask the President to bear in mind the appointment of our Harvard Professor, Mr. Soley, to fill the vacancy about to occur, in the Corps of Naval Professors, by the retirement of Professor Lockwood, who will go out, in a few days. The President had, I believe, decided to commission Professor Soley, when I last saw him, and the Secretary of the Navy also had the same idea. I know of no one, who would fill the place so well, and I think it very important for the Naval Academy, that Mr. Soley, should be a Naval Professor, instead of the Civil Professor he now is. Fearing our conversation may have escaped the President's memory, in the pressure of greater affairs, I venture to ask you to do me the favor to remind him of it. . . ."—ALS, DNA, RG 45, Letters Received From the President. On Dec. 12, USG nominated James R. Soley as professor of mathematics in the navy to replace Henry H. Lockwood.

1876, AUG. 14. USG veto. "For the reasons stated in the accompanying communications submitted to me by the Secretary of War, I have the honor to return herewith without my approval House bill No 36—entitled 'an Act to restore the name of Captain Edward S. Meyer to the active list of the Army'—" —Copy, DNA, RG 130, Messages to Congress. *HED*, 44-1-194; *SMD*, 49-2-53, 400. On Aug. 4, AG Edward D. Townsend had reported that Edward S.

Meyer's health compelled his retirement as capt., 9th Cav., and "no evidence has been filed in this office showing that he has sufficiently recovered."—*HED*, 44-1-194, 3; *SMD*, 49-2-53, 401. On Dec. 20, the House of Representatives sustained USG's veto. See *CR*, 44–1, 4518, 4912, 44–2, 323–24.

1876, AUG. 15.   USG veto. "For the reasons presented in the accompanying communications submitted by the Secretary of War, I have the honor to return herewith, without my approval, Senate Bill No 561, entitled—'An Act for the relief of Major Junius T. Turner—"—Copy, DNA, RG 130, Messages to Congress. *SED*, 44-1-93; *SRC*, 46-2-78, 3; *SMD*, 49-2-53, 404. On Jan. 12, 1877, USG wrote to the Senate. "On the eve of the adjournment of the last Session of Congress, I returned to the Senate Bill No 561, entitled 'An Act for the relief of Major Junius T. Turner' with my objections to its becoming a law—I now desire to withdraw those objections as I am satisfied they were made under a misapprehension of the facts.—"—Copy, DNA, RG 130, Messages to Congress. *SRC*, 46-2-78, 4; *SMD*, 49-2-53, 404. Junius T. Turner was unsuccessful in multiple attempts to obtain travel pay related to service in Mass. and Md. cav. regts. See *HRC*, 45-2-482; *SRC*, 46-2-78.

1876, AUG. 16.   USG endorsement. "Referred to the Sec. of War. I have no objection to the Surg. Gen. having the 2d & 3d vacancies occuring on the retired list."—AES, DNA, RG 94, ACP, 4456 1876. Written on papers related to retirements of army surgeons, including Col. Joseph J. B. Wright.—*Ibid.* Wright was retired as of Dec. 31.

1876, AUG. 16, Wednesday.   Culver C. Sniffen to Secretary of the Treasury Lot M. Morrill. "The President directs me to say that he will not leave the city until Saturday morning and if you will have the consolidation of Collection districts worked up any time before then, the President will go over the subject with you—"—Copy, DLC-USG, II, 3.

1876, AUG. 17.   USG endorsement. "I suggest that the Sec. of the Treas. should have some reliable employee of the Treas. examine whether Mr. Colein has not been improperly removed from his position, and whether he should not be restored to it."—AES, DNA, RG 56, Applications. Written on a petition of Aug. 14 from R. A. McAllister *et al.*, Baltimore, to Secretary of the Treasury Lot M. Morrill. "We the undersigned, Republican Citizens and Officers of the Republican Clubs, representing the whole Republican element of the City of Baltimore, respectfully represent, that we learn with deep regret, that our fellow citizen and useful and efficient co-worker Wm H. Colein, has recently been relieved from his position as Chief Engineer of the United States Treasury Building, and feeling that the services of each and every Republican, (especially those who are active) in this State, is eminently needed to overcome the corruptions, intimidation and frauds of the present Democratic organization, respectfully represent.—That,—*While* we do not doubt the wisdom, and shall not challenge the *justice* of the action of the Department, we respectfully and earnestly pray, that your decision in this matter may receive so favorable a reconsideration, as to restore him to his position, feeling assured from our knowledge of Mr Colein, that the Department will have no cause to be dissatisfied with his future conduct. . . ."—DS (21 signatures), *ibid.* On the same day, Archibald Sterling, Jr., U.S. attorney, Baltimore, wrote to Morrill requesting William H. Colein's reappointment despite "no doubt that he has been guilty of intemperance."—ALS, *ibid.* Related papers are *ibid.*

1876, AUG. 17.   USG endorsement. "Referred to the Com. of Int. Rev. for such consideration as he may be able to give this case."—AES, DNA, RG 56, Applications. Written on a letter of Aug. 16 from Miss Sidney Ann W. Dowd, Internal Revenue copyist, Washington, D. C., to USG. "In my *extremety* I am *compelled* to appeal to you.—I hear my name is on the list for *dismissal* from this Office.—I beg you will give your name in my behalf,—I am not young,—*have but one hand,* no home, money, or friends. I am the only one of my kindred in Goverment employ,—Had my life Insured to give my a decent burial—so if discharged—all would be lost. I will *modestly* hint that I have a *slight,* 'War Record,' too. Can you not communicate, with Genl Raum—(our Commissioner,) in my behalf? or some other *'Heads'?*"—ALS, *ibid.* Papers related to Dowd's service as a nurse at Rockville, Md., during the Civil War are *ibid.*

1876, AUG. 17.   Culver C. Sniffen to Attorney Gen. Alphonso Taft. "The President directs me to say that he thinks you had better not ask the Marshal of Virginia to resign.—If there is reason though, as the President understands there is, why the District Attorney should resign, you may ask that resignation—"—Copy, DLC-USG, II, 3. On the same day, USG wrote. "Write a note to the Atty Gn, asking him to come over to see me after dinner, about 8 p, m,"—AN, OHi. No changes followed.

1876, AUG. 18.   USG endorsement. "Referred to the Sec. of War. Received Aug. 16th 1876."—AES, DNA, RG 94, ACP, 5188 1872. Written on a letter of Aug. 15 from former 1st Lt. James W. Schaumburg, Washington, D. C., to USG requesting a court-martial to investigate his 1845 dismissal from the army.—ALS, *ibid.* Related papers are *ibid.* See *HRC,* 49-1-1178, 49-1-1376; *SRC,* 49-1-1476; *HD,* 58-3-238; *U.S. Statutes at Large,* XXXIII, part 1, pp. 803–4.

1876, AUG. 21.   Commodore Daniel Ammen, act. secretary of the navy, to USG reporting that Stanhope F. Wood could not be appointed to the U.S. Marine Corps because "no more appointments can be made for three or four years hence, under a recent law."—Copy, DNA, RG 45, Letters Sent to the President. See Wood to USG, Sept. 24, 1872, *ibid.,* RG 94, Unsuccessful Cadet Applications.

1876, AUG. 26.   Gen. William T. Sherman to USG, Long Branch. "Following just from General Upton. 'Have seen Russian Maneuvers; invited by Emperor to see Austrian. Has Berlin Legation been instructed to make application to see German.' Will you please enable me to reply"—Telegram sent, DNA, RG 107, Telegrams Collected (Bound). On July 22, J. C. Bancroft Davis, U.S. minister,

Berlin, had telegraphed to Secretary of State Hamilton Fish concerning an invitation for Lt. Col. Emory Upton.—Telegram received, *ibid.*, RG 59, Diplomatic Despatches, Germany. On the same day, Fish telegraphed to Davis. "President says not advisable to ask invitation."—Copy, *ibid.*, Diplomatic Instructions, Germany. For Upton's dispute with the State Dept. over authorization to observe German military maneuvers, see H. Fish to Nicholas Fish, Sept. 20, 1876, *ibid.*; N. Fish to H. Fish, Aug. 8, 25, 1876, *ibid.*, Diplomatic Despatches, Germany; N. Fish to Upton, Aug. 30, 1876, Davis to H. Fish, Sept. 16, 17, 1876, Feb. 15, 1877, DLC-Hamilton Fish; Upton, *The Armies of Asia and Europe:* . . . (New York, 1878), pp. iii–viii.

1876, AUG. 29.   To Maj. Gen. John M. Schofield, West Point, N. Y., from Long Branch. "Please inform me if there are any vacancies 'At large' at West Point"—Telegram received, USMA. On [*Aug.*] 30, USG telegraphed to Col. Thomas H. Ruger, superintendent, USMA. "Are there any alternates at West Point awaiting examination."—Telegram received, *ibid.* Ruger drafted a reply. "There are no alternates here."—AES, *ibid.* Schofield replaced Ruger on Sept. 1. See telegram to Alphonso Taft, March 7, 1876.

    On Aug. 31, Secretary of War James D. Cameron had telegraphed to USG. "If all the regularly appointed cadets at large are admitted now, there will be forty two (42) at large, or two (2) more than the law authorizes On this account the alternates for September were notified not to appear. Their names, as designated on the Office Register, are Louis W. Wilson, of Iowa; Thomas G. Stanson, of N. Y., J. B. Bernadeau, of Penn., Wm McEnaney, of N. Y., and John McLean, of N. Y."—LS (telegram sent), DNA, RG 107, Telegrams Collected (Bound). On the same day, USG telegraphed to Ruger. "you may examine Chas B Vogdes John McLean & Abercrombi for Cadetship The former is now at West Point the two latter I will send"—Telegram received, USMA. On Sept. 2, USG telegraphed to superintendent, USMA. "If a vacancy at large exists after the examination of Vodges Abercrombie & McLean you may have Breckinridge re-examined Answer"—Telegram received, *ibid.* John Breckinridge was admitted but did not graduate. See *PUSG*, 23, 473; *ibid.*, 26, 304–8.

    On Aug. 31, 1876, Cameron had telegraphed to USG. "Cadet James Todd Jr. of the 4th Class at the Military Academy is sentenced to be dismissed for using intoxicating liquor while at the Centennial Superintendent and Judge Advocate General recommend mitigation of Sentence to one years suspension Do you approve? It seems a proper case for clemency"—LS (telegram sent), DNA, RG 107, Telegrams Collected (Bound). On the same day, Jesse Root Grant, Long Branch, telegraphed to Cameron conveying USG's approval.—Telegram received, *ibid.*, RG 94, Correspondence, USMA. Suspended until July, 1877, James Todd, Jr., drowned at USMA on Aug. 29, 1878.

    On Sept. 2, 1876, Ellen E. Sherman, Washington, D. C., had written to USG. "Through your kind consideration you gave to the son of an old friend of mine L. Stambaugh (whose brother was killed on the plains) an appointment at West Point He has got into difficulty and cannot report for examination—Young Lusk has made through friends application for the vacancy—I sincerely hope that you will give it to him as a more intelligent upright industrious young man of good family could hardly be found. His appointment would confirm and strengthen the loyalty and regard of his friends to you. He is from Pennsylvania—May I ask you to give my love to Mrs Grant? She kindly invited me Long Branch but my California trip will interfere with my pleasure in that direction"—Copy, *ibid.* On Sept. 7, USG endorsed this letter. "Sec. of War. If a vacancy 'At Large' still exists at West Point this apt. may be made."—AES (facsimile), RWA Inc., Catalog No. 43, part 2, March 21 and 22, 1998, no. 1503. On Sept. 9, Henry T. Crosby, chief clerk, War Dept., telegraphed (twice) and wrote to USG. "The last, at large, vacancy filled, this day, by appointment of Charles S. Lusk to West Point." "Since telegram of this morning, it has been discovered that Lusk, appointed cadet at large, is over twenty two years of age. Particulars will be sent by mail, as a mistake is apparent" "Since the receipt of your order of September 7th 76, enclosed, directing the appointment, at large, of Charles S. Lusk, to a cadetship, I have received notice from Genl. Chas. Ewing, that it was not the intention of Mrs. Sherman to request an appointment at large, but *one to the Army,* in place of Mr. Stambaugh, who had been so designated but declined. In reviewing the details of Mr. Lusk's case, it is discovered that he is above the proper age for admission to the Academy, and that Mr. Stambaugh had not been designated by you for an appointment at large, and in view of these facts I have respectfully to request your instructions as to whether Mr. Lusk shall be directed to appear before the Board of Examination for a position as Second Lieutenant in the Army or not."—LS (telegrams sent), DNA, RG 107, Telegrams Collected (Bound); LS, *ibid.,* RG 94, ACP, 5648 1876. No appointment followed.

1876, AUG. 31. Secretary of War James D. Cameron to USG. "Herewith is submitted to you the report of the Judge Advocate General, upon the proceedings of a General Court Martial in the case of Captain Alexander Sutorius. He is convicted of drunkenness on duty while in charge of the pickets of the 3rd Regt. U. S. Cavalry, a portion of the expedition in the field against hostile Indians, and is sentenced to be discharged. . . ."—Copy, DNA, RG 107, Letters Sent, Military Affairs. On Sept. 7, USG approved this sentence.—Printed copy, *ibid.,* RG 94, ACP, 6139 1876. Related papers are *ibid.*

[*1876, Aug.*]. "Father Springer, the Judge of quick and the dead, of the present Power in Heaven, Earth, or Hell," to USG. "I in the name of the people of these United States, I summons you and your Cabinet to appear before me in the City of Oswego, on the 29th of August, to attend a convention that commences on the 28th, for the purpose of rendering a correct account of your stewardships as regards your rule and government of the people . . . and to establish a new form of Goverment, and annex the Canada's with the United States. . . . and establish the city of the New Jerusalem, which takes four towns. Oswego, Scriba, Volney and Granby, will be selected and chosen as the city of the most high here upon the earth, when the separation must be made upon the earth. . . ."—Copy (printed), OFH.

1876, SEPT. 2.   Secretary of War James D. Cameron to USG, Long Branch. "Your letter of twenty-fourth August about Major Mallery is only just received —This case is very much like that of Schriver and unless you have special reasons to the contrary I think it very much better that the order should be carried out. I have given this matter a great deal of attention and am convinced that it is best he should go."—LS (telegram sent), RG 107, Telegrams Collected (Bound). Capt. Garrick Mallery, bvt. maj., retired as of July 1, 1879.

1876, SEPT. 2.   Fanny Downing, Washington, D. C., to USG. "Please give your attention for a few moments, to a woman who in her deep trouble, comes to you as one of your people, & appeals to your goodness as a man & your magnanimity as a soldier. Two days ago, my daughter who, by testimony of her Chief Mr Patten, has served in the Treasury, with the utmost capacity, received her dismissal. She is the breadwiner for ~~four~~five person, & her dismissal means actual starvation. Oh! Sir, you who blessed with such good children, for whom you are able to provide as you desire, & they deseve, I beg you, let you love for them teach you how to pity me, in thus seeing all, all hope of a support for mine, destroyed, & induce you to aid us. One command from you, Sir, will restore us our happy little home, & save us from such suffering as I shrink to contemplate. Will you not be as good as you are great, & give such command? Not to have my daughter restored to her office, but that it or any other be given ME, I being better fitted to labor than she is, at present, from her close & most conscentious discharge of her official duties. . . ."—ALS, DNA, RG 56, Applications. No appointment followed. Downing had published *Nameless: A Novel* (1865) and contributed to *The Land We Love* (1866–69), edited by Daniel H. Hill, former lt. gen., C.S. Army.

1876, SEPT. 2.   Lt. Col. Horatio G. Wright, New York City, to USG, Long Branch. "I took the liberty of calling yesterday at your residence at Long Branch in the hope of seeing and interesting you in behalf of the widow of the late General Jos B. Hamblin, but as I unfortunately found you absent, and as I have to return to Washington tomorrow, I am forced to make my appeal by letter. General Hamblin was in the field during the entire war and rose through the various grades, by merit alone, to Brig Genl of Volunteers. During the last campaigns, from the Rapidan to to Appomattox C. H. he commanded a brigade of the 6th Army Corps, establishing for himself the reputation of being one of the best brigade commanders in that Corps or in the Army of the Potomac. For zeal and gallantry he had no superior. So far as the services of the husband can constitute a claim on the part of the wife for consideration by the government, Mrs Hamblin's is of the strongest. Her own official record is also of the best, as she entered the Internal Revenue Bureau, where she now is, in the lowest grade of clerkship and has risen, through competitive examinations to a grade which has attached to it a salary of $1,400, and has, I am assured, always given full satisfaction to her superiors in that office; but the reductions in clerical force about to take place in the various departments in Washington make her uneasy in regard to her tenure of office and hence she has asked me to make the above presentation of her case in the hope that it may save her from reduction or dismissal. Should you ever interpose in cases like this, I most sincerely hope you will do so in her behalf. I scarcely know Mrs Hamblin personally, but I believe she is without means of support for herself and mother, other than are derived from her present office."—ALS, DNA, RG 56, Applications. Related papers are *ibid.* Isabella Hamblin retained her clerkship; her husband, Joseph E., died in 1870.

1876, SEPT. 5. Brig. Gen. Benjamin Alvord, paymaster gen., to USG, Long Branch. "Learning that persons may be applying to you for appointment of Chief Clerk of Pay Department I ought to inform you that the Secretary of War who has left for California, said that on his return he will look into the question. I ask him to revoke his order for discharge of G D Hanson on tenth October. The injustice of this act to Mister Hanson I explain in the note by mail. If any change is made I desire the appointment of one in my office."—Copy (telegram sent), DNA, RG 99, Letters Sent. Grafton D. Hanson continued as chief clerk.

1876, SEPT. 6. Timothy C. Smith, Monkton, Vt., to USG. "The petitioner, Timothy C. Smith, a native of Vermont, graduate of Middlebury College, clerk in the Treasury Dept, at Washington, from 1849 to 1853, graduate of the Medical University of New York in 1855, and surgeon in the Russian army one year to 1856, married at the close of the Crimean War a lady of Odessa, Russia, and returned to Vermont. In June 1861, was appointed, by President Lincoln, Consul for Odessa—was recalled in June 1875—my successor, Mr Dyer of Tennissee, entering into functions last October. During all the time of my official service I was on the most friendly terms with the Russian authorities and many times received the thanks of the Department of State in approval of my official conduct. I was recalled in consequence of a mistake or misunderstanding, it being supposed by the Secretary of State Mr Fish, that the Russian Government was displeased with me and desired my recall. In August 1874 I had offended the new Post Master of Odessa in a dispute growing out of his refusal to deliver to me without a written certificate of my identity a letter officially addressed to me as Consul of the United States. . . . I believe Mr Fish would not be sorry but rather as he says *'glad'* to have me reappointed to Odessa but he does not like to undo, himself, what he himself has done."—ALS, DNA, RG 59, Applications and Recommendations, Hayes-Arthur. On Feb. 15, 1877, Secretary of State Hamilton Fish wrote to Smith. ". . . As to your restoration to the Consulate at Odessa I regret that I see no practical means thereto. There is no reason known for the removal of the present Consul—He has not resigned and, as to his transfer to some other place, it would be necessary to remove some one else to make a place for him and at this late period in the term of the President it has been thought not advisable to make changes in the foreign service of the Government unless some serious reason presented a necessity therefor."—Copy, *ibid.* Related papers are *ibid.*

1876, SEPT. 9. Susan M. Clay, Lexington, Ky., to USG seeking an army appointment for her son Thomas J. Clay ". . . in the name of his grandfather Henry Clay—bringing to your remembrance his greatness & goodness, his public services and pure patriotism, his undying love for his country and his death which was as truly in his country's service as if he had died on the bloody battle field— . . ."—ALS, DNA, RG 94, ACP, 1971 1877. An undated note referred to this case. "The President desires his appointment as 2nd Lt if it can properly be done—"—N, *ibid.* A related letter is *ibid.* Clay was appointed 2nd lt., 10th Inf., as of April 25, 1877.

1876, Sept. 11.   To President Boisrond Canal of Haiti acknowledging his election.—Copy, DNA, RG 84, Haiti, Instructions. On Aug. 10, Canal had written to USG on the same subject.—LS (in French), *ibid.*, RG 59, Notes from Foreign Legations, Haiti; translation, *ibid.* See *Foreign Relations, 1876,* pp. 333–35.

On Aug. 23, Adolphe H. Lazare, New York City, wrote to USG. "On the first day of September One thousand eight hundred and seventy four the Government of the Republic of Hayti granted to me a concession for the establishment of a National Bank. Under that concession and the modification of the same (made on the 11th May 1875) that Government undertook to perform certain duties, which it has neglected, although I, on my part, have carefully kept every covenant agreed on by me. . . . I have demanded a settlement of my claims against that Government and an arbitration under the Article above-recited, but this has been refused. I now ask that I shall have such protection as the laws of the United States can give me and I request the interposition of the United States Minister Resident in Hayti in my behalf. Such protection and such interposition are the more necessary to secure my rights in a country subject to sudden revolutions and where all law and justice are frequently set at defiance."— LS, DNA, RG 59, Miscellaneous Letters. A printed copy of Lazare's contract is *ibid.* See *SED,* 49-2-64, 21–43.

On Nov. 17, Heuvelman Haven & Co., New York City, petitioned USG concerning contracts to design and construct public buildings in Haiti. "Your Petitioners respectfully represent: . . . That the amount now due to your petitioners, together with the penalties and expenses of protests and the interest up to October 30, 1876, amounts in the total to $109,752.78/100. That Mr Heuvelman, the senior member of the firm, personally went to Hayti in reference to securing payment of the claim; and there he had several appointed interviews with the late, and with the present, members, of the Government of Hayti, including the President Boisrond Canal; and there presented the proofs of the claim. While that government does not deny the validity of the claim; yet, after waiting at Port au Prince thirty days for an answer to the demand for its payment, Mr Heuvelman had finally to abandon the attempt to get any satisfaction, and left the place without receiving any answer. . . ."—L, DNA, RG 59, Miscellaneous Letters.

1876, Sept. 12.   To Jesse H. Reno, collector of Internal Revenue, 2nd District, Ky., suspending him from office.—Copy, DNA, RG 56, Letters Sent. On Sept. 14, William H. Crook wrote to Oliver P. Johnson. "The President directs me to acknowledge the receipt of your letter of the 11th inst. and to say that the papers referred to, were sent to the Secretary of the Treasury who was then in Augusta Maine, that he has had a reply, and understand that your appointment was ordered, vice Mr. Reno to be suspended."—Copy, DLC-USG, II, 3. On Dec. 6, USG nominated Johnson.

1876, Sept. 12. Annie M. Wheeler, Delhi, N. Y., to USG. "My most valuable and truly sympathising friend, Hon S. B Ruggles who has so kindly interested himself in the sad, sad, fate of my noble son, ~~and~~ has encouraged me to believe that you kindly sympathise in my most heart rending affliction. He requests me to send you a statement of when my son died, and from what cause. In the hope that the Navy Department might deem it proper to have his precious remains brought home which I most earnestly desire. My son Lieut Comr William Knox Wheeler died at sea, on board the U. S. S. Alaska on the 14th of March 1876 on the West coast of Africa on the passage from Cape Coast Castle to the Gaboon river. His remains were taken to Gaboon, and buried in the Mission Cemetery there. He died of Brights disease of the Kidneys, contracted by a severe cold while working Ship, as Excutive Officer from Funchal, Maderia to Porto Grande De Verd Islands, in a very tremendous storm. . . ."—ALS, DNA, RG 45, Letters Received from the President. On Sept. 13, Samuel B. Ruggles, Delhi, wrote to USG concerning Lt. Commander William K. Wheeler. ". . . I personally knew him as a manly, upright, Christian gentleman well entitled to the kindest consideration of the Government he served. I have enjoyed while here, the melancholy satisfaction of examining the spirited photographs of the gallant but dangerous assault of the fortified city in Corea, where he was the second to scale the walls, but is represented as exerting his best efforts to spare, as far as possible, any useless, slaughter of the hordes of barbarians, that he was officially required to chastise. Passing from these distant seas, to waters and duties nearer home, I venture, as a citizen of the United States, to now repeat my earnest desire expressed at Long Branch, that in your next parting with Congress (*perhaps only for a season*) you may distinctly show the American people their great mistake (*not yet* wholly irreparable,) in omitting to secure a proper naval foothold, and at the same time a rich, seat of tropical commerce, in the *American* waters, so nearly adjacent, if not properly *appurtenant* to our continental Republic . . ."—ALS, *ibid.*

1876, Sept. 13. USG endorsement. "Returned to the Sec. of War. I told Mrs. English her ~~shoul~~ son should be appointed 2d Lt. with the understanding that his entire class had asked it, and supposing there was no legal disability."— AES, DNA, RG 94, Correspondence, USMA. Written on a letter of Sept. 5 from Mrs. Thomas C. English, Philadelphia, to Secretary of War James D. Cameron seeking the reinstatement to USMA of her son William, who had failed mathematics following his father's death on June 10.—ALS, *ibid.* On June 27, Mrs. English had written to USG on the same subject.—ALS, *ibid.* See Lt. Col. James W. Forsyth to Mrs. English, July 13, Aug. 24, 1876, Jan. 1, 8, 1877, DLC-Philip H. Sheridan. On March 5, 1873, and Jan. 20, 1874, Lt. Col. Thomas C. English, USMA 1849, had written to USG asking his son's appointment to USMA.—ALS, DNA, RG 94, Correspondence, USMA. William English was appointed 2nd lt. as of Sept. 1, 1879. See *SRC*, 45-3-576, 46-2-68; *HRC*, 50-1-3205.

1876, SEPT. 14.   William H. Crook to Frederic De Peyster. "I am directed by
the President to acknowledge the receipt of your invitation, in behalf of the
committee of the New York Historical Society, to be present at the celebration
of the Hundredth Anniversary of the Battle of Harlam Plains, and to express
his sincere regrets, that previous engagements will prevent his participation in
the pleasures of that occasion."—Copy, DLC-USG, II, 3. See *New York Times,*
Sept. 17, 1876.

1876, SEPT. 23.   Samuel F. Phillips, act. attorney gen., to USG. "The Attorney
General, at the time of his departure for Ohio, requested that a copy of a petition, received by him on the 21st inst., for the removal of United States Marshal Robert P. Baker, should be transmitted to you for your information, and
such action thereon as you might see proper to direct. In compliance with his
request the enclosed document is forwarded to you."—LS, DNA, RG 60, Letters from the President. In a petition to Attorney Gen. Alphonso Taft, circulated at a Sept. 16 rally in Huntsville, Ala., Samuel Lowery *et al.* charged that
Robert P. Baker was "not in sympathy with the Republican Party, nor the political interest of the colored people, who are nineteen twentieths of the Republican in this District:—and they have no confidence in him whatever, as a Republican."—Copy, *ibid.* Baker continued as marshal, Northern District, Ala.

1876, SEPT. 23.   W. M. Davidson, Cowansville, Pa., to USG asking for mathe-
matical experts to examine ". . . an important discovery in nautical science, . . . a
new and radical cystem, for *measuring triangles.* The facts, or Propositions upon
which it is founded, lie beyond the recognized '*circle of science.*' These are what I
claim as '*my discoveries,*' and of which both Admiral Davis, and Proffessor Coffin,
are in a state of child like ignorance. . . ."—ALS, DNA, RG 45, Letters Received
from the President.

1876, SEPT. 26.   Hugh S. Fullerton, Hillsboro, Ohio, to USG. "I have the honor
to report that the representative of the general government here, Jas W. Dog-
gett is in the calaboose for being drunk and abusing his family. This is no unusual thing with him but very indiscreet at present when the Republicans of
Ohio are endeavoring to prove that their party is immaculate. He holds the position of Deputy U. S. Marshal by appointment of one W. R. Thrall of Cincinnati to whom his general rascality and malicious worthlessness have been
well known for years but who persists in retaining him in office against the
indignant protests of our citizens. It is hard for us to ask people to vote the Republican ticket and have such men as these thrown up to us as 'specimens of
Republican Office-holders' If you desire reference as to my position and character I have the honor to refer you to Jno. A. Smith of this place, late M. C. or
to R. B. Hayes of Columbus this State."—ALS, DNA, RG 60, Letters from the
President.

1876, SEPT. 28.   Elihu B. Washburne to USG. "Knowing how you are hounded
by office beggars and how much you are pestered by office-*holders,* even, you
will bear me witness that I have not troubled you much in these regards. I am

sorry to say that now an appeal is made to me that I cannot well disregard. It is the case of Col. James M. Wilson, our present Consul to Nürnberg, who is a very old and highly esteemed friend of mine. He has just received a letter from Mr. Cadwallader saying that you deem a change necessary in his office and requesting his resignation. There can be no complaint against him, for he is a thoroughly competent officer and an honest, intelligent and incorruptible man, who served his country during during the war with great fidelity and acceptance as a Paymaster. He is quite poor and with the small salary he has, it is quite difficult to make the two ends meet. And what would make it worse for him to be removed now is that he has his house leased for several months yet. It would be a real distress to him and his family to be obliged to break up and go home this fall and when it would be impossible to procure any employment for the winter. As the public interest will not be subserved by a change and as it cannot be much of an object for any man to come over and take a little consulate of $1,500 a year with a good chance of going out on the change of administration, I hope you will, with this explanation of the matter, find it consistent with your sense of public duty to let my poor friend remain where he is. Excuse me, dear General, for thus troubling you, and begging to thank you in advance for any favor you may accord to Col. Wilson in respect of this affair, . . ." —ALS, DNA, RG 59, Applications and Recommendations, Hayes-Arthur; press, DLC-Elihu B. Washburne. On Nov. 1, Secretary of State Hamilton Fish recorded in his diary a conversation with USG. "I show him James M Wilsons Despatch #149 Nuremburg Oct 6th in reply to request for his resignation. The President has no recollection of the reason why he requested it but says it must have been some pressure which he may remember hereafter."—DLC-Hamilton Fish. James M. Wilson continued as consul, Nuremberg.

On Jan. 25, 1871, Wilson, Washington, D. C., had written to USG. "At the commencement of your administration I had the honor to receive the endorsement of the entire Delegation in Congress from my State—Mo, for the appointment of U. S. Consul to *Panama*—and was nominated to that position by the Hon E. B. Washburn—then Secretary of State. Failing to receive that appointment I returned to Missouri and have labored zealously for the interest of the party and the success of your administration. In the late Gubernatorial campaign I was honored with the unanimous nomination of the party for State Senator of my District. I now have the honor to apply for the appointment of U. S. Consul to *Melbourne*—I have the honor to refer to Hon D. T. Jewett U. S. S The Honl S. S. Burdett M. C. et al and to my recommendations, on file in State Department."—ALS, DNA, RG 59, Applications and Recommendations, Hayes-Arthur. Related papers are *ibid.* See *PUSG,* 21, 228.

1876, SEPT. 29. Bishop Pierre Bataillon of Central Oceania, Wallis Island, to USG alleging persecution at the hands of U.S. citizens.—ALS (in French), DNA, RG 59, Miscellaneous Letters; translation, *ibid.*

1876, SEPT. 30. Commodore John C. Howell, act. secretary of the navy, to USG recommending approval of sentence in the case of Capt. Joseph F. Baker, U.S. Marine Corps, court-martialed for drunkenness and facing dismissal.—

Copy, DNA, RG 45, Letters Sent to the President. On Oct. 4, Howell wrote to USG that "the Department has received the sad intelligence of the death of that Officer, who is reported to have been found dead in his bed, on the morning of the 2d Inst."—Copy, *ibid.* Baker purportedly died of apoplexy. See *New York Times*, Oct. 3, 1876.

[*1876, Sept.*].   USG endorsement. "The matter of Leave of absence is left entirely with the Heads of Departments. But they should not be granted to Societies except with loss of pay for the time absent, or by having the time charged to the usual leave allowed each Government employee during the year."—Copied in a Sept. 19 letter from William H. Crook to cabinet officers, DNA, RG 60, Letters from the President; *ibid.*, RG 94, ACP, 5147 1876. Alfred H. Gawler, War Dept. clerk, and other government employees, members of the Independent Order of Odd Fellows, had requested five days leave of absence to attend a Sept. 20 parade in Philadelphia.

1876, OCT. 2.   Maj. Gen. John M. Schofield, superintendent, USMA, to USG. "Being informed that a son of the late Genl Rodman of the Ordnance Corps, is an applicant for an appointment at large to the Military Academy, I beg leave to add my recommendation to those of other officers of the Army, in favor of the applicant, on the ground of his Father's distinguished services."—ALS, DNA, RG 94, Correspondence, USMA. Appointed from Ill., Addison B. Rodman did not graduate USMA.

1876, OCT. 6.   Culver C. Sniffen to Mrs. A. F. Johnson, New Orleans. "The President directs me to acknowledge the receipt of your letter of 27th accompanied by the commendatory letter of Governor Kellogg of the 30th ultimo— He remembers your late husband Col Johnson as a meritorius officer, but in answer to your request in behalf of your son, he requests me to inform you that it would be very improper in him to recommend, not only the son of Col Johnson, but any body else, as proper parties to receive Government contracts.—"— Copy, DLC-USG, II, 3.

1876, OCT. 6, Friday.   Culver C. Sniffen to John G. Nicolay, marshal, U.S. Supreme Court. "The President directs me to request that you will inform the Chief Justice and Associate Justices that he will be pleased to receive them on Monday next at the hour that it has been usual for them to call."—ALS, DLC- John G. Nicolay.

1876, OCT. 7.   USG endorsement. "Will the Sec of the Intr. please see Mrs. Washington when she calls."—Copy, OFH. Written on a letter of April 3 from Brig. Gen. Christopher C. Augur, New Orleans, to Secretary of the Interior Zachariah Chandler. "Mrs. Fannie Washington, a daughter of the late Colonel J. M. Washington a distinguished officer of the Army who was lost at sea some years before the late war, finds herself dependent upon her own exertions for a support, and is desirous of an appointment to some position in your

Dept. . . ."—Copy, *ibid.* Fannie V. Washington served as a laborer in the patent office.

1876, OCT. 7.   USG endorsement. "I would add my name to those given within for the retention of Mr. King in his present position."—AES, DNA, RG 56, Applications. Written on papers concerning Cyrus S. King, including a letter dated Sept. 9 from Horatio King, Oxford, Maine, to Secretary of the Treasury Lot M. Morrill. "My brother, Cyrus S. King, a $1200 clerk in the 2d Comptroller's office, writes me that his name is down 'for removal on the charge of Democracy,' and he says 'a removal now would ruin me, as I have a large amount to pay on my house, and have just taken an orphan to bring up.' You may recollect that you joined with my old friend Hamlin in a request for his retention, and I cannot think they would remove him under these circumstances. He is in no sense a politician, but acted during the war as a firm supporter of the war, . . ."—ALS, *ibid.* Cyrus King lost his clerkship.

1876, OCT. 10.   Joseph Adison, Winchester, Va., to USG. "I am a poor oled man of Color ignorant of the laws   I had worked for a man by the name of George. Ward and he refused to pay me   I warranted him for it and they still refuse to pay me   the law wont protect me in my rights   after I had warranted them they put me in jail contrary to law   the names of the men that put me in jail crebs is Magistrate Curts and Mesmore   they put me in for not giving up the receipt: my son paid two dollars for to get me out   John W. Gibbens drawed the warrant   I would like for you to make them pay $1500.00 fifteen hundred Dollars for false imprisonment . . . William barber has been doing the writing for me hertofore but cannot now on account of sickness   I have got another friend to write for me   Joseph Adison Accept againss George Ward $50.00"—L, DNA, RG 60, Letters from the President.

1876, OCT. 10.   William Burr, Oswego, N. Y., to USG. "With indignation towards my party in Oswego. N. Y. I take the liberty to enclose to you a list of persons drawing pay at this place and for what; I am a Republican *not a sore head.* (useing the term) And if I vote the Democrat tickt this fall it will be the first in silence & in shame. There are men in that list, that is a shame a disgrace to the party to the exclusion of respectable citizens   I mail you this for no other purpose than by your influence you may stop the tide that is surely seting against our party here. This list does not include all"—ALS, DNA, RG 56, Letters Received from the President. The enclosure is *ibid.*

1876, OCT. 14.   USG endorsement. "Referred to the Sec. of the Treas. The writer is a poor girl who has been some years in the Treasurers office, and is entirely dependent upon her own exertions for a support, having other members of her family less able to help themselves looking to her too."—AES, DNA, RG 56, Applications. Written on a letter of Sept. 23 from Mary L. Larner, Washington, D. C., to Secretary of the Treasury Lot M. Morrill. "I respectfully request a position in your department, as copyist, I have been employed in the

Treasurer's Office for two years, having been appointed by a special request of The President: I was dismissed on the 31st. day of August owing to the reduction of the force. I was born in this city in 1858, and have always lived here; I have a mother and two younger sisters who are entirely dependent upon me for their support. I promise to fulfil any duties that may be assigned me. Hoping this letter may meet with a favorable response."—ALS, *ibid.* No appointment followed. Probably in Sept., 1874, USG had written a note. "See the Sec. of the Treas. in regard to the apt. of Mary L. Larnar who passed the Civil service board (89) and was told that she would in all probability be apt. in Gen. Spinner's department"—AN (undated), *ibid.* On the back of this note, an official indicated Larner's appointment on Sept. 19.—N, *ibid.* On May 28, 1875, USG wrote another note concerning Larner's transfer from the Treasurer's Office to Internal Revenue. "Can the Com. of Int. Rev. exchange one of present employees so as to effect transfer requested on the reverse side of this."—ANS, *ibid.* Related papers are *ibid.*

1876, OCT. 14, Saturday.   Salem H. Wales, president, Dept. of Docks, New York City, to USG. "You did me the honor on thursday last to receive some papers and to listen courteously to some statements made by me on behalf of Commander Haxtun of the Navy, and at the same time you requested me to submit the matter to you in writing. In compliance I hand you herewith the following documents, . . ."—ALS, DNA, RG 45, Letters Received from the President. Related papers are *ibid.* At about this time, Wales and six others wrote to USG. "The undersigned, friends of Commander Haxtun and his family, in view of his recent abrupt dismissal from his command on the eve of her departure for a foreign station, without affording him an opportunity for refuting or explaining away any charges, would respectfully request that your Excellency would be pleased to intimate to the Hon. Secretary Robeson your desire for a reconsideration of the case, believing that such a course would be satisfactory to the latter and just to the commander."—LS (docketed Oct. 16), *ibid.* USG endorsed this letter. "Navy. Please have this matter examined."—AE (undated), *ibid.* On Dec. 9, A. V. Young, New York City, wrote to Secretary of the Treasury Lot M. Morrill. "In August last the U. S. Ship Vandelia, Commander Haxtun was ordered on a trial trip on the North River. There were about twenty five invited guests on board. Wives and relations of the Officers there were also four Ladies and Gentlemen invited by Commander Haxtun. For this he was detached by the department. . . ."—ALS, *ibid.*

On April 13, 1869, Annie A. Haxtun, Washington, D. C., had written to USG. "I have been waiting with all possible patience to see you for a few minutes. My letters of introduction were sent in this morning. My husband Commander Milton Haxtun entered the Navy in 1841 and has served faithfully the entire time, and during our own great war, he did faithfully and cheerfully what he was ordered to do, was at the attack on Fort Macon, and received very complimentary letters for his conduct under fire, and efficiency on the blockade. Now President Grant what I beg of you is that you will send name in to the Senate to be restored to his position on the Navy Register where he was past over in the unjust bill of 1866, . . ."—ALS, *ibid.*, Subject File, Div. NI. Annie Haxtun saw USG on April 17, and wrote twice more on the same subject.—ALS, *ibid.* No action followed.

1876, OCT. 16.   USG note. "Will the Sec. of the Treas. please see please see Mr. Brush, and if he can grant his request, strongly urged by Hon. John M. Frances, of Troy, N. Y I will be pleased."—ANS, DNA, RG 56, Applications. On Sept. 16, John M. Francis, *Troy Daily Times*, had written to USG. "May I again trouble you for a moment. It is about a small matter, and yet it takes right hold of my sympathies. My cousin Harmon M. Brush, has been for years a clerk in the Treasury department. He is a cripple, and has but one leg—has been a cripple from childhood. He behaved badly in a political way in 1872 and went off in the Greeley craze.—Subsequently, however, he returned to the Republican party, and has been true and right ever since. . . ."—ALS, *ibid.* A related letter is *ibid.* No reinstatement followed.

1876, OCT. 16.   Robert Crozier, Leavenworth, Kan., to USG. "I met your son here yesterday on his way west who informed me he understood it to be the design to assign to the Engineers this year the cadet who should have the highest standing on the general merit roll for scholarship, regardless of demerits. If such were the intention there must have been some oversight in assigning my son to the 4th artillery. . . ."—ALS, DNA, RG 94, ACP, 5173 1876. On Nov. 17, Gen. William T. Sherman telegraphed to Crozier. "Have seen the Secretary of war, who says the President has made no official order transferring Lieut Crozier from Artillery to Engineers—"—ALS (telegram sent), *ibid.*

1876, OCT. 17.   Culver C. Sniffen to Secretary of War James D. Cameron. "The President directs me to order the discharge from the Army of John Wade—Private, Co G. 1st United States Artillery.—"—Copy, DLC-USG, II, 3.

1876, OCT. 19.   USG note. "Will the P. M. G. see if position of Messenger or Watchman can be given to Mr. Lewis Rasten?"—ANS, Gallery of History, Las Vegas, Nev.

1876, OCT. 24.   USG pardon for Bernard Berendsen, convicted in Wis. of selling whiskey to an Indian and sentenced to ten days in prison and a $50 fine.—Copy, DNA, RG 59, General Records.

1876, OCT. 24.   Anthony J. Drexel, Philadelphia, to USG. "My Sister Mrs J. G. Watmough is very anxious that I should write to you in reference to her brother in law Dr Grier, who wishes your favorable consideration in connection with the vacancy to be created upon the retirement of Dr Beale on 31st Dec next as Surgeon General of the ~~Army~~ Navy. Dr Grier claims to stand next to Dr Beale on the active list & by seniority, and length of service giving him thus some claim to the position—When the time comes to act will you kindly give Dr Griers claims proper consideration which I hope will lead to a favorable

result for him"—ALS, DNA, RG 45, Letters Received from the President. On
Jan. 23, 1877, USG nominated William Grier to replace Joseph Beale as navy
surgeon gen.

1876, OCT. 26.   USG endorsement. "Reffered to Hds of Depts I would be very
glad if employment could be given to Mrs. Bradford."—Copy, DNA, RG 56,
Applications. Docketed with papers including a Feb. 24 testimonial from Gen.
William T. Sherman, St. Louis. "I take great pleasure in recommending for employment Mrs. Cynthia E. Bradford, widow of a Naval Officer, chiefly because
she is the daughter of Colonel Hildebrand who commanded a Brigade under me
at Shiloh and during the Corinth Campaign, and one of the bravest men I ever
saw in action. Colonel Hildebrand died in the Service long ago, and I contend
his children have a just claim on the generosity of the National Government."—
Copy, *ibid.* Cynthia E. Bradford later worked as counter, Treasury Dept.

1876, OCT. 26.   Ebenezer R. Hoar, Boston, to Secretary of State Hamilton
Fish. "I send you by to-day's mail a copy of the Boston Daily Advertiser, containing a scurrilous and vituperative letter of Benjamin F. Butler to me. I have
marked two passages;—and I wish to ask, if you think it not improper, that you
would shew them to the President, and ask him if he will authorise the public
statement of their falshood. He may remember that in our first interview after
I reached Washington, I spent most of our half-hour's conversation in urging
upon him to appoint Mr. Boutwell Secretary of the Treasury, and not to attempt
to patch up an arrangement for Mr. A. T. Stewart—This was before any decision of his to commission me as Attorney General. Will he authorise me to state
that fact? The second matter refers to the Democratic campaign slander of
1872, which Butler revives, that the Supreme Court was packed to reverse the
legal-tender decision. I refuted it in the newspapers in 1872, and on the floor of
the Ho. of Reps. in reply to Mr. Eldredge of Wisconsin. The nomination of Justices Strong and Bradley was made out on or before Saturday Feb. 5, 1870, and
sent to the Senate on Monday, Feb. 7, 1870, before the decision of the legal tender case of Hepburn v. Griswold was announced. . . ."—ALS, DLC-Hamilton
Fish. On Oct. 28, Fish recorded in his diary. "I accordingly call on the President
and read to him the letter. On the first point he made a written memorandum
as; follows, 'After Judge Hoars nomination and confirmation as Attorney General he visited me at my residence on "I" Street in this City, the ineligibility of
my nominee for Secretary of the Treasury had been ascertained. According to
my recollection Judge Hoar then recommended the Hon Geo. S. Boutwell for
the place saying that two members of the Cabinet coming from one State need
make no difference that he Judge Hoar was perfectly willing to go out or remain
without commission; that his appointment was a favor to him any way as it relieved him from his position on the bench in Mass which he was glad to give up.'
On the second point he said it would be difficult for him to make a statement
that although he required no declaration from Judges Strong & Bradley on the
Constitutionality of the Legal Tender Act, he knew Judge Strong had on the
bench in Pennsylvania given a decision sustaining its constitutionality and he

had reason to believe Judge Bradley's opinion tended in the same direction that at the time he felt it important that the constitutionality of the law should be sustained and while he would do nothing to exact anything like a pledge or expression of opinion from the parties he might appoint to the bench he had desired that the constitutionality should be sustained by the Supreme Court that he believed such had been the opinion of all his Cabinet at the time. I told him no that I had been decidedly of an opposite view and that I had supposed from conversation I had had with Bradley during several years when we were associated in the New Jersey Rail Road that his opinion would have been the other way and reminded him of some things said at the time which he could not recall to his recollection. To determine the date of the nomination of the Judges he sent the following memorandum to his Private Secty Mr Sniffen 'Find from the records the dates when Judge Strong's & Judge Bradley's nomination were sent to the Senate.' The following answer was sent in to the Presiden 'Feb 7, 1870' Mr Sniffen came in and remarked that did not show on what day the nomination had been sent in, he thought he could find it from their manifold copy, which however after search he failed to find and said that no manifold copy had been made until a later date, he produced the Executive Journal of the Senate of the 8th February showing that they were considered and referred on that date. The President authorized me to communicate to Judge Hoar on the first point what he had stated in the memorandum; on the second point however he said he would prefer to make no statement."—*Ibid.* On Oct. 29, Fish wrote to Hoar. ". . . there appears nothing to fix the actual time of sending the Messages to the Senate, or when they may have been brought to him for signature, & he cannot recall any thing to establish the date— . . . PS. I have read this letter to the President—he desires me to add a Postscript saying that the fact of the Announcement in the City Journals of the nominations, must be conclusive that they had then been sent to the Senate—inasmuch as nominations are never communicated to the Press, until after the Secretary shall have left the White House with the purpose of delivering them to the Senate—He adds however, that it has occasionally happened, that after the Secretary has left, & the nominations been announced to the Press, it has been found, that the Senate had adjourned before the arrival of the messages, & their actual delivery been thus delayed a day—"—ALS (press), *ibid.* See *PUSG,* 20, 55–57.

1876, OCT. 28.   Joshua S. Dye, "U. S. Invalid pensioner & Law Student," Kings Mountain, Ky., to USG accusing local officials in 1870 of "detaining me in the Lincoln county jail 22 days falsely for the purpose of giveing the Kuklux a chance to take me out and hang me for my political Sentiments which was only prevented by the interposition of the Colored Citizens of Lincoln count, and by United States troops . . . Now Therefore in the name of one who has been permanently Disabled in the regular army of the United States in the name of a republican in the name of the repubiclan party in the name of one of your Excellenci's highest prerogatives viz the enforcement of the Laws of the United States, I ask you . . . to call on the U. S. attorney General for a Critical investigation of this case . . ."—ALS, DNA, RG 60, Letters from the President. Related papers are *ibid.* Dye had served two months in 1869 as private, 14th Inf. His pension for heart disease was suspended after a Sept., 1876, investigation. See *HRC,* 47-1-667; *SRC,* 47-1-796.

1876, OCT. 30.   USG endorsement. "Will the Postmaster General please see Miss Gussie Gardner, the Grand daughter of Gen Wallach [*Walbach*] who died in the Service, and the daughter of a loyal Marylander. If any position could be given her I feel that it would be *worthily bestowed. I wish* you would oblige me by making room for her if necessary. Give her a good office if possible."—Copy, DNA, RG 56, Applications. Related papers are *ibid.* Gussie B. Gardiner served as temporary clerk, Post Office Dept.

1876, OCT. 30.   USG receipt for $90 paid by Gilbert Moyers, tenant at 1215 I Street, Washington, D. C.—DS, Gallery of History, Las Vegas, Nev. See *PUSG,* 21, 499.

Index

All letters written by USG of which the text was available for use in this volume are indexed under the names of the recipients. The dates of these letters are included in the index as an indication of the existence of text. Abbreviations used in the index are explained on pp. xviii–xxiii. Individual regts. are indexed under the names of the states in which they originated.

Burns, Thomas E. (U.S. marshal), 288n, 290n, 291n
Burnside, Ambrose E. (U.S. Senator), 17–18, 151n, 322n
Burr, Aaron, 46n, 52n
Burr, William (of Oswego, N.Y.), 445
Butler, Andrew P. (of S.C.), 331n
Butler, Benjamin F. (U.S. Representative), 118n, 145n, 448
Butler, James (U.S. Army), 374–75
Butler, John H. (of Md.), 265n
Butler, Mary E. C. (of Brooklyn), 374
Butler, Matthew C. (of S.C.), 198, 205n, 231, 233n–34n, 235n, 332n, 333n
Byers, Joseph K. (post trader), 67n
Byrne, Bernard M. (U.S. Army), 429
Byrne, Charles (U.S. Army), 429
Byron, Larkin A. (of Mount Vernon, Ky.), 349

Cadenhead, J. H. (of De Berry, Tex.), 387
Cadwalader, John (of Philadelphia), 364
Cadwalader, John L. (Asst. Secretary of State), 158n–59n, 168n–69n, 279n, 306n, 337n, 339n, 427, 443
Cain, Richard H. (of Charleston, S.C.), 235n
Cairo, Egypt, 304n, 305n, 325n
Cairo, Ill., 17, 19n, 269n–70n, 291n, 417
Calhoun, Edward (U.S. Navy), 95n
Calhoun, James (U.S. Army), 172n
Calhoun County, Ga., 213n
California: appointments from, 4n, 5n; Chinese immigrants in, 6n–8n; vols., 178n; Indians in, 178n; navigation improved, 271n; gold in, 293n; election in, 334n; U.S. Army in, 355; reservations in, 398; traveler to, 437, 439; mentioned, 299n, 319n
California Mining Co., 13, 15 and n, 16n
Callao, Peru, 341n, 426
Cameron, Angus (U.S. Senator), 111n
Cameron, Henry C. (USMA visitor), 357
Cameron, James D. (U.S. Secretary of War): administers dept., 74n, 82n, 133n–34n, 303 and n, 309, 310n, 411, 430, 434, 435, 437, 438, 447; appointed, 75n, 76n, 115, 116n, 121n, 142n; implements Indian policy, 125, 128n; advises traveler, 159 and n; after battle of Little Big Horn, 170n, 172n, 174n, 177n, 250, 250n–51n; involved in appointments, 196, 197n, 198n, 257n, 351, 407, 428–29; confronts racial violence, 202n–3n; during presidential campaign, 209n–10n; monitors La. unrest, 239n, 297, 297n–98n, 299n, 300n–301n; oversees

engineering projects, 269n, 270n–71n; administers USMA, 319n, 432–33, 436, 437, 441; monitors Miss. unrest, 320, 320n–21n, 324n; monitors S.C. unrest, 331n; reviews legislation, 418, 422, 433, 434; in pardon case, 419; investigates insanity case, 421; travels to Calif., 439
—Correspondence from USG: endorsement to, Oct. 14, 1876, 74n; endorsement to, June 13, 1876, 125; endorsement to, June 17, 1876, 133n–34n; endorsement to, June 26, 1876, 159; endorsement to, July 24, 1876, 196; endorsement to, July 22, 1876, 198n; telegram to, Sept. 4, 1876, 269n; endorsement to, March 2, 1877, 271n; letter to, Sept. 12, 1876, 303; endorsement to, Sept. 22, 1876, 320; endorsement to, Sept. 23, 1876, 320n; endorsement to, June 5, 1876, 407; endorsement to, [Aug. 5, 1876], 428; endorsement to, Aug. 7, 1876, 429; note to, Aug. 7, 1876, 430; endorsement to, Aug. 16, 1876, 434; endorsement to, Aug. 18, 1876, 435; endorsement to, Sept. 7, 1876, 437; endorsement to, Sept. 13, 1876, 441
Cameron, Simon (U.S. Senator), 55n, 111n, 116n, 118n, 121n, 142n, 295n, 304n, 393, 399, 415, 417
Cameron, Mo., 430
Camp Apache, Arizona Territory, 389
Campbell, Benjamin H. (U.S. marshal), 226n
Campbell, John A. (Asst. Secretary of State), 355
Campbell, Robert (of St. Louis), 38
Camp Douglas, Utah Territory, 225n
Camp Grant, Arizona Territory, 389
Camp Joe Holt, Ind., 291n
Camp Robinson, Neb., 389
Camp Sheridan, Neb., 389
Camp Verde, Arizona Territory, 389
Canada, 9, 57n, 58n, 134n, 154n, 177n, 182n, 360, 383, 386, 388, 437
Canal, Boisrond (Haitian president): letter to, Sept. 11, 1876, 440
Canals, 83, 83n–86n, 338, 338n–42n, 388
Canandaigua, N.Y., 176n
Candee, Lewis (paymaster applicant), 69n
Canterbury, N.H., 428
Capital University, Columbus, Ohio, 14n
Carbajal, José M. (Mexican insurgent), 354
Carbondale, Ill., 198n
Cárdenas, Adan (Nicaraguan minister), 338, 338n–41n
Cardiff, Wales, 393

Ovington, William H. (business associate of J. Russell Jones), 51
Owen, Philip A. (U.S. Army), 357
Owensboro, Ky., 286n
Owsley County, Ky., 286n
Oxford, Maine, 445
Oxford, Miss., 198, 231, 236n

Pacheco, Romualdo (Gov. of Calif.), 5n
Packard, Stephen B. (U.S. marshal), 237n–38n, 239n, 297n, 300n, 396
Paddock, Algernon S. (U.S. Senator), 133n, 174n, 270n, 379, 382, 401, 412, 428
Paddock, Franklin A. (brother of Algernon S. Paddock), 382
Paddock, Stephen G. (of Princeton, Ill.), 432
Paducah, Ky., 286n
Page, Horace F. (U.S. Representative), 271n
Page, Merritt C. (U.S. District Attorney), 394, 395
Pago Pago, Samoa, 96n
Pahlman, Herman J. (Chicago distiller), 226n, 228n
Paine, John K. (composer), 93n
Painter, Mrs. Hettie K. (of Lincoln, Neb.), 379
Palen, Joseph G. (New Mexico Territory Supreme Court), 349
Palermo, Sicily, 427
Palmer, Frederick A. (of S.C.), 332n
Palo Alto, Miss., 323n
Palo Alto, Tex., 429
Panama, 85n, 443
Panama Railroad, 340n
Pará, Brazil, 350
Pardons, 229n, 315n, 387, 392, 402, 410, 419, 420, 447
Parker (speculator), 388
Parker, Cortlandt (of Newark, N.J.), 116n, 118n–20n, 142n, 143n
Parker, David B. (U.S. marshal), 302n
Parker, Foxhall A. (U.S. Navy), 196n
Parker, Isaac C. (U.S. District Judge), 391
Parker, William H. (collector of Internal Revenue), 41, 50n
Paris, France, 160n–61n, 189n, 245n, 246n, 304n, 324n–27n, 340n, 362, 377, 388, 393, 416
Paris, Tenn., 358
Parnell, Charles Stewart (statesman), 336n–37n
Parrish, Samuel B. (Indian agent), 370
Parsons, Edward Y. (U.S. Representative), 354

Partridge, Frederick W. (U.S. consul), 109n–10n
Paschal (of Tex.), 396
Patents, 95n, 157n, 361, 445
Patrick, William (U.S. District Attorney), 229n
Patten, John D., Jr. (Treasury Dept. official), 438
Patterson, Carlile P. (U.S. Coast Survey): studies interoceanic canal, 84n–85n; note to, Jan. 10, 1876, 352; hires employees, 352
Patterson, Joseph (of Philadelphia), 116n, 120n, 121n
Pattison, George (of Jacksonville, Fla.), 432–33
Patton, Thomas M. (appraiser), 372
Pa'u Lauaki (Samoan), 101n–2n
Pawnees, 89 and n
Peabody, George (philanthropist), 422
Pearce, Frank W. (of Houlton, Maine), 353
Pearl (British navy), 100n
Pearson, Frank M. (Interior Dept. clerk), 351–52
Pearson, George L. (land office clerk), 352
Pearson, Richmond (U.S. consul), 404
Pease, R. M. (of Tex.), 218n
Pedro II (Emperor of Brazil), 108n–9n, 157n
Peirce, Grenville N. (of La.), 238n
Peirce, Henry A. (minister to Hawaii), 295n
Peixotto, Benjamin F. (U.S. consul), 326n
Peking, China, 4n
Peltz, George A. (*Sunday School Times*), 91n
Pemberton, H. A. (of Princeton, Minn.), 385–86
Pembina, Dakota Territory, 191n
Peña, Lucas (Pueblo), 365–66
Pennington, John L. (Gov. of Dakota Territory), 128n
Pennsylvania: crime in, 9, 419; physician in, 14n; cabinet prospects from, 75n, 115, 116n, 121n–22n; patronage involving, 120n, 121n, 349–50, 389, 392–93, 394, 399, 416–17; army appointment from, 256n–57n; USMA visitor from, 357; vols., 383, 422; schools in, 412–13; USMA applicants from, 436, 437; judge in, 448; mentioned, 216n, 370, 379
Pennsylvania, Historical Society of, Philadelphia, Pa.: documents in, 13–14, 15, 107–8, 280n–81n